THE WORLD BETWEEN THE WARS, 1919–39

THE WORLD BETWEEN THE WARS, 1919–39: An Economist's View

Joseph S. Davis *[handwritten: tandcliffe]* , *[handwritten: 1885–]*

THE JOHNS HOPKINS UNIVERSITY PRESS
BALTIMORE & LONDON

Copyright © 1975 by The Johns Hopkins University Press
All rights reserved. No part of this book may be reproduced or transmitted in any form or by any means, electronic or mechanical, including photocopying, recording, xerography, or any information
storage and retrieval system, without permission in writing from the
publisher.

Manufactured in the United States of America

The Johns Hopkins University Press, Baltimore, Maryland 21218
The Johns Hopkins University Press Ltd., London

Library of Congress Catalog Card Number 73-19339
ISBN 0-8018-1450-2

Quotations from *Recent Economic Changes in the United States*
(copyright McGraw-Hill Book Company, 1929) and from Joseph A.
Schumpeter, *Business Cycles* (copyright McGraw-Hill Book Company, 1939) are used with permission of McGraw-Hill Book
Company.

Library of Congress Cataloging in Publication Data

Davis, Joseph Stancliffe, 1885–
    The world between the wars, 1919–39: an economist's view [by]
Joseph S. Davis. [3] Baltimore, Johns Hopkins Univ. Pr. [c1975]
    viii, 436 p. ② 24 cm.
    Includes bibliographical references and index.
    1. Economic history—1918–1945. 2. Depressions—
1929. 3. Business cycles. I. Title.
HC57.D36 1975   330.9'04   74-6821
ISBN 0-8018-1450-2

CONTENTS

PREFACE

THIS BOOK is the product of research and pondering during the past decade, coupled with close observation of current affairs, which helped me better to understand an earlier quarter-century. Its preparation has involved consulting an enormous and still growing literature, laborious checking of facts and divergent opinions, and consistent efforts to see our complicated world in true perspective. It is offered as a contribution toward better answers to two basic questions, why the Great Depression, and why World War II? Though the positions taken must stand or fall on their own merits, a few background statements seem pertinent.

Most of my professional life has been devoted to the patient pursuit of significant truth. My researches have been mainly in history and what are termed the social sciences, often in areas where these overlap one another, or some of the natural sciences. Much of what I have published has won respect, if seldom full acceptance. For several decades I was active in three professional associations, in close touch with several federal agencies. For stretches of time I worked with research institutions other than Stanford's Food Research Institute and served on the Social Science Research Council, a few of its committees and conferences, and two boards of the National Research Council. I have taken no part in politics and never sought even appointive office, but have spent a total of seven years in the federal service, mostly in Washington, D.C., but at times in London, Paris, and Berlin. Professional duties have also taken me to these and other European centers and to Canada, Mexico, and Japan. I have known, more or less well, persons who played major and lesser roles in the interwar decades and many others who have written about that period then or later. My exceptional health and vigor have persisted in so-called retirement years, and I have continued to learn, unlearn, and share the results. Whatever its defects, in essentials this work stands up under my own critical scrutiny.

The book outgrew an early title, and the one finally chosen requires interpretation. The "world" is neither the universe nor the terrestrial globe, and no encyclopedic treatment is attempted. The focus is on Europe and the United States, and other huge areas are dealt with sparingly. In a few places it seemed essential to touch on events before 1919 and after 1939. I have never been "just an economist," and the "view" presented stretches well beyond my professional specialty.

I have relied mainly on publications in English, without wholly neglecting works in other languages. At a late stage I consulted several recently published books that provided additional details but involved no change in what was already written; not all of these are cited.

My indebtedness to Harvard and Stanford is inexpressibly great. My debts to many authors, editors, and publishers are amply indicated in footnotes. Particular thanks go to the President and Fellows of Harvard College for permission to quote from the *Review of Economics and Statistics* and its predecessors. A number of persons have kindly commented on drafts of portions of this book or have urged me to bring it to completion; these I leave unnamed to avoid embarrassing them. My personal library and extensive files have provided valuable materials. For many others I am grateful to Stanford University Libraries. I regret that I have found time to utilize only a small fraction of the enormous resources of the Hoover Institution on War, Revolution, and Peace.

For excellent typing assistance I owe much to my sister, Florence Davis Smith, and to Pauline Boyd Tooker. For unfailing support I am profoundly thankful to my wife, Florence Danielson Davis.

ABBREVIATIONS

AAA	Agricultural Adjustment Administration
AAAct	Agricultural Adjustment Act
AEA	American Economic Association
AER	*American Economic Review*
Amer. Labor Legis. Review	*American Labor Legislative Review*
ASA	American Statistical Association
AT&T	American Telephone and Telegraph Company
BIS	Bank for International Settlements
BLS	U.S. Bureau of Labor Statistics
Bus. Bul.	*Business Bulletin*
Citibank	National City Bank of New York, or First National City Bank of New York
C&FC	*Commercial and Financial Chronicle*
CTC	Cleveland Trust Company, Cleveland, Ohio
CWA	Civil Works Administration
ECP	*Economic Consequences of the Peace* (J. M. Keynes)
EJ	*Economic Journal*
Fed. Res. Bull.	*Federal Reserve Bulletin*
FRB	Federal Reserve Board
FRS	Federal Reserve System
HES	Harvard Economic Service (1922–27), Harvard Economic Society (1928–31)
Hist. Stat. U.S.	*Historical Statistics of the United States*
ICA's	International commodity agreements
ILO	International Labour Organization
JASA	*Journal of the American Statistical Association*
Jour. Ec. Hist.	*Journal of Economic History*
JPE	*Journal of Political Economy*
Jour. Roy. Stat. Soc.	*Journal of the Royal Statistical Society*
LCES	London and Cambridge Economic Service
N&A	*The Nation and the Athenaeum*
NBER	National Bureau of Economic Research
NICB	National Industrial Conference Board
NRA	National Recovery Administration
NYSE	New York Stock Exchange
Proc. Acad. Pol. Sci.	*Proceedings of the Academy of Political Science*
QJE	*Quarterly Journal of Economics*
Rev. Ec. Stat.	*Review of Economic Statistics* (1919–48), *Review of Economics and Statistics* (1948–)
RT	*Revision of the Treaty* (J. M. Keynes)
SCB	*Survey of Current Business*
Stat. Abstr. U.S.	*Statistical Abstract of the United States*
WSJ	*Wall Street Journal*

THE WORLD BETWEEN THE WARS, 1919-39

CHAPTER 1

INTRODUCTION

FORTY YEARS after the trough of the Great Depression, 1932–33, there is still no clear-cut agreement among historians and economists as to the part played by the extraordinary stock market boom and collapse, and many other factors, in the series of disasters culminating in the onset of World War II. Contemporary materials and a great abundance of other facts are available; excellent studies in this general area have been made by outstanding scholars, and many others have contributed much. Yet their conclusions—both explicit and implicit—are amazingly divergent.[1]

This lack of consensus is not only disturbing. Early in my study it seemed to me to have serious dangers in failing to provide adequate guidance for the future. As my work progressed, it was borne in upon me that various misinterpretations remained to be corrected and that, while multifarious blunders had been extensively exposed, more fundamental causal factors of permanent significance had been generally overlooked. What I came to regard as imperfect understanding of the turbulent quarter-century 1914–39 seemed partly responsible for the buildup of serious problems in the quarter-century after World War II.

The 1960s showed some striking similarities to the 1920s, including an even longer period of sustained prosperity and a few stock market crashes milder than that of 1929, but on the whole a very different combination of circumstances and conditions prevailed. Yet these eventually led to a series of crises the outcome of which is still in doubt. In the 1970s it is still pertinent to ask how we can do substantially better than our fathers and grandfathers—how we can develop our capacity to cope with domestic and international tensions and to meet effectively threats of monetary collapse, economic breakdown, a third world war, and lesser but still serious dangers.

[1]The variety of more or less contradictory explanations for the collapse and depression is the subject of comment by many competent writers. To cite only three, see Paul Einzig, *The World Economic Crisis, 1929–1931*, 2d ed. (London: Macmillan, 1932), foreword and p. 23; Chester W. Wright, *Economic History of the United States* (New York: McGraw-Hill, 1941), p. 975, and the revised edition (1948), p. 770; and Robert T. Patterson, *The Great Boom and Panic, 1921–1929* (Chicago: Regnery, 1965), preface and ch. 12, "Causes." There are even basic disagreements as to whether or not "inflation" characterized the period 1924–29 in the United States, how far the Federal Reserve practiced "gold sterilization" in these years, whether more serious efforts should have been made to curb the stock market boom, and whether those that were made were excessive. These disagreements persist, and recent writings by some prominent economists take positive positions on such points with inadequate consideration of strong adverse views expressed by reputable earlier writers, e.g., B. M. Anderson.

It has come to be widely believed that we have learned and applied important lessons from the experiences of the 1920s and 1930s, that both the United States and the world economies are far stronger today, that we have built-in safeguards against certain adverse developments, that we know so much more than we did in the 1920s, and that we are well prepared for appropriate and timely actions. Much of this may be true, but it is ominously reminiscent of the overoptimistic New Era thinking of the late 1920s. In the mid-1960s overconfidence again became a danger. The world today is even more complex than it was in 1914–39 and is still extremely difficult to understand clearly and comprehensively. Few concern themselves with the question of what combination of policies and actions would be adequate to prevent disaster, should a drastic and extended economic contraction be threatened, and what can be done in advance to ensure their adoption and successful application. In attempting to ward off severe depression, may we not underrate other risks, such as that of chronic or severe inflation? In our absorption with "social action" and government policies, are we overlooking the vast potential of individuals, of self-education, and of improvement in personal habits and standards at all levels?

Parts I and II of what follows deal with the events of 1914–29 and with the Wall Street crash and the subsequent decade. Part III examines the complex reasons for (I hesitate to say "causes of") the Great Depression and the drift toward a second world war.

The Speculative Crash of   The remarkable Wall Street boom of 1925–29
1929 and Its Precursors   and its crash and subsequent collapse are vividly remembered by a dwindling minority, but have been almost completely ignored by some recent scholars and are treated by others as only a dramatic episode. In 1955 John Kenneth Galbraith published a racy account of the great crash, the course of events that led up to it, and its early aftermath.[2] Admittedly hastily written, this did not pretend to be an exhaustive or definitive study, and none such has been published since its appearance.[3] Galbraith's discussion is illuminating and in large measure

[2]J. K. Galbraith, *The Great Crash 1929* (Boston: Houghton Mifflin, 1955, 1961, 1972). Written in the summer and autumn of 1954, the first edition was published on Apr. 21, 1955. Each of the later editions has a new introduction, but the pagination is unchanged. The third edition has a new foreword and a few slight changes in the final chapter. At various points he touched on similarities to and differences from the South Sea Bubble without attempting to do justice to that fascinating subject.

[3]Murray N. Rothbard's *America's Great Depression* (Princeton, N.J.: Van Nostrand, 1963) and Patterson's *Great Boom and Panic* contain much useful material but cannot be so characterized. The same is true of three later books that I consulted only at a late stage of my work: Goronwy Rees, *The Great Slump: Capitalism in Crisis, 1929–33* (London: Weidenfeld and Nicolson, 1970)—which contains photographs of many prominent figures in the period; C. B. Schedvin, *Australia and the Great Depression: A Study of Economic Development and Policy*

correct, so far as it goes. On a few crucial points and a number of lesser ones, however, his position strikes me as at best misleading and at worst quite wrong, and there are significant omissions in his treatment. Moreover, his conclusions as to the basic causes of the stock market boom and collapse and the degree of responsibility they bear for the Great Depression are neither clear-cut nor satisfying.[4]

For two centuries the classic cases of extreme stock speculation culminating in severe collapse had been the Mississippi and South Sea "bubbles," centering in Paris and London, respectively, which burst in 1720, when business corporations (then called joint-stock companies) and share ownership were still in an early stage of development.[5] The orgy of stock speculation that centered in New York in the late 1920s had a far greater scope, but financial manipulation, irresponsible flotations, and other forms of skullduggery were far less prominent,[6] though disgracefully prevalent: "Nothing in recent years . . . has touched the wild frenzy

in the 1920s and 1930s (Sydney, N.S.W.: Sydney University Press, 1970); and Charles P. Kindleberger, The World in Depression, 1929–39 (London: Allen Lane, The Penguin Press, 1973), reviewed by Alec Cairncross in EJ, December 1973, 83:1286–88.

[4]See his ch. 10, "Cause and Consequence," esp. pp. 173–74. After rightly saying that "the collapse in the stock market in the autumn of 1929 was implicit in the speculation that went before," he went on: "We do not know why a great speculative orgy occurred in 1928 and 1929." In an earlier paragraph he said: "On the whole, the great stock market crash can be much more readily explained than the depression that followed it. And among the problems involved in assessing the causes of depression none is more intractable than the responsibility to be assigned to the stock market crash."

[5]For a detailed account of the second and a briefer summary of the first, see John Carswell, The South Sea Bubble (Stanford, Calif.: Stanford University Press, 1960), ably reviewed by the British political scientist D. W. Brogan in New York Times, Jan. 22, 1961 ("Big Smash, Big Swindle"). Much more detail on the South Sea Bubble and the earlier history of many other companies is given in the monumental work of William Robert Scott, The Constitution and Finance of English, Scottish and Irish Joint-Stock Companies to 1720, 3 vols. (Cambridge: Cambridge University Press, 1910–12), esp. 1:1–14, 388–471; 3:288–360, 443–81. Some passages in Alfred Marshall, Industry and Trade (London: Macmillan, 1919), are also pertinent, esp. bk. 2, chs. 8–9.

In an earlier book I described at some length the emergence of security speculation in this country in 1791–92 and the brief panic in which it culminated. At the time numerous references were made to the South Sea Bubble, less than seventy-five years earlier (Essays in the Earlier History of American Corporations, Harvard Economic Studies 16, 2 vols. [Cambridge, Mass.: Harvard University Press, 1917], 1:174–212, 278–315, 428ff.; vol. 2, ch. 2, "Banking Companies"). W. R. Scott's review of this book is found in EJ, December 1917, 27:538–42. A. D. Noyes (The Market Place: Reminiscences of a Financial Editor [Boston: Little Brown, 1938], pp. 338–40) briefly discussed the similar "episode" in England that culminated in 1825, which Marshall also briefly touched upon (Industry and Trade, p. 313n). The Cleveland Trust Company (CTC) index of American Business Activity since 1790 (any recent annual edition) shows a peak in June 1825 and a protracted but not severe "secondary post war depression" in the United States in 1826–30.

[6]Lieutenant General Charles Ross, "one of the fiercest members" of its secret committee of inquiry into the 1720 crash, told the House of Commons early in its work that the committee had "discovered a train of deepest villainy and fraud Hell ever contrived to ruin a nation" (Carswell, South Sea Bubble, p. 227). Adam Smith termed his compatriot John Law's Mississippi scheme "the most extravagant project both of banking and stock-jobbing that, perhaps,

of the South Sea Bubble in England. But in range and volume, and consequently in its far-reaching results, the 1929 speculation has had no equal or rival in economic history. Never before in the history of the world has there been a public, to be numbered not by hundreds of thousands but by tens of millions, with both the will to speculate and the financial facilities to enable them to do so. It is a new and terrifying phenomenon."[7] The consequences of boom and collapse were severe and farreaching in all three instances. The early effects of the South Sea collapse were even more striking than those of 1929: "The economic confusion of the last three months of 1720 has perhaps no parallel in the history of England."[8]

Some Observations   This book is concerned with much more than busi-
on Business Cycles   ness cycles,[9] but it necessarily deals at length with
the major one that reached its peak in the crucial year 1929, and more briefly with lesser ones in 1914–39 (see the chart below). Some broad observations seem appropriate at this point, beginning with a few words on terminology.

Economists have seldom bothered to reach agreement on the precise meanings of terms, even of such common ones as "prosperity," "recession," "depression,"[10] "inflation," "money supply," and "standard of living." Largely in keeping with recent practice at the National Bureau of Economic Research, I shall use the terms "upturn," "expansion," "peak," "downturn," "contraction" (or "slump"), and "trough" for successive phases of the cycle and "prosperity" and "depression" for periods above or below some estimated norm of business activity or industrial production. The term recession is sometimes used to mean an early phase of contraction or, confusingly, a minor depression. I prefer to use "boom" for the later stages of a major expansion which is then typically (but not invariably) followed by a "bust," or marked downturn often accompanied by a sharp crisis or panic.

---

the world ever saw" (*Wealth of Nations* [1776], bk. 2, ch. 2). Smith also paid his respects briefly to the South Sea Company and the "knavery and extravagance of their stock-jobbing projects" (*ibid.*, bk. 5, ch. 1, pt. 3, art. 1).

[7]Sir Arthur Salter, *Recovery: The Second Effort* (New York: Century, 1932), p. 43. On the numbers involved in the 1929 speculation, see Chapter 4 below.

[8]Carswell, *South Sea Bubble*, p. 191.

[9]Like many others I must acknowledge great indebtedness to Gottfried Haberler, *Prosperity and Depression: A Theoretical Analysis of Cyclical Movements* (New York: Atheneum, 1963), p. viii. This classic has gone through various impressions and editions since it was first published by the League of Nations in 1937. This 1963 paperback edition is reprinted from the fourth edition, published in Harvard Economic Studies 105 (Cambridge, Mass.: Harvard University Press, 1958). The 1963 preface is reprinted from *Think* (IBM), April 1962, "Why Depressions Are Extinct."

[10]Especially confusing is the use of the term "depression." The term "Great Depression" has also been used to refer to the period 1873–96 in Great Britain. See D. J. Coppock's article and A. E. Musson's reply in *Economic History Review*, December 1964, 17:389–403.

CTC Index of American Business Activity and BLS Index of Wholesale Prices in the United States, Monthly, 1914–41

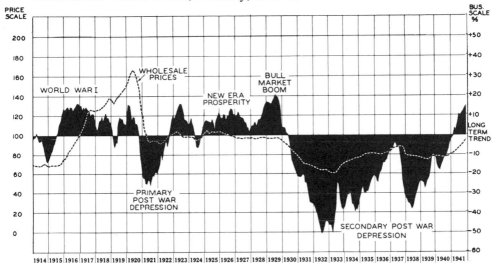

Source: adapted, by permission of the Cleveland Trust Company, from its chart, *American Business Activity since 1790.* For the BLS index, 1926=100.

Students of the business cycle recognize that often, perhaps usually, prosperity breeds contraction, and that often, perhaps usually, depression in turn breeds recovery, given time;[11] but that under some circumstances a vicious downward spiral develops to intensify the contraction and to delay recovery painfully, and that deep and protracted depression gives rise to new obstacles to recovery. The first case is well illustrated by the first postwar American business cycle, in which an early postwar boom was followed by severe contraction in 1920–21 and this in turn by quick recovery, in this country without significant governmental interposition.[12] The second case is best illustrated by the cycle of 1927–33.[13]

A highly pertinent question, understressed in business-cycle literature, is this: why do some cycles, even after drastic contraction, reverse direction fairly soon, as did the first cycle after World War I and the one of

[11]Cf. Warren M. Persons, *Forecasting Business Cycles* (New York: McGraw-Hill, 1931), p. 80.

[12]B. M. Anderson, *Economics and the Public Welfare: Financial and Economic History of the United States, 1914–1946* (New York: Van Nostrand, 1949), pp. 47–76.

[13]Cf. Arthur F. Burns, "Mild and Severe Depressions," in *The Frontiers of Economic Knowledge* (Princeton, N.J.: Princeton University Press, 1954), pp. 131–34. This book contains Burns' notable series of introductory essays to the annual reports of the National Bureau of Economic Research during his term as director of research (succeeding Wesley C. Mitchell), 1945–53.

1937–40, while others display a protracted cumulative spiral into prolonged depression, as in 1929–32?[14] In that period almost all close students of the current situation confidently expected the sustained upturn to come long before it did, and they were recurrently disappointed.

It is generally agreed that each business cycle is unique.[15] That of 1927–33 unquestionably was. Its distinctive features included (1) exceptional international interactions; (2) unusually important psychological or emotional factors, which not only fostered illusions but also gave rise to extremes of optimism in the expansionary period and of pessimism in the contraction and depression phases; (3) weak political leadership and an intricate interplay of politics with economics in all of the leading countries; (4) notable expansion, especially in the United States, in the prevalence of stock ownership and in the practice of buying stocks on margin; (5) the greatest speculative orgy, followed by the worst stock market collapse and economic depression, in two centuries; (6) a peculiar pattern of commodity prices, which declined mildly in 1925–29 and then fell drastically in 1929–32; (7) the first notable test of the new Federal Reserve System in this country; (8) serious efforts to enlarge statistical data, to intensify economic analysis, and to develop business forecasting; and (9) increasing intervention of governments in peacetime economic life, here and abroad.

Many of the studies I have examined appear to ignore or to minimize one or more of these features. Moreover, many do not look back far enough in their analyses. It is not enough to condemn what now appear—and what appeared to some perceptive observers at the time—as serious policy blunders, such as the United States' repudiation of Wilson's signature of the Treaty of Versailles with the Covenant of the League of Nations, its obdurate official position on interallied war debts, and the Hawley-Smoot Tariff Act of June 1930. One must seek to understand why these blunders were made.[16]

[14]See also Haberler, *Prosperity and Depression*, pp. ix–x.

[15]Thus Mitchell said: "Strictly speaking, every business cycle is a unique historical episode, differing in significant ways from all its predecessors, and never to be repeated in the future." Wesley C. Mitchell, *Business Cycles: The Problem and Its Setting* (New York: NBER, 1927), pp. 354–57. Here Mitchell briefly summarized some of the salient characteristics of the American cycles of 1878 to 1923.

[16]Milton Friedman and Anna J. Schwartz merit high commendation for asking, at the end of their study *The Great Contraction, 1929–1933* (1965) (a paperback reprint of ch. 7 of their *A Monetary History of the United States, 1867–1960* [Princeton, N.J.: Princeton University Press, 1963]), "Why Was Monetary Policy So Inept?" Their answers deserve careful consideration. Among the students of the interwar period, Schumpeter in particular tried to probe deeply into ultimate as contrasted with proximate causes. Haberler says: "Incredibly inept and timid anti-depression policies, on both the national and international level, must take much of the blame for the excessive length and severity of the Great Depression" (*Prosperity and Depression*, p. ix). No doubt. But why were these policies pursued? With A. J.

The great contraction and depression of the interwar period was worldwide—not in the literal sense but with respect to the economic world of the time.[17] As usual in business-cycle history, however, there were marked variations in the timing of the different phases in the various countries affected, in the course of development, and in degrees of severity.[18] The United States was by no means the first to succumb to contraction, but it experienced one of the severest contractions and depressions and was one of the slowest to begin sustained recovery and to return to normal business activity.[19] The Cleveland Trust Company indexes of industrial activity, on the base 1927–29, for eight leading industrial nations show Canada leading, with its contraction lasting about four years— from March 1929 to March 1933.[20] The United States showed the next longest contraction from peak to trough. Germany ranked third in severity. The average for the eight countries (weighted by population) ranked next, with a duration of slightly under three years, from the peak of September 1929 to the low of July 1932.[21]

The use of the 1927–29 average, however, is somewhat misleading, for the level of that three-year period was markedly subnormal for the United Kingdom and in lesser degree for Germany and some other countries. On the base 1929, the curves of industrial production in the United States and in the average for a number of foreign countries show very similar uptrends in 1921–29, identical troughs in 1932, and almost identi-

Hettinger, Jr. (quoted in Friedman and Schwartz, *Great Contraction*, p. 125), I am disposed to give much more weight to psychological and political factors than do Friedman and Schwartz or Haberler.

[17]See Einzig, *World Economic Crisis*, appendixes 1–11; *A Picture of World Economic Conditions* (New York: NICB, 1932), especially on unemployment in the several states of Australia in the third quarters of 1928–31.

[18]H. G. Moulton in his *Controlling Factors in Economic Development* (Washington: Brookings Institution, 1949), pp. 74–75, undertook to show graphically the course of the 1929–33 cycle in twenty-eight different countries by calendar quarters. His chart serves a useful purpose but is obviously rough and gives no indication of the different degrees of severity. Earlier history is extensively dealt with in Mitchell, *Business Cycles*, ch. 4, esp. pp. 424–50, with the aid of Willard L. Thorp's *Business Annals* (New York: NBER, 1926): "In the whole record there is no crisis which was equally severe everywhere" (Mitchell, *Business Cycles*, p. 439).

[19]Schumpeter observed that, in 1930, "the crisis was nowhere else anything like so severe as in the United States, the country most nearly free from injury by external factors" (Joseph A. Schumpeter, *Business Cycles: A Theoretical, Historical, and Statistical Analysis of the Capitalist Process*, 2 vols. [New York: McGraw-Hill, 1939], 2:911n).

[20]Canada also experienced a notable stock market boom and a severe collapse in 1927–31. Prices of industrial shares tended upward from mid-1922 to mid-1927, then rose sharply for six months; after a slump in the summer of 1928 they rose to higher levels in 1929; from a peak in September they fell drastically with only brief recoveries to the end of 1930 (see chart and brief text communicated by the Canadian Economic Service, McMaster University, Hamilton, Ontario, appearing in the Royal Economic Society's periodical *Report on Economic Conditions* by the London and Cambridge Economic Service).

[21]CTC, *Bus. Bull.*, June 15, 1933.

cal uptrends in 1932–37; sharper declines are recorded in 1929–32 in the United States and greater recoveries in 1932–37.[22]

Business cycles are complex phenomena. In the introduction to his *Forecasting Business Cycles* Warren M. Persons wrote:

The world of affairs in which we live is not a mechanistic world; it is a bewildering world of multiplicities, complexities, interactions, repercussions, and the vagaries of human wants, fears and hopes. It is a world in which, at times, facts and logic become subordinated to human emotions. At such times individuals, who by themselves are rational, join with other rational individuals to form an unreasoning mob. The business world then suffers from an epidemic of optimism, with hope, recklessness and indolence as its leading symptoms, or from an epidemic of pessimism, with fear, timidity and inertia as its leading features. It is also a world of wars, droughts, floods, earthquakes, and monetary changes. In such a world there can be neither a "sure-fire" system nor a reliable "trick" method of forecasting business cycles.

The range of alleged dominant causes of the boom, contraction, and depression of 1927–33 includes the war of 1914–18 and the resulting extreme disorganization and price inflation; serious defects in the peace arrangements of 1919; later policy blunders; excessive and unwise governmental intervention; the weakness and mistakes of the Federal Reserve System in the 1920s and in the early 1930s; inadequate international cooperation; inordinate stock speculation, reaching a veritable speculative mania in 1928–29; and extremes of optimism in the boom and its early aftermath and of deep pessimism after the stock market collapse. Surely it is necessary to recognize several powerful interacting causal influences.

Some reputable scholars hold that variations in degrees of severity of business contractions are primarily explained by preceding developments rather than by fresh complications arising in the course of the process.[23] Wesley C. Mitchell in 1933 ascribed the severity of the then-current depression to "a complex of factors" in which he emphasized both earlier and current developments.[24] As Joseph Dorfman has summarized his description of the 1927–33 cycle,

he declared that the characteristics of the expansion phase had been intense speculation in securities and urban real estate, the absence of a rise of commodity

[22]Hal B. Lary and Associates, *The United States in the World Economy* (Washington: U.S. Department of Commerce, 1943), p. 30; R. A. Gordon, *Business Fluctuations*, 2d ed. (New York: Harper, 1961), pp. 642–44.

[23]Arthur F. Burns, "Business Cycle Research and the Needs of Our Times," in *Frontiers of Economic Knowledge*, esp. pp. 180–81. Burns found this judgment reinforced by data on the interwar period. He had previously somewhat qualified it, however; see *ibid.*, p. 133.

[24]Wesley C. Mitchell, "Business Cycles: The Story of Rhythms in the Money-Making World," in *The World Today* (monthly supplement of the *Encyclopaedia Britannica*), October 1933, p. 28.

prices, and the drastic reduction in foreign loans on which countries in Europe and South America had become dependent. The unusual length and severity of the contraction he attributed to the liquidation of the stock exchange and real estate booms, the heavy fall in commodity prices, the severe agricultural depression, the mass of bank failures, and the "postwar snarl in international commerce and finance." The result was the gravest unemployment in American history. "The reduction in wage disbursements, coupled with reductions of profits, dividends, and even interest and rent payments reacted on consumer buying and further intensified the depression."[25]

Persons, another experienced scholar, also recognized that no two cycles are closely similar but held that their differences are due in large measure to "innumerable small accidents and some large ones," which may more or less cancel each other out but which may also determine a favorable or unfavorable outcome.[26] Without fully endorsing this view, I must give significant importance to a number of adverse factors, "special" or "accidental," no one of which was all-powerful in itself.

As early as 1867 John Mills had set forth the view that the basic cause of cycles is psychological. Good times breed optimism; this in turn leads to recklessness, which in turn breeds disaster; pessimism follows, breeding depression. Recovery follows when businessmen's spirits rise as they find the worst less bad than they had feared.[27] On the basis of some such view, A. C. Pigou in 1916 incorporated in a small volume this prophetic passage:

after the first few months of transition [after the end of the War], . . . it is practically certain that, to make good the havoc and the waste of war, there will be a strong industrial boom. This boom, if history is any guide, will generate in many minds an unreasoning sense of optimism leading to much wild investment. The result, some years afterward, will be failures, crisis, and depression. If this danger is to be obviated or mitigated, it is imperative that the Government and the banks should so act as to restrain and keep within limits the initial peace boom.[28]

---

[25]Joseph Dorfman, *The Economic Mind in American Civilization*, vols. 4–5: *1919–1933* (New York: Viking, 1959), 5:666.

[26]Persons, *Forecasting Business Cycles*, p. 80. See also W. L. Crum, "Review of the Year 1930," *Rev. Ec. Stat.*, February 1931, 13:1–2, for an impressive summary of a number of adverse developments, mostly unforeseen and unforeseeable, that led into the deep depression which most forecasters expected would be avoided. A year later, Crum observed that "chance played in 1931, as in 1930, a large part in controlling the course of economic conditions" (*ibid.*, February 1932, 14:13).

[27]John Mills, "On Credit Cycles and the Origin of Commercial Panics," *Transactions of the Manchester Statistical Society, 1867–68*, pp. 5–40, summarized in Mitchell, *Business Cycles*, p. 9.

[28]A. C. Pigou, *The Economy and Finance of the War* (London: Dent, 1916), pp. 87–88, quoted in C. A. Phillips, T. F. McManus, and R. W. Nelson, *Banking and the Business Cycle: A Study of the Great Depression in the United States* (New York: Macmillan, 1937), p. 35,

In 1920 Pigou set forth what was, in essence, John Mills' view, emphasizing that optimistic and pessimistic errors "give birth to one after another in an endless chain," both being overdone; but he also recognized the influence of other factors which modify this "dominant cause."[29] In his later work, *Industrial Fluctuations*, Pigou developed this explanation of business cycles,[30] and Keynes later accorded it significant weight.[31]

Mitchell and Haberler, in their reviews of theories of the business cycle, were in accord that the difference between psychological and other theories is a "distinction of emphasis rather than of kind."[32] Yet Haberler rejected Pigou's views on this matter, and endorsed as "probably correct" R. G. Hawtrey's opinion "that optimism and pessimism are wholly dependent on the policy of the banks. People are optimistic, he [Hawtrey] said, so long as credit expands and consequently demand rises; they become pessimistic when credit is contracted and demand flags."[33] Perhaps because of this rejection and endorsement, Haberler largely ignored the stock market boom in what he had to say about the cycle that included the Great Depression. For my part, with due recognition of their superior authority in general, I cannot accept Hawtrey's view, virtually endorsed by Haberler, nor agree in minimizing the significance of Pigou's position in 1927–29. Pigou made the important point that "the extent of the revulsion toward pessimistic error, which follows when optimistic error is disclosed, depends, in part, upon the magnitude of the preceding optimistic error. . . . But it is also affected by what one may call the detonation which accompanies the discovery of a given amount of optimistic error. The detonation is greater or less according to the number and scale of the legal bankruptcies into which the detected error explodes."[34]

---

with this comment (which I cannot wholly endorse): "The only flaw in his remarkable prevision is that the 'few years' extended to a decade; but he could not have foreseen, of course, that governments and banks, instead of restraining the investment boom and keeping it within limits, would aid and abet that boom by providing it with even more credit on which to feed."

[29]A. C. Pigou, *The Economics of Welfare*, 1st ed. (London: Macmillan, 1920), pt. 6, ch. 6, summarized in Mitchell, *Business Cycles*, pp. 17–19. Writing in 1932, Einzig closely followed Mills and Pigou in saying, "As is well known, periodic crises are mainly due to exaggerated optimism, which leads to excesses in some direction of economic activity, and which provokes a reaction in the form of excessive pessimism" (Einzig, *World Economic Crisis*, pp. 14–15). He applied this specifically to the current "crisis" (*ibid.*, pp. 50–51, 81–82, 86, 114–15).

[30]A. C. Pigou, *Industrial Fluctuations*, 2d ed. (London: Macmillan, 1929), especially chs. 6 and 7.

[31]J. M. Keynes, *General Theory of Employment, Interest, and Money* (New York: Harcourt Brace, 1936), ch. 22.

[32]Mitchell, *Business Cycles*, pp. 9, 17–20; Haberler, *Prosperity and Depression* (various editions, 1937–63), ch. 6; and cf. Gordon, *Business Fluctuations*, pp. 347–49.

[33]Haberler, *Prosperity and Depression*, p. 149.

[34]Pigou, *Industrial Fluctuations*, p. 94, quoted in Haberler, *Prosperity and Depression*, p. 148.

Privately, however, Mitchell came to recognize the profound importance of psychological factors. Writing to his wife on April 16, 1932, he said:

Now as to the business outlook: I feel sure that Americans are as emotionally unbalanced at the present as they were at the top of the stock-market boom in 1929. Then I expected the delusion to pass a year or more before it did. Now I expect a turn for the better; but the fact that there is no economic justification for the present depression aside from the almost universal discouragement may not prevent the depression from running on for another year. I don't think it will; but the wise course is to program for that contingency.[35]

And Hawtrey, in a later book (1937), went so far as to observe that "it would be difficult to put a limit to psychological influences on economic affairs."[36]

It is not necessary to adopt any psychological theory of the business cycle to recognize that degrees of optimism and pessimism, and shifts from one to the other, at times exert powerful influence on the expectations of businessmen, investors, and speculators and on the course of the fluctuations experienced. These are well illustrated in the period 1922–39 and in the shorter period 1927–32.[37] I cannot fully accept Warren B. Catlin's considered judgment that the fundamental explanation of business cycles is essentially psychological and that other factors are secondary.[38] Yet I believe that most analysts of the business cycle, and of the interwar cycles in particular, have put too little emphasis on various psychological factors.[39]

World War I gave rise to extraordinarily disturbed emotional states all over the Western world, and particularly in the belligerent countries; they bear a heavy responsibility for the blunders and delays in peacemaking and in early postwar economic recovery and for unfortunate political developments in this country and others. Excessive optimism as hostilities ended was quickly followed by extreme pessimism, which was itself

---

[35]Lucy Sprague Mitchell, *Two Lives: The Story of Wesley Clair Mitchell and Myself* (New York: Simon and Schuster, 1953), p. 388.

[36]R. G. Hawtrey, *Capital and Employment* (London: Longmans Green, 1937), pp. 107–8.

[37]Secretary Hoover early recognized the importance of psychological factors in booms and depressions. Herbert Hoover, *The Memoirs of Herbert Hoover*, vol. 2: *The Cabinet and the Presidency* (New York: Macmillan, 1952), pp. 174–75. President Hoover's efforts to maintain and revive public confidence, even when it seemed to entail suppression or distortion of facts, are discussed below (Chapters 8–9).

[38]Warren B. Catlin, *The Progress of Economics: A History of Economic Thought* (New York: Bookman Associates, 1962), pp. 647–49.

[39]Pigou is a notable exception, but his concept of the psychological factors seems to me unduly restricted. See his *Industrial Fluctuations*, especially ch. 7, "The Mutual Generation of Errors of Optimism and Errors of Pessimism." Einzig, as noted above, is another exception, yet neither of them neglects other factors.

a serious handicap in the readjustment process. After mid-1924 this was followed by increasingly excessive optimism, which rose to its zenith in the United States in 1929 but waned a little earlier in Western Europe. The ensuing depression was not, as some rashly asserted at the time, purely psychological; but excessive pessimism became a powerful factor accentuating the great contraction and delaying recovery.

PART I

BACKGROUND AND BOOM, 1914–29

CHAPTER 2

THE GREAT WAR AND THE PEACE TREATIES, 1914–20

MANY ABLE SCHOLARS and political leaders have concluded that the war of 1914–18 and the Peace Conference and treaties that formally ended it were fundamentally responsible for the drastic economic contraction of 1929–33, and that the "seeds of war" planted in Paris in 1919 combined with the Great Depression of the 1930s to bring on World War II. There are elements of truth in these views, but there are even more fundamental causal factors that call for illumination and emphasis.

The century preceding the outbreak of war in August 1914 was a period of unprecedented change. It was scarred by the American Civil War and numerous lesser wars and recurrently disturbed by business ups and downs of minor or major dimensions.[1] Yet the increasingly integrated world economy was never in grave danger of breakdown, and many segments of the growing world population experienced uptrends in their levels of living.[2] The United States, indeed, presented the outstanding example of "the western miracle of combining a phenomenal increase of population with rising standards of living."[3]

The four-year Great War was a multidimensional catastrophe.[4] It disrupted the world market. It broke down the international gold standard, gave rise to enormous inflations, and led to a drastic redistribution of gold reserves and of economic power in favor of the United States. It entailed vast destruction of human lives and of capital goods and brought into being a huge apparatus much of which peace rendered superfluous. It depleted European resources for lending abroad, and forced several nations to borrow instead. Even more important, the war destroyed or poisoned much of the delicate international fabric of human relations—eco-

[1]For example, see Willard L. Thorp, *Business Annals* (New York: NBER, 1926), and Cleveland Trust Company chart of *American Business Activity since 1790* (1971 edition).

[2]"According to the calculations of Sir Josiah Stamp, the level of real incomes in Great Britain in the years before the war was four times as great as in the Napoleonic period." Lionel Robbins, *The Great Depression* (London: Macmillan, 1934), pp. 1–2. Cf. Sir Josiah Stamp, *Jour. Roy. Stat. Soc.*, March 1926; Stamp, "Inheritance as an Economic Factor," *EJ*, September 1926, 36:339–74.

[3]W. K. Hancock, *Wealth of Colonies* (Cambridge: Cambridge University Press, 1950), p. 34.

[4]Robbins, *Great Depression*, pp. 3–6; H. V. Hodson, *Slump and Recovery, 1929–1937* (London: Oxford University Press, 1938), pp. 50–51. Kennan in 1960 considered this war "to have been *the* great catastrophe of Western civilization in the present century." George F. Kennan, *Russia and the West under Lenin and Stalin* (Boston: Little Brown, 1960), p. 47.

nomic, political, and cultural—which could be restored to health only by a painfully slow process.[5] In 1917, under the terrible strains of war and revolution, the shaky czarist regime disintegrated, Nicholas II abdicated, and the Russian armies crumbled. Late in the year the Bolsheviks under Lenin gained ascendancy among the revolutionary groups, but not yet dominance. These events were of momentous importance abroad as well as in Russia. The pre-Armistice breakup of the Austro-Hungarian Empire gave nationalism new scope and narrowed the range of the economic division of labor. In addition, the war also gravely weakened (especially in Great Britain, with the expansion of great industrial concerns and powerful labor unions) the former flexibility of the economic system, with adverse effects hard to overestimate. The peace settlements in some ways aggravated the disruption for a time, and gave rise to deep disagreements and profound ill-feeling among the former "Allied and Associated Powers" at a time when harmonious cooperation would have speeded recovery.

The United States   At the outbreak of war in Europe on August 4, 1914,
and World War I   President Wilson proclaimed United States neutrality, and in his message to the Senate on August 19 he called for "neutrality in fact as well as in name," and for impartiality "in thought as well as in action."[6] This proved impossible for increasing numbers of citizens as the war dragged on, after German expectations of quick victories were disappointed. The interventionists increased in numbers and influence, while the neutralist, pacifist, Anglophobe, and Germanophile groups declined. But Wilson only narrowly won the 1916 election, aided by a serious slip by the California managers of his opponent (Hughes) and the slogan "He Kept Us Out of War."[7] In the next three months he earnestly strove to bring about a compromise peace. As Morison says (p. 858), "most of the country supported his every effort to evade or avoid war." On February 3, 1917, two days after the Germans instituted unrestricted submarine warfare, the president broke off diplomatic relations with Germany. The infamous Zimmermann telegram, offering Mexico terms, at the expense of

[5]Schumpeter adverted to the "moral disorganization brought about by the war and by inflation," which he considered "mainly responsible for the lack of stamina that was displayed by the ruling strata in some countries and that suddenly forced issues into practical politics for which evolution was providing, but had not yet provided, the necessary conditions." Joseph A. Schumpeter, *Business Cycles: A Theoretical, Historical, and Statistical Analysis of the Capitalist Process*, 2 vols. (New York: McGraw-Hill, 1939), 2:701-2.

[6]For the discussion here I have leaned heavily on Samuel Eliot Morison, *Oxford History of the American People* (New York: Oxford University Press, 1965), pp. 848-60. See also M. J. Bonn, *Wandering Scholar* (New York: John Day, 1948), pp. 176-82; Bernadotte E. Schmitt, "The First World War, 1914-1918," *Proceedings of the American Philosophical Society*, June 1959, 103:321-31.

[7]Commenting on Wilson's victory, the famous editor of the *Emporia* (Kansas) *Gazette* minimized the influence of the slogan, did not mention the California episode, and said "that the defeat of Hughes came about because he did not understand the divisory issues of the day." *The Autobiography of William Allen White* (New York: Macmillan, 1946), p. 532.

the United States, to draw her into a German-Mexican alliance, soon came to light.[8] This was followed by the sinking of American merchant ships without warning and with heavy loss of life. Public sentiment then quickly mounted to go beyond armed neutrality or quasi-war; the special session of the new Congress, opening on the evening of April 2, responded overwhelmingly to Wilson's appeal for a declaration of war, which the president signed with a heavy heart on Good Friday, April 6. But many die-hard pacifists and anti-war liberal intellectuals, who had warmly supported him through 1916, felt tricked[9] and persistently opposed him throughout the next four critical years.

Prior to the United States entry into the war in April 1917, Herbert Hoover had devoted his enormous energies mainly to organizing and directing the work of the Commission for the Relief of Belgium, which from November 1914 on provided food, medical aid, and clothing to some 10 million people in Belgium and northern France during the five years of German occupation and its aftermath. This "enterprise of compassion" was carried out by a large staff of American, Belgian, and other volunteers and was financed by private charity and by subsidies from the American, British, and French governments.[10] Hoover necessarily dealt with Allied war leaders. He moved freely across enemy lines to Allied and enemy capitals and to army headquarters on both sides, taking no part in military intelligence but sharing his "appraisals of the state of mind in the combatant countries" freely with United States ambassadors and with President Wilson's trusted representative, Colonel Edward M. House. Though Hoover had "no sympathy with the Allied food blockade of Germany," which impelled Germany to resort to unrestricted submarine warfare, he eventually came around to the view that the blockade must continue until the fighting stopped.[11] On May 19, 1917, Hoover was made U.S. Food Administrator, directly responsible to the president; and on August 10 he became head of the new U.S. Food Administration. He also served on the American War Council, the establishment of which he suggested, from its first meeting on March 20, 1918, to the end of hostilities.[12]

[8]Barbara Tuchman, *The Zimmermann Telegram* (New York: Viking, 1958); W. Lionel Fraser, *All to the Good* (Garden City, N.Y.: Doubleday, 1963), pp. 53–54; R. Ernest Dupuy, *5 Days to War, April 2-6, 1917* (Harrisburg, Pa.: Stackpole Books, 1967).

[9]For more recent testimony on this point, see Bernadine Kielty Scherman, *Girl from Fitchburg* (New York: Random House, 1964), pp. 106–7.

[10]This is the subject of the first volume of Herbert Hoover, *An American Epic: Famine in Forty-Five Nations*, 4 vols. (Chicago: Regnery, 1959–64). A Quaker, Hoover was reluctant to see the United States enter the war; after it did, he participated actively in its conduct. W. A. White's attitude was closely similar; see his *Autobiography*, pp. 543, 640–42.

[11]*American Epic*, 2:xi, 2–5, citing *War Memoirs of David Lloyd George*, 6 vols. (Boston: Little Brown, 1933–37), 3:199–200.

[12]*American Epic*, 2:5, 7, 47; *The Memoirs of Herbert Hoover*, vol. 1: *Years of Adventure, 1874–1920* (New York: Macmillan, 1951), p. 263; and Herbert Hoover, *The Ordeal of Woodrow Wilson* (New York: McGraw-Hill, 1958), pp. v–vi. In this book he mistakenly said that he served on the Council "throughout our participation in the war." Baruch, another member,

On February 13, 1917, at Colonel House's request, Hoover wrote a letter to the president giving his views as to "immediate steps to be taken in case we go to war with Germany." These included utilizing all the country's "resources to supply England, France, and Italy with food-stuffs and munitions" and some control of domestic food consumption to meet the threat of a food shortage before the next harvest. Shortly after this, he talked with the president, who commented favorably on his letter, welcomed an additional suggestion, and asked Hoover to "study the Allied organizations in the conduct of the war."[13] When Hoover's departure for Europe was delayed, he called on the president at Wilson's request early in March, and these subjects were again discussed. On being recalled from Europe he next saw the president on May 4, and at that time Wilson confirmed that he wished Hoover to "organize the food for war."[14] He was to provide food for Allies and neutrals during the war[15] as well as carry out related Food Administration policies and measures.

The crop year 1917–18 was the worst food year of the war—the result of very poor wheat crops in the United States, France, and Italy, an extreme shipping shortage because of the submarine sinkings, a severe winter, and other adverse factors which culminated in the powerful German drive on the Western front in March and April 1918. Both United States and Allied officials were alarmed over the threat of a severe food shortage and consequent weakening of French and Italian morale. From December 1917 through March 1918, as Hoover put it, "the spectre of famine was more terrifying than at any previous period": "starvation was threatened in all three Allied countries before the end of the summer." Because of many factors, including improved Allied organization of shipping, food, and other matters, good prospects for grain crops which the 1918 harvest justified, reduction in submarine sinkings, and increased output of ships in the United States, the threatened "great food crisis" failed to materialize.[16]

---

termed it "the War Cabinet." Bernard M. Baruch, *Baruch: The Public Years* (New York: Holt, Rinehart and Winston, 1960), pp. 85–86. See also my article, "Herbert Hoover, 1874–1964: Another Appraisal," *South Atlantic Quarterly*, Summer 1969, 68:295–318.

[13]Hoover, *Ordeal*, pp. 5–9; *American Epic*, 2:5, 7–10, and ch. 4. This work he started soon after reaching Paris and London late in March. He was shocked by the complexity of the existing Allied organization.

[14]Hoover, *Memoirs*, 1:219–25.

[15]Hoover, *American Epic*, 2:1–236.

[16]*Ibid.*, vol. 2, chs. 15–18; Hoover, *Memoirs*, vol. 1, ch. 27; and J. A. Salter, *Allied Shipping Control: An Experiment in International Administration* (Oxford: Clarendon Press, 1921), especially pp. 156–58, 197–98. Salter was secretary to the Allied Maritime Transport Council and chairman of the Allied Maritime Transport Executive, both set up in March 1918. Hoover became chairman of the Allied Food Council, set up in July 1918. From early 1918 I was in London on the staff of the American Shipping Mission, and after the AMTC was set up I worked under Salter as its statistician.

In deference to the traditional fear of entangling alliances, and on Hoover's strong advice through Colonel House to President Wilson, the United States joined the Allies only as an Associated Power.[17] Because of the president's eagerness to avoid involvement in the war, preparations for active military participation had been extremely restricted up to April 1917.[18] For more than a year thereafter, U.S. aid was largely limited to moral, financial, economic, shipping, and naval support, all of which were of the highest importance.[19] For the time this was acceptable to the Allies; but General Pershing, commander of the American Expeditionary Force, persistently called for more and more American troops. Some 180,000 of these reached France in July through December 1917; they first saw action, under French command, in February 1918.[20]

The military situation soon changed radically. On March 3, 1918, after protracted negotiations following the Bolshevik Revolution in the fall, 1917, the Soviet government accepted harsh peace terms from the Germans at Brest-Litovsk. The great German spring offensive started on March 21 and almost succeeded. On April 5, the Allied prime ministers urged President Wilson to speed the flow of American troops. On April 14, at the height of the military crisis, General Foch was made supreme commander. On June 5 Foch, Lord Milner, and Pershing cabled President Wilson for more combat troops even if insufficiently trained, and a week later the Allied prime ministers strongly seconded this request. By November the AEF numbered two million.[21]

Allied plans, however, still called for a gigantic final campaign in 1919. Hoover feared the consequences of stretching out the war for another year and found that the food situation warranted the release of vital shipping for troop transport. On August 6 he saw Pershing, and they success-

---

[17]See Hoover's letter of Feb. 13, 1917, to Colonel House. *Ordeal*, pp. 4–7, 12–31; *American Epic*, 2:3 5.

[18]Morison, *Oxford History*, pp. 861–67.

[19]Keynes wrote with authority in late 1919: "The financial history of the six months from the end of the summer of 1916 up to the entry of the United States into the war in April 1917, remains to be written. Very few persons, outside the half-dozen officials of the British Treasury who lived in daily contact with the immense anxieties and impossible financial requirements of those days, can fully realise what steadfastness and courage were needed, and how entirely hopeless the task would soon have become without the assistance of the United States Treasury. The financial problems from April 1917 onwards were of an entirely different order from those of the preceding months." J. M. Keynes, *The Economic Consequences of the Peace* (London: Macmillan, 1919), p. 256n, and the American edition, identical except for paging (New York: Harcourt Brace, 1920), p. 273n, hereafter cited as *ECP*, L., or *ECP*, N.Y. Cf. Keynes' radio talk in *Nation and Athenaeum*, May 5, 1928, quoted in his *Essays in Persuasion* (New York: Harcourt Brace, 1932).

[20]Morison, *Oxford History*, p. 865.

[21]Leonard P. Ayres, *The War with Germany: A Statistical Summary*, 2d ed. with figures revised to Aug. 1, 1919 (Washington, D.C.: U.S. Government Printing Office, 1919), ch. 1. The Selective Service Act was signed on May 19, 1917. During the war the army was built up from two hundred thousand to four million men.

fully urged on President Wilson, and the Allied High Command, a crash program involving large U.S. forces in an all-out effort to end the war in 1918 or early 1919. Allied plans were so revised, and on August 10 Pershing obtained Allied consent to his plan for an independent American army.[22]

The turn of the tide came suddenly. By August 28, if not as early as July 18, the German inner circle knew that the war was lost, though the German people still expected victory.[23] Disintegration of German morale was accelerated by shortages of food and other civilian goods, to which the Allied blockade contributed heavily, and by the spread of President Wilson's series of speeches on war objectives and peace terms, speeches which were "worth armies." Harassed by these critical developments and military setbacks, Field Marshal Hindenburg and General Ludendorff[24] urged German civilian leaders to seek an armistice before Germany was invaded. Early in October the chancellor of the new democratic government (Prince Maximilian of Baden) formally sought peace on the basis of Wilson's Fourteen Points and his subsequent addresses. After difficult negotiations, toward the end of which Kaiser Wilhelm II abdicated and found refuge in Holland, the Republic of Germany was proclaimed, Social Democratic party leader Friedrich Ebert became chancellor, and hostilities were ended by the Armistice signed on November 11, 1918.[25]

The Armistice Period, 1918–19   The signing of the Armistice produced a wave of joy and relief everywhere, even in Germany,

[22]Hoover, *American Epic*, vol. 2, ch. 18, "The Revolution in Allied Military Strategy and Its Effect on Food Supply"; Hoover, *Memoirs*, vol. 1, ch. 27; Morison, *Oxford History*, pp. 871–72.

[23]Hoover, *American Epic*, 2:169–70; Morison, *Oxford History*, pp. 872–73; Bonn, *Wandering Scholar*, pp. 182–93. Bonn helped by contributing memoranda to the German Foreign Office and by his two booklets published in Munich, *The United States as an Enemy* and *What Are Wilson's Aims?* On arriving in Berlin on Mar. 15, 1917, after nearly three years in America, Bonn's strongest impression was that "Germany is going to lose the war." See also Thomas A. Bailey, *Woodrow Wilson and the Lost Peace* (New York: Macmillan, 1944), pp. 5–33.

[24]A Canadian officer and military historian, D. J. Goodspeed, author of *Ludendorff: Genius of World War I* (Boston: Houghton Mifflin, 1966), rated Ludendorff "one of the very greatest military organizers of all time" but unfortunately "completely unequipped . . . to cope with political problems." *Foreign Affairs*, January 1967, 45:366.

[25]Hoover, *Memoirs*, 1:275–76; Hoover, *Ordeal*, chs. 4–6; Bailey, *Lost Peace*, pp. 34–54; Sidney Edward Mezes, "Preparations for Peace," in Edward M. House and Charles Seymour, eds., *What Really Happened at Paris* (New York: Scribner, 1921), pp. 8–14; Morison, *Oxford History*, p. 873; Alma Luckau, *The German Delegation at the Paris Peace Conference* (New York: Columbia University Press, 1941), ch. 1, "The Pre-Armistice Agreements . . . ," and documents 1–12, pp. 137–47; and Bonn, *Wandering Scholar*, pp. 193–200. Bonn considered Ludendorff chiefly responsible for the "dictated peace" to Russia, for failure to agree to a compromise peace early in 1918, and for losing his nerve in pressing for an armistice in September-October. *Ibid.*, pp. 188–89, 240.

where invasion and devastation were averted[26] and there was hope of peace terms far milder than Germany would have imposed if she had won.[27] In all the victorious nations victory celebrations were among the factors that helped to delay the opening of the Peace Conference for two months. Idealism burned brightly. President Wilson was acclaimed as a second Messiah. A new golden age seemed within reach, if not at hand. The end of big wars, the abolition of want, "homes fit for heroes," and vast enlargement of opportunities for all were eagerly anticipated.[28] Buying sprees, coupled with fresh postwar currency and credit expansion, drove prices up. A business boom, in this country and in Europe, was fast developing even while disillusion began to grow.[29]

The exultation was shortlived. Even before the preliminary session of the Peace Conference got under way on January 12, 1919, Europe seemed in chaos. Bolshevist moves there were alarming and puzzling. Multiple interallied disagreements delayed decisions on urgent matters. Wrangles among the Allied and Associated Powers continued over several points as the Armistice terms were altered on three renewals (December 13, January 16, and February 16)—in particular, moderation of the food blockade (not substantially relaxed until March 14, after Lloyd George's crucial intervention), the surrender of merchant vessels in German ports, the use of German gold to pay for food imports, and the organization of international cooperation during and after the Armistice.[30]

[26]What Germany escaped by the sudden ending of the war Churchill vividly described in *The Aftermath* (published Jan. 1, 1929), quoted in Winston S. Churchill, *The Second World War*, vol. 1. *The Gathering Storm* (Boston: Houghton Mifflin, 1948), pp. 39–41.

[27]See C. H. Haskins, "The New Boundaries of Germany," in House and Seymour, *Paris*, pp. 40–41, citing Ludendorff's *War Memoirs*, 1:320. The British historian of the Peace Conference termed the treaty of Bucharest (May 7, 1918) "the most damning evidence available of what a victorious Germany would have been." H. W. V. Temperley, *A History of the Peace Conference at Paris*, 6 vols. (London: Oxford University Press, 1920–24), 1:233.

[28]Keynes' comment, written in the fall of 1919 (*Economic Consequences*, p. 2), is quoted in Chapter 3 below. See also Hoover, *Memoirs*, 1:282–86, and *American Epic*, 2:286–88; Moritz J. Bonn, *The Crisis of European Democracy* (New Haven, Conn.: Yale University Press, 1925), pp. 88, 91, 93.

[29]Gustav Cassel wrote from Stockholm on Dec. 9, 1919 (*Economist*, Dec. 20, 1919, p. 1141): "The peoples of Europe generally seem to believe that the time has come for high living and reduced work." A. L. Bowley made the same point in his book *Some Economic Consequences of the War* (London: Butterworth, 1930), pp. 25–27. Hodson wrote: "The cessation of warfare was followed by a tremendous boom, with soaring prices, feverish industrial activity, wild dreams of wealth; less was earned than was spent, less was saved than was spent on capital goods. Then in 1920 and 1921, the boom collapsed, and prices too, with demoralizing swiftness." *Slump and Recovery*, p. 34. On the subsequent fall in prices, see *ibid.*, pp. 34–36.

[30]These subjects are dealt with in many sources in addition to those cited in the next two footnotes. Noteworthy are Keynes' posthumous memoir on Dr. Melchior in his *Two Memoirs* (London: Rupert Hart-Davis, 1949), and a personal reminiscence in Sir Arthur Salter, *Personality in Politics: Studies of Contemporary Statesmen* (London: Faber, 1947), pp. 44–45.

In its relations with the Allies the Wilson administration was sorely handicapped by strong domestic tendencies toward aloofness from and suspicions of Allied leaders and bureaucrats in Europe, complicated by an anti-British feeling that was not limited to Irish-Americans. By degrees, as more and more Americans—civilian, military, and naval—served on inter-allied agencies in London and elsewhere, this handicap was reduced, but it had not yet vanished when hostilities ended. Indeed, Hoover, who had long had close contact with the British, shared these sentiments and did much to disseminate them.[31]

Hoover had cordially supported the successful evolution of the inter-allied organization under the Allied Maritime Transport Council and its Executive in the last year of hostilities.[32] In October 1918 the Executive (headed by J. A. Salter) worked out a scheme for promptly converting the AMTC into a general economic council to cope with different but difficult requirements of the transition to peace. The British, French, and Italian governments agreed, as did American economic representatives in London. When the proposals reached Hoover in Washington on October 22, his immediate reaction was strongly negative. With the president's approval, on November 7 he cabled the Food Administration's European representative, Joseph P. Cotton, that "this Government will not agree to any programme that even looks like inter-Allied control of American resources after peace" and that the relevant discussions "must await Mr. Hoover's arrival in Europe." On Armistice Day it was announced that the president had requested Hoover to go over to take charge of an international relief organization, as Colonel House had suggested in his cable of November 8. (Early in January Hoover was formally appointed director general of relief.) Discussions in London on November 22 through 24 failed to yield a compromise solution, and it was not until December 12 that agreement was reached to establish a Supreme Council of Supply and Relief, under Lord Reading, with only limited scope. Set up in January 1919, this body first met on January 12, but soon proved unsatisfactory. On February 8, at Hoover's suggestion to Lord Robert Cecil, it was merged into and replaced by a Supreme Economic Council, to which the AMTC became subordinate. Salter considered the SEC to be essentially what the AMTC Executive had proposed in the revised but still tentative document that reached Wash-

---

[31]See Herbert Heaton, *A Scholar in Action: Edwin F. Gay* (Cambridge, Mass.: Harvard University Press, 1952), pp. 102–23, especially pp. 116–18. I cannot escape the conclusion that Hoover and Keynes unwittingly contributed to the breakup of wartime unity, to the desertion of Europe by the United States, and to strengthening the antipathy between France and Germany. Each great in his own way, these two men were powerfully influenced by emotions which helped distort their judgments in the first year after hostilities ended.

[32]Salter, *Allied Shipping Control*, pp. 134–215, 226–39; Hoover, *American Epic*, 2:14–16, 156–58.

ington on November 13; Hoover considered it something completely different. The three-month delay was costly, and the protracted discussions revealed and accentuated a basic divergence of viewpoints. Hoover finally won out, became the most powerful figure in the SEC but minimized its significance, and reported direct to the Council of Four of the Peace Conference.[33]

Hoover and key members of his Food Administration staff had shared the roseate outlook in their discussions on shipboard and with old friends (British and American) on their first evening in London after arriving on November 21. Within a month he had shed his illusions. On December 15, soon after President Wilson reached Paris as head of the American Peace Commission, Hoover shocked him by a gloomy reply to Wilson's question about the situation in Paris:

I remarked that the whole air had suddenly become impregnated with currents of indescribable malignity. There had been a let-down in the whole *élan* of the war. All Europe was faced with desperation. I said I could describe these attitudes in persons as the spirits of greed, robbery, power, sadistic hate and revenge. . . . Certainly the bonds of private integrity, generosity or sportsmanship would have no count in the forthcoming battle of national ambitions toward the enemies alone— that they would embrace advantages over one's partners. I said the deference to American views and wishes was already pretty weak. I was convinced America was accepted in Europe as the golden-egged goose—as such our life would be safe, but not the eggs.[34]

Wartime propaganda was heavily to blame, Salter said in mid-1924: "During the War every combatant nation had to exploit, develop and inflame national patriotism into national passion, in order to secure the motive power required for a vigorous prosecution of the war. These inflamed sensibilities and inflamed passions, together with, in some cases, suddenly

---

[33]See Salter, *Allied Shipping Control*, esp. pp. 216–46; R. F. Harrod, *The Life of John Maynard Keynes* (New York: Harcourt Brace, 1951), pp. 234–35. Hoover, *American Epic*, 2:251–352, esp. p. 284n; 3:31, 52–53, 85–97; Hoover, *Memoirs*, 1:276–79, 287–99, 310–12; and Hoover, *Ordeal*, pp. 263–75. The AMTC became subordinate to the SEC, but its chairman, Lord Robert Cecil, most often chaired the SEC, and Salter was secretary of the British SEC delegation as well as of the AMTC. The truth about the SEC lies somewhere between Hoover's belittling representation and Ray Stannard Baker's laudatory description in his *Woodrow Wilson and World Settlement*, 3 vols. (New York: Doubleday Page, 1923), 2:335, which Harrod quoted in his *Keynes*, pp. 234–35. The minutes of the SEC (which show that Keynes did not attend regularly) suggest that the Council served useful purposes. For several months before it expired, the SEC sponsored the *Monthly Statistical Bulletin*, which the League of Nations took over in mid-1920.

[34]Hoover, *America's First Crusade* (New York: Scribner, 1941), pp. 29–30; Hoover, *Memoirs*, 1:437–52; Hoover, *Ordeal*, p. 68; Hoover, *American Epic*, 2:261–62, 282. Three months later Wilson wearily remarked to him: "I have often agreed with you." On the state of mind of Americans, Germans, French, and British in October-December 1918, see Bailey, *Lost Peace*, pp. 34–70.

revived national aspirations after centuries of oppression, remain as a major difficulty in the maintenance of peace at present."[35]

In the United States the official Committee on Public Information (CPI), headed by George Creel, produced highly effective propaganda which unfortunately "oversold" the president's Fourteen Points, but Creel was embarrassed by the hate campaign of super-patriotic organizations— contrary to official policy—which the CPI vainly tried to curb.[36] In Germany and France the buildup of hatred was of longer duration. The Germans had earned the bitter enmity and fears of the French, not only by the Franco-Prussian War of 1870, the "rape" of Alsace-Lorraine, and the indemnity then exacted, but also by humiliating diplomacy under Bismarck and his successors, the 1914 invasion through Belgium, and wanton destruction by the retreating German armies in 1918.[37] In Great Britain the climate was further poisoned by arrant demagoguery in the "khaki election" campaign in December 1918.[38] The propaganda of all the combatant nations also whipped up "unrealizable expectations."[39] Count Harry Kessler, a liberal German diplomat, termed "the worst devastation wrought by the war . . . the poisoning of the moral atmosphere," but he also emphasized (as Hoover did not) the pacifist counterforces that had gained headway even during the war.[40]

In lurid terms Hoover wrote later: "Impoverishment, famine, revolution, hate, nationalism and all the other plagues" sat at the peace table:[41]

The future of twenty-six jealous European races was there. The genes of a thousand years of inbred hate and fear of every generation were in their blood. Revenge for past wrongs rose every hour of the day. It was not alone the delegates that were thus inspired. These emotions of hate, revenge, desire for reparations, and a righteous sense of wrong were at fever heat in their peoples at home. England

---

[35]Sir Arthur Salter, *Europe's Recovery: What It Means to World Peace* (remarks before the Institute of Politics, Williamstown, Mass., August 1924) (New York: League of Nations Non-Partisan Association, 1924), p. 24.

[36]See George Creel's autobiography, *Rebel at Large* (New York: Putnam, 1947), esp. ch. 25, "High Priests of Hate," and the president's commendatory lettter of Mar. 20, 1919, on p. 221. See also Bailey, *Lost Peace*, pp. 27–29. Morison condemns Creel, ignoring or declining to accept his defense against the charges. *Oxford History*, pp. 873–74, 886.

[37]In his lecture at the Institute of Politics (Williamstown, Mass.) in the summer of 1923, Lord Birkenhead stressed this. See *Approaches to World Problems* by Birkenhead, T. H. Bliss, and P. H. Kerr (New Haven, Conn.: Yale University Press, 1924), esp. pp. 14–15; William MacDonald, *Reconstruction in France* (New York: Macmillan, 1922), pp. 41–46.

[38]David Lloyd George, in *The Truth about the Peace Treaties*, 2 vols. (London: Gollancz, 1938), 1:157–79, naturally stressed other aspects of the campaign. Cf. C. L. Mowat, *Britain between the Wars, 1918–1940* (London: Methuen, 1955), pp. 2–3.

[39]Bailey, *Lost Peace*, pp. 243–45.

[40]*Germany and Europe* (New Haven, Conn.: Yale University Press, 1923), pp. 12–19. Cf. also James Bryce (Viscount Bryce), *International Relations* (New York: Macmillan, 1927), pp. 255–56.

[41]*America's First Crusade*, pp. viii, 9–10.

after the Armistice had just re-elected Lloyd George on a platform of 'Hang the Kaiser' and wringing from the enemy fantastic indemnities for Britain. Clemenceau had secured a vote of confidence from the French National Assembly with a blood-thirsty program to render Germany innocuous for all time, and collect every centime of French losses. The oppressed races were there, with their recollection of infinite wrong. Every warring nation in Europe was exhausted, economically desperate, and most of them hungry.

Their officials naturally wanted every atom of advantage for their people that could be secured. Their delegations at Paris had to go home to governments still in these fevers and get subsequent parliamentary approval of their actions. Moreover, every Allied official had a high regard for his future political life.

The statesmen were shackled by these malign forces. None of them were free to make peace on the twenty-five points even if they had wanted to. Moreover, the governments of the Allies were committed to a maze of secret treaties dividing the spoils of victory.[42]

Clearly the psychological climate was far from conducive to writing the kind of peace treaties that were desperately needed. Moreover, the dislocation caused by the war was far more serious than the actual destruction, and the element of good will, dependent on trade connections and good credit, which received the severest blows, could be restored only by a slow and painful process.[43]

In his customary vigorous language, Hoover repeatedly painted a dire picture of what the Allied and Associated Powers faced in the liberated and enemy countries at the moment of the Armistice: threat of chaos, imminent danger of economic collapse, the most terrible famine since the Thirty Years' War, racial hatreds of centuries reaching white heat, dismembered transportation systems, paralysis of production and interchange of commodities, food-hoarding become a mania, cities and towns in acute need, strikes, seizure of private property by government, general let-down of discipline. "The whole mass of urban humanity formerly under enemy domination seemed headed directly for Bolshevism, or anarchy."[44] More extravagantly still, Hoover wrote much later: "Even before the Armistice was signed it was obvious that a gigantic famine would follow." Then "the curtain was lifted on the greatest famine of all times."[45] This he presumably believed, and persuaded Keynes and many others to believe, at the time.[46]

[42]*Memoirs*, 1:437–38. The "twenty-five points" were Wilson's famous "Fourteen Points" plus eleven drawn from his later addresses. *Ibid.*, pp. 434–35. See also Bailey, *Lost Peace*, pp. 333–36.

[43]Bowley, *Economic Consequences*, pp. 93–97.

[44]"The Economic Administration during the Armistice," in House and Seymour, *Paris*, pp. 336–38; Hoover, *American Epic*, 3:241–42 (a condensation of Colonel Carlson's report of June 27, 1919, "The Condition of the Children").

[45]*American Epic*, 2:239, 241.

[46]Keynes, who came to know and admire Hoover in their work on the Supreme Economic Council in January through June 1919, was greatly influenced by Hoover's gloomy views

Sir Arthur Salter put the situation more soberly, but starkly enough, when he wrote in 1932:

When, in 1919, at the Supreme Economic Council in Paris, we surveyed a world shattered in over four years of the most destructive war in history; the grave shortages of food and raw materials; the breakdown in communications by sea and land; the loss by death of many millions of workers in their prime; the disorganization of currencies and public finances; the staggering load of debts; the dislocation of the channels of trade and the mechanism of industry; the profound changes in the habits and desires of man; revolutions and actual starvation in several countries, and the grave impoverishment in many others; the inflamed passions and new political grievances which threatened new wars as soon as there were again the energy and resources to wage them. . . .

Many, indeed, of those best qualified to judge, believed that the foundations on which the fragile, precarious, and soaring fabric of Western civilization had been built were fatally undermined; that the delicate and intricate mechanism of money and finance which alone enabled man to find a market for his goods in every continent, and enrich his daily life with the products of every clime, was irremediably destroyed. Prophecies of universal bankruptcy, of a return to the conditions of barter, of a rapid or gradual sagging of standards and modes of life to the levels of the days before the Industrial Revolution, were frequent and sometimes, apparently, authoritative.[47]

In the face of urgency to avert such a fate, prompt agreement on peace terms seemed imperative, and the two-month delay in assembling the Peace Conference and the five and a half months required to formulate the treaties and get them signed seemed far too long. Considering the magnitude and complications of the peacemaking task and the divergence of viewpoints and prior commitments (through public pronouncements and secret treaties) that had to be compromised, the time was remarkably short. Foch, House, and Hoover were among those who urged that there be two peace treaties, one preliminary and another final. Morison later wrote: "it is now clear that the Allies could and should before the new year dawned, have lifted the blockade, fed the hungry, and drafted a preliminary treaty leaving the working out of a definitive treaty and league to professional diplomats at a plenary conference with those of the defeated powers."[48] In mid-April 1919, this idea was abandoned as impractical for a variety of reasons,[49] though several solutions were wisely deferred. But the speed of

when, in August and September, he dashed off the manuscript of his famous *ECP* (see, e.g., the London edition, pp. 2, 5, 209, 211, 233).

[47]*Recovery: The Second Effort* (New York: Century, 1932), pp. 27–28. The conditions existing in Europe at the end of hostilities are touched upon in various papers in House and Seymour, *Paris*, and extensively in Hoover's address, "Economic Administration."

[48]*Oxford History*, p. 877.

[49]See Ray Stannard Baker, *The Versailles Treaty and After* (New York: Doran, 1924), p. 31; and Bailey, *Lost Peace*, pp. 210–14, 323.

the process inevitably resulted in blunders that were relentlessly magnified and distorted at the time and afterward.[50]

The Peace Conference, January–June 1919 For our purposes it is unnecessary to summarize fully the complicated story of the Peace Conference which formally opened in Paris on January 12, 1919; the drafting of the peace treaties and the forcing of the German signature on June 28; the widespread furor over the peace terms; President Wilson's efforts to arouse the American people to support the Versailles treaty and the covenant of the League of Nations, his collapse on September 25, 1919, and his stroke soon after; the initial decisions of the Senate not to approve the treaty on November 19; Wilson's obdurate refusal to accept any reservations to the covenant; the narrow failure of the treaty to win a two-thirds majority of the Senate on March 19, 1920; and the shock to the Allies from this "betrayal."[51] Yet several points must be made, first about the Peace Conference itself.

A large number of nations were involved. There were five principal Allied and Associated Powers: the British Empire, comprising the United Kingdom and five dominions—Canada, Australia, New Zealand, South Africa, and India—France, Italy, Japan, and the United States. There were twenty-two lesser powers on the same side. Of the Central Powers, only Germany was allowed a small part at the end. The Soviet Union was not formally represented, but its disturbing presence was felt throughout the Conference, and a rebellious Ukrainian delegation was among many that sought to have its position heard and considered.

There was no real meeting of minds on the precise nature of the "agreed" armistice terms.[52] In the absence of a joint statement of war aims, which Wilson had failed to secure, the armistice terms were based on his eloquent addresses in January through September 1918 containing

[50]The "blunders" made before, at, and after the Peace Conference are dealt with meticulously and at length in Bailey, *Lost Peace*, at the end of which he stressed "certain basic principles which the American people should keep in mind at the end of a great world conflict" (pp. 322–25). Cf. also Churchill, *Gathering Storm*, ch. 1, "The Follies of the Victors."

[51]This sorry story is forthrightly told, in great detail and with excellent citations, in Bailey's *Lost Peace* and in his *Woodrow Wilson and the Great Betrayal* (New York: Macmillan, 1945). Despite my admiration for these works, I have to disagree with Bailey's judgments on several points. Many later publications add to or modify his treatment in important respects, e.g., the first volume of Hoover's *Memoirs*; his *Ordeal* and *American Epic*; Salter's *Personality in Politics* and *Memoirs of a Public Servant* (London: Faber, 1961), esp. ch. 7 of the latter; and *Encyclopedia Americana* (1958 ed.), s.v. "War, European."

[52]Bailey, *Lost Peace*, chs. 2–3 and pp. 332–37; Harold Nicolson, *Peacemaking, 1919: Being Reminiscences of the Paris Peace Conference* (Boston: Houghton Mifflin, 1933), pp. 12–17. Then an able young diplomat in the British delegation to the Peace Conference, Nicolson (1888–1968) kept a diary major portions of which were appended to his *Peacemaking*. This book describes the atmosphere of the conference and shows how many specific decisions were arrived at, but is not above censure as hypercritical and often unfair.

his famous "Fourteen Points" and later additions. These were "rained" on
Germany and Austria-Hungary, and generally aroused hopes impossible of
fulfillment[53] which were exaggerated by Wilson's speeches in England and
Italy in December and January. In October and November 1918 the Allied
governments agreed to make peace on the basis of these points (excepting
only the one on "freedom of the seas"), and the Germans did also. In the
course of the pre-Armistice discussions, Colonel House had submitted to
the Supreme War Council of the Allied Powers a commentary on Wilson's
Fourteen Points and later addresses, largely the work of Walter Lippmann
and Frank Cobb, Wilson's close friend and adviser. The president approved
the text on October 30, adding that "details of application mentioned
should be regarded as merely illustrative suggestions and reserved for the
peace conference." In the hectic last fortnight of active hostilities, however, this vital document could not be thoroughly considered by the staffs
of the Allied Powers. It was apparently not shown to the Germans, and
was not published until 1928. Hence not only were the "points" used for a
purpose for which they were not designed, but there was wide leeway for
differences in their interpretation. This inevitably gave rise to friction in
drafting the peace treaties, to charges of flagrant violation of promises
made,[54] and to lasting bitterness.

Serious divergence of viewpoints among the victorious powers soon
came to light. The French, British, and Italians realized that massive
American financial, economic, and military participation in the war had
been decisive for victory and that Wilson's diplomacy had brought about an
early armistice, but were understandably unwilling to have this powerful
but remote Associated Power dictate the peace terms. Most basic was the
well-founded, deep-seated French fear and distrust of the Germans, which
dominated their attitudes on almost every issue and of which President
Wilson seemed inadequately aware. Obsessed by the paramount need for
security against future aggression, the French sought to exact reparations
in ways that would keep Germany weak. Idealism and realism were not
easily reconciled. Wilson opposed the balance of power idea which
Clemenceau strongly supported. Irreconcilable conflicts grew out of
numerous secret treaties made during the war.[55] Compromises were

---

[53]Widely quoted slogans were "a just peace," "open covenants of peace openly arrived
at," "make the world safe for democracy," and "self-determination of peoples."

[54]Nicolson undertook to show that nineteen out of twenty-three of Wilson's points were
"flagrantly violated" in the draft treaty. Keynes, Lippmann, Hoover, and many others also
voiced their deep unhappiness privately and publicly.

[55]After Russia's collapse, the Bolshevik government released some of these, which the
Manchester Guardian Commercial (and other journals) published late in 1917. See André
Tardieu, *The Truth about the Treaty* (Indianapolis, Ind.: Bobbs-Merrill, 1922), p. 88;
Temperley, *Peace Conference*, 6:1–22; Charles Seymour, ed., *The Intimate Papers of
Colonel House*, 4 vols. (Boston: Houghton Mifflin, 1926–28), 3:38–51, 61–63, 4:265, 272, 364–
65; Nicolson, *Peacemaking*, chs. 6–7, esp. pp. 146–52, 171; Bailey, *Lost Peace*, pp. 31, 141–49.

worked out with great difficulty and delay,[56] and some decisions were
made which were adverse to strong commitments by political leaders.
There were repeated crises and threats of blowup and breakdown. Within
each national group sharp differences of opinion emerged, even between
top leaders and their chief advisers—such as Wilson, Lansing, House,
Hoover, and Baruch—some of which led to strains on and breaks in personal relations.

Though not supermen, the prestigious war leaders who dominated
the Peace Conference were very able men with divergent personalities
and strongly clashing views and commitments who were forced to cope
with personal, domestic, and international crises while reaching agreement
on peace terms. Clemenceau, Lloyd George, and Wilson were the Big
Three of the conference.[57] Each had outstanding strengths and weaknesses. Each had "certain personal qualities which irritated and antago-
nized to an extraordinary degree those people who did not like him."[58] All
had "whipped up unrealizable expectations."[59] Each had to face changing
public and political opinion in his own country, was watched closely
throughout the Peace Conference, and was incessantly attacked in legislative chambers and in the press. None dominated all decisions; each won
points but had to give in on others. Tensions among them at times became
acute.

Georges Clemenceau, an old political war horse ("The Tiger") who
had been French premier in 1906–9, again came to power late in the fall of
1917. With Marshal Foch and President Poincaré he was regarded as
having a major responsibility for the Allied victory, and late in 1918 he

[56]Bailey perhaps too harshly observed: "One tragedy of the Peace Conference was that
men compromised when they should have stood up, and they stood up when they should have
compromised. But," he rightly added, "they were mortal men, and it was not given them to
see the future." *Lost Peace*, p. 270. On the organization to deal with relief and reconstruction during the armistice Hoover, backed by Wilson, soon won out over Allied opposition led
by the British. On the continuance of the blockade to ensure German acceptance of the
peace terms, the French lost out only after four months' delay, and then only partially.
French pressures for a new frontier on the Rhine and partial dismemberment of Germany
were eventually met by agreement on an Anglo-American-French security treaty—which the
Senate later pigeonholed. Over the reparations provisions of the treaty, the eventual compromise satisfied no nation. Related to this, though American representatives refused to
admit the fact, was the obdurate American resistance to pressure from the French and British
for a joint settlement of the Allied war debts with substantial reductions. Lesser but still
important issues included Upper Silesia, the Saar, Fiume, Austria, the Tyrol, and Shantung, on most of which workable deferred solutions were reached.

[57]Keynes, *ECP*, ch. 3; Robert Lansing, *The Big Four and Others of the Peace Conference*
(New York: Houghton Mifflin, 1921); and Bailey, *Lost Peace*, ch. 10, "The Olympians";
Salter, *Personality in Politics*, chs. 3, 11, 14, et passim (see index). The Salter book is excep-
tionally perceptive.

[58]Anderson later said this of Wilson, whom he greatly admired. B. M. Anderson, *Economics and the Public Welfare: Financial and Economic History of the United States, 1914–
1946* (New York: Van Nostrand, 1949), p. 90.

[59]As Bailey said of Lloyd George. *Lost Peace*, p. 203.

won a decisive vote of confidence in the Chamber of Deputies. A cynical realist above all, he personified the dominant French attitude toward the Germans.[60] He was absent for a time after an assassin shot him in the lung on February 19.

David Lloyd George, long a leading minister in British Liberal governments, had been prime minister for the last two years of the war, heading a coalition government in which the Tory Andrew Bonar Law served as his deputy. In mid-December 1918 the government sought a new mandate from the people, since the old Parliament had been elected in 1910. Though Labour members and Asquith Liberals deserted the coalition, it won an overwhelming victory with predominantly Conservative members, and the badly split Liberal Party never regained power. A wily, agile, resourceful politician, with a statesman's experience, Lloyd George was often forced to go to London to respond to his critics,[61] as well as to struggle with serious problems in Ireland and India.[62]

President Wilson, against the advice of several of his closest advisers, took the unprecedented step of going to Paris as head of the American Commission to Negotiate Peace, where he arrived on December 13. At the outset he overshadowed Clemenceau, Lloyd George, and Orlando like a veritable Colossus.[63] The opening plenary session of the Conference on January 25 resolved that a League of Nations be created and its covenant incorporated in the peace treaties. Inauspiciously, in the November 1918 elections, after Wilson's ill-starred appeal to elect Democrats, the Republicans had won majorities in both houses of Congress, and Senator Henry Cabot Lodge, his *bête noire*, became chairman of the Senate Committee on Foreign Relations, which he packed with senators hostile to the League.[64] This political setback was promptly made known in Europe, and ex-president Theodore Roosevelt, "who next to Wilson was

[60]In his *ECP* (L., pp. 24–33, esp. p. 29) Keynes characterized this eminent Frenchman with considerable accuracy and sympathy, though he viewed his influence on the treaty as pernicious. Mantoux called this characterization "masterly, and it is beyond anyone's power to equal it." Étienne Mantoux, *The Carthaginian Peace, or the Economic Consequences of Mr. Keynes* (London: Oxford University Press, 1945), quoted in Harrod, *Keynes*, p. 268. Salter called it "both incomplete and unjust." *Personality in Politics*, p. 191.

[61]In 1919 Keynes wrote a rather savage appraisal of Lloyd George, whom he had bitterly criticized in private and who had largely ignored him in Paris; but he left most of this out of his *ECP* and published it years later (*Essays in Biography* [London: Macmillan, 1933]) after they had collaborated on various political issues. Harrod, Keynes' biographer, recently wrote that Lloyd George never forgave him for it. *EJ*, December 1971, 81:336–39. Cf. Salter, *Personality in Politics*, pp. 38–53 et passim.

[62]See Mowat, *Britain between the Wars*, pp. 57–66, 110–11.

[63]Keynes' picture of Wilson at the Conference (*ECP*, L., pp. 33–50) contained elements of truth but was based on inadequate evidence and struck those better informed as flagrantly in error—indeed, a caricature. Keynes' friend Salter had vainly urged him to omit or change it. Salter, *Personality in Politics*, pp. 141–42.

[64]Bailey, *Great Betrayal*, pp. 70–75.

the most influential American abroad," and who "hated Wilson and all his works," publicly asserted that the president's leadership had already been emphatically repudiated by the American people. On February 15, the day after a commission draft of the covenant had been agreed upon, Wilson sailed home and was gone for a month. On his return he was unhappy over developments in his absence and with Colonel House's part in them.[65] A revised draft, proposed by a new commission, was unanimously approved at a plenary session on April 25. Meanwhile, several crucial issues came to a head. For several days in early April Wilson was laid up by a severe cold with complications.[66] Yet he continued to play an important role in decisions until the German treaty was signed.[67]

Prime Minister Orlando of Italy was also a member of the Council of Four, which from late March 1919 dominated decisions on the draft treaty, but he played only a small part. He could not speak English; he was frequently absent; on April 23 he bolted the Conference over the Fiume decision adverse to Italian claims; he returned just before the treaty was presented to the Germans, only to be replaced before it was signed.[68]

Exceptional preparations for the Conference had been made, and large numbers of able personnel were assembled.[69] The British and U.S. delegations included government officials of high rank, outstanding civil

[65]Bailey, *Lost Peace*, p. 57 and ch. 14.

[66]*Ibid.*, pp. 221–23. There are diverse views as to the nature of this illness. Hoover later reported medical testimony that there was a painful infection of the prostate gland. *Ordeal*, pp. 198–99. William C. Bullitt and Sigmund Freud collaborated in writing, over a period of ten years (1922–32), a study of Woodrow Wilson of which an agreed version was completed in 1938 but published only years later: *Thomas Woodrow Wilson: Twenty-Eighth President of the United States—a Psychological Study* (Boston: Houghton Mifflin, 1967). Advance excerpts from this appeared in *Look*, Dec. 13, 1966, pp. 36–48. Allen W. Dulles, a one-time Princeton student and life-long admirer of Wilson, contributed to the same issue his criticisms of the Freud-Bullitt article.

Both Bullitt and Dulles were with the American delegation at the Peace Conference. Bullitt, who had been deeply offended by Wilson's ignoring of the Lenin peace proposal that he had negotiated, attacked the peace treaty before the Senate Committee on Foreign Relations in September 1919. Dulles says that Wilson "never was himself after a heavy attack of the flu in April, 1919"—the illness which, at its outset, Freud and Bullitt graphically described (p. 46). They claimed that when the president boarded the *George Washington* on February 15 to return home, "he was close to nervous collapse" (p. 44), and that his actions and reactions after his return to Europe on March 14 were "evidence of a divorce from reality that was beginning to characterize Wilson's mental life" (p. 46).

[67]This is made clear in Bailey, *Lost Peace*, House and Seymour, *Paris*, and many other books, even when the writers disagreed with the decisions. As Bailey put it, "John Maynard Keynes and Harold Nicolson have done the cause of truth no service by stereotyping Wilson as an ignorant fumbler who was 'bamboozled' by the European frock coats. He made his errors, as they all did, but his average of constructive achievement was high." *Lost Peace*, p. 83. Cf. Morison, *Oxford History*, p. 879n.

[68]Bailey, *Lost Peace*, pp. 137, 159–60, 262–64, 268–69, 312.

[69]See especially House and Seymour, *Paris*, esp. chs. 1–2: Mezes, "Preparations for Peace," and Clive Day, "The Atmosphere and Organization of the Peace Conference." Mezes, the director of the inquiry, apparently did not recognize the weakness on the eco-

servants and diplomats of large experience, lawyers, bankers, and experts in almost every field. The whole French government was on tap and had a disproportionate voice in program and machinery. The list of key personnel certainly must include Marshal Foch, André Tardieu, Captain Paul Mantoux, and Léon Bourgeois; Lord Robert Cecil, Sir Maurice Hankey, Philip Kerr, Sir Eric Drummond, and J. A. Salter; Colonel House, Herbert Hoover, Bernard Baruch, Joseph C. Grew, Thomas W. Lamont, C. H. Haskins, Isaiah Bowman, and J. F. Dulles; General Jan Smuts of South Africa; and Premier Venizelos of Greece. Professional economists figured minimally. Keynes had not won Lloyd George's confidence and was given no place on the commission on reparations. Allyn A. Young, a prominent economist, was very belatedly included in the American delegation, and Wilson's economic advisory group consisted of non-economists: Hoover, Baruch, Norman Davis, Vance McCormick, and Henry M. Robinson.[70] Inevitably there were divergences of opinion, personality clashes, and serious imperfections of communication, yet Young stressed the "unity of spirit and purpose" and "common loyalty to high leadership."[71]

The staff of the U.S. delegation included able historians, political scientists, geographers, and legal specialists, many of whom had been active under Colonel House's leadership in doing research on issues expected to arise at the Peace Conference.[72] It also included wartime officials, persons experienced in relief work, and officers detached from military duty because of special qualifications. Its work proved of great value. Individual experts were frequently called upon for specific advice, but their experiences were often frustrating, they were often unhappy, even bitter, over decisions made against or without their advice, and several quit before the final session.[73]

The Peace Conference labored under many special handicaps. Paris was shattered, crowded, underfed, and underheated; it sometimes seemed a veritable madhouse.[74] The French press was corrupt, corruptible, and servile to the government, which leaked to favored newspapers. The city swarmed with reporters who worked diligently within the confines of the

nomic side, which was probably the basis for Felix Frankfurter's exaggerated statement in the *New Republic* of early 1919 that Wilson's "unpreparedness" was the secret of his "failure" in Paris. Heaton, *Scholar in Action*, pp. 432–35.

[70]Hoover, *America's First Crusade*, esp. pp. 34–48.

[71]House and Seymour, *Paris*, p. 294.

[72]See L. E. Galfand, *The Inquiry: American Preparations for Peace, 1917–18* (New Haven, Conn.: Yale University Press, 1963).

[73]A. M. Schlesinger, Jr., *The Crisis of the Old Order, 1919–1933* (Boston: Houghton Mifflin, 1957), ch. 2, mentioning Adolf A. Berle, Jr., William C. Bullitt, and Samuel E. Morison.

[74]Bailey (*Lost Peace*, p. 243) quoted Churchill as describing the conference as "a turbulent collision of embarrassed demagogues." Many others, including Clemenceau, Lloyd George, Keynes, and Nicolson, made similarly exaggerated statements.

highly restrictive publicity policy early decided upon.[75] In addition to the large delegations of the principal Allied and Associated Powers, official and unofficial delegations from many other countries arrived and insisted on having a hearing. Germany and the broken remnants of the Austro-Hungarian Empire were in political and social turmoil as well as economic distress. Russia, still in the throes of revolution, was the source of distracting problems which were faced with only limited success. The worldwide influenza epidemic, which began in the autumn of 1918, played havoc in the armed services and raised death rates and lowered birth rates almost all over the world. It raged furiously among the British delegation, putting Keynes out of action for weeks.[76] Others were ill at crucial times with the flu or other causes. Nicolson rightly stressed the confusion that prevailed in Paris, "the appalling dispersal of energy," "the eternal inadequacy of human intelligence," the facts that "human error is a permanent factor in history" and that under the conditions of the first half of 1919 "it would have been impossible even for supermen to devise a peace of moderation and righteousness."[77]

Though no advance agreement on how the Conference should function was reached, workable procedures were evolved, largely under the guidance of the French and British. Wilson and Lloyd George virtually ignored draft plans of conference procedure which were worked out by the French under Tardieu's supervision and which Ambassador Jusserand handed to Wilson on November 29, 1918. After revisions in January, when Colonel House was ill with the flu, and informal negotiations among the Great Powers, a substitute for the French plans was ready when the Conference opened. From January 13 to March 25, 1919, the Council of Ten, with two representatives each from France, Britain, Italy, the United States, and Japan, was the official source of authority; it set up commissions to prepare reports on special subjects and heard many minor delegations present their pleas. Thereafter the Council of Four, composed of Wilson, Lloyd George, Clemenceau, and Orlando, took over.[78]

---

[75]In a memorandum of July 12, 1919, to the secretary general (Sir Eric Drummond) urging the importance of admitting the press to the League council meetings from the start, Raymond B. Fosdick said: "The decision to curtail the privileges of the press representatives at the Peace Conference in Paris, and to inform the public of the proceedings only through emasculated communiques did more than any other single factor to shake the confidence of the United States in the good faith of the peace negotiations and in honesty of the treaty itself." *Letters on the League of Nations* (Princeton, N.J.: Princeton University Press, 1966), pp. 6–8. Cf. Bailey, *Lost Peace*, pp. 127–33.

[76]Harrod thought it conceivable that, "but for the influenza, we might have had a slightly better peace treaty." *Keynes*, p. 234.

[77]*Peacemaking*, ch. 1.

[78]Baker, *Woodrow Wilson and World Settlement*, 2:56–63; Tardieu, *Truth about the Treaty*, pp. 88, 91; Seymour, *House Papers*, 4:271–73; Clive Day, "Peace Conference."

The hundreds of articles of the Versailles Treaty were drafted by some sixty commissions (many of them with subcommissions), each made up of representatives of the Allied and Associated Powers, in frequent consultation with their top leaders. Each of the U.S. plenipotentiaries was a member of one or more commissions, and other Americans were drawn partly from those who had worked in Colonel House's inquiry group and partly from other key personnel called to Paris. Draft sections, and eventually completed drafts, came to the Council of Four for review, modification, and approval.[79]

Gradually the draft treaty took shape. On January 25, the Conference resolved that a League of Nations should be created and that its covenant should be incorporated in the peace treaties. Wilson chaired the commission then set up to draft this document, which was completed just before he sailed for home on February 15. On April 28 a revised draft was unanimously approved in plenary session.[80] Sir Eric Drummond was promptly agreed upon as its secretary-general, with R. B. Fosdick and Jean Monnet his deputies; steps were taken to set up its provisional organization in London until it could be moved to Geneva, the permanent seat agreed upon on April 10.[81]

By mid-April most of the other sections had been approved by the Council of Four. On April 18 the Supreme Council wired the German government an invitation to send a delegation to Versailles to receive the draft treaty on April 25, which proved too early. The delegation arrived in Paris late on April 29. For their protection the delegates and experts, technical staff, and press were barricaded in three hotels. Credentials were formally exchanged at noon on May 1.[82] Finally, after major crises had caused further delays, the entire draft was unanimously approved at a plenary session of the Conference on May 6, over protests by Marshal Foch and others. Next day it was made available for the first time to all concerned. It precipitated a flood of criticisms, completed the disillusionment of liberal insiders such as Nicolson, Keynes, Smuts, and Hoover,[83]

[79]The treaty-drafting process is well described by several of the contributors to House and Seymour, *Paris*, e.g., Charles Seymour, Thomas W. Lamont, and Allyn A. Young.

[80]Seymour, *House Papers*, 4:424, 426n; Bailey, *Lost Peace*, chs. 12–13 and pp. 214–18, 352–55; Bailey, *Great Betrayal*, p. 288. For good political reasons, Wilson opposed prompt organization of the League, but important progress had been made when the council first met on Jan. 16, 1920.

[81]Fosdick, *Letters on the League*, passim. Fosdick resigned on Jan. 19, 1920.

[82]Luckau, *German Delegation*, p. 59, and docs. 17–18, 22–26, 29–30; Bonn, *Wandering Scholar*, pp. 226–28. Though not on the "Preliminary List of the German Peace Delegation," Bonn's name later appeared as a member of a subcommission of the Legal Commission. Luckau, *German Delegation*, doc. 18, June 6, 1919.

[83]See Hoover, *America's First Crusade*, pp. 50–51; Hoover, *Memoirs*, 1, ch. 52. Vance McCormick was chairman of the War Trade Board and, after he arrived in Paris early in February 1919, chairman of the Superior Blockade Council. With Hoover and Baruch, he was

and was violently attacked by others who considered its terms too soft. The German reaction was "bitter in the extreme," and the German president, Ebert, called it a "monstrous document."[84]

After weeks of acrimonious discussions and repeated crises, the draft treaty of more than two hundred pages was ceremoniously presented to the German peace delegation on May 7, 1919, introduced in a brusque speech by Clemenceau. Count Ulrich von Brockdorff-Rantzau, chairman of the delegation, tactlessly remained seated while he read a lengthy reply, poorly put together from several drafts, in which he bluntly stated the German position on some of the issues.[85] Interim notes on specific points followed, to which Allied notes replied. During this interval Lloyd George, after a stormy visit to London led him to fear his political downfall, tried to get the terms softened, but Clemenceau and Wilson would not countenance a last-moment rewriting of the pact.[86] The detailed comments by the German delegation on the peace terms were submitted on May 29. The 35,000-word Allied reply on June 16 made a few minor concessions and also provided for a plebiscite on Upper Silesia (Art. 88). On June 19 two hundred copies of the printed text with corrections, alterations, and comments on alleged discrepancies were sent to the German delegation.[87] Next day the German chancellor (Scheidemann) and Brockdorff-Rantzau resigned rather than accept the terms. For a few days there was renewed alarm that the Germans might refuse to sign, and Marshal Foch prepared to march into Germany.[88]

Despite their grievances, the Germans were soon forced to sign the treaty. They had many grounds for complaint, some of them well-founded: hardening of the Armistice terms in three successive renewals, and violation of several of those terms; long continuance of the food blockade; ex-

one of the president's key advisers. McCormick's diary of June 14, 1919, mentions a "hot discussion" at lunch with other American advisers in his room "on treaty and blockade": "Hoover and Bliss think it too hard. Baruch and I think it just and workable. Hoover says if blockade [is] imposed he will resign." Hoover, *American Epic*, 3:52, 96.

[84] Bailey, *Lost Peace*, p. 292.

[85] House wrote that day: "If I had been in his position I should have said: 'Mr. President, and gentlemen of the Congress: War is a great gamble; we have lost and are willing to submit to any reasonable terms.' " Seymour, *House Papers*, 4:456–58, quoted in Bailey, *Lost Peace*, p. 291.

[86] See especially Baruch, *Public Years*, pp. 118–21. This was the basis for Keynes' assertion (*ECP*, ch. 3) that "in the last act the President stood for stubbornness and refusal of conciliations." Hoover had previously won Wilson over on many points but shared Keynes' initial reaction to the draft treaty and tried to get Wilson to agree to modify the terms; this succeeded only in alienating the president. Hoover, *Memoirs*, 1:433, 463–67, 473–78.

[87] Luckau, *German Delegation*, pp. 31–40, 46, 55, docs. 28–60, and pp. 472–79; Mantoux, *Carthaginian Peace*, pp. 47, 61–64.

[88] Reimposition of the blockade was prepared for, over Hoover's strong protest, but not publicly threatened, and the Supreme War Council decided on June 13 that its enforcement would depend on a further decision by the Council of the Principal Powers. Hoover, *Ordeal*, pp. 229–32.

posure of French efforts to foment separatist movements; Allied denial of the opportunity for oral arguments over the treaty provisions; and compulsion to admit full responsibility for the war[89] and to sign what Germany viewed as a blank check for reparations far beyond its capacity to honor. The German representatives could not but be aware of the hatred their actions during the war had earned, made no defense of the invasion of Belgium contrary to their own commitments, made no objection to full compensation to that country, admitted their liability for restoring devastated areas in northern France, and sourly accepted the fact that they had lost the war—itself a new and shattering experience. Unconvinced by the Allied notes in reply, they magnified the evil consequences of the treaty and regarded Germany's future as hopeless.

Nevertheless, the new German chancellor and foreign minister (Bauer and Erzberger), faced with certain military occupation and the threat of secessions of the Rhineland and Bavaria, rejected the advice of the German High Command and on June 23 agreed to sign. Having reached this decision, with the grudging consent of the legislative body, on June 24 the German government appealed to its people to "bend every effort to fulfill it."[90] The signing ceremony took place on June 28, on the spot where in 1871 the Germans had proclaimed Wilhelm I the emperor of United Germany.[91]

Aftermath of the   The Allied reply to the German counterpro-
Versailles Treaty, 1919–20   posals on June 16, 1919, signed by Clemenceau, had expressed the Allies' "desire that the passions engendered by the war should die as soon as possible, and that all nations should share in the prosperity which comes from the honest supply of their mutual needs. They wish that Germany shall enjoy this prosperity like the rest, though much of the fruit of it must necessarily go, for many years to come, in making reparation to her neighbors for the damage she has done."[92] These

[89]For dissident German views on this point, see Bonn, *Wandering Scholar*, pp. 195–224, 238–40, esp. p. 206.

[90]Luckau, *German Delegation*, doc. 70, pp. 496–97.

[91]Keynes, *ECP*, L., p. 272; Bailey, *Lost Peace*, pp. 299–306; Bonn, *Wandering Scholar*, ch. 13, "Versailles." The Chinese, embittered over the Shantung decision (Art. 156), refused to sign. The full list of signatures is given in 66th Cong., 1st sess., Sen. Doc. 49, *Treaty of Peace with Germany*, submitted by Senator Lodge, July 10, 1919, pp. 3–7. *Encyclopedia Americana* (1958 ed.), s.v. "War, European," gives the texts of the German, Austrian, Bulgarian, and Polish treaties and a summary of the Turkish. Also included are the texts of the separate treaty between the United States and Germany signed at Berlin on Aug. 25, 1921, and approved by the Senate on Oct. 18, 1921, and a summary of the Brest-Litovsk Treaty signed Mar. 3, 1918, between the Central Powers and the Bolsheviks.

[92]Luckau, *German Delegation*, doc. 60, pp. 411–19, esp. p. 417. An accompanying memorandum amplified this and the delegation of ample powers to the Reparation Commission. David Hunter Miller (legal adviser of the American Peace Commission), in his articles on Keynes' *ECP* in the *New York Evening Post* for Feb. 6 and the *Sun* for Feb. 18,

noble sentiments were slow to be translated into action. The *Economist* of May 10, 1919, said: "If we are to approach the consideration of the terms of the Peace in the proper spirit, we must first remind ourselves what the document is and what were the tasks faced by those who framed it." This wise counsel was conspicuously ignored in the furor over the treaty, which some deemed too soft, others too hard.

On the first page of the treaty the powers expressed the desire that the war "should be replaced by a firm, just and durable Peace." Smuts, on signing for South Africa, expressed the feeling "that in the Treaty we have not yet achieved the real peace to which our peoples were looking." Foch said after the signing, "This is not Peace. It is an Armistice for twenty years."[93] Clemenceau said gloomily to Hoover as he left Paris in September 1919, "There will be another world war in your time and you will be needed back in Europe."[94] These dark forecasts proved accurate, but went much too far in implying that the blunders of the Peace Conference, serious though some proved, ensured another world war. "Seeds of war" are ever present, but their germination and development can be speeded, retarded, or terminated.

Germany ratified the Versailles treaty on July 16, Great Britain on July 31, Italy and France on October 7 and 13, Japan on October 30, and all the lesser powers including China (with a reservation over Shantung) by November. Only the United States lagged. President Wilson, struggling to win popular support for the League of Nations, collapsed on a speaking tour in mid-September 1919, suffered a stroke shortly thereafter, and never regained his health or influence. On November 19, however, after four months of debate, the U.S. Senate voted 55–39 against approving the treaty with the controversial Lodge reservations to the League covenant, and then 53–38 against approval without reservations. No constructive proposal had been able to win even a simple majority vote.[95] For a time the German government refused to sign the protocol needed to bring the treaty into effect, but on January 10, 1920, ratifications were formally exchanged in Paris by the ratifying powers, and the war officially ended among them.[96] The League of Nations automatically came into existence at once; its council first met on January 17, upon Wilson's formal summons from

1920, rightly added that the treaty repeatedly stated that the commission was to take account of the German economic situation, even so far as permitting any part of the initial credit of about $5 billion for German state properties, foreign investments, coal mines, etc., to be reloaned to Germany for food, raw materials, and other payments.

[93]Churchill, *Gathering Storm*, p. 7.

[94]Hoover, *Memoirs*, 1:482, and *American Epic*, 3:537.

[95]Bailey, *Great Betrayal*, chs. 10–11.

[96]*Ibid.*, pp. 206, 224. On Dec. 3, 1919, Clemenceau begged Undersecretary of State Frank Polk to put off the scheduled departure of the American delegation from Paris until the Germans signed this protocol. Bowman, in House and Seymour, *Paris*, pp. 165–66.

his sickbed; the Peace Conference was wound up on January 21; and an embittered Clemenceau, passed over for the presidency of France on the 20th, resigned as premier and retired.

Treaties with the other enemy states—Austria, Bulgaria, Hungary, and Turkey—were drawn up by representatives of the Paris delegations on the same lines as the German one; they were all signed by August 1920.[97]

Meanwhile, furious battles over the terms of the treaty raged in the United States. Drastic changes in public sentiment occurred. Now criticism of the peace terms as too severe contrasted sharply with the insistence on a stern peace in late 1918. Many groups of hyphenated Americans came out against the treaties. Soldiers returned home with anti-French prejudices and fresh respect for the German people. Hoover later wrote of the second half of 1919: "The daily echo of the continuing wrangles and conflicts in Europe coming to the American people and the Congress plus home problems and recovery, had driven our people to disgust with all Europe." Morison, writing when opposition to U.S. involvement in Vietnam was in its infancy, said that "World War I was the most popular war in our history while it lasted, and the most hated after it was over."[98]

On February 9, 1920, the Senate voted to reconsider the treaty, but on March 19 the final vote on it with revised reservations on the covenant was 49-35, seven votes short of the necessary two-thirds,[99] with twelve senators not voting. The Senate merely pigeonholed the tripartite security treaty. In the election of November 1920 the voters overwhelmingly confirmed the repudiation of Wilson and all his works, ensuring that the country would not join the League of Nations, which had had strong bipartisan support. In July 1921 the new Congress declared peace by joint resolution, and late in August the Harding administration negotiated separate peace treaties with Germany, Austria, and Hungary.[100]

Hypercriticism of the Peace Treaties   At sea en route to France in December 1918 President Wilson soberly remarked: "People will endure their tyrants for years, but they tear their deliverers to pieces if a millennium is not created immediately."[101] This glum observation became pertinent all too soon. Each nation expected too much of its leaders and expected the impossible of the Versailles treaty. Its good points were minimized and its defects magnified; personal antagonisms, internal political divisions, and widespread propaganda distorted its features and

---

[97]Bailey, *Lost Peace*, pp. 269-70.
[98]Hoover, *American Epic*, 3:236-37; Morison, *Oxford History*, p. 886.
[99]Bailey, *Great Betrayal*, chs. 15-16.
[100]*Ibid.*, ch. 21.
[101]Quoted in George Creel, *The War, the World, and Wilson* (New York: Harper, 1920), p. 163.

led to wholly unwarranted forecasts. Bryce said in August 1921, "One hears people say all over Europe: 'The sort of peace these negotiations have given us is just as bad as war,' "[102] and this sort of exaggeration was typical of the period. The treaties and their framers were subjected to vitriolic attack, much of it extreme, unfair, and unjustified. The critics made much of the "hypocrisy" displayed at the Peace Conference, but they were equally guilty of "hypercrisy" in their attacks.

A prime example of such an attack was J. M. Keynes' *The Economic Consequences of the Peace (ECP)*. Utterly frustrated and disillusioned, Keynes left Paris in mid-June 1919. In August and September he dashed off this brilliant book—an amazing performance. It was published in London in December. The *New Republic* promptly published excerpts and an inexpensive edition; the hard-cover New York edition appeared late in January 1920. It was quickly translated into several languages and became a worldwide nonfiction best seller, was widely reviewed, and exerted enormous influence.[103]

Several early reviewers, and many other readers, were influenced by their recognition of Keynes as an outstanding young economist. It was assumed that *ECP* was, for the most part, a factual economic analysis that could be trusted, even if other aspects of the book might be less reliable.[104] In fact, it was essentially a strongly worded polemic. The knowledge displayed was imperfect, its emotional biases were powerful, many of its judgments of key persons and provisions were unreliable, and its forecasts were seriously in error. In large measure the author proved a false prophet who was believed—a Cassandra in reverse.

Keynes' portrayal of Wilson was impressionistic, based on wholly inadequate knowledge (as competent reviewers soon pointed out). To me and many others, it seemed a cruel caricature that gave ammunition to Wilson's enemies at home and abroad. Keynes concentrated on the Big Three, largely ignoring the highly important contributions of the experts in the framing of the League covenant (in which he reposed little confidence even before the United States backed out), on territorial issues (some of which he criticized), and on many other points. He did pay high tribute to Hoover's notable relief activities. His expectations of the Peace Conference itself, and of Americans, were excessive and led him to urge

[102]Bryce, *International Relations*, pp. 39–40.

[103]See the long, incomplete list of early editions of *ECP* and press notices in pages following the index to its sequel, *A Revision of the Treaty* (New York: Harcourt Brace, 1922), cited below as *RT*. M. J. Bonn made the German translation; see his *Wandering Scholar*, p. 321. *ECP* has recently been reprinted as vol. 2 in the Royal Economic Society's standard edition of Keynes' collected writings. See E. A. G. Robinson's first Keynes Lecture of the British Academy in *EJ*, June 1972, 82:531–46.

[104]E.g., *Economist*, Dec. 27, 1919, pp. 92–93; F. W. Taussig, in *QJE*, February 1920, 34: 381–87; and Allyn A. Young, *New Republic*, Feb. 25, 1920, pp. 385–89.

(naively, as the Harvard economist F. W. Taussig put it in his review of *ECP*) the cancellation of all interallied indebtedness incurred for the purposes of the war (a wise solution which both U.S. officials and the public strongly opposed) and a huge international loan (for which the time was not ripe, as Keynes himself realized).[105] He condemned the territorial and reparations provisions of the treaties and uncritically endorsed German viewpoints, ignoring Allied responses. He made little or no allowance for the conditions under which the treaties had to be formulated, and failed to recognize forces that could and did come into play to mitigate the evils and make for progress.

ECP stimulated other attacks on conference personnel and the treaties, did much to bring about a remarkable shift from anti- to pro-German sentiment in Britain and America, and promoted the German recalcitrance and Anglo-French estrangement which were crucial in the next few years. Though it could not affect the Senate's votes in November 1919, the book did much to swell the clamor against Wilson which came to a head in March and November 1920. On the whole, as Sir Arthur Salter, his great friend and warm admirer, eventually concluded, *ECP* did more harm than good.[106]

---

[105]*ECP*, L., pp. 33–50, 135, 211–12, 236–37, 240–44, 252–70. In his next book (*RT*, ch. 6) and in later articles (e.g., "The Inter-Allied Debts," *Nation*, Jan. 10, 1925, pp. 516–17) Keynes renewed his appeal for American cancellation. See further Chapter 5 below.

[106]Salter, *Personality in Politics*, pp. 138–48, esp. pp. 141–42; Mantoux, *Carthaginian Peace*. Mantoux, son of the general secretary of the Peace Conference, researched and wrote his book largely at the Institute for Advanced Study from July 1941 to the end of 1942. In the summer of 1944, on leave from the Fighting French Forces, he added a last chapter or part of it; he died in battle on Apr. 29, 1945. His father's foreword and R. C. K. Ensor's introduction were dated October 1945. This important work was not widely reviewed. If Keynes read it, which is doubtful, his biographer does not refer to his reactions, but Harrod takes exception to several of Mantoux's points. Harrod, *Keynes*, pp. 275–80.

The following brief citations should be added: Thorstein Veblen, in *Political Science Quarterly*, September 1920, reprinted in Veblen, *Essays in Our Changing Order*, ed. Leon Ardzrooni (New York: Viking, 1934), pp. 462–70; C. H. Haskins, in House and Seymour, *Paris*, p. 65n; Bailey, *Lost Peace*, pp. 83, 171, 338–39, and *Great Betrayal*, p. 373; Harrod, *Keynes*, pp. 186, 255, 270, 274, 282, 332; Mowat, *Britain between the Wars*, pp. 4, 53; Baruch, *Public Years*, pp. 124–25; Lord Salter, *Memoirs*, pp. 148–50, 156–65; Sir Andrew McFadyean, *Recollected in Tranquility* (London: Pall Mall Press, 1964), p. 71; Morison, *Oxford History*, p. 879n; Harold Macmillan, *Winds of Change, 1914–1939* (New York: Harper and Row, 1966), p. 123; Fosdick, *Letters on the League*, pp. vii–viii, 118, 121; Herbert Stein, *The Fiscal Revolution in America* (Chicago: University of Chicago Press, 1969), pp. 133–35, 480–81; R. S. Sayers, "The Young Keynes," *EJ*, June 1972, 82:591–99, esp. pp. 596–98.

I cannot endorse all of the highly complimentary opening words in Taussig's generally balanced review; Bailey's praise of *ECP* as on the whole a "farsighted analysis" (*Lost Peace*, p. 338); Churchill's acceptance of Keynes' economic judgments (*The Aftermath*, p. 156, and *Gathering Storm*, pp. 7–11); Sir Josiah Stamp's favorable opinion in *Foreign Affairs*, October 1934, 13:112); or a number of statements in Schumpeter's 1946 obituary of Keynes (reprinted in his *Ten Great Economists* [New York: Oxford University Press, 1951], pp. 266–68) and in Harrod, *Keynes*, both of which recognize the less admirable elements in Keynes' makeup, which he often displayed.

Though Keynes concentrated his diatribe on the Versailles treaty, he devoted a footnote to the treaty with Austria.

The terms of the Peace Treaty imposed on the Austrian Republic bear no relation to the real facts of that State's desperate situation. The *Arbeiter Zeitung* of Vienna on June 4, 1919, commented on them as follows: "Never has the substance of a treaty of peace so grossly betrayed the intentions which were said to have guided its construction as is the case with this Treaty . . . in which every provision is permeated with ruthlessness and pitilessness, in which no breath of human sympathy can be detected, which flies in the face of everything which binds man to man, which is a crime against humanity itself, against a suffering and tortured people." I am acquainted in detail with the Austrian Treaty and I was present when some of its terms were being drafted, but I do not find it easy to rebut the justice of this outburst.[107]

Keynes devoted many pages to the dismal state of continental Europe, political, economic, and social— in this he must have relied heavily on Hoover's information without sufficient awareness of its inevitable limitations. In summary: "An inefficient, unemployed, disorganised Europe faces us, torn by internal strife and international hate, fighting, starving, pillaging, and lying. What warrant is there for a picture of less sombre colours?" He found some comfort in "the fact that, even to the minds of men who are desperate, Revolution offers no prospect of improvement whatever. There may, therefore, be ahead of us a long, silent process of semi-starvation, and of a gradual, steady lowering of the standards of life and comfort."[108]

In September 1919, while Keynes was writing this, a Harvard economist wrote with a sounder perspective:

Of the difficult conditions which European and American industries faced in November 1918, none were more fundamental than the prevailing social unrest. In Russia, chaos; in eastern Europe, intense suffering and economic disorganization bordering on the chaotic; in Germany and Austria, the throes of political revolution; in France, England, and Italy, severe war strain and a condition aptly described as that of political and social shell shock. The revolutionists were busy everywhere with their propaganda, the dangers of the situation were very evident, and those with whom the wish was the father to the thought were vociferously prophesying an industrial and social upheaval. Today, while there are still many clouds upon the horizon and many problems yet unsolved, the process of readjustment in Europe seems to be under way and there is every prospect that our political Cassandras will once more turn out to be false prophets. There is trouble enough

---

[107]*ECP*, L., p. 233n. This treaty was handed to the Austrians on June 2, signed at St. Germain Sept. 10, and ratified by the Austrian National Assembly on Oct. 17, 1919. *Encyclopedia Americana* (1958 ed.), s.v. "War, European." Cf. Charles Seymour, in House and Seymour, *Paris*, ch. 5, and Bryce, *International Relations*, pp. 48–49.

[108]Keynes, *ECP*, L., pp. 216–35, esp. pp. 233, 277.

on every hand, but, upon the whole, the civilized world is returning to the pursuits of peace about as rapidly as could be expected; and the danger of a European *débâcle*, while not at an end, is much less than it was last January. The profound unrest which has prevailed has undoubtedly retarded the return of industry to a peace basis, but it has not prevented the process from getting under way and does not seem likely to prevent its successful completion.[109]

In *A Revision of the Treaty (RT)*, the sequel to *ECP* published early in 1922, Keynes acknowledged some of his errors: "There is little prospect now of the disastrous consequence of the fulfillment" of the Versailles treaty, he said, and saw "indications that the worst has passed" for European nations, which were "settling down to a new equilibrium" (pp. 14, 181–82). But he did not foresee the events of the next two years.

The Treaties   In view of the magnitude and complexity of the tasks of
in Retrospect   making peace, the conflicts of commitments and strong ideas of the peacemakers, their limitations and fallibility, the chaotic conditions during the Peace Conference, and the time pressure under which it was drafted, the treaty with Germany was a surprisingly respectable document. At the time several of those who took part in its construction admitted its imperfections but concluded that its virtues outweighed its defects, that it was better than the world had a right to expect, and that if it contained some "seeds of war" it also contained elements by which its errors could be corrected in due course, if only a "proper spirit" could be developed and maintained.[110] This was Salter's mature view expressed in 1947.[111]

Keynes strongly believed, as did Churchill and many others, that it "was right and expedient that the terms of peace should be magnanimous,"[112] but such terms could not have been agreed upon under the circumstances. Inevitably, the treaties reflected the many compromises worked out between advocates of a hard peace and of a soft one. Keynes

---

[109]*Rev. Ec. Stat.*, September 1919, 1:8. The author was probably C. J. Bullock, but several of his associates in the Harvard University Committee of Economic Research doubtless considered it in draft. My later articles in 1921–23 provided a stream of evidence; see Chapter 3 below, passim. Six months earlier Federal Reserve Board member A. C. Miller said: "It is even likely that in Europe the process of reconstruction and recuperation will be speedier and more complete than many now expect. . . . Indeed, the rapidity of Europe's industrial recovery is likely to be one of the economic marvels of all time." *Annals*, March 1919, 82: 306–22. Paul M. Warburg, a recent FRB member, was also optimistic about financial reconstruction. *Ibid.*, pp. 347–73.

[110]See *Economist*, May 10, 1919, pp. 770–73; several contributors in House and Seymour, *Paris*; Tardieu, *Truth about the Treaty*; and memoirs of Lloyd George and others.

[111]Salter, *Personality in Politics*, pp. 141–42.

[112]Harrod, *Keynes*, pp. 263–64, citing *ECP*, L., pp. 23, 135, 209–10. Harrod also (p. 265) quoted Winston Churchill (*The Aftermath*) on his mood on the evening of the Armistice signing.

failed to stress the many respects in which, even with regard to reparations, the terms of the treaty were flexible.[113] Moreover, Keynes argued throughout on the assumption that the treaty terms would be rigidly and implacably enforced.[114] Subsequently he went much too far in explaining the failure of his dire predictions to be realized on the ground that no serious attempt was made to enforce the treaty. In most respects, the treaty was carried out. On the thorny issue of reparations, it would surely have been wiser to have fixed a sum clearly within Germany's capacity to pay and to have provided incentives for such payment. This proved impossible, and it was therefore left to the Reparation Commission to fix the figure, which in due course it did.

On January 25, 1919, the Peace Conference created a fifteen-member commission to determine the responsibility for the war. It unanimously determined that the war was due to Austria-Hungary, aided and abetted by Germany. This was the basis for the unfortunate war-guilt Article 231 of the Versailles treaty. Article 227, adopted under strong pressure from Britain and France over the objections of the United States and Japan, provided for the former Kaiser's arraignment and trial. Early in 1920 the Supreme War Council called on the Dutch government to surrender him, but the request was respectfully declined.[115] There was no disposition to try him in absentia; the trial never came off, the movement to "Hang the Kaiser" evaporated, and he died in exile at Doorn on June 4, 1941.

[113]See Miller's articles cited in n. 92.
[114]In *RT*, pp. 180–82.
[115]James Brown Scott, "The Trial of the Kaiser," in House and Seymour, *Paris*, pp. 221–38.

CHAPTER 3

EUROPEAN AND INTERNATIONAL DEVELOPMENTS, 1919-29

WE MUST BRIEFLY review the extraordinarily tangled decade 1919–29. Its key events included official United States retreat into isolation from Europe in 1920; the collapse of the postwar boom in 1920–21 and the fall of international commodity prices; the failure of the ambitious Genoa Conference in the spring of 1922, wrecked by the bombshell Rapallo treaty; the continued failure of political negotiations over German reparations in 1920–23, culminating in the Franco-Belgian occupation of the Ruhr and the end of the Anglo-French entente in 1923; hyperinflation in Germany, ended late in 1923; the Anglo-American debt settlement in 1923; the Dawes committee report and its implementation in 1924; the British return to the gold standard in April 1925; the Locarno international agreements of late 1925; the great British coal strike of 1926; de facto stabilization of the French franc late in 1926; completion of international debt settlements in 1927–29; and international influences from the Wall Street superboom of 1925–29.

The Hectic Years, By slow degrees progress in pacification was made.
1919–23 Five separate attempts during the Peace Conference to smooth thorny relations with the Russians all came to naught. The bumbling interventions by Allied forces in North Russia and Siberia were painfully liquidated. Civil war in Soviet Russia ended in Bolshevik domination early in 1920. Polish-Soviet hostilities from May through August ended in Polish victory on August 14, but the ensuing Treaty of Riga (March 18, 1921) was a compromise which Lenin regarded as an outstanding victory and led the Poles to feel that they had lost the peace.[1] Sporadic civil disorders in Germany and elsewhere, some of them fomented by the Soviets, were quelled by various means.

Early in 1921, faced with serious economic breakdown, the Soviets launched their New Economic Policy. The terrible Russian famine of 1921–23 was due to causes other than the war and the peace treaties; Hoover's American Relief Administration did much to mitigate it. The repudiation of czarist debts cost the French a large part of their international invest-

---

[1] This war was fateful for both parties and powerfully influenced the course of European history for two decades. See Norman Davies, *White Eagle, Red Star: The Polish-Soviet War of 1919–20* (London: MacDonald, 1972; foreword by A. J. P. Taylor). British historian Taylor commends this recent book without reserve for elucidating an important subject that has been much misunderstood.

ments and made it impossible for the Soviet Union to attract significant amounts of foreign credits. The confiscation of foreign investments and concessions in Russia hurt influential business groups, especially in Britain. The loss of Russian trade was a severe blow to Germany and other countries. Steps were secretly taken for collaboration between German and Russian military and industrial establishments and for the drafting of what became the Treaty of Rapallo. Some trade with Western countries developed despite old debts, frictions over new credits, and Western anger over subversive efforts, hostile Soviet propaganda, and provocative official rhetoric.[2] The Allied Treaty of Sèvres with Turkey (signed August 10, 1920) had not ended strife between Greeks and Turks. This flared up again in 1922, widened the Anglo-French rift, almost involved Britain in another war, and was ended only in July 1923.[3]

Cooperation among Great Britain, France, and the United States had been essential in winning the war and writing the peace treaties, and its continuance seemed imperative to restore peace and to promote recovery.[4] For four years this was lacking: in 1920 America officially backed out; in 1920–22 Franco-British relations went from bad to worse, and these two governments were seriously at odds through the summer of 1923.[5]

The Versailles treaty was never revised, as Keynes and other critics urged and the Germans demanded. In large part its terms were carried out, though not always perfectly; plebiscites were duly held in 1920–21; the Saar arrangement proved workable; and the various agencies provided for were set up and functioned. In certain respects the treaty was gradually modified,[6] either in ways that its authors and defenders had anticipated, or otherwise, as in the case of the Fiume agreement between Italy and Yugoslavia in August–September 1923, embodied in a treaty early in 1924.

The Reparation Commission was organized early in 1920, without an American voting member. Poincaré became an early chairman of this four-member body, with a deciding vote in case of a tie. He resigned after

[2] Harold H. Fisher, *The Famine in Soviet Russia, 1919–23* (New York: Macmillan, 1927); C. L. Mowat, *Britain between the Wars, 1918–1940* (London: Methuen, 1955), pp. 41–42; George F. Kennan, *Russia and the West under Lenin and Stalin* (Boston: Little Brown, 1960), chs. 4–15; and Adam B. Ulam, *The Bolsheviks: The Intellectual and Political History of the Triumph of Communism in Russia* (New York: Macmillan, 1965), and *Stalin: The Man and His Era* (New York: Viking, 1973).

[3] Mowat, *Britain between the Wars*, pp. 54–56, 114–15, 117–19, 156–57.

[4] C. H. Haskins, "The New Boundaries of Germany," in Edward M. House and Charles Seymour, eds., *What Really Happened at Paris* (New York: Scribner, 1921), p. 66.

[5] On September 19, 1923, Britain's new prime minister, Stanley Baldwin, had a friendly conference with Poincaré in Paris which purportedly ended in "a common agreement of views." Mowat, *Britain between the Wars*, p. 160. Carl Bergmann later termed this "an empty phrase" (*The History of Reparations* [London: Benn, 1927], p. 219).

[6] Cf. "Ten Years of Peace," *Economist*, July 6, 1929, p. 5; and James T. Shotwell's foreword to Alma Luckau, *The German Delegation at the Paris Peace Conference* (New York: Columbia University Press, 1941), p. vii.

a few months (May 19, 1920) but continued to exert his influence through his French successors. He and Lloyd George were antipathetic in temperament, and friction between them severely hampered progress in a series of conferences in 1920–22 that were marked by all sorts of disputes, proposals and counterproposals, and explosions. In order to force Germany to accept unwelcome ultimatums, Allied troops occupied Frankfurt and Darmstadt on April 6, 1920, and Duisberg, Ruhrort, and Düsseldorf on March 8, 1921. Late in April 1921 the commission fixed the Germany reparation obligation at 132,000 million gold marks (£6,600 million), subject to deductions and an additional 6,000 million marks for the Belgian debt.[7] A schedule of payments was agreed on in London on May 5, superseding that in the so-called Paris Resolution of January 29. Finally, early in 1923, over British objections, Franco-Belgian forces occupied the Ruhr, as had been earlier threatened, to force payment of reparations. This ended the Franco-British postwar entente, was met by organized passive resistance in Germany, and was accompanied by the final stages of depreciation of the mark.[8]

High hopes were pinned on the economic and financial conference that opened in Genoa on April 10, 1922, at which twenty-nine nations were represented, along with British dominions. Its prime mover, Lloyd George, viewed it as "an urgent and essential step towards the economic reconstruction of Central and Eastern Europe." In his opening speech he called it "the greatest gathering of European nations which has ever been assembled," its purpose being to seek "the best methods of restoring the shattered prosperity of this continent." Poincaré, who had succeeded Briand as French premier on January 12, insisted that reparations be excluded from the agenda and declined to attend. Soviet Russia and Germany were both represented, implying de facto recognition of the U.S.S.R. Ill health prevented Lenin from attending, but he supervised the preparations of the Russian delegation and kept in close touch with its proceedings through his deputy, G. V. Chichirin.[9] The German delegation was headed by Chancellor Dr. Josef Wirth and Foreign Minister Walther Rathenau (Rathenau was murdered a few weeks after the conference ended). The United States declined representation but sent observers. On April 16 the Russo-German Treaty of Rapallo was hastily signed—Kennan termed it "the first great victory for Soviet diplomacy."[10] This explosive event

[7]Keynes (RT, p. 185) considered 36,000 million the proper figure.

[8]Keynes, RT, chs. 2–4 and appendix of documents (pp. 203–39); Bergmann, History of Reparations, chs. 3–26; Sir Andrew McFadyean, Reparation Reviewed (London: Benn, 1930), chs. 1–3; and Eleanor L. Dulles, The Bank for International Settlements at Work (New York: Macmillan, 1932), passim.

[9]Evgeny Chossudovsky, "Genoa Revisited: Russia and Coexistence," Foreign Affairs, April 1972, 50:554–77.

[10]Russia and the West, ch. 15, esp. pp. 222–23.

wrecked the conference, though it dragged on until May 19 and produced some resolutions which, as Keynes wrote in June 1929, "voiced the reasonable fears and wise counsels of the most prudent opinion in Europe."[11] Its failure was momentous for Europe and the world[12] and contributed heavily to Lloyd George's downfall later in the year.

Public opinion and fiscal considerations had forced demobilization of British and American armed forces so rapidly that the French feared that the ability of the Allies to enforce the peace terms would be jeopardized. Under strong public pressure, the huge apparatus of controls that were built up during the war was also quickly dismantled.[13] In the spring of 1919 the United States and British governments ended their financial support to their wartime allies, whose currencies weakened as a result. Late that year Keynes wrote: "The inflationism of the currency systems of Europe has proceeded to extraordinary lengths. . . . It is a continuing phenomenon of which the end is not yet in sight."[14] Early in 1920 I wrote that Germany was "moving at a headlong pace to the currency *debacle* which has already engulfed Russia and Austria-Hungary," where no sign of improvement was visible, and that France was still "making progress in the wrong direction."[15] Inflation was relatively moderate in Great Britain, the European neutral nations, and most non-European countries. It was substantial in France, Italy, and the Balkan countries, where prices rose to six to ten times prewar levels. It went to extremes in Soviet Russia and in Germany, where the Ruhr occupation in 1923 finally made the mark virtually worthless, but it was also severe in Poland, Austria, and Hungary before it was arrested. In the chaos of the exchanges gullible Americans and other foreigners made large purchases of depreciating currencies, which provided unexpected resources to the nations whose currencies were involved, especially Germany.[16]

Great Britain emerged from the war with much reduced international assets and export trade but with great prestige and high confidence in her basic strength—a confidence that Americans shared. Her people looked forward, Keynes wrote late in 1919, "not only to a return to the comforts of 1914, but to an immense broadening and intensification of them. All classes alike thus build their plans, the rich to spend more and save less,

---

[11]*A Treatise on Money*, 2 vols. (New York: Harcourt Brace, 1930), 2:389.

[12]Sir James Grigg later expressed the belief that had it succeeded there might have been no Ruhr occupation, no Hitler, no World War II. P. J. Grigg, *Prejudice and Judgment* (London: Jonathan Cape, 1948), p. 82.

[13] Mowat, *Britain between the Wars*, pp. 22–24, 28–30.

[14]*ECP*, L., pp. 223, 232.

[15]"World Currency Expansion during the War and in 1919," *Rev. Ec. Stat.*, January 1920, 2:8–20, esp. pp. 16, 20.

[16]The second (McKenna) committee of experts, in its unanimous report to the Reparation Commission on Apr. 9, 1924, estimated the amount at 7,000 to 8,000 million gold marks, lost by more than one million foreigners.

the poor to spend more and work less."[17] Britain was harassed by industrial strife, which also afflicted other nations. In the early postwar boom, British wholesale prices rapidly rose until in May 1920 the index was 325 percent of the prewar level (compared with 270 in the United States). From this peak it fell below 160 by the end of 1922.[18] The severe slump hit Britain hard, and unemployment rose to around 15 percent of the labor force in 1921 and 1922.

The British were most eager to see normal international relations—financial, economic, and political—restored as quickly as possible in order that British trade could recover, yet they feared severe competition from Germany. They earnestly strove to be conciliatory in international affairs; the effort was, for the time, unsuccessful with France and Germany. They stuck to orthodox fiscal and monetary policies, working toward a return to the gold standard at the old parity between the pound and the dollar.

At the nine-power Washington conference (November 1921–February 1922) two agreements were reached: a five-power treaty for scrapping capital ships and a ten-year "holiday" on new construction and a four-power treaty guaranteeing the status quo in the Pacific, ending Britain's historic naval superiority and the Anglo-Japanese alliance.[19] Serious disagreements between the British and French blocked any reduction of land forces, and failure to make other progress toward disarmament long remained a sore point with Germany.

When United States officials resisted persistent efforts of Allied war debtors to get all-round cancellation of debts incurred for prosecuting the war and were adamant in their opposition to linking reparation and debt settlements or joint consideration of the debts, Great Britain declared, in the Balfour note of August 1, 1922, that she would ask of her debtors no more than the United States demanded of her.[20] Proud of her financial strength and reputation, she was the first major debtor to negotiate, early in 1923, a settlement with the United States, on terms that were publicized here as generous but seemed hard to her leaders. The Bonar Law government most reluctantly approved this Mellon-Baldwin agreement on January 30; it was signed for Great Britain on June 18 (after Baldwin had

[17]ECP, L., pp. 2, 237–39.

[18]A. L. Bowley, *Some Economic Consequences of the War* (London: Butterworth, 1930), pp. 70–73.

[19]Mowat, *Britain between the Wars*, pp. 115–16, and chapter 5 below. The United States, Britain, France, and Japan signed both; Italy signed only the first. Belgium, the Netherlands, Portugal, and China were also represented at the conference.

[20]J. T. Gerould and Laura S. Turnbull, *Selected Articles on Interallied Debts and Revision of the Debt Settlements* (New York: Wilson, 1928), pp. 1–47, 189–217, 228–81, 311–38, 391–94, 471–73; H. G. Moulton and Leo Pasvolsky, *War Debts and World Prosperity* (Washington, D.C.: Brookings Institution, 1932), chs. 1–4. See also HES, *Weekly Letter*, Nov. 11, 1922, pp. 283–84; Mowat, *Britain between the Wars*, pp. 161–62; and Harold Macmillan, *Winds of Change, 1914–1939* (New York: Harper and Row, 1966), p. 133.

succeeded Bonar Law) and was formally accepted by the United States on June 19.

France gave top priority to the restoration of her war-devastated areas and to exacting from Germany the large sum that this entailed, rejecting Germany's offers to do the job with her own materials and labor, and accepted the consequent enlargement of her huge national debt.[21] France was comparatively free from unemployment and felt the postwar slump much less than Britain, and French businessmen were more progressive than their British counterparts.[22] By the end of 1923, about 62 percent of the war damage had been repaired, but French relations with Germany, Britain, and the United States were in almost complete disarray.

Extreme political turmoil racked Germany in the first four years of the Weimar Republic, despite the able leadership of President Friedrich Ebert. Proportional representation resulted in a large number of political parties; since none of these could command a majority in the Reichstag, coalitions were necessary. Top leaders and cabinet members changed frequently, and successive governments were weak.[23] In France the political situation was almost equally unstable, though Poincaré held the premiership from 1922 to 1924. In Great Britain the Lloyd George coalition endured with difficulty until October 1922, and the successor Conservative governments lasted only to January 1924. On October 30, 1922, after the Fascist march on Rome, Mussolini became premier. As virtual dictator, he provided a stable government at the cost of severe curtailment of civil liberties, which outraged the liberals but permitted economic progress. In all four countries personal antagonisms among leading politicians found frequent expression in harsh words, delaying action, and changing governments and policies. Similar frictions seriously hampered progress in international negotiations.[24]

[21]Dwight W. Morrow, *Memorandum on the Economic and Financial Condition of France* (New York: privately printed, 1921), on which I worked with Morrow in February through April (see Harold Nicolson, *Dwight Morrow* [New York: Harcourt Brace, 1935], pp. 244–45); J. S. Davis, "Recent Economic and Financial Progress in France," *Rev. Ec. Stat.*, July 1921, 5: 223–48; William MacDonald, *Reconstruction in France* (New York: Macmillan, 1922); and R. C. Dawes, *The Dawes Plan in the Making* (Indianapolis, Ind.: Bobbs-Merrill, 1925), p. 26.

[22]Clarence Bertrand Thompson, an early scientific management specialist who had spent fifteen years in Europe, wrote enthusiastically of French businessmen, in comparison with German and British, in *Sixth Report* of the class of 1908, June 1933, pp. 696–701. Cf. also *Harvard Class of 1908: Fiftieth Anniversary Report* (Cambridge, Mass.: Harvard University Printing Office, 1958), pp. 633–37.

[23]In lectures at the Institute of Politics in the summer of 1924, Moritz J. Bonn ably discussed the crisis of European democracy (see his book of the same title [New Haven, Conn.: Yale University Press, 1925]), with special but not exclusive reference to Germany before the Dawes Plan. Also illuminating is H. A. Turner, *Stresemann and the Politics of the Weimar Republic* (Princeton, N.J.: Princeton University Press, 1963), chs. 1–4.

[24]See especially Sir Arthur Salter, *Personality in Politics: Studies of Contemporary Statesmen* (London: Faber, 1947).

Germany in 1920–23 was severely affected by pressure for reparation payments in kind and in cash, by humiliations repeatedly inflicted on her by the French, by the Ruhr occupation, by grave internal dissension, by lax fiscal policies, and by currency inflation. Nevertheless, the worst internal disorders were quelled; the extreme postwar food shortages were overcome, in part by partial agricultural recovery and in part by the unexpected foreign purchases of her depreciating currency mentioned earlier. Her economic organism was not destroyed, her captains of industry displayed astonishing vitality, and her trade unions were exceptionally docile and cooperative. Significant gains were made in industrial output and in capital investment, although some investment was misdirected during the "flight from the mark." Liberal diplomat Count Harry Kessler, in lectures at the Institute of Politics (Williamstown, Massachusetts) in the summer of 1923, recognized a few of these positive factors while he damned the Versailles treaty and French postwar policy and emphasized the physical, intellectual, and moral degradation of the German people.[25] He did not recognize the remarkable change in public sentiment toward Germany, from extreme hostility to warm sympathy, which took place in 1919–23, especially in Great Britain and America, nor did he foresee that the Ruhr occupation would pave the way for "Germany's restoration to a place of honor in the society of nations."[26]

Despite disordered currencies, political turmoil, international discord, and the impact of the depression of 1920–23, economic rehabilitation proceeded in Europe. Shortages of food, coal, and shipping soon turned into surpluses. The marked decline in international commodity prices, which was so hard on exporting countries, proved a boon to the peoples of the importing countries of Europe.

Clemenceau, Lloyd George, Keynes, and Robert Lansing were among the many in 1919 who were skeptical about the practical value of the League of Nations in executing the treaty and dealing with problems left unsolved at Paris.[27] The Senate debates in the fall spread grave concern over it, which deepened when Senate votes in March 1920 seemed to insure

[25]*Germany and Europe* (New Haven, Conn.: Yale University Press, 1923).

[26]Paul Einzig, *Germany's Default: The Economics of Hitlerism* (London: Macmillan, 1934; preface dated November 1933); editors' note to Hitler, *Mein Kampf* (New York: Reynal and Hitchcock, 1939), p. 922, n. 16; and Winston S. Churchill, *The Second World War*, vol. 1: *The Gathering Storm* (Boston: Houghton Mifflin, 1948), pp. 12–13.

[27]Clemenceau, however, wrote Colonel House and Lloyd George on September 4, 1919, expressing hope. Charles Seymour, ed., *The Intimate Papers of Colonel House*, 4 vols. (Boston: Houghton Mifflin, 1926–28), 4:401–3. Germany was suspicious of the League and did not apply for admission; her admission was delayed until September 1926. In the interwar period "many thoughtful Europeans and Americans" believed that "the very concept of the League was a delusion. It promised more than it could possibly perform in a world of sovereign nations." Robert Murphy, *Diplomat among Warriors* (Garden City, N.Y.: Doubleday, 1964), p. 363.

the indefinite abstention of the United States. Yet the League recovered from this seemingly mortal blow and in three years went far to confound the skeptics.[28] It quickly developed the best civil service the world had ever known. It contributed to solving difficult problems with coal, internal transport, and shipping. It sponsored the great Brussels financial conference at which, in September 1920, representatives of thirty-nine countries unanimously agreed on the outlines of financial policy best adapted to the conditions of the postwar world; and some progress was gradually made in this direction. In 1922–23, after other attempts had failed, the League succeeded in raising divided Austria from the verge of starvation and dissolution to a position where she was prosperous, self-supporting, and politically secure. Similar steps were soon taken in Hungary, and an agreement was reached for settling the disputes with her neighbors which had long embittered Hungarian international relations.

The League also helped to resolve the obstinate economic problems in the Saar, which was governed by a commissioner responsible to the League; to settle the dispute over the division of Upper Silesia between Germany and Poland, after the plebiscite of March 1921; and to get agreement on a stable currency in the free city of Danzig. It arranged for the resettlement of more than a million Greek refugees from Turkey after the Greco-Turkish war of 1921–23. It played a helpful role in settling the ominous Greek-Italian incident over Corfu in summer of 1923. Irving Fisher even went so far as to say in late 1924: "In four years the League has snuffed out, or headed off, six wars, any one of which might otherwise have developed into another World War."[29]

Gloom and Reality, 1920–23   The gloom that pervaded most of 1919 persisted.[30] Widespread dissatisfaction with the peace treaties in 1919–20; the United States rejection of the Versailles treaty and the League Covenant in March 1920 and of President Wilson himself in the November election; the consequent extreme bitterness of the French and

---

[28]Sir Arthur Salter, *Europe's Recovery: What It Means to World Peace* (remarks before the Institute of Politics, Williamstown, Mass., August 1924) (New York: League of Nations Non-Partisan Association, 1924), esp. pp. 17–30; Salter's articles in *Foreign Affairs*, 5:630–43, 6:91–102; Lord Salter, *Memoirs of a Public Servant* (London: Faber, 1961), ch. 9.

[29]*America's Interest in World Peace* (New York, Funk and Wagnalls, 1924), p. 99.

[30]Two earlier expressions should be recalled. Sir Edward Grey, Britain's Liberal foreign secretary in 1905–16, looked out on St. James Park on the evening Britain declared war and remarked: "The lamps are going out all over Europe. We shall not see them lit again in our lifetime." Quoted in *Encyclopedia Americana* (1958 ed.), s.v. "Grey of Falloden." Withers in 1916 summarized the views of "pessimistic observers, with a pacifist turn of mind" who held that "war will inevitably leave Europe so exhausted and impoverished that its financial future is a prospect of unmitigated gloom." While conceding that such gloomy forecasts may be right, he hoped and believed that "they will be found to have been nightmares, evolved by depressed and prejudiced imaginations." Hartley Withers, *International Finance* (London: Murray, 1916; reprinted in June 1918), p. 176.

British over this desertion;[31] the collapse of the postwar boom in 1920–21; the drastic shrinkage of commodity prices in the stronger countries and renewal of price inflation in the weaker ones; wide-ranging currency instability and unemployment; the failure of the Reparation Commission and successive conferences, in the absence of official U.S. participation, to arrive at workable agreements on German reparations; the Franco-Belgian occupation of the Ruhr in early 1923; the collapse of the German mark in the late summer; and political instability in Britain, France, Germany, and elsewhere—all these bred pessimism.

In August 1921 Lord Bryce[32] gave eight lectures on international relations at the Institute of Politics. He sought to answer three questions: why "ill feeling continues still so rife?"; why "before the clouds of the Great War have vanished from the sky new clouds are rising over the horizon?"; and "what can be done to avert the dangers that are threatening the peace of mankind?" His answers were gloomy in the extreme.[33] T. E. Gregory, an able British economist, wrote in 1921: "Ours is a weary and disillusioned generation, dealing with a world which is nearer collapse than it has been at any time since the downfall of the Roman Empire."[34] In an address on December 1, 1921, Paul M. Warburg, president of the American Acceptance Council, said: "It admits of no doubt that Germany's present course must lead to financial and social chaos in Central Europe within an ominously short time."[35]

By the end of the depression year 1921, though there was yet no general agreement on whether the worst was passed or a general collapse was imminent, Keynes concluded that the perils he had seen two years earlier had been safely passed and that the time had almost come to turn from "the avoidance of calamity to the renewal of health." My own conclusion in April 1922 was that "1921 was a year of distinct progress toward the reestablishment of normal relations of prices, industry, trade, and finance, within and among the nations," however powerful and incomplete the necessary readjustments and "however aggravated by blunders of omission and commission." I also noted that "most of the dismal prophecies of catastrophe, collapse, and degeneracy which have been rife during the past

[31]Raymond B. Fosdick, *Letters on the League of Nations* (Princeton, N.J.: Princeton University Press, 1966), pp. 98–123: "Our generation in America has betrayed its own children and the blood of the next war is on our hands" (p. 123).

[32]For an illuminating brief appreciation of Bryce, see Salter, *Personality in Politics*, pp. 109–12.

[33]*International Relations* (New York: Macmillan, 1927), pp. 112–13, 124, 255–56. The lectures were first published by the Institute in February 1922, a few weeks before Lord Bryce's death at eighty-three, and reprinted in July 1923 and July 1927.

[34]*Foreign Exchange Before, During, and After the War*, 3d ed. (Oxford: Oxford University Press, 1925), p. 9. Cf. Churchill, *Gathering Storm*, pp. 14–15.

[35]*The Federal Reserve System: Its Origin and Growth: Reflections and Recollections*, 2 vols. (New York: Macmillan, 1930), 1:743.

three years have proved false."[36] Over most of the Continent, despite currency inflation, dislocated exchanges, and unbalanced budgets, production had improved since 1919, living conditions were better, and appreciable gains had been made in reconstruction, reconditioning, and restoring trade to normal channels.

The failure of the Genoa conference in the spring of 1922, continuing tensions between Lloyd George and Poincaré, the fall of Lloyd George after the elections of October 1922, and economic warfare in the Ruhr gave fresh impetus to pessimism. At the Institute of Politics in the summer of 1923, the Earl of Birkenhead discussed the problems left by the war. In his conclusion he expressed the hope and belief that "some common effort shall be made to alleviate and correct the misery under which Europe is groaning to-day and before which Europe may so easily succumb," but he was pessimistic enough to say that "unless some change unforeseen by me, unforeseeable by me, occurs in the present situation, all Europe must grow progressively worse."[37] Sir Philip Kerr, who had been Lloyd George's private secretary, was equally gloomy. Speaking on world problems, he said:[38]

> The truth is that the world presents a picture of almost inextricable confusion. . . . To-day, however, international chaos is more intense than it has ever been. . . .
> I do not think it requires any argument to show that we have reached a crisis in international history, and that, unless the civilized nations set to work to establish some better method of conducting the world's affairs than the one we have at present, there is not the slightest chance of peace, prosperity, or stability in human affairs.

Supposedly competent observers considered Europe, after "three years of a progressive drift toward anarchy," on the verge of a "catastrophe of the first magnitude."[39] Four years after the Armistice was signed, Churchill "was deeply under the impression of a future catastrophe." He wrote: "In their loss of purpose, in their abandonment even of the themes they most sincerely espoused, Britain, France, and most of all, because of their immense power and impartiality, the United States, allowed condi-

---

[36] Keynes, *RT*, pp. 5, 180–82. My view was set forth at somewhat greater length in HES, *Weekly Letter*, Apr. 8, Aug. 12, Nov. 11, 1922, pp. 85–92, 193–200, 281–88. These were the first of an unsigned series that continued through Jan. 10, 1925 (pp. 15–18). My longer articles appeared in the *Review of Economic Statistics* from 1919 to 1925.

[37] *Approaches to World Problems* (New Haven, Conn.: Yale University Press, 1924), pp. 3–21, esp. pp. 20–21.

[38] *Ibid.*, pp. 75–120, esp. pp. 81, 87.

[39] G. P. Auld, *The Dawes Plan and the New Economics* (Garden City, N.Y.: Doubleday, 1927), pp. 29, 31. Auld, an American, was the accountant-general of the Reparation Commission in 1920–24. Under the pen name "Alpha" he published "Reparations and the Policy of Repudiation: An American View," *Foreign Affairs*, October 1923, 2:55–83.

tions to be gradually built up which led to the very climax they dreaded most."[40]

Actually, much of the pessimism of 1920–23 was as excessive as was the unbounded optimism that had prevailed briefly after hostilities ended. The reality was far different from the impressionistic generalizations that continued to appear in print.[41] As it had been before the war, Europe was "a congeries of nations, each far from unified internally, extremely diverse in language, characteristics, ideals, ambitions, and interests, jealous and suspicious of one another, muddling along together after a fashion, but clashing frequently in war and in peace, with many a chip on shoulder and much powder and tinder waiting for a spark."[42] Normality was far from attained, yet by the end of 1923 the nations of Europe had achieved significant economic gains. I wrote on September 8, 1923: "Europe's constitution is tough; she is inured to hardships; her present position, on the whole, is far from desperate." As for Germany and France in particular, "even Western Europe has stood the strain surprisingly well, and is adjusting trade and industry to the situation with considerable facility; while elsewhere in Europe, perhaps even in Russia, fair progress generally continues." The recent Austrian settlement suggested "a possible solution of the fundamental difficulties in Germany and Western Europe."[43] The European harvests were remarkably good.[44] In May 1924 I wrote: "Undoubtedly, the year 1923 must be regarded as a year of economic recovery throughout Europe, save in Germany, despite the handicap of the Ruhr occupation and the German crisis, and despite a delining tendency in most European exchanges, particularly serious in France and Belgium."[45] In August 1924 Salter said of Europe: "Progress toward European recovery during the last few years has been very real."[46] This was the foundation for the striking transformation of public opinion in the next two years.

[40]Churchill, *Gathering Storm*, pp. 38–41, quoting from his book *The Aftermath*, published on Jan. 1, 1929.

[41]See, for example, the exaggerated contrast between 1918–23 and 1924–27 made by an able young economist, James W. Angell, "The Interallied Debts and American Policy," *International Conciliation*, May 1927, pp. 16–30.

[42]From my summary appraisal ("Forecasting Conditions in Europe," in W. M. Persons, W. T. Foster, and A. J. Hettinger, Jr., eds., *The Problem of Business Forecasting* [Boston: Houghton Mifflin, 1924], pp. 277–96, esp. pp. 282–83). This conclusion rested mainly on my continuing studies of European economic and financial developments, mentioned in n. 36. After hearing this, my former student Paul H. Douglas told me he thought me overoptimistic. (C. O. Hardy's views at the same session [*ibid.*, pp. 310–11] were pessimistic.) Since I underestimated the success of the Dawes Plan, not yet then formulated, my forecast proved somewhat too conservative. Shortly after I gave this paper I was asked and agreed to be one of the "technical assistants" to the U.S. members of the Dawes committee and with another assistant, E. W. Kemmerer, was briefed by Secretary Hughes before we sailed for Paris.

[43]HES, *Weekly Letter*, pp. 243–50.

[44]*Ibid.*, pp. 249–50, and Dec. 8, 1923, pp. 323–30.

[45]*Ibid.*, May 10, 1924, pp. 123–30.

[46]*Europe's Recovery*. More detailed material is included in my article "Economic and Financial Progress in Europe, 1923–24," *Rev. Ec. Stat.*, July 1924, 5:205–42. I cannot

In the summer of 1923 it was clear that the Ruhr occupation was a costly failure, most conspicuously for Germany and France. On August 12 Chancellor Wilhelm Cuno resigned and Gustav Stresemann succeeded him, with initial support from the Social Democrats. With great moral courage he ended passive resistance in the Rhineland on September 24. Serious political disorder followed. His cabinet resigned on October 3, but he carried on with a rump cabinet until November 23, when Wilhelm Marx became chancellor, Hans Luther minister of finance, and Stresemann foreign minister. First steps toward stabilization of the currency had been taken with the setting up of the Rentenbank, a scheme of Karl Helfferich (leader of the Prussian junkers), which was established October 15 and opened for business on November 15. After Reichsbank President Rudolf Havenstein died on November 20, Dr. Hjalmar Schacht succeeded him. He and Luther had the ruthlessness necessary to balance the budget and stabilize the currency. From utter fiscal chaos a temporary equilibrium had emerged, but its permanence depended on a reasonable reparations settlement.[47]

On November 30 the Reparation Commission appointed two committees of nonpolitical "experts," the first of which was to consider ways of balancing the German budget and stabilizing the German currency. Such a step had been suggested by Secretary of State Hughes in his New Haven address late in 1922. President Coolidge reiterated the suggestion on October 11, 1923. The British Foreign Office approached France and Italy and got their approval in principle, and precise terms were eventually agreed upon.[48] As we shall see, the Dawes committee wisely chose to interpret the terms liberally and soon made a major contribution.

The Dawes Plan Formulated   A noteworthy change in spirit took place in 1924. The year began in anxiety tinged with hope, and ended in confidence based upon substantial achievements.[49] It is generally agreed that the outstanding events of the year were the formulation of the Dawes Plan in the first four months and its acceptance and implementation in the

accept Angell's 1929 conclusion (*The Recovery of Germany* [New Haven, Conn.: Yale University Press, 1929], ch. 2) on Germany's position at the end of 1923.

[47]Bergmann, *History of Reparations*, ch. 26; Auld, *Dawes Plan*, ch. 6; Moritz J. Bonn, *Wandering Scholar* (New York: John Day, 1948), pp. 280–86. Bergmann credited the resumption of negotiations at so crucial a moment primarily to the Belgian and British delegates to the Reparation Commission and to Colonel Logan, the U.S. "unofficial observer": "These men continued, even in the darkest days, their great and persistent labours to repair the mistakes and follies of high politics" (p. 216).

[48]Bergmann, *History of Reparations*, pp. 219–22; Dawes, *Dawes Plan*, app. 1 ("The Evolution of the Terms of Reference to the Committees of Experts"), by Leon Fraser; Auld, *Dawes Plan*, pp. 67–72; McFadyean, *Reparation*, ch. 4; Charles G. Dawes, *A Journal of Reparations* (London: Macmillan, 1939; forewords by Lord Stamp and H. Brüning), pp. vii–x et passim. On Morrow's role, see Nicolson, *Morrow*, pp. 272–73.

[49]J. S. Davis, "European Economic and Financial Progress," in HES, *Weekly Letter*, Jan. 10, 1925, pp. 15–18.

next six months. The ensuing transformation of the world situation—psychological, political, and economic—paved the way for "the return march to civilization after the war."[50] The difficulties involved in this process, however, have been too much ignored or minimized, and call for careful illumination.

Political leaders had attempted for four years, largely without success, to deal constructively with the German reparations problem; economists disagreed radically in their solutions; and there had been much distortion and demagoguery. Now nonpolitical businessmen were given a chance to try to reach, if possible, with comparative freedom from political interference,[51] a workable provisional solution. Already, at biennial "congresses" in 1921 and 1923, the International Chamber of Commerce had laid the groundwork. After the official aloofness of 1920-23, semi-official initiative and leadership from this country were vital.

The United States members of the two committees of experts were chosen, after much consultation, by Secretary of State Hughes, Treasury Secretary Andrew Mellon, and Commerce Secretary Hoover on November 5, 1923.[52] Charles G. Dawes, a Republican, had become highly popular in France while he was chief of supply procurement for the American Expeditionary Force; early in 1923 he published an article predicting a reasonable settlement of reparations within two years and said that the Ruhr "invasion" had made this possible. For such reasons the Reparation Commission designated him chairman of the first committee, which became known by his name. Owen D. Young, an independent Democrat, a lawyer and corporation executive, was suggested as a committee member by Dwight Morrow, who was aware that his wartime friend Dawes would need such a colleague. Dawes and Young first met in Secretary Hughes' office to be briefed three days before they sailed for France on December 29.[53] Hoover doubtless suggested his close friend, the Los

---

[50]J. S. Davis, "Economic and Financial Progress in Europe, 1924-25," *Rev. Ec. Stat.*, April 1925, 6:61-85; McFadyean, *Reparation*, chs. 4-5, esp. pp. 110-11; J. Harry Jones, *Josiah Stamp, Public Servant: The Life of the First Baron Stamp of Shortlands* (London: Pitman, 1964), chs. 20-21; Macmillan, *Winds of Change*, pp. 200-201, 341; Arthur Salter, *Slave of the Lamp* (London: Weidenfeld and Nicolson, 1967), pp. 115, 264; J. W. Wheeler-Bennett, *The Wreck of Reparations: Being the Political Background of the Lausanne Agreement* (New York: William Morrow, 1933), p. 255.
     The brief paragraph in Morison's *Oxford History of the American People* (New York: Oxford University Press, 1965), pp. 923-24, does scant justice to the facts and contains a few slips of the kind which are present in most of the works on which (together with my own published papers and personal memories) this presentation is based. The chief sources used here are Bergmann's *History of Reparations*, the two Dawes books, that of Auld (no index), the two McFadyean books, four Salter books, and Jones, *Stamp*.
     [51]McFadyean, *Reparation*, pp. 74-75.
     [52]Hoover, *The Memoirs of Herbert Hoover*, vol. 2: *The Cabinet and the Presidency, 1920-1933* (New York: Macmillan, 1951), pp. 181-82.
     [53]Dawes, *Journal*, pp. 1-2.

Angeles banker Henry M. Robinson, for the second committee, which a leading British banker, Sir Reginald McKenna, was appointed to chair, to ascertain how much German capital had been exported and how it could be brought back.

Most members of the Dawes committee were highly respected bankers (Dawes himself, Sir Robert Kindersley, Jean Parmentier, Emile Franqui) and industrialists (Young, Sir Josiah Stamp, Alberto Pirelli), each of whom had other important qualifications. There were two professors (Edgard Allix, Federico Flora) and one older man of broad experience (Baron Maurice Houtart). All were nominated by their respective governments and appointed by the Reparation Commission, to which their report would be submitted. They were naturally wary of one another at first, but most of the members developed highly congenial working relationships.[54]

Young and Stamp were in many senses the big men of the committee. Each had overcome an early feeling of inferiority without developing the "superiority complex" which characterized several key men of their time. Young was invaluable as strategist, negotiator, and harmonizer; Stamp for his knowledge, experience, skills, and unflagging industry. Dawes was a unique "character," with his underslung pipe and "Hell and Maria" expressions, who proved an able chairman. He greatly admired and constantly consulted Young and Stamp, who were early made chairmen of the two subcommittees, but he did not pretend to contribute to the substance of the evolving report. He was successful in developing the *esprit de corps* of the committee, and resolutely maintained an air of cheerful confidence in the face of delays, friction, and pessimism. He took pains to talk with many individuals and groups outside the committee, especially the French, whose cooperation he recognized as vital to a solution, and carefully prepared both his formal speeches and informal talks. Parmentier was another key member; he had Poincaré's confidence but was given his head, and at times was confronted by a conflict of loyalties to Poincaré and the committee. Kindersley, Franqui, and Pirelli also played substantial parts, as did Henry M. Robinson, when he was informally drawn into the service of the Dawes committee.

In addition to the members, Sir Arthur Salter of the League staff was called upon to contribute to the substance and form of the report. Andrew McFadyean, his successor as secretary-general of the Reparation Commission, was invaluable as secretary of the committee and as Stamp's col-

---

[54]Bergmann, *History of Reparations*, p. 223; Auld, *Dawes Plan*, pp. xvi xvii, 72–78, 252–55, 304; Dawes, *Journal*, pp. 18, 30; Jones, *Stamp*, pp. 220, 222; Sir Andrew McFadyean, *Recollected in Tranquillity* (London: Pall Mall Press, 1964), pp. 89–94. Stamp experienced a great deal of friction with Franqui, whose personality he found difficult, and with Allix and Houtart, whose names appear in Jones, *Stamp*, as "Allen" and "Hontart."

laborator in drafting the main body of the report.[55] Louis Barthou, president
of the Commission, Colonel James A. Logan, Jr., the astute American
unofficial observer, and Carl Bergmann, the personable representative of
the German minister of finance, rendered important services to the committee before, during, and after its work.[56] The British and U.S. ambassadors in Berlin, Lord D'Abernon and A. B. Houghton, assisted in various
ways.[57] Some witnesses and drop-in visitors were helpful (e.g., Dr. Schacht,
W. M. Acworth), while others were not (e.g., Governor Norman, Keynes).[58]

The technical assistants to the various members were useful but
played little part in the outcome. Dawes and Young selected Dawes'
brother, Rufus C. Dawes, as chief of staff and Young's assistant at General
Electric, Stuart M. Crocker, as secretary. Hoover must have suggested
Colonel Alan G. Goldsmith, the Commerce Department specialist on
reparations, and the commercial attachés to the U.S. embassies in
London, Paris, and Berlin (W. S. Tower, C. L. Jones, and C. E. Herring).
Morrow and others suggested E. W. Kemmerer and me. Robinson brought
with him the banker and statistician Colonel Leonard P. Ayres. Ayres
and Kemmerer, already famous as a "money doctor," deserved the title of
expert. The rest of the group of assistants were simply useful to have
around. In no sense was the entire group of assistants a team of experts;
they did not attend committee meetings, saw little or nothing of the maturing draft report, and were never given a chance to scrutinize and comment on it.[59] When the report was about to come out, most of them were
gloomy over it and pessimistic about its acceptance, especially in France.[60]

[55]On the parts played by Salter and McFadyean, see Dawes, *Journal*, pp. 103, 131, 179–80,
205; Sir Arthur Salter, *Recovery: The Second Effort* (New York: Century, 1932), pp. 164–68,
and *Memoirs of a Public Servant*, pp. 170–71; Jones, *Stamp*, p. 209n.

[56]On Barthou, Logan, and Bergmann, see Dawes, *Journal*, pp. 12–15, 50–51, 70–71, 104–5,
109–10, 126–27, 209, 220–22, 229, 247–61, 267–68; Bergmann, *History of Reparations*, Stamp's
foreword, author's preface, and pp. 235–36; McFadyean, *Recollected*, pp. 83–84. Others
included Sir Frederick Leith-Ross, Gaston Bergery, and Arthur N. Young, assistants to Bradbury, McFadyean, and Logan, respectively, and Maurice Frère, a Belgian. Leith-Ross and
Frère were especially valuable then and later.

[57]Dawes, *Journal*, pp. 15, 71, 88, 103; Turner, *Stresemann*, pp. 5–6, 87n, 92, 105, 115, 130,
148, 168, sometimes citing Stresemann's good friend since 1921, Viscount d'Abernon (*An
Ambassador of Peace*, 3 vols. [London: Hodder and Stoughton, 1929–30], with historical notes
by Maurice Alfred Gerothwohl). The second and third volumes of this valuable work are sub-
titled *Lord D'Abernon's Diary*; they deal with June 1922 through December 1923 and January
1924 through October 1926, respectively. See also McFadyean, *Recollected*, pp. 111–12.

[58]Auld, *Dawes Plan*, p. 128; Dawes, *Journal*, pp. 49–53, 58–60, 64, 68, 75, 83–88, 91–93, 119;
Jones, *Stamp*, pp. 210, 216–17, 222–23, 225.

[59]Dawes, *Dawes Plan*, pp. 20–22 et passim. This book and Dawes' *Journal* contain many
references to this staff, some overcomplimentary. In one exceptional instance, a Kemmerer
memorandum dated Berlin, February 9, was endorsed by the other U.S. technical assistants
and was given serious attention by Dawes and Stamp. Dawes, *Journal*, pp. 86–93. An
illuminating entry in *ibid.*, pp. 204–8, for April 1 gives no support to a paragraph in
McFadyean, *Recollected*, p. 93, which I feel sure is in error. Cf. also McFadyean's observation
in another connection in his *Reparation*, p. 114.

[60]At a private dinner attended by most of the U.S. technical assistants toward the end
of the work, I noted an atmosphere of gloom. I knew too little to share it and still had great

Dawes and Young had certainly discussed their task with key persons in New York and Washington and together on shipboard with Goldsmith and others. In their initial statement to the press on January 8, 1924, they said they had no preconceived plans. In his keynote address to the Commission and the committee, Dawes expressed the desire of the U.S. team "to be helpful to you who, with superior knowledge and longer experience, will take the initiative in the search for a common-sense agreement"; the committee's success, he said, would depend "chiefly upon whether, in the public mind and conscience of the Allies and of the world, there is an adequate conception of the great disaster which faces each Ally and Europe unless common sense is crowned King."[61]

The committee members realized that their task was fully as much diplomatic as technical, took it most seriously, and worked long hours under severe strain. Their meetings were in Paris except for a fortnight in Berlin (January 31 to February 13), where they conferred with high-level German officials, businessmen, and others. They undertook to propose means of stabilizing the German currency and balancing the German budget in such ways as to promote German recovery and yield optimum reparation payments—the last was the real crux of the matter. Young's subcommittee held fifty-one sessions, Stamp's sixty-three, and the whole committee fifty-four.

The atmosphere was charged with pessimism.[62] The German situation was precarious, if not desperate, with mass unemployment in the wake of hyperinflation. In February only a timely communiqué indicating progress toward agreement on the bank and currency plans saved the Rentenmark from collapse. The French situation was very weak, and in February and March a "battle of the franc" was won only with the aid of loans from New York and London bankers on the strength of the prospect that the committee would come up with an acceptable plan.[63] As at Paris

faith in Young and Stamp. Like the others present, I did not appreciate the importance of Dawes' role until later and was unaware of Salter's major contribution.

[61]Dawes, *Dawes Plan*, pp. 42–51; Dawes, *Journal*, pp. 18–31, 180. Poincaré's speech in the Chamber of Deputies on January 18, which Dawes interpreted as "designed to help us," is partially quoted in his *Journal*, pp. 40–48. Cf. Auld, *Dawes Plan*, pp. 109–11.

[62]Sir John Bradbury, the British member of the Reparation Commission, had persistently expressed Keynes' views (against which the Americans were on guard) and was pessimistic before ("prescribing a pill for an earthquake," he called it) and during the committee's work. So were Ambassador Houghton and his commercial attaché. See Auld, *Dawes Plan*, pp. 102–3; McFadyean, *Reparation*, pp. 25, 34n, 72, 73, 216, and *Recollected*, pp. 45–46, 64, 74–75, 82–83; Dawes, *Journal*, pp. 14, 15, 72, 73, 137, 229.

[63]HES, *Weekly Letter*, Mar. 22, May 10, 1924, pp. 72, 123, 128; Mar. 15, 1930, p. 72; *Rev. Ec. Stat.*, July 1924, 5:232–34; Bergmann, *History of Reparations*, pp. 216, 220, 229–30; Dawes, *Journal*, pp. 14, 53–54, 72–74, 91–95, 108–9, 113, 159–60; McFadyean, *Reparation*, pp. 61–65; Jones, *Stamp*, p. 218; Turner, *Stresemann*, ch. 5. My July 1924 article contained this paragraph (p. 207): "Early in 1924 the French and Belgian francs, which had been falling gradually in 1923, suffered a precipitous decline, under the influence of speculative operations encouraged by the weakness of the fiscal and financial position. With the aid of domestic

in 1919, the press presented problems; leaks had to be guarded against—
one was traced to a member—and erroneous rumors squashed.[64] Only six of
the ten members spoke English and six or seven French; hence time-
consuming translation was necessary.[65] Illnesses and absences interrupted
the preparation and revision of drafts of a document that had to appeal
not only to the French and Germans but to world opinion as well. Personality clashes and friction were inevitable, and at times a breakdown
seemed imminent. Stamp, who bore the heaviest burden, on March 27
drafted a minority report that he was promptly induced to scrap.[66] Only
after a fortnight of "hideous nightmare" were difficult compromises
finally reached, and hitches came up even in the last days before the report
was presented, weeks later than Dawes had hoped.

The committee early reached certain basic decisions. No attempt
would be made to estimate Germany's ultimate capacity to pay reparations,
and the huge figure set in May 1921 was ignored. The interests of Germany
and her creditors required the rehabilitation of the country, which involved
stabilizing the currency on a gold basis[67] and budget balancing, both protected against excessive reparation burdens. Representatives of German
labor, industry, and banking recognized as just the principle that she must
bear a tax burden commensurate with that borne by the Allied nations. The
plan was to facilitate the normal operation of the German economy, provide incentives for its return to prosperity, give its reparation creditors
(the French especially) reasonable assurance of adequate reparations, and
provide acceptable guarantees. As the work progressed, agreement was
reached on details and important additional elements: the consolidation of
all sums due by Germany into one, the size of the foreign loan to be issued,
the schedule of annual payments and the sources of each, the formulation
of a control system acceptable to both Germany and her creditors, and
several other points.[68]

---

measures supported by large liquid credits from America and England, a striking recovery
occurred, from which there has been a partial reaction. The repercussions of the 'battle'
were severely felt, both financially and industrially, not only in France and Belgium, but in
most of Western and Central Europe, and especially in Germany and Austria."

[64]Bergmann, *History of Reparations*, p. 229; McFadyean, *Reparation*, p. 74n; Dawes,
Journal, pp. 90–93, 122, 137; Jones, *Stamp*, pp. 217–18, 220, 222.

[65]Jones, *Stamp*, pp. 216, 219, 230.

[66]Bergmann, *History of Reparation*, p. 223, 253; Dawes, *Journal*, pp. 183–84; Jones,
Stamp, pp. 222, 227.

[67]The decision to place the reorganized Reichsbank on a gold basis with a 33 and 1/3 percent gold reserve (later somewhat relaxed) was reached on March 19 (the day the Gold Discount Bank Act was passed by the Reichstag), under pressure from New York bankers and the
U.S. State Department and over objections from the British, French, and Italians, who were
not yet back on the gold standard. Dawes, *Journal*, p. 172.

[68]Auld, *Dawes Plan*, pp. 128–31; McFadyean, *Reparation*, pp. 67–85; Dawes, *Journal*,
pp. 95–101, 104–10.

The most crucial decision concerned the size of the reparation annuity in the "standard year." A wide range of figures was considered. The British apparently urged that it not be over 2,000 million gold marks. As late as March 20 Young was inclined to a figure of 3,000 million. With great difficulty the compromise figure of 2,500 million was agreed to, subject to increase by a crude "prosperity index" and to further adjustment up or down if the purchasing power of gold should vary by 10 percent or more.[69] The thorny problem of getting French and Belgian troops out of the Ruhr concerned the committee greatly but was not specifically mentioned in the report. At the outset, however, stress was laid on the basic assumption "that the fiscal and economic unity of the Reich will be restored."

With appropriate ceremonies, the committee's 124-page report was handed to the Reparation Commission on April 9.[70] On the same day the McKenna committee submitted its report. It had first met on January 21, held thirty-eight meetings in Paris and Berlin, and arrived at estimates of several categories of German exported capital. The committee emphasized permanent stoppage of inflation and giving effect to the recommendations of the Dawes committee as a means to induce the return of this capital.[71]

The committee provided a rare example of superb "social engineering."[72] Its report offered a skillfully designed, somewhat flexible plan for a sensible way out of a veritable morass. It had flaws but approached perfection as nearly as existing conditions permitted. Though open to criticism at many points, it proved on the whole "most too dear to take and most too cheap to leave."[73] As Dawes later wrote, the report was "a compromise between economic principles and political necessities, but it was a compromise whose finding was dominated by economic experts."[74] As Stamp commented, "It was not in itself, and could not be,

[69]Bergmann, *History of Reparations*, pp. 36–37, 226–27, 234–38, 246–47; Dawes, *Journal*, pp. 174, 181–86; Bonn, *Wandering Scholar*, pp. 252–53; Jones, *Stamp*, pp. 223–25. Cf. McFadyean, *Reparation*, ch. 4; B. M. Anderson, *Economics and the Public Welfare: Financial and Economic History of the United States, 1914–1946* (New York: Van Nostrand, 1949), pp. 105–9.

[70]Dawes, *Journal*, pp. 212–22, 280–488. On March 23 three members of the McKenna committee urged that the report be held back until after the German elections on May 4, but this proposal was quickly rejected. *Ibid.*, pp. 176–78.

[71]*Ibid.*, pp. 489–511; Bergmann, *History of Reparations*, pp. 224–26, 253–56. Both reports were published in Dawes, *Dawes Plan*, and also in Harold G. Moulton, *The Reparation Plan* (New York: McGraw-Hill, 1924; preface dated June 1924), which contains a useful "Index to the Experts' Reports" prepared by the Brookings Institute of Economics (pp. 317–25).

[72]This is most clearly brought out in the books by Auld and McFadyean. See also Roland W. Boyden, "The Dawes Report," *Foreign Affairs*, July 1924, 2:583–97.

[73]McFadyean, *Reparation*, p. 67.

[74]Dawes, *Journal*, pp. vii–ix.

for it was not allowed to be, a solution of the Reparation policy—but it was a substantial step away from lunacy."[75]

The Dawes Plan was built of elements already available but conceived in a new spirit and presented in a way to appeal strongly to world opinion. In essence, it was intended to enable Germany to regain her financial and industrial equilibrium, and move from distress to prosperity; to provide the confidence which would stimulate the flow of American and other foreign capital to aid German and European recovery; and at the same time to assure that substantial reparations, at a level that Germany and her creditors would find acceptable, would be paid over the next few years, without upsetting her economic equilibrium or imposing excessive burdens on her people's level of living. It fixed annual payments (to cover all German obligations for Allied and European claims arising out of the war) on a rising scale for five years, to reach a maximum in the fifth or "standard" year. In the first year no burden would be placed on the German budget, and the amount required was to be met out of a proposed international loan and interest on railway bonds to be issued. In the standard year only half the payment was to come out of the budget, the rest out of other pledged sources.[76] Provision was made for increase in the scheduled payments in accordance with a crude index of prosperity, such as the Germans had proposed (*Besserungsscheine*) at the Spa conference of July 1920.[77] It was also provided that if the purchasing power of gold should vary by more than 10 percent, the scheduled payments should be adjusted accordingly.[78] Since the extent to which the payments could be transferred to the creditors depended on the willingness of the creditors to receive payment in forms available to Germany, it was provided that full compliance would be registered when the specified sums were paid into the reorganized Reichsbank for the account of the creditors' agent. This important "innovation" had been a feature of the League's arrangement for the financial rehabilitation of Hungary in late 1923, in which Salter had played a leading part.[79] A fairly complicated system of controls, in which foreigners would have a large role, was designed to protect Germany as well as her creditors.[80]

From the outset Dawes had insisted that the report must be read and understood by the general public. Under his urging, Young drafted a long,

[75]*Ibid.*, p. xviii.

[76]Bergmann, *History of Reparations*, pp. 238–42. See chart in *Report of the Agent General for Reparation Payments* (published in Berlin), Dec. 10, 1927, p. 5.

[77]Bergmann, *History of Reparations*, pp. 36–37, 236–38, 243; McFadyean, *Reparation*, pp. 69–70; Bonn, *Wandering Scholar*, pp. 232–33. Ayres worked with Stamp on the index.

[78]McFadyean, *Reparation*, p. 199.

[79]Bergmann, *History of Reparations*, pp. 242–48; Moulton and Pasvolsky, *War Debts and World Prosperity*, pp. 166n, 239; Salter, *Memoirs*, p. 181.

[80]Bergmann, *History of Reparations*, pp. 248–52; McFadyean, *Reparation*, pp. 75–79.

readable introduction, helped by Salter, and prepared a digest to precede it. Toward the end some members wanted this introduction eliminated, but their objections were overborne, and it had a powerful effect.[81] In the final section of the report, the committee made several points. It was to be regarded as "an indivisible whole." The plan was to be "strictly dependent upon the restoration of Germany's economic sovereignty." The committee was confident that the German people could carry the burdens imposed and refused to speculate on how fully the payments could be transferred. The reconstruction of Germany was "only part of the larger problem of the reconstruction of Europe." The plan was "so framed as to facilitate a final and comprehensive agreement as to all the problems of reparations and connected questions as soon as circumstances make this possible."

The public reception of the plan was overwhelmingly favorable,[82] as the committee had hoped, and this was of great importance in France, Germany, and the United States, where Dawes was nominated for the vice presidency in June. It was promptly praised by critical individuals. Keynes published in his weekly a highly commendatory review, with only mild reservations and no hint of the savage criticism that he would express six months later.[83] B. M. Anderson pronounced the report "a masterly document," "an enduring monument to the able, patient, fair-minded, upright men who produced it" and "an adequate basis for the solution of the reparations problem, if loyally accepted and intelligently and courageously administered." He predicted that its acceptance in good faith by the interested countries would constitute the turning point in Europe's economic life.[84] Moulton's early analysis of the plan was clear-cut and friendly, though in his last two chapters he gave reasons for anticipating only limited success for it. Similar comments were made by many others. At the Institute of Politics in July and August, Louis Aubert discussed it very favorably at length.[85]

Of course, there were criticisms and misgivings. Many Frenchmen considered the plan too lenient to Germany and questioned German will-

[81]Bergmann, *History of Reparations*, p. 253; Dawes, *Journal*, pp. xvii (Stamp foreword), xxvii (Brüning foreword), 85, 101, 141, 155–58, 173, 175, 179–81, 203–4, 207–14, 284–347.

[82]It is unnecessary to cite all the sources for this statement or the passages in journals and books which touch on it, but see *Economist*, Apr. 12, 19, 26, 1924, pp. 773–74, 824–28, 861–62; HES, *Weekly Letter*, Apr. 19, May 10, 1924, pp. 99–100, 123–24, 128–30, both written while I was in Europe.

[83]*N&A*, Apr. 12, 19, 1924, pp. 40–41, 76–77, and below, p. 68. On March 24 Stamp wrote his wife after a chat with him: "Keynes I found pretty critical and sceptical but obliged to admit that the main immediate problems have been secured beyond his expectation. But he is particularly sceptical of the Yankees living up to their promises." Jones, *Stamp*, p. 225.

[84]"The Report of the Dawes Committee," *Chase Economic Bulletin*, Apr. 22, 1924. In *ibid.*, Aug. 31, 1922, Anderson had proposed his "detailed scheme." Later he was critical of some provisions of the plan.

[85]Moulton, *Reparation Plan*; Louis Aubert, *The Reconstruction of Europe* (New Haven, Conn.: Yale University Press, 1925), pp. 82–111.

ingness to carry it out if accepted. On February 3 Dawes had noted:
"Many feel that if Germany is made strong enough to pay she will be
strong enough to refuse to pay." When Dawes and Young spent an hour
with Clemenceau on April 18, he was pessimistic about the future of
France and Europe and doubted that Germany would show good faith in
accepting the plan and carrying it out.[86] Many Germans considered it too
demanding; the British leaned to this view, as did Morrow, who had other
misgivings.[87] The highly uncertain political situation in France and
Germany made the British skeptical about its acceptance by these countries.[88] Economists such as Keynes and Moulton, who placed extreme
emphasis on the necessity of payment through German exports, gravely
underestimated the potential of capital movements; what Moulton called
"simply an illusion" was to become a reality.[89] Kemmerer in mid-1925
admitted that the scheduled payments were larger than most American
and British economists thought economically desirable but argued that they
were not impossible for a vigorous Germany to meet if she had a strong
incentive to pay them and if all countries welcomed imports of German
goods and services.[90] Schacht held similar views. I cannot accept Schumpeter's later assessment that "the Dawes tribute was *morally* inacceptable
to Germany and *economically* inacceptable to the recipient countries."[91]

Implementation   McFadyean wrote in 1930, after discussing the con-
of the Dawes Plan   ditions under which the Dawes committee was set up,
that "any report which the Experts chose to produce unanimously was
practically assured beforehand of acceptance, and, indeed, if it was sea-
worthy, of success."[92] So it turned out, but this was far from clear in mid-
April 1924. For months the outcome was uncertain,[93] and five years of its
operation constituted a great experiment.

[86]Dawes, *Journal*, pp. 73, 124, 229.

[87]Nicolson, *Morrow*, p. 273.

[88]See *Economist*, passim, and reports on British economic conditions in HES, *Weekly Letter*, June 7, July 5, Aug. 2, Sept. 6, Oct. 4, 1924, pp. 157, 189, 221, 257, 289.

[89]Dawes, *Dawes Plan*, pp. 186–204; Auld, *Dawes Plan*, pp. 155–86; McFadyean, *Reparation*, pp. 138–39. *Editorial Research Reports* hastily published (in Washington on Apr. 11, 1924) "The Dawes Report—An Economic Analysis" (mimeographed), by Guy Greer, formerly for four years on the Reparation Commission's interallied staff. He remarked that the report was "fundamentally different from the forecasts which have appeared in the press" and was skeptical of its successful functioning.

[90]*Annals*, July 1925, 120:7–10, reprinted in Gerould and Turnbull, *Interallied Debts*, pp. 386–91. In another connection, McFadyean remarked: "It is reported that Dr. Schacht would have been willing to undertake the standard Dawes annuity of 2½ milliard marks if he could have been assured of free markets for German exports." *Reparation*, pp. 211–12.

[91]Joseph A. Schumpeter, *Business Cycles: A Theoretical, Historical, and Statistical Analysis of the Capitalist Process*, 2 vols. (New York: McGraw-Hill, 1939), 2:704n.

[92]McFadyean, *Reparation*, pp. 66–67.

[93]*Economist*, April-November 1924, passim; Bergmann, *History of Reparations*, pp. 256–327; McFadyean, *Reparation*, pp. 82–92; Dawes, *Journal*, pp. 230–75. In HES, *Weekly Letter*,

Inspired by the Dawes committee work, the Reparation Commission followed through in exemplary fashion.[94] On April 11 it notified the German government that it considered the Dawes report "a practical basis for the rapid solution of the reparation problem" and asked assurances of "its willingness to cooperate in the execution of the Plan." On April 16 full German consent was given in a brief note, and despite partisan opposition from extremists of the right and left and the election of May 4, the Reichstag and Reichsrat repeatedly confirmed the Marx cabinet's endorsement. On April 17 the Commission advised the other governments involved that it had accepted the report and recommended that they take favorable action. On April 24 Britain, Belgium, and Italy responded affirmatively, but Poincaré's note of the next day was inconclusive and necessitated delay. Before and after the crucial election of May 11, with Poincaré's encouragement, the Commission did its utmost to speed preparations for putting the plan into operation, setting up organization committees on the Reichsbank, railways, and industrial bonds and drafting a protocol to develop the plan into a binding treaty between the Allies and Germany.

For two months political crises in Germany and France delayed action on the Dawes Plan. In the Reichstag elections on May 4 the Social Democratic Party (Sozialdemokratische Partei Deutschlands; SPD) dropped from 171 seats to 100; all the parties supporting Marx's minority coalition (including Stresemann's Deutsche Volkspartei; DVP) lost seats; gains were made by the opposition Nationalist, Communist, and extreme rightist Nazi Racist parties, which emerged with 106, 62, and 32 seats, respectively; a host of splinter parties also gained seats. With great difficulty Marx formed a new cabinet on June 1, which included the indispensable Stresemann.[95]

Liberal Ramsay MacDonald, who became Britain's first Labour prime minister early in 1924, was in close touch with Poincaré. In the May 11 elections to the Chamber of Deputies, however, Poincaré's Bloc National was unexpectedly and decisively defeated by a left coalition led by Radical-Socialist Edouard Herriot and Paul Painlevé. Poincaré did not resign until June 1, two days after publication of his correspondence with MacDonald. Activist President Millerand was a die-hard supporter of Poincaré's foreign policy, and Herriot refused to take office under him. The Chamber forced Millerand to resign in mid-term and elected Gaston

May 10, Sept. 13, 1924, pp. 123–30, 267–70; Jan. 10, 1925, pp. 15–18, I touched on these developments, covered more fully in my "Progress in Europe, 1923–24" and "Progress in Europe, 1924–25."

[94]Davis, "Progress in Europe, 1923–24," pp. 207–9; HES, *Weekly Letter*, Sept. 13, 1924, p. 267; Bergmann, *History of Reparations*, pp. 256–60; McFadyean, *Reparation*, pp. 85–92.

[95]*Economist*, May 10, 1924, pp. 945–46, and later issues; Turner, *Stresemann*, ch. 5, esp. pp. 163–78.

Doumergue to replace him. Herriot was installed as premier in mid-June. On the new foreign policy he had strong support, but he proved a somewhat timorous leader, and in April 1925 he lost office on a domestic issue and was succeeded by Painlevé.[96]

During the maneuverings of these hectic weeks, Colonel Logan (the so-called unofficial observer of the United States on the Reparation Commission) visited Berlin and talked with Stresemann on June 4 in company with Ambassador Houghton, reporting by letter to Dawes, Barthou, Bradbury, and others; back in Paris he talked with Herriot, whom he knew well.[97] Gaston Bergery, McFadyean's strongly anti-Poincaré assistant, also lent Herriot "powerful aid."[98]

The cordial conference of Herriot and MacDonald at Chequers on June 22 and 23 led to the calling of an Allied conference in London on July 16. Meanwhile, probably thanks to Logan's suggestions, Herriot made a friendly move on one sore point by authorizing the return of some 140,000 Germans who had been expelled from the Ruhr and the Rhineland for what the Germans deemed political reasons. Also in June, on motion of the French and Belgian representatives, Germany was welcomed into the International Chamber of Commerce; its Committee on Economic Restoration, which included five members of the two experts' committees (Stamp, Alberti, Pirelli, Robinson, and Young), was active in the next few years.[99]

MacDonald soon visited Paris to clear up misunderstandings, and on July 9 an Anglo-French memorandum was published stating that the Dawes Plan should be put into operation as soon as possible and summarizing the matters to be decided at a London conference, at which all governments concerned would confirm their acceptance of the plan.[100] When this all-important conference opened, it included the British, French, and Belgian prime ministers; special delegates from Italy and Japan; and others from Portugal, Greece, Romania, and Yugoslavia. On behalf of the United States, the ambassador to Great Britain, Frank Kellogg, and Colonel Logan "unofficially" participated; the ambassador to Germany, A. B. Houghton, and Owen D. Young were also there, and Secretary Hughes was in London on holiday. Poincaré continued to make trouble for Herriot, who had to return to Paris for support before the German delegation could be invited. It arrived on August 5, led by Chancellor

[96]*Economist*, issues of June 1924; Dulles, *BIS*, p. 511. Most of the books cited omit important details.

[97]Logan to Dawes, June 12, 1924, in Dawes, *Journal*, pp. 252-61; Jones, *Stamp*, p. 234.

[98]McFadyean, *Reparation*, p. 60n. Earlier Bergery had contributed significantly by his "Lycurgue" articles in *L'Europe nouvelle* from July 1922 to February 1923.

[99]Davis, "Progress in Europe, 1924-25," pp. 62-65.

[100]Bergmann, *History of Reparations*, p. 260; *Economist*, July 12, 1924, pp. 43-44, 54-55. On February 20 Logan told Dawes that he felt "very sure that a conference of premiers over the report will be productive not only of delay but of unnecessary political controversy," Dawes, *Journal*, p. 14. But it proved unavoidable.

Marx and the key ministers Luther and Stresemann. Four days later the Reparation Commission signed an agreement with the German government for the execution of the Dawes Plan, and further agreements were reached, after some difficulty, before the conference ended on August 16.[101]

Withdrawal of foreign troops from the Ruhr began on August 14 and was to be completed in a year. The requisite German laws for putting the plan into effect were promulgated on August 30. On September 1 the first year of operation began. In the first month the Franco-Belgian customs control was ended and the French ceased to operate the German coal mines. On October 10 the loan agreement was signed; on October 14 it was successfully floated. The new Reichsbank Act was passed on October 11. On November 15 controls over the Ruhr and Rhineland railways were turned over to the new German National Railway Company, which had begun operation October 1 and from the start was an unqualified success.[102]

Meanwhile, a serious difficulty had arisen over the appointment of an American to the key post of agent general for reparation payments, the top man in the control organization. Early in June Houghton and Stresemann were under the impression that Logan wanted and expected to be appointed; so was McFadyean, who distrusted Logan and did all he could to frustrate this ambition. Late in June, however, the Reparation Commission unanimously selected Dwight W. Morrow, whom leaders in Europe and America recognized as uniquely qualified. However, at a White House dinner conference on July 2 Houghton brought word from Berlin to President Coolidge, Secretary Hughes, Dawes (now the Republican nominee for the vice presidency), and Young that the appointment of a Morgan partner (even if he quit the firm, as Morrow seemed ready to do) would arouse so much political opposition in Germany as to jeopardize the plan. The administration reluctantly—and too hastily[103]—concluded that his appointment was inadvisable. Young agreed to serve for a few weeks to get the plan started, but many weeks actually elapsed before the permanent appointment, which the bankers felt essential before floating the Dawes loan, could be made. A bright young lawyer, S. Parker Gilbert, Jr., was appointed early in September and took over on October 31. He was conscientious and capable, but Morrow's incomparable strengths, such as he was soon to demonstrate in Mexico, were sadly lacking, and the history of 1927–29 would probably have been far different if he had been in this post in Berlin.[104]

[101]HES, *Weekly Letter*, Sept. 13, 1924, pp. 267–70; Bergmann, *History of Reparations*, pp. 260–65; McFadyean, *Reparation*, pp. 89–91; Dawes, *Journal*, pp. 234–35, 261–68; Turner, *Stresemann*, pp. 168–78.

[102]Angell, *Recovery of Germany*, pp. 204–46.

[103]Houghton's judgment was fallible and may well have been wrong. The need for a quick decision was less urgent than it appeared at the time.

[104]Salter, who was extremely eager for Morrow's appointment, would, I presume, agree. My conclusion rests mostly on my fairly close acquaintance with Morrow, with whom I had

As the Dawes Plan machinery took over, the Reparation Commission shrank its staff and operations but continued to function (with an American voting member, which it appointed by unanimous vote) until it was superseded by the Bank for International Settlements in May 1930.[105] The agent general made elaborate semiannual reports to the Commission, which were published in Berlin and given wide circulation.

On the eve of the loan agreement Keynes published an article in which he declared the control system "not compatible with civilization or human nature," called its object "to extract from the German people the last drop of sweat," and flatly predicted failure of the scheme.[106] London newspapers voiced hostility. Lord Rothermere's *Daily Mail*, which had strongly supported the French occupation of the Ruhr, "led an even more furious campaign against the loan."[107] The German External Loan, a twenty-five-year, 7 percent sinking fund issue, was offered at 92. The flotation on October 14 in New York and London was a brilliant success: more than half was taken in the United States, more than a quarter in England, for a nominal total of about 960 million gold marks, to yield 800 million net. The bonds soon rose above par, and the proceeds served many purposes.[108] The reorganized Reichsbank began operations on the 15th, under a law passed four days earlier. The old mark currencies were retired at the rate of a million million to 1, and the Rentenmark currency began to be retired at par. Over the next few weeks other difficulties regarding deliveries in kind, British and French levies on imports from Germany, and the distribution of reparation payments among the creditors were gradually resolved.[109]

C. W. Guillebaud, a younger colleague of Keynes, wrote after another visit to Germany: "the change from the conditions of a year ago is almost unbelievable. The miracle has actually occurred: the currency has been stabilized. . . . The old virtues of the German people—diligence, probity, and thrift—have in a large measure returned." He noted that Stresemann

---

worked in London (in 1918–19), Paris (1921), and Mexico (1928), and with whom I had visited in New York and Washington.

[105]Bergmann, *History of Reparations*, p. 282; Auld, *Dawes Plan*, pp. 247–48, 256n; McFadyean, *Reparation*, pp. 75–76, 194; Moulton and Pasvolsky, *War Debts and World Prosperity*, p. 199.

[106]*N&A*, Oct. 4, 1924, pp. 7–9, partially quoted in McFadyean, *Reparation*, pp. 77–78, with a scathing comment, and in Étienne Mantoux, *The Carthaginian Peace, Or the Economic Consequences of Mr. Keynes* (London: Oxford University Press, 1945), p. 146. Keynes repeated his dismal prediction in *New Republic* for Aug. 3, 1927 ("the Dawes Plan will break down according to schedule"). Quoted in Auld, *Dawes Plan*, p. xv. Keynes' inveterate hostility and erroneous predictions continued through 1929. On the control system, see Bergmann, *History of Reparations*, chs. 30–31; Auld, *Dawes Plan*, pp. 132–40. On the whole it worked very smoothly.

[107]*Economist*, Oct. 18, 1924, pp. 600–601; McFadyean, *Reparation*, p. 48. On the British press in the interwar period see Mowat, *Britain between the Wars*, pp. 244–46.

[108]Bergmann, *History of Reparations*, pp. 280–81; Auld, *Dawes Plan*, pp. 140–43.

[109]Bergmann, *History of Reparations*, pp. 271, 282–94.

argued, in his campaign speech at Dortmund on November 19, that acceptance of the Dawes Plan had conferred more solid benefit on Germany than had any other line of policy, and he referred to current negotiations for a commercial treaty with France as promising "one of the most vital instruments for the pacification of Europe during the next decade."[110] Early in 1925 a dispute over German fulfillment of the military terms of the Versailles treaty delayed the French evacuation of Cologne scheduled for January 10 and acutely inflamed German public opinion, and this incident caused a temporary departure from the amicable spirit that had developed during the London conference.[111]

Meanwhile, despite his success over the Dawes Plan, MacDonald's minority government fell on October 8, 1924, over unrelated issues. The tense and dirty campaign, in which the sensational (and probably forged) Zinoviev letter figured heavily, ended in a decisive Conservative victory, and Stanley Baldwin resumed the top post.[112] The new foreign secretary, Austen Chamberlain, soon rejected two of MacDonald's key moves but reinforced the newly re-established Anglo-French entente and cooperated heartily with Briand and Stresemann in progressive international efforts, of which the Locarno agreements of 1925 were outstanding.[113] Even in Britain the mood slowly changed from anxious caution to modest confidence.[114] The European outlook seemed so promising early in 1925 that I wrote: "The danger now lies not in pessimistic underrating of the sound elements in the European position, but in excessive optimism."[115]

Genuine But Checkered The breakthrough year 1924 was followed by
Progress, 1925–29 five years of impressive progress on many fronts in Europe.[116] A crude "international business index" combining indexes of monthly data for iron, steel, and coal output and rail-freight

[110]C. W. Guillebaud, "The Fruits of Stabilization of Germany," *N&A*, Nov. 22, 1924, pp. 288–89, and his later book, *The Economic Recovery of Germany from 1933 to the Incorporation of Austria in March 1938* (London: Macmillan, 1939), pp. 4–5. This treaty finally came into force on Sept. 6, 1927, as the agent general for reparation payments noted in his report (Dec. 10, 1927, p. 136).

[111]*N&A*, Jan. 3, 10, 17, 1925, pp. 486, 511–12, 542–43, and later issues. That of June 13, 1925, pp. 311–14, asserted that if the mid-May joint note had been issued in January, Marx would have won the election.

[112]Mowat, *Britain between the Wars*, pp. 183–97; Kennan, *Russia and the West*, ch. 16 and pp. 278–80.

[113]Mowat, *Britain between the Wars*, pp. 197–200. Cf. McFadyean, *Reparation*, p. 110: "Without the Dawes Plan there would have been no Locarno; without Locarno the further evolution of the plan would have been thwarted."

[114]See successive reports on British economic conditions in HES, *Weekly Letter*, for 1924 and 1925.

[115]*Ibid.*, Jan. 10, 1925, pp. 15–18. In concluding my longer review ("Progress in Europe, 1923–24," pp. 240–42) I had already referred to "a tendency to excessive optimism, blind to the inevitable delays and further adjustments that lie ahead."

[116]McFadyean, *Reparation*, chs. 5–8; Salter, *Recovery* and *Security: Can We Retrieve It?* (New York: Reynal and Hitchcock, 1939); and numerous other sources.

volume for eight countries (United States, Canada, Great Britain, France, Belgium, Germany, Italy, and Japan), weighted by population, showed a gradual advance of 30 percent in calendar year averages 1924-29; the rise from the low of mid-1924 to the peak in September 1929 was nearly 50 percent, with the most marked gains in the second half of 1924, the second and third quarters of 1926, and the first three quarters of 1929.[117] Salter wrote in 1960: "Everywhere in the Western world pre-war standards of prosperity had been surpassed. . . . The average standard of living, even in Europe, was in 1928 higher than it had ever been."[118] But the progress was uneven, and contemporary observers generally understressed weaknesses and exaggerated gains in their generalizations and forecasts. It looked as if the world had gone back to "normalcy" and this illusion was cherished in what Bonn called "Indian Summer,"[119] when the few who saw clearly were not believed.

The Dawes Plan fulfilled the hopes of its framers, never broke down, and operated without severe test until it was superseded, prematurely, by the Young Plan of 1929-30. In mid-September 1929 a writer in Keynes' own weekly credited the Dawes Plan not only with having "first brought sanity into the treatment of the Reparations problem," but also with having provided "an essential condition of the progress which has since been made in the sphere of political appeasement."[120] International tensions and political instability were notably diminished but did not disappear.

The newly generated spirit of international good will bore early fruit in the Locarno agreements of 1925, and harmony among Britain, France, and Germany persisted despite interruptions. A veritable "pactomania" followed, marked by "noble illusions and grave errors."[121] The Kellogg-Briand Pact of August 1928 was an extreme example of such an agreement.

Great Britain put the pound sterling back to prewar par with the dollar in late April 1925, made some regional economic gains despite depression in older industries, endured excessive unemployment, suffered a disastrous coal strike from May to December 1926, and made a modest recovery in 1927-29. With much League and central bank assistance, most continental European nations returned to some form of the gold standard.

Inept fiscal and financial management led to another grave crisis of the French franc, which fell as low as 2 cents in the spring of 1926.

[117]CTC, *Business Bulletin*, Oct. 15, 1932 (1924 = 100). From September 1929 the combined index fell almost continuously until mid-1932, by a total of almost 50 percent; it was then about 70 percent of the 1924 average.

[118]*Memoirs of a Public Servant*, pp. 194-96.

[119]Bonn, *Wandering Scholar*, ch. 17.

[120]*N&A*, Sept. 14, 1929, pp. 754-55, quoted in part in Jones, *Stamp*, pp. 250-51.

[121]Sorbonne Professor J. B. Duroselle's illuminating recent article ("Reconsiderations: The Spirit of Locarno: Illusions of Pactomania," *Foreign Affairs*, July 1972, 50:752-64) ably summarizes (albeit with a few slips) the flood of international agreements in 1924-29 in an amazing prevalence of optimism.

Poincaré returned to power and stabilized it de facto by the end of the year at about 4 cents (roughly one-fifth of prewar parity), where it was stabilized de jure in July 1928; this proved too low, relative to sterling. France then went on to achieve a high level of prosperity and financial power, which she used none too wisely. Late in July 1929, under extreme pressure from Poincaré shortly before ill health forced his resignation as premier, the French chambers finally ratified the Mellon-Berenger debt settlement which had been signed April 27, 1926.[122] This virtually completed the American war debt settlements; the British had also settled theirs. Germany, in the five years of the Dawes Plan, made what was regarded as an extraordinary recovery, but there were many internal and external strains.

Individual Americans participated extensively in European affairs, with encouragement from Washington and New York. Most of this, but by no means all of it, was helpful: some Americans contributed to the obsessions and euphoria that characterized the later 1920s and others to the overextension of private lending to continental Europe.

The League of Nations was warmly supported and functioned constructively, despite some setbacks, with Germany as a full member (after several months' delay) from September 1926.[123] Under League auspices a world economic conference at Geneva from May 4 to 23, 1927, reached unanimous agreement on sound commercial policies, but the national followups were disappointing, and the influence of the League began to wane before 1930.[124] International trade grew, even between Western nations and Stalin's Russia, and there were halting approaches toward normal economic and political relations with the Soviet Union.[125] Italy's dictator, Mussolini, though often truculent, was generally cooperative for the time.

[122]*Economist*, July 27, Aug. 3, 1929, pp. 115, 222–23; Anderson, *Economics and the Public Welfare*, chs. 21, 25.

[123]Harold Nicolson, *King George the Fifth, His Life and Reign* (London: Constable, 1952), pp. 410–13; Mowat, *Britain between the Wars*, pp. 343–44. Internal dissension had prevented Germany from applying for admission years earlier. Aubert, *Reconstruction*, pp. 156–58, citing a letter of Lord Robert Cecil in the *Morning Post* (London). On the League in this period, see *Foreign Affairs*, especially three articles by Eduard Beneš (4:295–310, 8:212–24, and 11:66–80); and Harriet E. Davis, ed., *Pioneers in World Order* (New York: Columbia University Press, 1944), in which a number of Americans who were associated with the League's work discuss its successes and failures.

[124]Salter, *Recovery*, pp. 196–200, 231–37; *Memoirs of a Public Servant*, pp. 195–206.

[125]Some of these approaches are touched upon in my papers of 1924–25 which have been cited. They are discussed at greater length in various articles in *Foreign Affairs*, e.g., 5:650–62, 8:260–73; in Xenia J. Euden and H. H. Fisher, *Soviet Russia and the West, 1920–1927: A Documentary Series* (Stanford, Calif.: Stanford University Press, 1957), pp. 228–415; in Kennan, *Russia and the West*, ch. 16; and briefly in Mowat, *Britain between the Wars*, pp. 187–97, Macmillan, *Winds of Change*, pp. 151–52, Turner, *Stresemann*, pp. 203, 220–21, 227–28, and Chossudovsky, "Genoa Revisited," p. 567. Henry Shapiro, who spent nearly

Some Major   *Lessened political instability.* Prime Minister
Topics Elaborated   Stanley Baldwin's new government lasted from
November 7, 1924, until June 1929, with Austen Chamberlain at the
Foreign Office and Winston Churchill as chancellor of the exchequer.
In view of the improving international situation Churchill supported the
basic doctrine of "no war for ten years," fought for strict economy in public
expenditures, even on the Navy, and agreed with his predecessor and successor, Philip Snowden, on the main principles of financial and commercial
policy.[126] Chamberlain, though he reversed two of MacDonald's recent
decisions (on Russian policy and the Geneva protocol), ably cooperated
with Briand and Stresemann on major issues in 1925-28.

Stresemann continued as foreign minister in successive German cabinets, though he failed to win Nationalist support for the Locarno agreements and was persistently hampered by political turmoil. President Ebert
died on February 28, 1925, four months before his seven-year term was to
expire. On April 26 the national hero Field Marshal Paul von Hindenburg
was elected over ex-chancellor Wilhelm Marx and was inaugurated on
May 12. Hindenburg gave Stresemann more cordial support than the latter
had expected, and this went far to allay misgivings abroad.[127] Belatedly
Stresemann won French consent to early evacuation of all occupied zones,
but he was ill for a year before he died on October 3, 1929; the evacuation
took place in June 1930, five years ahead of the treaty schedule.[128] Briand,
the most European-minded French statesman of the period, was foreign
minister for most of this period. When Poincaré was premier from mid-
1926 until ill health forced his retirement late in July 1929, he concentrated his efforts mainly on finance, but he sometimes hampered Briand
in conducting foreign policy.[129] In May 1930 Briand put forward the intriguing but highly premature idea of a United States of Europe, which
was widely discussed in the 1920s and early 1930s.[130]

---

forty years in Moscow, almost without interruption, in December 1972 published a series of
newspaper articles based on his Kremlin-watching since 1933.

[126]Churchill, *Gathering Storm*, pp. 50-51; Macmillan, *Winds of Change*, pp. 199-200.

[127]*Economist*, May 2, 1925, pp. 1848-49, soberly said: "we do not regard the result as a
disaster, but it definitely means delay in the pacification of Europe." As noted in n. 111 above,
Marx might have won if early evacuation had been assured before the election.

[128]McFadyean, *Reparation*, pp. 106-7, 212; Viscount D'Abernon, "Stresemann," *Foreign
Affairs*, January 1931, 8:208-11; Churchill, *Gathering Storm*, pp. 26-27; and Turner,
Stresemann, passim.

[129]Salter, *Personality in Politics*, pp. 197-201, and in other books comments on Briand and
Poincaré.

[130]Lenin wrote an article in 1915, "On the Slogan for a United States of Europe."
Chossudovsky, "Genoa Revisited," p. 557. American and foreign periodicals contained many
articles on the subject. Cf. Salter, *Recovery*, pp. 207, 212-19; Sir Arthur Salter, *The United
States of Europe and Other Papers* (London: Allan and Unwin, 1933), pp. 83-124; Mowat,
Britain between the Wars, p. 372. Briand circulated his plan among the European govern-

Locarno. MacDonald's government had pressed an ambitious and far-reaching protocol for the pacific settlement of international disputes, which the League Assembly approved on October 2, 1924, at a session attended by seven prime ministers and seventeen foreign ministers. The smaller European powers and Latin American countries were enthusiastic, but the Conservative press in England denounced it and the British dominions objected to it; on March 12, 1925, Chamberlain announced to the League Council the British rejection which killed it.[131] However, he supported a more limited proposal that was already under serious consideration, with important support from Lord D'Abernon, the British ambassador in Berlin. Lengthy diplomatic exchanges to overcome difficulties finally led to a seven-nation conference at Locarno on Lake Maggiori on October 5 through 16.

The agreements there adopted included a treaty of mutual guarantee of Germany's western borders, the demilitarization of the Rhineland, undertakings by Germany, France, and Belgium not to go to war with one another and to settle disputes by arbitration, and commitments by England and Italy to aid the victim of any violation. Also, the powers agreed to welcome Germany into the League of Nations and to support her interpretation of her obligations under Article 16 of the Versailles treaty. The all-important Locarno treaties were ratified by the Reichstag on November 27 by a vote of 291 to 174. These and the "Locarno spirit" were hailed as bringing in a new era of peace. In their aftermath the Allies withdrew their military control commission from Germany early in 1927.[132]

Britain returns to gold. In the greatly improved international atmosphere, with sterling exchange appreciating toward prewar parity with the dollar, the Baldwin government late in April 1925 took the long-delayed step of getting back to the gold standard with the pound at $4.8665.[133] The prestigious Cunliffe committee had recommended this in

ments in May 1930. Governor Norman of the Bank of England was among those who were intrigued by the idea.

[131]Manley O. Hudson, "The Geneva Protocol," *Foreign Affairs*, January 1926, 3:226–35. In "Progress in Europe, 1924–25," p. 63, I said in part: "Initiated by a group of private American citizens, modified by counsel from many sources, the plan was proposed by the Czechoslovakian prime minister, Beneš, and strongly supported by the British and French premiers present at the Assembly as well as by leaders of other delegations." Shotwell, who was active in promoting the protocol, later wrote, overstating the case by far, that the League never recovered "from this fatal blow." J. T. Shotwell, "Security," in Davis, *Pioneers*, pp. 34–39.

[132]McFadyean, *Reparation*, pp. 104–13; Churchill, *Gathering Storm*, pp. 27–31, 47; Mowat, *Britain between the Wars*, pp. 198–99; Turner, *Stresemann*, chs. 6–7; Macmillan, *Winds of Change*, pp. 201–2.

[133]This highly condensed paragraph is based on samplings of a vast literature. Reviewing D. E. Moggridge, *British Monetary Policy, 1924–1931: The Norman Conquest of $4.86*

two reports in 1918–19; Labour Chancellor Snowden's Chamberlain-Bradbury committee of 1924–25 had endorsed it; and the Bank of England under Governor Norman regarded it as a crowning achievement. It was overwhelmingly supported by political, financial, and economic opinion, with very few dissenters, of whom Keynes was the most vocal.[134] Federal Reserve Board member A. C. Miller hailed it as "one of the most important steps achieved since the Armistice toward world economic restoration," one which could not "easily be exaggerated," "bringing to an end a condition which has affected British business adversely since the close of the war."[135]

The early results were disappointing: British exports were handicapped, strong trade unions resisted reductions in wage rates, and the U.S. price level stubbornly failed to rise as many British had hoped and expected. Keynes, who had warned for weeks before the decision that it would be rash and premature, soon published in *The Evening Standard* three strongly worded articles, which were soon made into a pamphlet, *The Economic Consequences of Mr. Churchill.* He then blasted the report of the Bradbury committee (of which his Cambridge colleague Pigou was a member) and the Gold Standard Act of 1925.[136] Churchill did not reply to Keynes but later came to accept the general conclusion that here was a crucial blunder, not only for Britain but for the world, and angrily blamed Governor Norman for misleading him about the matter.[137]

British coal and general strikes, 1926. The return to gold at a figure which was some 10 to 12 percent too high in relation to the dollar was among the factors that brought on the disastrous coal strike of May through December 1926,[138] but its relative importance was exaggerated by Keynes and others. Industrial strife was endemic in Great Britain after the war, and coal

---

(London: Cambridge University Press, 1972), Edward Nevin, in *EJ*, September 1972, 92:1100–1101, termed it "a masterpiece of its kind." An earlier version is cited in Chapter 16, n. 20, below.

[134]Others included Keynes' friend, the influential banker Sir Reginald McKenna, who recognized the decision as politically inevitable; Vincent Vickers, V.C., who resigned from the board of the Bank of England in protest; and Lloyd George, who had already lost his influence. Stamp, in a New York address of Apr. 13, 1932 (*Proc. Acad. Pol. Sci.*, May 1932, 15:136), reported a conversation with a British labor leader in which the union viewpoint was expressed.

[135]Address of May 23, 1925, Federal Reserve Board Press Release X-4337, and HES, *Weekly Letter*, May 2, 1925, pp. 134–35. Miller later saw his error.

[136]*N&A*, e.g., Mar. 21, 1925, pp. 866–68; *EJ*, June 1925, 35:299f., 312f.

[137]See Austin Robinson's review of Andrew Boyle, *Montagu Norman* (London: Cassell, 1967), in *EJ*, June 1968, 78:392–98.

[138]Mowat, *Britain between the Wars*, chs. 1, 6, et passim; Sir Josiah C. Stamp, "The Coal Mining Deadlock in Great Britain," *Foreign Affairs*, July 1926, 4:547–55; articles by D. H. Robertson and Alfred Morgan in *EJ*, September, December 1926, 36:325–93, 563–76; Philip Kerr, "Can We Learn from America?" *N&A*, Oct. 16, 1926, pp. 76–77, and Keynes' contemporary articles in the same weekly; A. J. Youngson, *The British Economy, 1920-1957* (Cambridge, Mass.: Harvard University Press, 1960), pp. 36–43, 70–74.

crises were frequent. Nationalization of the mines, which the Labour Party demanded and which in 1920 had seemed to some Conservatives as inevitable as that of transport and electricity, was averted by Lloyd George but continued to be urged. The Sankey Coal Industry Commission made three reports in 1919 which lacked unanimity. Several legislative acts were passed, but mine owners and workers felt betrayed. A wage settlement in 1921 lasted until early 1924; heavy exports during the Ruhr occupation were a windfall. But for years the contending groups pursued what a colliery official (Alfred Morgan) called "a suicidal policy," which brought "the miners to starvation wages and the mines to bankruptcy." In July 1925, threat of a general strike was averted by Baldwin's concessions and, after the summer holidays, by the appointment on September 7 of a prestigious royal commission chaired by Sir Herbert Samuel. When it presented its report on March 11, 1926, negotiations deadlocked and governmental mediation efforts failed.

The general strike that marked the early stages of the coal strike was promptly declared illegal, its effects were alleviated by governmental moves and a host of volunteer workers, and it lasted only from May 4 to 12. With it ended the threat of possible revolution, and it only briefly interrupted "the inexorable advance of social welfare" despite the persistence of unemployment.[139] But the coal strike dragged on, with profound domestic and international effects. The miners started drifting back to work in November, and the strike was gradually terminated rather than settled. After the exhausting, disillusioning experiences of 1926, strikes and lockouts were few in the next two years, and in 1927–34 British industrial relations were exceptionally peaceful, as they had been in 1900–1907.[140] Though reported unemployment never fell below one million as employment increased in the later 1920s, Keynes and others repeatedly voiced satisfaction with the diminution of poverty, the improvement in real wages, and the relatively high level of living of the British people.

Interallied war debt "settlements." Most settlements of war debts were completed by July 1929.[141] The American ones generally followed the pattern of the Anglo-American agreement of 1923, which in April 1926 Newton D. Baker (a highly respected citizen who had been Wilson's secretary of

[139]Mowat, *Britain between the Wars*, esp. pp. 284–85, 331, 338–43. Reminiscent of Disraeli's long Tory regime in the 1870s, the Baldwin government's "record of useful social legislation was greater than that of any of the interwar governments save Lloyd George's coalition of 1918–22" (p. 338).

[140]J. Henry Richardson, "Industrial Relations," in *Britain in Depression* (London: Pitman, 1935), pp. 59–79, esp. p. 60. Working days lost in 1927–34 averaged only one-eleventh as many as those lost in 1919–20.

[141]Summarized in Moulton and Pasvolsky, *War Debts and World Prosperity*; Gerould and Turnbull, *Selected Articles*, reprint a large collection of relevant papers. See also Churchill, *Gathering Storm*, pp. 23–25.

war) termed a "magnificent disaster," but on terms much more lenient in that they overtly recognized the "capacity-to-pay" principle, which the English negotiators had not invoked.[142] The British settlement with continental debtors followed the principle laid down in the Balfour note of August 1, 1922, which Keynes, in an article published early in 1925, blasted Churchill for endorsing.[143] The American settlements left hard feelings, in England as well as France and elsewhere. Snowden, Labour chancellor of the exchequer in 1924 and in 1929-31, wrote in September 1926:

No American who has visited Europe occasionally during the last few years, and who has come in touch with public opinion, can have failed to be impressed by the growing antipathy to the United States. . . .

The unpopularity of America is due to her postwar attitude to European resettlement. Rightly or wrongly, she has managed to create the impression that, when her fear of the German menace was removed, she left Europe in the lurch, devoted herself to taking advantage of Europe's misfortunes, and was concerned only in her own material interests.

This view, so general throughout Europe, is, I believe, largely, if not wholly, without foundation. But it exists, and nothing has done so much to give to it apparent justification as America's policy on the matter of interallied debts.[144]

McFadyean wrote in 1930 that the French debt settlements with Britain and America "were regarded by the general body of Frenchmen with passionate resentment." The several Anglo-American frictions were the subject of a broadly successful summit conference of MacDonald and President Hoover in Washington from October 4 to 16, 1929.[145]

The Kellogg-Briand Pact, 1928. On July 20, 1927, when Franco-American relations were somewhat strained, Briand wrote a note suggesting a pact of perpetual friendship between the two countries. Secretary of State Kellogg's reply of December 29 proposed inviting other nations to join such an agreement. On August 27, 1928, plenipotentiaries of fifteen leading nations signed the resulting Pact of Paris, renouncing war as an instrument of national policy and agreeing to settle all disputes by peaceful means. U.S. speakers at the American Academy of Political Science on

---

[142]Richard A. Newhall edited the proceedings of the 1927 sessions of the Institute of Politics and summarized the roundtable discussions in a mimeographed document (Williamstown, Mass., 1927). The summary of my round table on "International Debts, Retrospect and Prospect" is on pp. 109-31. My own views were set forth in "The War Debt Settlements," *Virginia Quarterly Review*, January 1928, 4:1-27.

[143]*N&A*, Jan. 24, 1925, pp. 575-76, reprinted in Gerould and Turnbull, *Selected Articles*, pp. 391-94.

[144]*Atlantic*, 138:400-8, reprinted in Gerould and Turnbull, *Selected Articles*, pp. 439-55. Here Snowden may have minimized his own share in this feeling.

[145]McFadyean, *Reparation*, p. 170; *Foreign Affairs*, October 1928, 5:6-27; Hoover, *Memoirs*, 2:242-48; Macmillan, *Winds of Change*, p. 241.

November 23 were predominantly enthusiastic but displayed a wide spectrum of opinion: some considered it "the most far-reaching agreement that the United States has ever been called to enter into," while others thought it had no significance. The United States Senate gave its consent; President Coolidge signed it late in January 1929; some sixty-three nations, including the U.S.S.R. and Japan, accepted it. As Macmillan later wrote, this "seemed to all but the most skeptical a definite turning-point in the history of human endeavor and the search for peace." Unhappily, the treaty was open to different interpretations, had no teeth in it, and soon proved illusory. Its supporters highly overrated the power of world opinion to make its utopian declarations effective.[146]

Substantial but checkered German recovery. Under the Dawes Plan Germany made a recovery, which seemed to many observers phenomenal in speed and comprehensiveness, into what seemed general prosperity in 1927–29. Her currency was effectively stabilized, her credit amazingly restored, and much German capital abroad repatriated. Foreign investors and speculators bought German securities and deposited heavily in German banks. These and a flood of foreign loans permitted some replenishment of working capital, expansion of industrial equipment, and increases in state and local construction and services. The Germans' will to work and industrial adaptability were abundantly manifested, and their hopes were raised. Industrial output, exports, and real wages increased. The fundamental structure of industry and commerce, after a sweeping reorganization, appeared by 1928 to be so sound that the remaining obstacles to regaining a progressive equilibrium seemed sure to be overcome, given time. Both in Germany and abroad, the future of the country looked highly promising as the 1920s ended. But these genuine strengths were coupled with grave weaknesses that were recognized but underemphasized. In combination, they made Germany unexpectedly vulnerable to the strains that developed in 1929–30.[147]

[146]See Levinson's initial article, "Morals and the Conduct of War," *New Republic,* Mar. 23, 1918, pp. 232–34; Claudius O. Johnson, *Borah of Idaho* (New York: Longmans Green, 1936), ch. 20, "A Venture in Idealism"; Marian C. McKenna, *Borah* (Ann Arbor, Mich.: University of Michigan Press, 1961), ch. 14, "In Search of a Peace Plan"; *C&FC,* Sept. 1, 1928, p. 1195, Jan. 31, 1929, pp. 505–6, July 27, 1929, pp. 531, 557–59; *Proc. Acad. Pol. Sci.,* January 1929, 13:218, 243–57; Salter, *Recovery,* pp. 303–19, *U.S. of Europe,* pp. 228–51, and *Security,* pp. 146–52; H. A. Garfield, *Lost Visions* (privately printed, 1944), pp. 270–73; Hoover, *Memoirs,* 2:335–36, 343–46, 353–54, 363–79; Macmillan, *Winds of Change,* p. 202; Duroselle, "Reconsiderations," pp. 754, 757, 764; and numerous articles in *Foreign Affairs,* esp. vols. 7 and 10–12.

[147]There is almost a superabundance of factual material on Germany in 1924–29, assembled and presented in the agent general's semiannual reports to the Reparation Commission (*AGR*); in many German, British, French, and United States bank and government agency publications, journals, and economic services; and in books published at the time

The German economy actually experienced a series of ups and downs. Carl T. Schmidt's National Bureau study reported two post-inflation cycles, with troughs in the winter of 1923–24 and the spring of 1925 and high points in March 1925 and the spring of 1928.[148] These were exceptional in the extent of their expansion and contraction, in the shortness of the first cycle, and in the length of the contraction in the second to its trough in the summer and fall of 1932. The disastrous hyperinflation left serious maladjustments that had to be painfully corrected. Many thousands of small businesses failed in the sharp setback of 1925–26, which was marked by swelling numbers of protested bills and bankruptcies. The gigantic Stinnes combine collapsed in June 1925 (Stinnes died in 1924), and out of its wreckage the United Steel Works Company was built in 1926. Widespread combinations and cartelization created rigidities and frictions. The British coal strike temporarily stimulated German industry and exports, and the extensive industrial reorganization and rationalization in 1925–27 favored exports, which expanded despite obstacles set up by importing countries, yet the balance of payments continued strongly adverse. The year 1927 was one of marked business improvement, but a mild recession began in the summer of 1928, and there was a severe iron and steel strike in the Ruhr in November. The level of business activity and industrial production was relatively high in 1928–29 but far from stable.

A great boom in stocks on the Berlin bourse from the end of 1925 to early May 1927 was partially the result of heavy purchases by foreign speculative investors. It ended in an unprecedented panic on May 12 when the Berlin Bankers Association decided to restrict loans for stock purchases and Reichsbank Governor Schacht attempted to regain the bank's control over the money market and urged curtailment of borrowing abroad. Some recovery of stock prices followed the slump, but the 1927 peaks were not again reached.[149]

---

and later. But many of the interpretations and forecasts based on it were seriously defective. Several broad statements in Angell's valuable *Recovery of Germany* fit badly with his detailed discussion and with the agent general's reports that he utilized. Even the realistic McFadyean, in concluding his *Reparation*, found "much ground for encouragement and even reasoned optimism." Early in 1930 (January 10, pp. 107–8) the *Economist* reported it difficult to understand "the extreme pessimism pervading the German business world," in contrast to the general optimism of the "fat years." The generally perceptive and reliable B. M. Anderson was surely wrong in later crediting Germany with "nearly three years [1926–29] of strong, sustained industrial activity with excellent business profits" and "full employment" (*Economics and the Public Welfare*, ch. 20, esp. p. 152).

[148]*German Business Cycles, 1924–1933* (New York: NBER, 1934), ch. 4, esp. pp. 266–67.

[149]Robert Crozier Long, in *Annalist*, June 3, June 10, 1927, pp. 787, 789, 791, 829; *AGR*, Dec. 10, 1927, pp. 95–96, 203–4; Angell, *Recovery of Germany*, pp. 197–203; and *Rev. Ec. Stat.*, June 15, 1932, 14:4. Long, Berlin correspondent of the *Economist*, soon published *The Mythology of Reparations* (London: Duckworth, 1928), which McFadyean critically reviewed in that journal and later called "a farrago of nonsense" in his *Recollected*, pp. 98–99.

In 1919–23, as inflation permitted Germany to escape the first general postwar depression, unemployment was abnormally low until mid–1923, when it shot up until, about the turn of the year, one-fourth to one-third of German workers were jobless. Substantial improvement in the first half of 1924 (surprising in retrospect) reduced it to moderate levels for more than a year. From late in 1925, as business concerns drastically pared staffs, it rose to extreme levels in the winter, and remained high for a year or more. From February 1927 it fell strongly under the influence of industrial revival and expanded public programs, but registered unemployment, under the new system of insurance adopted in 1927, averaged 1,353,000 in 1927 and 1928, and the slump in the last quarter of 1929 raised the 1929 average to 1,892,000. In short, as in Great Britain, heavy unemployment, however patiently endured, was an obstinate problem in the later 1920s.[150]

Drastic fiscal measures at the inauguration of the Dawes Plan yielded a relatively large budget surplus in fiscal year April to March 1924–25. Later, political pressures forced expenditures up faster than revenues, until in 1928–29 the Reich deficit reached a figure much more than double the advance estimate and exceeding the reparation charge for the standard year. In February 1927 an internal loan for 500 million gold marks was floated, and extensive short-term borrowing had to be resorted to in the spring of 1929. The agent general was deeply worried by these developments and late in 1927 exchanged memoranda with the finance minister on the subject of overspending and overborrowing. Dr. Kohler acknowledged in his response that the country was "full of political excitement and internal unrest." James W. Angell soon came to consider the most serious source of internal tension "the conflict between the socialist and the anti-socialist groups in the German state."[151]

There were other sources of strain, internal and external. The extreme shortage of working capital was alleviated but never overcome. The middle class made only limited recovery from its financial devastation by hyperinflation. The agricultural sector, though its earlier indebtedness had been wiped out by the inflation, was seriously depressed, in spite of increasing protection after Germany recovered her freedom from treaty restrictions on tariff duties in 1925, and accumulated large new debts; farming practices continued to be backward. Strong trade unions, with

[150]This paragraph is based largely on the agent general's reports; on Angell, *Recovery of Germany*; and on Guillebaud, *Economic Recovery of Germany*, ch. 1. Partly on demographic grounds, Angell in mid-1929 made an astonishing prediction: "For at least the next 15 or 20 years the average rate of unemployment will almost certainly continue to fall." *Recovery of Germany*, pp. 263–65.

[151]See esp. *AGR*, June 10, Dec. 10, 1927, and later reports; Angell, *Recovery of Germany*, pp. 308–18 et passim.

political support, kept forcing up wage rates, and a vicious spiral of rising wages and rising prices began to appear. The growth of foreign debt and debt charges seemed inexorable. Though Germany had increased its export of services—for transport, insurance, and tourism—her balance of international payments continued adverse. The large short-term debt made Germany vulnerable to foreign withdrawals on little or no notice.

The Young Plan, 1928-29. The Dawes committee had considered its frankly provisional plan "so framed as to facilitate a final and comprehensive agreement as to all the problems of reparation and connected questions as soon as circumstances make this possible." Quoting this passage, the agent general late in 1927 expressed the view that, while the testing period was not yet over, these problems could not be "finally solved until Germany has been given a definitive task to perform on her own responsibility, without foreign supervision and without transfer protection."[152] A combination of fears and hopes led to the Allied decision, reached at Geneva in September 1928, with the approval of Poincaré and Briand, to call into being a new committee of experts to formulate a plan for a definitive settlement. There were fears that the inflow of foreign capital would dry up and short-term debts not be renewed; that the transfer of reparation payments would be blocked, which no party wanted; and that the budget deficits would further increase and price inflation would reappear. There were hopes that the reparation annuities could be materially reduced, that the somewhat humiliating foreign control system could be ended, evacuation of the Rhineland speeded, and substantial "commercialization" of the reparation obligations achieved. What became the Young committee framed its recommendations in February through June 1929, and the Young Plan was approved with modifications at Allied conferences at The Hague in August 1929 and January 1930.[153]

Outlook, summer 1929. Despite the strains that had recently developed and deep misgivings on the part of a very few, the future of Europe as well as America looked bright to most observers in the summer of 1929, on the basis of the gains achieved since 1923 and the momentum that seemed clearly evident. Salter wrote in 1960:

> For five years it looked as if the world's central financial problems had perhaps been solved. In this period Europe stabilized her finances, increased her production and trade; and with prosperity came political progress too. Locarno, and the entry of Germany into the League of Nations, seemed to offer a prospect of stable peace. Economic chaos in Germany, which had previously threatened the Weimar

---

[152]See *AGR*, Dec. 10, 1927, pp. 169-73, and a comparable passage in that of June 7, 1928.
[153]McFadyean, *Reparation*, ch. 9.

Republic, and when it returned in later years was destined to give Hitler his opportunity, had for the time come to an end. During these five years Hitler, and all the forces on which his power to convulse the world depended, seemed to have disappeared from the picture.[154]

To an extraordinary degree these and other illusions were widely cherished, few realized how insecure were the foundations of the present prosperity, and the danger of imminent economic breakdown went largely unperceived.

---

[154]*Memoirs of a Public Servant*, p. 171. Cf. Churchill, *Gathering Storm*, pp. 31, 38; Youngson, *British Economy*, pp. 75–78; McFadyean, *Recollected*, p. 213.

CHAPTER 4

ECONOMIC AND SPECULATIVE DEVELOPMENTS IN THE UNITED STATES, 1914–29

WORLD WAR I drastically altered the position of the United States in the world economy.[1] In the period 1914–18 it ceased to be a net debtor nation and became a net creditor nation. When the war ended, the major European belligerents were impoverished and disorganized, the Soviet Union and most of Eastern Europe were in a still more desperate state, and the neutrals were relatively minor factors. The United States, which had suffered least and prospered most, became the outstanding world economic and financial power. These changes came about so quickly that our financiers, statesmen, and the public could not readily readjust their minds to the new status and greatly enlarged responsibilities. Moreover, the war ended so suddenly that the complex problems of transition to new peacetime norms were magnified. The disillusionments and bitterness of 1919–20, both at home and abroad, created a climate in which consistently rational attitudes and actions were impossible.

The absences of President Wilson at the Peace Conference, growing bitterness toward him, and his illnesses and obstinacy led to a deadlock between the president and the Congress and deprived the country of an effective federal government for the last two and a half years of his second term.[2] The country repudiated the president and retreated into isolation from the rest of the world. Warren G. Harding's election to the presidency in November 1920, Bernard Baruch well said later, "symbolized the state

[1] W. P. G. Harding, *The Formative Period of the Federal Reserve System* (Boston: Houghton Mifflin, 1925), chs. 12–16 and pp. 273–79; Moritz J. Bonn, *Prosperity: Myth and Reality in American Economic Life* (London: Martin Hopkinson, 1931); Moritz J. Bonn, *The Crisis of Capitalism in America* (New York: John Day, 1932; introduction by George S. Counts), pp. 1–32; E. M. Patterson, "The United States and the World Economy," in *Economic Essays in Honour of Gustav Cassel* (London: Allen and Unwin, 1933), pp. 479–90; Simon Kuznets, "Foreign Economic Relations of the United States and Their Impact upon the Domestic Economy: A Review of Long-Term Trends," *Proceedings of the American Philosophical Society*, October 1948, 92:228–43, reprinted in Joseph T. Lambie and Richard V. Clemence, eds., *Economic Change in America* (Harrisburg, Pa.: Stackpole, 1954), pp. 575–99, esp. pp. 588–90; Lester V. Chandler, *Benjamin Strong: Central Banker* (Washington, D.C.: Brookings Institution, 1958), ch. 5, "Aftermath," and p. 262. Harding and Strong were outstanding men in the Federal Reserve System (FRS) during Harding's six-year term as governor of the Federal Reserve Board (FRB) from Aug. 9, 1916, and Strong's as governor of the Federal Reserve Bank of New York (FRBk-NY) from the outset to his death in October 1928.

[2] Harding, *Formative Period*, pp. 277–78.

of cynicism and disillusion into which our Republic fell after the war, as Woodrow Wilson had symbolized the idealism of the New Freedom and the war years."[3]

Commodity price inflation of major proportions had taken place in the United States before it entered the war, as European wartime demands for U.S. exports were made effective by gold imports (some $1.1 billion from December 1914 through April 1917[4]), sales of foreign-owned U.S. securities, large extensions of private U.S. credits, and important bank credit expansion under the new Federal Reserve System; costs of imported goods were further raised by foreign competition, shortages, and high ocean freight rates. The official Bureau of Labor Statistics (BLS) wholesale price index (1913 average = 100) rose in nineteen months from 100 in September 1915 to 172.9 in April 1917, about 73 percent.[5]

During the nation's active participation in the war, commodity price inflation continued at a slower pace: in the twenty-one months from April 1917 to November 1918 the BLS price index rose by only 17 percent. Controls imposed by wartime federal agencies were partly responsible for retarding inflation in the face of huge federal expenditures. More important was the Treasury policy of floating Liberty bonds and Victory notes, which raised the federal gross debt to $26.6 billion at its peak on August 30, 1919. Five effective campaigns, aided by liberal bank credits to those who borrowed to buy, induced large personal savings and held down personal spending.[6]

Postwar Reaction, Revival, and Boom, 1918–20   Following the signing of the Armistice there was a sharp reaction in U.S. business activity (see Table 1) as war production ceased, payrolls declined, business loans were reduced or paid off, government controls were removed or relaxed, employment dropped, industrial readjustment began, and commodity prices broke or eased. The BLS wholesale price index fell to 193.4

[3]*Baruch: The Public Years* (New York: Holt, Rinehart and Winston, 1960), pp. 186–90.

[4]B. M. Anderson, *Economics and the Public Welfare: Financial and Economic History of the United States, 1914–1946* (New York: Van Nostrand, 1949), pp. 19–20.

[5]The BLS monthly data are available in the various issues of the Department of Labor *Bulletin* and *Federal Reserve Bulletin*; they are summarized for 1915–22 in Anderson, *Economics and the Public Welfare*, p. 25.

[6]Anderson, *Economics and the Public Welfare*, chs. 3, 5; the Leffingwell address of Apr. 30, 1920, is in Harding, *Formative Period*, app. A. The Treasury had persistently insisted that one-third of the current war expenditures should be met from current taxes. The fraction of total expenditures met by current taxation was about one-fourth—a larger percentage than Great Britain achieved, and the British record was better than that of the continental belligerents. This policy succeeded in limiting wartime price inflation in the United States, where the cost of living increased less than in any of the belligerent or neutral countries of Europe. Extreme wartime demands for goods and services greatly raised price and wage levels. Methods of financing the war enormously increased the number of people who bought and held war bonds and notes, and left many in debt to banks for much of their purchases.

Table 1. CTC Index of American Business Activity

Month	1917	1918	1919	1920	1921	1922	1923	1924	1925	1926	1927	1928	1929
Jan.	14	2	2	15	–22	–17	7	6	7	9	10	5	17
Feb.	13	3	–1	15	–22	–15	10	8	7	9	10	5	16
Mar.	14	7	–7	12	–25	–10	12	6	7	10	12	7	16
Apr.	13	8	–4	7	–25	–13	14	3	7	10	9	4	17
May	14	9	–4	9	–23	–8	16	–2	6	8	9	6	19
June	13	7	4	9	–23	–3	16	–7	6	10	9	8	20
July	12	9	9	6	–26	–3	13	–7	8	9	6	8	20
Aug.	13	11	9	6	–21	–6	10	–5	6	11	6	10	20
Sep.	9	9	8	3	–21	–2	7	–3	3	13	4	11	17
Oct.	11	9	6	0	–19	3	7	–1	7	13	4	13	15
Nov.	11	6	5	–8	–19	8	7	1	9	11	1	15	10
Dec.	6	6	5	–16	–19	10	4	5	11	10	3	17	4

Source: Cleveland Trust Company, *American Business Activity since 1790*, 1971 ed. The chart in Chapter 1, from the same source, covers the years 1914–41. A broadly similar course is shown by the American Telephone and Telegraph Company's latest series on U.S. industrial production as related to long-term growth, in percentage deviations from a calculated trend of the Federal Reserve index of industrial production, 1957–59 = 100. Monthly data for both series for the years 1920–69 were published in a supplement to AT&T, *Business Conditions* for February 1970, "Measuring the Industrial Sector."

in February 1919, less than 5 percent below the high of 202.9 recorded for November 1918. The business contraction was very short-lived, and in April 1919 there began a revival that developed into the unsound boom which reached its peak early in 1920.[7]

Important among the many factors responsible[8] was the one-sided export trade to Europe, financed first by government credits and then by private credits, supplemented by speculative purchases of foreign currencies and securities. A second factor was the 25 percent expansion of U.S. bank loans and investments in the year ending April 9, 1920, under the influence of abnormally low rediscount rates of the Federal Reserve Banks, rates maintained under Treasury pressure through most of 1919. A third important factor was the marked expansion of speculation in commodities, farm real estate, and common stocks, based on seriously erroneous appraisals of the present and near future, which led to grossly excessive increases in prices, farm values (centering in Iowa), and business costs. A fourth factor was huge federal expenditures, which increased nearly 50 percent in the fiscal year ending June 1919 as compared with the one preceding.[9] A fifth factor was exuberant purchases by consumers, in "a

[7]See Cleveland Trust Company, *American Business Activity since 1790* (April 1971 ed.). This index dropped from +11 in August 1918 to –7 in March 1919, then rose to +15 in the first two months of 1920.

[8]Anderson ably discussed numerous factors in his *Economics and the Public Welfare*, ch. 7, but did not touch on the one I have called "fifth."

[9]*Historical Statistics of the United States, Colonial Times to 1957: A Statistical Abstract Supplement* (Washington, D.C.: U.S. Department of Commerce, 1960), ser. Y 350. Treasury

time of fatuous optimism and of reckless extravagance,"[10] "a period of expansion, speculation, and extravagance, the like of which has never before been seen in this country or perhaps in the world."[11] A sixth factor was the serious physical and financial plight of the railways, still under government operation with freight rates held at low wartime levels; railway congestion became acutely critical in the early part of 1920.[12]

Foodstuffs, raw materials, and manufactured goods went to Europe on a grand scale. At their monthly peak in June 1919 U.S. exports totaled over $1 billion. The exports were largely financed by Treasury loans: some $7 billion had been loaned to European governments before the Armistice was signed; almost $3 billion more had been loaned by June 30, 1919. These postwar loans helped to ease the shock of demobilization in the European countries and enabled them to meet commitments on canceled war contracts, but they exerted no pressure on the recipients to get their economies and finances back to normal. J. P. Morgan & Company, the principal financial agent of the British and French governments, pegged the pound sterling until March 20; when it broke, the European exchanges followed. When government credits ceased, however, private credits took their place. From January 1, 1919, to September 15, 1920, the unfunded debt of Europeans to Americans grew to astounding size; B. M. Anderson's estimate at the time was $3.5 billion.[13]

Speculation in stocks naturally expanded in the months after the Armistice, and in December and January 1918–19 Treasury Secretary Glass expressed anxiety over the "wave of stock market gambling,"[14] and this anxiety continued in the ensuing months. A memorandum of October 25, 1919, from Carter Glass to R. C. Leffingwell, assistant secretary of the Treasury, stated that "the labor situation has become so acute as gravely to threaten production and the speculative mania has been allowed to proceed to such an extent as gravely to threaten our credit structure." It adverted to the "abuse of the facilities of the Federal Reserve System in support of the reckless speculation in stocks, cotton, clothing, foodstuffs and commodities generally."[15] In retrospect, the great buildup

---

Secretary Carter Glass, in his annual report for fiscal 1919 (dated Nov. 10, 1919), roundly criticized the postwar extravagance of the executive departments and agencies and the Congress as well: "All sense of values seems to have departed from among us." Quoted in Rixey Smith and Norman Beasley, *Carter Glass: A Biography* (New York: Longmans Green, 1939), pp. 190–92, 467, 469. See also Harding, *Formative Period*, pp. 276–79.

[10]Harding, *Formative Period*, p. 163.

[11]*Ibid.*, pp. 297–98, quoting the Joint Commission of Agricultural Inquiry *Report on Credit* issued in January 1922.

[12]Harding, *Formative Period*, pp. 276–79; Anderson, *Economics and the Public Welfare*, p. 62.

[13]Anderson, *Economics and the Public Welfare*, pp. 52–53.

[14]Smith and Beasley, *Glass*, pp. 159–60.

[15]*Ibid.*, pp. 178–85.

of excessive business inventories, based on bad appraisals of commodity positions, appears to have been the most damaging form of "speculation."

In this critical period many holders of Liberty bonds and Victory notes, bought as a patriotic duty, cashed them in and spent the proceeds. There was "feverish speculation in European currencies, credits, and securities," including those of Germany. Leffingwell went so far as to say that price inflation here was due "in no small degree to the inflation of the Continental European currencies operating upon the optimism of the American people" and that "many of our own people have turned gamblers and wasters."[16]

As in Great Britain, serious labor disturbances marred the early postwar period here. Labor union membership rose sharply in 1915–20 to its peak of 5 million in 1920 out of 41 million "gainful workers" aged sixteen and over. More than 4 million employees were involved in numerous industrial disputes in 1919, more than one-fourth of these in strikes in the coal and steel industries and the railroads. In 1920 the anthracite coal miners struck, and there were "outlaw" strikes by railway switchmen and yardmen. In 1921 the marine workers in all principal ports struck, and there were conflicts in the clothing, building, and packing industries. In 1922 strikes of coal miners and railway shopmen raised the total number of reported strikers to 1.6 million. Both the number of disputes and the number of employees involved were much lower in 1923–29.[17]

Collapse, Depression, and Recovery, 1920–22; Prosperity, 1923–29   The broad course of the American economy in the 1920s is well indicated by the Federal Reserve index of industrial production shown in Table 2.[18] On a 1947–49 base, its annual averages were 40 in 1920, 30 in 1921, 50 in 1926 and 1927, 52 in 1928, and 58 in 1929. The

---

[16]Harding, *Formative Period*, pp. 257–79, esp. pp. 275–78.

[17]*Hist. Stat. U.S.*, ser. D 36–45, 735–36, 746–78; and Leo Wolman, "Labor: Industrial Disputes," in Edward Eyre Hunt, ed., *Recent Economic Changes in the United States: Report of the Committee on Recent Economic Changes of the President's Conference on Unemployment, Herbert Hoover, Chairman, Including the Reports of a Special Staff of the National Bureau of Economic Research, Inc.*, 2 vols. (New York: McGraw-Hill, 1929), 2:490–92 (the data were compiled by Ben M. Selekman). For the position in construction and transportation, see *ibid.*, 1:251–52, 279–84. Work stoppages averaged 3,727 a year in 1916–20, but fell off sharply after 1921; they averaged only 1,250 in 1922–26 and only 754 in 1927–32. Data are, unfortunately, very limited before 1927.

[18]This index, revised to include electric and gas utilities, covers the years beginning with 1919. *Fed. Res. Bull.*, December 1959, 45:1451–74. Indexes prior to 1947 were not otherwise revised. The earlier series, not strikingly different in the period 1920–36, is plotted in the FRS *Chart Book* for September 1958, p. 90. The revised index is shown on a 1957–59 base in the FRS *Hist. Chart Book, 1971*, pp. 86–91. This valuable annual has long been published, usually in October, by the Federal Reserve Board and its successor, the Board of Governors of the Federal Reserve System. For considerable periods the paging is the same in successive issues, as the same charts are brought more up to date. The FRS also publishes a monthly *Chart Book*.

Table 2. Federal Reserve Index of Industrial Production in the United States (1947–49 average = 100)

Month	1919	1920	1921	1922	1923	1924	1925	1926	1927	1928	1929	1930	1931	1932
Jan.	37	43	30	33	44	45	47	49	51	50	57	53	42	35
Feb.	36	43	30	34	45	46	47	49	51	50	57	53	42	34
Mar.	34	42	29	36	46	45	47	50	52	51	57	52	43	33
Apr.	35	40	29	35	47	44	47	50	51	50	58	52	43	31
May	35	41	30	37	48	42	47	49	51	51	59	51	43	30
June	38	41	30	39	48	40	47	50	51	52	60	50	41	29
July	40	40	29	39	47	40	48	50	50	52	60	47	41	28
Aug.	40	40	31	38	46	41	47	51	50	53	60	46	39	29
Sept.	40	39	31	40	45	42	46	52	49	54	59	45	38	31
Oct.	39	38	32	42	45	43	48	52	49	55	58	44	36	32
Nov.	39	35	32	44	45	44	49	51	48	56	56	43	36	32
Dec.	39	32	32	45	44	46	50	51	49	57	53	42	36	31
Year	*38*	*40*	*30*	*38*	*46*	*43*	*48*	*50*	*50*	*52*	*58*	*48*	*40*	*31*

Source: *Federal Reserve Bulletin*, December 1959, 45:1469.

monthly series, seasonally adjusted, stood at 60 in June–August 1929—the high point of the 1920s, not again reached until November 1936. The monthly series shows the marked uptrend from 1919 through 1929, broken only by a severe drop from 43 in January–February 1920 to 30 a year later, and merely interrupted by minor declines in June–December 1923, February–June 1924, and March–November 1927. The rise in July–December 1928 was continuous but slow, and further modest gains were registered in the spring of 1929. The total index declined gradually from 60 in June–August 1929 to 56 in November and to 53 in December, where it stood through February 1930 before falling slowly in subsequent months. Especially striking were the rise in the subindex of durable goods production (motor vehicles and others) from late 1927 through mid-1929 and the sustained high rate of increase in gas and electricity output in 1921–29.[19]

The postwar boom collapsed in the spring and summer of 1920, following the collapse of the Japanese silk market.[20] Consumer resistance to

---

A valuable statistical compendium of annual data for the United States is given in "A Record of Salient Economic Changes, 1923–1939," appended to Arthur F. Burns, *Economic Research and the Keynesian Thinking of Our Times*, Annual Report of the National Bureau of Economic Research (New York: NBER, 1946), pp. 30–38. Data for 1923, 1929, 1937, and 1939, expressed as relatives on a 1929 base, are given in *ibid.*, pp. 14–16.

[19]The net value of plant and equipment in electric light and power companies and in telephone companies more than doubled in 1921–29. *Hist. Stat. U.S.*, ser. V 208, 210. See also chart and table in C. A. R. Wardwell, "Energy Output and Use Related to the Gross National Product," *SCB*, February 1961, pp. 28–29.

[20]On Japanese developments in the first half of 1920, see *Economist*, Jan. 3, Feb. 7, Apr. 17, May 15, June 12, pp. 19–20, 263, 815, 1001, 1298; Harding, *Formative Period*, pp. 163, 304–5; and Anderson, *Economics and the Public Welfare*, pp. 75–76.

high retail prices helped to check it. The New York stock market had turned down late in 1919, as usual preceding the business downturn.[21] The BLS wholesale price index reached its peak in May 1920 at 247 percent of the 1913 average, after an increase of about 21.5 percent over eighteen months; by July 1921 it was down to 141. Caused mainly by the collapse of foreign demands, the price debacle was most severe in farm products in the United States and abroad; farmers and farmland values were extremely hard hit.[22] Unemployment rose sharply. Though no indexes were available at the time, Lebergott's later estimates (1956) show a rise in average annual unemployment from 560,000 in 1918 to 950,000 in 1919 and to a high of 5,000,000 in 1921—almost 12 percent of the labor force.[23] Nonfarm wage rates declined, but far less than did consumer prices, and new immigration restrictions helped maintain them much above prewar levels. Extensive liquidation occurred, and the business failure rate rose sharply, from an abnormal low of 37 per 10,000 concerns in 1919 to 120 in 1922.[24] Business activity continued subnormal from November 1920 through September 1922.

The revulsion of public sentiment in 1920 was reflected in the election returns of that fall. It was aggravated by the marked decline in the price of Liberty bonds and Victory notes, which had been touted as the safest investments anyone could have; by complaints of the high cost of living; by continuing labor unrest, strikes, and the onset of farm distress; by the severe business contraction and the striking rise of unemployment from spring to fall; and by the intensification of bickering over Federal Reserve policy and actions, as well as many other matters.

The 1920–21 contraction in industrial production and employment was unprecedentedly severe but very short. With little governmental interposition, and in the face of discouraging conditions abroad, it was met by a drastic cleanup of credit weaknesses and a sharp reduction in costs of production, initially in construction.[25] From July 1921 into June 1923 the CTC index of American business activity rose from –26 to +16, and nonfarm physical output, both total and per wage earner, increased strikingly. The Federal Reserve contributed to this advance by expanding bank credit through lower rediscount rates and, mostly in 1922, by buying government securities. A heavy inflow of gold provided much of the basis for bank

[21]Anderson, *Economics and the Public Welfare*, ch. 8. See curves of common stock prices, industrial production, and wholesale commodity prices, monthly, 1919–39, in R. A. Gordon, *Business Fluctuations*, 2d ed. (New York: Harper, 1961), fig. 39, p. 400.

[22]Cf. L. C. Gray, "The Responsibility of Overproduction for Agricultural Depression" (Nov. 15, 1930), *Proc. Acad. Pol. Sci.*, January 1931, 14:376–96, esp. pp. 380–88.

[23]*Hist. Stat. U.S.*, pp. 68, 73, and ser. D 46–47.

[24]*Ibid.*, ser. V 2.

[25]Anderson, *Economics and the Public Welfare*, ch. 8.

credit expansion.[26] By 1923, except for farmers, "extraordinary prosperity" was general.[27]

The sustained high level of business activity after the sharp recovery of 1921–23 (as shown, for example, by the Cleveland Trust Company index, which is adjusted for trend) was and is highly impressive, despite minor setbacks in 1923–24 and 1927. Increases in new corporate stock issues in 1922, 1924, 1925, and 1927 contributed much to the business recovery that followed, and they rose still more spectacularly in 1928 and 1929, enabling strong corporations greatly to improve their financial position.[28] The strong stimuli of long-term investment opportunities, for both business and consumers, figured heavily among the powerful expansionary forces that culminated in 1929. A high level of capital formation was reached by 1923 and was maintained for seven years. Both producers' and consumers' durables, R. A. Gordon has pointed out, "formed a larger fraction of the GNP during the 1920's than during any period before World War I."[29] This prolonged investment boom was largely responsible for the sustained prosperity of the decade, but all too few realized that its pace could not be sustained indefinitely.

The Federal Reserve System, despite severe criticism at the time and later, followed a policy of providing liberal credit at high rates to "sound" concerns and contributed to restoring stable credit conditions.[30] The organized commodity exchanges met the shock "amazingly well," and hedging protected grain millers and cotton spinners.[31] By mid-1921, much earlier than in Europe, industrial production had begun to increase, and it rose sharply in the next two years.[32] Aided especially by drastic reductions in interest rates and an upsurge in residential building construction, recovery was remarkably rapid except in agriculture, and by the end of 1922 a level of moderate prosperity had been attained.[33]

[26]Milton Friedman and Anna J. Schwartz, *A Monetary History of the United States, 1867–1960* (Princeton, N.J.: Princeton University Press, 1963), pp. 279–87.

[27]E. A. Goldenweiser, *American Monetary Policy* (New York: McGraw-Hill, 1951), p. 137.

[28]Harold L. Reed, *Federal Reserve Policy 1921–1930* (New York: McGraw-Hill, 1930), pp. 126–28, 175, 182–83; J. M. Keynes, *A Treatise on Money*, 2 vols. (New York: Harcourt Brace, 1930; preface dated Sept. 14, 1930), 2:194–95; Leonard P. Ayres, *Turning Points in Business Cycles* (New York: Macmillan, 1939), ch. 6; N. J. Silberling, *The Dynamics of Business* (New York: McGraw-Hill, 1943), pp. 291, 411–15, especially the chart on p. 412 covering 1906–40.

[29]Gordon, *Business Fluctuations*, pp. 406–14, 444–46, esp. p. 408.

[30]Harding, *Formative Period*, chs. 13–16. Until November 1919 its rates had been kept abnormally low under pressure from the Treasury, which thereby was enabled to raise funds cheaply.

[31]Anderson, *Economics and the Public Welfare*, p. 71.

[32]FRS, *Hist. Chart Book, 1971*, p. 86.

[33]*Ibid.*, pp. 4, 26, 57–61, 94, 96, 98, 101–2, 104–5; Anderson, *Economics and the Public Welfare*, chs. 5–6; E. A. Goldenweiser, *Monetary Management* (New York: McGraw-Hill, 1949), pp. 46–49; and the CTC chart reproduced on p. 5 of this volume.

Moreover, despite tariff rate increases in 1921 and 1922, the physical volume of U.S. imports grew in 1922-29 at an average rate of 3.9 percent a year, fully equal to the growth of domestic production, while exports grew at a significantly higher rate of 6.5 percent. The postwar advance was dominated by exports of finished manufactures (which about doubled in aggregate value in this period) and semimanufactures. Private foreign loans stimulated and facilitated this expansion.[34] The net outflow of capital averaged $451 million a year in 1922-29, enough to offset most of the sum of the export surplus ($150 million) plus payments on debts to U.S. creditors ($339 million), in contrast with a net inflow of capital averaging $53 million a year in 1896-1914.[35] Agricultural exports, though large at times, lost in relative position, largely because of the unexpectedly early restoration of European agricultural output by 1925 and increasing protection of European producers of farm products, by a variety of devices, in 1925-29.

Developments in the 1920s provided solid grounds for satisfaction with the U.S. economy and optimism for the future. Among the evidences that were both highly gratifying and highly promising[36] were these: the strong upward march of the economy despite slowing population increase; the brevity of the first postwar depression and the mildness of later contractions; the general stability of commodity price indexes in 1923-29;[37] great technological advances in industry and agriculture;[38] marked gains in

[34]HES, *Weekly Letter*, Mar. 30, 1929, pp. 74-75; Frederick C. Mills, *Economic Tendencies in the United States* (New York: NBER, 1932), pp. 516-17. "If it was a forced draught that kept up our expanding volume of exports during this period, this was the form that the draught took." For details, mostly on 1922-27, see James Harvey Rogers, "Foreign Markets and Foreign Credits," in *Recent Economic Changes*, 2:709-25.

[35]Mills, *Economic Tendencies*, p. 472; revisions of these figures would not alter the broad picture.

[36]Ably discussed in Mills, *Economic Tendencies*, and Gordon, *Business Fluctuations*, ch. 14, both with many additional references. Annual data on most of them can now be found in *Hist. Stat. U.S.* Many of these and other relevant series are shown graphically in long perspective in the annual FRS *Hist. Chart Book*.

[37]Cf. Joseph A. Schumpeter, *Business Cycles: A Theoretical, Historical and Statistical Analysis of the Capitalist Process*, 2 vols. (New York: McGraw-Hill, 1939), 2:693 (chart). In June 1922 and November 1925 the HES undertook to appraise the outlook for the level of commodity prices over the next few years. *Weekly Letter*, June 10, 1922, pp. 133-40; Nov. 18, 1924, p. 337; Nov. 28, 1925, pp. 358-60. In both instances it provisionally forecast a horizontal trend as probable, at about 50 percent above the prewar level. There were occasional interruptions, e.g., a drop from January 1926 to the spring of 1927, which Reed found significant. Reed, *Federal Reserve Policy*, pp. 97-98. In a mid-March 1930 review of the outlook for commodity price levels in the 1930s, the HES noted that the 1922 forecast had "turned out to be substantially correct for the United States," and emphasized the profound effect of the New York money rate, largely influenced by Federal Reserve policy, on "the movement of commodity prices throughout the world." *Weekly Letter*, Mar. 15, 1930, pp. 70-75.

[38]On the relative importance of capital employed per manhour and the level of technology in U.S. manufacturing in the 1920s in promoting increases in output per manhour, see Benton F. Massell, "Capital Formation and Technological Change in United States Manufacturing," *Rev. Ec. Stat.*, May 1960, 42:182-88, esp. charts 3-4.

productivity per worker or per manhour in manufacturing;[39] the smooth expansion of employment in trade, service, and financial occupations; what was deemed, with grossly inadequate data, a tolerable if commonly underrated level of unemployment;[40] exceptionally peaceful industrial relations after 1921, when the labor movement was weak, all but "paralyzed";[41] despite marked variations among different groups of workers,[42] a substantial rise in real wages (according to early computations, real wages rose to 136.4 percent of the 1913 average in 1929);[43] notable progress in per capita consumption;[44] widely expanded ownership of automobiles, radios,

[39]In an impressive article, Clarence D. Long presented a chart which shows, for the 1920s in long perspective, the marked rise in GNP per manhour, the rise in factory real hourly wages, and the decline in factory unit labor cost. "The Illusion of Wage Rigidity: Long and Short Cycles in Wages and Labor," *Rev. Ec. Stat.*, May 1960, 42:140–51, esp. p. 141. See also charts in Gordon, *Business Fluctuations*, p. 200 (Solomon Fabricant's data), and Citibank, *Monthly Letter*, November 1962, p. 129.

[40]Gordon went too far in saying, "From 1923 to 1929 the economy operated at close to full employment, with mild declines in 1924 and 1927." *Business Fluctuations*, p. 315n. Mills later asserted: "Even before the period of expansion was terminated in 1929 a widening margin of unemployed was accumulating." *Economic Tendencies*, p. 481. An early attempt to construct an annual index of unemployment for the period 1897–1920 led Douglas and Director to conclude that on the average 10 percent of those employed in manufacturing, mining, construction, and transportation were out of work, 8 percent if those ill and disabled were excluded, and that there was no clear trend for unemployment percentages in these industries to increase or decrease. Paul H. Douglas and Aaron Director, *The Problem of Unemployment* (New York: Macmillan, 1931), ch. 2. In ch. 4 these authors undertook to explain why unemployment was relatively high in the United States and low in France.
American Federation of Labor data indicated that unemployment in building trades unions was 16 percent in July 1929. In that month the U.S. Department of Agriculture reported the largest supply of farm labor for any month on record (103.4 percent of normal)—swelled by unemployed industrial workers—whereas demand for such labor was only 81.4 percent of normal, chiefly because of a shrinkage resulting from low prices of farm products. AT&T, monthly *Summary*, Aug. 6, 1930, pp. 1–2. Cf. HES, *Weekly Letter*, Mar. 17, 1928, pp. 66–67; Irving Bernstein, *A History of the American Worker, 1920–1933: The Lean Years* (Boston: Houghton Mifflin, 1960); and reviews in *AER*, June 1961, 51:480–82 (J. P. Goldberg), and *Jour. Ec. Hist.*, June 1961, 21:231–33 (G. G. Somers), esp. pp. 58–63, 241–42.

[41]*Hist. Stat. U.S.*, ser. D 764–78; and Bernstein, *Lean Years*, especially prologue and chs. 1–4, pp. 59, 84–90, 97, 241.

[42]*Hist. Stat. U.S.*, ser. D 642–53; *Stat. Abstr. U.S., 1930*, pp. 335–42, 347–50; Mills, *Economic Tendencies*, pp. 290–99.

[43]*Stat. Abstr. U.S., 1932*, p. 311; Mills, *Economic Tendencies*, pp. 476–81. Rees' careful later study concludes that real wages had risen in 1890–1914 at the much lower average annual rate of 1.3 percent. Albert Rees, *Real Wages in Manufacturing 1890–1914* (Princeton, N.J.: Princeton University Press, 1961).

[44]The gains in U.S. levels of living in 1913–28 are stressed in Leo Wolman's opening chapter in *Recent Economic Changes* ("Consumption and the Standard of Living," which includes a long subsection on food consumption written by me). They are summarized in Edward Eyre Hunt, *An Audit of America: A Summary of Recent Economic Changes in the United States* (New York: McGraw-Hill, 1930; foreword dated Jan. 1, 1930), esp. pp. 7–23, 26, 42–43, 46, 47, 57–60, 75–78, 80, 109, 163, 175, 179, 181. Commerce Secretary Hoover's annual reports in the 1920s went beyond the review of events to present indicators of improved levels of living, to discuss the causes of the remarkably long period of prosperity, and occasionally to mention dangers ("the orgy of speculation and ultimate collapse") and important issues ("the reversal

and electrical household equipment, facilitated by what seemed an extraordinary growth of consumer installment credit; enormous increase in the production, sale, and use of automobiles and motor trucks; marked growth of other relatively new industries such as electric power; a notable swelling of savings;[45] an "elastic credit supply"; a sustained high level of construction and total capital investment, despite a decline in residential construction in the later 1920s; persistently high and rising corporate profits after taxes (the 1929 peak was almost 50 percent above the 1923 level); the doubling of corporate dividend payments between 1923 and 1929, from $4.6 billion to $9.2 billion—a figure not exceeded until 1948;[46] and a broad advance in real gross national product per capita, from $710 in 1919 and $660 in 1921 to $857 in 1929 (1929 prices).[47] Such burgeoning industries as public utilities, communications, road transport and related services, and entertainment, rather than manufacturing (except of motor vehicles), made the major contribution to the growth of the economy.[48]

In the fiscal year 1929, federal, state, and local public expenditures on social welfare, including education, totaled $4.3 billion, having risen more than four-fold since 1913. In terms of 1959–60 prices, they represented almost $60 per capita,[49] a significant supplement to personal consumption expenditures of lower-income groups.

In every fiscal year of the decade 1920–30 a surplus was realized in the federal budget, and the gross national debt was reduced from its midyear peak of $25.5 billion on June 30, 1919, to its midyear low of $16.2 billion eleven years later. The per capita debt went from $242.56 to $131.51.[50] Federal tax rates were repeatedly reduced. Individual income

of the gold movement"). See also Charles A. Dice, *New Levels in the Stock Market* (New York: McGraw-Hill, 1929; foreword dated Aug. 1, 1929), ch. 17, "A New Standard of Living"; and the concluding paragraphs in Mills, *Economic Tendencies*, p. 481.

[45]In 1922–29 savings "were an increasing proportion, and probably an unprecedentedly large proportion, of an unprecedentedly large national dividend." "The total," Clark says, "was sufficient to finance a large export of capital and an enormous increase in our domestic capital equipment, and to leave something over for sheer speculative inflation of security values." J. M. Clark, *Strategic Factors in Business Cycles* (New York: NBER, 1935; introduction dated November 1933), p. 99. This valuable book could be cited at many points in this chapter.

[46]CTC, *Bus. Bull.*, May 15, 1930, Feb. 15, 1932, Nov. 15, 1935, Jan. 15, 1936.

[47]*Hist. Stat. U.S.*, ser. F 4.

[48]*Jobs Profits Economic Growth* (New York: NICB, 1963), p. 31; Daniel Creamer, *Capital Expansion and Capacity in Postwar Manufacturing*, NICB Studies in Business Economics (New York: NICB, 1961), p. 8.

[49]Official data summarized in NICB, *Road Maps of Industry*, no. 1357, Dec. 29, 1961; *Hist. Stat. U.S.*, ser. H 1–29; and *Stat. Abstr. U.S., 1962*, pp. 274–75. Today, of course, they are vastly larger; cf. *ibid.*, 1973, pp. 286–316.

[50]*Hist. Stat. U.S.*, ser. Y 256, 368–69. The rise which followed continued through the depression decade and beyond, and the previous peak in per capita debt was exceeded as early as mid-1936.

taxes, at their pre-depression peaks in 1928 and 1929, yielded only a little over $1 billion a year.[51] Total federal internal revenue collections declined in fiscal years 1920–23 but rose, with slight dips in 1925 and 1928, to a modest peak in 1930.[52]

The resiliency of the economy was repeatedly tested, with reassuring results. The collapse of the amazing Florida land boom late in the winter of 1926,[53] the nationwide decline of new residential construction after 1925–26, the threat of overdoing consumer installment buying, repeated transitory setbacks in the stock market, recurring weakness in one or another particular industry, and chronic difficulties of agriculture, coal mining, and textile manufacturing—all seemed to be taken in stride, and the pessimists were proved wrong for the time being. Despite accelerating contraction in the fourth quarter of 1929, the year as a whole was the best of the decade—as F. C. Mills later wrote, it was the climax of "a period of prosperity, marked by increasing industrial productivity, rising living standards, generally advancing wages and rapidly increasing profits."[54] And pride was taken in the national commitment to high wage rates, corporate encouragement of employee stockholding,[55] and workers' pensions.[56] The performance of the U.S. economy in the 1920s was impressive even in comparison with that in 1960–65.[57]

Except for strident appeals from agrarian spokesmen for "equality for agriculture," the public generally accepted the record of 1922–29 with

[51]*Ibid.*, ser. Y 307.

[52]*Ibid.*, ser. Y 259, 261; *Stat. Abstr. U.S., 1930*, p. 185.

[53]H. B. Vanderblue, "The Florida Land Boom," *Journal of Land and Public Utility Economics*, March August 1927, 3.113–31, 252–69. Cf. J. K. Galbraith, *The Great Crash: 1929* (Boston: Houghton Mifflin, 1955), pp. 8–13; and Wyatt Blassingame, *The Golden Geyser* (New York: Doubleday, 1960).

[54]Mills, *Economic Tendencies*, pp. 414–16.

[55]The movement to interest employees in owning stock in the company they work for got under way after the depression of 1921–22 and gained momentum in the succeeding years. Foerster and Dietel, after studying 306 plans in use, conservatively estimated that substantially $700 million worth of stock (market value as of Apr. 15, 1926) was so owned. R. F. Foerster and Else H. Dietel, *Employee Stock Ownership in the United States* (Princeton, N.J.: Princeton University Press, 1926), favorably reviewed by James A. Bowie in *EJ*, March 1927, 37:94–96.

[56]Abraham Epstein began his commendatory review of Murray W. Latimer's two-volume *Industrial Pension Systems in the United States and Canada* (New York: Industrial Relations Counselors, 1932) with the sentence: "Only a short while ago it was commonly believed that American employers were bringing about the millenium for their workers," but "most of the earlier hopes of pension plans have disappeared." *AER*, September 1939, 23:547–50. Latimer gave a paper on "Old Age Pensions in America" at the December 1928 meeting of the ASA which was published in *Amer. Labor Legis. Rev.*, March 1929, 19:55–66.

[57]Paul W. McCracken made this point on Feb. 23, 1966, at the economic symposium of the Joint Economic Committee on the occasion of the twentieth anniversary of the passage of the Employment Act of 1946. *Proceedings*, p. 69. In 1922–29, McCracken said, unemployment averaged about 4 percent, the price level rose at the rate of only 0.2 percent per year, and the average rate of increase of output was 4.7 percent per year, as compared with the 4.5 percent average from 1960 to 1965. See my comments in n. 40 above.

satisfaction, even with complacency. It was only later that the sharp contrast between the income gains of labor and those of corporate stockholders were brought out clearly;[58] it was still later that alleged maldistribution of income was accorded large blame for the severe setback of 1929–33.[59] Such experiences helped to sustain the remarkable "wave of optimism" which was an independent factor among those responsible for the notably high level of real investment in the 1920s.[60]

The dominant view, reiterated by responsible business, economic, financial, and political observers, was that the economy in 1929 was fundamentally sound in spite of recognized weaknesses and speculative excesses. The evidence upon which this view was based included the broad stability of commodity price indexes, the smooth absorption of record production into consumer use, the apparent absence of excessive commodity inventories, the lack of conspicuous surpluses of productive capacity, and the paucity of failures of important industrial and financial companies.[61] Ayres, surely a competent analyst, later asserted that "during the long prosperity before this depression . . . production, prices, and employment were in better balance with one another than in almost any other period of which we have records."[62]

The complex, complicated, and changing agricultural situation in the 1920s was diversely appraised in those years, and extreme views about it at the time and in the years that followed have been voiced with seeming authority. In accepting the presidential nomination in August 1928, Herbert Hoover said: "The most urgent economic problem in our nation today is in agriculture. . . . A nation which is spending ninety billions a year can well afford an expenditure of a few hundred millions for a workable program that will give to one-third of the population their fair share of the nation's prosperity." Moritz J. Bonn wrote in 1930: "Agriculture had for some years been in a state of crisis that was becoming more and more acute." Alvin H. Hansen wrote in 1951 that "from 1920 to 1939 we had

---

[58]Mills, *Economic Tendencies*, pp. 501–3.

[59]Galbraith, *Great Crash*, p. 182, and n. 62 below.

[60]Gordon, *Business Fluctuations*, p. 410. Yet soon Clark could write that the evidence of growing excess in productive capacity in 1922–29 was "overwhelming in some instances, though no adequate measure of real excess capacity exists." *Strategic Factors*, p. 104.

[61]For total failures of business concerns, see *Hist. Stat. U.S.*, ser. V 1–3. For a long perspective, see the various charts for the 1920s in J. Frank Gordon, *Growth Patterns in Industry: A Reexamination*, NICB Studies in Business Economics 75 (New York: NICB, 1961). The most impressive instances of rapid growth were in production of primary aluminum, asphalt, copper, Portland cement, and paper and paperboard; in consumption of cigarettes, lead, motor fuel, and rubber; and in life insurance in force and motor vehicle registrations. See also Y. S. Leong, "Indexes of the Physical Volume Production of Producers' and Consumers' Goods" (compiled on a monthly basis for 1919–29), *JASA*, March 1932, 27:21–36.

[62]CTC, *Bus. Bull.*, Sept. 15, 1934, discussing "seven economic fallacies that have wide current acceptance": industrial overproduction, concentration of wealth, redistribution of income, profit margins, government debts, inflation, and purchasing power.

agricultural hard times." Gilbert C. Fite and Jim E. Reese wrote in 1959 that "at the end of the decade farmers were still floundering in a depression that had hit them in 1920." Baruch, an "agricultural fundamentalist," as late as 1960 had no doubt that "the great depression had its origins, in part, in the agricultural malaise of the 1920's" and that "if we had had the foresight to come to grips with the farm question, we might have been spared the decade of the 1930's."[63] As a close student of agriculture whose views underwent changes during the interwar period, I consider most of these generalizations seriously wrong.

U.S. agriculture had emerged from its severe postwar depression in 1924–25, and net income of farmers from farming reached its peak in November 1925 but showed a roughly horizontal trend in the next five years. Wartime prosperity and early postwar illusions had led to a rise in farm mortgage debt from the prewar peak of $4.7 billion on January 1, 1914, to an all-time high of $10.8 billion nine years later (a figure not exceeded until 1959). Through abnormally heavy foreclosures and forced sales, for the most part, it had shrunk to $9.6 billion on January 1, 1930. Farmland values had increased by $10 billion in 1912–22, then declined by $6.6 billion to $34.9 billion in 1929, while nonfarm land values rose from $35.2 billion to $60.2 billion. Farmers' interest charges and taxes were burdensome, much above prewar levels. Yet use of farm equipment had greatly expanded and levels of living had improved. In December 1929 not only President Hoover but also leading agricultural economists and farm spokesmen viewed the situation with real, if ill-founded, optimism. In the ensuing deep depression the agricultural level of 1925–29 seemed a plateau of prosperity.[64]

It is still occasionally asserted (as it was so often in the depression years) that the world-famed "Coolidge prosperity" was a myth. On the contrary, there is ample evidence that it was very real. At the time, however, its extent was often exaggerated: even responsible observers called it unparalleled, unprecedented, extraordinary, immense, colossal, stupendous. It was so only for the limited number of persons who were reaping

[63]Herbert Hoover, *The New Day: Campaign Speeches of Herbert Hoover, 1928* (Stanford, Calif.: Stanford University Press, 1928), pp. 17, 22; Bonn, *Prosperity*, p. 70, and *Crisis*, p. 93; A. H. Hansen, *Business Cycles and National Income* (New York: Norton, 1951), p. 72, Gilbert C. Fite and Jim E. Reese, *An Economic History of the United States* (Boston: Houghton Mifflin, 1959), pp. 547, 561; Baruch, *The Public Years*, ch. 9, esp. pp. 167–68; and my 1934 paper on "Agricultural Fundamentalism" in J. S. Davis, *On Agricultural Policy, 1926–1938* (Stanford, Calif.: Food Research Institute, 1939), pp. 24–43.

[64]*Hist. Stat. U.S.*, ser. F 216–18, K 116–17, 125–28, 134–35, 150–52, 162, 172; John D. Black's unsigned reviews of "The Agricultural Situation and Outlook" in HES, *Weekly Letter*, esp. June 15, Dec. 14, 1929, pp. 146–48, 298–303, and his articles in *Rev. Ec. Stat.*; several papers in Davis, *On Agricultural Policy*; Silberling, *Dynamics of Business* chs. 7–8—valuable for charts and discussion; and Chapters 6 and 8 below.

enormous capital gains.[65] The prosperity of the mass of Americans was moderate, yet substantial. True, it was uneven, unbalanced, as prosperity usually is;[66] then, as today, there were great disparities in wealth and income, and poverty coexisted with affluence.[67]

While there were marked differences in wage rates among different groups, comparisons with prewar rates were broadly favorable,[68] and advances in levels of living were fairly general. Through the 1920s the level of money wage rates remained more than double the 1913 level, with a slightly rising trend in 1925-29. From the monthly low of 211 percent of the 1913 average in April and May 1925, there was about a 7 percent rise to 226 in June through December 1929.[69]

Leading Federal Reserve banker Benjamin Strong, speaking in March 1927 to a group of economists on whom he called for policy advice, said that "a more equitable distribution of the returns of industry" among capital, the employer, and labor was "the only advantage gained from the war"; it had contributed to the general contentment and thereby consti-

---

[65]Statistics of the Internal Revenue Service reveal that in 1929 there were 513 individuals each of whose *net income* exceeded $1 million. This record was not approached again until the mid-1960s, in spite of the marked increase in population and the substantial decline in the purchasing power of the dollar. Treasury Secretary Mellon's annual report for fiscal 1929 (p. 4) noted that capital gains on stock transfers accounted for the larger part of increased federal revenue from individual taxpayers. The high profits of 1928-29 were due in part to the extraordinary stock market advance, which they helped to accentuate, but their most ominous significance lay in promoting excessive expectations that they would continue.

[66]Schumpeter rightly emphasized (*Business Cycles*, 1:142) that times of prosperity are not typically associated with universal gains in welfare and that times of prolonged depression are not typically associated with increasing wretchedness. Persistence of poverty and misery despite broad improvement in income and in average consumption was true in the 1920s and again in the 1960s, as we keep being reminded; indeed, important vital statistics show larger gains in the 1930s than in the 1920s, and slackening gains in the 1960s. Schumpeter referred, as had David A. Wells four decades earlier, to "the progress of the standard of life of the working classes, 1873-1897," in which depression years slightly exceeded prosperous years (see the CTC index covering that quarter century).

[67]See Bernstein, *Lean Years*, especially the prologue and ch. 1; and *Economic Report of the President*, January 1964, ch. 3.

[68]*Stat. Abstr. U.S., 1930*, pp. 335-42, 347-50, and *Hist. Stat. U.S.*, ser. D 642-53. The AT&T chart of weekly wage earnings in manufacturing industries shows a severe drop from August 1920 until early 1922, briefly interrupted early in 1921; a marked increase in 1922-23 to a level equal to that in early 1921; and a moderate uptrend in 1923-29, followed by a severe decline from late in 1929 to March 1933 (*Summary*, Dec. 6, 1933, p. 11; chart of seasonally adjusted data for 1914-33, 1914 = 100). See also Leo Wolman, in *JASA*, March 1930, suppl., 25 (169A):158-63; Rufus S. Tucker, "Gold and the General Price Level," *Rev. Ec. Stat.*, Jan. 15, 1934, 16:8-16, 25-27, esp. chart 5 ("Indexes of Wages in the United States, 1791-1932)", pp. 14, 27.

[69]See Lionel Robbins, *The Great Depression* (London: Macmillan, 1934), p. 224, giving an index of composite wages (1913 = 100) worked up by the Federal Reserve Bank of New York, monthly from January 1925 through October 1933, "based on indexes of *either* wages or earnings in 12 different industries, with seasonal fluctuations eliminated." In 1930-33 there was a gradual downdrift to the low of 168 in March 1933, a net loss of 26 percent.

tuted "a great factor in the sustained prosperity."[70] Unfortunately, the illusion came to be cherished, here and abroad, that we had achieved "the miracle of a permanent prosperity which no crisis could destroy."[71]

As the year 1929 began, reviewers of the business situation and outlook were almost unanimous, according to AT&T, in forecasting a recession in the spring, largely because of the cumulative effect of dear money and the probability that the level of output in the automotive industry expected in the early months would be too high to be sustained.[72] Later forecasts, such as those of Brookmire's and the Harvard Economic Society,[73] broadly concurred as the onset of contraction was delayed.[74] June-August indexes of business activity were on a high plateau; a mild contraction followed in the next two months.[75]

The burgeoning speculation prevented the Harvard Curve A ("speculation") from giving its usual advance warning of business contraction; it reached its peak after instead of before its Curve B ("business").[76] The weekly sensitive price index, designed to aid in forecasting intermediate fluctuations in business, worked strikingly well in a test period 1923-25,

[70]Schumpeter, one of those present, so wrote Mitchell on Mar. 10, 1927, as cited in Joseph Dorfman, *The Economic Mind in American Civilization*, vols. 4-5: *1919-1933* (New York. Viking, 1959), 4:281. The words quoted are Dorfman's.

[71]Bonn, *Prosperity*, p. 7. Stuart Chase discussed the subject in a popular vein in his book written on the eve of the stock market crash, *Prosperity: Fact or Myth?* (New York: Boni, 1929); this drew heavily on the recently published two volumes on *Recent Economic Changes* and on Robert S. and Helen M. Lynd, *Middletown: A Study in Contemporary American Culture* (New York: Harcourt Brace, 1929).

[72]AT&T, *Summary*, Feb. 5, 1929, p. 1.

[73]These, with Babson's, were prominent among the serious and influential economic "services" which flourished in the 1920s. Brookmire's weekly issues concentrated on analysis of "fundamental conditions and of individual stocks" and included *The Brookmire Analyst, The Brookmire Forecaster*, and *Brookmire Special Reports*. The Harvard University Committee on Economic Research (initiated in 1917) in 1919 began publishing the quarterly *Review of Economic Statistics* (the name was changed in 1948 to the *Review of Economics and Statistics*) and a *Weekly Letter* (published from 1922 through 1931), neither of which gave any attention to individual stocks. Both undertook to make economic forecasts. See also Chapter 15 below.

[74]In his cogent and competent paper given late in 1929 Franz Schneider, Jr., held that it would have been better if the contraction had begun in the spring. AEA, *Papers and Proceedings*, published in *AER*, March 1930, 20(1):102-7. Schumpeter (*Business Cycles*, 2:793) later took April 1929 to mark the peak of prosperity in his short (Kitchin) cycle.

[75]For pertinent comments on the mildness of the contraction in the summer of 1929, in contrast with the sharpness of that in September through December, see C. A. Phillips, T. F. McManus, and R. W. Nelson, *Banking and the Business Cycle: A Study of the Great Depression in the United States* (New York: Macmillan, 1937), p. 160; HES, *Weekly Letter*, e.g., June 22, July 20, 1929, pp. 152, 176; AT&T, *Summary*, e.g., Sept. 5, 1929.

[76]See CTC subchart, "Typical Sequences in a Typical Business Cycle," in its *Business Cycles since 1831*. In typical business cycles, common stock price indexes reach their peak a few months before the peak of business activity. In 1929 the series did not perform as a "leading indicator" of a business downturn. At the time June seemed to be the peak of business; as later revised, "business" was on a plateau in June-August, but the stock market rose until September.

but the results in later years were less gratifying.[77] Only in retrospect, with newer tools of analysis, did the moderate decline in the "comprehensive diffusion index" of the National Bureau of Economic Research, in the first half of 1929, and its sharp and extreme fall in the second half, appear to warn that serious trouble lay ahead.[78] The protracted very low level of this index from late 1929 into early 1932 is consistent with the continued declines in business activity and prices of common stocks in 1930–32. Despite later encouraging advances, the art of business forecasting is by no means perfected, as experience has amply demonstrated even in the past decade.[79]

The Great American   The broad course of stock market prices is
Bull Market, 1922–29   well shown in long perspective by Standard
and Poor's price index of a large number (in recent years, 500) of common stocks (1941–43 average = 10) monthly, from 1917 to a recent date, together with the volume of brokers' loans and the average daily volume of trading on the New York Stock Exchange.[80] From a high level of 9–10 in late 1919, the total index slumped to about 6 in mid-1921. By early 1923 it had regained its former high. After a moderate decline, late that year it began a fairly sustained advance which continued, with only shortlived setbacks,[81] to the middle of 1929. Then it rose sharply to an extraordinary peak of about 30 in September.[82] Measured from low to high, the index rose almost fivefold in eight years![83]

[77]See the chart covering the years 1921–31 in Samuel J. Dennis, "The Sensitive Price Index," *Rev. Ec. Stat.*, Jan. 15, 1932, 14:12–44.

[78]Gordon, *Business Fluctuations*, pp. 519–21; Geoffrey H. Moore, "The 1957–58 Business Contraction: New Model or Old?" AEA, *Papers and Proceedings, AER*, May 1959, 49(2):292–308, esp. p. 298. See also Bureau of the Census, *Business Cycle Developments*, April 1964, pp. 2–3, 33–39; Leo B. Shohan, *The Conference Board's New Diffusion Indexes*, Technical Paper 13 (New York: NICB, 1963).

[79]Cf. Gordon, *Business Fluctuations*, ch. 17.

[80]FRS, *Hist. Chart Book, 1971*, pp. 32–33; CTC, *Bus. Bull.*, Nov. 15, 1929. The computation of the standard statistics stock price indexes was described by H. Dwight Comer late in 1928 in "Measurement of Stock Prices and Stock Values," *JASA*, March 1929, suppl., 24(165A):9–19. A chart covering 1926–28 (p. 14) shows the close correspondence between the market value of the 392 stocks then in the *weekly* composite SSC index and the market value of all stocks listed on the New York Stock Exchange. At that time weighted *daily* indexes were being computed for fifty industrials, twenty utilities, and thirty rails.

[81]Severe ones in early December 1928 and in early and late March 1929 are not perceptible in the curve of monthly averages.

[82]This level was not reached again until mid-1954. The index touched 60 late in 1959 and 72 briefly late in 1961. After a severe slump in the spring of 1962, it passed the previous high in September 1963. For later annual data, see *Economic Report of the President*.

[83]Gordon, *Business Fluctuations*, p. 400 (chart). The truly extraordinary rise in prices of common stocks in 1923–29 and the sharp decline in 1929–32 are shown in still longer perspective in charts of the Cowles Commission price indexes of all common stocks annually for 1871 to 1940 and monthly for 1906–40. Alfred Cowles III and Associates, *Common Stock Indexes*, 2d ed. (Bloomington, Ind., 1939), and supplements. Cf. Silberling, *Dynamics of Business*, pp. 397n, 399, 412 (chart).

The influences basically responsible for this long and striking advance were the rising tide of confidence, here and abroad, in the future of the U.S. economy; a pronounced increase in investors' desires and preference for common stocks; and enormous expansion in the spread and use of facilities and credit for buying stocks, both for cash and on margin. Investment in common stocks in the 1920s was encouraged by reasoned arguments that they deserved inclusion, along with bonds, even in conservative portfolios and that they were often superior to bonds for careful investors.[84] One striking consequence was that dividend yields on common stocks trended downward to lows of around 4 percent in most of 1928–29, when for nearly two years they were lower than yields on highest-grade corporate bonds.[85] Both investment and speculation were promoted by broadened facilities offered for buying stocks on margin, which all sorts of people came to use.

Very low margins for brokers' loans and bank loans on stock collateral—as low as 20 percent of market value, or even 10 percent for favored customers—had greatly stimulated stock speculation in 1927 and 1928, and even these margins were not rigidly enforced as the market rose. Without legislative or overt Federal Reserve pressures, however, such requirements were raised considerably in the first half of 1929, and New York Stock Exchange questionnaires revealed that in that period margins averaged 40 percent on customers' accounts and 65 percent on debit balances with brokers.[86] This increase failed to restrain the frenzied purchasing in July and August 1929 but eventually rendered vulnerable the great bulk of speculative accounts and even the accounts of the average investor.

[84]Edgar Lawrence Smith, *Common Stocks as Long-Term Investments* (New York: Macmillan, 1924, reprinted frequently until 1928); and Kenneth S. Van Strum, *Investment in Purchasing Power* (Boston: Barron's, 1926). Keynes was much impressed by Smith's book. He reviewed it for the *N&A* (London), May 2, 1925, pp. 157–58, and urged that a comparable study should be made of British shares and bonds.

[85]Conveniently shown in long perspective in charts in CTC, *Bus. Bull.*, e.g., November 1971, p. 4. The then recent low, late in 1961, was slightly under 3 percent, as it has been at times in recent years. See charts in *Economic Indicators*, e.g., September 1971, p. 34. (This official monthly is prepared for the Joint Economic Committee by the Council of Economic Advisers.) In that month dividend yields on the thirty stocks in the Dow-Jones industrials averaged 3.55 percent, less than one-half the 7.48 percent yield on Barron's best-grade corporate bonds. *WSJ*, Oct. 7, 1971.

[86]Irving Fisher, *The Stock Market Crash—and After* (New York: Macmillan, 1930; preface dated Dec. 15, 1929), pp. 50–51; E. H. H. Simmons, *The Principal Causes of the Stock Market Crisis* (New York: NYSE, 1930), address of the president of the NYSE, Jan. 25, 1930; F. W. Hirst, *Wall Street and Lombard Street: The Stock Exchange Slump of 1929 and the Trade Depression of 1930* (New York: Macmillan, 1939), p. 26; Galbraith, *Great Crash*, p. 37. Galbraith rashly said: "An increase in margins to, say 75 percent in January 1929, or even a serious proposal to do so, would have caused many small speculators and quite a few big ones to sell. The boom would have come to a sudden and spectacular end." Even if such a move would have been wise, as hindsight suggests, its effect might have been small, considering the "climate" of the period; for the same reason, it would have seemed too extreme a proposal to make.

Loans to brokers for purchase of or carrying securities, mostly common stocks, rose considerably in 1922 and much more in 1925 and 1927. By early 1928, when the volume had reached $4.4 billion, it was widely but not universally held that the expansion had gone to an undesirable extent. Moreover, much of the recent increase was provided by nonbank lenders, mostly corporations which had excess liquid funds, in part raised by new security flotations; and investment companies loaned on call sizable sums awaiting investment. This whole process continued apace in the next twenty-one months, as call-loan rates kept rising, at times reaching the extraordinary heights of 12 to 20 percent. Annual average rates on call-loan renewals rose from 4.06 percent in 1927 to 6.04 percent in 1928 and to 7.61 percent in 1929.[87] Monthly averages of daily rates were above 6 percent from mid-1928 through September 1929, and above 9 percent in two months of this period.[88]

In 1928, the volume of brokers' loans rose to $6.4 billion, and practically all of the increase was supplied by nonbank lenders. In 1929, with only a shortlived interruption in the spring, the volume went on up until, on September 30, the total exceeded $8.5 billion,[89] and more than three-fourths of this was then supplied by nonbank lenders. Though changes in the statistical series make precise comparisons difficult, it appears that this level has not been closely approached since 1929.[90]

Nor was this the whole story. Commercial banks loaned their customers large sums on stock and bond collateral, and other sources also were tapped. For loans on securities, the several estimates differ widely. Late in 1928, Norman Merriman, of S. Ungerleider and Company, reported his calculation that the sum of reported brokers' loans and bank loans on securities came to about $15,250 million, 25 to 30 percent of all banking resources of the nation.[91] H. V. Roelse and Shaw Livermore, in their two later careful estimates, reached totals of $16,660 million and $18,400 million, respectively, for the peak date of October 4, 1929.[92]

As rates on call loans ran above other market rates by wide margins, funds were drawn into the New York stock market from all over the coun-

[87]*Hist. Stat. U.S.*, ser. X 307–8.

[88]FRS, *Hist. Chart Book, 1971*, p. 36; Robbins, *Great Depression*, pp. 47, 223.

[89]Chandler, *Strong*, pp. 426–27.

[90]The roughly corresponding but somewhat larger present-day series, "Customers' Debit Balances" of NYSE member firms, reached a postwar peak of $4.3 billion at the end of 1961. *SCB*, September 1962, p. S–20. This peak was exceeded in 1963.

[91]Point made at an ASA dinner meeting on Dec. 6, 1928, reported in *JASA*, June 1929, 24:73.

[92]*Rev. Ec. Stat.*, August 1930, 12:109–11; and Nov. 15, 1932, 14:191–94. Keynes cited Roelse's figures in his *Treatise on Money*, 2:196n. Harris seems to have overlooked these studies when he later made his "very rough" estimate of $12 billion. Seymour E. Harris, *Twenty Years of Federal Reserve Policy*, 2 vols. (Cambridge, Mass.: Harvard University Press, 1933), 2:455–58.

try and from financial centers abroad. Though no reliable data on the foreign inflow are available, the London *Economist* was probably right in asserting, late in 1928, that "an appreciable proportion of loans from 'others' really consisted of foreign short money which comes to New York to take advantage of the high call rates." After mid-1928, largely for this reason, the flow of U.S. capital to Europe had been severely curtailed, with consequences not then widely recognized. According to the *Economist*, "Wall Street speculation ceased to be a national and became an international problem, and one that affected London, the world's financial center, most of all."[93]

An extraordinary volume of new issues of common stock was floated toward the end of the boom—$2.1 billion in 1928 and $5.1 billion in 1929, as compared with a total of $3.3 billion in 1921–27 and the later postwar peak of $4.5 billion ($2.65 billion "net change") in 1961.[94] As Franz Schneider put it, business profits in 1928 were "most satisfactory; but those of the first half of 1929 showed striking increases. . . . Record-breaking production and brilliant earnings inspired almost unlimited optimism." In September alone, new capital issues reached the extraordinary total of $1,615 million.[95]

In the later stages of the boom, speculation was unwholesomely heightened by a rash of mergers and holding companies, especially in public utilities.[96] Recorded mergers in manufacturing and mining rose from a low of 309 in 1922 to extraordinary peaks of 1,058 and 1,245 in 1928 and 1929, respectively.[97] The merger boom reached its peak in the spring of 1929 (mergers fell sharply in the next two quarters). Formerly confined largely to manufacturing, transportation, and utilities, the movement broadened its scope, even to include banking.[98] The president of Bank-

---

[93] Dec. 7, 1929, pp. 1069–71; Gordon, *Business Fluctuations*, pp. 420–22; and Harris, *Twenty Years*, 2:480–87.

[94] *Hist. Stat. U.S.*, ser. X 371, *Stat. Abstr. U.S., 1965*, p. 474, and *ibid., 1970*, p. 456. (The 1961 high was exceeded in 1969.) Cf. D. W. Ellsworth, "The Unprecedented Volume of New Stock Issues: A Statistical Analysis," *Annalist*, Oct. 25, 1929, pp. 813–14; Reed, *Federal Reserve Policy*, pp. 126–28. However, as Silberling pointed out (*Dynamics of Business*, pp. 428–29), the "really *productive* (new capital) portion of the total issues of stocks and bonds, as estimated by Moody's Investors Service," was surprisingly small—in 1929 only 22 percent.

[95] Schneider, in AEA, *Papers and Proceedings*, pp. 103–6.

[96] M. C. Waltersdorf, "The Holding Company in American Public Utility Development," *EJ*, December 1926, 36:586–97; a series of papers from divergent viewpoints, given Apr. 11, 1930, in *Proc. Acad. Pol. Sci.*, June 1930, 14:1–210 (one extreme critic called state commission regulation "a farce"); Leslie T. Fournier, "Regulating the Power and Light Industry," in J. G. Smith, ed., *Facing the Facts: An Economic Diagnosis* (New York: Putnam, 1932), pp. 222–23; and J. C. Bonbright and G. C. Means, *The Holding Company, Its Public Significances and Its Regulation* (New York: McGraw-Hill, 1932).

[97] *Hist. Stat. U.S.*, ser. V 30.

[98] Willard L. Thorp and several other speakers discussed this at an ASA dinner meeting in New York City on Dec. 5, 1929, reported in *JASA*, March 1930, suppl., 25(169A):80–89.

shares National Corporation, F. C. Thomas, admitted, shortly after the Wall Street crash: "The fact that bank mergers have enabled banks to engage in security speculation has probably contributed to the sharpness of the recent decline in the stock market."[99] The almost insatiable demand for securities, the huge profits many concerns were making, decisions to use much of these for expansion rather than for dividends, the hopes for both economies and some degree of price control, and especially the activities of stock promoters, were mainly responsible.[100] Frank A. Fetter, an eminent Princeton economist, in 1932 expressed no doubt that "one of the major factors in causing and intensifying the boom" was "the stupendous merger movement with the very real added power it gave to stock-security manipulation and monopolistic price control, and with the deluded public faith in the inordinate profits to be obtained by mergers."[101]

The demand for stocks from endowment funds and individual investors and speculators was heavily supplemented by purchases of investment "trusts" and trading companies, which multiplied amazingly in 1928–29.[102] The New York correspondent of the London *Economist* wrote on August 21:

The popularity of the investment trusts is a not unnatural consequence of the long-sustained bull market in shares. Some misgivings are created in conservative minds, however, by the manner in which some of these holding companies and trusts are being "pyramided." The holding companies purchase shares of subsidiaries in the open market and thus advance the prices of the subsidiaries. The rise in the subsidiaries thereupon stimulates strength in the shares of the holding company. Frequently the holding company will then sell more of its own shares to the public at the higher prices and then repeat the process by buying more of the shares of the subsidiaries. Instances are not lacking in which this holding company "pyramiding" has been carried through several stages with an accumulation of paper profits throughout. The practice has been much more prevalent in the utility field than in any other, and is to a considerable degree responsible for the low yield and earnings ratios at which utility shares are selling.[103]

[99]*Ibid.*, p. 89.

[100]Willard L. Thorp, "The Persistence of the Merger Movement," AEA, *Papers and Proceedings, AER*, March 1931, 21(1):77–89.

[101]"Big Business and the Nation," in Smith, *Facing the Facts*, pp. 186–214, esp. pp. 203–5. Cf. Walter Lippmann's columns of Apr. 4 and May 30, 1935, in Lippmann, *Interpretations, 1933–1935*, ed. Allan Nevins (New York: Macmillan, 1935), pp. 119, 276.

[102]Charles F. Speare, in *Journal of the American Bankers' Association*, February 1929; Fisher, *Stock Market Crash*, pp. 214–17; and Hugh Bullock, *The Story of Investment Companies* (New York: Columbia University Press, 1954). Mutual funds were few and relatively insignificant in the 1920s. Some pertinent comments on the British counterpart of the Wall Street superboom can be found in W. Lionel Fraser, *All to the Good* (Garden City, N.Y.: Doubleday, 1963), pp. 97–99.

[103]Aug. 31, 1929, p. 394. Cf. CTC, *Bus. Bull.*, Nov. 15, 1929.

The same correspondent wrote again on October 8, 1929: "The persistent and sharp rise in brokers' loans during September, in the face of a declining stock market, is attributed to further large-scale exercising of rights of shareholders and to the boom in investment trust fluctuations."[104] Three weeks later, shortly after the "Wall Street tornado" had hit, he wrote: "The factors that are considered immediately responsible for the decline are the excessive flotations of 'investment trust' securities during the past several months and the great boom that was staged in public utilities during June, July, and August."[105] In the last months before the crash, prices of utilities stocks rose most strikingly: from a little over 200 (1926 average = 100) in February through May 1929 they zoomed to monthly highs of 304 in August and 321 in September.[106] In the summer of 1929 "frenzied finance" indeed reached heights that soon seemed incredible in retrospect; various forms of skullduggery ran rampant; and influential men in high positions made irresponsible statements, pursued reprehensible courses, or both (see Chapter 14 below).

The volume of trading on the New York Stock Exchange was a sort of thermometer registering the speculative temperature of the stock market.[107] In 1919 a high of 317 million shares was traded, and the low in 1921 was 173 million. In 1922–24 trading was moderate, but in 1925 and 1926 it ran above 450 million shares. In the next three years the volume rose sharply to 920 million in 1928 and to 1,125 million in 1929,[108] when the number of shares traded exceeded the number of shares listed—a record not since approached.[109] The 1929 total was first exceeded in 1963, when more than 8,000 million shares were listed, as compared with 946.4 million in September 1929.[110]

Here is quantitative evidence of the mounting, widespread, and feverish speculation in common stocks before the crash, when stock ownership had increased remarkably but was far less prevalent than nowadays.[111] Probably fewer than a million persons actively participated in the

[104]Oct. 19, 26, 1929, pp. 714, 765.

[105]Nov. 9, 1929, p. 867.

[106]Standard Statistics Indexes, in FRS, *Chart Book*, Nov. 9, 1930, p. 26.

[107]See a little brochure (*Is the Market High?*) published June 30, 1934, by the National Securities and Research Corporation, 120 Broadway, New York City.

[108]*Hist. Stat. U.S.*, ser. X 373.

[109]CTC, *Bus. Bull.*, April 1971.

[110]*Stat. Abstr. U.S., 1965*, p. 471, and *ibid., 1970*, 142:455.

[111]There are no reliable estimates of the number of *different* stockholders in the 1920s. In a 1928 article John Moody quoted an estimate that more than 15 million Americans then owned "stocks, bonds, and government obligations" as compared with only half a million in 1908. John Moody, "The New Era in Wall Street," *Atlantic*, August 1928, p. 261. (In his *Wall Street and Lombard Street*, p. 41, Hirst seems to have used this figure for those "directly interested in the stock markets.") But all such estimates must be distrusted because care was not taken to

"speculative orgy."[112] Much of the public participation took the shape of ill-informed gambling, but Galbraith probably went too far in asserting that "it became central to the culture." There was also a large volume of more or less studious investment in equities.[113] This contributed heavily to the upsurge of prices of common stocks, the consequent decline of dividend yields below bond yields,[114] and the even more striking shrinkage of earnings/price ratios in 1925–29.[115]

A host of true investors were recurrently concerned over the height to which the stock market rose, even if they were not borrowing to buy at a wide rate differential between interest paid and dividends received.[116] Most of them, however, were loath to sell out, to stay out of the market, or to shift from stocks to bonds—even after Treasury Secretary Mellon wisely suggested, in a press conference on March 14, 1929, that "now is the time to buy good bonds."[117] Mere inertia was partly responsible, even if by no means everyone accepted the prevalent New Era philosophy. Important

---

allow for the many individuals who owned two or more securities. The subject is dealt with in Edwin Burk Cox, *Trends in the Distribution of Stock Ownership* (Philadelphia: University of Pennsylvania Press, 1963), reviewed by R. J. Lampman in *JASA*, June 1964, 59:606–7. Cox estimated that the number of stockholders rose from 1 million in 1900 to 5 million in 1927 and to 10 million in 1930.

For various years beginning with 1956 the New York Stock Exchange has attempted careful estimates, excluding duplications. Its sixth "national census of shareholders," as of early 1965, gave a total of 20 million, up 3 million in three years, and up 11.4 million since 1956. *Stat. Abstr. U.S., 1965*, pp. 475–76. The 1970 figure was 30,850,000. *Ibid., 1972*, p. 457. But the rate of increase in shareholder numbers in the 1920s was surely more rapid than in the 1960s.

[112]Galbraith said: "there is probably more danger of overestimating rather than underestimating the popular interest in the market. . . . only one and a half million people, out of a population of approximately 120 million and of between 29 and 30 million families, had an active association of any sort with the stock market. And not all of these were speculators. . . . However, it is safe to say that at the peak in 1929 the number of active speculators was less— and probably was much less—than a million." *Great Crash*, pp. 82–83.

[113]Keynes wrote in 1930: "The investment boom in the United States in 1929 was a good example of an enormous rise in the price of securities as a whole which was not accompanied by any rise at all in the price of the current output of new fixed capital." *Treatise on Money*, 1:249.

[114]A good chart covering the years 1915–65 is given in CTC, *Bus. Bull.*, September 1965.

[115]FRS, *Hist. Chart Book, 1971*, p. 37. In recent years it has become commoner to express this in reverse, as price-earnings ratios.

[116]A New York friend who was an officer in an international banking house wrote me on Nov. 12, 1928: "As you know, opinion in even the best informed cricles here has been extremely divided and perplexed regarding the course of the stock market. There seem to exist at present only the same old reasons for a recession and as these have failed to work, during the last two or three years, everybody, even the most conservative observers, is beginning to wonder whether the recession is really coming at all in the near future."

[117]*C&FC*, Mar. 16, 1929, p. 1607, citing *New York Times*. The secretary, however, "would not enter into a general discussion of present day speculation in stocks." Praising his advice, the *Chronicle* referred to "the unbridled speculation in the stock market" and extravagantly observed: "The public has got the idea that the rise can be continued indefinitely." Brookmire's *Investment Opportunity Bulletin* of June 24, 1929 noted that corporate bond prices were at their lowest since late 1925, and added: "Good bonds are undoubtedly at bargain prices."

also was the experience of those who saw the market go on up after they had sold, especially in the sharp breaks of December 1928 and March 1929.

Moreover, many investors were reluctant, in the summer of 1929, to subject themselves to taxes on the capital gains they would realize by cashing in all or most of their holdings. At its meeting early in October 1928, the American Bankers Association passed a resolution calling for repeal of the capital gains tax.[118] The National City Bank of New York, in a special bulletin of April 18, 1929, argued that reduction in the capital gains tax rate might be the key "to unlock the funds heretofore imprisoned in the stock market by a tax policy which discourages liquidation except under force of the most drastic measures," and might thus prove "one of the most promising avenues of escape from the present impasse" and "an important help toward restoring normal credit conditions."[119] But no such action was taken, and it is doubtful that if it had been, then or earlier, it would have seriously weakened the upsurge in prices of common stocks.[120]

In reply to critics who blamed the banks for the subsequent depression, the chairman of the board of the Chase National Bank testified before the Senate Committee on Manufactures on October 30, 1931, that, although excessive credit for speculative uses was a factor in bringing on the crisis, the bankers could not have stopped excessive speculation when "the demand of the public was just surging over the whole country."[121]

Throughout the summer of 1929, despite the onset of a check to business expansion, industrial and business news continued predominantly good to excellent.[122] The optimism thus encouraged helped to promote the final rise of the market to its September peak while European stock markets were sagging. The "heaviness" of particular stocks was recurrently noted, as was the possibility that "the speculative movement may be overdone." The long-delayed increase in the discount rate of the New York Federal Reserve Bank from 5 to 6 percent on August 9 hardly affected bullish sentiment, since its effect was offset by lowering the buying rate for bankers' acceptances. The market continued to rise for another month. The *Annalist* reported on September 13 extraordinary irregularity in prices on the New

[118]*C&FC*, Oct. 6, 1928, pp. 1875–76.
[119]In this bulletin the unnamed authors (probably George E. Roberts and his son, George B.) discussed three proposed remedies, an "easy money solution," "aggressive discount rate control," and the "middle ground" policy which the Federal Reserve had been pursuing, but could endorse none. The chairman of the Chase National Bank, in his report to stockholders on Jan. 13, 1930 (pp. 8–9), discussed this subject, argued that existing law intensified swings in the stock market and caused violent fluctuation in federal revenues, and urged that a more moderate rate (a maximum of 7.5 percent regardless of the time between purchase and sale) "would eliminate the serious menace to market stability."
[120]M. Slade Kendrick, "The Tax on Capital Net Gains," *AER*, December 1929, 19:648–51. The rate was then 12.5 percent, but the provisions were complex, as they are today.
[121]Dorfman, *Economic Mind*, 5:609, citing testimony of Albert H. Wiggin.
[122]*Economist*, July–October 1929, passim, and numerous U.S. sources already cited.

York Stock Exchange. The next issue said: "The stock market has righted itself. . . . The credit situation remains comfortable, but with new stock offerings, mostly of investment trusts, perpetually increasing, the problem of credit control seems bound to recur later on in a new form." In short, "the stock market has apparently resumed its upward course."[123] It is significant that brokers' loans tended to rise even faster than the stock market, eventually reaching their peak on October 4.[124]

The last year of the extraordinary stock market boom was marked by Federal Reserve efforts to restrain it (see Chapter 5 below) and by a few warnings of more or less severe collapse which would endanger the economy as well as over-bullish individuals (see Chapter 7). But the tide of events repeatedly controverted such skeptical, pessimistic, and alarmist assertions, and the buoyant optimism of the public (see Chapter 6) persisted into October 1929. Indeed, it resisted the shock of the Wall Street crash, and vanished only as the forward momentum of the economy ceased in 1930–31 (see Chapters 8 and 9).

[123]*Annalist*, Sept. 20, 1929, pp. 537–38.
[124]Chandler, *Strong*, p. 426; Fisher, *Stock Market Crash*, pp. 221–25.

CHAPTER 5

ADMINISTRATION AND FEDERAL RESERVE POLICIES, 1918–29

THE POSTWAR transition period was hectic, in this country as elsewhere.[1] At the end of hostilities the American economy had to convert war-based production to very different peacetime objectives and to absorb into peacetime employment millions released from civilian and armed service at home and abroad. Disillusionment with Europe grew as overseas veterans returned home, after delays caused by shipping shortages, prejudiced against the French, cool to the British, and somewhat more friendly toward the Germans; as a violent controversy raged over the peace terms; and as resentment mounted at foreign efforts to get the war debts canceled. Failure to reach agreement on ratification of the peace treaty with its League of Nations covenant resulted from Wilsonian errors of judgment, exacerbated personal bitterness, and popular revulsion against foreign commitments and internationalism.[2]

Public opinion hastened the scrapping of war controls. The railroads, which had been federally operated since January 1, 1918, were returned to private hands on March 1, 1920. Many federal decisions were exceptionally difficult to arrive at because of President Wilson's loss of support in the Congress after the 1918 elections, his absences at the Peace Conference, his absorption in its problems, and his subsequent disabling illness. From September 1919 to the end of his administration the country was politically leaderless. In the same period the young Federal Reserve System was handicapped by inexperience and by its subservience to the Treasury, which as quickly as possible terminated financial commitments at home and abroad, successfully floated the Victory loan (oversubscribed by 16 percent in the early spring of 1919), and ended the embargo on gold exports on June 7.[3] The banks were burdened by loans secured by war bonds and notes. Inflation, strikes, speculation, and demagoguery were followed by collapse into depression, which was most severe in agriculture.

---

[1]See Chapters 4 and 7; Samuel Eliot Morison, *The Oxford History of the American People* (New York: Oxford University Press, 1965), pp. 880–87 and ch. 53; Herbert Hoover, *The Memoirs of Herbert Hoover*, vol. 2: *The Cabinet and the Presidency, 1920–1933* (New York: Macmillan, 1951), pp. 10–13, 35–37, 47–60.

[2]Thomas A. Bailey, *Wilson and the Peacemakers* (New York: Macmillan, 1947); Herbert Hoover, *The Ordeal of Woodrow Wilson* (New York: McGraw-Hill, 1958).

[3]W. P. G. Harding, *The Formative Period of the Federal Reserve System* (Boston: Houghton Mifflin, 1925), chs. 10–12 and app. A (Leffingwell address of Apr. 30, 1920).

The Harding and Coolidge The elections of late 1920 brought in a pre-
Administrations, 1921–29 dominantly Republican Congress (with
the majority riven by factions) and a very weak president, Warren G.
Harding. He took pains to bring into his cabinet three strong men as secre-
taries of State, Treasury, and Commerce. Hughes, Mellon, and Hoover
were outstanding exceptions to the mediocre to shoddy level of most
Harding appointments, and each took the lead in certain policy fields.[4]
Vice President Calvin Coolidge duly presided over the Senate but played
no role in the administration until Harding's death in August 1923 precipitated him into the White House, shortly before the scandals hatched in
the Harding regime broke into the open. Harding and his political backers
stood for a "return to normalcy," which in broad terms meant prewar
laissez-faire except for "protection" in various forms, and Coolidge essentially agreed. Both were characteristically indolent, averse to enlarging the
role of the federal government, and disposed to defer to businessmen.
Neither took any active steps toward improving the effectiveness of regulatory agencies or uncovering and checking abuses that became rampant in
the financial world of the period.[5]

In contrast to both his chiefs, Hoover was a glutton for work and an
"activist" in several areas, to an extent that annoyed Coolidge. He was
firmly opposed to expansion of government ownership and operation but
favored more vigorous government regulation than was achieved, and in
1926 he strongly urged the need to restrain speculative excesses until
Coolidge and Mellon silenced him. On his advice in 1921 Harding appointed
the President's Conference on Unemployment, which he chaired to the

[4]On Harding, Coolidge, and Hoover, see Morison, *Oxford History*, exp. pp. 885–86,
918–40, 983–84; Thomas A. Bailey, *Presidential Greatness* (New York: Appleton-Century-
Crofts, 1967), pp. 312–20 et passim; and my later paper, "Herbert Hoover, 1874–1964; Another
Appraisal," *South Atlantic Quarterly*, Summer 1969, pp. 295–318. Walter Lippmann's *Interpretations, 1931–1932* and *Interpretations, 1933–1935*, both edited by Allan Nevins (New York:
Macmillan, 1932, 1936), contain trenchant comments on the three presidents, their characteristics, policies, and failures, and the situations with which they dealt.

Coolidge's Amherst classmate and lifelong admiring friend Dwight W. Morrow and
Hoover, his loyal cabinet member, both termed him exceptionally well qualified for the presidency. If he was not (as I believe) so qualified, he was in tune with his time and proved surprisingly popular with the voters. See Harold Nicolson, *Dwight Morrow* (New York: Harcourt
Brace, 1935), pp. 229–34, 269–72, 348; Hoover, *Memoirs*, 2:55, 217, 221.

[5]Harvard Professor W. Z. Ripley published in 1927 his *Main Street and Wall Street*; when,
early that year, he urged on the president the need for regulation of the securities markets,
Coolidge was relieved to hear him say that this was a matter for state rather than federal
action. See Arthur M. Schlesinger, Jr., *The Crisis of the Old Order, 1919–1933* (Boston:
Houghton Mifflin, 1957), p. 70. Governor Roosevelt of New York made no move to investigate
or regulate the New York Stock Exchange. The Exchange took a few steps in the summer of
1929, particularly with reference to investment trusts, most of which were not listed on the
Exchange, but these steps were too feeble and too late to affect the situation at the time. See
Bernhard Ostrolenk, "Stock Exchange Takes Lead in Securing Publicity on Investment
Trusts," *Annalist*, Sept. 20, 1929, pp. 540–41.

end of his secretaryship in July 1928. This body set up several committees, most of which Hoover also chaired, and on which he persuaded businessmen and others to serve, to promote studies and issue reports on unemployment and other problems, with the aid of research done under the leadership of the recently established National Bureau of Economic Research. The Congress, it is important to add, took the lead in several policy areas and sometimes thwarted White House efforts.

President Harding "wobbled" on the League of Nations, and the official policy throughout the decade continued strongly isolationist (except as to Latin America), despite moderating influences from several key men and important private organizations and journals (see Chapter 15 below). Treasury funds heavily supplemented private contributions toward relief of the disastrous Russian famine of 1921–22, in which Hoover's American Relief Administration did a difficult job well. But recurrent pressures for U.S. recognition of the Soviet government were thwarted until 1933.[6] Secretary Hughes won Senate consent to the naval limitation treaty signed on February 6, 1922, put pressure on Japan to return Shantung to China, and thereby "gave China a chance to recover her full sovereignty."[7] Overwhelming ratification of the Kellogg-Briand Pact on January 15, 1929, by a vote of 81 to 1 "was obtained upon the argument that it contained no commitments to action." Three successive presidents vainly urged Senate approval of U.S. participation in the World Court, which did appoint an American to serve as one of its judges. Nevertheless, there was increasing (if carefully guarded) collaboration with the League of Nations in its nonpolitical activities.[8] Participation by individual Americans in European recovery moves was encouraged; on Secretary Hughes' own suggestion, prominent Americans served on the Dawes and Young committees of experts; and the Federal Reserve System played an important part in the rehabilitation of European currencies.[9]

From 1919 on, the United States consistently refused to recognize the practical interrelationship between the debts incurred by foreign nations for war supplies and the legally separate issue of German reparations, to take official part in reparations discussions, or to enter into any debt conference with the group of debtor nations; all suggestions for outright cancellation of war debts were adamantly rejected. President Coolidge's narrow-minded query, "they hired the money, didn't they?" won undeserved popularity. An able World War Foreign Debt Commission, com-

[6]Hoover, *Memoirs*, 2:23–26, 177, 182; George F. Kennan, *Russia and the West under Lenin and Stalin* (Boston: Little Brown, 1960), pp. 179–81, 206–7.

[7]Hoover, *Memoirs*, 2:179–81.

[8]Morison, *Oxford History*, pp. 921–25; Hoover, *Memoirs*, 2:181–82, 330–31, 335–37.

[9]Cf. R. L. Wilbur and A. M. Hyde, *The Hoover Policies* (New York: Scribner, 1937), pp. 348–58.

posed of key cabinet members (Mellon, Hughes, and Hoover), Senator Reed Smoot, and Congressman Theodore E. Burton of Ohio, was appointed early in 1922 to negotiate debt-funding agreements with each of the former Associated Powers.

The first major settlement, with Great Britain, was signed in June 1923, on terms that were basically stiff because of American public opinion, British pride, and American and British overconfidence in Britain's economic and financial strength. By early 1927 more lenient terms had been worked out with nearly all other debtor nations which, like the British settlement, provided for payments over sixty-two years; all but one (that with France) had been signed and ratified; and the commission expired. Ostensibly, under the "capacity-to-pay" principle, the settlements were open to revision if and when any were found unduly burdensome, but, in the absence of specific provisions and with no country taking the initiative, no such step was ever taken. When the Senate approved the Hoover moratorium late in 1931 it rejected his recommendation for reconstitution of the Debt Commission and went on record against any modification of the terms. The whole subject was thoroughly and heatedly discussed, in the United States and abroad, without achievement of a meeting of minds, and war debts and reparations continued one of the "festering sores" that embittered international relations through much of 1919–32.[10]

Enormous shipbuilding activities initiated during the war, in which America had played a major role, left the postwar world with a grave surplus of tonnage, much of it ill suited to peaceful trade and uneconomical to operate. Idle tonnage reached huge dimensions. Political pressures prevented the U.S. Shipping Board from quickly disposing of more than a few of its two thousand ships for scrap or private use, and its postwar attempts at operation were costly. Its willingness to release tied-up ships when rates rose, during the British coal strike of 1926, helped to check these advances. Domestic costs of building and operating ships were high compared with foreign costs, yet both were subsidized as a means of national defense,

---

[10]Valuable materials on this subject are gathered in J. T. Gerould and Laura S. Turnbull's handbook, *Selected Articles on Interallied Debts and Revision of the Debt Settlements* (New York: Wilson, 1929). Several Brookings Institution studies dealt with specific aspects; the last and most comprehensive was Harold G. Moulton and Leo Pasvolsky, *War Debts and World Prosperity* (Washington, D.C.: Brookings Institution, 1932). My summary paper on "The War Debt Settlements" (*Virginia Quarterly Review*, January 1928, pp. 1–27) was the outgrowth of a round table at the Institute of Politics in the preceding summer. See also C. W. Whittlesey, "Reparations, War Debts, and Foreign Investments," in J. G. Smith, ed., *Facing the Facts: An Economic Diagnosis* (New York: Putnam, 1932), pp. 98–125; W. S. Myers and W. H. Newton, *The Hoover Administration: A Documented Narrative* (New York: Scribner, 1936), pp. 152–55, 248, 882–87; R. L. Wilbur and A. H. Hyde, *The Hoover Policies* (New York: Scribner, 1937), pp. 506–23; Sir Henry Clay, *Lord Norman* (London: Macmillan, 1957), pp. 145–146, 172–79; Hoover, *Memoirs*, 2:177–79; Lester V. Chandler, *Benjamin Strong: Central Banker* (Washington, D.C.: Brookings Institution, 1958), pp. 142–47, 264, 268–69, 282–84, 294–95, 474–79.

because of public pressure to keep the American flag prominent on the seas. The White-Jones Merchant Marine Act of early 1928 provided liberal mail subventions and loans on liberal terms to U.S. shipping companies building in U.S. shipyards. These efforts were an almost complete failure, but they complicated the problems of the British and other maritime powers which were consistently able to build and operate ships more economically.[11]

Justified fears of a postwar flood of immigrants led to a drastic reversal of the traditional open door policy, which had been already eroded by various specific acts from 1882 to 1917. The Johnson acts of May 1921 and May 1924 imposed quota restrictions severely limiting the number of newcomers from Asia (almost completely excluded already), southern and eastern Europe, and the Near East, while not limiting those from North and South America, and cut the total influx to low levels in 1925–29, with profound effects. Hoover strongly supported the general policy but urged "humanizing" changes.[12]

American farmers in the 1920s were plagued by serious troubles which grew out of the wartime expansion of output and exports, overestimates of peacetime exports, the postwar commodity price and land price inflation which collapsed in 1920, and heavy burdens of debts and increased taxes. Under pressure from farm organizations and the bipartisan "farm bloc" in Congress, numerous steps were taken to alleviate farm distress,

[11]There is a vast and highly uneven literature on this subject, of which I venture to cite only E. S. Gregg, "Shipping," in *Recent Economic Changes in the United States* (New York: McGraw-Hill, 1929), 1:309–19; Wilbur and Hyde, *Hoover Policies*, pp. ??? 28; L. Isserlis, "British Shipping since 1934," and H. M. Hallowolth, "The Shipbuilding Industry," in *Britain in Recovery* (London: Pitman, 1938), pp. 323–60; Hoover, *Memoirs*, 2:135–38, 387; Carl E. McDowell and Helen M. Gibbs, *Ocean Transportation* (New York: McGraw-Hill, 1954); Samuel A. Lawrence, *United States Shipping Policies and Politics* (Washington, D.C.: Brookings Institution, 1966), esp. pp. 1–79, 198–99, 253–55, 369–76. The principal merchant marine acts in 1914–39 were those of 1916, 1920, 1928, and 1936. Perennial criticism of the government program was muted in the boom years of the later 1920s but mounted in 1929–35. Lawrence wrote (p. 45): "As the findings of the several investigatory groups were made public in the spring of 1935, a pattern of opportunism, shoddy performance, and both public and private irresponsibility emerged." He then quoted from the 1935 report of a select committee chaired by Senator Hugo Black (*Investigation of Air Mail and Ocean Mail Contracts*, 74th Cong. 1st sess., 1935, S. Rept. 898, pp. 39–40): "Private ownership of merchant and aerial transportation with government subsidy has resulted in a saturnalia of waste, inefficiency, unearned and exorbitant salaries, and bonuses and other so-called 'compensation,' corrupting expense accounts, exploitation of the public by sale and manipulation of stocks, the 'values' of which are largely based on the hope of profit by robbing the taxpayer, and a general transfer of energy and labor from operating the business to 'operating on' the taxpayer. Measured by results, the subsidy system, as operated, has been a sad, miserable, and corrupting failure."

[12]W. W. Husband, "A Rational Immigration Policy," in Louis I. Dublin, ed., *Population Problems in the United States and Canada* (Boston: Houghton Mifflin, 1926), pp. 167–75; Wilbur and Hyde, *Hoover Policies*, pp. 143–45; George H. Soule, Jr., *Prosperity Decade: From War to Depression, 1917–1929* (New York: Rinehart, 1947), pp. 208–11; Chester W. Wright, *Economic History of the United States* (New York: McGraw-Hill, 1941), pp. 553–59; Irving Bernstein, *A History of the American Worker, 1920–1933: The Lean Years* (Boston: Houghton Mifflin, 1960), pp. 50–52, 322–23; Morison, *Oxford History*, pp. 813–14, 827–28, 897–99.

ease farm credit, and promote agricultural recovery. These included the revival of the War Finance Corporation early in 1921, which continued into 1923 and did much to relieve distress in the agricultural sections; amendments to the Federal Reserve Act to liberalize terms for loans to farmers and to add a Board member specifically representing agriculture; and a 1923 act creating twelve intermediate credit banks to supplement the federal land banks set up under a 1916 act.[13]

A Joint Commission of Agricultural Inquiry was appointed early in the Harding administration. Chaired by Congressman Sydney Anderson of Minnesota, it began exhaustive hearings on August 2, 1921. The first section of its comprehensive report, submitted in December 1921, dealt with the agricultural crisis and its causes. The other three parts were submitted later: a section on credit was submitted in January 1922 and two others, one on transportation and the other on distribution and marketing, in March 1923.[14]

Federal and state departments of agriculture, with the far-flung experiment stations, extension services, and county agents, continued to promote rapid improvements in farming techniques and practices of many kinds, and the federal Bureau of Agricultural Economics developed an Outlook Service. Mechanized farming made great strides; trucks and hard-surfaced roads promoted marketing efficiency; and the spread of electricity in rural areas and the multiplication of radios made signal contributions to output and levels of living. Despite such progress, farmers did not enjoy the level of prosperity that they argued they deserved. And President Coolidge, with strong support from Secretary Hoover, vetoed two successive McNary-Haugen bills which agrarian leaders vigorously urged to bring "equality" to agriculture. Other radical proposals did not reach this stage.[15]

The Emergency Tariff Act of June 1921 (Wilson had vetoed a similar bill on March 2) was passed primarily in response to demands from farming interests. The Fordney-McCumber Tariff Act of 1922 was a general revision which raised rates to or above the 1913 high levels but put on the "free list" certain products, including some used by farmers in production. The results were disappointing to farmers, partly because some duties

[13]Harding, *Formative Period*, pp. 120–21, 218–23, 238, 296–305; Wright, *Economic History*, pp. 633–35, 851–52.

[14]Harding, *Formative Period*, pp. 218–24, 253, 296–305.

[15]Edwin G. Nourse, *American Agriculture and the European Market* (New York: McGraw-Hill, 1924, preface dated Apr. 22, 1924), esp. chs. 2–3, and his "Agriculture," ch. 8 in *Recent Economic Changes*, 2:547–602; J. S. Davis, *The Farm Export Debenture Plan* (Stanford, Calif.: Food Research Institute, 1929); John D. Black, *Agricultural Reform in the United States* (New York: McGraw-Hill, 1929), esp. chs. 3, 7–10. 13–15, 21; Archibald McIsaac, "Whither Agriculture?" in Smith, *Facing the Facts*, pp. 289–321; Wright, *Economic History*, pp. 701, 851–52.

were ineffective but mainly because, as rates were revised, concessions to industrial interests tended to cost farmers more than they gained. The new provision authorizing the president to raise or lower rates on recommendation of the Tariff Commission led mostly to increases.[16]

The Bureau of the Budget was established in 1921, with Charles G. Dawes as its first director.[17] Secretary Mellon in the Harding and Coolidge administrations persistently strove to hold down federal expenditures and to reduce the war-swollen federal debt. As prosperous years yielded surplus revenues, successive cuts were made in income tax rates. These popular policies promoted economic growth, and facilitated expansion of state and local indebtedness for improved roads, schools, and other public buildings, floating corporate securities, and private spending for homes, cars, and other durable goods; they also fed speculation in securities and real estate. These policies have been severely criticized, and in some details deserve to be, but I consider them on the whole appropriate and wise.

The federal policies of the 1920s were a mixture of good, bad, and indifferent, as we have to expect in a democracy in which ill-informed and emotional public opinion often counts heavily in decisionmaking.[18] The high tariff policies were unwise, especially in view of the international creditor status and insistence on payment of the war debts to the United States, but they were less damaging than has often been charged. The generally probusiness policy was broadly sound but carried to extremes. The merchant marine policy was a costly failure, with undesirable international and domestic influences. The policies with respect to war debt settlements were shortsighted and pursued too rigidly. The foreign loan policy was basically good but was administered imperfectly and with insufficient regard for the consequent buildup of heavy foreign commitments for payments on interest and principal. A conspicuous mistake was the failure to come to grips with the rising tide of speculation in 1925–29, in which administration as well as Federal Reserve action was needed.

---

[16]F. W. Taussig, *The Tariff History of the United States*, 8th ed. (New York: Putnam, 1931); F. W. Fetter, "Tariff Policy and Foreign Trade," and Archibald McIsaac, "Whither Agriculture?" in Smith, *Facing the Facts*, pp. 72–97; B. M. Anderson, *Economics and the Public Welfare: Financial and Economic History of the United States, 1914–1946* (New York: Van Nostrand, 1946), chs. 12, 16; Wright, *Economic History*, p. 701. In its *Weekly News Letter*, Jan. 11, 1923, the American Farm Bureau Federation voiced its conclusion that under the existing tariff acts farmers were paying $426 million a year for $125 million of benefits.

[17]An early account is a Brookings study by W. F. Willoughby, *The National Budget System* (Baltimore: Johns Hopkins Press, 1927). See also Harley L. Lutz, "Budgets, Bonds and Ballots," in Smith, *Facing the Facts*.

[18]See the introduction and various chapters in Smith, *Facing the Facts*. I consider inaccurate and strongly biased the comprehensive adverse judgment expressed in W. E. Leuchtenburg, *The Perils of Prosperity, 1914–32* (Chicago: University of Chicago Press, 1958), p. 246. This entertaining book on the New Era and its "smashup" contains much that is true and significant but is marred by a few important slips and some significant omissions.

On the whole, however, the American people were well satisfied with the record of the Republican administrations in the 1920s. Under President Coolidge the amazing scandals that came to light after Harding's death were weathered with surprisingly little political damage. As a presidential candidate, Hoover overpraised his two predecessors' policies, attributed to them the remarkable progress of the postwar decade, and all too confidently asserted that their continuation would assure extended prosperity and pave the way for the abolition of poverty in America.[19]

The Federal Reserve   The Federal Reserve Act, of which Carter Glass
System, 1921-29   considered himself the proud father, was approved late in 1913 after long consideration and many compromises, and was frequently amended thereafter.[20] Political pressures prevented the establishment of a central bank, such as the First (1791-1811) and Second

---

[19]See especially his 1928 campaign addresses in Hoover, *The New Day: Campaign Speeches of Herbert Hoover, 1928* (Stanford, Calif.: Stanford University Press, 1928). In my recent paper cited in n. 4 I included this among the "understandable but serious misjudgments" that contributed to his overwhelming defeat in 1932.

[20]See the excellent, well-annotated official publication *The Federal Reserve Act . . . as Amended through December 31, 1956, With an Appendix Containing Provisions of Certain Other Acts of Congress Which Affect the Federal Reserve System* (Washington, D.C.: FRS, [1957]).

Below are listed, in alphabetical order, the works on which my condensed account largely rests: Anderson, *Economics and the Public Welfare*; G. L. Bach, *Making Monetary and Fiscal Policy* (Washington, D.C.: Brookings Institution, 1971), esp. ch. 4; W. R. Burgess, *The Reserve Banks and the Money Market* (New York: Harper, 1927; rev. ed., 1935); Chandler, *Strong*; Lawrence E. Clark, *Central Banking under the Federal Reserve System, with Special Consideration of the Federal Reserve Bank of New York* (New York: Macmillan, 1935); Federal Reserve Board, *Annual Report* and monthly *Federal Reserve Bulletin*, various issues; Milton Friedman and Anna J. Schwartz, *A Monetary History of the United States, 1867-1960* (Princeton, N.J.: Princeton University Press, 1963), esp. chs. 5-6; A. D. Gayer, ed., *Lessons of Monetary Experience: Essays in Honor of Irving Fisher* (New York: Farrar and Rinehart, 1937); E. A. Goldenweiser, *Monetary Management* (New York: McGraw-Hill, 1949), and *American Monetary Policy* (New York: McGraw-Hill, 1951); Harding, *Formulative Period*; Charles O. Hardy, *Credit Policies of the Federal Reserve System* (Washington, D.C.:Brookings Institution, 1932); C. A. Phillips, T. F. McManus, and R. W. Nelson, *Banking and the Business Cycle: A Study of the Great Depression in the United States* (New York: Macmillan, 1937); Harold L. Reed, *Federal Reserve Policy, 1921-1930* (New York: McGraw-Hill, 1930; Elmus R. Wicker, *Federal Reserve Monetary Policy, 1917-1933* (New York: Random House, 1966). Several of these books include extensive bibliographies.

Despite a measure of agreement among these and other writers, there is substantial disagreement on crucial questions and lesser ones. My interpretation differs from that of Friedman and Schwartz (*Monetary Policy*, ch. 6) on a number of significant points: (1) they interpret "inflation" to mean only *price* inflation and ignore other aspects of inflation; (2) they exaggerate the extent of "gold sterilization" in the 1920s; (3) they almost completely ignore what other scholars term the "investment credit inflation" and its effects, and the writings of Anderson, Phillips et al., and others who stress this. I cannot accept their denial of "the widespread belief . . . that the United States experienced severe inflation before 1929 and [that] the Reserve System served as an engine of it" (p. 298) or their assertion: "Far from being an inflationary decade, the twenties were the reverse."

(1816–36) Banks of the United States.[21] The complex Federal Reserve System (FRS), set up under the act in August–November 1914, consisted of twelve regional Federal Reserve Banks owned by the member banks; over them a Federal Reserve Board (FRB) of five presidential appointees (six, after provision was made on June 3, 1922, for an additional member specifically to represent agricultural interests) plus the secretary of the treasury (named chairman) and the comptroller of the currency, both ex officio; and a Federal Advisory Council composed of one member annually elected by the board of directors of each bank. The FRS was superimposed on "a crazy quilt of banking authorities" which fostered "competition in laxity."[22] National banks were required to be members, but the more numerous and heterogeneous state-chartered banks and trust companies were permitted to join, not to join, and to change their status almost at will, and they exercised these options freely.

Though commonly termed a centralized system the FRS was hardly this, but the drift was in the direction of centralizing the policymaking power. The banks were largely autonomous, and the stockholding member banks elected six of the nine directors of each. The FRB appointed three class C directors of each bank, one of whom was chairman and federal reserve agent, and fixed his compensation. The Board also had the authority to approve or disapprove proposed changes in rediscount rates by the banks, and in one instance forced the Chicago Reserve Bank to lower its rate from 4 to 3.5 percent (on September 7, 1927) over the objection of the Bank's own board of directors. In law and in fact, the Board's duties, Goldenweiser wrote, were "to supervise the System, coordinate regional policies, and take the lead in the formulation of national monetary policies."[23] However, because of the outstanding importance of New York as a financial center and the character and prestige of its first governor, Benjamin Strong, the Federal Reserve Bank of New York took on some attributes of a central bank, especially in international dealings. Its predominance gave rise to jealousy and friction, which reached its peak during Strong's final illness and after his death in October 1928.[24]

[21]W. P. G. Harding, an early governor (1916–22), said flatly: "The plain intent of the law was to create a regional as opposed to a central banking system." *Formative Period*, p. 29. Benjamin Strong originally favored a single "real central bank" rather than the complex system then set up, but in less than three years he had come to believe that such a bank could not "be kept alive in the face of political attack today any more than it could in 1836." Letters of Dec. 19, 1913, and Nov. 14, 1916, quoted in Chandler, *Strong*, pp. 37–39. Cf. Clark, *Central Banking*, esp. pp. 34–36, 326, 387–99.

[22]Goldenweiser, *Monetary Management*, ch. 3, esp. pp. 38, 42, 44.

[23]Goldenweiser, *American Monetary Policy*, p. 79; Clark, *Central Banking*, passim; Chandler, *Strong*, pp. 444–50.

[24]Carter Glass, as congressman, secretary of the treasury, and senator, was intimately informed on the origin and operation of the FRS. A man of strong opinions and sharp tongue and pen, he was repeatedly critical of the Board and of Governor Strong; but he had "a deep

The FRS got under way in the period before the United States entered the war in April 1917, and it gradually solved difficult organizational problems. It functioned virtually as an adjunct to the Treasury during the war and early postwar periods. As the author of the most detailed account of these formative years, W. P. G. Harding, wrote in 1925: "No banking system has ever experienced so many vicissitudes as has the Federal Reserve System since its establishment." Indeed, it was not until 1921–22 that the FRS was free to develop and apply its policies, accumulating experience and evolving its ideas in the midst of unprecedented problems.[25] Board member Adolph C. Miller, in an address late in 1918 on "After-War Readjustment," argued: "Where there has been inflation, there must follow deflation, as a necessary condition to the restoration of economic health."[26] He was not, however, speaking for the Board, which "was never in favor of a policy of deflation," particularly of radical or drastic deflation, as was made clear in its annual report for 1919.

In its early years the FRB was racked by serious internal dissension and by friction with the Treasury.[27] Board members were profoundly disturbed by political attacks during the early postwar years, in particular by charges that the FRB had failed to support war bonds when they dropped in price and was responsible for the unsound boom of 1919–20, the severe collapse of 1920–21, and the distress of farmers. Under pressure from the Treasury, rediscount rates were kept at 4 percent until November 4, 1919, when the New York rate was raised to 4.25 percent; it was sharply raised to 6 on January 23 and to 7 in June 1920.[28] In January 1922 Glass gave in the Senate a "masterly" address in support of the FRS, to which the Banks gave wide circulation.[29]

---

affection" for Strong, and considered him "a man of such unusual ability, whose usefulness to the Federal Reserve System can scarcely be overestimated." Letter of Sept. 29, 1927, quoted in Chandler, *Strong*, pp. 449–50. Anderson (*Economics and the Public Welfare*, pp. 116–18) was highly critical of Strong, whom Friedman and Schwartz (*Monetary History*, pp. 225–28, 411–14, 692–93) warmly commend. These two authorities also differ greatly on Governor Harding.

[25]Harding, *Formative Period*, p. 252; Goldenweiser, *American Monetary Policy*, ch. 7, "Evolution of Federal Reserve Ideas," and pp. 131–34; B. H. Beckhart's review of Wicker, *Federal Reserve Monetary Policy*, in *AER*, December 1967, 57:1372–74.

[26]Quoted in part in Harding, *Formative Period*, pp. 134–38, with his own comments on pp. 139, 166–67.

[27]Goldenweiser, *American Monetary Policy*, pp. 113–14; Wicker, *Federal Reserve Monetary Policy*, ch. 1.

[28]On these matters judgments differ. See Harding, *Formative Period*, chs. 12–13, 15–17, and appendixes C and E, esp. pp. 218–23, 253, 296–305; Reed, *Federal Reserve Policy*, pp. 44–45; Anderson, *Economics and the Public Welfare*, chs. 7–8; Goldenweiser, *American Monetary Policy*, pp. 134–37; Friedman and Schwartz, *Monetary History*, pp. 225–39. I cannot concur in Friedman and Schwartz's conclusion (p. 228), though I agree that the delay in raising rates was unfortunate and that the sharp advances to 6 and 7 percent were too drastic.

[29]Harding, *Formative Period*, pp. 237, 306–9.

During the years 1922–29, when the U.S. economy was enjoying a period of remarkable prosperity with only minor interruptions, the FRS faced many difficult problems, hampered by several erroneous ideas, under conditions so unprecedented that it is not surprising that the complex young institution did not cope with all of them successfully.[30]

The FRS was designed to be largely insulated from day-to-day political pressures such as those to which the president and the Congress are inevitably subjected.[31] The FRB was not put into the Treasury Department, nor was it formally under the control of the president. He, however, appointed its members (for ten-year terms, after the staggered terms of the early years) and its governor, who was the executive head. The secretary of the Treasury, one of the two ex officio members, was designated chairman of the Board. Its "independence" was thus tempered. Presidents Wilson, Harding, and Coolidge kept their hands off, though Harding responded to political pressures not to reappoint Governor Harding when his eight-year term expired. Coolidge occasionally broke out with statements that must have embarrassed the Board.[32] Secretary Mellon, busy with other official duties, missed all or part of many Board meetings, sometimes voted in a minority, and seems to have made no effort to dominate the Board, but he too made occasional public statements that bore upon its actions. Secretary Hoover in 1925–26 spoke out in criticism of the Board's policies, but he kept silent when Mellon and Coolidge gave him no support. As a presidential candidate Hoover's speeches contributed, on the whole not happily, to the climate in which Federal Reserve decisions were made. As president, he talked often with Board members Miller and Young, whom he trusted, and his strong views presumably carried some weight, but he too made no attempt to dominate the decisions. While the Reserve authorities could not ignore the president's ideas or wishes, from 1922 through 1929 they enjoyed a large measure of independence.[33]

Two of President Wilson's initial appointees to the FRB were reappointed and served for twenty-two years: Charles S. Hamlin, a Boston lawyer, was the first governor, a member from 1914 through 1935, and special counsel in 1936 to 1938; Adolph C. Miller, a California-born economist of wide experience, served on the Board from 1914 to 1936. Two

---

[30]Goldenweiser, *American Monetary Policy*, chs. 8, "Policy Decisions from 1917 to the Collapse of 1932," and 12, "Review of Principles of Monetary Policy"; Friedman and Schwartz, *Monetary History*, ch. 6, "The High Tide of the Federal Reserve System." These references should be supplemented by the accounts of Clark, Hardy, Reed, Wicker, and others. Here I attempt no full discussion.

[31]Bach, *Making Monetary and Fiscal Policy*, pp. 66–69; Bach, *Highlights of Making Monetary and Fiscal Policy*, Brookings Research Report 114 (Washington, D.C.: Brookings Institution, 1971), p. 5.

[32]Anderson, *Economics and the Public Welfare*, p. 188.

[33]See a thoughtful relevant article by Lindley H. Clark, Jr., in *WSJ*, Aug. 25, 1971.

of the original appointees were not reappointed when their short terms expired: Paul M. Warburg, a broadly informed German-born New York banker, fell under public suspicion because of his German connections, and served only in 1914–18; and W. P. G. Harding, a Birmingham banker, ably served as governor from 1916 to 1922 but fell under political attack. Other members died or resigned, and served for less than full ten-year terms.

Soon after his inauguration in March 1921 President Harding appointed an Ohio crony, Daniel R. Crissinger, as comptroller of the currency, and promoted him to FRB governor on May 1, 1923. Two years later President Coolidge reappointed him, and he served until his resignation on September 15, 1927. Ill fitted for the post, Crissinger was succeeded in October by Roy A. Young, who came from the governorship of the Federal Reserve Bank of Minneapolis, strongly endorsed by Mellon and Hoover. He served until September 1930, when he was eased out and succeeded the late W. P. G. Harding as governor of the Federal Reserve Bank of Boston. He was in turn replaced by Hoover-appointee Eugene Meyer.[34]

The weakness of the Federal Reserve Board in the period 1922–29 is indisputable. There were several reasons: the salary scale fixed by the Congress was far below levels prevailing in the Federal Reserve Banks; the membership changed frequently; its members were exposed and sensitive to violent and often intemperate criticism from Congress, a few high federal officials, and the public; and the Crissinger appointment and reappointment hurt the Board's morale. Yet there were honest and more or less basic differences of opinion; difficulties in right timing of decisions were inevitable; and friction with the Federal Reserve Bank of New York reached a high level in 1928–29. The level of ability of Board members was probably above that of most federal statutory boards and commissions, and it is too easy to blame incompetence (as Galbraith did) for such mistakes and blunders as were made.

Staff-building and economic intelligence work began under Adolph C. Miller and H. Parker Willis. Willis, a Massachusetts-born economist, political scientist, and journalist, had been an expert for two leading Congressional committees in 1911–13, helped to draft the Federal Reserve Act, was the Board's first secretary (1914–15), and then became its director of research (1916–22). Later he became a severe critic of Board policies and actions. Walter W. Stewart, a Kansas-born economist, succeeded Willis and greatly expanded the staff and work of the Division of Analysis and Research, which he headed in 1922–25. E. A. Goldenweiser, a Russian-born

[34]Chandler and Friedman and Schwartz made much use of Hamlin's diary and the papers of Goldenweiser and George L. Harrison—Strong's successor as governor of the New York Bank—and Wicker of other primary sources which throw valuable light on several of these men and others.

economist, ably carried on this work in 1926–45.[35] Both men, and such staff members as Carl E. Parry, W. W. Riefler, and Woodlief Thomas, contributed information and counsel to the Board, which of course reached or failed to reach its own decisions. The *Federal Reserve Bulletin* and the Board's annual reports owed much to this staff. Similar but smaller research groups were developed in the several Federal Reserve Banks; these emphasized regional "intelligence."[36]

The principal original objective of the Federal Reserve Act was the prevention of monetary stringency culminating in financial panics such as that of 1907. To this end the FRS was to centralize monetary reserves in the regional Reserve Banks, arrange for rediscounting commercial paper at rates set by them with a view to accommodating industry and commerce, and thus to provide elasticity of the currency. But the System was also designed to facilitate Treasury operations, to provide for telegraphic transfers of funds, to promote a system of par collection of checks, to maintain a system of inter-district clearance, and to compile and publish significant statistical data—a group of service functions. The framers of the act clearly hoped that the FRS would curtail the financial predominance of New York City, discourage excessive speculation, moderate geographical differences in interest rates, and bring about lower average levels of those rates.

As the System matured and its thinking evolved in the 1920s, its objectives were added to, amplified, and rephrased.[37] It actively sought to develop an American acceptance market. It undertook to help nations return to the gold standard. It aimed to keep domestic banking and credit conditions "sound." Governor Young said on October 1, 1928: "A healthy banking situation must be forever the primary concern of the managers of the Federal Reserve Banks and of the Federal Reserve Board."[38] This concern did not lead the System to grapple with the problem of numerous bank failures, but it did arouse anxiety over the growing influence of speculation in 1928 and 1929.[39] It resisted pressures to compel it to make price level

---

[35]Stewart was later economic adviser to the Bank of England (1928–30) and had a distinguished career. See *Who Was Who in America*, 3:821. Goldenweiser dedicated his *American Monetary Policy* to "Walter W. Stewart, who made central bankers aware of economics and economists better able to advise central bankers"; he devoted ch. 6 to the Board's economic intelligence, rightly observing, "Over the years the economic intelligence service of the Federal Reserve System has made a great contribution to national economic policy, official and private, in the United States" (p. 100).

[36]Carl Snyder was long a key member of the New York Bank staff, as was W. Randolph Burgess, who became deputy governor in 1930 and vice president in 1936.

[37]Hardy, *Credit Policies*, chs. 1, 4–6, 10, 12, 15; the official publication, *The Federal Reserve System: Its Purposes and Functions* (Washington, D.C.: FRS, 1939); Goldenweiser, *American Monetary Policy*, chs. 4, 7; Wicker, *Federal Reserve Monetary Policy*, ch. 4 et passim.

[38]Hardy, *Credit Policies*, p. 79.

[39]*Ibid.*, pp. 344–48; Clark, *Central Banking*, pp. 402–4.

stability an overriding objective, but was given, and took, credit for contributing to this end.[40] Later it could be said: "The achievement of stable economic progress has been the underlying and ultimate objective of Federal Reserve policy from the beginning of the System."[41]

Nearly all students, J. W. Angell wrote in 1937, would agree on the principal broad goals of monetary policy—"not only to deal with acute booms and collapse after they have occurred, but also to counteract as far as possible the less extreme fluctuations in which booms and collapse presumably originate, while at the same time securing continuously a reasonably full utilization of the existing factors and techniques of production." But, he added, "there is an amazing diversity of opinion on just what the specific content of that policy should be." He also observed that, despite general agreement that irreducible fluctuations in economic activity are inevitable and "have a persistent tendency . . . to degenerate into the extreme phenomena of boom and collapse," "opinion is again divided on how great and inevitable" is the part that monetary and banking phenomena play in this degenerative process.[42] Actually, the FRS undertook to moderate economic fluctuations, though it stopped short of setting as its goal the prevention of economic crises and depressions.[43]

Keynes in 1923 praised the Federal Reserve for pursuing, "half consciously and half unconsciously," methods much along the lines he advocated for Great Britain, with "the object of maintaining stability in prices, trade, and employment."[44] He spoke of the Board as accepting gold "out of convention and conservatism" and as burying it "out of prudence and understanding," thus combining "new wisdom with old prejudice." He did not call the process "sterilization," or claim that it was complete.[45] He

---

[40]"During the years beginning with 1922 the Federal Reserve banking authorities embarked on a misguided attempt to keep up the price level artificially by a further inflation of bank credits in consequence of which the war inflation was carried over to the depression which began in 1929." Phillips, McManus, and Nelson, *Banking and the Business Cycle*, p. 36. These authors called this "the proximate cause of the depression"; "the ultimate controlling influence was the war and the war-time inflation."

[41]*The Quest for Stability*, a pamphlet published about 1954 by the Federal Reserve Bank of Philadelphia, p. 53.

[42]"The General Objectives of Monetary Policy," in Gayer, *Lessons of Monetary Experience*, pp. 53–54.

[43]In an excellent paper read on Nov. 22, 1929, Lionel D. Edie said that, whereas European central banks more or less commonly viewed it as their primary function to prevent economic crises, in this country this responsibility had not been "clearly and definitely acknowledged." "Putting the So-Called New Era to the Test," *Proc. Acad. Pol. Sci.*, January 1930, 13:514–23.

[44]*Monetary Reform* (New York: Harcourt Brace, 1924), pp. 213–21. Though he spoke of the Board, he must have meant the System. Keynes favored cooperation between the Federal Reserve and the Bank of England, each aiming at the stability of its own currency.

[45]Thus he said: "The influx of gold could not be prevented from having *some* inflationary effect because its receipt automatically increased the balances of the member banks. . . . But the gold was not allowed to exercise the multiplied influence which the prewar system presumed" (p. 215n). See Hardy, *Credit Policies*, ch. 9, "Reserve Credit and the Gold Supply."

warned against inferring that the FRS could maintain its independence against the farmers "or other compact interests possessing political influence"; he also warned against expecting the reversal or defeat of the current FRS policy, and the depreciation of the dollar through inflation (for which many English authorities had long hoped), and said that such inflation would have to be prolonged and substantial to raise U.S. commodity prices enough to help the British solve their exchange problems.

Reserve requirements as set in the original act were revised under that of June 21, 1917 (Sec. 19), to allow member banks to count as reserves only deposits with the district bank.[46] The percentages then fixed against demand deposits (13, 10, and 7 percent for central reserve city, reserve city, and country banks, respectively), and time or savings deposits (3 percent) remained unchanged until mid-August 1936, when the Board exercised new authority given by the Banking Act of August 23, 1935, to alter them (see Chapter 12 below). The much lower rate on time deposits gave member banks the incentive to expand these disproportionately: they swelled from $11 billion to $20 billion in 1922-29 while demand deposits increased from $17 billion to $23 billion and deposits in mutual savings banks grew from $6 billion to $9 billion.[47]

The Banks in turn were required to hold in gold, gold certificates, or U.S. treasury deposits 35 percent of their deposits and 40 percent of their outstanding Federal Reserve notes (Sec. 16). Since the Banks were not conducted primarily for profit—beyond cumulative dividends of 6 percent, all profits went to the Treasury—the System could and did maintain reserve percentages against deposits well above the statutory minimums.[48] Deposits in the Banks were "high-powered dollars." If reserves were in excess of requirements, member banks were free to expand their loans severalfold, as they tended to do. If their reserves threatened to fall below the minimum, they were constrained to reduce lending; but they could replenish them by selling owned securities or by getting the Bank to rediscount part of their commercial paper holdings. The FRS could ease credit by lowering rediscount rates or buying government securities, and tighten credit by raising rediscount rates or selling from its portfolio.[49]

[46]Goldenweiser, *American Monetary Policy*, pp. 43-46.

[47]Phillips, McManus, and Nelson, *Banking and the Business Cycle*, pp. 23-28; Anderson, *Economics and the Public Welfare*, pp. 129-31, 138-40; Friedman and Schwartz, *Monetary History*, pp. 270-77, 710-12. Keynes wrote late in 1930: "It was the great growth of time deposits in the Federal Reserve System between 1925 and 1929 which made possible the great increase in the loans and investments of the Member Banks without a corresponding increase in their reserve requirements and, at the same time, without an increase in commodity prices." *A Treatise on Money*, 2 vols. (New York: Harcourt Brace, 1930), 2:14-18.

[48]Goldenweiser, *American Monetary Policy*, pp. 64-67.

[49]Phillips, McManus, and Nelson, *Banking and the Business Cycle*, p. 29; FRS, *Federal Reserve System*, p. 43.

The principal techniques for easing and tightening credit that were available to the system[50] were setting and changing the rates for rediscounting commercial paper,[51] setting rates for buying acceptances ("bills") offered to the Banks, and, in fact far more important, open market purchases from and sales of government securities to the member banks.

The initiative in setting rediscount rates ordinarily rested with the individual Banks, but their proposals were subject to approval by the Board and this was often refused. In the summer of 1927 the Board insisted that the Chicago Bank lower its rate to 3.5 percent; it finally did so, against the judgment of its board of directors, and the right of the Board to do so was not subsequently challenged.[52] For several months in 1929 the Board refused approval of Bank efforts to raise rates (see p. 125 below). Contrary to the practice of the Bank of England, rediscount rates were held somewhat below rates charged by major banks to their "prime customers." This tended to expansion of credit, but was much less of a factor than aggressive open market operations in inducing a great expansion of credit in 1922-28.[53] The New York Bank was usually the leader, but its lead was not always followed by all the other Banks and, if so, often after some delay. There was a drift toward uniformity of these rates, but it was only a tendency.[54] No other Bank followed the rise to 6 percent in New York on August 9, 1929, and by the end of 1929 only five other Banks had followed New York's move of November 15 to reduce its rate from 5 to 4.5 percent.

A great gold influx in 1920-27 resulted from abnormal social, political and economic conditions in Europe. Contrary to the hopes and expectations of many Europeans, it did not lead to commodity price inflation here, in part because U.S. businessmen were fearful of repeating the errors of 1919-20 by building up inventories. The FRS undertook to neutralize the gold inflow somewhat, though by no means resorting to complete "steriliza-

[50]Hardy, Credit Policies, ch. 2.

[51]Prior to 1922 different rates were generally in effect for different classes of paper; they can be found in an official pamphlet, Discount Rates of the Federal Reserve Banks, 1914-1921 (Washington, D.C.: FRS, 1922). Changes in discount rates at each of the Federal Reserve Banks in the calendar years 1922-29 are conveniently shown in a table in the Federal Reserve Board Annual Report for 1929 (pp. 89-90). Later data can be found in subsequent annual reports and, from 1922 through June 1932, in Hardy, Credit Policies, pp. 358-62.

[52]Goldenweiser, American Monetary Policy, pp. 146-48.

[53]Anderson, Economics and the Public Welfare, chs. 11, 18, 19. As early as July 20, 1921, Anderson (ibid., p. 86) had urged in the Chase Economic Bulletin (vol. 1, no. 5) that rediscount rates should always be held above the market. The Joint Commission of Agricultural Inquiry, in its report on credit (January 1922), also considered this the normal practice. Harding, Formative Period, p. 296. Such views did not prevail. Cf. Goldenweiser, American Monetary Policy, p. 115.

[54]Hardy, Credit Policies, ch. 15. One must not take literally Goldenweiser's flat statement (American Monetary Policy, p. 83): "Over the years it has become the general practice to have a uniform discount rate at the twelve Federal Reserve Banks."

tion." The influx first permitted the member banks to reduce their debt to the FRS, but then led to a great expansion of bank credit: in the five years ending in mid-1927 the gold stock rose about $800 million and total loans and investments of the country's banks increased about seventeen and one-half times as much. This "gold inflation" did much to promote both prosperity and speculation.[55]

Carl Snyder of the New York Bank staff argued that the volume of credit should be allowed to increase at "close to the working maximum increase of trade that can be maintained year after year"—something like 4 percent a year (anticipating Milton Friedman). Less would definitely check prosperity; more would give rise to undue speculative activity, and even mania, rising prices, and all the familiar ills attendant upon inflation or monetary depreciation. The Federal Reserve authorities chose not to adopt any such formula but to exercise their fallible discretion, as Goldenweiser considered essential.[56]

A momentous decision was taken in the summer of 1927, under the influence of the domestic business contraction and pressures to aid currency rehabilitation and economic recovery in Europe: credit was eased by lowering rediscount rates and adding to Bank portfolios of government securities and bank acceptances.[57] It was realized that this might promote speculation, but not that the momentum acquired would be so hard to check, as the event proved. The policy was reversed early in 1928, under the influence of the booming stock market; in January through August portfolios were reduced and rediscount rates raised from 3.5 to 4.5 or 5 percent.[58]

Though Governor Strong had worried over the growth of speculative activity in the mid-1920s, the FRB did not seem to view it seriously until 1928, when "repression of excessive stock speculation became the leading immediate objective of policy."[59] The steps taken in January through August failed to achieve this and were not intensified or persisted in.

[55]As Reed pointed out in 1930 (*Federal Reserve Policy*, p. 188), the huge security operations of 1928 and 1929 were financed largely by more rapid credit turnover and involved little draft on the supply of bank credit. Wicker (*Federal Reserve Monetary Policy*, pp. 122–23, 129–30) rightly emphasized the large role played by nonbank leadership in 1928–29.

[56]Carl Snyder, "New Measures of the Relations of Credit and Trade," Nov. 21, 1929, *Proc. Acad. Pol. Sci.*, January 1930, 23:468–86. This paper was the fruit of a decade of work. Phillips, McManus, and Nelson include it in a list of Snyder's papers for 1929–35, which supplements Snyder's own list of 1921–29. *Banking and the Business Cycle*, pp. 267–68. Goldenweiser's view is stated in his *American Monetary Policy*, pp. 129–30.

[57]Board member Miller, in his January 1931 testimony before a subcommittee of the Senate Committee on Banking and Currency, viewed this as a crucial blunder, and Lionel Robbins (*The Great Depression* [London: Macmillan, 1934], pp. 53–54) quoted and followed Miller. This view became widely accepted, but has been disputed.

[58]Data in Hardy, *Credit Policies*, pp. 353–54, 359–60.

[59]*Ibid.*, pp. 94–95 and chs. 8–9. Galbraith said (*The Great Crash 1929* [Boston: Houghton Mifflin, 1955], p. 37), I think wrongly, that the Board "was helpless only because it wanted to

Governor Strong's absence abroad, then his fatal illness and death (October), prevented his pressing for more drastic action early, to be followed by easing when the speculative momentum had been checked. Memories of too drastic action early in 1920, and its aftermath of collapse, were still vivid.[60] Political conditions were not favorable to risking a serious check to the current prosperity. The Board was loath to ask Congress for additional powers.[61]

The consequences of failure to stem the powerful speculative tide were gravely underestimated. Dissension outside and within the Board, and quarrels between the Board and the New York Bank, were important factors which grew much worse in the first half of 1928. Early in 1929 the Board shifted from quantitative controls to efforts at qualitative discrimination, which proved largely futile. The speculative coterie gradually became convinced, as W. L. Crum observed in September 1929, "that the system would take no action which would hurt productive enterprise, and the realization that no other action could long withhold from them a share in the great remaining store of reserve credit gave a feeling of security which had not been possible in 1923–26."[62] So the stock market superboom rose to its frenzied climax. In this major area the System failed.

Clearly the Board and the System were unequal to the demands of the times, as most of the persons involved would have admitted if pressed. In an article published in November 1929, George E. Roberts of the National City Bank wrote: "As to divided councils, I think we must accept the conclusion that this is one of the penalties of having so complicated an organization. There have been divisions within the Federal Reserve Board, divisions between the Federal Reserve Board and the Boards of the Reserve Banks, and divisions within the Bank Boards. Probably nothing else is to be expected but majority rule, with the compromises that usually attend upon such conditions."[63]

Not only at the time, but also in retrospect, presumably competent experts held strongly divergent views as to what Reserve policy should

be." It was deeply concerned but perplexed and bewildered. See A. C. Miller's testimony in the congressional hearings on stabilization, from Mar. 19 through May 29, 1931, pp. 105–26, 162ff., esp. pp. 119, 162; and Wicker, *Federal Reserve Monetary Policy*, pp. 116, 136.

[60] See Goldenweiser, *Monetary Management*, pp. 46–56.

[61] Sprague in October 1928 suggested authority to impose a penalty addition to the rediscount rate on rediscounts of member banks lending on the Stock Exchange. C. E. Mitchell in April 1929 urged removal of the capital gains tax. Reed, *Federal Reserve Policy*, pp. 178–79. Galbraith later (*The Great Crash*, pp. 37–38) held that the Board should have sought authority to set margin requirements.

[62] Crum, *Interpretation of the* [Harvard] *Index of General Business Conditions* (reprint from supplement to *Rev. Ec. Stat.*, September 1929), p. 18. See also various issues of the HES *Weekly Letter*, e.g., Aug. 31, 1929, pp. 206–7 ("Bank Credit Expansion and Reserve Policy"). See Wicker, *Federal Reserve Monetary Policy*, chs. 8–10. On p. 118 he summarized Senator Glass' influential views.

[63] *Rev. Ec. Stat.* 11:197–202.

have been in 1928–29. Late in 1930 Keynes (I believe wrongly) blamed the credit restraints of the late 1920s for having checked and reduced real investment, and by implication criticized efforts "to control the enthusiasm of the speculative crowd" and "to bring this speculative fever somehow to an end." Reed, also in 1930, analyzed Federal Reserve policy in 1928 and 1929 and considered various remedies without reaching very positive conclusions. Hardy, in 1932, was critical and illuminating but not very conclusive.[64]

A. C. Miller wrote a candid and illuminating paper in mid-1935 on the developments of 1927–29 with special reference to Federal Reserve policy and actions. The crucial error, he held, was the easy money policy of July through September 1927, which he had vainly opposed. It was concurred in by all but a few of the Banks, who were persuaded or forced into line. It achieved its immediate objectives but had serious consequences: it so stimulated speculation that the situation got out of hand; the momentum was grossly underestimated. The restrictive policy pursued in the first half of 1928 proved ineffective in a period of "optimism gone wild and cupidity gone drunk." So entrenched had the speculative boom become that increased rediscount rates no longer sufficed to check it. The generally passive policy in the second half of 1928, the result of lack of strong conviction in a presidential election year, was followed in the hope that the seasonal demand for funds would be a restraining influence. Miller complained that the initiative for raising discount rates lay with the Federal Reserve banks, and that their request was belatedly made early in February 1929. When the 6 percent rate was urged, however, it was repeatedly vetoed by the Board—initially unanimously, then by diminishing majorities. Five members, said Miller later, "took the responsibility of formulating the attitude and policy for the Federal Reserve System," over the opposition of a notable minority including the secretary of the Treasury, and twelve Reserve Banks, the Federal Advisory Council, and many of the largest member banks.[65]

Much later, Friedman and Schwartz came to the view that the Board "should have paid no direct attention to the stock market boom," but that "it followed a policy which was too easy to break the speculative boom, yet too tight to promote healthy economic growth." They added: "A vigorous restrictive policy in early 1928 might well have broken the stock market boom without its having to be kept in effect long enough to constitute a serious drag on business in general"—as Strong and his successor Harrison believed.[66]

[64]*Treatise on Money*, 2:196, 381, 385; Reed, *Federal Reserve Policy*, ch. 5; Hardy, *Credit Policies*, chs. 7–8.

[65]A. C. Miller, "The Banking Bill Considered in the Light of 1927–29," FRB Press Release, June 24, 1935. Cf. his address of Nov. 18, 1925, in Press Release X 4451.

[66]Friedman and Schwartz, *Monetary History*, ch. 6, esp. pp. 254–66, 289–92, 297–98. Goldenweiser's views (*Monetary Management*, pp. 54–56; *American Monetary Policy*, pp.

Without endorsing all the positions these authorities took, I am constrained to believe that Keynes, Reed, and Hardy were justified in the caution they exercised in judging the policy pursued and in suggesting how the errors might have been avoided.[67] Moreover, it seems clear that the Federal Reserve alone should not have been expected to avert the disaster without much more help from social scientists, businessmen, the administration, and the Congress than was forthcoming or could have been obtained. Under the circumstances, not only mistakes but serious misjudgments were inevitable.

Despite the conspicuous failure to check the speculative orgy, and lesser failures as well, the FRS had to its credit by 1929 a number of achievements.[68] It had pooled the nation's reserves, resulting in economy in the use of gold. It had ended the former inelasticity of credit and averted "general monetary stringencies" called panics—the Panic of 1907 was not repeated even in 1929. It had made some progress in the integration of the nation's banks and presented a united front to foreign countries. It largely eliminated the burden of exchange charges so that most checks passed at par, thus facilitating wider use of checks. It reduced extreme geographical variations in interest rates, lowered the level, and was able to lend aid in regional and local emergencies. It facilitated the operations of the Treasury in many ways. Indeed, its service functions were well performed.

The official publication which described the System stated in 1939: "The Federal Reserve System has successfully overcome certain difficulties that formerly beset American economic life and imposed upon it great losses; the System still has constantly to meet new problems and difficulties. . . . Federal Reserve policies must be constantly adapted to conditions in an ever-changing world." Such statements, which could have been written in 1929 or in 1971, do not go far toward a balanced appraisal.

In his lengthy paper published in September 1929, W. L. Crum of the Harvard Economic Society attributed the "maintenance of a fairly uniform and moderately high level of general business activity" since 1923 to "the systematic regulation of credit by the federal reserve system," facilitated "by the strikingly responsive temper of the business community, by the restoration of transportation efficiency, by . . . the existence of excess

148–54) are broadly in harmony with most of this, but not with the Friedman and Schwartz position that the Board should have ignored the stock market.

[67]See also J. A. Schumpeter's summary in his *Business Cycles: A Theoretical, Historical, and Statistical Analysis of the Capitalist Process*, 2 vols. (New York: McGraw-Hill, 1939); 2:894–903.

[68]E.g., it failed to prevent further concentration of banking power in New York City, to popularize trade acceptances, and to prevent abuses in the bank-acceptance system which it undertook to establish; and the elasticity of the currency it achieved was mainly upward. However, see Clark, *Central Banking*, ch. 14, "Twenty Years of the Federal Reserve System"; Goldenweiser, *American Monetary Policy*, pp. 70–73.

capacity in some lines, and . . . by large holdings of gold in the United States." He recognized "exceptionally active speculation in stocks, with a consequent development of credit strain," but saw no evidence of "unstable equilibrium in the whole economic situation." "The extensive reserve of unused credit," Crum said, "encouraged a much more vigorous wave of speculation, unaccompanied by boom conditions in general business, than any which had developed in 1922–26." While he wrongly judged it "unlikely that a prolonged decline in the general price level will develop within the next few years," he held it probable that the present period of regulated prosperity would ultimately terminate in another period of depression, but he considered it "impossible now to foresee the termination of the present business cycle" and concluded that our new banking system "will mitigate the severity and diminish the frequency of business depressions rather than abolish them for all time—a thing which centralized control of banking has never yet accomplished in any country." Hopeful as he was on this score, he stated: "Little progress has been made toward preventing the development of those trains of events which ordinarily precipitate business crises." His summary of the economic situation in the summer of 1929 showed him insufficiently aware of serious weaknesses in the situation here and especially abroad.[69]

Despite many specific criticisms, there was an approach to a consensus in 1929 that the Federal Reserve System had not only justified its existence but fully "proved its worth" up to, and even for a time after, the Wall Street crash.[70]

First Months under Hoover,   Hoover brought to the presidency a strong
March-September 1929   personality imbued with an activist spirit
but with limited political aptitude or experience. A profound believer in American individualism, he was eager to have the federal government play a much larger role in the nation than Harding or Coolidge favored. As presidential candidate he extravagantly extolled the virtues of Republican policies and held out roseate hopes from their continuance, but he also urged a number of actions to deal with obstinate problems. Upon his inauguration in March 1929, he started by pushing a vigorously positive farm policy, including tariff rate increases, and put forward an extensive program to reconstruct America. When the Wall Street crash came in the fall, he overrode Treasury Secretary Mellon's views and accepted, for the first

[69]Crum, *Interpretation*, pp. 14, 1, 2. See also pp. 10 (chart), 12–22. Clearly the members of the Harvard group, to which Crum belonged, were not believers in the New Era, permanent-prosperity philosophy.

[70]See quotations from Baruch, Burgess, Warburg, and Whitaker in Chapters 6–7 below. Whitaker was an acute and critical thinker whose unqualified testimony is especially impressive. Even Friedman and Schwartz, who were extremely critical of its operations in 1929–33, were far less so on FRS policies in 1922–29. *Monetary History*, pp. 296–98, 407–19.

time in the nation's history, federal responsibility for ending the economic contraction and restoring prosperity.

Early in his inaugural address Hoover warned that the country's "majestic advance should not obscure the constant dangers from which self-government must be safeguarded," and asserted: "The strong man must at all times be alert to the attack of insidious disease." Among these dangers and diseases he did not specify rampant speculation, which he saw, or the threat of economic breakdown, which he probably did not foresee; but he did recommend positive government efforts in "the direction of economic progress and the further lessening of poverty."[71] The stage was thus set for active interposition to meet the challenges of the crash and its aftermath of contraction into depression.

From his Food Administration days and the post-Armistice struggle to dispose of food surpluses produced with liberally guaranteed farm prices, Hoover had developed views on postwar agricultural policies, which he expressed in a press statement on December 1, 1920.[72] One point called for development of farmer cooperative buying and selling. During the farm relief agitation in the mid-1920s he had encouraged President Coolidge to veto two different McNary-Haugen bills, which had much farmer support, effectively opposed the export-debenture plan which the National Grange favored, and came to support a third proposal which stressed cooperative marketing and a federal farm board financed by liberal federal appropriations. These were stressed in the Republican platform of 1928, in Hoover's acceptance speech, and in his campaign addresses of August 21 and November 2, 1928.[73] To redeem those pledges he called the Congress to meet in special session on April 16, 1929.[74]

The Agricultural Marketing Act became law on June 15, 1929,[75] and was acclaimed by the president as "the most important measure ever passed by Congress in aid of a single industry." A month later the Federal Farm Board was constituted. Hoover and Alec Legge, its able first chairman, viewed its major purpose to be the building up of farmer-owned and farmer-controlled cooperative marketing organizations, over a period of years, as essential to the "permanent realization of our hopes of a new day for agriculture." The act also permitted resort to price stabilization measures, and the Board's fateful commitments of October 1929 virtually ensured its overall failure.[76]

[71]Hoover, *The State Papers and Other Public Writings of Herbert Hoover*, ed. William Starr Myers, 2 vols. (Garden City, N.Y.: Doubleday Doran, 1934), 1:3–13.

[72]Wilbur and Hyde, *Hoover Policies*, pp. 146–47.

[73]*Ibid.*, pp. 146–54; Hoover, *New Day*, pp. 17–24, 53–58, 102–4.

[74]Hoover, *State Papers*, 1:13–14, 31–37.

[75]Myers and Newton, *Hoover Administration*, p. 24. The act is reprinted in appendixes to the Farm Board's annual reports.

[76]See below, Chapters 6, 8, and 9.

Hoover's fear of the consequences of unbridled speculation in stocks continued as the superboom rose to its climax.[77] Political considerations, however, weighed against his publicly taking a strong position on the subject during the campaign, after his election, or in his first six months in the White House. In his *Memoirs* he noted that his first interest was to get the Wall Street boom "under restraint," but his actions toward that end had negligible effects, and he considered it futile to ask the Congress for "powers to interfere in the stock market." In his message to the Congress early in December 1929 he could say: "Fortunately, the Federal Reserve System had taken measures to strengthen the position against the day when speculation would break, which, together with the strong position of the banks, has carried the whole credit system through the crisis without impairment."

It might seem that, by the end of 1927 or early in 1928, the more responsible bankers, investment leaders, and businessmen could have led in promoting the view that the stock market boom had already gone to dangerous lengths and urged suitable moves to check it.[78] Failing this, it might seem that President Hoover, early in his term, could have called together a group of such leaders with a view to issuing an emphatic warning, taking steps to put brakes on the still growing Wall Street boom, and formulating plans appropriate to meet the eventual crisis. Even better, as presidential candidate he might have used his 1928 campaign speeches to alert the public to the seriousness of this danger and to promise such a move if elected, and then have followed up this commitment in his inaugural address. Unfortunately, the requisite wisdom and courage were lacking in New York, in Washington, and in the country at large.

---

[77] Hoover, *The Memoirs of Herbert Hoover*, vol. 3: *The Great Depression, 1929–1941* (New York: Macmillan, 1952), chs. 1–2.

[78] Samuel Spring, a New York lawyer specializing in investment law who in 1919 had published a book on Blue Sky laws, adverted to this possibility in his candid article "Whirlwinds of Speculation," *Atlantic*, April 1931, pp. 477–86. He concluded: "To escape succeeding decades of similar distress we must look, in a \democratic state, to the greater wisdom and more foreseeing courage of our financial leaders. Little help will come from expecting aid from governmental agencies, or from hoping for a miraculous forebearance on the part of the public in the face of exploitation."

CHAPTER 6

NEW ERA OPTIMISM, GROWING INTO OVERCONFIDENCE, 1924–29

THE DOMINANT MOOD of the American people in the sustained economic advance of 1922–29 was one of remarkable and growing optimism and confidence, which became widespread as the stock market boom rose to its climax in the summer of 1929. In order to understand the evolution of this attitude in the 1920s, it seems essential to summarize certain long-observed characteristics of Americans, the testimony of foreign visitors, the experience of the decade as interpreted by Americans and Europeans, the positions taken by several prominent and less prominent Americans and Europeans, the part played by European developments in 1924–29, and, finally, three important factors reinforcing high confidence in 1929. These go far to support the conclusion that the most basic cause of the stock market superboom, and the accompanying extreme speculation in stocks and real estate, was the extraordinary development of overoptimism about American business, profits, and economic stability in the years ahead.

American Characteristics   David M. Potter devoted a stimulating book to the thesis that "the United States [has always] enjoyed a richer endowment than other countries and that this physical heritage has influenced our past history and our present society in distinctive ways. . . . this wealth stimulated our technology and our entire productive system in such a way that we developed an unparalleled aptitude for converting many previously inconvertible materials and sources of power into forms that also constituted wealth."[1] Potter also endorsed one of Margaret Mead's central ideas, that Americans "have a supremely strong compulsion to achieve success, . . . measured not by what one possesses in wealth or position but by what one has gained."[2] These convictions I consider pertinent to the interpretation of the 1920s, but other factors were also influential.

In a paper given in June 1954 I undertook to distinguish salient characteristics of U.S. standards of living for early, deferred, or ultimate attainment which, though not universal here, are common enough to be identified by groups and in more detail and to be distinguishable from corresponding "standards" of other peoples.[3] Several of these help to explain

---

[1] *People of Plenty: Economic Abundance and the American Character* (Chicago: University of Chicago Press, 1954), p. 139.
[2] *Ibid.*, pp. 67–72, esp. p. 68.
[3] "Economic Potentials of the United States," in Robert Lekachman, ed., *National Policy for Economic Welfare at Home and Abroad*, Columbia University Bicentennial Conference

the course of developments in the two interwar decades, as well as in the quarter-century after World War II.

We crave a liberal and varied level of consumption, including waste. We have a powerful urge to work, and we regard work as normal, *not* a curse. We prize change and flexibility. We rate enterprise high, and enjoy taking risks. We set relatively little store by status, and are loath fatalistically to accept our "lot in life." We have a profound faith in "progress," and think we know what the word means. Individually and collectively, we tend to set higher goals when one set has been achieved. We resent being bossed, are not conspicuously law-abiding,[4] and have strong predilections for freedom of all sorts. We prize independence and shun dependence. We are gullible—highly susceptible to influence by propaganda of all sorts, including advertising and patriotic appeals. We are addicted to tall stories, strong language, boasting, and exaggeration of all sorts, and are willing to entertain millennial ideas. We are prone to cherish illusions and hence to suffer disillusionment. While typically optimistic, we can swing to extreme pessimism; we tend to go to extremes in confidence, optimism, and enthusiasm and to the opposite extremes of pessimism and something approaching despair. Closely related to this is our tendency to overdo and underdo. Our volatility in sentiment and in action has been repeatedly demonstrated, seldom more conspicuously than in 1925–35.[5]

"Two of the most distinctive traits" of human nature, James Truslow Adams wrote in 1929, "are love of distinction and the need to follow leaders." In the 1920s big businessmen attained the highest distinction and became "the genuine leaders of our people," and business ideals had become dominant in American culture. In 1930 Adams lamented: "The Protestant churches . . . are bankrupting themselves as fast as they can by their appeal to Caesar, and are so fast becoming political lobbyists instead of moral leaders that we may ignore them in the latter role."[6]

When Paul Einzig, a London financial journalist, made a crowded four-week visit to New York in the spring of 1926, he found "sweeping optimism" the chief characteristic of most of the financiers whom he met:

Series (Garden City, N.Y.: Doubleday, 1955), pp. 104–74, esp. pp. 129–32. I also adverted (p. 172) to a few significant differences. Cf. also James Truslow Adams, *The American: The Making of a New Man* (New York: Scribner, 1943), pp. 372–85.

[4] See James Truslow Adams, "Our Lawless Heritage," *Atlantic*, December 1928, pp. 732–40, and "Our Deep-Rooted Lawlessness," *New York Times Magazine*, Mar. 9, 1930, pp. 1–2.

[5] Witness the "meteoric rise and fall of technocracy" in 1932–34. Joseph Dorfman, *The Economic Mind in American Civilization*, vols. 4–5: *1919–1933* (New York: Viking, 1959), esp. 5:647–49.

[6] *Forum*, May 1930, p. 301; Adams, *Our Business Civilization: Some Aspects of American Culture* (New York: Boni, 1929), pp. 14–16. Adams had been in Wall Street for a dozen years before he quit his membership in a firm in 1912 to become one of the most prolific and respected essayists and historians of the interwar period. One of his earliest books was *Speculation and the Reform of the New York Stock Exchange* (Summit, N.J.: Summit-Herald Press, 1913).

"With very few exceptions they were convinced that the period of prosperity then being experienced was everlasting, and they refused to listen to arguments to the contrary. Although just then there was a minor slump in Wall Street, and the Florida real-estate boom had just collapsed, everybody I met was convinced that the boom would be resumed and would continue indefinitely."[7] He noted, however, that none of the many "really big bankers or business men I came across . . . indulged in overstatements, which was erroneously regarded on this side of the Atlantic as an integral part of the American character," though they did not "share the British habit of understatement."[8]

In his later summary of the "crisis" in the United States[9] Einzig stressed the American tendency to "exaggerate everything"; he noted that the "great prosperity" "gave rise to a wave of optimism," when it "was widely, almost generally, believed that prosperity would last forever and would go on increasing." It seemed that "possession of a huge gold reserve and an improved credit system" would permit notable exploitation of American natural resources in the next decade or two; that the "optimism was encouraged . . . by leading bankers and statesmen"; that the demand created by installment buying stimulated abnormal "extension of the productive capacity of American industry"; and that the expanding "earnings of business concerns was largely responsible for the boom and overspeculation in Wall Street," in which "millions" had participated.

Testimony of   Einzig was one of a veritable flood of inquiring
Foreign Observers   foreign visitors who came to the United States in the
1920s; "books, reports, and articles, in many languages, describing, explaining or criticizing the economic and social situation in the United States, . . . appeared in unparalleled quantity" in 1922–29. In his introduction to *Recent Economic Changes* Edwin F. Gay, who had entertained many of these visitors, ably summarized their conclusions with the aid of his study of their published work.[10]

[7] *In the Centre of Things* (London: Hutchinson, 1960), ch. 7. Einzig's articles on his New York observations appeared in the London *Financial News* from Apr. 9 to June 4, 1926. A prolific writer, Einzig is still writing books, articles, and book reviews; see indexes to *EJ*.

[8] *Ibid.*, p. 73.

[9] *The World Economic Crisis, 1929–31*, 1st and 2d eds. (London: Macmillan, 1931, 1932), app. 2. A third edition was published.

[10] *Recent Economic Changes in the United States*, 2 vols. (New York: McGraw-Hill, 1929), 1:1–10. An extraordinary man of many great talents, Gay was an outstanding economic historian who had spent more than twelve years of study in Germany, Switzerland, Italy, and England (1890–1902); he spoke several languages. He was the first dean of Harvard's pioneer Graduate School of Business Administration (1908–17); a key economist in Washington in 1917–19; one of the founders (1919) of the National Bureau of Economic Research, its first president, and, with Wesley C. Mitchell, its co-director of research in 1924–33; a founder

It is not surprising that these visitors, mostly from countries that were far from prosperous, spoke in extravagant terms of the "immense advance in America" and of its "great" and "ebullient prosperity" even as early as 1926 and 1927, when U.S. observers were using more moderate terms than they would do in 1928 and 1929. Thus the prestigious editor of the London *Observer* said in the issue of March 21, 1926: "The United States, by contrast with Great Britain, is the thing nearest to El Dorado that actual human society has seen."[11]

Many of the visitors earnestly sought the causes. Though they differed on various points, and particularly in emphasis, there was a considerable approach toward a consensus. Gay's summary covered several factors: (1) America's unrivaled natural resources, "especially those . . . fundamental to modern large-scale industrialization," though some weighted more heavily "the energy and organization which has utilized them"; (2) the facts that labor was relatively scarce and wages were relatively high; (3) the resulting "progressive development of labor-supplementing machine equipment, in agriculture, transportation and industry, and also a remarkable utilization of power"; (4) "the great domestic market, untrammeled by barriers of tariffs, language, or tradition of local or national jealousies," and the "resulting 'mass consumption' [which] makes mass production possible and profitable"; (5) the "high premium on management and organizing capacity" and the emergence of far-sighted management as a new profession; (6) the great improvement in industrial relations and even the "achievement of industrial peace between labor, capital and management"; (7) the "open-mindedness of American management" and "increasing support of scientific research." Lastly (8) , the foreign visitors in the 1920s unanimously stressed the "dominant national trait of optimistic energy, as an underlying element in . . . American economic activity" and found "strongly persistent" the "spirit of indomitable hopefulness."[12]

Gay mentioned four previous "periods of marked acceleration," "efflorescence," and "unprecedented prosperity"—1825-37, 1849-57, 1879-93, and 1898-1907—and concluded: "Finally, throughout all the four great

(1921) and first president of the Council on Foreign Relations and the "moving spirit in launching its quarterly journal, *Foreign Affairs*, in 1922, and in 1927 became chairman of its research and publishing committee." Herbert Heaton, *A Scholar in Action: Edwin F. Gay* (Cambridge, Mass.: Harvard University Press, 1952).

[11] J. L. Garvin, quoted in an advertisement for *English Life* in *N&A* (London) of June 26, 1926. It went on to review a new book by "two young and expert engineers who went to America last autumn at their own expense," *The Secret of High Wages*, by Bertram Austin and W. Francis Lloyd, published in New York by Dodd Mead, with a foreword by Walter T. Layton, editor of the *Economist*. The July issue of *English Life* contained the first of a new series, "Prosperity in Our Time."

[12] *Recent Economic Changes*, 1:1-6.

waves of advance, and even in the troughs between, there has always been felt that upward movement of forceful energy, of optimistic ambition, which our foreign observers have so constantly noted."[13] It is impressive that this outstanding scholar voiced no warning based on the troughs that had followed earlier peaks, apparently because "prognostications" were outside the terms on which the arrangements with the Committee on Recent Economic Changes were made.[14]

Sir Reginald McKenna, chairman of the Midland Bank, addressing its annual meeting in London early in 1927, contrasted the "great and increasing prosperity" of the United States in the past six years with the British "depression and unemployment of almost unparalleled severity," and found a partial explanation in the wide divergence of monetary policies.[15] McKenna's good friend Keynes commended this diagnosis, and observed that the disequilibrium that had existed two years earlier had grown worse instead of disappearing.[16]

Moritz J. Bonn, an especially acute foreign visitor in the 1920s, stressed in 1931 a factor which Gay did not list:

> The World War was the final and determining cause of the stupendous boom in the United States. . . .
>
> Three causes—natural resources, revolutionary temperament, and deliberate technical aspiration—have shaped the economic and social life of the United States of the past. The fact that in the last ten years they have produced something like a new revolution is due not so much to the acceleration of their tempo or to the widening of their range, as to the transformation of the world and the modifications in the proportionate strengths of the various countries throughout the globe, resulting from the war.[17]

Consequently, Bonn reasoned, the transformation which could perhaps have taken twenty-five years if the catastrophe of war had not come was compressed within a decade—too short a period for the generation that had grown up under the old regime to develop the qualifications needed in the new order. Bonn also wrote in 1931: "An economic boom of such extent and such duration as the prosperity of the last five years had never before been

---

[13]*Ibid.*, 1:9–10. In December 1924 Strong warned Montagu Norman "that 'our enthusiastic, energetic, and optimistic population' might generate speculative tendencies to such a degree as to require restrictive action." Lester V. Chandler, *Benjamin Strong: Central Banker* (Washington, D.C.: Brookings Institution, 1958), pp. 310–11, 424.

[14]*Recent Economic Changes*, 1:12.

[15]*Economist* (London), Jan. 29, 1927, pp. 229–32.

[16]*Annalist* (New York), Mar. 11, 1927, pp. 363–64.

[17]*Prosperity: Myth and Reality in American Economic Life* (London: Martin Hopkinson, 1931), pp. 11, 14–15. The American edition, with an introduction by George S. Counts, was entitled *The Crisis of Capitalism in America* (New York: John Day, 1932). Though Bonn does not cite or refer to *Recent Economic Changes*, his reference to "tempo" and "range" implies that he had read at least the Committee report and disagreed with one of its main points.

witnessed, either by the world at large or the American world in particular. All experiences tended to show that it could not continue without interruption or disturbance. But all the ambitions and longings of the nation set themselves in opposition to experience, and clung almost passionately to the determination that it must last because it dare not collapse."[18]

Einzig, about the same time, also stressed the war as a factor, saying: "During the boom the view was widely held that the war had fundamentally changed our economic system, so that prosperity need not be followed by relapse, and could go on increasing forever."[19] And in 1937 he wrote: "The unwarranted degree of optimism about everlasting prosperity resulted in a boom in Wall Street which brought about an increase in fictitious wealth through the fantastically high level to which stocks and shares had risen as a result of the practices of carrying securities largely with the aid of borrowed money."[20]

Interpretations of the   The postwar disillusionment of Americans with
American Experience   Europe, and their painful realization that the
foundations for a new era of durable peace and international cooperation had not been securely laid, were accompanied by fresh optimism over the realizable potentials of the United States, now by all odds the strongest nation in the world. We had won the Great War—so the braggarts put it. Clearly, the United States had provided the food, materials, finance, and armed forces to ensure victory to the Allied and Associated Powers and the utter defeat of the Central Powers. The nation had suffered little, and farmers, bankers, and industrialists had profited greatly.

Economic developments in 1921–29 provided substantial bases for both gratification and optimism. From a severe postwar depression recovery was speedy; except in agriculture, which lagged, full prosperity had been regained by 1923, in striking contrast to most of the rest of the world. The mild contraction in the first half of 1924 was promptly succeeded by notable expansion. By 1926 "prosperity" was at a level that responsible observers called "hitherto undreamed of," "extraordinary," "overwhelming," though careful U.S. observers deemed it only moderate;

[18]*Prosperity*, p. 142. Cf. also J. W. Krutsch, *The Modern Temper: A Study and a Confusion* (New York: Harcourt Brace, 1929).
[19]*World Economic Crisis*, 1st ed., p. 69; 2d ed., p. 81. In 1937 Marriner Eccles made a similar statement in his paper, "Controlling Booms and Depressions," in A. D. Gayer, ed., *Lessons of Monetary Experience: Essays in Honor of Irving Fisher* (New York: Farrar and Rinehart, 1937), p. 5.
[20]*World Finance, 1935–1937* (London: Macmillan, 1937; preface dated March 1937), p. 21. He added: "The Wall Street slump of 1929 brought about a severe depression in the United States, a depression which spread over Europe and the rest of the world and which culminated in the financial crisis of 1931."

and the stock market came to be watched as a prime index of prosperity.[21] Despite a moderate shrinkage of business activity in 1927, due in considerable part to the Ford shutdown from May into November to permit retooling for Model A and other new models,[22] the conviction spread, at home and abroad, that Americans had learned the secret of perpetual prosperity. The stock market superboom of 1928–29, in part a result of this belief, was interpreted as a confirmation of it.

A. D. Noyes said in his reminiscences: "Illusion or not, the American idea of the country's unlimited resources seemed to be adopted, even by conservative European financiers."[23] They expected an eventual collapse, such as had occurred in commodity speculation in 1920 and in Florida land speculation in 1925, but the reactions in the stock market later in the decade were short-lived until the crash. Moreover, the 1920s were a virtually "defaultless era in foreign lending," abroad as well as in the United States[24]—a remarkable fact. Though conservative bankers were concerned over some of the issues floated by their less cautious competitors, they did not advertise their worries and were swept along with the tide of opinion that prosperity would be permanent.[25] It is true that agriculture, coal mining, the textile industries, and some others were not sharing fully in the general prosperity, but "the boom in other industries was so tremendous that . . . many people had visions in which the blessings of eternal prosperity would ultimately be shared even by backward industries."[26]

The belief in a New Era had emerged soon after hostilities ended. Herbert Hoover wrote the foreword to Elisha M. Friedman's *America and the New Era: A Symposium on Social Reconstruction*. Johns Hopkins economist Jacob H. Hollander, one of its contributors, had published in October 1914 his *Abolition of Poverty*, which he quoted in the Friedman volume and continued to view it as an attainable objective. As the decade wore on, a remarkable "New Era psychology" evolved, came to be widely accepted, and pervaded or powerfully influenced the thinking of

[21]James Truslow Adams, *The Tempo of Modern Life* (New York: Boni, 1931), p. 280, and *Our Business Civilization*, p. 35.

[22]Leonard P. Ayres, *Turning Points in Business Cycles* (New York: Macmillan, 1939), p. 45.

[23]*The Market Place: Reminiscences of a Financial Editor* (Boston: Little Brown, 1938), pp. 290–91, 317–18.

[24]Ilse Mintz, *Deterioration in the Quality of Foreign Bonds Issued in the United States, 1920–1930*, NBER Publication 52 (New York: NBER, 1951), p. 25. She noted a few minor exceptions.

[25]Cf. Moritz J. Bonn, *Wandering Scholar* (New York: John Day, 1948), p. 309, regarding J. P. Morgan and T. W. Lamont at Young committee meetings early in 1929. Much later (1952) Herbert Hoover referred to a long memorandum that Lamont sent him "that makes curious reading today." *The Memoirs of Herbert Hoover*, vol. 3: *The Great Depression, 1929–1941* (New York: Macmillan, 1952), p. 17.

[26]Bonn, *Prosperity*, pp. 89–94.

many who were not convinced that long-accepted generalizations had become obsolete. In his *Memoirs*, in a passage written less than three years after he left the White House, Hoover adverted to the "American wave of optimism, born of continued progress over the decade," which "gave birth to a foolish idea called 'The New Economic Era' " which "spread over the whole country"; he seemed unaware, however, of the extent to which he had helped its spread (see pages 140–41 below).[27]

Economic, financial, and business analysts in 1929 were almost unanimously optimistic,[28] though many would not have endorsed the more extreme views. Even those who voiced the most vigorous criticisms and warnings, such as Anderson, Noyes, and Warburg, revealed after the stock-market crash their basic confidence (see Chapter 7 below). And even Sir George Paish, who did not, found grounds for hope of the restoration of "prosperity to Great Britain, Europe and the world in general" and could conclude: "All trustworthy signs indicate a very great change of outlook, and it is abundantly obvious that an unprecedented expansion of both buying power and income is in store for the nations as soon as they abandon their present policies and take advantage of the great opportunities which await them."[29]

Much later Arthur F. Burns observed that "the optimism of the time was general and financial specialists did not escape infection." "Each of the successive cyclical waves during this decade [the 1920s] carried further the belief in a 'new era' of boundless prosperity. As speculative fever mounted, even the business declines that occurred were ignored or explained away."[30] This was not quite true of scholars such as Burns' senior

---

[27]Friedman, ed., *America and the New Era* (New York: Dutton, 1920); Hollander, *Abolition of Poverty* (Boston: Houghton Mifflin, 1914); Hoover, *Memoirs*, 3:v, 5.

[28]In saying this I rely in part on the opinion of a long-time friend (F. Ernest Richter) who wrote the January 1929 issue of the AT&T *Summary of Business Conditions*, shortly thereafter joined the staff of a Stock Exchange firm, and later served as economist to a big corporation, and who was an active member of two or three groups of outstanding analysts in the 1920s and 1930s. Robert T. Patterson may have been right in saying: "Most of the economists who served the larger banks and industrial corporations, as well as many economists in academic life, helped foster the New Era illusion." *The Great Boom and Panic, 1921–1929* (Chicago: Regnery, 1965), p. 28. The economist of the Chase National Bank was a prominent exception. For an interesting comparison between two "new eras," 1921–28 and 1896–1903, see B. M. Anderson in *Chase Economic Bulletin*, Feb. 11, 1929, and the same author's *Economics and the Public Welfare: Financial and Economic History of the United States, 1914–1946* (New York: Van Nostrand, 1949), pp. 202, 503–6. This book, with a foreword by Henry Hazlitt and a preface dated November 1948, was published soon after the author's death on Jan. 19, 1949. Perhaps because of the subordination of its subtitle, it has been overlooked by many scholars, and for different reasons others have ignored it.

[29]*The Road to Prosperity* (London: Benn, 1927), p. 133; see also pp. 1, 118, 136–37.

[30]"New Facts on Business Cycles" and "Business Cycle Research and the Needs of Our Times," reprinted in his *The Frontiers of Economic Knowledge* (Princeton, N.J.: Princeton University Press, 1954), pp. 132, 178–79.

colleague and predecessor Mitchell, or Mitchell's National Bureau co-director Gay, or of the Harvard group including C. J. Bullock, W. M. Persons, and W. L. Crum. Yet their critical and skeptical reservations were muted, and they calmly envisaged a mild or moderate business contraction, avoided strong warnings, and appeared to feel sure that no severe depression lay ahead.

By 1929 four views had become prevalent, if not always in their most extreme form: (1) that the U.S. economy was "fundamentally sound"; (2) that another major depression like that of the 1890s was at least highly improbable, if not impossible; (3) that the upward trend of the economy would be indefinitely sustained, despite temporary setbacks; and (4) that the broad course of prices of common stocks would continue upward.

America's progress and prosperity in the 1920s amazed the rest of the world. The liberal Spanish internationalist Salvador de Madariaga wrote late in 1929: "The whole world is now fascinated by the United States—by its wealth, its power, its speed. With that eagerness to believe which is one of the most pathetic features of the human race, the world wants to discover the higher principle of success responsible for the turbulent prosperity of the American nation and her marvelous expansion. So American life becomes the model which, consciously or unconsciously, all life is now imitating."[31] In mid-1930 R. L. Buell commented: "Our vast industrial and financial strength casts a shadow over the whole of mankind."[32] Bonn wrote in 1931:

> The stupendous economic development of the United States in the years 1924–29 engendered in many parts of the world, and above all in Germany, the belief that there, by the agency of a reasoning intelligence, had been achieved the miracle of permanent prosperity which no crisis could destroy. . . .
>
> Anyone who wants to understand the meaning and significance of the present American crisis must study the causes and forces which for a few short years shaped that phantom of eternal prosperity which infatuated America and Europe.[33]

In *The Epic of America* James Truslow Adams wrote of the "American Dream . . . of a better, richer and happier life for all our citizens of every rank which is the greatest contribution we have as yet made to the

[31]"Our Muddling World: The U.S. of Europe," and "America's Stake in European Recovery," *Forum*, January-February 1930, pp. 19–23, 110–13. Madariaga wrote enthusiastically of U.S. contributions to Europe's recovery. Cf. also Frank Bohn, "The U.S. of Europe," *ibid.*, May 1930, pp. 290–93 (Bohn called the United States "a first draft of the U.S. of Europe"); and Edouard Herriot, *The United States of Europe*, trans. R. J. Dingle (New York: Viking, 1930), reviewed by H. D. Gideonse in *JPE*, June 1931, 39:417–18.

[32]Raymond Leslie Buell, "The Naval Fumble," *Forum*, June 1930, pp. 358–62. Buell viewed the London Naval Conference of early 1930 as a "fumbling failure," rather than the success that President Hoover termed it.

[33]*Prosperity*, pp. 7, 10.

thought and welfare of the world."[34] To many observers the 1920s witnessed signal progress toward realization of that dream. Adams disagreed. He observed in 1929 that "the gulf between the average man and the rich man has widened with appalling rapidity."[35] This may have been true, yet there is no doubt that the "average man" in the 1920s enjoyed a rising level of living in terms of his own standards, and this concerned most people more than the gulf between rich and poor. Adams seemed unaware of the extent to which luxury spending by the rich had helped to bring used and even new cars and much new household equipment within reach of middle- and lower-income people, including those on farms.

Sixteen of Adams' essays written between 1927 and 1931 were collected in a volume entitled *The Tempo of Modern Life* published late in 1931. He recognized, but decried, the "mere emotional optimism and hope" in which the country "wallowed" (page 260), "that vast American optimism with its refusal to recognize and wrestle with the problem of evil" (page 146), and the worship of "Pollyanna, Our Patron Goddess" (page 259). In his view, a "dehumanized economic system" (page 32), a "perpetually increasing tempo" (page 84), and "prosperity-bitten Americans" (page 12) "working to the limit to buy to the limit" (page 166) had led to the "complete confusion of our present-day social, intellectual, and spiritual life" (page 255). "Our civilization is becoming warped out of shape" (page 56), he concluded, and lamented the trends of the past century in the substitution

of self-expression for self-discipline; of the concept of prosperity for that of liberty; of restlessness for rest; of spending for saving; of show for solidity; of desire for the new or novel in place of affection for the old and tried; of dependence for self-reliance; of gregariousness for solitude; of luxury for simplicity; of ostentation for restraint; of success for integrity; of national for local; of easy generosity for wise giving; of preferring impressions to thought, facts to ideas; of democracy for aristocracy; of the mediocre for the excellent. . . .

With an ingenuity that would have been fiendish had it not been so unthinking and ignorant, the leaders of the new era used every resource of modern psychology to warp the unformed character of the people, to provide the greatest possible profit to the individuals and corporations that made and purveyed the new "goods." Our best and worst qualities, our love of wife and children, our national pride, our self-respect, our snobbery, our fear of social opinion, our neglect of the future, our lack of self-restraint and discipline, our love of mere physical comfort have all been played upon to make mush of our characters in order that big business

[34](Boston: Little Brown, 1931), p. vii, quoted in Granville Hicks' review of Frederic I. Carpenter's *American Literature and the Dream* (New York: Philosophical Library, 1955), p. 5. Carpenter reported that Adams was the first to use this exact term but found the earliest statement of the notion in Captain Edward Johnson, *A History of New England . . .* (London, 1654). *New York Times*, Feb. 19, 1956.

[35]*Our Business Civilization*, pp. 37, 53.

might thrive. Even our national government, whether wittingly or not, undertook to inflame our American love of gambling and our desire to "get rich quick" regardless of effect on character.[36]

Adams was not alone in voicing such sour observations, but such diatribes had little impact until after the New Era had ended and were mostly written after the stock market crash. Then, indeed, opinions were voiced to the effect that our vaunted prosperity had been "sham," "phony," or "illusory," as well as inadequate. These views were unwarranted, for the prosperity was real and general, if not universal. Only its indefinite continuance was illusory (see Chapter 4 above).

Herbert Hoover, *The New* **Day and** *Recent Economic Changes*   As the secretary of commerce in both the Harding and the Coolidge administrations, Herbert Hoover was much concerned over the taming of the business cycle, and in 1921–26 he was occasionally outspoken in his warnings about speculation (Chapter 7 below). Privately he scorned much of the New Era philosophy, yet his public utterances in the later 1920s gave it no little support. Thus he began his message of June 14, 1928, to the Republican National Convention which had just nominated him for the presidency on the first ballot: "A new era and new forces have come into our economic life and our setting among nations of the world. These forces demand of us constant study and effort if prosperity, peace, and contentment shall be maintained."[37] The volume of his 1928 campaign speeches, which were devoted to this theme, was entitled *The New Day.* In accepting the presidential nomination on August 11, 1928, he said:

One of the oldest and perhaps the noblest of human aspirations has been the abolition of poverty. By poverty I mean the grinding by undernourishment, cold, and ignorance, and fear of old age of those who have the will to work. We in America today are nearer to the final triumph over poverty than ever before in the history of any land. The poorhouse is vanishing from among us. We have not yet reached the goal, but, given a chance to go forward with the policies of the last eight years, we shall soon with the help of God be in sight of the day when poverty

[36]Adams, *Tempo of Modern Life.* Specific page references are given in the text. He had already adverted to the "vast amount of Polyanna literature" in *Our Business Civilization,* pp. 35, 59. B. M. Anderson later wrote: "We had seen for years the appalling spectacle of the President of the United States [Coolidge] and the Secretary of the Treasury, Mr. Mellon, giving out interviews to encourage the stock market whenever prices seemed to flag." *Economics and the Public Welfare,* p. 182. He referred to Ralph Robey's "brilliant and justly indignant paper," "Capeadores in Wall Street" (*Atlantic,* September 1928, pp. 388–97), and to the more complete story in William Allen White, *A Puritan in Babylon* (New York: Macmillan, 1938).

[37]Hoover, *The Memoirs of Herbert Hoover,* vol. 2: *The Cabinet and the Presidency, 1920–1933* (New York: Macmillan, 1951), p. 195.

will be banished from this nation. There is no guarantee against poverty equal to a job for every man. That is the primary purpose of the economic policies we advocate.[38]

At Elizabethton, Tennessee, he said on October 6: "Our country has entered into an entirely new era."[39] In various campaign speeches he made much of our economic and social gains in the 1920s, and his comments were permeated with optimism for the future, while he made only a few brief references to the stock speculation which was rampant in the months of the campaign. His overwhelming victory at the polls in November 1928 seemed to many to ensure both stability and continued economic advance. In concluding his inaugural address on March 4, 1929, President Hoover said: "I have no fears for the future of our country. It is bright with hope." And the mid-1929 report of his Committee on Recent Economic Changes,[40] as we shall see, broadly supported the prevailing overoptimism.

Hoover's able and trusted aide in the Department of Commerce, E. Dana Durand, soon published *American Industry and Commerce*, in the introduction to which he felt it possible to say:

For the first time in history man has reached a height whence he can dimly see ahead the Promised Land. From the material standpoint, at least, the Utopia of the Philosophers and the romancers seems no longer an altogether idle dream. . . [The] real prosperity and progress of the country and the real well-being of the masses of the people (as judged, of course, by comparison with other peoples and other periods of time) do constitute strong arguments in support of the general soundness of American economic and political institutions and policies.[41]

The Committee on Recent Economic Changes[42] was set up late in 1927 by the President's Conference on Unemployment, of which Hoover was chairman. Composed of a group of prominent men, also under his chairmanship, this committee arranged for a series of basic studies to be made under the leadership of the National Bureau of Economic Research, with extensive collaboration from able persons outside the Bureau and with "the assistance of an unprecedented number of governmental and private

[38] *The New Day: Campaign Speeches of Herbert Hoover, 1928* (Stanford, Calif.: Stanford University Press, 1928), p. 16. Cf. Hollander's views cited on p. 136 above.

[39] *Ibid.*, pp. 97–98.

[40] In his brief reference to this committee in his *Memoirs* (2:176), he spoke of Arch W. Shaw as chairman and omitted five names (Brown, Dunlap, Lawrence, Raskob, and Woolley) from the full list of members given in the foreword to the published volumes (see n. 42 below).

[41] (Boston: Ginn, 1930), pp. xvi, xvii. It was reviewed by Willard L. Thorp in *JASA*, March 1932, 27:111–12. For Durand's optimistic outlook late in 1929, see Chapter 8 below.

[42] The title of the committee may have been suggested by a book by David A. Wells, *Recent Economic Changes and Their Effect on the Production and Distribution of Wealth and the Well-Being of Society* (New York: Appleton, 1890–93; preface dated August 1889), which was largely a collection of papers, published earlier in *Popular Science Monthly* (New York) and in *Contemporary Review* (London), which had been rewritten, revised, and brought up to date.

agencies."[43] This important "analysis of post-war developments in economic life, particularly those since the recovery from the depression of 1920–21" was begun in January 1928, completed in February 1929, and published in book form on June 10.[44] The committee was "directed to make a critical appraisal of the factors of stability and instability; in other words, to observe and describe the American economy as a whole, suggesting rather than developing recommendations." The attempt was noble, and the results were impressive;[45] but the job had to be rushed, and the next four years revealed serious defects and inadequacies of analysis and appraisal.

In the two volumes of *Recent Economic Changes* the committee's own report and extensive acknowledgements were followed by Gay's introduction, fifteen monographs, and Mitchell's summary review.[46] The numerous authors mentioned many limitations of available data and pointed to many shortcomings and weaknesses in the U.S. economy, though without adequate emphasis, summarization, or judgments as to their significance for the future. Their net effect was to give restrained support to the optimism that prevailed so widely before the stock market crash and that persisted for months after the crash had shocked participants and sobered observers.

The committee report emphasized the "speed and spread" of economic changes in the 1920s and "intensified activity" rather than

---

As listed at the end of the committee report (p. xxvi), its members were Herbert Hoover, chairman, Walter F. Brown, Renick W. Dunlap, William Green, Julius Klein, John S. Lawrence, Max Mason, George McFadden, Adolph C. Miller, Lewis E. Pierson, John J. Raskob, Arch W. Shaw, Louis J. Taber, Daniel Willard, Clarence M. Woolley, Owen D. Young, and Edward Eyre Hunt, secretary. My friend Hunt was very close to Hoover and was the main channel through which Hoover influenced the report. In the committee's later deliberations Shaw served as acting chairman because President-Elect Hoover was unable to take part. The committee continued to exist for several years with slightly altered membership, under Shaw's chairmanship, and sponsored other studies by the National Bureau of Economic Research, e.g., Frederick C. Mills, *Prices in Recession and Recovery* (1936). In its list of members (p. vii), the names of Hoover and Brown are missing, and that of Samuel W. Reyburn is added.

[43]See list in *Recent Economic Changes*, 1:xxvi–xxx.

[44]The NBER *News Bulletin* of June 10, 1929, reported the document "just off the Press." The committee's own report had appeared on May 13 or 15 and was reprinted and critically commented upon in *C&FC* for May 18, 1929, pp. 3246–48, 3257–60. The *Survey Graphic* devoted most of its June 1, 1929, issue (pp. 279–308, 322–23) to summary articles by various authors, which were mainly expository, with few reservations or critical notes. The cover was headed: "Why Prosperity Keeps Up: Mr. Hoover's Pocket Domesday Book of American Land and Folk." *Recent Economic Changes* was not widely reviewed. Charles O. Hardy's long, able review appeared in *JPE*, April 1930, 38:213–27. Jewkes' review, published late in 1930, is summarized in Chapter 13 below.

[45]C. W. Wright somewhat overgenerously termed *Recent Economic Changes* the "best general economic survey of the decade of the twenties." *Economic History of the United States* (New York: McGraw-Hill, 1941, 1949), 1st ed., p. 1094; 2d ed. (1949), p. 917, W. E. Leuchtenburg likewise called it "an invaluable compendium." *The Perils of Prosperity, 1914–32* (Chicago: University of Chicago Press, 1948), p. 293.

[46]Gay, who read the manuscripts and proofread the whole, was unhappy over this undertaking and had "a very poor opinion of the book." Heaton, *Scholar in Action*, pp. 202–3.

"structural change" (page ix). Though spottiness of this activity was noted (page x), it was concluded that "equilibrium has been fairly well maintained" (page xxi). Some dangers were touched upon:

> During the later months of the period covered by the survey a new tendency has been observed. Investors, as well as a large body of speculators, have invested through the Stock Exchange not only their savings, but the proceeds of loans secured through banks and brokers, until the credit structure of the country has been sufficiently weighted to indicate a credit stringency, resulting in an abnormally high rate for call money and an appreciable increase in the rate of interest for business purposes. The consequences of this process can not be measured at this time, but they are factors in this problem of maintaining economic balance which will be touched on later in this report. . . . (page xii)
>
> The forces that bear upon our economic relationships have always been sensitive. All parts of our economic structure from the prime processes of making and of marketing to the facilitating functions of finance, are and have been interdependent and easily affected. And therein lies the danger: That through ignorance of economic principles, or through selfish greed, or inadequate leadership, the steady balance will be disturbed, to our economic detriment. . . . (page xx)
>
> If natural resources, especially the land, are wastefully used; if money in quantity is taken out of production and employed for speculation; if any group develops a method of artificial price advancement which puts one commodity out of balance with other commodities; if either management or labor disregards the common interest—to this extent equilibrium will be destroyed, and destroyed for all. . . . (page xx)
>
> . . . Until recently we have not diverted savings from productive business to speculation.[47] There has been a balance between the economic forces not perfect balance, but a degree of balance which has enabled the intricate machine to produce and to serve our people.[48] (page xxi)

All these mildly worded forebodings were to be borne out, all too soon.

One crucial passage was headed "Remote Saturation Points" (pages xviii–xix). Subsequent history proved every word of it true for the next generation but false for the near and intermediate future. The rising volume of what is now termed "discretionary income"[49]—income beyond the satisfaction of urgent needs and therefore available for "optional consumption"—was touched upon (pages xv–xvi); but its important implications, for

---

[47]This was a widely prevalent misconception. See Chapters 8, n. 16, and 15 below.

[48]*Recent Economic Changes*, 1:ix–xii, xx–xxi.

[49]The National Industrial Conference Board computations of "discretionary income" run back only to the year 1939, and quarterly only from 1946. See NICB, *Business Record*, March 1961, p. 13. C. F. Roos and Victor von Szeliski had utilized this concept, termed "supernumerary income," in their paper on forecasting demand for passenger cars, given at a joint meeting of the American Statistical Association and the Econometric Society on Dec. 27, 1938. See the General Motors publication, *The Dynamics of Automobile Demand* (Detroit, Mich.: GMC, 1939), esp. pp. 41–42, 51–52.

possible changes in consumer disposition to buy and for possible deferment of consumer spending on durable goods in particular, were not pursued.

The importance of maintaining "the organic balance of our economic structure," if increasing activity was to be prolonged indefinitely, was rightly emphasized. But the report contained only a few hints of the serious lack of such balance in the U.S. economy of 1928–29 which was shortly to be revealed. Furthermore, it gave wholly inadequate recognition to the weaknesses in the U.S. and European economies and their consequent vulnerability to shock and stress; the detailed discussions brought out this point but never properly summed up its implications. Hence the optimism pervading the committee report was well-nigh unrestrained. Its glowing account of the 1920s included this prophetic passage: "We have the power to produce and the capital to bring about exchange between the producing and consuming groups. We have communication to speed and spread the influence of ideas. We have swift and dependable transportation. We have an educational system which is steadily raising standards and improving tastes. We have a great national opportunity. . . . We seem only to have touched the fringe of our potentialities."[50] For the long run this was perfectly true, but for the near future it was thoroughly misleading. The final paragraph, conspicuously lacking in penetration, read simply: "Our situation is fortunate, our momentum is remarkable. Yet the organic balance of our economic structure can be maintained only by hard, persistent, intelligent effort; by consideration and sympathy; by mutual confidence, and by a disposition in the several human parts to work in harmony together."[51]

The *Commercial & Financial Chronicle* of May 18, 1929, which reprinted the full report, complained that the first impression of the average reader would be "not only that the United States is tremendously prosperous, but also that its capacity for continued prosperity is wellnigh unlimited." The committee, it held, "would have been better advised if it had pointed out fearlessly the dangers of the pace that is being set, instead of giving to its criticisms and warnings, all of them excellent so far as they go, so small and incidental a place as to cause them, we fear, to be largely overlooked."[52] These points were well taken.

I find no clear evidence that the committee report and the book as a whole contributed appreciably to prolonging the great boom that was ap-

[50] *Recent Economic Changes,* 1:xviii–xix. A quarter-century later, Woytinsky quoted this with a trenchant comment: "The nation awoke to the realization that it was living in a fog of unwarranted self-confidence and self-admiration." W. S. Woytinsky and Associates, *Employment and Wages in the United States* (New York: Twentieth Century Fund, 1953), p. 15.

[51] *Recent Economic Changes,* 1:xxii.

[52] Pp. 3246, 3248. The editorial also criticized the Sprague-Burgess chapter (see Chapter 15 below), a preprint of which had just come out, for the "one-sided way in which some of the matter is presented" (p. 3234).

proaching its climax in the summer of 1929.[53] Its chief significance lies rather in the facts that it represented a serious effort to size up the U.S. economic position and broad outlook as of early 1929 and that it embodied so much of the current New Era psychology without giving clear warnings that serious trouble might be in the offing.[54] It was broadly in harmony with President Coolidge's last State of the Union message, submitted on December 4, 1928, in which he asserted that the Congress and the nation might "regard the present with satisfaction and anticipate the future with optimism." He went on: "No Congress of the United States ever assembled, on surveying the state of the Union, has met with a more pleasing prospect than that which appears at the present time."[55]

Other American T. N. Carver had published in September 1925 *The*
Views, 1925-29 *Present Economic Revolution in the United States.*
In 1928, with his son-in-law, Hugh W. Lester, he published *This Economic World and How It May Be Improved.* The final chapter was entitled: "How Long Will This Diffusion of Prosperity Last, and What Will It Do to Us?" He did not really answer this question; but he did say, somewhat rashly, though with misgivings: "For the first time in history the masses themselves, in this country, are emerging into a condition of prosperity comparable to that of the aristocracies of any previous age. They have neither practical experience, nor a religion, nor a moral discipline that was ever designed to fortify them against these new dangers. . . . There are no longer any poor as that word was once understood."[56]

Paul M. Mazur, a young partner in Lehman Brothers, wrote a glowing book on American prosperity in which he expressed great faith in the ability of the Federal Reserve System to eliminate "periodic eruptions of business conditions," by applying brakes to check excesses of "over-optimistic business men." He foresaw a continuing trend, for one or more

[53]Charles A. Dice (see p. 149 below) may have skimmed it before finishing his *New Levels in the Stock Market* (New York: McGraw-Hill, 1929) but did not mention or cite it. Noyes drew upon it for his monthly financial articles in *Scribners* in June-October 1929. Stuart Chase drew heavily upon it for his popular book *Prosperity: Fact or Myth?* (New York: Boni, 1929).

[54]In a brief article in the *Forum* ("Self-Concerned Business: America, England, Germany," August 1929, pp. 124-28), E. E. Hunt referred to roughly similar investigations in Great Britain under prominent industrialist Sir Arthur Balfour and in Germany (initiated in 1925). The Balfour committee, which was directed to inquire into "the conditions and prospects of British industry and commerce, with special reference to the export trade," made its final report in 1929 after publishing several reports on particular aspects. See C. L. Mowat, *Britain between the Wars, 1918-1940* (London: Methuen, 1955), p. 260. In his paper of Nov. 22, 1929, Lionel D. Edie remarked that in this elaborate two-volume work on the new era only one chapter was devoted specifically to recent *financial* changes, and in this only four pages to the security market. "Putting the So-Called New Era to the Test," *Proc. Acad. Pol. Sci.*, January 1930, 13:514.

[55]Quoted in J. K. Galbraith, *The Great Crash 1929* (Boston: Houghton Mifflin, 1955), p. 6.

[56](Chicago: Shaw, 1928), pp. 413-14.

decades, to lower yields on good bonds, preferred stocks, and common stocks. He considered the bull market already relatively "venerable," and called it "undoubtedly a psychological factor that promoted the confidence and enthusiasm of business men. If optimism is an element in prosperity, then surely cheap money and the stock market have contributed their share as causes of that prosperity." He rightly forecast the eventual "loss of our favorable balance of trade," but mistakenly regarded this as "the greatest single threat to American business which it is possible to foretell for the near future"[57] (see Chapter 7 below).

A vice president of McGraw-Hill Publishing Company coined the phrase "long-time guarantees of prosperity," and Robert M. Davis of his staff published a paper on this subject in June 1928. Several long-term basic factors developed since the war and "largely American in character," he said, "strongly presage a continuance of our general [sic] prosperous condition for some time to come." He emphasized "significant industrial balance," with pig iron and steel production no longer dominant and other industries greatly expanded in importance. He found five "underlying" reasons for his prediction: "increased use of power per worker," "the receptivity of the public to new commodities," "modernized distribution techniques," "increased purchasing power of the public," and "industrial research."[58]

An essentially similar view was expressed in mid-1928 by the vice president of Standard Statistics Company (New York) in the British *Economic Journal.* "Barring a monetary stringency, barring inflation in bank credit or commodity prices, barring an unexpected national disaster such as a great war or a general crop failure"—his optimistic forecast was further tempered only by one concluding sentence: "The only danger point of immediate importance which we may discern is the speculative situation: the props beneath the speculative price structure appear to be steadily growing less secure."[59]

The president of Moody's Investment Services in New York shortly thereafter contributed to the *Atlantic* an article in which he said, "All the European calamity prophets have been continually discredited. . . . In fact, a new age is taking form throughout the entire civilized world." But he concluded: "There is still as much truth as ever in the axiom that what is pushed up in speculative Wall Street is certain sooner or later to be pushed down." Rash "stock speculation is as dangerous as ever."[60]

[57] *American Prosperity* (New York: Viking, 1928).

[58] *JASA*, June 1928, 23:138–39.

[59] Laurence H. Sloan, "The Business Prospect in the United States," *EJ*, June 1928, 38:175–92. Sloan also noted: "We are in an era of business consolidations," some of which were induced by the profits of those who floated the stocks.

[60] John Moody, "The New Era in Wall Street," *Atlantic*, August 1928, pp. 255–62, esp. pp. 260, 262. Moody published three years earlier *Profitable Investing* (New York: Forbes Publishing Co., 1925), in ch. 2 of which he discussed investment vs. speculation.

In early October 1928 Colonel Ayres, addressing the American Bankers Association in Philadelphia, adverted to the transition to "a new economic era" in which heavy imports of gold would no longer provide a stimulus to the economy, but held that its difficulties could be surmounted:

We appear to be leaving behind us the wonderful golden age that we have enjoyed most of the time since the depression of 1921, during which prosperity has promised to be perpetual, the old-fashioned business cycles with their recurrent booms and depressions have been in abeyance, and the trend of stock prices has been almost constantly upward.

We may look forward to the longer future with confidence, for we shall have a larger gold supply in proportion to our needs than has any other country, and we have a central banking system that is probably more effective and efficient than that of any other country.[61]

Bernard M. Baruch was an avowed speculator who had made his fortune in Wall Street by the age of thirty and had won great acclaim, at home and abroad, for his leadership of the powerful War Industries Board in 1917–18. Early in 1929 he gave Bruce Barton a long interview, which was published in *The American Magazine* for June.[62] Its present significance lies primarily in the highly optimistic convictions that such a respected public figure had come to hold. Baruch stressed several factors in postwar American prosperity. These included the Federal Reserve Act, "which gave us coordinated control of our financial resources and made credit the servant of business instead of its master," and "a unified banking system"; "vastly expanded productive capacity and self-confidence"; the "shorter day and the increased wages . . . recognized by almost everybody as essential elements in prosperous business"; cooperation "within the ranks of business," and between government and business, "with results that are beyond measure"; standardization and simplification, and elimination of "wasteful inventories and interruptions of work"; and a "far wider fund of statistical knowledge than business men had ever had before."[63]

Baruch refused to be drawn into appraisals of the stock market or the short-run outlook, on which his private views were by no means wholly optimistic. On the dangers of financial panics and business depressions, however, he said: "we now have certain safeguards which never existed before: the Federal Reserve Bank [*sic*]; the better understanding and use of statistics by the nations, by banks, and industries, and by individuals; the coordination of the financial systems of all the leading nations; and the

---

[61]Fully reported in *Annalist*, Oct. 12, 1928, pp. 555–56.

[62]Pp. 26–27, 133–38. See *Baruch: My Own Story* (New York: Holt, 1957), chs. 7–11, and *Baruch: The Public Years* (New York: Holt, Rinehart and Winston, 1960), pp. 217–29. In neither book does he mention the Barton interview.

[63]A little later Albert Shaw, editor of the *Review of Reviews* (New York), went so far as to say (February 1930, p. 42): "We now run the country statistically."

great increase of human wants and ambitions throughout the world which, with occasional and temporary setbacks, ought to provide a huge volume of business for many years to come." Two of his concluding passages read: "There will, of course, be temporary setbacks due to causes perhaps more or less avoidable. Finance will be a limiting factor until that subject is better understood and worked out, but I am not speaking in terms of weeks or months when I say I think the great economic surge is forward. . . . When a man has made up his mind to believe in the country and its industries, and to go forward with them, he must be willing to take the temporary setbacks with the progress."

As Baruch much later set forth at length, he was characteristically apprehensive about the stock market from 1926 on, and by 1928 he had begun to liquidate his holdings. But the course of events repeatedly proved his sour predictions wrong, if only premature, and he kept on buying and selling stocks. Only near the end of September 1929 did he begin to sell everything he could in anticipation of the break that he now felt to be imminent. Like most others, however, he "never imagined, in those last months of 1929, that the collapse of stock prices was the prelude to the great depression."[64]

Baruch well knew the obstacles to world economic progress that were created by the ill-fated "making of the peace" and the obstinate problems of war debts and reparations, despite formal settlements gradually agreed upon. But he anticipated some such revision as was shortly arranged by the apparently definitive Young Plan that was initially reached in June 1929. In his Barton interview, indeed, he went so far as to say that "the economic condition of the world seems on the verge of a great forward movement" "which future historians may call the 'industrial renaissance.' " "We are within sight of the day," he said with amazing optimism, "when everybody in the world will have enough food all the time."

In his annual report for the year ending May 1, 1928, E. H. H. Simmons, president of the New York Stock Exchange, remarked "how great have been the steps toward financial stability and greater economic prosperity taken during the past three years"; "even in Berlin, Milan, and Vienna vast progress toward this goal has obviously been made." A year later he noted that "on the whole European finance perceptibly strengthened its position," commented on "the extraordinary security markets," the effect of the financial and business revolution, and blithely concluded: "With every due allowance for the factor of artificial manipulation, or for the occasional vagaries of excited public opinion, it still remains true that the stock market, considered as a collective mechanism, reflects basic economic forces and conditions much more accurately and

[64]*Baruch: The Public Years*, p. 229, published also in *Saturday Evening Post*, Oct. 1, 1960.

dependably than do the opinions or assertions of individuals, however experienced, gifted or profound." In the next year's report he belatedly acknowledged that the "New Era" phrase had been "productive of exaggerated notions of many kinds."[65]

In mid-July Emerson W. Axe, then a financial writer of repute and later an investment executive, held that the bull market was likely to peak in the fall, and that "there is a possibility of a serious decline." He concluded: "the political atmosphere is more favorable, from a Wall Street viewpoint, than it has been for a long time, possibly than ever before. The European situation is on the whole good—certainly better than at any time since the war. Finally, we are a creditor nation, and there is no telling how low long-term interest rates may finally go or how high investors' buying may push stock prices. . . . With the Reserve Board . . . powerless to tighten money further, the stock market is free, for several months at least, to work out its destiny in its own fashion."[66]

Benjamin Baker, another financial journalist, reviewing the business outlook late in July, found "no excuse for pessimism unless the observer takes with great seriousness . . . the threatening inflation in stock market prices and the inflation of member bank credit to which brokers' loans on high price levels have given rise."[67]

In August 1929 the *Ladies Home Journal* published an interview by Samuel Crowther with John J. Raskob entitled "Everybody Ought To Be Rich."[68] Raskob was the Du Pont-General Motors tycoon who had been a member of Hoover's committees, was chairman of the Democratic National Committee in 1928–32, and was an outstanding "bull" in the stock market.

One of the most extensive presentations of the New Era psychology appeared in September 1929, on the very eve of the stock market crash. Charles A. Dice, professor of business organization in the College of Commerce at Ohio State University, was the author of a widely-used textbook, *The Stock Market*, which went through seven printings in the 1920s, the last in August 1929. In that month Dice wrote the preface of his new book, *New Levels in the Stock Market*, which began by pointing to "a mighty revolution in industry, in trade, and in finance" which "has been making all things new in the United States." After "five years of the most extraordinary advances in the prices and the activity on the stock market," it had dawned upon the public that "a new day had come in the market; that a marvelous reconstruction was taking place in the economic fundamentals of our time;

[65]NYSE, *Annual Report* (1927–28), p. 20; (1928–29), pp. 5–7; (1929–30), p. 3.

[66]*Annalist*, July 19, 1929, pp. 95–96.

[67]*Ibid.*, July 26, 1929, pp. 153–54.

[68]Patterson, *Great Boom and Panic*, pp. 24–28, 47–49, 207. Raskob later turned against Roosevelt as he had against his predecessor. See Hoover, *Memoirs*, 2:296, 3:19, 128, 219–21, 232, 454–55.

and that the market was but registering the tremendous changes that were in progress."[69]

At the end of the first chapter, Dice mildly disclaimed membership in the club of " 'new-era' enthusiasts"; yet even there, and in the book as a whole, he made clear that he was one of them. He explicitly denied any implication "that we are through with major declines and advances" in the stock market—or in business. Yet his thesis was that "stocks have moved from a lower level, occupied from 1906 to 1923, to a relatively much higher level which will be permanent for some years to come." Though at times it "appears that average prices have discounted the growth of the country for some years into the future," he asserted: "The new level of prices is not fictitious, fundamentally. . . . the tremendous advances made since 1923 have been based for the most part on unprecedented fundamental developments in wealth, in the habits of people, in mass production, in efficient distribution, in the world of finance, in the attitude toward investments, and in public confidence." He explored the "new worlds" of industry, distribution, finance, and banking and the "new standard of living." He emphasized the "new trend of investments," argued that "the day of the small investor" had come, and viewed the investment trust movement as an outstanding financial development which is "loaded with tremendous possibilities for progress but is also fraught with many dangers." The book's concluding paragraph was a mixture of insight and blindness:

> Whatever accusations socialists may hurl; whatever criticisms labor leaders may raise; and however faulty and unsoundly based our confidences and faiths may be, the fact remains that they do exist as masterful elements in the stock market and business situation of our time. It is this sublime faith which furnishes the pillars for the new levels in the stock market and in business. How long this faith will continue to be a dynamic constructive factor depends upon the attitude of the scientists, the engineers, and the business and financial leaders. If they betray the confidence placed in them the wheel will turn quickly.[70]

Stuart Chase, already a prolific popular writer on economic affairs, wrote in the summer of 1929 *Prosperity: Fact or Myth*, drawing on two new works, *Recent Economic Changes* and the Lynds' *Middletown*. Chase recognized unsatisfactory aspects of the vaunted prosperity, and correctly saw

---

[69]Both *Stock Market* and *New Levels* were published by McGraw-Hill. The latter was advertised in *Annalist*, Oct. 18, 1929 (p. 767), six days before the panicky trading on October 24, when the volume reached a then unprecedented total of 12.9 million shares. Wilford J. Eiteman was joint author of the second, third, and fourth editions of *Stock Market*, published in 1941, 1952, and 1966, respectively.

[70]*New Levels*, passim, esp. pp. 3, 232, 260.

that it was real, but did not foresee its early end.[71] One of the few business economists who forecast the business contraction of 1929–30 well said, late in December 1929, "The increase of stock prices to unreasonable heights was based on the belief in a new era in which outstanding companies among those most successful would continue to increase their earnings forever, with, of course, increasing dividends forever, thus bringing about constantly increasing stock prices for such securities."[72] In 1939 Ayres accurately summed up the 1929 position thus: "Prosperity lasted so long, and permeated so many kinds of business, that it came to be rather generally believed that we had entered upon a genuine new era in which the problems of production had been largely solved, while those of equitable distribution were well on their way toward solution."[73]

Impressive European Developments, 1924–29   Beginning in mid-1924, the new spirit in Western Europe, the general return to the gold standard, the new arrangements on reparations and intergovernmental debts, and the progress of the League of Nations gave rise to a notable upsurge of optimism, there and here, replacing the stark pessimism over Europe that had been dominant for five years since mid-1919.[74] This strongly reinforced the New Era psychology in this country, led to great expansion in private loans to European central and municipal governments and in loans to and investments in private European enterprises, and encouraged European belief in permanent prosperity here. Despite some European skeptics, cautious appraisals by some Americans, and a waning of enthusiasm after mid-1928 in Western Europe, the growth of what later appeared as overconfidence continued through the summer of 1929. Baruch's

[71] In his later book, *The Nemesis of American Business and Other Essays* (New York: Macmillan, 1931), Chase said (p. 14): "Many of us at the time saw no reason why a stock market collapse should necessarily undermine business, and indeed there was none; but what most of us did not see was the extent of the black cloud over Detroit which had been gathering all summer." In an earlier book, *Men and Machines* (New York: Macmillan, 1929), he had written (p. 228): "If we should cease to buy automobiles at the present rate, what would happen to prosperity; would it go down like a house of cards?" As we have seen (Chapter 4 above), this was the subject of a discussion in a dinner meeting of the American Statistical Association in the spring of 1929, when the prospect of reduced output and sales was faced without deep concern.

[72] John G. Thompson of Simonds Saw and Steel Company, in *JASA*, March 1920, suppl., 25 (169A):50. Pertinent comments on the New Era psychology were made by several speakers at the Nov. 22, 1929, sessions of the Academy of Political Science, New York; see its *Proceedings*, January 1930, 13:456–57 (Hollander), 481 (Snyder—"the quite mythical 'new era' of the last five or six years"), 487 (Edgar Lawrence Smith), 494 (A. D. Noyes), 514–23 (Edie, "Putting the So-Called New Era to the Test").

[73] Ayres, *Turning Points*, pp. 43–44.

[74] Cf. John Moody, quoted above (p. 146). Some, of course, were slow to abandon their gloomy outlook; see Chapter 3 above.

good friend Churchill later summed up the situation as he saw it in May 1929:

> At the end of the second Baldwin Administration, the state of Europe was tranquil, as it had not been for twenty years, and was not to be for at least another twenty. A friendly feeling existed towards Germany following upon our Treaty of Locarno, and the evacuation of the Rhineland by the French Army and Allied contingents at a much earlier date than had been prescribed at Versailles. The new Germany took her place in the truncated League of Nations. Under the genial influence of American and British loans Germany was reviving rapidly. Her new ocean liners gained the Blue Riband of the Atlantic. Her trade advanced by leaps and bounds, and internal prosperity ripened. France and her system of alliances also seemed secure in Europe. The disarmament clauses of the Treaty of Versailles were not openly violated. The German Navy was non-existent. The German air force was prohibited and still unborn. There were many influences in Germany strongly opposed, if only on grounds of prudence, to the idea of war, and the German High Command could not believe that the Allies would allow them to rearm.[75]

In a valuable article on European government bonds written late in July 1928, the London *Economist* acclaimed the "soundly constructive results achieved . . . in the last few years in the political, economic and financial spheres. . . . The general return to the gold standard, the restoration of balanced national budgets, and the increasing productivity of European industry and agriculture, have all appreciably raised the value of . . . the 'equity' of good government on the Continent of Europe. . . . The Dawes Scheme and the Locarno Pacts have severally exerted noteworthy influence to that end."[76] Six months later a writer in the New York *Annalist* called attention to the ratification of the Kellogg-Briand Pact and observed: "During the last ten years . . . the Reich has staged one of the spectacular German come-backs. . . . Common sense, instead of bombastic rhetoric has become the dominating factor in Europe's international relations."[77]

[75]Winston S. Churchill, *The Second World War*, vol. 1: *The Gathering Storm* (Boston: Houghton Mifflin, 1948), ch. 2, "Peace at Its Zenith," esp. p. 31. He ended: "On the other hand, there lay before us what I later called the 'economic blizzard.' Knowledge of this was confined to rare financial circles, and these were cowed into silence by what they foresaw." Cf. Harold Macmillan, *Winds of Change, 1914–1939* (New York: Harper and Row, 1966), pp. 200, 202.

[76]*Economist*, July 28, 1928, pp. 184–85 (slightly altered in order). On the general return to the gold standard, see the glowing opening paragraph in O. M. W. Sprague's paper of Nov. 22, 1929, "The Working of the Gold Standard under Present Conditions," *Proc. Acad. Pol. Sci.*, January 1930, 13:524–34. Keynes gave a roseate summary of the period 1925–29 in the first of his two lectures in Chicago in June 1931. Quincy Wright, ed., *Unemployment as a World Problem* (Chicago: University of Chicago Press, 1931), pp. 4–5.

[77]Emil Lengyel, "The Economic Shaping of History Visible in Europe," *Annalist*, Jan. 25, 1929, pp. 231–32. Cf. *C&FC*, Mar. 9, 1929, pp. 1449–50. The Kellogg-Briand Pact of Paris was the subject of a session of the Academy of Political Science, New York, on Nov. 23, 1928, reported in *Proc. Acad. Pol. Sci.*, January 1929, 13:195–325.

The annual report of the Federal Reserve Board for 1928, dated February 25, 1929, expressed almost unqualified gratification over developments at home and abroad and stressed the fact that "much progress was made in monetary and financial reconstruction in foreign countries, and the reestablishment of the international gold standard was practically completed" (pages 1, 14–16). In his commencement address at George Washington University on February 22, 1929, President Coolidge gave a glowing account of the state of our foreign relations, seeing no important questions awaiting settlement and no clouds on the horizon.[78]

On the whole the "decade of recovery, progress and stability," 1919–29, witnessed remarkable achievements in continental Europe, both economic and political.[79] Agriculture in Western Europe, though still in financial straits, had largely recovered in output by 1925. Currencies had been restored and linked to gold; the world had once more a stable medium of exchange; national finances had been stabilized; trade and employment had greatly increased; unemployment had been reduced, and the unemployed were maintained at public expense "on a scale previously unknown." Germany had emerged from economic chaos into what seemed notable prosperity, and her relations with her neighbors had improved impressively. Apparently final settlements of reparations and war debts had been made. Progress in removing obstacles to international trade seemed promised by the "remarkable unanimity of the Economic Conference of 1927." "The broken countries of Central and South-eastern Europe were restored. . . . Capital was flowing freely to countries that needed development. The entry of Soviet Russia into the League seemed not far distant. Except in Italy, parliamentary government was extended. By 1928 the average level of living was generally higher than ever before.

Despite the absence of formal participation by the United States, both the League of Nations and the World Court made notable progress in their first ten years,[80] though without giving to the world the sense of security that hearty and full-fledged U.S. cooperation might have assured. By 1928, indeed, the League had "grown in strength and authority," was thoroughly established as a highly constructive world institution, and was at the peak

[78]Coolidge's account is summarized and partially quoted in *C&FC*, Feb. 23, 1929, p. 1273. Cf. Hoover's less roseate yet not wholly somber summary of the state of the world when he was inaugurated, in his *Memoirs*, 2:331.

[79]Ably summarized in Lord Salter, *Memoirs of a Public Servant* (London: Faber, 1961), pp. 171, 194–99. Similar views were expressed by Macmillan in his *Winds of Change*, ch. 8, esp. pp. 202 and 341.

[80]See *Ten Years of World Co-operation*, by the Secretariat of the League of Nations, with a foreword by Sir Eric Drummond (later Earl of Perth), its able secretary-general (Geneva: League of Nations, 1930), reviewed by H. D. Gideonse in *JPE*, October 1931, 39:684–85. It should be noted that Presidents Harding, Coolidge, and Hoover all urged United States membership in the World Court, but the Senate was obdurate in its opposition.

of its power and influence.[81] General Jan Smuts, one of the drafters of the covenant, said at Oxford on November 9, 1929:

Looked at in its true light, in the light of the age and of the time-honoured ideas and practice of mankind, we are beholding an amazing thing—we are witnessing one of the great miracles of history. . . .

The League may be a difficult scheme to work, but the significant thing is that the Powers have pledged themselves to work it, that they have agreed to renounce their free choice of action and bound themselves to what amounts in effect to a consultative parliament of the world. . . . The great choice is made, the great renunciation is over, and mankind has, as it were at the one bound and in the short space of ten years, jumped from the old order to the new, across a gulf which may yet prove to be the greatest break or divider in human history.[82]

Of special importance was the current appraisal of Germany's progress. S. Parker Gilbert's favorable interim report as agent general for reparations for the nine months ending May 31, 1929, published in July 1929,[83] registered confidence that Germany could meet the obligations embodied in the Young Plan on which the financial experts had agreed in June. Worked out on the then accepted assumption of continuing U.S. prosperity, this plan was widely viewed as providing a workable solution of the stubborn problems of reparations and interallied debt, and as inaugurating "a new era of international economic stability and prosperity."[84]

J. W. Angell's book on the recovery of Germany, written for the Council on Foreign Relations with a preface dated August 16, 1929, concluded with confidence and optimism. While recognizing that various factors will "hinder future growth in a number of directions, and discourage too roseate predictions," his final paragraph began: "But that Germany's expansion will continue in coming years seems assured." It ended with this sentence: "The road marked out for Germany through the coming decades is not easy, but it is a road which climbs steadily upward, and at its end lies the prize of assured national strength and prosperity."[85] It is significant that

[81]Salter, *Memoirs of a Public Servant*, ch. 9, esp. p. 200.

[82]Quoted in Sir Eric Drummond's foreword (pp. vi–vii) to *Ten Years of World Co-operation*. This impressive volume faithfully summarizes the organization and extensive activities of the League in 1920–30. Its annex 1 contains the League covenant as amended. See also Sir Philip Gibbs, "The League: A Ten-Year Record," *New York Times Magazine*, Jan. 5, 1930, and Lord Robert Cecil, "Ten Years of the League," *Living Age* (New York), Oct. 15, 1929, pp. 202–8.

[83]*Fed. Res. Bull.*, September 1929, 15:613–23; *Annalist*, July 26, 1929, p. 151.

[84]James W. Angell, "America's Role in the International Economic Situation," Nov. 14, 1930, in sessions titled "The Young Plan in Operation," published in *Proc. Acad. Pol. Sci.*, January 1931, 14:280–90. Angell said that "most people undoubtedly believed" this at the time.

[85]*The Recovery of Germany* (New Haven, Conn.: Yale University Press, 1929), p. 361. Sir Andrew McFadyean, then a key member of the staff, and Lady McFadyean became warm friends of the Angells. See McFadyean, *Recollected in Tranquillity* (London: Pall Mall Press, 1964), pp. 124–25.

Angell said in his preface that his book had been read in manuscript by E. F. Gay, by W. C. Mitchell, and by Charles P. Howland (who wrote the introduction) and the concluding chapter, "The Young Plan and Germany's Future," by John Foster Dulles; and that he acknowledged aid from a large number of well-known men, including Paul M. Warburg of New York, M. J. Bonn and Melchior Palyi (then of the Berlin Handelshochschule), Josef Schumpeter (then of the University of Bonn), Ernst Wagemann and Otto Nathan of the German Federal Statistical Office, and "various members of the staff of the Office for Reparation Payments, Berlin."

When the subject of German recovery was discussed at the year-end meeting of the American Economic Association, Angell and John H. Williams agreed that Germany's economic recovery in 1924–29 had been "perhaps the most remarkable . . . in the world's annals," and Williams expressed no reservations about Angell's conclusion as to the future. Reviewing Angell's book in June 1930, the Englishman W. J. Dawson called it "a sound piece of workmanship," adding that "in both diagnosis and prognosis Dr. Angell is backed by most well-informed opinion abroad." H. C. Simons, in his belated review of this book, called it a remarkably fine piece of journalism based on intensive investigation of less than a year, "a critical synthesis of competent German opinion in numerous fields." He noted a few points on which careful readers would dissent (pages 35, 36, 53, 211, 253, 272) and pointed to the meager attention given to the "transfer problem," but did not specifically comment on Angell's highly optimistic conclusion.[86]

Factors Reinforcing High Confidence, 1929   It remains to mention three factors which reinforced the remarkable superconfidence in 1929: the improved position of U.S. agriculture, the high reputation of the Federal Reserve System, and the extraordinary prestige of President Hoover.

Much was made in the 1920s of the plight of the American farmer,[87] after the great farm prosperity in wartime and the immediate aftermath, and in spite of the export stimulus provided by U.S. flotations of foreign loans in the middle 1920s. The common view long persisted that agriculture had never emerged from the depression that started in 1920–21.[88] Yet gross and net income in real terms in 1925–29 were not low compared with the prewar "golden years," when agriculture had enjoyed its greatest relative peace-

[86]Angell and Williams, *AER*, March 1930, 20(1):76–91; Dawson, *EJ*, June 1930, 40:290–93; Simons, *JPE*, April 1931, 34:263–66.

[87]William Allen White headed his contribution to the *Survey Graphic* of June 1, 1929 (pp. 281–83), "The Farmer—and His Plight." See my two reviews of several recent books on the agricultural situation in *QJE*, May 1929, 43:532–43; November 1929, 44:138–59.

[88]See Chapter 4 above. My own views underwent changes in the 1920s, as my published and unpublished papers reveal, but I never endorsed the more extreme views.

time prosperity, and outstanding agricultural economists had come to the conviction that the agricultural depression had ended in mid-decade. J. D. Black of Harvard wrote authoritatively in the winter of 1929:

> Although specific data are lacking, there is little doubt that the plane of living of farm families is considerably higher now than in 1910 to 1914. It has risen appreciably even since 1921. More farm families have motor cars now than in 1921, and probably fewer of them have cheap cars. There has been a rapid increase in the last 10 years, no doubt halted for a while in 1921 and 1922, in the number of farm homes with telephones, radios, lighting systems, water systems, furnaces, and electricity. Farm people are wearing much more nearly the same sort of clothes as city people than was true 10 years ago. There are sections of the country where no doubt these changes have not been very pronounced; but in others they have been little short of revolutionary.[89]

It was correctly argued, however, that farmers did not fully share in the prosperity of the decade; and agrarian agitation encouraged farmers to expect higher prices and incomes than economic forces could bring about, and to demand federal "action programs" to secure "fair prices" and "equality for agriculture." President Coolidge vetoed two McNary-Haugen bills, in February 1927 and May 1928. The National Grange's favorite proposal, the export debenture bill, failed to pass. Finally, early in his term, President Hoover pushed through the Congress the Agricultural Marketing Act of June 15, 1929 (without the export debenture provisions), and set up the Federal Farm Board on July 15 with Alexander Legge, president of the International Harvester Company, as chairman and with a revolving fund of $500 million. This was the forerunner of the far more ambitious New Deal program for agriculture.[90]

Late in 1929 three reputable agricultural economists summed up the farm situation fairly optimistically. Black referred to the "emergence from agricultural depression five or six years ago," the fairly stable level of net cash income in the three crop years ending June 30, 1929, and the improvement in the agricultural land situation despite "a vast volume of foreclosures still in process."[91]

A. B. Genung of the Department of Agriculture, summing up the 1929 agricultural season late in the year, concluded that "the current conditions of supply and markets this fall are as stable and about as favorable to

---

[89] *Agricultural Reform in the United States* (New York: McGraw-Hill, 1929; preface dated April 1929), p. 11.

[90] Anderson, *Economics and the Public Welfare*, pp. 220–22.

[91] HES, *Weekly Letter*, Dec. 14, 1929, pp. 298, 303. Earlier and later, Black wrote other unsigned issues of the *Weekly Letter* and signed articles in *Rev. Ec. Stat.* on the agricultural situation and outlook. In March 1929 R. J. McFall went so far as to say that "the purchasing power of the farmers' personal income is as good as in the postwar boom and materially better than in the best prewar years." *Annals*, 142:149.

farmers as they were in 1925 and except for that year are the best since 1920." "Agriculture," he said, "is undoubtedly in position to contribute a stabilizing element to the general business situation this winter. It will be a help, not a drag on business as was true in 1921."[92]

From the same department, Louis H. Bean observed that the "recent upward tendency in agricultural product prices" had restored the relative level to "above the long-term upward trend, or about 112 in 1928 and 1929 compared with the same level in the war years" 1918–19. He rashly added that it was quite likely that the long-time upward trend in the relative position of agricultural prices would continue, despite "temporary recessions lasting several years."[93]

President Hoover had said in his first State of the Union message (December 3, 1929): "The agricultural situation is improving. . . . The slight decline in general commodity prices during the past few years naturally assists the farmers' buying power. The number of farmer bankruptcies is very materially decreased below previous years. The decline in land values now seems to be arrested and rate of movement from the farm to the city has been reduced. . . . Responsible farm leaders have assured me that a large measure of confidence is returning to agriculture and that a feeling of optimism pervades that industry."[94]

Despite many and varied criticisms of Federal Reserve policy, actions, and inaction in 1927–29, there developed extraordinary confidence that the System could be relied upon to meet a recession and reverse it before it had gone to excess. Warburg, one of its severest critics in March 1929 (see Chapter 7 below) referred in his 1930 book to the country's "unbounded confidence in the unequaled strength of the Federal Reserve System and the availability of its vast resources to the country's banks."[95] This conviction underlay the well-nigh unanimous agreement of the analysts that the anticipated setback would be moderate and short-lived. It pervaded the able presentations by the Harvard Economic Society in 1929, and the paper written by its key staff man, W. L. Crum, in August–September 1929.

Other clearheaded students of financial developments lent support to this view. Two of these were key senior staff men in the Federal Reserve Bank of New York. Carl Snyder late in 1928 referred to "our now centralized and unified banking system"[96]—though it was actually neither "centralized" nor "unified," despite steps in this direction under the Federal

[92]*JASA*, March 1930, suppl., 25(169A):58–63. By and large, Genung's position was supported in Black's careful articles.

[93]Louis H. Bean, "Agriculture in the Post-War Decade," *ibid.*, pp. 155–57.

[94]Hoover, *State Papers and Other Public Writings of Herbert Hoover*, ed. William Starr Myers, 2 vols. (Garden City, N.Y.: Doubleday, 1934), 1:146–47.

[95]Paul M. Warburg, *The Federal Reserve System: Its Origin and Growth: Reflections and Recollections*, 2 vols. (New York: Macmillan, 1930), 2:501–17.

[96]In his ASA presidential address, Dec. 28, 1928, *JASA*, March 1929, 24:141.

Reserve System. W. Randolph Burgess, usually reliable if somewhat restrained in such writings as his *The Reserve Banks and the Money Market*, wrote in the spring of 1929:

> Just how important the influence of the Reserve System has been in retarding speculative booms and in relieving business depression and unemployment, no one can say. . . .
>
> But it may safely be asserted that the Reserve System has been a powerful force toward business stability and toward the stability of employment. The Reserve System has been lauded for its aid in the return of Europe to the gold standard and to monetary stability. It has been lauded for its prevention of money panics. But over a long term of years it seems reasonable to expect that more important than any of these may be its influence toward leveling out the booms and depressions which in past times have brought with them so much of human unhappiness and distress.[97]

Stanford's respected A. C. Whitaker, an acute and critical student, said without qualification in his paper at the American Economic Association meetings late in 1929: "Despite the two great price booms and collapses we have experienced since its foundation, one in commodities and one in stocks, the Federal Reserve system is one of the most brilliant successes among our political and economic institutions."[98]

As early as 1920 Herbert Hoover was widely recognized as an outstanding "engineer-economist-organizer" and as good presidential timber, and some influential Democrats (among them young F. D. Roosevelt) wanted him to be given that party's nomination.[99] After he announced himself as a Republican, the party politicians never warmed to him: they saw victory so assured that there was no reason to nominate so independent a figure, who had spent much of his mature life abroad. He enhanced his public reputation, notably among businessmen, by an outstanding record as secretary of commerce from 1921 to 1928. Though he was amazingly loyal to Presidents Harding and Coolidge, his abilities quite dwarfed theirs, and after two extremely weak administrations the public seemed ready for another strong president. Effective publicity had built up his reputation, until he came to be hailed as the "greatest Republican of his generation," the "symbol of a prosperity created by enlightened economic statesman-

[97]"The Balance Wheel of Gold," *Survey Graphic*, Apr. 1, 1929, pp. 23–24, 82–84, esp. p. 84. The Sprague-Burgess chapter in *Recent Economic Changes* had been completed in the autumn of 1928. The first edition of Burgess' *Reserve Banks* was published by Harper in 1927.

[98]*AER*, March 1930, suppl., 20(1):97.

[99]See Joseph S. Davis, "Herbert Hoover, 1874–1964: Another Appraisal," *South Atlantic Quarterly*, Summer 1969, pp. 295–318. In his latest book, published after my paper was written, a veteran journalist expressed views in broad harmony with mine: Arthur Krock, *Memoirs: Sixty Years on the Firing Line* (New York: Funk and Wagnalls, 1968), esp. ch. 10, "Hoover," pp. 122–43. See also Gene Smith, *The Shattered Dream: Herbert Hoover and the Great Depression* (New York: Morrow, 1970), pp. 85–86.

ship"—indeed, a veritable "miracle worker." There were doubters and snipers, of course, and Hoover himself realized the danger of excessive confidence in him,[100] but his overwhelming election in November 1928 was commonly viewed as ensuring indefinite continuation of prosperity and advance. As a leading journalist wrote early in March 1930: "We were in a mood for magic."[101]

In short, it is hardly possible to exaggerate the extent to which Americans and foreigners agreed, at least into September 1929, that the United States was outstandingly strong, prosperous, sound, and resilient, and that the momentum of its progress was unstoppable. This conviction strengthened the hope that the world had entered a new era of peace, prosperity, and progress. Here and abroad, people were utterly unprepared for the stock market crash and the drastic contraction and depression that followed.

[100]To the Gridiron Club he said on Apr. 13, 1929: "One of the primary difficulties of a new administration is the over-expectation which is aroused in political combat. The hopes for immediate solution of long-deferred problems of extraordinary difficulty are always raised to the anticipation that some magic or miracle is about to take place which will realign the whole social and economic system." Hoover added that the only miracle of his engineering profession was "constant and everlasting building with brick on brick and stone on stone." Hoover, *State Papers*, 1:27–31, esp. p. 30.

[101]The opening sentence of Anne O'Hare McCormick's "The First Year of the Hoover Method," *New York Times Magazine*, Mar. 2, 1930. She ended: "We no longer look for miracles and infallible economic solutions of political problems. That may be a valuable preface to the new political primer."

CHAPTER 7

SIGNIFICANT WARNINGS, LARGELY UNHEEDED

MANY OF THOSE who were predominantly optimistic in the 1920s voiced incidental reservations and mild warnings, as we have seen. It was generally accepted that there would be ups and downs in business activity, even though another severe depression came to seem highly improbable. Minor and substantial fluctuations in the stock market were viewed as inevitable, even normal. Careful students of business and the stock market tried to foresee and forecast their courses, with limited success, and at times issued warnings of recession or market declines. But only a few individuals and journals voiced trenchant criticism of private practices, public policies, and economic trends; really significant public warnings were scarce even in midsummer 1929; and almost no one foresaw the drastic collapse that came in the year 1930 or the subsequent catastrophic course of events. J. W. Angell was substantially right when he wrote, early in 1932, before the contraction had reached bottom: "*I know of no competent student who anticipated a world depression of such cataclysmic magnitude as the years actually brought.*"[1]

After the stock market crash, some claimed that ample warnings had been given. Walter Lippmann, in mid-1930, wrote that Hoover "took office at a time when the most experienced business men, bankers, and economists were pointing out the symptoms of extreme danger."[2] E. W. Kemmerer wrote in 1932: "Of course, such a speculative boom could not last indefinitely, and, when the collapse should come, not only the participants but practically everybody else would have to suffer. Countless warnings of the danger were given by prominent economists and financiers and by our Federal reserve authorities, but they were unheeded by the great masses of the people."[3] We have almost no means of knowing what professors of economics said to their classes, but careful exploration of the literature of the period—books, pamphlets, periodicals, and association proceedings— fails to bear out these statements. Very few warnings were either emphatic

---

[1] J. W. Angell, *The Recovery of Germany*, 2d ed. (New Haven, Conn.: Yale University Press, 1932), p. 372 (italics added).

[2] Walter Lippmann, "The Peculiar Weakness of Mr. Hoover," *Harper's*, June 1930, pp. 1–7. In the *Atlantic* in June 1929 (pp. 52, 54), R. A. Thorndike had referred to "the alarmist school of bankers and financial men."

[3] E. W. Kemmerer, "The Gold Standard in the United States," in J. G. Smith, ed., *Facing the Facts: An Economic Diagnosis* (New York: Putnam, 1932), p. 7.

or thoroughgoing. A stock market decline was expected, sooner or later, but its severity and manifold repercussions were not forthrightly predicted.

J. T. Adams, who later called the 1920s "a mad decade," went so far as to write: "As the decade drew toward its end, America was living in the fantastic dreams of opium or delirium."[4] In the prevailing climate of opinion, the discordant voices of a critical minority were drowned out. Yet it is pertinent here to mention various warnings that were sounded in 1925–29.

Herbert Hoover's Views   Because of his key positions in the federal government in 1921–33, and because he was an outstanding victim of the "economic blizzard," Herbert Hoover's views have special importance. As his *Memoirs* make clear, he was long concerned over the business cycle and worried by the course of speculative activities.[5] "Reduction of the great waste of booms and slumps of the 'business cycle' with their intermittent waves of unemployment and bankruptcy" was among the "major directions for national effort" outlined by the Department of Commerce early in his secretaryship.[6] On September 12, 1921, the President's Business Conference appointed a Committee on Business Cycles and Unemployment, which Hoover also chaired. At its first meeting he rightly sized up this problem thus: "Booms are times of speculation, overexpansion, wasteful expenditures in industry and commerce, with consequent destruction of capital. . . . It is the wastes, the miscalculations and maladjustments, grown rampant during the booms, that make unavoidable the painful process of liquidation. The obvious way to lessen the losses and miseries of depression is first to check the destructive extremes of booms. Mitigation of depressions is a further task of relief and reconstruction." In reviewing the progress of the committee's investigation in a report to the Congress, Hoover added: "The 'business cycle' of course is not based alone upon purely economic forces. It is to some considerable degree the product of waves of confidence or caution—optimism or pessimism. Movements gain much of their acceleration from these causes, and they in turn are often the product of political or other events, both domestic and foreign, and even climatic conditions may play an important part."[7]

Late in 1925, when Benjamin Strong, Montagu Norman, and continental European central bank governors were discussing a program of central bank actions to ease money and expand credit, Secretary Hoover

---

[4]James Truslow Adams, *The March of Democracy*, 2 vols. (New York: Scribner, 1932–33), 2:393.

[5]See the last two volumes of *The Memoirs of Herbert Hoover* (New York: Macmillan, 1951–52): *The Cabinet and the Presidency, 1920–1933*, esp. pp. 62–63, 174–76, and 388, and *The Great Depression, 1929–1941*, pp. 5–19.

[6]Hoover, *Memoirs*, 2:62–63.

[7]*Ibid.*, pp. 174–75.

vigorously protested to Federal Reserve Board Governor D. R. Crissinger, and prepared drafts of a series of letters which Wisconsin Senator Lenroot passed on to Crissinger. One, dated November 25, 1925, referred to "the proposed American-British financial understanding" and to the speculative atmosphere in the United States and included the "ominous prophecy" that these policies meant "inflation with inevitable collapse which will bring the greatest calamities upon our farmers, our workers and legitimate business."[8] For the time, these warnings exerted an influence.

During 1926, in speeches at Staunton, Virginia, on March 20 and at Caldwell, Idaho, on August 17, Hoover warned that "reckless speculation would undermine our prosperity." His annual report as secretary of commerce dated November 2, 1926, included his blunt observations, based on his conviction that the Federal Reserve System (under the influence of Governor Strong) was deliberately creating credit inflation: "Many previous crises have arisen through the credit machinery through no fault of either the producer or consumer. . . . That the Federal Reserve System should be so managed as to result in stimulation of speculation and overexpansion has received universal disapproval."

When he failed to win President Coolidge and Secretary Mellon to his alarmist views, however, Secretary Hoover's public warnings ceased. In deference to the president's position, he kept silent as the movement developed apace in 1927–29. In a significant passage in his *Memoirs*, he noted Coolidge's reluctance "to take any action in advance of the actual explosion of trouble," which left him "wholly unprepared" when this arrived with "such momentum that it spelled disaster. The outstanding instance," he went on, "was the rising boom and orgy of mad speculation which began in 1927, in respect to which he rejected or sidestepped all our anxious urgings and warnings to take action."

The political conditions of 1928 and 1929 were highly unfavorable both for attacks on speculation and for official warnings or gloomy predictions. The outgoing president delighted in the phrase "Coolidge prosperity," and, as his term approached its end, embarrassed his successor by pronouncing stocks cheap at current prices.[9] The Republican candidate for this office could not be expected to seek votes by voicing criticisms of the strangely popular incumbent, by pointing to significant or critical weaknesses in the U.S. economy, or by rubbing the gloss off the picture of an absolutely prosperous country. Nor could the Democratic candidate hope to win by voicing alarm, and he chose as chairman of the Democratic National Committee a rampant Wall Street bull, the tycoon J. J. Raskob.

    [8]William Starr Myers and Walter H. Newton, *The Hoover Administration: A Documented Narrative* (New York: Scribner, 1936), pp. 9–10.
    [9]Hoover, *Memoirs*, 2:16.

Finally, President Hoover's first half year was packed with programs for development and reform, in high confidence that the economy was truly basically sound. In his inaugural address he said: "The strong man must at all times be alert to the attack of insidious disease." He was "fully alive" to the dangers inherent in the stock boom, but his attempts "to stop the orgy of speculation" were so gentle as to be futile.[10] He doubtless believed, in 1920–29, what he said on May 1, 1929: "All slumps are inexorable consequences of the destructive force of booms."[11] But he did not touch on this national problem in his inaugural, which ended on a highly optimistic note.

Moreover, he gave no public sign of recognizing—and probably did not recognize—the "destructive extremes" of the business boom which was approaching its climax when he succeeded to the presidency, and he evinced no eagerness to restrain it. On the contrary, he quietly but firmly resisted Federal Reserve efforts to check the speculative orgy in the early months of his administration (see Chapter 5 above). Nor did he follow his favorite practice of assembling a group of leaders to consider the problem and make recommendations. After the Wall Street crash the president was particularly concerned to restore the public confidence that had been severely shaken, and early in December 1929 he rashly asserted his conviction that that confidence had been reestablished (see Chapter 8 below). Like his predecessor, indeed, he repeatedly laid himself open to Adams' scornful charge of uttering "Pollyanna nonsense."[12]

One can made a reasonable guess at the reasons for Hoover's failure to give high priority, in 1928–29, to what proved to be the crucial problem of his presidency, which he seems never to have publicly explained or even admitted. This much is fairly clear: he was convinced that the U.S. economy was fundamentally sound and strong; he viewed a collapse of the "orgy of speculation" as inevitable; he urged that the Federal Reserve System prepare to meet this shock; and he felt confident that its impact could be kept within tolerable limits. On these points he relied on a large body of what he considered competent opinion, and he was naturally unwilling to begin his term by making statements that might precipitate a reversal of the prosperity to which he had recently pointed with great pride.

[10]*Ibid.*, pp. 56, 223ff.; *ibid.*, vol. 3, ch. 2; J. K. Galbraith, *The Great Crash 1929* (Boston: Houghton Mifflin, 1955), pp. 18–22, 57–58; Charles A. Dice, *New Levels in the Stock Market* (New York: McGraw-Hill, 1929), p. 9.

[11]Address to the U.S. Chamber of Commerce, in Hoover, *State Papers and Other Public Writings of Herbert Hoover*, ed. William Starr Myers, 2 vols. (Garden City, N.Y.: Doubleday, 1934), 1:289–96, esp. p. 290. He added: "The effect of them is to divert capital and energy from healthy enterprise—the only real source of prosperity."

[12]James Truslow Adams, *The Tempo of Modern Life* (New York: Boni, 1931), esp. pp. 259–300. This paper preceded by about two years Adams' articles "Presidential Prosperity" (*Harper's*, August 1930, pp. 257–67) and "Pollyanna: Our Patron Goddess" (*Forum*, November 1930, pp. 237–62), both reprinted in *Tempo*, pp. 259–300, which deal also with Hoover's statements.

Other Warnings, Mild and   A single group of foreign visitors in the mid-
Trenchant, 1925–28   1920s—German trade unionists—voiced the
belief that U.S. prosperity had within it "the seeds of its later undoing."[13]
Moritz J. Bonn, Paul Einzig, and Sir George Paish were among the few
other foreign observers who recurrently took exception to the prevailing
optimism over the domestic and foreign situations in the second half of the
1920s.

Bonn's sober analyses of the European situation were not always
welcome to his audiences and readers in this country or his own. He
warned, as did the agent general for reparations in his official reports and
as Dr. Schacht did repeatedly, of the dangers of reckless German state and
municipal borrowing for nonproductive projects and of "irrational rationalization" in a period of "borrowed prosperity." In the summer of 1926, Bonn
wrote much later,

the era of permanent prosperity was dawning. It intoxicated everybody, even those
who had not yet been toppled over by the equally exhilarating stimulants of Pro-
hibition. As usual I was deeply impressed by the marvelous technical strides America was taking; yet I was disturbed by its cocksure optimism and its carbonated
swagger. My friends assured me that the second industrial revolution had found the
key to permanent prosperity; but when I asked to have a look at it, nobody could
produce it. Behind all the braggadocio and the boasting, I could hear the still small
voice of fear; when people had time to think they were worried. Some of my Continental colleagues, who had come to the United States for the first time, were
swept off their feet. One of them felt bound to write the customary book on America, rightly called *The American Economic Miracle*, for he could neither understand nor explain it.[14]

At the Institute of Politics in the summer of 1926 Bonn correctly predicted
as inevitable the impending fall of prices. His book *The Destiny of German
Capitalism*, published in 1927, warned of the "impending catastrophe,"
and closed with the words: "Surely the fate of German capitalism is in very
weak hands." But his words fell on deaf ears.[15]

In mid-May 1925 the Harvard Economic Service observed "the existence of a considerable excess of capacity in many branches of industry,

---

[13]E. F. Gay, in his introduction to *Recent Economic Changes*, 1:1–2, citing *Amerikareise
deutscher Gewerkschaftsführer* (1926). For Keynes' views on this point in 1930, see his *A
Treatise on Money*, 2 vols. (New York: Harcourt Brace, 1930), 2:378–82, and in 1933, in his
Means to Prosperity (London: Macmillan, 1933), p. 19.

[14]M. J. Bonn, *Wandering Scholar* (New York: Day, 1948), pp. 300–301, 305–6.

[15]This "was republished four years later in an enlarged edition" and was "a great
literary success," but "had no influence on those to whom my warning was addressed."
Bonn later admitted that he lacked some essential qualifications of a prophet, but concluded
that if his writings had been more effective they "would not have diverted the course of history. Those who swim against the current may occasionally reach dry land: eventually they
may even discover the source of the river. But they cannot turn the flood." *Ibid.*, pp. 299, 306,
392.

especially in those producing basic materials or staple commodities intended for sale to ultimate consumers."[16] This point received little or no emphasis in the next four years, as industrial expansion continued apace, and its scope was not widely appreciated in mid-1929.

On May 21, 1925, Benjamin Strong, the outstanding governor of the leading Federal Reserve Bank (New York), wrote a memorandum to his trusted aide, Carl Snyder, in which he correctly noted three disturbing developments: "One is overbuilding and real estate speculation. Another is too much enthusiasm in automobile production, and the third, of course, is the ever-present menace of the stock exchange speculation." And on November 7, 1925, he wrote to Governor Norman of the Bank of England: "It seems a shame that the best sort of plans can be handicapped by a speculative orgy, and yet the temper of the people of this country is such that these situations cannot be avoided." Their anxiety and bafflement continued as all three tendencies persisted, but apparently neither ever spoke out strongly in public about it. Strong's biographer noted that "rising stock speculation was a major reason for initiating mildly restrictive [Federal Reserve] policies in 1925, in early 1926, and again in late 1926."[17] Yet for other major purposes, mainly to combat domestic contraction and to relieve European financial strains, and despite the admitted risk of stimulating speculation, Strong led the movement to ease money rates in 1927, when from July 29 to mid-September all Federal Reserve Banks bought securities and acceptances and lowered their discount rates from 4 to 3.5 percent (see Chapter 5 above).

Illness severely handicapped Strong during the following year, and he died on October 16, 1928, before the most crucial months of the speculative advance. As early as May 7, 1928, he had written:

There are of course, always two dangers confronting us. One is a serious, violent and calamitous collapse of stocks. I regard that as rather slight so long as there is always a supply of funds at some price. The other is that either advancing rates for money or a combination of advancing rates for money and a collapse of stock prices will have an adverse effect upon business. That is where discretion must be shown as to the extent to which aggressive action is taken. There is, of course, another remote danger, but one of which I have little fear just now, namely that the high money rates would so restrict our loan market as to have a definitely adverse effect upon our foreign trade at the same time that large balances were returning to this country from Europe. That danger is much less than it was, and is one that can be promptly remedied after a wholesome dose of medicine has been administered in curing the domestic situation.

[16]HES, *Weekly Letter*, May 16, 1925, pp. 149–50.
[17]Lester V. Chandler, *Benjamin Strong: Central Banker* (Washington, D.C.: Brookings Institution, 1958), ch. 12, esp. pp. 423, 428, 435. See also Sir Henry Clay, *Lord Norman* (London: Macmillan, 1957), esp. ch. 6. Norman's concern was manifested as early as December 1924, and increased through October 1929.

The really fundamental difficulty in a number of these matters is lack of courage to act effectively or sufficiently effectively and with sufficient promptness so that the remedy is accomplished without damaging consequences.[18]

Actually, the more "remote danger" materialized in mid-1928, so far as foreign loans were concerned; the other dangers materialized within eighteen months, despite the abundance of Federal Reserve credit.

On July 14, 1928, Strong wrote S. Parker Gilbert, the agent general for reparation payments: "No one realizes more than I do that the continued maintenance of very high rates in New York may ultimately present a real hazard to the smooth operation of the Dawes Plan. It may indeed provoke the very crisis which you seek to avoid, and which should be avoided if it does not involve unreasonable sacrifices at home."[19]

While successful in its immediate aims, the 1927 easing of credit greatly stimulated advances in the stock market. The Reserve System's open-market sales of government securities, and three successive increases in the New York Bank's discount rate in February–July 1928, were ineffective in checking further "inflation" of security prices. The annual report of the secretary of the treasury for fiscal 1928 (dated November 20) somewhat surprisingly observed with reference to this Federal Reserve action that it "unquestionably was not effective with reference to speculation, partly due to the activities of powerful groups of speculators, and partly due to the fact that *the public in general believed and acted as if the prices of securities would indefinitely advance.*"[20] Secretary Mellon may have repeatedly urged caution, but his best-publicized action was to suggest to "prudent investors," in mid-March 1929, that "now is the time to buy good bonds."[21]

The conservative Lawyers Mortgage Company ran advertisements in July–September 1922, and in many later months of 1923–26, warning of "a day of reckoning in mortgage securities."[22] Irving Allen contributed to

[18]Letter to Professor O. M. W. Sprague, with whom he frequently consulted, in Chandler, *Strong*, pp. 432–35.

[19]*Ibid.*, p. 459. See Gilbert's reports in *Fed. Res. Bull.*, e.g., February, September 1929, 15:126–47, 613–23, and *C&FC*, July 27, 1929, pp. 564–65.

[20]P. 5 (italics added). Noyes, after citing this in his reminiscences (*The Market Place: Reminiscences of a Financial Editor* [Boston: Little, Brown, 1938], p. 358), also said that Secretary Mellon voted unsuccessfully as a member of the Federal Reserve Board for more urgent restriction of speculative use of credit. Adolph C. Miller, another Board member who dissented on its 1927 action, severely criticized it before a Senate committee in 1931, and Lionel Robbins virtually accepted Miller's extreme view in his book *The Great Depression* (London: Macmillan, 1934; preface dated June 1934), pp. 52–54. As we have seen (Chapter 6 above), Miller was a member of the Committee on Recent Economic Changes. Noyes discusses the action in *Market Place*, pp. 315–16.

[21]*C&FC*, Mar. 16, 1929, p. 1635. In his *Memoirs* (3:17) Hoover later wrote, "Secretary . . . Mellon and others, at my request, issued repeated statements urging the public to convert their stocks into bonds and advising other forms of caution. This also had no effect."

[22]E.g., *Annalist*, Sept. 10, 1926, p. 240, and *ibid.*, June 14, 1927, pp. 52–54.

The Annalist in May–September 1926 a series of articles on elements of unsoundness in financing real-estate development, but in his mid-June 1927 article he overoptimistically reported "progressive elimination of unsound practices." Actually, they persisted.

Edgar Lawrence Smith contributed to the *Atlantic* of October 1927 a big article, "British Investment Trusts—A Warning," on the very eve of the mushroom growth of U.S. investment companies.[23] Kenneth S. Van Strum, the financial analyst whose 1926 book on the virtues of common stock investments was cited above (see Chapter 4, above), wrote this highly prophetic paragraph in his second book, published in 1927, under the heading "Prosperity Will Not Be Eternal":

Since 1921 business has been neither very active nor very dull. It has been a period of moderate prosperity, during which the idea has become prevalent that business extremes—severe depressions and periods of intense prosperity—are things of the past. Such prolonged periods of moderate prosperity as this, however, are not new in the history of industry, for they have occurred frequently in many different countries. *And it generally happens that as the impression becomes more universal that prosperity is to continue indefinitely, a period of intense prosperity followed by a severe depression approaches.*[24]

But as this impression came to be widespread in 1927–29, though under attack in a few respected quarters and never universally held, even this author apparently forgot his own warning (see Chapter 8 below).

Early in 1927 the financial editor of the *Brooklyn Eagle* said: "The fundamentals of American finances and industry are sound as the year turns. . . . The seeds of danger lie in overextended stock and real estate speculation, and in the too rapid expansion of installment buying. There is little pessimism."[25] Other able commentators believed, as Noyes then put it: "Experience is wholly against perpetual continuance of uninterrupted trade activity." Yet the New York *Sun*'s Franz Schneider, Jr., concluded that "analysis of prevailing economic and financial factors reveals no convincing ground for expecting depression. On the contrary, such an analysis encourages the belief in continued prosperity." Colonel Ayres of the Cleveland Trust Company observed: "The outlook is for restrained good times rather than for speculative prosperity." And B. M. Anderson of the Chase National Bank said there was "no certainty that the extraordinary period of activity which the last two and a half years have witnessed may not con-

---

[23]Quoted in his paper of Nov. 22, 1929, "The Bank and the Investment Trust," in *Proc. Acad. Pol. Sci.*, January 1930, 13:487–93. Smith was then listed as "President, Irving Investors Management Company, Inc."

[24]*Forecasting Stock Market Trends* (Boston: Barron's, 1927), p. 299. His phrase "moderate prosperity" was out of tune with then-current foreigners' exaggerations.

[25]Selected New Year appraisals quoted in *Annalist*, Jan. 7, 1927, p. 2, in a summary signed by Benjamin Baker.

tinue for a time." Later figures showed a persistent contraction in industrial production and business activity in April–November 1927, which had not been forecast early in the year; yet both curves turned up before the situation became serious.[26]

The Harvard Economic Service recognized the "new high levels" of stock prices as early as October 1925, and Crum had recently asserted "the likelihood that the present period of prosperity will ultimately terminate in another period of depression," at some unforeseeable date. It seems surprising that the HES did not take more seriously the very high and rising level of its Curve A, "Speculation," in 1927–29, which necessitated repeated revisions in its charts. In its 1928 midyear review it commented on the "fundamentally healthy condition" of the banks despite "a spectacular outburst of speculative activity and the extremely rapid outward movement of gold"; and unseasonably high money rates in August were attributed to "speculative excesses and not business unsoundness."[27] But the "speculative excesses" were not openly treated as truly dangerous.

There must have been many in the 1920s who regarded the extreme New Era doctrines as a delusion;[28] yet very few forthrightly said so at the time, and I have been unable to find any careful analysis of this concept in the pre-crash or early post-crash literature.

As president of the American Statistical Association, Carl Snyder prevailed upon Paul Clay, of Moody's Investors Service, to present a paper on currently injurious financial fallacies on December 28, 1928. Clay said in part: "First among these fallacies is the new era delusion as typified by the famous dictum, 'This is a new era. Statistics of the past don't count.' Every period of great prosperity is considered to be a new era and so much better fortified as to give promise of permanence. However, each experience has been that the improvement in commercial and financial methods has ultimately been overcome by credit inflation and business rashness, resulting in another backward movement." His general conclusion was that "investors should focus their attention upon economic forces, and especially upon those forces which have promoted the growth of American industries."[29]

Having said this, however, Clay was among the restrained optimists in 1929. At a dinner meeting of the American Statistical Association on March 14, 1929, he saw "depression . . . in the offing." "The boom in

---

[26]See Cleveland Trust Company charts, 1940 and 1971 editions.

[27]HES, *Weekly Letter*, Oct. 31, 1925, p. 330; June 30, Aug. 18, Oct. 20, 1928, pp. 156, 187–88, 263–64. See also W. L. Crum, "The Interpretation of the Index of General Business Conditions," *Rev. Ec. Stat.*, September 1925, suppl., 7:217–35, esp. pp. 218, 224, 232–34. The revision of this paper four years later is discussed above, pp. 126–27.

[28]Among these was Wesley C. Mitchell; see Chapter 13 below.

[29]Clay, "Blither and Blah," *JASA*, March 1929, suppl., 24(165A):144–45.

stocks," he said, "will last just as long as optimism and confidence continue, for it is purely psychological in nature." He reminded his hearers "that overconfidence has always been followed by fear." Yet he predicted that the coming depression would "probably be short-lived because . . . the underlying supports of industry are at present so well buttressed," and that after a deflation of 15 to 25 percent of mid-March stock prices "business will be left in a thoroughly secure position."[30]

William Trufant Foster, pioneer president of Reed College (1910–20), and Waddill Catchings, his Harvard classmate, who was with Goldman, Sachs and Company in 1918–30, collaborated in producing a series of books in the 1920s aimed at persuading the public that the U.S. economy would sooner or later founder on the shoals of inadequate purchasing power. These books, and Foster's many articles on the same theme, had something of a vogue, but were never taken very seriously by economists or the financial community.[31]

From the late 1920s into the 1970s, E. C. Harwood has recurrently voiced warnings of dangerous tendencies and impending troubles or disasters, with special emphasis on inflation.[32] In January 1928 he set forth reasons for asserting that "Inflation Is Here," contrary to the still widely accepted view that the course of the index of wholesale prices indicated a surprising absence of price inflation. Capital investment, facilitated by credit arrangements, had exceeded savings. That spring he warned that the tendency of banks to increase the proportion of nonliquid assets might cause trouble, though he considered the banking organization excellent and saw no danger of a financial panic or serious banking crisis if the Federal Reserve managed properly. He considered that underconsumption because

---

[30]*JASA*, June 1929, 24:182–83.

[31]*Money* (1923), *Business without a Buyer* (1927), *The Road to Plenty* (1927), *Profits* (1928), *Progress and Plenty* (1930). The Pollak Foundation for Economic Research, of which Foster was director in 1920–50, published most of these as well as other books. An outstanding British economist, Dennis H. Robertson, wrote a critical review of their views in "The Monetary Doctrines of Messrs. Foster and Catchings," *QJE*, May 1929, 43:473–99. Joseph Dorfman was more favorably impressed by their work; see his *The Economic Mind in American Civilization*, vols. 4–5: *1919–1933* (New York: Viking, 1959), pp. 339–51, 708–11, 742, et passim.

[32]In his 1932 book—*Cause and Control of the Business Cycle* (Boston: Financial Publishing Co., 1932; preface dated June 1932)—Harwood presented his "index of inflation" and his conviction that inflation (as he defined it) was responsible for the economic breakdown, and asserted that his index had predictive value. The eighth edition of this book appeared in 1961, and on p. 37 of the 1963 reprint the index is plotted from mid-1914 into 1963 except for a gap from mid-1932 to early 1934. For years the index figured prominently in the analyses of the American Institute of Economic Research (Great Barrington, Mass.), of which Harwood has long been director, and his views have been repeated at intervals in circulars advertising the investment advisory service of the AIER. Carl Snyder, whose paper of Dec. 12, 1930, is quoted on pp. 127–28, was impressed by Harwood's ideas, but the latter's work has been largely ignored by professional economists. When price inflation got out of control in the early 1970s, Harwood felt vindicated and won recognition long denied him.

of lack of purchasing power would prove the immediate cause of depression, and asserted that business forecasters were paying little attention to this. He also charged them with "failure to foresee the continuing decline in long-term interest rates." In midsummer, apropos of Seligman's book "whitewashing" installment selling, he warned that this practice of "super-stimulated sales" had accelerated the approach to a "satisfaction point" (the term he preferred to "saturation point"), for automobiles in particular, and that the automobile industry was already "vastly over-equipped."[33]

In an article in the *Atlantic* in September 1928, Bonn saw great danger ahead "if ever there were a real hitch." He contrasted the diverse European views of the United States: while some spoke of its "marvelous prosperity" and the "economic miracle," others found it exemplifying "everything vile in modern industrial civilization." He said its "dream of reforming the world has evaporated," and that Americans were "wedded to political isolation"; "a gulf between the United States and Europe is deepening and widening."[34]

Speaking at the Philadelphia meeting of the American Bankers' Association early in October 1928, Colonel Ayres observed that stocks were "selling on expectations" and warned: "All the experience of the past points clearly to the conclusion that prices are too high, and must come down. . . . The American public are in a mood of invincible optimism."[35] The *Chronicle* said that brokers' loans had reached "a really appalling magnitude"—over $5.5 billion. Both stock prices and brokers' loans rose much higher in the next twelve months. Yet the general tone of the ABA meeting was one of complacency and satisfaction, and Federal Reserve Board Governor Young's address lent support to this tone. The chairman of the House Committee on Banking and Currency (L. T. McFadden) said: "Apparently New York is now the money center of the world."[36]

In his *American Prosperity*, Paul Mazur tempered his broadly optimistic views (see Chapter 6 above) by predicting trouble when "the changed international financial status of America and Europe will create

[33]*Annalist*, Jan. 20, pp. 165–66; April 13, pp. 643, 650; July 6, p. 10.

[34]Moritz J. Bonn, "The American Way," *Atlantic*, September 1928, pp. 300–308.

[35]*C&FC*, Oct. 6, 1928, pp. 1843–45, 1863–76, and *Annalist*, Oct. 12, 1928, p. 556. J. T. Adams, in his *March of Democracy*, 2:397, 404, reproduced excerpts from the *New York Times*, Oct. 3, 26, 1928. Cf. Chapter 6 above.

[36]Paul Einzig, in *The Fight for Financial Supremacy* (London: Macmillan, 1931; prefaces to 1st and 2d eds. dated November 1930 and March 1931), summarized the advantages and disadvantages of the three leading centers, and concluded that "notwithstanding the spectacular progress made by both New York and Paris—thanks to exceptional circumstances—London will be able to hold her own in the long run." "London is still the most important banking center in the world." *Ibid.*, 2d ed., pp. v, vii, 120.

a surplus of imports in America's international balance of trade." He went on:

The results of a loss of our favorable balance of trade constitute the greatest single threat to American business which it is possible to foretell for the near future. If the eventual existence of a surplus of imports is accepted as a fact, then surely there can be no doubt that foreign competition and serious tariff questions will be consequences of that import balance. Nor is anyone likely to deny the probability that such an excess of imports will impose onerous and possibly dangerous burdens upon those American industries which will most feel the competition with European industries.[37]

Carl Snyder of the Federal Reserve Bank of New York devoted his American Statistical Association presidential address late in 1928 to "The Problem of Prosperity." He resisted the temptation to expose New Era delusions personally and couched a strong warning in gentle language. He reviewed the sequences of prosperity, boom, collapse, depression, and recovery since the Civil War, with special reference to the depressions of the 1870s and 1890s and the preceding "high industrial and constructional activity . . . accompanied by a period of intense speculative activity which approaches, at times, a national mania." He went on:

It seems not improbable that this seizure of the national mind has been one of the chief contributing causes to the disasters and disillusionments which followed. In the earlier periods this speculative fervor related more distinctly to land booms and to the building of railways, which in many cases gave rise to the booms. With the disappearance of great areas of unoccupied land and the diffusion of population over all of the habitable areas of the country, these great land booms, once so picturesque a part of our developmental history, have largely disappeared. They have given place to the eras of widespread industrial consolidation and excited speculation in the shares of these great corporations.[38]

Thus Snyder came to the brink of stressing imminent danger and urging timely steps to avert the threatened catastrophe, but he did not say: "Here we are now." Instead, he found comfort in "a parallel outburst of the statistical mania" (page 9), and expressed his belief that "the Cinderella of the sciences may offer a solution" (page 2). "We have learned to measure the rate of our industrial growth." We can also "measure the rate of credit expansion." He considered "the most important contribution which statistical investigation has made to economic theory" the evidence

[37]*American Prosperity* (New York: Viking, 1928), p. 256.
[38]*JASA*, March 1929, 24:1–14, esp. p. 7. Snyder dropped into my Stanford office one day, I think in the fall of 1928, and said: "Davis, do you believe we are in a new era in which past experience doesn't count?" I do not recall how I worded my negative reply, nor the details of the ensuing discussion.

"that an excess of the rate of credit expansion over the growth of production and trade results merely in the familiar forms of over-stimulation, inflation and speculation."[39] He added that "its recognition as a working rule of banking and credit policy may prove the greatest gain which we have derived from our now centralized and unified banking system" (itself a serious overstatement); but he was silent as to measures that the Federal Reserve System should apply under this "rule."

George B. Roberts of the National City Bank of New York discussed "The Price-Earnings Ratio as an Index of Stock Prices" at the December 1928 meeting of the American Statistical Association. He noted that ten times annual earnings had long been regarded as a fair selling price for stocks, but that in 1928 the ratio had risen nearly to twenty to one. He gave reasons for refusing to endorse the inference that stocks were inflated by some 85 percent.[40] Yet he considered the present apparently abnormal ratio "dependent upon the permanence of conditions in business and credit," which "has not yet been thoroughly demonstrated." He therefore suggested that "it is the part of conservatism to regard them [the ratios] with suspicion and to be prepared against unpleasant surprise should they not be continued."

The Berlin Institute for Business Cycle Research correctly foresaw that the German downturn in 1928 would be long and severe, recognized the depression as no short-term affair, and attributed its severity to the excess capacity to which the German rationalization movement had led. It was later critical of the Brüning government's resort to wage cuts in 1931–32 in an attempt to improve Germany's international competitive position, and favored low interest rates and work creation, methods which the Nazis soon adopted in their own ways.[41] Late in 1928 the corresponding Austrian Institute[42] interpreted its three major indicators (adapted from the Harvard ones) as presaging an economic downturn, and it became increasingly pessimistic in 1929–30. Its statistical analysis showed the international weakness of the Austrian economy.

[39]Elaborated in his paper of Nov. 22, 1929, "New Measures of the Relations of Credit and Trade," *Proc. Acad. Pol. Sci.*, January 1930, 13:16–34.

[40]*JASA*, March 1929, suppl., 24(165A):21–26. Speaking on Nov. 22, 1929, Rufus S. Tucker observed, with reference to such views and Clay's (see pp. 108–9 above), that many expected that "a serious reaction in the stock market might occur in any single month from May, 1928 to November, 1929 inclusive, and that there was practically as good reason for picking one month as there was for picking another." *Proc. Acad. Pol. Sci.*, January 1930, 13:536–37.

[41]E. Coenen, *La "Konjunkturforschung" en Allemagne et en Autriche 1925–1955* (Louvain, 1964), reviewed by C. T. Saunders in *EJ*, December 1967, 77:892–94.

[42]F. A. Hayek and Oskar Morgenstern were the first two directors of the Austrian Institute, and Fritz Machlup was one of its senior staff. All three soon emigrated to Great Britain or the United States.

The outlook for 1929 as viewed by the National Bank of Commerce in New York late in 1928 contained the following paragraphs, which ended with a warning:

The basic price situation is notably sound. Commodity markets are free of speculative price inflation, and with but minor exceptions they have been freed also of those restrictions and measures of artificial control[43] which, as with rubber this last year, carry a constant threat of disaster to the industries involved. Employment has regained a very high level,[44] and the conjunction of good wages and good profits is resulting not simply in a record volume of current holiday buying, but in the prospect of a well-stabilized volume of demand in the new year.

In manufacture, the great problem is to attain and hold a nice ratio of output to the fluctuating volume of demand. In more and more lines of enterprise the attempt is being made to secure this adjustment by volitional control of output rather than the blind forces of competitive struggle. Desirable as such a method is, the long record of past failures must warn against a too-easy hope of its success. *Danger comes from business that is too good rather than too poor—from the active demands, rising prices and high profits that tempt an overjudgment of the market, leading to increased output and enlarged capacity that in the end means its undoing.* It is in this fashion that the most serious threat to next year's ultimate prosperity lies. The year may start so well as to cause an overestimate of its possibilities.[45]

There were some who argued, even after the marked improvement in the position of U.S. agriculture in the middle of the decade, that its depressed condition would force a breakdown in American prosperity. These arguments contributed to the agrarian agitation for "action programs" which eventually led Hoover to his fateful commitments to raise tariffs on farm products, press the Agricultural Marketing Act, and set up the Federal Farm Board; but they were never firmly based and appear to have carried little weight with economists, bankers, and the investing and speculative public.

Prominent Cassandras, Alexander Dana Noyes, the weekly *Commercial*
1925-28   *and Financial Chronicle*, B. M. Anderson of
the Chase National Bank, the Englishman Sir George Paish, and his more eminent compatriot Sir Josiah Stamp voiced grave warnings in 1925-28, as did a few others.

Noyes, who was financial editor of the New York *Evening Post* in 1891-1920 and of *The New York Times* from October 1920, was able to

---

[43]This was inaccurate. The breakdowns of coffee and copper controls were yet to come.
[44]This too I consider inaccurate (see Chapter 4, n. 40, above).
[45]Statement issued Dec. 29, 1928, and quoted in *C&FC*, Jan. 5, 1929, pp. 22-23 (italics added).

view the developments of the 1920s with exceptional perspective. In the *Post* columns he had braved hostile opinion to attack the widely held illusions that led to the shortlived speculative mania of 1901.[46] In the *Times* he continued to do so in the 1920s. As he later remarked, he did his utmost to warn, "in the strongest and most emphatic language, against the prevalent illusion of perpetually rising [stock] prices and perpetually increasing prosperity"; but he was denounced for "trying to discredit or stop American prosperity," and was of course condemned by those who had lost by accepting his bearish judgment too soon.[47]

As the boom approached its climax in the summer of 1929, however, Noyes muted his warnings and almost admitted the possibility that the "enthusiastic panegyrists" of the New Era might be right after all.[48] The "almost invariable midsummer slackening of pace was thus far virtually absent"; high money rates had not checked it, nor had they hurt corporations which, because of the shift of investors' preference from bonds to stocks, could obtain funds cheaply by floating new issues of stock. He noted that wages had risen more than the cost of living, giving increased buying power even to those with small means. Even to conservative experts, America's "immense prosperity" appeared "not an illogical sequel to the extraordinary change in the country's position in the financial world during the ten or twelve past years." Though all experience indicated that indefinite continuation of the movement was improbable, no date for the potential reaction could be assigned. On the very eve of the crash Noyes noted increased strain in the international market, and quoted an eminent British economist as having warned at Williamstown that Wall Street was "reasserting its old role of disturber of the peace of Europe."[49] Not until the October issue of *Scribner's*, however, did he see signs of "distinct relaxation from the pace of July and August" and mildly ask whether the superstructure had been raised so high as to have become unwieldy.[50] And in December his concluding comments were broadly reassuring (see Chapter 8, n. 128, below).

Two years later, Noyes was to write and speak in equally strong terms against the illusions of overpessimism. In a 1931 address he said in part:

[46]Noyes, *Market Place*, pp. 194–200.
[47]*Ibid.*, pp. 322–23. Speaking on Nov. 22, 1929, Royal Meeker said: "I remember distinctly at least two years ago that a great many prophets . . . were predicting this calamity. They said that prices of stocks were altogether too high. I took their advice and sold some and the stock went up 150 points after I sold it. . . . Everybody expected the calamity, but everybody except the very wise, or the very lucky, hoped that the calamity would be postponed until the next high peak was reached and passed." *Proc. Acad. Pol. Sci.*, January 1930, 13:498–99.
[48]See his columns on "The Financial Situation" *Scribner's*, July and August 1929, pp. 119–20.
[49]*Ibid.*, September 1929, pp. 473–74ff.
[50]*Ibid.*, October 1929, pp. 591ff.

Bishop Butler once asked if it was possible for a whole nation simultaneously to go mad. Our own experience of 1928 and 1929 strongly suggested that we should have to answer yes.[51] If any doubt about the answer had been left, it has been removed by 1931. The greater part of the community has pretty nearly gone mad this past season in its ideas about investments. It is my own belief that, when we shall have emerged from this depression period as we have emerged from a dozen others, there is a great and notable financial future ahead of the United States.[52]

The *Commercial and Financial Chronicle* persistently castigated the views of spokesmen for "Prosperity Unlimited," volubly warned about the course of the stock market, and liberally quoted from addresses and reports that were critical of the credit and speculative "debauch." On May 18, 1929, the *Chronicle* stated: "Speculative proclivities are inherent in human nature. They should not be suppressed, and in fact, cannot be, but they should at all times be held within bounds, lest they run to dangerous excesses, such as has been the case during the last two years, under the easy money policy of the Federal Reserve authorities."[53] And it called the Sprague-Burgess chapter in *Recent Economic Changes* (published that week) onesided.

Arnold G. Dana, of New Haven, Connecticut, contributed to its columns in December to March 1928–29 five articles with the title, "Is Not Group Speculating a Conspiracy, Working for Sham Prosperity?" Countrywide stock gambling, he said, "is aggravating and threatens to render malignant business conditions which are generally accepted as beneficial, but which rightly diagnosed appear in the nature of an insidious national malady, a new sort of selective inflation, masquerading as expanding prosperity." He argued at length that stock speculation was furthering "an insidious type of business inflation—presumably a luxury inflation," and that "as a nation we are living and spending far beyond our income in a manner possible only through a progressive and inflationary expansion of artificial purchasing power."[54]

The New Republic, Bliven remarked in his recent autobiography, had for years been warning of the danger of severe depression, "thanks chiefly

---

[51] For an analyst's later views of the emotional influences on the stock market, see E. S. C. Coppock (founder and director of the Trendex Research Group), "The Madness of Crowds," *Barron's*, Oct. 15, 1962, pp. 5, 16–17.

[52] Noyes, *Market Place*, p. 355.

[53] P. 3235. Cf. *C&FC*, Apr. 6, 13, 1929, pp. 2176–78 ("Economic Effect of Widespread Speculation"), pp. 2353–54 ("The Relation of Speculation to Prosperity").

[54] *Ibid.*, Dec. 16, 23, 1928, pp. 3303, 3461; Jan. 12, 26, Mar. 16, 1929, pp. 161, 455, 1624, 1627. Dana quoted this extreme statement made at a Lumberman's Association meeting in New York on Jan. 22, 1929: "Never in recent years has the outlook for the future based on tangible existing facts been so universally optimistic among the country's industrial and financial leaders including the building materials industry" (p. 1625). In the *Yale Review* for June 1932 (pp. 841–43), C. Reinold Noyes reviewed Dana's recent book, *"Prosperity" Prob-*

to the foresight and economic knowledge of George Soule";[55] but after the Wall Street crash Soule was among those who mistakenly viewed it as on the whole beneficial.

B. M. Anderson, the respected economist for a big New York bank, vigorously warned in the *Chase Economic Bulletin* of August 8, 1925, that the dangers of the course which had been pursued since 1922 were "increasingly grave." The cheap-money policies, in his view, had led to the expansion of bank credit by $11.5 billion. Unneeded by commerce, these funds had flowed into real estate mortgages on a great scale, into installment finance paper on easing terms, into startling increases in loans on securities and bank investments, and into an ominous growth of foreign loans which financed U.S. exports for the time. Speculation in real estate and securities was growing rapidly, and capital gains were being treated as ordinary income and spent on luxuries. Prolonging this course, with no tariff reductions, could only create "a desperately difficult situation" later. He went on to forecast the troubles of 1929 (page 16). Increasingly in 1925–29 Anderson emphasized this danger,[56] though his work was by no means focused upon the matter. For reasons not altogether clear, his influence on contemporary opinion was much less than his writings and speeches justified, and they have been unduly ignored or slighted by most later students.

Sir George Paish, long on the editorial staff of the London weekly *Statist* (as joint editor in 1900–1916), was the leading Cassandra in the second half of the 1920s. His emphatic warnings and urgent pleas were for the most part well founded but largely disregarded. In his little book published in London early in 1927, *The Road to Prosperity*, Paish briefly, but on the whole competently, analyzed the position of each of a large number of countries (chs. 5–15), and stressed the matters of trade restrictions, interallied debts, reparations, the restoration of confidence, and the expansion of buying power (chs. 16–20). The "immense increase in income in the long period prior to the war," he said, came from "a policy of great courage." Now, he went on, "one of the very first things to be done to preserve the world from bankruptcy is to replace the present pusillanimous policy of the nations by one of courage, and for every nation to sell and to buy freely without restriction or impediment of any kind" (pages 17–19). Noting the "unexampled trade activity" in this country he warned that

America's present prosperity is built upon her capacity to sell unprecedented quantities of her products to foreign nations, and a collapse of foreign buying power

---

lems; referring to a long essay published in 1926, Noyes commented that "the author seems to have had hold of the right idea all the time."

[55]Bruce Bliven, *After Five Million Words*, (New York: John Day, 1970), pp. 214–15.

[56]B. M. Anderson, *Economics and the Public Welfare: Financial and Economic History of the United States, 1914–1946* (New York: Van Nostrand, 1949), ch. 18, esp. p. 136.

would be felt from one end of the United States to the other. The great edifice of banking . . . credit will be in jeopardy. . . . So long as America is prepared to grant credit, so long she can continue to sell, but the more credit she grants the greater will be the subsequent contraction. . . . At the present moment America is presenting every possible obstacle to the payment in goods by other countries for her products or of her interests.

He cited immigration restrictions, subsidies to U.S. shipping, and the rapid increase in Europe's and the world's debt to the United States as tending toward "a complete collapse both in Europe's buying power and in America's selling power involving a financial crisis in the United States far more severe than any crisis America has yet experienced. . . . America cannot remain prosperous in a world not only impoverished, but overwhelmed by debt" (pages 20–25).

Current U.S. policy, he went on, is rendering the world's "problems more difficult and more dangerous." Its continuance would have "especially grave and momentous" consequences for British prosperity. "As long as America lends freely to the world, and thus gives the nations greater buying power than otherwise they would have, Great Britain will be able to continue to buy from America and to sell to other nations. But should anything occur to cause American investors and bankers to stop their loans to foreign countries, Great Britain's position would become most precarious" (pages 34–37). Paish did not forecast the drastic reduction in foreign loans by U.S. investors from mid-1928 in consequence of the stock market's powerful influence in raising short-term money rates, but he was prophetic in saying: "So long as Germany can raise credit in the United States and Great Britain, so long will the disastrous consequences of her relative lack of buying power be averted, but if a time should come when her credit is exhausted and she is forced to reduce her purchases to the limit of her selling power, less her reparation and interest payments, then the full consequences of the impoverishment of the German people will be experienced by other nations" (page 53).

Sir Josiah Stamp, at the peak of his prestige following the success of the Dawes Plan, wrote a commendatory foreword to Paish's *Road to Prosperity*. He raised the question, which he considered of vital importance in the international situation, of "whether America will go on indefinitely exchanging real wealth for promises, in a ledger, of real wealth to be paid back after the crack of doom; for a whole set of commercial tendencies now established are dependent on the continuance of this policy" (page vii). Keynes and Moulton repeatedly sounded a similar note, with pessimistic conclusions which proved wrong with specific reference to the Dawes Plan. It was only during the crash that Stamp publicly expressed the view that "the state of affairs in New York for the last twelve months had been a menace to financial stability everywhere, and had upset the working of the international gold standard."[57]

Paish considered that "the task of restoring prosperity to Great Britain, Europe, and the world in general" was rendered feasible by the Locarno treaties and the entry of Germany into the League of Nations. Yet he stressed serious dangers:

> The present disorganisation is extraordinarily great. . . . Only by the most whole-hearted and loyal cooperation will it be possible to place the world in a condition of soundness and solvency . . . there are few signs of trade revival, and any further great expansion of credit is not warranted under existing conditions. This position is in itself one of the greatest dangers. . . . the refusal of new credits would induce efforts to be made to collect existing debts and a world crisis of unprecedented proportions would be precipitated. . . . no time should be lost in taking measures which will effectually avert the crisis to which every nation without exception is exposed. . . . Probably never was the condition of so many manufacturing, mining and mercantile corporations as precarious as it is today. . . . The present crisis is unique because the nations have become interdependent to an extent never before experienced. . . . [It] is quite unprecedented in its danger, and in its far-reaching consequences, and urgently demands remedies both fundamental and comprehensive such as were never needed in the past" (pages 6, 14–15; order of quotations slightly altered).

Confidence, said Paish, "is the basis of prosperity. Without it credit is impossible, and without credit . . . business would be rendered impossible." "A universal breakdown of credit is the imminent danger now confronting the nations" (page 112). This proved a correct prophecy, though the breakdown was deferred. Many Americans, including Hoover, firmly held this view of "confidence," but most of them refused to believe the prophecy, and sought to bolster confidence without giving significant weight to Paish's diagnosis or prescriptions, including his appeal for a "financial Locarno" (ch. 21).

Freer international trade was a subject on which Paish and Stamp saw eye to eye. In the spring of 1925 Stamp had been invited to address the United States Chamber of Commerce, but could not do so. In June he gave a forthright speech on this topic at the Brussels meeting of the International Chamber of Commerce. President Coolidge read a press report of this, and publicly took occasion to "rebut vigorously" what he considered Stamp's suggestion that the United States should modify its tariff. By letter on July 3, Stamp undertook to clarify the matter, and warmly defended his frank speaking. This instance, and another in 1926 in which his good friend General Dawes (then vice president) had involved him in discussing

[57]As summarized by F. W. Hirst in *Wall Street and Lombard Street* (New York: Macmillan, 1931), pp. 29–30, on the basis of Stamp's cable of Oct. 24, 1929, published in the New York *Evening Post*. See Chapter 8 below.

the controversial McNary-Haugen plan, revealed "the sensitiveness of American officialdom . . . to anything which savoured of interference from outsiders in the formation of American public opinion."[58] This sensitiveness was especially acute in connection with American attitudes and policies on war debt settlements. It goes far to explain why American officials and the public were so resistant to warnings and prophecies from overseas.

In October 1926 Stamp had been one of the forty British signers of the impressive "Plea for the Removal of Restrictions upon European Trade" (often miscalled the "Bankers' Manifesto"), which was signed by a large number of leading bankers, manufacturers, and businessmen of fifteen European countries, as well as by six prominent Americans, including J. P. Morgan, President Albert H. Wiggin of the Chase National Bank, and Gates W. McGarrah, chairman of the Federal Reserve Bank of New York. This was at once a grave warning and a powerful appeal.[59] It helped to pave the way for the League's great International Economic Conference in May 1927, which reached a high degree of unanimity in this field[60] but whose promise was never fulfilled.

Various Warnings in 1929   Warnings of trouble ahead increased in January–September 1929, but most of them were mild or tempered. Such notes were sounded from time to time in weeklies such as *The Economist* and in the monthly bulletins of the Federal Reserve Bank of New York, the National City Bank of New York, and the Cleveland Trust Company; but on the whole these supported the common and official view that the U.S. economy was strong and healthy despite speculative excesses. By and large, this was also true of the economic services. Even those who were most forthright in some of their utterances on the developing dangers stopped far short of depicting their true magnitude, muted their warnings as the crash approached, and became reassuring after it had occurred.

[58]J. Harry Jones, *Josiah Stamp, Public Servant: The Life of the First Baron Stamp of Shortlands* (London: Pitman, 1964), pp. 306–9. On Jan. 6, 1927, the Associated Press published the whole correspondence in a pamphlet. On this subject, it should be noted, Stamp was *not* qualified by "prolonged study" to speak with authority.

[59]*C&FC*, Oct. 23, 1926, pp. 2057–60, with comments by several signers. Chicago banker J. J. Mitchell took pains to say that it "pertains exclusively to Europe," and Dr. Schacht agreed. See also Sir George Paish, *The Road to Prosperity* (London: Benn, 1927), pp. 83–87, 138–49. Paish commented (p. 138): "No warning ever published has been so grave, and . . . so authoritative." The French and Italian signers characteristically expressed reservations which were on the whole appropriate (pp. 141, 146). The Council of the International Chamber of Commerce applauded the "Plea." The *Nation and Athenaeum* (Oct. 23, 1926, p. 103) called it "a remarkable manifesto," but said that the greatest service it could render would be "to give a strong lead in the right direction" to the forthcoming economic conference.

[60]Lord Salter commented in his memoirs: "No international conference within my experience had ever been so elaborately and carefully prepared; and the fruits of it seemed in sight." *Memoirs of a Public Servant* (London: Faber, 1961), p. 198.

The *Annalist* of January 4, 1929, quoted three respected observers. One of them, Carl Snyder, had made a brief pessimistic reference to the speculative situation in his contribution to *The Evening Post Annual* early in 1929, saying in part: "Years of unusual expansion are paid for by lean years of depression and unemployment, often involving widespread suffering. High hopes are brought low, fortunes are wrecked, and worst of all, the business and economic morale of the nation seriously impaired." This proved an exceptionally accurate prediction. Noyes in the *New York Times* of January 1 cautiously prophesied that violent speculation would lead to great stringency, but concluded: "As to the underlying strength of the American economic situation, however, there is only one opinion." Schneider in *The Sun Annual* noted that "business is on a firm foundation and that the conditions essential to a business depression or a real bear market in stocks are lacking."

One of the most powerful financiers of the day was Charles E. Mitchell, president of the National City Bank of New York, which followed the course of economic and financial news in its monthly *Letter*. Mitchell's year-end statement, published January 1, 1929, recognized the ever-present danger that roseate expectations underlying the great rise in stocks might discount the future too freely, but he expressed the common view in saying that complaints of the level of stock prices were justified only "from the standpoint of credit strain." His bank *Letter* in December 1928 had said: "Undoubtedly a severe break in securities would throw a chill over the situation, but business appears too sound fundamentally to be more than temporarily thrown off balance by any such development." The January 1929 *Letter* mildly warned that "it behooves business men to be watchful lest prosperity overreach itself and prove its own undoing"; but it concluded that the "sharp corrective movement in the stock market" in early December 1928 had "cleared the situation of some unwholesome features," and the subsequent recovery of good stocks had "demonstrated anew the widespread confidence in the business outlook."[61]

H. Parker Willis, the respected editor (from 1919 to 1931) of the New York *Journal of Commerce* who had been prominent in the establishment of the Federal Reserve System, was forthright. In an address to the District of Columbia's Bankers' Association on January 23, 1929, he said: "It is quite clear that the general market and speculative situation is quite out of the hands of the Federal Reserve system, just as the agricultural credit and land speculation of 1919 and the early part of 1920 had escaped from control." He was highly critical of the Federal Reserve for permitting "the development of an unparalleled era of overspeculation, which had resulted in the extravagant money rates that have prevailed on the New York mar-

[61]Cf. Noyes, *Market Place*, p. 324.

ket for the past few weeks and months." There should be a moratorium on the issue of new securities, and the Federal Reserve "must go out of the business of furnishing bargain counter credit or bootlegging its accommodation to the stock market."[62]

In an address on January 28, 1929,[63] after happily reviewing eight years of the federal budget system, President Coolidge took occasion to refer to "the alarming increase in the cost of State and local governments." Overlooking the fact that much of the increase was for highway construction, an aid to prosperity, he found it "such a heavy drain on the earnings of the people that it is the greatest menace to the continuance of prosperity." Such observations reflect his preoccupation with economy rather than with economics.

The Federal Reserve Board issued its famous major warning on February 7, 1929,[64] but it did not "validate" this by further discount rate action. Instead it tried "moral suasion" and "direct action" against banks making "speculative" loans. Both accomplished all too little. The rate increases of February–July 1928 had failed to stem the speculative tide; the Board was mindful of the serious charges that its vigorous actions had precipitated the collapse of 1920; and its counsels were divided. For nearly six months it resisted all pressures to take vigorous action. To quote Chandler:

By February, 1929, every interest rate in the open market was appreciably above the discount rate. This, the officers and directors of the New York Bank believed, was an open invitation to borrowing and further credit expansion. At eleven meetings between February 14 and May 23, the New York directors voted to raise their rate from 5 to 6 per cent. The Federal Reserve Board disapproved every time, despite a visit from a committee of the New York directors in March, unanimous agreement at the Governors Conference early in April that all Reserve Banks in major financial centers should go to 6 percent, and a similar resolution by the Federal Advisory Council on April 22.[65]

Not until August 9, 1929, and then to the surprise of almost everyone, was the New York Bank allowed to raise its rate to 6 percent; but this was

---

[62]*C&FC*, Jan. 26, 1929, p. 503. The same page reported an address of January 17 before the Detroit Stock Exchange by David Friday, an economist who was the dominating figure in the management of an investment trust sponsored by A. G. Becker and Company (Domestic and Foreign Investors Corporation). Friday made a very bullish prediction for the second half of 1929, and asserted: "The greatest fallacy extant in the United States is the belief that brokers' loans constitute money withdrawn from industry."

[63]Summarized and partially quoted in *C&FC*, Feb. 12, 1929, pp. 610–11. The gross debt of state and local governments rose from $10.1 billion on June 30, 1922, to $17.2 billion seven years later, or nearly $1 billion more than federal gross debt declined in this period. *Hist. Stat. U.S.*, ser. Y 257,545, and *Stat. Abstr. U.S., 1952*, p. 537.

[64]*Fed. Res. Bull.*, February 1929, 15:93–94 (quoted in part in Galbraith, *Great Crash*, p. 39). See also *Fed. Res. Bull.*, March 1929, 15:175–77, and later issues.

[65]Chandler, *Strong*, p. 466, and Hoover, *Memoirs*, 3:16–19. See also Milton Friedman and Anna J. Schwartz, *A Monetary History of the United States, 1867–1960* (Princeton, N.J.: Princeton University Press, 1963), pp. 256–66.

coupled with a reduction in the buying rate on bankers' acceptances, which effectually offset its restraining influence.[66]

The outstanding banker to sound a strong warning was Paul M. Warburg, who had served on the Federal Reserve Board in 1914–18. His annual report as chairman of the board of the International Acceptance Bank, which appeared early in March 1929, contained a trenchant and what the *Chronicle* termed a "refreshing discussion of the whole credit situation." The following quotations indicate his views:

the Federal Reserve System, pursuing a well conceived and farsighted policy, rose to a position of world leadership. Yet within the short span of a year it lost that leadership owing to its failure promptly and effectively to reverse the engines at the critical moment.

The rudder then passed into the hands of Stock Exchange operators, who have now for many months governed the flow of money, not only in the United States, but in the principal marts of the world. History, which has a painful way of repeating itself, has taught mankind that speculative over-expansion invariably ends in over-contraction and distress. If a Stock Exchange debauch is quickly arrested by prompt and determined action, it is not too much to hope that a shrinkage of inflated stock prices may be brought about without seriously affecting the wider circle of general business. If orgies of unrestrained speculation are permitted to spread too far, however, the ultimate collapse is certain not only to affect the speculators who sell, but also to bring about a general depression involving the entire country.[67]

In the Cleveland Trust Company's *Business Bulletin* of March 15, 1929, its vice president, Colonel Ayres, wrote in a similar vein. He noted that the "stock market appears to be taking business for a ride," that the Federal Reserve Board's warning whistle "has gone unheeded," and that "the Reserve authorities have the appearance of being baffled and perhaps thwarted." Ayres continued: "A vigorous bull market of large volume exercises a potent influence in sustaining the prosperity of general business . . . in three main ways": it "creates and sustains business confidence and optimism," it generates large profits that are "gained easily" and "spent freely," and it creates "so great a public demand for stocks that corporations are enabled to float and sell new stock issues and with the proceeds to retire their bonds, pay off their bank loans, and add to their working capital." He concluded: "Probably the degree to which the market succeeds in assuring increased loans from corporations and individuals during the next two months will determine whether both business and the stock market are to be subjected to proximate bumps, or are to go on until they are victims of an ultimate crash."[68]

[66]Discussions in August–October 1929 issues of the *Annalist* are illuminating.

[67]Discussed and quoted at length in the *C&FC*, Mar. 9, 1929, pp. 1443–44. It was reprinted in Paul M. Warburg, *The Federal Reserve System: Its Origin and Growth: Reflections and Recollections*, 2 vols. (New York: Macmillan, 1930), 1:823–26. Cf. *ibid.*, 1:508–19.

[68]Quoted in *C&FC*, Mar. 23, 1929, p. 1830.

Such strong warnings must have helped bring about the severe market break on March 25–26, 1929, when call-money rates rose to 20 percent, the high for the boom. Then President Mitchell of the National City Bank, a director of the Federal Reserve Bank of New York, boldly intervened to check the market decline. He told the press: "We feel that we have an obligation which is paramount to any Federal Reserve warning, or anything else, to avert any dangerous crisis in the money market."[69] On March 27 the bank "announced that it would insure reasonable interest rates by putting $25 million into the stock market—$5 million when the rate was 16 percent, and $5 million additional for each percentage point." But the attitude of the bank was doubtless much more influential than were the small sums it put up. Its monthly *Letter* of April 1929 said in virtual justification: "The National City Bank fully recognizes the dangers of overspeculation and endorses the desire of the Federal Reserve authorities to restrain excessive credit expansion for this purpose. At the same time, the bank, *business generally, and it may be assumed the Federal Reserve Banks . . . wish to avoid a general collapse of the securities markets such as would have a disastrous effect on business.*"[70]

Mitchell's action aroused the ire of peppery Senator Carter Glass, who charged that he was defying the Federal Reserve Board, which Glass defended against the pressures from the Federal Reserve Bank of New York for higher rates.[71] Actually, however, the Board did not disapprove so much of Mitchell's action, which Governor Roy Young thought "100% right," as of his press statement.[72]

The stock market recovered, and soon resumed its advance. The position and action of this leading bank may well have postponed the crash for six months, in which the course of events went far to ensure that it would be far more severe.[73] The bank's special bulletin of April 18, however, put the matter more strongly and specifically: "The existing credit situation is already having its effect upon business and threatens to undermine the natural and justifiable prosperity of the country to an increasing degree unless a corrective is promptly found. . . . if the rate of credit in-

[69]*Ibid.*, Mar. 30, 1929, pp. 1967–68, 2015–16; *New York Times*, Mar. 28, 29, 1929; Myers and Newton, *Hoover Administration*, pp. 14–15; Galbraith, *Great Crash*, pp. 40–45, 104; Friedman and Schwartz, *Monetary History*, pp. 260–62.

[70]Citibank, *Monthly Economic Letter*, April 1929 (italics added).

[71]Rixey Smith and Norman Beasley, *Carter Glass: A Biography* (New York: Longmans Green, 1939), pp. 289–90, 400–401. President Hoover privately endorsed Senator Glass' denunciation. Hoover, *Memoirs*, 3:18–19.

[72]Anderson, *Economics and the Public Welfare*, pp. 206–8; Friedman and Schwartz, *Monetary History*, pp. 258–61.

[73]This was Franz Schneider's view late in 1929; see Chapter 4, n. 74, above. Early in 1937, S. H. Slichter held that by March–April 1929 the stock market position was widely recognized as "dangerous," and that many businessmen "began to fear that there may be a more or less serious collapse" and "were led by this expectation to reduce commitments." Slichter, "The Period 1919–36 in the United States: Its Significance for Business Cycle Theory," *Rev. Ec. Stat.*, February 1937, 19:1–19, esp. pp. 12–13.

crease rises above the rate of business growth, we have a condition of inflation which manifests itself in rising prices in some departments of the business structure." Despite this accurate analysis and forecast, the eventual crash upset the bank's plan to merge with the Corn Exchange Bank Trust Company,[74] caused huge losses to President Mitchell on his heavy purchases of National City stock, and led in time to his resignation and disgrace.[75]

In the spring of 1929, Paish sarcastically complimented the politicians of the world "for their extraordinary success in hampering trade by every means in their power, and more particularly by the imposition of tariffs," and said, much as the late chairman of the Westminster Bank (Dr. Walter Leaf) had said to the International Chamber of Commerce in the autumn of 1925, that "it means the economic suicide of the World." He recognized the "great monetary stringency in the United States," attributed it "to speculation in securities upon a scale never before witnessed," emphasized the part played by loans to purchase stocks, and warned of the consequent prospect of lower prices of commodities. He concluded that "we are face to face with the most difficult and dangerous financial situation the world has ever confronted."[76]

In an article published in many newspapers on May 12, 1929, Irving Fisher held "that the so-called 'Hoover Boom' in the stock market had about reached its climax," and intimated that so large an upward departure from Karsten's long-range forecast line could not be expected long to persist. But only in retrospect did he "appreciate that preliminary symptoms of the crash were not lacking."[77]

The Investment Research Bureau wrote me on June 16, 1929: "The Stock Market is in a perplexing position for the uninformed or ill-advised investor or trader. The coming months will be fraught with possibilities of grave danger for anyone who merely dabbles in securities—in fact, for anyone who deals in them except upon the advice of competent and experienced forecasters. . . . During the next few months thousands of people will suffer staggering losses. Others, who buy or sell the RIGHT stocks at the right time, will be rewarded handsomely." This was a fairly typical market letter of the period, and Brookmire's took essentially the same position. Van Strum's forecast of the stock market turned bearish in July, as did that of Emerson W. Axe.[78]

[74]See Citibank, *Monthly Economic Letter*, for October and December 1929, pp. 151, 175–77, and Noyes, *Market Place*, p. 331.

[75]Galbraith, *Great Crash*, pp. 155–59.

[76]Pamphlet entitled *World Economic Suicide* (London General Press). Though undated, internal evidence indicates that it was written in or about April 1929. Leaf had been elected ICC president in June 1925.

[77]Fisher, *The Stock Market Crash—and After* (New York: Macmillan, 1930), pp. xvi–xviii.

[78]Van Strum Financial Service, *How To Make and Keep Stock Market Profits*, 6th ed. (New York: Van Strum Financial Service, 1930), p. 45; *Annalist*, July 19, 1929, pp. 95–96.

The London *Statist* of June 22, 1929, urged that something be done "to dissociate world credit and world prices from the deflationary influences" emanating from the United States. In this view, the gold standard was effectively prevented from operating. The writer (perhaps Sir George Paish) attributed the undervaluation of European currencies to three causes: the vast mass of unproductive debt owed to the United States, the United States tariff, and the recent decline of capital exports from the United States, which in the past had offset the other two factors.

In a long article in early August 1929, E. C. Harwood asserted that inflation had been increasing ever since 1925, that bank assets were becoming more and more fixed, and that the use of bank credit for capital purposes was more excessive than in 1920, and saw as "phenomena which need no emphasis" the speculative building boom, the ebullient stock market, and "possibly an artificial level of commodity prices." Here he found "a more satisfying explanation of the prosperity of the past few years than the 'new-era' brand of reasoning; and further, . . . the time may not be far distant when the country will realize, in the light of the cold gray 'morning after,' that it has just been on another credit-splurging spree."[79]

Edgar Lawrence Smith, author of the influential 1925 book on common stocks as long-term investments, in August 1929 issued the rather belated warning, "Share Investment Can Be Overdone," saying that "when current interest rates are high, the larger part of any conservatively invested fund will be in short maturities."[80]

On September 5 Roger Babson uttered his final warning of the coming crash, which he said "may be terrific."[81] This had an immediate impact on the market, as the *Annalist* admitted. "The upward movement of stock prices has met a sudden and serious check." But Babson had not won the confidence of economists or the financial community, and his record on predictions had been, and continued to be, spotty. At his "annual national business conference" in September 1926 he had spoken of installment buying as "eating into the vitals of business" and said: "I am distinctly bearish on the stock market for the long pull."[82] The next year he had warned that a crash would come sooner or later, and in September 1928 he had forecast a business depression if the voters elected Al Smith and a Democratic Congress. *Barron's* financial weekly, which at first denounced

---

[79]*Annalist*, Aug. 2, 1929, pp. 203–5.

[80]*Ibid.*, Aug. 23, 1929, p. 351.

[81]*Ibid.*, Sept. 6, 21, 1929, pp. 442, 1800. Another headline in the September 6 issue was (p. 445): "Economic Depression Increases in Australia and Deflation the Only Cure," after two years in progress, with wool prices down 30 percent. Cf. chart in C. B. Schedvin, *Australia and the Great Depression* (Sydney, N.S.W.: Sydney University Press, 1970), p. 111. Had this book come out earlier, it would have been cited at several points because it stresses the international setting; but I have not attempted to cover developments in countries with small populations.

[82]*C&FC*, Sept. 11, 1926, p. 1309.

Babson as a scaremonger, in October 1928 began charging him and those like him with causing the crash.

In the spring of 1929 Wesley C. Mitchell ended his cautious review of *Recent Economic Changes* with the warning that "all is not well. . . . The condition of agriculture, the volume of unemployment, the textile trades, coal mining, the leather industries, present grave problems." Several uncertainties were mentioned and several suggestions made for maintaining business prosperity. He would not say that no serious setback would occur "for years to come"; on the other hand, he did not emphasize the respects in which the U.S. economy had become vulnerable to shocks and strains or to the mounting threats of breakdown.[83]

In the summer of 1929, then, there was a fairly general expectation (1) that an economic contraction was in prospect from the peak that was at hand or near, and (2) that a more or less severe fall in the stock market from the heights to which it had risen was inevitable. Neither prospect was viewed with alarm generally, and the timing seemed unpredictable. Both were commonly regarded as normal corrections of excesses. The Federal Reserve, with its extremely strong gold holdings, and the Hoover administration, with a reputed superman at its head, were trusted to prevent either contraction or fall from going to extremes and to reverse the contraction in good time, if indeed the economy and the stock market did not recover without substantial government interposition, as they had in 1921–23.

All in all, the country was amply forewarned of coming events, except on vital points. The severity of the stock market crash, the repercussions of that crash on the economy, the crumbling of the commodity price structure, the drastic economic contraction in 1930, the international consequences, and extreme deflation of superconfidence: not many foresaw all these, fewer still spoke out, and those who did were commonly disbelieved. Had the outlook been rightly appraised, quite different decisions would surely have been made by investors and speculators, by bankers and businessmen, and by the Federal Reserve and the administration in mid-1927, early in 1928, and in the course of 1929. Moreover, as we shall see, highly erroneous appraisals of the economic position and outlook persisted for six months after the crash. The country was ill-prepared for catastrophe, and the prevailing overconfidence was so deepseated that the initial crash merely weakened without destroying it.

---

[83]*Recent Economic Changes* (June 1929), 2:909–10. The contributors to the two volumes, most of whom had completed their manuscripts in the fall of 1928, had devoted little attention to these matters, which became increasingly important in subsequent months.

PART II

CRASH, CONTRACTION, DEPRESSION, AND RECOVERY, 1929–39

7

CHAPTER 8

CRASH AND AFTERMATH, OCTOBER 1929–APRIL 1930

PRICES of industrial and railroad common stocks on the New York Stock Exchange weakened early in September 1929,[1] though September prices averaged higher than in August. They fell precipitously on October 24, 28, and 29, and declined further to a new low on November 13, when they averaged 40 to 50 percent below the recent highs. Stocks of public utilities, investment companies, and banks—the "glamour stocks" of the late 1920s—had risen in September and suffered conspicuously heavily in the all-inclusive crash. The avalanche of selling on the worst days was accentuated by serious overload on the facilities of the Exchange.[2] There were more or less parallel declines in stocks listed on other exchanges throughout the country and in over-the-counter stocks.

Some recovery to the end of 1929 and a marked rise in the first four months of 1930 were commonly interpreted as the return of the bull market, but proved only a fairly sustained rally in a long bear market. Late in April a marked downtrend in prices of common stocks began; it continued, with occasional interruptions, until extreme lows were reached in mid-1932. The crash in the fall of 1929 thus proved to be only the first phase of a collapse that extended over a period of some thirty-three months but was clearly severe by the end of 1930.

Contrary to precedents, the stock market decline in 1929 followed, rather than preceded, the onset of recession in indexes of business activity and industrial production. According to some contemporary indexes, such as that of the American Telephone and Telegraph Company, the business boom reached its crest in June 1929, and eased off in the next three months. Later revisions showed the level remaining high through August, and falling only a little lower in September. But even these indexes declined sharply in October-December and went down a little further in the first six

---

[1]The HES *Weekly Letter* of Sept. 7, 1929 (p. 213), noted the new peak of stock prices reached on Tuesday the 3d, followed by a considerable reaction on Thursday (the "Babson Break"), but said that no prolonged decline was in sight. The more comprehensive Standard Statistics index reached its high on September 7. In *Only Yesterday* (New York: Harper, 1931), F. L. Allen reprinted parts of the *New York Times* financial pages for Sept. 3 and Oct. 29, 1929. These do not appear in the paperback edition (New York: Harper and Row, 1959).

[2]*Economist*, Nov. 9, 23, Dec. 7, 1929, pp. 867, 976–77, 1081; Franz Schneider, Jr., Nov. 22, 1929, in *Proc. Acad. Pol. Sci.*, January 1930, 13:568–75; E. H. H. Simmons, "The Principal Causes of the Stock Market Crisis of Nineteen Twenty Nine" (address of the president of the NYSE, Philadelphia, Jan. 25, 1930), in Simmons, *Financing American Industry and Other Addresses* (New York: NYSE, 1930), pp. 303–31.

months of 1930. Then began a drastic fall into what became a severe depression by the end of the year.[3] Wholesale price indexes, here and abroad, fell almost continuously from November 1929 through 1930 and 1931.

**The Crash, October-   A fully detailed and authoritative story of stock
November 1929   market developments in the crucial months of
September-December 1929 apparently remains to be written. Abundant materials are available in New York dailies; weeklies such as the *Commercial and Financial Chronicle*, the *Annalist*, the *Economist* (London), and the *Weekly Letter* of the Harvard Economic Society; and monthlies such as the AT&T *Summary of Business Conditions in the United States* and the National City Bank *Monthly Letter*. Irving Fisher and Francis W. Hirst wrote useful early accounts, and A. D. Noyes and F. L. Allen briefer ones.[4] Galbraith, Rothbard, and Patterson published much later ones.[5]

As early as September 1929 some investors and speculators took their profits and quit the market, as Baruch did. In late September and early October nonbank lenders began calling their loans rather than renewing them, and such action reached its peak in the week ending October 30. Superconfidence waned in September and October as foreign and domestic news became increasingly unfavorable.

In the financial section of the *Nation and Athenaeum* (the London weekly controlled by Keynes, to which he often contributed) of October 5, 1929, the London Stock Exchange was reported as "suffering from three

---

[3]This course is also shown by the Cleveland Trust Company chart of *American Business Activity since 1790* (April 1971 ed.). For 1929-30 the first edition of the chart, then entitled *Business Cycles since 1831* (October 1940), showed a somewhat different course, with slight declines in June-August reaching a subnormal level in December 1929 rather than in May 1930. Current issues of the AT&T *Summary* showed a broadly similar course.

[4]Irving Fisher, renowned as an economist but noted also for erratic ideas, had rashly made several predictions that quickly proved false during the crash. He then rushed into print a short book entitled *The Stock Market Crash—and After* (New York: Macmillan, 1930; preface dated. Dec. 15, 1929). Fisher included several useful charts of stock prices, including his own index. Others, including daily prices of various indexes, were published in the *AT&T* monthly summaries (then marked "confidential" but given considerable circulation).

Francis W. Hirst, an able former editor of the *Economist*, was convalescing from a severe illness, first in a New York hospital and then at Atlantic City, in October-December 1929. In his book *Wall Street and Lombard Street: The Stock Exchange Slump of 1929 and the Trade Depression of 1930* (New York: Macmillan, 1931), Hirst first discussed the market crash (pp. 1-73) with the aid of personal observations, reading, and conversations. His part 2, "The Trade Depression of 1930," was not treated seriatim.

For Noyes' account, see Alexander Dana Noyes, "The Stock Market Panic," *Current History*, December 1929, 31:618-23; for Allen, see *Only Yesterday*, ch. 13.

[5]J. K. Galbraith, *The Great Crash 1929* (Boston: Houghton Mifflin, 1955), chs. 6-8; Murray N. Rothbard, *America's Great Depression* (Princeton, N.J.: Van Nostrand, 1936); Robert T. Patterson, *The Great Boom and Panic, 1921-1929* (Chicago: Regnery, 1965), chs. 5-7 and bibliography.

necessary evils—the Hatry collapse, the rise in Bank rate [September 26], and the break in New York. . . . The New York market is considered to be passing through more than a technical reaction occasioned by the rise in brokers' loans. If the present recession in the automobile industry, apart from Ford, is followed by a reaction in autumn business generally, the 'bull' market in New York will suffer the long awaited 'major' break" (page 30). A week later, in the same section, this break was believed to have occurred—actually, the decline was reversed within a week. Relief was expressed: "The London Stock Exchange should rejoice to see the break in New York, for it hastens the return of sterling balances to London, which the 6-1/2 per cent. bank rate has set in motion, and brings nearer solution of our monetary troubles" (page 64). On October 26, however, after the panicky selling of the 24th, it was stated: "The New York Stock Exchange has been heading for a major break for some considerable time" (page 156). It was attributed largely to excessive issues of investment trusts.

On November 2, on the heels of the debacles of October 24, 28, and 29, the *N&A* editorially commented: "The persistent buoyancy of the American stock markets, which has now come to so decisive and so drastic an end, has been one of the dominating facts in the international economic situation during the past three years. Its influence upon our economic life has been far-reaching and profound, operating in various ways, some of them direct and palpable, others of psychological and intangible description" (pages 162–63). This "buoyancy," it continued, had entailed a long period of dear money in the United States. The Federal Reserve Bank authorities had early decided that it was undesirable, and with very doubtful wisdom had tried to check it by raising rediscount rates at a time (early 1928) when stock prices were "in no way excessive." Dear money in the United States was one of the main causes of dear money in Britain. British investors "were suddenly converted to the view that as the boom had continued so long it might continue indefinitely. . . . All the reactions which we have so far considered, of the prolonged Wall Street boom on British trade, have been of an unfavourable kind; and the consequences of the collapse ought to be correspondingly beneficial." While some unfavorable reactions were anticipated, these were not expected to be "very serious or very lasting." "The imagination of the whole world has been dazzled of recent years by the phenomenon of American 'prosperity.' It is possible that the world may now discern that the prosperity was only partly a reality and partly an illusion created by the soaring prices of stocks." This was the setting in which Keynes and Sir Josiah Stamp cabled their comments to the New York *Evening Post* of October 25, in which both viewed the break as salutary (see page 193 below).

To an important degree—the full extent was not known, at the time or later[6]—foreigners were heavily involved in the New York market, chiefly through ownership of U.S. stocks and through lending of short-term funds attracted especially by high call-loan rates.[7] Sales of such securities and recall of short-term funds, begun in late September and early October, must have exerted considerable influence, along with profit-taking by prudent investors and speculators, in precipitating the severe crash. Once it started, the weakening of margins on collateral loans, extensive calling of loans, accompanying short selling, and fear of more sales under pressure all made for a downward spiral.

The decline was somewhat cushioned, between October 24 and November 13, by the concerted action of several New York bankers under the leadership of J. P. Morgan and Company, who, contrary to the hopes of many, sought merely to bring order into the market movement after the panicky selling of October 24.[8] Despite purchases by the bankers' consortium, however, such selling was resumed on October 28 and 29. During the crash, the New York banks courageously took over the loans which apprehensive out-of-town banks and corporations had called; the banks increased their collateral loans by over $1 billion in the week ending October 30 and rates on new call loans fell from 10 percent on the 1st to 5 percent on the 29th.[9]

The volume of trading on the New York Stock Exchange reached an extraordinary peak on October 29, at 16,410,030 shares.[10] This extreme record was not later approached, despite an enormous increase in the number of shares listed,[11] until the spring of 1968. In the peak week another 7,046,300 shares were traded on the Curb (later American) Exchange. The New York Stock Exchange opened at noon on Thursday, October 31, "to allow members' offices to catch up on work and for relief of personnel and to straighten out trades." Throughout November the Exchange closed all day on Saturdays and on two Fridays, November 2 and 29; on most other

---

[6]Calendar year data summarized in *Hist. Stat. U.S.*, ser. U 185–90, are not very helpful. Governor Norman wrote to the governor of the Bank of Canada on June 19, 1935: "The 'panic' money which grew to such large proportions in the 'twenties, and which was the prime agent in wrecking the gold standard, is still (as recent events have shown) capable of putting a severe strain without warning and perhaps without adequate cause upon almost any currency." Sir Henry Clay, *Lord Norman* (London: Macmillan, 1957), p. 419. Clay died in a road accident in Holland on July 30, 1954, before this book was finished.

[7]*C&FC*, Oct. 26, Nov. 2, 9, 16, 23, 1929, pp. 2617, 2800, 2949, 3104–6, 3253–54; Hirst, *Wall Street and Lombard Street*, pp. 80–81.

[8]*C&FC*, Oct. 26, 1929, pp. 2617–18; Hirst, *Wall Street and Lombard Street*, pp. 23, 27, 28, 33.

[9]B. H. Beckhart, in *Proc. Acad. Pol. Sci.*, January 1930, 13:501; Lionel D. Edie, in *ibid.*, pp. 520–21.

[10]*C&FC*, Nov. 2, 1929, p. 2728.

[11]Second to it was the 14,910,000 shares traded on Mar. 10, 1967. Third was the 14,746,000 shares traded on May 29, 1962, on the rally during the severe slump of that spring.

days it closed at 1 P.M. for the same reasons.[12] The curtailed hours "undoubtedly contributed greatly to the restoration of more orderly trading."[13]

Most contemporary judgments in the midst of the crash, whether domestic or foreign, proved seriously in error, especially as to its consequences, as a few illustrations clearly show.[14] Keynes and Stamp, in their cabled comments after the severe break of October 24, reflected current English financial opinion that the slump should be healthy for the United States and still more so for the rest of the world.[15] Keynes even predicted that credit would be freed for industry,[16] that commodity prices would recover, and that farmers would find themselves in better shape. The crash was even termed "a bull point for world prosperity." They were gifted with no more foresight into the coming repercussions than less prominent observers.

For the time, the public turned blind eyes and deaf ears to Sir George Paish's simultaneous assertion, published in the New York *World* of October 25: "Due simply to overspeculation. . . . we are now traversing the biggest financial crisis the world has ever seen." And President Hoover's statement of that afternoon was reassuring.[17] Babson now asserted that only an orderly decline was to be expected, and even the *Chronicle* expected nothing so bad again.[18] On October 31 the Ford Motor Company announced reductions in its car and truck prices, expressed its belief that industry and business were basically sound, and confidently predicted "that

[12]NYSE, *Year Book, 1931–1932*, pp. 41, 45.

[13]AT&T, *Summary*, Dec. 7, 1929, p. 6.

[14]See also Anon. [Robert S. Allen and Drew Pearson], *Washington Merry-Go-Round* (New York: Liveright, 1931), pp. 75–76; W. S. Myers and W. H. Newton, *The Hoover Administration: A Documented Narrative* (New York: Scribner, 1936), pp. 21–22; Arthur M. Schlesinger, Jr., *The Crisis of the Old Order, 1919–1933* (Boston: Houghton Mifflin, 1957), p. 138; Joseph Dorfman, *The Economic Mind in American Civilization*, vols. 4–5: *1919–1933* (New York: Viking, 1959), 5:607–8; H. G. Warren, *Herbert Hoover and the Great Depression* (New York: Oxford University Press, 1959), pp. 103–12.

[15]Reported in the New York *Evening Post* of Oct. 25, 1919, summarized and partially quoted in Hirst, *Wall Street and Lombard Street*, pp. 28–30. Keynes began one paragraph: "I may be a bad prophet. . . . " Similar views were expressed in editorials in the *Times* (London), the *Manchester Guardian*, and the *Nation and Athenaeum*, reprinted in *Living Age* (New York), Dec. 1, 1929, 337:394–400.

[16]This misapprehension, largely but not wholly unfounded, was shared by the Federal Reserve, President Hoover, and many others. Cf. Lionel Robbins, *The Great Depression* (London: Macmillan, 1934), p. 40: "The idea that the boom on the Stock Exchange keeps money from industry is of course the exact opposite of the truth."

[17]C&FC, Nov. 2, 1929, p. 2807, quoted in Hirst, *Wall Street and Lombard Street*, pp. 30–31. On the basis of Department of Agriculture releases on the reduction in world wheat output in 1929, Hoover rashly predicted for wheat "a very low carryover at the end of the harvest year." This proved a gross error. See Wheat Studies of the Food Research Institute 7 (Stanford, Calif.: Food Research Institute, 1930), pp. 107–10, 177–78. The 1928 carryover figures were later revised upward.

[18]Hirst, *Wall Street and Lombard Street*, p. 31, and C&FC, Oct. 26, 1929, pp. 2579, 2620.

general conditions would remain prosperous."[19] In its editorial of November 1 the *New York Times* rejoiced "that a wild and abnormal chapter in financial history has been definitely closed and a new chapter in financial sanity opened."

Irving Fisher on October 15 had asserted that stock prices were on "a permanently high plateau." On October 23 he assured the District of Columbia Bankers' Association that the market decline was only temporary. On November 3 he expressed the view that unexampled prosperity had justified the stock market boom, that foolish panic was responsible for the recent crash, and that prices were absurdly low; and he foresaw no break in the nation's record prosperity.[20] On November 6 John D. Rockefeller was reported as saying that the destruction of security values was unjustified and that he and his son were buying substantial amounts of stock. On the day that the market touched bottom, a broker acting for Rockefeller made a firm bid for a million shares of Standard Oil of New Jersey at fifty dollars a share.[21] By this time European investors too were attracted back into the market.

After the severe market break of October 28, Hirst later reported: "In response to the general wailing and groaning of the unlucky clients and customers, who were now bankrupt or on the verge of bankruptcy, bankers and brokerage houses now joined in a compassionate movement to lower margin requirements from 50 to 25 per cent of market valuation. This was only reasonable in view of the deflation in spot prices."[22] Canadian banks, which for some time had limited loans on stock collateral to 30 to 40 percent of market values, and after the sharp decline had cut this to 25 percent, announced on November 13 that they would lend up to 85 percent of the value of shares selling for over thirty dollars.[23] For the lenders, call loans justified their reputation as "the safest and most liquid investment in American banking," but for the borrowers the liquidation was extremely costly. Many were just sold out.

The New York Stock Exchange on November 13 required all banks and brokers to make daily reports on their market operations, including short sales; and short selling ended for a time.[24] By this time also, call-loan

[19]Quoted in Hirst, *Wall Street and Lombard Street*, p. 39.

[20]*C&FC*, Oct. 26, Nov. 16, 1929, pp. 2618-19, 3106; George H. Soule, Jr., *Prosperity Decade: From War to Depression, 1917-1929* (New York: Rinehart, 1947), pp. 305-7, 310; Hirst, *Wall Street and Lombard Street*, pp. 41-42.

[21]*C&FC*, Nov. 16, 1929, p. 3106, citing New York *Journal of Commerce*, Nov. 14; Hirst, *Wall Street and Lombard Street*, pp. 38, 46.

[22]*Wall Street and Lombard Street*, pp. 33-34.

[23]*C&FC*, Nov. 16, 1929, p. 3106.

[24]*Ibid.*, pp. 3051-52; Fisher, *Stock Market Crash*, pp. 53-55. Simmons (*Financing American Industry*, pp. 322-23) said short selling was "extraordinarily small."

rates and bank rates had come down drastically,[25] margin requirements had been liberalized, and the fortunate ones who had liquidated their holdings early were in funds to buy stocks for cash. The stage was set for the irregular recovery and advance that marked the next five months, during which the bankers who had intervened to ensure an orderly market could liquidate their purchases, if they chose, without sustaining significant losses.

Proximate Causes   The proximate cause of the severe but shortlived stock market crash in the fall of 1929 was the frenzied rise of the market in the preceding months, and the extraordinary increase of investment and speculation in common stocks, including many that were not listed on the New York Stock Exchange, under the influence of the prevailing super-optimism.[26] Stock prices were pushed up far out of line with current corporate earnings; brokers' loans rose to extraordinary heights; call-money rates rose to exceptionally high levels, though the rates were lower as the crisis was approached; and funds were attracted from all over the United States and Europe, subject to rapid withdrawal when the mood and situation changed. These developments made the stock market highly vulnerable to bad news and severe pressures of any kind from any quarter.[27] Though it had previously resisted and recovered from many similar pressures, when depressing factors were reinforced by others which, if present, were not apparent until the fall of 1929, crumbling of stock prices ultimately precipitated an extreme crash.

Even soon after the event it was painfully clear that the stock market had risen too fast and too far in 1928–29, following the marked price gains of 1922–27.[28] Advances in particular stocks were predicated on a number of fragile assumptions: the continuing heavy purchase of durable goods by

[25]Call-money rates, which had already fallen far from their peak in March 1929, began falling again in October. Except for a temporary high at the turn of the year, they trended downward in 1930 and in most of 1931. See table of daily highs and lows from May 3, 1919, to Sept. 30, 1932, in NYSE, *Year Book, 1931–1932*, pp. 87–95. Cf. Hirst, *Wall Street and Lombard Street*, pp. 7, 25, 48, 51, 55, 93–95.

[26]See esp. Simmons' address of Jan. 25, 1930, in his *Financing American Industry*, pp. 305–31. The "Big Board" was overwhelmingly dominant, but there were numerous other stock exchanges throughout the country, as well as the Curb Exchange in New York City. See Leonard Kuvin, "Stock Price Indexes of the New York Curb Exchange," *JASA*, March 1930, 25:51–62. In addition many stocks were unlisted and traded "over the counter."

[27]This view was held by contemporaries Carl Snyder, E. H. H. Simmons, J. M. Keynes, Sir Josiah Stamp, the *Commercial and Financial Chronicle*, and others. See Fisher, *Stock Market Crash*, pp. 34–38; Hirst, *Wall Street and Lombard Street*, pp. 29–31; *C&FC*, Jan. 18, 1930, stated (pp. 18–19): "The speculative mania in this country, and the consequent high rates for money attracted funds from all parts of the United States and . . . were exerting a disturbing influence on business and credit conditions throughout the world."

[28]For example, see several papers given before the Academy of Political Science, New York City, on the heels of the crash, Nov. 22, 1929 (*Proc. Acad. Pol. Sci.*, January 1930,

consumers and of machinery by farmers, high and rising business profits, further large new investment in modernization of and additions to business plant, and early realization of economies of consolidation. The enormous expansion of brokers' loans, the extremes to which call-loan rates rose, and the abnormally "large inverse spread" between bond yields and dividend yields on common stocks[29] all were warnings that were taken far too lightly. Eventually the superoptimists were caught in the trap of their own extrapolations!

The timing of the crash was strongly influenced by adverse events in London and Berlin, where security liquidation had been under way for months before the peak was reached on the New York Stock Exchange.[30] As late as August 31, 1929, reports from both the London and the New York stock exchanges were reassuring, but September brought bad news from abroad: the failure of an important German insurance concern (Frankfurter Allgemeine), affected by serious weakness in rayon shares;[31] the scandalous collapse of the Clarence Hatry group in London—announced on September 20, soon followed by Hatry's arrest and, within five months, by his conviction for forgery of stock certificates; and the largely coincidental rise of the Bank of England rate from 5.5 to 6.5 percent on September 26.[32] Heavy withdrawals of foreign funds from the United States thereafter were important. The decline in stock price indexes in late 1929, indeed, was sharpest in London, where it was comparable to that in the serious Baring crisis of 1890.[33]

13:455-575), including excellent discussions by J. H. Hollander, B. H. Beckhart, Carl Snyder, W. R. Burgess, Lionel D. Edie, George E. Roberts, O. M. W. Sprague, and Franz Schneider, Jr., and Schneider's paper and several others given at the American Economic Association meetings in late December 1929.

[29]Keynes said on October 25: "The relative yield of stocks and loans was an impossibility as a permanency. I consider this to be the root cause of the crash." This was a rash judgment.

[30]See Fisher, *Stock Market Crash*, pp. 31-33, which includes a chart of New York, London, Paris, and Berlin stock price indexes for 1927-29.

[31]*Economist*, Aug. 24, Sept. 21, 1929, pp. 352, 509-10. The Hatry crash was handled with remarkable skill and celerity. Cf. Joseph A. Schumpeter, *Business Cycles: A Theoretical, Historical, and Statistical Analysis of the Capitalist Process*, 2 vols. (New York: McGraw-Hill, 1939), 2:908.

[32]*Economist*, Sept. 28, Oct. 5, 1929, pp. 556-57, 627; Jan. 11, 18, 25, Feb. 1, 22, Mar. 29, 1930, pp. 79, 124-27, 168-69, 180, 223-24, 244, 417-18, 714; Fisher, *Stock Market Crash*, pp. xiii, 4, 31, 230; Economicus, "The Hatry Scandal," *Review of Reviews* (London), February 1930, pp. 115ff.; Hirst, *Wall Street and Lombard Street*, pp. 8-9, 61, 80, 89. Fisher dated the Hatry failure as "in August," or "August 30," and miscalled the group a "banking house." In his comment on Oct. 24, 1929, Stamp expressed the belief that this had nothing to do with the New York situation. Hirst, *Wall Street and Lombard Street*, pp. 30, 80-81. Like various others, I cannot accept this extreme opinion, though the Hatry affair was only one of many factors. In his discussion of recent events on Nov. 22, 1929, Rufus S. Tucker gave reasons for calling the Hatry failure the "occasion" of the fall in the stock market, which had already risen "to a dangerous height and stood just ready to topple over at a slight touch." *Proc. Acad. Pol. Sci.*, January 1930, 13:533-37.

[33]A. D. Noyes, *Forty Years of American Finance* (New York: Putnam, 1909), pp. 157-58.

Many factors contributing to the crash were mentioned, at the time and later,[34] though most of the later commentators concentrated on the ensuing economic contraction. The exceptionally large volume of "undigested securities"—securities held by underwriters or sold to buyers who expected to resell to ultimate investors; the unprecedented and unanimous refusal (October 11) of the Massachusetts Department of Public Utilities to permit Boston Edison Electric to split its stock; the existence of the federal capital gains tax, which had helped to make holders of common stocks reluctant to cash in large paper profits; uncertainties over the outcome of the struggle over the tariff bill: these were some of many items of adverse import which offset such favorable news as increases in corporate dividends.[35] The pre-crash decline in construction, the concurrent reduction in steel and automotive output, the threat of contraction of exports, the weakening of commodity prices, the breakdown in Brazil's efforts to control prices of coffee on October 11,[36] and the break in California's oil production restriction on October 21: all helped dissipate excessive bullishness in September and October but were not major bearish influences.[37] The financial and economic weaknesses in overseas countries, in part consequences of the U.S. stock market boom, were very inadequately recognized even after the Hatry collapse and the rise in the Bank of England rate.[38] And one must not overlook the American tendency, more or less shared in other countries, to swing from excessive optimism to excessive pessimism.[39]

Early Consequences   The Wall Street crash was of unprecedented severity. The relative shrinkage of market values of common stocks from the

[34]G. A. Anderson and D. W. Ellsworth, in *Annalist*, Oct. 25, 1929, pp. 811-14; E. C. Harwood, in *ibid.*, Nov. 29, 1929, pp. 1052-53, 1096; Fisher, *Stock Market Crash*, ch. 2, "Causes of the Panic"; Simmons, *Financing American Industry*, pp. 303-31; Hirst, *Wall Street and Lombard Street*, ch. 5, "Causes and Remedies"; T. W. Lamont, Nov. 14, 1930, *Proc. Acad. Pol. Sci.*, January 1931, 14:90-91; Leonard P. Ayres, *The Chief Cause of This and Other Depressions* (pamphlet published in April 1935); Robert T. Patterson, *The Great Boom and Panic, 1921-1929* (Chicago: Regnery, 1965), ch. 12, "Causes"; E. R. Ellis, *A Nation in Torment: The Great American Depression, 1929-1939* (New York: Coward-McCann, 1970), ch. 6.

[35]See chart in CTC, *Bus. Bull.*, Feb. 15, 1932.

[36]See J. W. F. Rowe's discussion in Royal Economic Society *Memorandum 23*, October 1930, p. 25, and *Memorandum 34*, February 1932, pp. 49-57, 86.

[37]In its *Weekly Letter* of Sept. 21, 1929 (p. 228), the Harvard Economic Society observed: "Recent developments have tended to emphasize the unfavorable elements in the business (as distinguished from the financial) structure. . . . But no sharp decline has occurred in general business and activity remains high."

[38]Simmons rightly observed (*Financing American Industry*, p. 317): "We must consider European conditions more closely and more critically in the future as a regular factor in the New York securities market." Keynes later wrote in his 1933 pamphlet *The Means to Prosperity* (London: Macmillan, 1933), p. 19: "The chief agency in starting the slump" was "the collapse of expenditures financed out of loans advanced by the United States, for use both at home and abroad."

[39]See Paul Einzig, *The World Economic Crisis, 1929-1931*, 2d ed. (London: Macmillan, 1932), pp. 81-82.

peaks of August and September to the low of November 13, 1929, was the largest in U.S. history, even to the end of 1972. The various indexes of stock prices—none of them adequately representative[40]—showed divergent percentages. Thus the Dow-Jones index of industrials showed a drop of 48 percent and that of rails 32 percent (from their late August high). The *New York Times* index of leading industrials declined 50 percent, and that of leading stocks 47 percent. The Standard Statistics index of public utility shares, which had risen exceptionally far in May-September, registered a fall of 56 percent.[41] Shrinkages were also unusually large in bank stocks and investment trust shares, which were commonly traded over the counter.

Abroad, stock markets had peaked in Berlin in the spring of 1927, in London and Brussels in April and May 1928, in Tokyo in midsummer 1928, in Switzerland in September 1928, and in Paris and Amsterdam early in 1929. The "staggering avalanche of liquidation" in New York in October 1929 accelerated declines in foreign centers and precipitated a colossal world-wide liquidation of securities.[42] Soule later put it thus: "This volcanic explosion set in motion a tidal wave that also overwhelmed the markets in London, Paris, Berlin and was felt throughout the world."[43] Phillips, McManus, and Nelson well spoke of the "percussive character" of the crash, and said, with only limited exaggeration, "The whole character of the ensuing depression was colored and shaped by what happened in Wall Street in October 1929."[44]

The losses from the crash were spectacularly large and widespread, and hordes of small speculators were wiped out.[45] Yet such direct consequences can easily be exaggerated, and have been.[46] Even if the losers lost all they put into stocks they bought on margin, a large proportion of them had other assets and were by no means "ruined." Galbraith took pains to destroy the myth that the suicide rate shot up sharply.[47] For the great ma-

---

[40]Simmons (*Financing American Industry*, p. 307) urged the need for better indexes.

[41]AT&T, *Summary*, Dec. 5, 1929, p. 5.

[42]Fisher, *Stock Market Crash*, p. 33; N. J. Silberling, *The Dynamics of Business* (New York: McGraw-Hill, 1943), p. 303.

[43]Soule, *Prosperity Decade*, p. 309.

[44]C. A. Phillips, T. F. McManus, and R. W. Nelson, *Banking and the Business Cycle: A Study of the Great Depression in the United States* (New York: Macmillan, 1937), pp. 151–52. Cf. Hirst, *Wall Street and Lombard Street*, pp. vi, 154.

[45]Lead editorials in *C&FC*, Oct. 26, Nov. 3, 1929; AT&T, *Summary*, Nov. 7, 1929, pp. 1, 5; Hirst, *Wall Street and Lombard Street*, pp. 24–25, 39–40, 50.

[46]The American propensity to exaggerate found many illustrations in this period, but many later writers who pointed out these instances fell into the same trap themselves.

[47]*Great Crash*, pp. 133–36. The crude suicide rate for the nation was only slightly higher in 1929 than in 1928. *Vital Stat. U.S., 1950*, 1:219; *Hist. Stat. U.S.*, ser. B 128. The age-adjusted suicide rate, as computed by the Statistical Bureau of the Metropolitan Life Insurance Company, showed slight *declines* in 1929 and in 1930 from the 1922–28 plateau but showed sharp increases in 1930–34 and again in 1938–40. Yet one must distrust suicide data, for many true suicides are reported as accidental deaths or erroneously assigned to other specific causes. Cf. W. S. Pinkerton, Jr., "The Lethal Impulse," *WSJ*, Mar. 6, 1960, pp. 1, 12.

jority, the biggest losses of shareowners were paper losses, since many investors merely sat tight. These profoundly affected spending attitudes for the time, for "paper losers" felt poor even if they were not. Hence sales of cars, jewelry, silk goods, furs, and many other luxuries and semi-luxuries were especially depressed, and the 1929 Christmas sales fell short of pre-crash expectations. Moreover, caution in spending replaced recklessness even on the part of many who had not been in the market, for recognition and intensification of the economic contraction that was under way engendered uncertainties about future profits and employment. Installment purchasing was restrained by reluctance on the part of both borrowers and lenders.

Patterson's good chapter, "Human Aspects of the Panic,"[48] stressed the emotional strain, the highly varied responses, and the crop of disclosures of defalcations and embezzlements. He also called attention to instances in which companies or individual multimillionaires, including Julius Rosenwald and Samuel Insull, protected employees from being wiped out by margin calls.[49] Particularly important, however, was the loss of prestige and reputation suffered by big businessmen, bankers, brokers, investment analysts, and economists, who had been trusted far beyond their merits. The full effect of this, however, was spread over the next two or three years.

Capital gains had figured heavily in the rising volume of income subject to tax prior to the crash.[50] They shrank drastically in the last quarter of 1929, and many wealthy taxpayers took such heavy capital losses that they paid no income tax for 1929. Yet the total number of individuals whose net income exceeded $1 million reached its peak at 513 in that year—a record not broken until 1965, if then.[51]

The Wall Street crash profoundly altered the mood of the American people and of businessmen in particular. The shock took various forms and engendered fears that successive experiences intensified; recurrent disillusionments changed for the worse the entire climate of opinion. Confidence was shaken, in the United States and abroad, in stocks and commodity values; in business forecasts; in businessmen and bankers; in one's ability to hold one's job or get a new one; in banks and the Federal Reserve System; in the honesty of individuals and business leaders; in the reliability of utterances by leaders in business, finance, and government; and in President Hoover himself. Purchasing power was not lacking, but those

---

[48]*Great Boom and Panic*, pp. 161–74.

[49]To protect the good name of the London financial community, members of the London Stock Exchange decided, on Jan. 15, 1930, to subscribe $5 million to buy up worthless shares to ensure that no loss fall on the general public in consequence of the Hatry crash. *Ibid.*, p. 93; *Economist*, Jan. 18, Feb. 22, 1930, pp. 129, 417.

[50]U.S., Secretary of the Treasury, *Annual Report, 1929*, p. 4.

[51]In recent years the basis for the figure reported has been in terms of adjusted gross income, and that number first exceeded 513 in 1965, when 596 were reported.

who had it were afraid to use it lest they need it even more later. Credit soon became abundant and increasingly cheap, but with fears predominating over hope, relatively little was used. Naturally enterprise shrank. It was persistently held that "the all-important object of sound public policy today should be a restoration of confidence."[52] But how to do this was far from clear.

In sharp contrast to his reassuring public statements to the press and his State of the Union message of December 3, President Hoover frankly said in his off-the-record talk to the Gridiron Club on December 14, with what doubtless was unconscious exaggeration: "Fear, alarm, pessimism, and hesitation swept through the country, which, if unchecked, would have precipitated absolute panic throughout the business world with untold misery in its wake. Its acute dangers were far greater than we are able to disclose at the present time."[53] These private sentiments go far to account for the president's public show of optimistic confidence, which he defended in his *Memoirs*,[54] and also for the actions which he took in November (see pages 208-9 below).

The climate of investment markets, like that of consumer markets, was radically altered for the worse. New security issues had been extremely large in the first nine months of 1929, but dropped sharply in the last two months of the year. Investment company issues fell drastically from their September peak to extreme lows in November and December, and continued very low through 1930.[55] Foreign securities offerings, which in the third quarter of 1929 were the lowest since 1923, fell much lower in the fourth quarter.[56]

An unforeseen consequence of the crash was an intensification of previously mild declines in commodity prices, followed by a gradual crumbling of the whole price structure that extended throughout 1930 and gave rise to severe strains here and abroad.[57] This gravely weakened the position of the country banks which had loaned too liberally on farm products. As

[52]E. W. Kemmerer, "The Gold Standard in the United States," in J. G. Smith, ed., *Facing the Facts: An Economic Diagnosis* (New York: Putnam, 1933), pp. 20-33.

[53]Hoover, *State Papers and Other Public Writings of Herbert Hoover*, ed. William Starr Myers, 2 vols. (Garden City, N.Y.: Doubleday, 1934), 1:187-93, esp. p. 191.

[54]Hoover, *The Memoirs of Herbert Hoover*, vol. 3: *The Great Depression, 1929-1941* (New York: Macmillan, 1952), pp. 58, 480. See further Chapter 9 below.

[55]See chart and brief discussion in HES, *Weekly Letter*, Nov. 29, 1930, p. 293. Other corporate issues rose sharply in January-May 1930, after which they fell to low levels in August-October. Even foreign issues were much higher in February-June 1930 than in all but two months since mid-1928.

[56]AT&T, monthly summaries for the last four months of 1929, the latest published Jan. 7, 1930.

[57]The details are extensively discussed, with useful tables and charts, in the HES *Weekly Letter* in the issues of 1929 and 1930. That of Nov. 16, 1929 (p. 295), noted that "our sensitive price index has been falling sharply in the past four weeks." See also Hirst, *Wall Street and Lombard Street*, ch. 3, "The Collapse of Prices and the Plight of the Cultivator."

stock market losses and new caution in expectations put a crimp in sales of all sorts of luxuries and semi-luxuries, prices of raw silk dropped sharply, and soon led to a marked decline in Japan's chief export.[58] The crash was by no means the only factor that made for falling commodity prices. Wool prices, so important for Australia and other surplus-producing countries, had declined some time earlier.[59] So had coffee prices; but the breakdown in São Paulo's coffee-defense mechanism, announced on October 28, led to intensified price declines that sharply affected Latin American coffee-producing countries.[60]

The crash also precipitated emergency actions by the recently constituted Federal Farm Board, on October 21 and 26, to save over-loaned country banks, and cotton and wheat growers, from severe losses on unsold parts of their crops. These fateful decisions, under extreme pressures, preceded the worst declines in prices of industrial stocks[61] and were to wreck the Board's chances of succeeding in its primary purpose (see discussion on pages 204-5, 236, below). The subsequent descent of wheat prices was due largely to accumulating evidence that carryovers and crops (especially European and Argentine) had been underestimated and international demand overestimated; but in the course of the crop year "pessimism was engendered by breaks in stock prices and by other evidence of the growth and spread of general economic depression."[62]

"The stock market crash itself produced an unbalanced situation which quickly degenerated into depression."[63] Even more important, it forced a drastic revaluation of the economic situation. This gradually revealed a number of vulnerabilities hitherto unrealized, at least in degree: in commodity prices, real estate values, high consumer inventories; altered dispositions to spend on consumer durables and luxuries, on new residential construction, and on industrial plant and equipment; and declines in business and stock market profits. As this revaluation proceeded it came to light that financiers, industrialists, and political leaders had not been truly far-sighted and sound of judgment, and that far too many had been unworthy of the trust they had enjoyed (see Chapter 14). And it had to be

[58]AT&T, monthly summaries for September 1929-January 1930, touching also on other commodities.

[59]Noted in *Annalist*, Sept. 6, 1929, p. 445.

[60]AT&T, *Summary*, Dec. 7, 1929; Hirst, *Wall Street and Lombard Street*, pp. 34-35, 119, 152-54. In December 1929 the price of No. 7 Rio fell as low as 9 cents a pound, less than half the price in February. What was termed the abandonment of São Paulo's coffee-defense policy came in April 1930. *N&A*, Apr. 19, 1930, p. 298.

[61]See chart in Wheat Studies of the Food Research Institute 6 (Stanford, Calif.: Food Research Institute, 1930), p. 137.

[62]*Ibid.*, pp. 89-90 *et seq.*; Federal Farm Board, *First Annual Report, 1930*, pp. 28-39, and *Third Annual Report, 1932*, pp. 63-65.

[63]Phillips, McManus, and Nelson, *Banking and the Business Cycle*, p. 171. Cf. *ibid.*, p. 9: "when the stock boom eventually collapsed, it loosed business activity from its false and insecure moorings and the descent into the maelstrom of disaster began."

recognized that the Federal Reserve System had failed to check pre-crash credit inflation and to prevent excesses that led eventually to the market collapse.[64]

For such reasons the mild contraction in industrial output and business activity was accentuated in October-December,[65] as reflected in the contemporary indexes of the Federal Reserve Board, the American Telephone and Telegraph Company, the Cleveland Trust Company, and others. Some of these were later revised upward, implying that the true degree of contraction was not as large as some contemporary observers believed.

There were no monthly indexes of overall employment and unemployment, but indexes of factory employment fell significantly, and those of factory payrolls and wage earnings more extremely, in the last three months of 1929.[66] Miscellaneous and total freight car loadings, which had been on a high level in January-September 1929, were notably reduced by the end of the year.[67] Marked shrinkages occurred in production of electric power, crude petroleum, pig iron, passenger cars, and many others. Commodity stocks and industrial inventories began a significant rise.[68]

Some early financial effects on foreign countries were favorable, as Keynes and Stamp had foreseen. The inflow of gold slackened in September and changed in October to an outflow that lasted into January. But the international repercussions of the sequential developments were highly adverse, as we shall see (see Chapter 9 below). Hirst was right in saying, late in 1930, that "from a purely financial point of view, the difficulties of the world have been very much increased by the *boom and slump* in Wall Street."[69]

After the stock market crash, there were some who claimed to have foreseen the end of our "unparalleled" prosperity. Anne O'Hare McCormick wrote, with typical exaggeration: "Everybody knew that the paper

---

[64]W. R. Burgess, "The Money Market in 1929," *Rev. Ec. Stat.*, February 1930, 12:15–20.

[65]Cf. Phillips, McManus, and Nelson, *Banking and the Business Cycle*, p. 160. In his 1930 discussion of the extent of the influence of the stock market crash in causing the severe business contraction of 1930, Harold L. Reed seems to me to have gone too far in minimizing that influence. *Federal Reserve Policy, 1921–1930* (New York: McGraw-Hill, 1930), pp. 193–201. If, indeed, "the business depression was born largely of causes independent of the stock-market crash" (p. 195), it is pertinent to stress the importance of the crash in bringing to light and intensifying weaknesses theretofore inadequately recognized (see Chapter 13 below).

[66]See the valuable charts appended to the AT&T monthly summaries and the tables, charts, and discussions therein and in the HES weekly letters. The American Federation of Labor was reported as saying, early in 1930, that about 3 million were unemployed, most of them only recently. *Review of Reviews* (New York), February 1930, p. 46. All later references in this chapter are to this journal, not to the London one of the same name cited in n. 32 above.

[67]Weekly data on total freight car loadings in 1929–30 (to July 1930), in percentage deviations from normal, showed the decline sharpest in November, moving to low levels from mid-November to the end of the year. AT&T, *Summary*, Aug. 6, 1930, pp. 10, 13.

[68]HES, *Weekly Letter*, Sept. 14, Oct. 5, 12, 19, 1929, pp. 221, 237, 241, 249, 252.

[69]Hirst, *Wall Street and Lombard Street*, pp. 108–22, 152–55 (italics added).

pyramid was unsubstantial as a pillar of cloud and that the betting at last was no more than a fantastic gamble on how long it could stand."[70] General Dawes wrote at sea on Armistice Day 1929: "To me it seems that the signs of the coming of the present panic were more pronounced than those of any other through which the United States has passed."[71] But he had not publicly voiced this opinion earlier, nor did he then. Some observers in late 1929 predicted severe depression as the aftermath or the consequence of the crash,[72] partly on "boom-bust" assumptions, partly on the assumption that saving had been overdone, partly for other reasons; but these were distinctly in the minority. Indeed, for a period of several weeks in the winter of 1929–30 there was an amazing revival of optimism and confidence, which was reflected in the stock market and the economy.

Federal Actions Taken   The stock market crash gave rise to significant actions by the Federal Reserve authorities, the Federal Farm Board, and the White House. The Federal Reserve System had prepared for the crash by shrinking its portfolio of government securities and by raising rediscount rates. The New York Bank took "timely and effective" actions on its own initiative, and other Reserve Banks followed suit. In the hectic last week of October 1929 the New York Bank radically expanded its security holdings and its rediscounts, and the System expanded credit enormously. As nonbank lenders declined to renew their call loans, and as brokers' loans "on account of others" shrank drastically in the later stages of the crash, member banks notably expanded their loans on securities and borrowed as needed from the Federal Reserve Banks. Beginning October 25, the New York Bank reduced its buying rates for bankers' acceptances. On November 1 and 15 it reduced its rediscount rate, first from 6 to 5 and then to 4.5 percent. "This easing of money," said the Harvard Economic Society on November 2, "is itself evidence of the soundness of the present business situation."[73]

These steps were widely praised, even by most of those who had been critical of Federal Reserve policies in 1927–29. The System seemed to have fulfilled its high promise. There was no money or credit panic; there were almost no significant banking, exchange, or business failures;[74] and, con-

---

[70]*New York Times Magazine*, Mar. 2, 1930, pp. 1–2.

[71]Charles G. Dawes, *Journal as Ambassador to Great Britain* (New York: Macmillan, 1933), pp. 98–99. See also quotations from Lippmann and Kemmerer in Chapter 7 above.

[72]Briefly adverted to in *N&A*, Dec. 7, 1929, p. 339.

[73]HES, *Weekly Letter*, Nov. 2, 1929, pp. 257–60; Reed, *Federal Reserve Policy*, pp. 186–93; Milton Friedman and Anna J. Schwartz, *A Monetary History of the United States, 1867–1960* (Princeton, N.J.: Princeton University Press, 1963), pp. 167–68, 335–39.

[74]One exception was the collapse of the $20 million W. B. Foshay conglomerate, with headquarters in a thirty-two-story "Washington Monument of the Northwest" in Minneapolis, which was announced a few days after the worst selling on October 29. *C&FC*, Nov. 2, 1929, p. 2794; Galbraith, *Great Crash*, pp. 125–26.

sidering the extreme stock market liquidation, it seemed that the financial impact of the "detonation" was well cushioned.[75]

Paul Warburg had been extremely critical of the Federal Reserve Board in the spring of 1929 for its weakness and indecision (see Chapter 7 above). After the "convulsion" in the fall he noted two outstanding facts: "the impressive demonstration of the System's structural strength and . . . the inadequacy of its form of administration." The "desperate fight to avert a further spread of the disaster could never have been hazarded and won," he said, "had it not been for the country's unbounded confidence in the un-equaled strength of the Federal Reserve System and the availability of its vast resources to the country's banks. . . . Bank credit remained unshaken, because it rested on the rock foundation of the Federal Reserve System. . . . Unlike the panic of 1907, the convulsion of 1929 did not shake the people's confidence in our banking and currency system."[76] New York City member banks in particular were given a share of the credit.[77]

In his extensive analysis, *Wheat under the Agricultural Marketing Act: Some Problems of the Federal Farm Board*, Alonzo E. Taylor evinced sober concern over excessive expectations of the act. He recognized that "the Farm Board would take exceptional measures in the direction of stabilization and price enhancement under circumstances of unusual emergency," but expressed disbelief "that such measures will be adopted as routine policy."[78] The stock market crash forced these exceptional measures while the Board was still in its infancy, with as yet no economic staff. Price declines in cotton and wheat, accompanying the crash, created an emergency; and the threat to country banks that had loaned heavily on these products, plus political pressures on behalf of their producers, virtu-ally forced the Board to promise to lend specified sums on cotton (October 21) and wheat (October 26) to farm cooperatives.[79] This step was motivated

[75]Lionel D. Edie, Nov. 22, 1929, in *Proc. Acad. Pol. Sci.*, January 1930, 13:514–23, esp. p. 520; B. M. Anderson, in *Chase Economic Bulletin*, Nov. 22, 1929, vol. 9, no. 6; Hoover, State of the Union address, Dec. 3, 1929, in Hoover, *State Papers*, 1:145; *N&A*, Dec. 7, 1929, pp. 338–39; Hirst, *Wall Street and Lombard Street*, p. vi and chs. 3–4; Reed, *Federal Reserve Policy*, p. 190; Phillips, McManus, and Nelson, *Banking and the Business Cycle*, p. 152; B. M. Anderson, *Economics and the Public Welfare: Financial and Economic History of the United States, 1914–1946* (New York: Van Nostrand, 1949), ch. 30.

H. Parker Willis, however, attacked the System's resort to open-market purchases, which he considered contrary to the original intent of the Federal Reserve Act. His editorial of Nov. 14 was quoted in *C&FC*, Nov. 16, 1929, pp. 3072–73. Cf. Friedman and Schwartz, *Monetary History*, pp. 368, 470–71.

[76]Paul M. Warburg, *The Federal Reserve System: Its Origin and Growth: Reflections and Recollections*, 2 vols. (New York: Macmillan, 1930), 2:501–17 ("The Stock Exchange Crisis of 1929").

[77]Anderson, *Economics and the Public Welfare*, pp. 214–17.

[78]Taylor, in Wheat Studies of the Food Research Institute 5 (Stanford, Calif.: Food Re-search Institute, 1929), pp. 347–425, esp. p. 354.

[79]For Chairman Legge's statement on Feb. 25, 1930, his letter to President Hoover dated Mar. 6, 1930, and Hoover's reply dated Mar. 15, 1930, see Myers and Newton, *Hoover Ad-ministration*, pp. 37–39, and Forrest Crissey, *Alexander Legge, 1866–1933* (Chicago: privately

in considerable part by the fear of extensive failures of banks which had made liberal loans on cotton and wheat.[80] It served its initial purpose for a time, cushioning the fall of wheat and cotton prices, saving some banks, and assuring many wheat and cotton growers better returns on their 1929 crops than they might otherwise have received.[81] But it failed to prevent severe declines in farm prices, reduced exports, saddled the government with heavy stocks and eventual losses, and in due time discredited the Farm Board and the act by which it was created.[82]

The day the stock market reached its lowest point, November 13, Secretary Mellon announced that agreement had been reached to recommend a cut of one percentage point in individual and corporate income tax rates.[83] Reporting this, the *Chronicle* commented editorially: "The President is handling Government problems with rare skill and judgment." The reduction was too small to be of much consequence, but it was widely welcomed, and was presumably designed and timed for maximum psychological impact. The House and Senate both approved promptly.

The Hoover administration had expected a stock market crash sooner or later. Secretary Mellon, Hoover later reported, "felt that the government must keep its hands off and let the slump liquidate itself." Broadly speaking, this had been the practice in previous crises, even including the early postwar crash of 1920–21.[84] Hoover and other cabinet members, as well as Governor Young of the Federal Reserve Board, strongly believed that all the powers of government should be used to cushion the impact of the shock, even though there was no experience to guide them and no one, not even the president, could see clearly what the true situation was or what

printed, 1936), pp. 191–93. I had accepted the post of chief economist of the Board before the commitments of Oct. 21 and 26, but my tenure began only on Dec. 2, 1929. The appointment was announced in *C&FC*, Dec. 21, 1929, p. 3896.

[80]See Crissey, *Legge*, pp. 189–90, 193–200; M. K. Bennett, Helen C. Farnsworth, and Alonzo E. Taylor, *Survey of the Wheat Situation, December 1930 to March 1931*, Wheat Studies of the Food Research Institute 7 (Stanford, Calif.: Food Research Institute, 1931), pp. 295, 318–27. They were right in saying that the "compelling motive" for the Federal Farm Board's "stabilization" (or "valorization") steps initiated after mid-October 1929 was "support of public psychology in the downward phase of the trade cycle, and support of banking institutions—not support of wheat [and cotton] prices alone."

[81]See Federal Farm Board, *First Annual Report*, December 1930, pp. 24–42, esp. pp. 27, 33–34, 36–39; *Second Annual Report*, December 1931, pp. 36–58, esp. pp. 37, 44–48, 53, 55, 57.

[82]A. H. Hurst early in 1930, in his book *The Bread of Britain* (London: Oxford University Press, 1930), went so far as to say (p. 21) that the Board "has already been unusually effective." J. A. Venn, reviewing Hurst's book eight months later (*EJ*, September 1930, 40:484–86), referred to "the impotence of the Federal Farm Board in the face of steadily falling prices when backed by almost unlimited financial aid."

[83]*C&FC*, Nov. 16, 1929, pp. 3051, 3108–9; Hoover, *State Papers*, 1:143; Galbraith, *Great Crash*, p. 142. Current rates were then 1.5 to 5 percent on individual incomes and 12 percent on corporation incomes.

[84]Hoover, *Memoirs*, 3:30–31. On this important issue B. M. Anderson agreed with Mellon, though he warmly commended the initial actions of the Federal Reserve System, as noted above. See his *Economics and the Public Welfare*, ch. 31, "The New Deal in 1929–1930."

would be the consequences of alternative courses of action. Though Hoover knew the weaknesses of the European economies better than most, even he could not gauge their vulnerability, and Mellon, he later said, "would not take the European situation seriously." At the time everyone, including Hoover and Mellon, underestimated the weaknesses in the banking system, which Hoover later called "the weakest link in our whole economic system."[85]

These moves seemed to most observers wise at the time, and were paralleled abroad, as central banks eased money rates with a view to checking liquidation and as other forms of government support became prevalent. When it soon became clear that the economic and financial maladjustments were gravely underrated and the duration of the contraction vastly underestimated, what had seemed wise policy helped to make matters worse.[86]

President Hoover welcomed the Federal Reserve moves in October and November 1929.[87] He reluctantly approved the October commitments of the Federal Farm Board. He sought to stem the spread of panic and pessimism by making and encouraging others to make public utterances that must often have taxed his own conscience. He certainly played a part in getting agreement of legislative leaders on the reduction in the income tax rate announced by Secretary Mellon on November 13. He soon went much further and undertook to lead the government in playing an active role,[88] initially in his own characteristic way.

---

[85]Hoover, *Memoirs,* 3:21–28. In his State of the Union address of Dec. 3, 1929, Mr. Hoover suggested the creation of a joint commission to investigate the banking system and recommend legislation. Hoover, *State Papers,* 1:154–55; R. L. Wilbur and A. M. Hyde, *The Hoover Policies* (New York: Scribner, 1937), pp. 332–34.

[86]See Robbins, *Great Depression,* esp. pp. 72–75. Wesley C. Mitchell, in his review of this book (*QJE,* May 1935, 49:503–7), was critical of Robbins' views; and in his recent *Autobiography of an Economist* (New York: Macmillan, 1971) Lord Robbins expressed regret that he had published it (p. 154). Anderson, in ch. 31 of his *Economics and the Public Welfare,* also argued, as he had earlier in various issues of the *Chase Economic Bulletin,* that it would have been far better to take the bitter medicine in 1929 and early in 1930, as had been done in 1921–22, and as Mellon had advised. It is conceivable that they were right.

[87]See his press statement of Nov. 15, 1929, in *State Papers,* 1:133–34, from which two sentences merit quoting: "The magnificent working of the Federal Reserve System and the inherently sound condition of the banks have already brought about a decrease in interest rates and an assurance of abundant capital—the first time such a result has been so speedily achieved in similar circumstances. In market booms we develop over-optimism with a corresponding reverse into over-pessimism." Similar passages appeared in his first annual message of Dec. 3, 1929, in *ibid.,* pp. 144–46, and in his important address of Dec. 5 to the National Business Survey Conference, in *ibid.,* pp. 181–84. In the *Annalist* for Nov. 29, 1929 (pp. 1052–53, 1090), E. C. Harwood criticized the president's earlier statements as giving "an entirely erroneous conception of the financial situation."

[88]Hoover, *Memoirs,* 3:29–32, 42–52. Though he typically defended his foresight and actions, and rarely admitted making mistakes, in this passage (p. 29) he reiterated that "it is not given even to Presidents to foresee the future. . . . We could have done better—in retrospect."

On November 15 an Associated Press dispatch reported: "Leaders of industry, labor and agriculture will be called into conference by President Hoover next week to lay preliminary plans for concerted action looking toward business progress."[89] And the president was reported to have commented on the unfortunate tendency for the extreme optimism of the market boom to be followed by acute pessimism. Undoubtedly one of his purposes was to check this dangerous reversal.

These major White House conferences, closed to the press, were duly held: on November 17 with a few railroad presidents; on the 21st with major industrialists in the morning and outstanding labor leaders in the afternoon; on the 22d with representatives of the construction industries; on the 25th with national farm organization leaders; and on the 27th with leading public utility executives.[90] At the close of each conference, brief press releases were issued,[91] and the press reported remarks of a number of participants. These were typically reassuring. Even farm leaders told the president that the morale of farmers was "better than it had been for years."[92]

At the second of the confidential conferences Hoover spoke with great seriousness.[93] This was no mere stock market crash. Already two or three million were unemployed. Though the depth of the disaster could not yet be judged, the country faced a long and difficult depression period at best. There must be much liquidation of inflated values, debts, and prices. The boom and its reversal were worldwide, and Europe was still far from fully recovered. The president urged that wage rates be maintained for the present; that the work week be shortened temporarily to spread the available work; that each industry look after distress among its employees; that constructive plans be worked out; and that government agencies expand public construction to increase employment. With a view to maintaining employment, railway and public utility companies were urged to proceed with proposed construction projects and to consider expanding them. The industrialists expressed major agreement, and accepted the proposed program subject to the agreement of labor leaders not to initiate strikes or demands for increased wage rates. That same afternoon the president spoke in a similar vein to a conference of outstanding labor leaders, and won their support for this program. To a remarkable degree it was carried

[89]*C&FC*, Nov. 16, 1929, p. 3108.
[90]*Ibid.*, Nov. 23, 30, pp. 3261–67, 3361; Myers and Newton, *Hoover Administration*, pp. 25–34.
[91]Hoover, *State Papers*, 1:134–37.
[92]*Magazine of Wall Street*, Dec. 14, 1929, p. 264.
[93]Presidential secretary Walter H. Newton, who was present, summarized the president's statement, as quoted in Wilbur and Hyde, *Hoover Policies*, pp. 129–31. Similar statements were probably made at the other conferences. See also Myers and Newton, *Hoover Administration*, pp. 24–31; Hoover, *Memoirs*, 3:43–46.

out in 1930, and even in lesser degree later, and the country enjoyed unparalleled labor peace in 1930–32.[94]

In addition, on November 18 the president got Secretary Mellon to urge Congress to increase the public buildings program by $423 million. On the 23d telegrams were sent to state governors and city mayors urging them to expand public works, in every practicable direction, to give employment; and the next day the president directed the secretary of commerce to set up an organization for federal cooperation with them. In his State of the Union address on December 3, the president's recommendations included increased public works, expansion of the merchant marine, and an investigation looking toward banking reform.[95] Shortly afterward, industrial and labor leaders were called into a joint conference to follow up the earlier separate conferences.[96] A national Business Survey Conference was set up under Julius H. Barnes, a trusted friend of Hoover, formerly president of the U.S. Grain Corporation, and then chairman of the board of the Chamber of Commerce of the United States. The president addressed this conference, held in Washington on November 5, and the Chamber promptly published a summary of its remarkably comprehensive reports, *Business Conditions and Outlook*.[97]

Contemporary opinion on these conferences and actions was strongly favorable.[98] They surely contributed to improved business sentiment. This was reflected in slowing the economic contraction for a few months and promoting the mid-November to mid-April rise in the stock market.[99] On the assumption, which respected analysts firmly accepted, asserted, or endorsed, that only a minor depression lay ahead, most of these moves were well-advised. When this assumption proved ill-founded (as Hoover himself had feared it might be) because of blindness to or underestimation of serious domestic and foreign weaknesses, the results of these new initiatives were disappointing and in some respects were unwise.

International affairs also claimed the president's attention during these momentous weeks. In his *Memoirs* Hoover stressed his presidential ambition "to lead the United States in full cooperation with world moral

---

[94]Wilbur and Hyde, *Hoover Policies*, pp. 133–34, 142–43; Hoover, *State Papers*, 1:134–35. Cf. *Hist. Stat. U.S.*, ser. D 764–78.

[95]Myers and Newton, *Hoover Administration*, pp. 28–31, 33, 414–19.

[96]*Ibid.*, p. 34.

[97]Hoover, *State Papers*, 1:181–84.

[98]For examples, see the discussions by J. M. Clark, F. G. Dickinson, and others at the late December meeting of the American Economic Association, published in its *Papers and Proceedings*, May 1930, esp. pp. 15–28; W. T. Foster and Waddill Catchings, "Mr. Hoover's Road to Prosperity," *Review of Reviews*, January 1930, pp. 50–52; and M. G. Rukeyser, "Why Prosperity Will Return," *ibid.*, May 1930, pp. 47–51. Galbraith, who quoted some items from *Literary Digest*, Nov. 30, 1929, derisively called the Hoover conferences "no-business meetings," but declined to endorse later allegations that they had been a failure. *Great Crash*, pp. 142–46.

[99]See CTC, *Bus. Bull.*, Jan. 15, 1935, summarizing six upturns and setbacks in 1930–34.

forces to preserve peace," despite the handicap of isolationist sentiment that led the Senate to resist unreserved U.S. participation in the World Court (as recommended by Presidents Harding, Coolidge, and Hoover himself) and led to stormy protests against official collaboration with the League even in its nonpolitical activities.[100] He was disturbed by friction between Great Britain and the United States, and welcomed a visit from Labour Prime Minister Ramsay MacDonald (October 4-14, 1929) to discuss these matters and to develop coordinated ideas for the Naval Limitation Conference planned for early 1930.[101] He was surely sympathetic with the Owen D. Young committee's efforts to work out a "final settlement" of the thorny reparations problem, which was finally approved at The Hague on January 20, 1930. In his notable Armistice Day address (1929), Hoover said that "the world is comparatively at peace, with the outlook for a peaceable future more bright than for half a century past." Yet, noting that there were nearly thirty million men under arms (including active reservists), he observed: "There are fears, distrusts and smoldering injuries among nations which are the tinder of war. . . . To maintain peace is as dynamic in its requirements as the conduct of war."[102]

Moreover, on November 12 a bankers' committee selected by the central banks succeeded, after six weeks of work, in drafting the agreed charter and statutes of the Bank for International Settlements, a notable feature of the Young Plan.[103] Congressional hostility to official U.S. involvement in this institution prevented formal participation by the Federal

[100]*Memoirs*, 2:330-31. In his first message to Congress (Dec. 3, 1924) President Coolidge recommended adherence to the "Hughes reservations," but the Senate approved (Jan. 27, 1926) only with stiffer reservations which at the time were unacceptable to other nations. Early in his first message to Congress (Dec. 3, 1929), President Hoover urged adherence and asked Senate approval of a revised protocol (dated Sept. 14, 1949), worked out with Elihu Root's aid, that met and went beyond the earlier Senate reservations; on Dec. 8, 1931, he renewed his appeal, but Senate opposition kept the issue from coming to a vote during his term. President Roosevelt fared no better. Hoover, *State Papers*, 1:125-29, 138-39, 238-40, 460-66, 2:80-81, 503; Wilbur and Hyde, *Hoover Policies*, pp. 587-88; Claude M. Fuess, *Calvin Coolidge: The Man from Vermont* (Boston: Little Brown, 1940), pp. 403-4; Hoover, *Memoirs*, 2:50, 330, 335-37.

[101]Hoover, *Memoirs*. 2:345-52, and Hoover, *State Papers*, 1:106-9. The *N&A* of Oct. 19, 1929 (pp. 95-99), called this "an errand of first rate importance," and reported that the French premier (Briand) had cabled Hoover his pleasure over its "brilliant success," though it dismissed the joint statement at its conclusion as "composed mainly of platitudes and pious aspirations."

[102]*C&FC*, Nov. 16, 1929, pp. 3057-59, 3065-67, 3111-13; Hoover, *State Papers*, 1:125-32, esp. p. 130; Wilbur and Hyde, *Hoover Policies*, pp. 598-99. In this address he put forward his proposal for international agreement that food ships should be free from interference in time of war—to which the official European responses were almost all unfavorable.

[103]*C&FC*, Nov. 16, 23, 1929, pp. 3054-57, 3081-86, 3211. Two U.S. bankers, Jackson E. Reynolds and Walter Lichtenstein, were chairman and secretary, respectively, of the bankers' committee which worked these out. Cf. *N&A*, Oct. 12, 1929, p. 37. Also relevant are the lectures and commentaries on Sept. 17, 1970, at the seventh lecture meeting convened in Basel by the Per Jacobsson Foundation, *Toward a World Central Bank*, at which William McChesney Martin was the lecturer.

Reserve System; but Gates W. McGarrah, who had been chairman and federal reserve agent at the New York Bank, resigned this post to accept the BIS presidency. Sir Charles Addis, a respected British banker, became vice president. The key position of general manager, however, was assigned to a Frenchman, Pierre Quesnay.[104]

Encouraging   In the weeks after the stock market touched bottom
Developments,   in mid-November 1929, the key question was whether
December 1929–   the United States faced "a prolonged spell of severe
April 1930   trade depression" or the resumption of "her triumphant course of industrial expansion after a transient, partial, and altogether minor setback."[105] For several months presumably competent Americans favored the optimistic answer, and foreign observers appeared to agree.[106]

The Harvard Economic Society confidently asserted in mid-November that "a severe depression like that of 1920–21 is outside the range of possibility. We are not facing protracted liquidation of huge inventories, worldwide demoralization in commodity markets, and rising money rates."[107] Shortly after the crash, B. M. Anderson—no Pollyanna—gave a reassuring summary of the financial situation, saying: "We have been through trying times, and there are unpleasant facts to face, but the general situation is strong, and we can face the facts." He undertook to analyze "the causes which led up to the wild stock-market speculation which culminated in the stupendous stock market crash," and paid warm tribute to the foresight and prudence of banks and brokers during the preceding boom.[108] The *Chronicle* said in its lead editorial next day that "things are rapidly returning to normal. Evidences of this are met with on every side."[109]

Several respected speakers before the Academy of Political Science on November 22 voiced similar views.[110] Among them was the financier Herbert H. Lehman, lieutenant governor of New York State. Franz Schneider, Jr., concluded his able paper by saying that "a relatively brief period of rest and recuperation should leave business in excellent condi-

---

[104]See papers on the Young Plan in operation (Nov. 13, 1930) in *Proc. Acad. Pol. Sci.,* January 1931, 14:211–328; Paul Einzig, *The Fight for Financial Supremacy* (London: Macmillan, 1931), ch. 11; and Eleanor L. Dulles, *The Bank for International Settlements at Work* (New York: Macmillan, 1932).

[105]Posed in a good article in *N&A*, Dec. 7, 1929, pp. 338–39.

[106]Cf. *ibid.*, Nov. 2, 1929, p. 163. Silberling (*The Dynamics of Business*, p. 303) quoted Stuart Chase as saying in November 1929: "We probably have three more years of prosperity ahead of us before we enter the cyclic tailspin which has occurred in the eleventh year of each of the four great previous periods of commercial prosperity."

[107]*Weekly Letter*, Nov. 16, Dec. 21, 28, 1929, pp. 276, 305–11.

[108]*Chase Economic Bulletin*, Nov. 22, 1929, vol. 9, no. 6.

[109]*C&FC*, Nov. 23, 1929, pp. 3207–8.

[110]*Proc. Acad. Pol. Sci.*, January 1930, 13:494–97, 562–75.

tion. We still have the strongest and most promising situation in the world." Harvard professor Sprague voiced the conviction then prevalent, that the gold standard was here to stay and that there was no promising substitute for it "in the maintenance of a reasonable measure of international financial stability." But he held that the standard could not work as automatically as in prewar times, and that postwar conditions required more cooperation among and more conscious efforts by central banks, including "the adoption of concerted policies based upon intelligent foresight and adopted well in advance of the appearance of emergencies." He viewed the U.S. market for short-term funds as "a more disturbing factor in the international situation" than ever before. But he did not "expect the depression to be so serious or so prolonged as if it followed unsound development in industry." Nor did he anticipate a repetition, "at all events during the lifetime of most of us here present," of the stock market superboom and supercrash—and his conclusion was not based solely on the assumption that the Federal Reserve would probably take more drastic action at an earlier date in future emergencies.[111]

President Hoover opened his State of the Union message of December 3 with a glowing paragraph, which concluded: "The problems with which we are now confronted are the problems of growth and of progress." After touching on the steps he had already taken, he said: "I am convinced that through these measures we have reestablished confidence." He also spoke optimistically of international relations, adverting to the Kellogg-Briand Pact and the Young Plan. The president of the New York Stock Exchange ended his Philadelphia address on January 25, 1930: "Overoptimism may be dangerous but it is important to remember that the present difficulties of American finance rise, not from weakness, but from the profound strength of our country."[112]

The foreword of Edward Eyre Hunt's *Audit of America* (which summarized the two-volume *Recent Economic Changes*), dated January 1, 1930, adverted to the "dip in the business cycle, followed by a stock market crash," and continued: "As a result of these events and at the suggestion of President Hoover, a large amount of public works, federal, state, and municipal, has been set in motion, and the railroads, the telephone and telegraph companies, the electric light and power companies and other industries have inaugurated programs of construction and maintenance.

[111]O. M. W. Sprague, "The Working of the Gold Standard under Present Conditions," *ibid.*, pp. 496, 524-30. Sprague strangely ignored the fact that the gold exchange standard of the 1920s was not the same as the prewar gold standard, a point that Jacques Rueff stressed afresh in his article, "Last Twitches of the International Monetary System," *WSJ*, June 5, 1969.

[112]Simmons, *Financing American Industry*, p. 331. Discussing Sprague's paper, Robert B. Warren well said: "At what point has a wave of commendable optimism turned into a wave of unjustifiable speculation? So far as I know, there is no way of telling that until afterwards and then it is pretty late." *Proc. Acad. Pol. Sci.*, January 1930, 13:532.

These efforts have already exerted an influence in the direction of economic balance."[113] Accumulating evidence of industrial and business contraction did not deter the Harvard Economic Society from seeing "orderly readjustment and prompt recovery" in prospect at the year end.[114] Almost concurrently the AT&T said: "The constructive efforts of industrial leaders and others to temper the readjustment promise assurance that it will be effected with a minimum of economic disturbance."[115] Though the numerous year-end predictions varied somewhat as to the timing of the return of business to normal, stress was laid on the elements of strength in the situation, and the consensus was essentially optimistic.[116] The Van Strum Financial Service, in the sixth edition of *How To Make and Keep Stock Market Profits*, published early in 1930, went so far as to assert: "Today investors in common stocks need not fear a general reduction in dividends paid by corporations" (page 32).

Despite the "swift and terrifying" stock market crash and its early repercussions at home and abroad, as 1929 came to an end it was judged a truly extraordinary business year.[117] In most industries activity was intense and profits were exceptional.[118] U.S. Steel Corporation profits for 1929 almost equaled the sum of its net earnings in 1927 and 1928. Corporations typically maintained or increased their dividends until mid-1930.[119] Willford I. King's preliminary estimate of the national income in 1929, based on reports for January-October, was that per capita realized income would be greater than in 1928 by 4 percent in current dollars and by 8 percent in 1913 dollars.[120] Though unemployment increased in the last quarter of 1929, the much later officially accepted estimate of the average for the year was only 3.2 percent of the labor force, equal to the low in the prosperous year 1923.[121]

---

[113]*An Audit of America: A Summary of Recent Economic Changes in the United States* (New York: McGraw-Hill, 1930), p. vii. Actually, investment in railroad, telephone, electric power, and all regulated industries was indeed higher in 1930 than in 1929. *Hist. Stat. U.S.*, ser. Q 103–5, V 203–16.

[114]*Weekly Letter*, Jan. 4, 1930, pp. 1–4.

[115]*Summary*, Jan. 7, 1930, p. 6.

[116]See especially the *Annalist*'s summaries of year-end reviews early in 1930, and Howard Florance in *Review of Reviews*, February 1930, pp. 112–16. The *Westminster Bank Review* (London) for January 1930 commented on the persistence of optimism at the beginning of every calendar year, and rightly added: "The ephemeral nature of New Year optimism is equally proverbial." It quoted (p. 21) the Bank of Montreal as reporting on Dec. 23, 1929, that, despite the slowdown of business in Canada, "what may appear as a quiet condition would two years ago have been regarded as one of unwonted briskness."

[117]See HES, *Weekly Letter*, Nov. 16, 1929, pp. 275–76; and W. L. Crum, "Review of the Year 1929," *Rev. Ec. Stat.*, February 1930, 12:1–14, and subsequent articles.

[118]C. W. Sills, in *Review of Reviews*, March 1930, p. 110, citing the National City Bank of New York.

[119]CTC, *Bus. Bull.*, Feb. 15, 1932, covering 1929–31 by quarters, for stocks registered on the New York Stock Exchange.

[120]Willford I. King, in *JASA*, March 1930, suppl., 25(169A):73–75.

[121]*Hist. Stat. U.S.*, ser. D 46, 47; *Fed. Res. Bull.*, November-May 1929–30.

The dollar value of U.S. industrial inventories rose by 11 percent in 1929, reaching a level slightly in excess of that of the end of 1920, although agricultural and nonagricultural prices fell substantially in 1929 to levels much lower than in 1920 and the practice of hand-to-mouth buying had expanded notably in the 1920s.[122] Dealers' stocks of used cars were higher than ever, and the rate of turnover was the smallest in years.[123] Tire stocks, already high, increased in December. But these developments did not seem serious at the time; indeed, the absence of swollen inventories was widely considered a favorable factor.

The drastic curtailment of foreign lending beginning in mid-1928 had not suddenly curtailed U.S. exports.[124] Nor did the stock market crash have a striking immediate effect on the nation's international trade. Both exports and imports increased in 1929. Partly because of the threat of tariff rate increases, imports increased more than exports, so that the export surplus declined from $1,038 million in 1928 to $850 million in 1929. The largest import gains were in raw silk and copper, the largest export gains in machinery.[125] E. Dana Durand, Hoover's highly competent lieutenant, was vocal in his optimism concerning the foreign trade outlook at the end of the year.[126]

Early indications were that the wreckage from the crash was less than the pessimists had thought. Apart from the Foshay case (n. 74 above) there were no major failures of stock exchange houses, banks, or business concerns, and no runs on banks.[127] Even those who had warned of the coming crash, such as Babson, Noyes, Anderson, and Warburg, agreed in viewing the year ahead with reasonable confidence.[128] Experienced business forecasters were nearly unanimous in predicting upturns in the spring of 1930. At the late December meetings of the American Economic, Farm Economic, and Statistical Associations the participants were broadly in accord on this crucial issue; and evaluations of economic forecasts at the meeting

[122]AT&T, *Summary*, Apr. 5, 1930, pp. 9–11.

[123]*Ibid.*, Feb. 6, 1930, pp. 1, 6.

[124]On Nov. 14, 1930, Carl Snyder wrote: "Before the crisis there was no marked slump in American exports." "Overproduction and Business Cycles," *Proc. Acad. Pol. Sci.*, January 1931, 14:377.

[125]AT&T, *Summary*, Feb. 6, 1930, p. 10, and the four preceding issues.

[126]"The Foreign Trade of 1929," *JASA*, March 1930, 25(169A):51–55. He concluded: "Without attempting to make a very definite forecast for 1930 it may be stated with some confidence that the . . . upward trend of exports of the United States is likely to continue in most years of the near future. Exports of manufactures have now become the dominant factor in our foreign sales and the world demand for these tends to increase steadily."

[127]*C&FC*, Nov. 16, 1929, p. 3105; Hirst, *Wall Street and Lombard Street*, pp. 50–51; W. R. Burgess, "The Money Market in 1929," *Rev. Ec. Stat.*, February 1930, 12:15–20; and Warburg, *Federal Reserve System*, 2:501.

[128]E.g., Noyes, in *Scribner's*, December 1929, concluded: "It is not at all impossible that, in the long run at any rate, the stock market's collapse and the release of its strangle-hold on credit will turn out to have removed a shadow of doubt from the industrial prospects." Cf. Schumpeter, *Business Cycles*, 2:793–94.

of the American Statistical Association were misleadingly reassuring.[129] E. A. Goldenweiser of the Federal Reserve Board senior staff summarized credit developments in 1929 and concluded on this cheery note: "I feel that we are entering the year 1930 under more favorable credit conditions than we have had for at least two years, and while there are many phases of the situation that need to be watched and much that might develop that will not be so favorable, I think I can on the whole view the future in an optimistic light."[130]

The *New York Times* said editorially on February 12 that "the patient" had begun to recover. A few days later the Hoover cabinet agreed that the danger of a general panic in finance and industry had definitely passed.[131] Also in mid-February the Harvard Economic Society concluded that unemployment, though larger than early in 1928, was in general less, and less serious, than in the 1927 recession, and did not expect it to be "more lasting."[132] At about the same time the American Federation of Labor said there were about three million unemployed and that most of the loss of jobs was quite recent.[133] In March Hoover said that the worst effect of the crash on employment would be ended in sixty days.[134] In December-April 1929-30, indeed, many significant U.S. statistical series fell more slowly, ceased to fall, or even rose.

The first two issues of the Cleveland Trust Company *Business Bulletin* in 1930 stated: "One conclusion which seems justified is that this period of slow business will probably be of only moderate severity and duration" (January 15). "The bottom of the business decline appears to have been reached" (February 15). On April 19 the Harvard Economic Society said: "The essentially sidewise movement of our B curve last month probably marked the end of the business recession." As late as May 17, indeed, it concluded that "general business, as reflected in Curve B, is likely to improve continuously, or nearly continuously, through the rest of the year," with the most rapid gains in the third quarter.[135] This proved a conspicuously misleading forecast.

---

[129]*JASA*, March 1930, suppl., 25(169A):31–50.

[130]*Ibid.*, pp. 69–72.

[131]Myers and Newton, *Hoover Administration*, p. 35; and a similar statement in Wilbur and Hyde, *Hoover Policies*, p. 402. The latter statement continued: "The balance of the year 1930 [after mid-February] was a period of moderate economic readjustment and by the opening of 1931, the whole situation showed a turn for the better." As will shortly appear, this appraisal was seriously wrong.

[132]*Weekly Letter*, Feb. 15, 1930, p. 46. Reflecting the concern of workers, the "voluntary quit rate" in December had been the lowest ever reported. AT&T, *Summary*, Feb. 6, 1930, pp. 8–9.

[133]*Review of Reviews*, February 1930, p. 46.

[134]*C&FC*, Mar. 15, 1930, p. 1731; Allen, *Only Yesterday*, p. 283.

[135]*Weekly Letter*, pp. 101, 127–28. In view of the mutual respect of Keynes and the Harvard economists, and the formal relations between the Harvard and the London and Cambridge economic services, it is surprising that apparently the gist of Keynes' May 10 article quoted below (Chapter 9) was not conveyed to the HES before this statement was formulated.

Early in 1930 overproduction in the motor vehicle industry was regarded as the sorest spot in the business situation, but the construction
industry—the other prime mover and chief support of sustained prosperity
in the 1920s—was expected to cushion declines in business activity and
stimulate general recovery.[136] Even passenger car production, which had
dropped very low in December 1929, rose in January-April 1930, approximately to the level of these months in 1928, and motor truck output approached the record level of the first four months of 1929.[137]

The idea that the cataclysmic shake-out in Wall Street was on the
whole healthy was prevalent, here and abroad, for several months.[138] Many
investors and speculators rushed in to buy stocks at the "bargain prices" of
mid-November and later. From the low on November 13 the stock market
rose moderately for two months and then advanced sharply to an April
1930 peak that was not far below the high average of the first half of
1929.[139] During this period, though commercial failures increased in number and volume of liabilities, there were still no important failures of banks,
stock exchange firms, or business corporations; and respected analysts as
well as business and political leaders reasserted that the general business
situation was fundamentally sound. The stock market upswing from mid-
November to mid-April 1929–30 seemed to many the start of a new bull
movement, rather than the bright interlude in a protracted bear market
which it soon proved to be. The rise in stock prices was accompanied by a
fresh expansion in brokers' loans on account of New York City reporting
member banks and out-of-town banks, which more than offset further
declines in loans "for account of others."[140]

New issues of corporate and government securities, which had been
sharply curtailed in the last three months of 1929, rose impressively in the
first few months of 1930.[141] During these months money rates eased further,
not merely because of lower demand but also because the Federal Reserve,
perhaps under political pressures, pushed them down.[142] The Reserve Bank

[136]Citibank, *Monthly Economic Letter*, January 1930; W. C. Clark, "The Construction
Industry: Outlook for 1930," *Rev. Ec. Stat.*, February 1930, 12:23–29. In his late 1929 paper at
the ASA meetings, Thomas S. Holden of the F. W. Dodge Corporation had earlier expressed
similar optimism. *JASA*, March 1930, suppl., 25(169A):64–68.

[137]AT&T, *Summary*, June 5, 1930, p. 5; *Automobile Facts and Figures, 1930*, and *Motor
Truck Figures, 1930*.

[138]Friedman and Schwartz, *Monetary History*, p. 691.

[139]Even by March the stock market had regained about 40 percent of the ground lost in the
crash, and average prices of industrial stocks were nearly up to the level of February 1929
when the Federal Reserve Board issued its serious warning. AT&T, *Summary*, Apr. 5, 1930,
p. 3.

[140]See chart covering 1926 to July 30, 1930, in *ibid.*, Aug. 6, 1930, p. 3. Under-collateraled
loans in country member banks in the Second Federal Reserve District in July 1930 were
almost negligible, according to a study summarized in the Federal Reserve Bank of New York
Monthly Review for Aug. 1, 1930.

[141]See AT&T monthly summaries for the first six months of 1930 and charts in Leonard P.
Ayres, *Turning Points in Business Cycles* (New York: Macmillan, 1939), pp. 127, 150.

[142]Anderson, *Economics and the Public Welfare*, pp. 222–23.

of New York further reduced its rediscount rate from 4.5 to 4 percent on February 7 and to 3.5 percent on March 13, 1930. The Banks' buying rate for ninety-day bankers' acceptances was reduced by gradual steps from 4 percent on January 1 to 3 percent on March 19. At the time the System was criticized for these reductions, on the plausible ground that they encouraged the revival of the speculative boom.[143] Professor Reed argued, on the other hand, that the rediscount rate should have been reduced faster and further, say to 3 percent, "just as soon as it was clear that the boom was definitely terminated"; but he admitted that such rapid reduction would have used up its revival stimulus prematurely and that early low rates would have accelerated the gold outflow, which had reached sizable dimensions in November-December 1929.[144]

The interval between the crash and the renewed decline of the stock market in April-May 1930 was marked by numerous reassuring assertions and optimistic predictions, some of them by no means responsible.[145] As late as May 1, 1930, the president said to the United States Chamber of Commerce, "I am convinced we have now passed the worst and with continued unity of effort we shall rapidly recover."[146] Editor Albert Shaw wrote in the May *Review of Reviews*: "there is not a single member of the federal union today that is languishing or discouraged" (page 17). In June he headed a section on world progress "Business Trends Encouraging," and said that "the best authorities believe that conditions will soon show marked improvement" (page 29). He went on to say: "If Mr. Hoover could be made dictator of the United States for the next ten years, we should have before us a period of social progress and of diffused well being, such as no country has ever known since the Middle Ages. . . . Relationships with foreign governments have never been more uniformly agreeable than they are at this moment" (page 29). The same issue noted the recent report of the U.S. Treasury that July-March tax collections in 1929-30 were $140 million more than in the same months of 1928-29.

The true picture was distorted by selection of favorable facts, ignoring or minimizing others, and even "bending" the facts, often under the influence of a serious misjudgment that bolstering of public confidence was the prime essential. President Hoover repeatedly stressed the strength and

[143]Reed, *Federal Reserve Policy*, p. 101.

[144]*Ibid.*, pp. 101-3. I would add that it was by no means clear *to all* that either the stock exchange boom or the economic boom was "definitely terminated" by the end of 1929. Friedman and Schwartz virtually endorsed Reed's opinion, and said: "The New York Reserve Bank favored more rapid reductions . . . than those made." *Monetary History*, p. 341.

[145]Schlesinger, "The New Era at Bay," *Crisis of the Old Order*, pp. 161-65; Allen, *Only Yesterday*, ch. 14; Galbraith, *Great Crash*, pp. 123-24, 140-46.

[146]Hoover, *State Papers*, 1:289-96. On May 28 he forecast that business would be normal by fall.

soundness of the banks and the credit system, in stark contrast to the caustic criticisms he expressed years later in his *Memoirs*.[147]

In the first quarter of 1930, in short, it was not merely a hope but a common belief that the direct and indirect effects of the stock market crash would be so neutralized, localized, and minimized that return to normal, if not high prosperity, would be fairly prompt.[148] This belief rested in large part on exaggerated confidence in the basic soundness of the U.S. economy; on excessive faith in European recovery, the League of Nations, the Federal Reserve System, and President Hoover; and on inadequate recognition of subtle weaknesses that had developed in the long prosperity period.

In December–April 1929–30 little or no effort was made, so far as I can ascertain, to tackle the job that had been neglected before the crash, namely, to re-examine three basic assumptions: (1) that U.S. business was fundamentally sound; (2) that easing money would provide adequate stimulus to recovery; and (3) that the administration would be able to prevent a severe contraction. Furthermore, no serious attempts were made to reappraise the weaknesses in the domestic and international situation, political as well as economic, that might conceivably make, as they in fact did, for a downward spiral in the near future.

In this same period, indeed, there were a few encouraging items of news from Europe. In Great Britain, because of the high level of output in the iron and steel, coal, and paper industries, in the first quarter of 1930 the index of industrial production was higher than in the first quarters of 1929 and 1928. In other industries, however, unemployment increased almost every week, and in mid-April unemployment was considerably larger than in mid-March.[149] Moreover, British foreign trade continued at a low level, and an extraordinarily large tonnage of shipping was idle. The seasonally adjusted index of the value of exported manufactures in March was the lowest since December 1926, and no improvement was registered in April.

An English baronet, surveying the first ten years of the League of Nations early in 1930, called it a "success—despite many failures and much weakness."[150] By the end of February all the member states of the League

[147]Schlesinger, *Crisis of the Old Order*, p. 474; Hoover, *Memoirs*, 3:21–28.

[148]Cf. AT&T, *Summary*, July 7, 1930, p. 1; Julius Barnes, "Business in the New Year," *Review of Reviews*, January 1930, pp. 48–49: "It is becoming reasonably apparent that business has emerged from the confusion riding on a fairly even keel." On March 16 and April 23 Barnes issued further reassuring statements. See also Rukeyser, "Why Prosperity Will Return."

[149]*Westminster Bank Review* (London), January 1930; HES, *Weekly Letter*, May 3, 1930, p. 113.

[150]Sir Philip Gibbs, "The League: A Ten-Year Record," *New York Times Magazine*, Jan. 5, 1930, pp. 2, 21. In *ibid.*, Feb. 2, 1930 (pp. 1–2, 19), S. J. Wolff quoted General Pershing to a similar effect, though he felt that our country should stay out of the League. Cf. also Chapter 6, n. 73, above.

of Nations had approved the Kellogg-Briand Pact which had been signed on August 27, 1928.[151] Its American co-author, Frank B. Kellogg, who had received the Nobel peace prize in 1929, viewed the international outlook optimistically late in April 1930.[152]

On January 20, 1930, in a second conference at The Hague, representatives of the governments concerned adopted, with seemingly minor modifications, the ambitious Young Plan for "final settlement" of the reparation problem.[153] The leading German delegate, Dr. Hjalmar Schacht, who had signed the Young Plan on June 7, 1929, turned against it six months later, fought it as beyond Germany's capacity to fulfill, and on March 7 resigned as head of the Reichsbank rather than share in the responsibility for carrying it out. Having survived a German referendum on December 22, however, the plan was approved by the Reichstag on February 1 and by the Reichsrat on March 12, and shortly signed by President Hindenburg.[154] Such responsible specialists as J. W. Angell, J. H. Williams, M. J. Bonn, and W. J. Dawson considered that it almost ensured the continuation of Germany's remarkable recovery.[155] Not everyone (Schacht

[151]*Economist*, Mar. 1, 1930, pp. 448–49. See also "The Preservation of Peace" (Nov. 23, 1928), *Proc. Acad. Pol. Sci.*, January 1929, 13:195–325, and Hoover's address of July 24, 1929, in Hoover, *State Papers*, 1:78–80.

[152]S. J. Wolff, "Kellogg Sees Peace Advancing," *New York Times Magazine*, Apr. 27, 1930, pp. 1–2.

[153]The earlier Hague conference of Aug. 6–31, 1929, was a difficult one. Philip Snowden, Churchill's successor as chancellor of the exchequer, won popularity at home by his insistence on modifying the plan to reverse a hard-won compromise by Stamp and Schacht which sacrificed a small portion of the British share of reparation payments which had been previously agreed upon. A financial agreement was reached (Cmd. 3392), but acceptance of the Young Plan as a whole was deferred. *Economist*, Aug. 31, 1929, pp. 383–84, Jan. 18, 23, 1930, pp. 109–10, 118–19, 162–63, 172–73; Dulles, *BIS*, pp. 290–307, 512–15; and J. Harry Jones, *Josiah Stamp, Public Servant: The Life of the First Baron Stamp of Shortlands* (London: Pitman, 1964), pp. 247–52.

[154]See chronology in Dulles, *BIS*, pp. 513–14; *Review of Reviews*, January-June 1930; Sir Andrew McFadyean, *Reparation Reviewed* (London: Benn, 1930), chs. 9–10; Hjalmar Schacht, *The End of Reparations*, trans. Lewis Gannett (New York: Jonathan Cape and Harrison Smith, 1931; 2d printing July 1931), largely based on his lectures in the United States in the fall of 1930 (published "first in New York, then in March 1931 in Germany"), and his autobiography, *Confessions of "The Old Wizard,"* trans. Diana Pyke (Boston: Houghton Mifflin, 1956), chs. 30–35; Moritz J. Bonn, *Wandering Scholar* (New York: John Day, 1948), pp. 306–9; Clay, *Lord Norman*, pp. 196, 268–71; and Sir Andrew McFadyean, *Recollected in Tranquillity* (London: Pall Mall Press, 1964), pp. 101–3.

Though Schacht did not mention the fact, the then-prestigious international financier Ivar Kreuger doubtless influenced Germany's acceptance of the Young Plan. In October 1929 his Swedish company, Kreuger and Toll, sought to acquire a match monopoly in Germany and offered in exchange a 6 percent loan of $125 million, subject to German acceptance of the Young Plan. *Economist*, Sept. 14, Oct. 26, 1929, pp. 484–85, 780; Mar. 1, 1930, pp. 460–63; *C&FC*, Mar. 29, 1930, p. 2123; and Robert Shaplen, *Kreuger: Genius and Swindler* (New York: Knopf, 1960), p. 129.

[155]See Chapter 6 above and contemporary discussions by Angell and Williams late in 1929 in *AER*, March 1930, suppl., 20(1):76–91; Owen D. Young's Charter Day address at the University of California, Berkeley, Mar. 24, 1930, in *C&FC*, Mar. 28, 1930, pp. 2131–33; Alzada Comstock, "Reparations Payments in Perspective," *AER*, June 1930, 20:199–209.

excepted) was convinced of this at the time;[156] but it was only much later that Guillebaud wrote, with exaggeration induced by hindsight, that by the end of 1929 "it was apparent to everyone that the stage was set for an economic depression" in Germany.[157]

Late in July 1929, the French premier, Poincaré, resigned because of ill health after pushing through the Chamber of Deputies the approval of debt agreements with the United States and Great Britain. Briand took over as premier for four months, then was succeeded by another member of Poincaré's cabinet, André Tardieu. Tardieu was lauded for striking a new note: "Let us go forward joyfully and confidently into the future."[158] He took the lead in winning the Chamber's consent (by a narrow margin on March 29, 1930) to the Young Plan, with its commitment to withdraw French forces from all occupied German zones in June, five months ahead of schedule; and the Senate overwhelmingly agreed on April 3.[159] The plan went into effect on May 9; the Bank for International Settlements opened its doors on May 30; and the big German international loan was floated, not without difficulty, on June 12.[160]

The protracted five-power naval conference in London from January 21 to April 22, 1930, resulted in a three-power naval limitation treaty which was ratified by the United States on July 22, by Great Britain on August 1, and by Japan on October 2; it entered into force on January 1, 1931.[161] Basic disagreements between France and Italy prevented their signing it, but on April 11 they agreed to halt battleship construction until 1936. Unreconciled and, for the time, irreconcilable conflicts of public opinion frustrated high hopes. President Hoover overstated its significance when he said that it marked "an important step in disarmament and in world

[156]See Marcus Nadler's late 1929 paper in *JASA*, March 1930, suppl., 25(169A):170–76.

[157]C. W. Guillebaud (citing the *Frankfurter Zeitung* annual survey written early in 1930), *The Economic Recovery of Germany from 1933 to the Incorporation of Austria in March 1938* (London: Macmillan, 1939), p. 17. The *Economist*'s corresponding review early in 1930 was cautious as to the German situation.

[158]Percy Philips, in *New York Times Magazine*, Feb. 9, 1930, pp. 3, 17. Cf. *Journal of Commerce, C&FC.*

[159]Cf. Emil Langyel, "The Rhineland Occupation," *Current History*, February 1930, 21:927–33; Harold Callendar, "The Tricolor Leaves the Rhine," *New York Times Magazine*, June 15, 1930.

[160]See Einzig, *Financial Supremacy*, chs. 11–12.

[161]Hoover, *State Papers*, 1:230–33, 274–85. Frank H. Simonds contributed a series of illuminating articles on this conference to the *Review of Reviews*, January-June 1930. Harold Nicolson's *Dwight Morrow* (New York: Harcourt Brace, 1935) has a valuable chapter (17) on Morrow's notable contributions to its limited success.

Laborious advance preparation for the naval conference (in which President Hoover had effective cooperation from Ambassador Dawes in London), wise selection of the U.S. delegation, and skillful conduct of the negotiations played important parts in this achievement, as Dawes made clear in his valuable *Journal as Ambassador*, pp. 1–200. The Hoover record in this instance was markedly superior to his successor's record at the London conference of mid-1933 (see Chapter 11 and n. 7 above). Cf. also Harold Nicolson, *King George the Fifth, His Life and Reign* (London: Constable, 1952), pp. 438–40.

peace" and was "a further long step toward lifting the burden of militarism from the backs of mankind."[162] However, it ended "forever" the danger of Anglo-American naval rivalry, provided an excellent temporary solution of the Japanese problem, saved these signatories very substantial naval expenditures, and considerably improved international feeling among the powers involved. To one able commentator it seemed of "enduring importance," exceeding that of the Treaty of Versailles.[163] But it made no appreciable contribution toward checking the economic contraction.

Sources of Concern   The general, persistent, and severe decline in commodity prices and the accompanying swelling of stocks of primary commodities, both in the United States and overseas, were sources of genuine concern in the first quarter of 1930,[164] but were given little weight. Weakness in prices of farm products was especially worrisome. Wheat prices fell spectacularly from December 5 to March 14. In January the Federal Farm Board took another fateful step: it set up the Grain Stabilization Corporation, which soon exercised its authority to buy cash wheat and wheat futures. Early in 1930, moreover, the gold price of silver fell to new low records, causing crises in Shanghai and Hong Kong. This was attributed to demonetization of silver in India and replacement of fractional silver currency in many countries.[165] There were crises also in Japan, due in part to the decision to get back onto the gold standard at what proved too high a figure, and in part to the shrinkage in overseas demand for silk; in India, where the fall in prices of silver and jute had serious consequences and Gandhi's civil disobedience program got under way in April;[166] and in Brazil, where coffee was in dire trouble and the coffee-defense mechanism, severely shaken in the preceding October, was saved by securing a loan of £20 million.[167] Adventitiously, crop and trade developments and forced reappraisals of commodity positions helped depress prices of wheat, silk, and coffee.

---

[162]See his message to the Senate in May and his statement on signing July 22, in Wilbur and Hyde, *Hoover Policies*, pp. 590-97, and Hoover, *State Papers*, 1:351-60.

[163]Simonds, in *Review of Reviews*, June 1930, pp. 52-54. Britain's weakened economic position had helped her public to accept naval parity with the United States.

[164]AT&T, *Summary*, Feb. 6, 1930, pp. 1-2, 4, 14; *Economist*, Feb. 8, 1930, pp. 289-90; W. L. Crum, "Review of the First Quarter . . . ," *Rev. Ec. Stat.*, May 1930, 12:49-58, esp. pp. 53-54; BIS, *Annual Report for 1939-40*, p. 9. In its monthly supplement for Mar. 1, 1930, the *Economist* lamented "that the collapse of what after all was an unsound speculative movement should have come at a time when the world was overstocked with many staple commodities, and so should have had such a prejudicial effect upon production and employment. It must, however, be admitted that the stock market collapse was a most important contributory factor."

[165]Hirst, *Wall Street and Lombard Street*, pp. 82-85, 108-22, 153.

[166]*Review of Reviews*, May 1930, p. 80; June 1930, pp. 39-40.

[167]Rowe, in Royal Economic Society, *Memorandum 34*, February 1932, pp. 54-57.

In an extended discussion of the commodity price outlook for 1930, published in mid-March, the Harvard Economic Society attributed the recent declines chiefly to the high interest rates brought about by great stock speculation,[168] noted the marked decline in money rates, and held that a prospective easing of money "will presently stabilize commodity markets and then lead to an upturn of prices," followed by a restoration of the horizontal trend or a temporary reaction from a downward trend. And the writers found "reasons for believing that there is some prospect of international cooperation in stabilizing commodity prices," for which conditions seemed "obviously" more favorable than ever before.[169] In late March and April an encouraging upturn in prices got under way, and the first quarter was considered to have seen the "termination of the recession."[170] This inadequate and misleading analysis soon proved false.

Another ominous change was maturing in the early months of 1930. President Hoover developed good relations with the Republican-controlled House of Representatives in the 71st Congress in the first half of his term. Not so with the Senate, where by no means all of the forty-two regular Republicans were sympathetic to him, while the thirty-nine Democrats, fourteen Progressives, and one Farmer-Labor senator tended "to act as a coalition of obstruction." Difficulties had arisen in the special session called in April 1929, and continued unabated in the following regular session.[171] Especially serious squabbles arose over the tariff bill, particularly the flexible provision and the effort to incorporate the export-debenture plan in it—on both of which issues Hoover won his point—and the bill was greatly delayed in running its congressional course.

By the end of his first year in office the president was in serious trouble with the Congress. One able journalist, reviewing that year, wrote early in March: "Seldom has a situation existed in Congress as chaotic as at present. Since the last term of Wilson no such open war has been waged between the Senate and the Executive."[172] Yet in his editorial comments in the *Review of Reviews* for April 1930, Albert Shaw adverted to "the inces-

[168]Rufus S. Tucker, in a forthright later article on "Gold and the General Price Level" (*Rev. Ec. Stat.*, Jan. 15, 1934, 16:8–16), made this pertinent comment (p. 14): "This present depression came after eight years of unusually stable wholesale commodity prices, and many economists believe that the most important cause was that central banks of many countries, including our own, had deliberately attempted to prevent commodity prices from declining and had thereby brought about, or prevented the removal of, an excessive debt structure which finally collapsed of its own weight."

[169]HES, *Weekly Letter*, Mar. 15, 1930, pp. 70–75.

[170]*Ibid.*, Mar. 29, Apr. 5, 12, 19, 26, 1930, pp. 82, 83, 88, 93, 101, 104, 108.

[171]Myers and Newton, *Hoover Administration*, pp. 32–33 and pt. 2, chs. 1–2.

[172]Anne O'Hare McCormick, "A Year of the Hoover Method," *New York Times Magazine*, Mar. 2, 1930, pp. 1–2, 17. Cf. Myers and Newton, *Hoover Administration*, pp. 32–33 and pt. 2, chs. 1–2; *Review of Reviews*, February 1930, pp. 73–74 (Simonds).

sant bickerings and jabberings that pass for debate in the United States Senate" (page 25) but also said, "The fine record of the first year has been praised with justice, not only by Republicans, but also by Democrats. . . . The New York *World*, which is Democratic without being narrowly partisan, declared that Mr. Hoover 'is in the line of the great Presidents.'[173] . . . Clear-headed people are grateful for a President who can both think and act" (pages 33-34). Miss McCormick also said, somewhat prematurely: "We no longer look for miracles and infallible economic solutions of political problems."[174] This in itself was wholesome, as the president would have agreed;[175] but Hoover's reputation, still bright in November 1929, was already dimmed.

As secretary of commerce, Hoover had been "unquestionably the favorite of the Washington correspondents," who "got his views on what was going on here and everywhere else, and relied upon his judgment and perfect candor." When he became president, he could no longer afford the time for such an intimate relationship, nor could he be wholly frank.[176] Within a year, though he had "the best editorial press of any President in recent years," he lost the favor of many reporters, which President Coolidge, surprisingly, had retained,[177] and some of his severest critics during his presidency were newspaper men. Much of this was the result of the Raskob-Shouse-Michelson campaign—well-financed, relentless, and outrageous—to discredit him for political purposes.[178] But there is little doubt that the pains he took to avoid publicly voicing his felt apprehensions and the nonfulfillment of his numerous reassuring statements during the crash and for months thereafter did much to undermine newsmen's confidence. Years later Galbraith sourly observed: "Hoover had converted the simple business ritual of reassurance into a major instrument of public policy."[179] Though Hoover later acknowledged that he had gone too far, he defended

[173]Walter Lippmann, then editor of the New York *World* (until Feb. 27, 1931), nevertheless soon published a highly critical article, "The Peculiar Weakness of Mr. Hoover," *Harper's*, June 1930, pp. 1-7.

[174]"A Year of the Hoover Method," p. 17.

[175]See his comments to the Gridiron Club on Apr. 13, 1929, quoted in Chapter 6, n. 100, above.

[176]Herbert Corey (an able reporter), *The Truth about Hoover* (Boston: Houghton Mifflin, 1932), pp. 62-64. Erwin D. Canham, editor of the *Christian Science Monitor*, much later expressed the same view at Stanford. *Palo Alto Times*, Mar. 9, 1967. Corey's book was largely devoted to exposing the falsity of many vicious charges against Hoover.

[177]McCormick, "A Year of the Hoover Method," p. 2.

[178]Hoover, *Memoirs*, 3:218-30, 232; Frank Kent, "Charley Michelson," *Scribner's*, September 1930, pp. 290-96; and Corey, *The Truth about Hoover*, ch. 5. Kent called Michelson a man "of high intelligence and unquestioned character," and apparently viewed his campaign in the light of the maxim "all's fair, in love, war, and politics."

[179]*Great Crash*, p. 149.

his practice on the ground of "sustaining morale in the people."[180] He seems not to have realized the serious sacrifice of credibility which this course was bound to entail.

Moreover, as Simonds had written in August 1928, "official Europe" disliked and distrusted Hoover, even while the peoples who had benefited from his great relief operations considered him "the American superman . . . Providence and Santa Claus combined"; and there was genuine fear that with Hoover in the White House, "American efficiency, already a dread phenomenon, might become a tenfold greater menace."[181] His blunt speech and what seemed domineering ways had rubbed many Europeans the wrong way in 1918–19, and so did his later harsh comments on Europe and Europeans. The prejudices of many were reinforced by his adamant stand on the interallied debts, his sharp criticisms of rubber and other commodity controls, and his tariff policy. So did his Armistice Day address in 1929, proposing unobstructed passage of food-bearing ships in time of war.[182]

---

[180]*Memoirs*, 3:32–37. Addressing the American Bankers Association in Cleveland on Oct. 2, 1930, he said that "no one can occupy the high office of President and conceivably be other than completely confident of the future of the United States." Hoover, *State Papers*, 1:375–84; Myers and Newton, *Hoover Administration*, pp. 46–47. See also Chapter 9 below.

[181]Frank H. Simonds, "What Europe Expects of Our Election. II. Hoover as Europe Sees Him," *Review of Reviews*, August 1928, pp. 144–46.

[182]*C&FC*, Nov. 16, 1929, pp. 3057–59, 3065–67, 3111–13; Hoover, *State Papers*, 1:413–17. See n. 102 above.

COLLAPSE INTO SEVERE DEPRESSION, APRIL–DECEMBER 1930

ONE OF THE KEENEST U.S. analysts active in the interwar period wrote in the trough of the major cycle of 1927–33, with the advantage of hindsight: "Probably no nation ever faced a business decline more optimistically than we did this one. For six months we experienced a truly typical minor depression, and then suddenly the major depression was upon us. American confidence and optimism were submerged by superior economic forces. Within a very brief time it became entirely clear that this depression was not merely or mainly psychological."[1] Colonel Ayres perhaps overstated the suddenness of the reversal, but he was right in stressing its reality. In the spring of 1930 American business sentiment gradually turned apprehensive, then pessimistic, as declines in business activity, employment, output, and stock prices gathered momentum, and as stocks of primary commodities rose steeply in 1930 and remained high while prices declined inexorably. From about the middle of 1930 the "normal liquidation" of recession turned into the "abnormal liquidation" of depression, and the vicious circle began its two-year operation.[2] The illusions which pervaded the boom period, and were cherished even after the stock market crash, were reluctantly moderated (but not yet wholly surrendered) under the pressure of accumulating evidence. Severe contraction in May–December 1930 brought widespread and severe depression by the end of the year, when the first of three U.S. banking crises erupted.

Perspective, 1931–39   To put these events in perspective, a few later developments will be summarized here.[3]

     After a hopeful interlude of four months early in 1931, serious European financial crises marked the last two-thirds of that year. These were

---

[1]L. P. Ayres, *The Economics of Recovery* (New York: Macmillan, 1933), p. 3. He also said (p. 25): "This is primarily a debt depression."

[2]Joseph A. Schumpeter, *Business Cycles: A Theoretical, Historical, and Statistical Analysis of the Capitalist Process,* 2 vols. (New York: McGraw-Hill, 1939), 1:9–25, 2:911–17.

[3]The course of the world economy in 1929–39, with charts and tables for the world and for the leading industrial countries, is ably discussed in the various annual reports of the Bank for International Settlements, especially those published on May 9, 1938 (pp. 5-18), and in the two following years.

accompanied and followed by deepening depression to mid-1932. From that low trough, far below that of late 1930, irregular recovery took place in Europe and, in general, outside the United States. With great variations among the several countries, increasing international tensions, and important rearmament activities in Europe, many nations emerged from depression—some by mid-1937, and most of them before World War II broke out early in September 1939. The United States and Great Britain lagged.

International trade shrank strikingly in value in 1929–33, as the fall in unit prices combined with a shrinkage in quantities exported and imported. From its 1929 peak the decline in volume was substantial in 1930, devastating in 1931.[4] From January 1930 to at least the end of June 1933 the aggregate value of international trade in every month was lower than in the same month of the preceding year.[5] In 1931 the value was only 60 percent, and the volume only 74 percent, of the 1925–29 average.[6] Here was a "contracting spiral," "the most vicious of vicious circles." Trade fell even lower in 1932 and 1933.[7] The growing business contraction, the persistent fall of commodity prices, and increasing barriers to trade were jointly responsible.

Extreme deterioration of spirit, domestically and internationally, followed the Wall Street crash and accompanied the economic contraction of 1929–32. The "era of good feeling" that had come to predominate in 1925–29 was followed by a period of increasingly bad feeling. The Young Plan for settling reparations, devised in 1929–30 on the assumption of continuing U.S. prosperity, broke down under the stress of widespread contraction and financial crises in 1930–31; and the virtual end of reparations and war debt payments in mid-1932 left a legacy of ill will while it removed one long-persistent source of international friction. Excessive faith was replaced by excessive distrust.[8] International cooperation diminished, and the League of Nations retrogressed from weakness to impotence. Another charismatic figure, Adolf Hitler, arose to lead Germany

---

[4]H. V. Hodson, *Slump and Recovery, 1929–1937* (London: Oxford University Press, 1938), p. 60.

[5]League of Nations, *World Economic Survey, 1932–33* (Geneva: League of Nations, 1933), p. 8, reproduced in J. B. Condliffe, *The Commerce of Nations* (New York: Norton, 1950), p. 495.

[6]G. B. Roorbach, in *Proc. Acad. Pol. Sci.*, January 1933, 15:224–34, esp. p. 225, citing League of Nations, *World Economic Survey, 1931–32* (Geneva: League of Nations, 1932), p. 155.

[7]League of Nations, *World Economic Survey, 1933–34* (Geneva: League of Nations, 1934).

[8]E.g., Herbert Feis, *The Diplomacy of the Dollar, 1919–1932* (New York: Norton, 1966; orig. publ. 1950), pp. 1–3. I think Hoover was misleading, if not wrong, in saying, in 1952: "By the time Roosevelt took office the fears from abroad had disappeared." *The Memoirs of Herbert Hoover*, vol. 3: *The Great Depression, 1929–1941* (New York: Macmillan, 1952), p. 478.

relentlessly toward a second world war. Salter put it accurately when in 1961 he wrote of "powerful disruptive forces": "the stock market crisis of October 1929, [was] followed . . . in 1931 by the collapse of the world's financial structure. Thereafter the tide of disruption gathered an irresistible force which destroyed first the hopes for a better future, then the measure of recovery already achieved, then the financial foundations of any tolerable economic progress—and then of peace itself. . . . The decade of recovery, progress and stability was succeeded by the decade of disruption and destruction."[9]

In the United States, banking difficulties continued to be serious into 1933; political controversies reached their worst in the 1932 presidential campaign; a virtual impasse in Washington existed through the four-month interval between Hoover's overwhelming defeat in the November 8 elections and the Roosevelt inauguration on March 4, 1933; and the U.S. economy continued to scrape bottom, although the stock market never again declined to its mid-1932 low.

Beginning with his stirring inaugural address, President Roosevelt succeeded in persuading the public of a complete change of spirit and attitude, and went on to get congressional approval of an astounding number of hastily drafted measures for recovery and reform. The "New Deal" administration launched a vigorous drive for recovery, ignored important campaign promises, tried many bold experiments, and achieved some valuable results, yet experienced important rebuffs. A severe short-term contraction and depression in 1937-38 had substantial repercussions in Great Britain and several other countries. The administration failed to attain its avowed objectives of restoring the pre-crash price level, bringing "equality" to agriculture, eliminating excessive unemployment, and ending federal budget deficits. The Democratic Party and its charismatic leader nevertheless retained the favor of the voters and won the elections of 1936 and 1940 with the aid of temporary improvement in business. Only with the huge defense buildup of 1940-41 was the goal of general prosperity achieved, and the percentage of the labor force unemployed remained above 4 percent until some time in 1942.

Some vocal contemporary writers in 1930-33 were (and many later ones have been) contemptuous of the optimistic utterances, from the president down, that marked the Wall Street crash and its aftermath and the "great contraction" in 1929-30 and later.[10] True, there were some

[9]Lord Salter, *Memoirs of a Public Servant* (London: Faber, 1961), pp. 198-99.

[10]For example, see James Truslow Adams' "Presidential Prosperity," first published in *Harper's*, August 1930, pp. 257-87, and "Pollyanna, Our Patron Goddess," *Forum*, November 1930, pp. 237-62, both reprinted in his book *The Tempo of Modern Life* (New York: Boni, 1931), pp. 259-300; Edward Angly, *Oh, Yeah?* (New York: Viking, 1931); and J. K. Galbraith, *The Great Crash 1929* (Boston: Houghton Mifflin, 1955), pp. 147-48 et passim.

disciples of Emil Coué[11] who proceeded on the assumption that putting up a smiling front and radiating cheer were essential to improvement of a difficult situation. True also that there were numerous irresponsible assertions, from the president down, which lacked adequate factual basis at the time. In view of the national tendency to swing from great optimism to extreme pessimism, which became a major factor from mid-1930, however, the urge to dispel or neutralize gloom was neither surprising nor altogether irrational. It is important to add that reputable, objective analysts were more or less seriously in error in their appraisals, forecasts, and judgments.

We do well in later decades to recall Hoover's candid comments in his *Memoirs*: "Presidents cannot be pessimistic in times of national difficulties. They must be encouraging. . . . Presidents must be cheerful and optimistic. To be the reverse would bring new disasters."[12] In his campaign address at Des Moines on October 4, 1932, President Hoover dealt with the strenuous battle to save this country from the consequences of European financial crises, and observed: "It had to be fought in silence, for it will be evident to you that had the whole of the forces in motion been made public at the time there would have been no hope of victory because of the panic through fear and destruction of confidence that very disclosure would have brought."[13]

As presidential candidate, Roosevelt naturally attacked instances of what had proved mistaken optimism, but as president he followed his predecessor's practice in this respect.[14] Though subjected to similar criticisms, he managed to escape the consequences that dogged Hoover in the early 1930s.[15] Both presidents believed that restoration of confidence was a prime essential. In the conditions of 1929–33 Hoover signally failed to achieve this objective. In the more favorable conditions of cyclical uptrend in 1933–39, Roosevelt's successes in this respect were greater, but were shortlived and limited rather than durable and comprehensive; in contrast to his predecessor, however, President Roosevelt proved a consummate politician and reaped his reward.

[11]See F. L. Allen, *Only Yesterday* (New York: Harper, 1931), p. 83, with special reference to early 1923. The paperback edition (New York: Harper and Row, 1964) is differently paged.

[12]Hoover, *Memoirs*, 3:58, 480.

[13]R. L. Wilbur and A. M. Hyde, *The Hoover Policies* (New York: Scribner, 1937), pp. 403–8; Hoover, *The State Papers and Other Public Writings of Herbert Hoover*, ed. William Starr Myers, 2 vols. (Garden City, N.Y.: Doubleday Doran, 1934), 2:447–49.

[14]Examples of Roosevelt's "comforting optimism" in 1934–36 are quoted in Hoover, *Memoirs*, 3:479–82.

[15]In large part this may be attributed to striking differences in personality. Hoover, despite his designedly cheerful utterances and typically sound arguments, tended often to radiate gloom. F. D. R., on the contrary, generally succeeded in radiating hope and cheer in private and public alike. See Edgar Eugene Robinson, *The Roosevelt Leadership, 1933–1945* (Philadelphia: Lippincott, 1955).

Severe Contraction The remarkably hopeful interlude of the early
in the United States, months of 1930 was followed by adverse devel-
May–December 1930 opments in the rest of the year.[16] For some time
far too little attention was paid to the declines in retail sales and industrial
production, the rise of unemployment and short-time employment, other
evidences of continuing contraction at home and abroad, and especially to
the worldwide fall in wholesale prices of foodstuffs and raw materials
which Keynes, late in January 1930, publicly asserted "has now taken on
the character of a world-wide disaster."[17] Here, despite the vigorous
"stabilizing" measures initiated by the Federal Farm Board in October 1929,
which were expanded early in 1930, the fall of prices of farm products was
especially severe.[18] Commodity price declines continued, with catastrophic
consequences abroad and at home.[19] Apparent "stabilization" of commodity prices twice proved shortlived, in April and again in September.
Several commodity price stabilization undertakings broke down, and the
Federal Farm Board lowered its new-crop price supports.[20] Excessive accumulation of commodity stocks and overexpansion of productive capacity
became evident.

Nearly all the significant U.S. economic indicators kept falling: production of pig iron, steel, crude petroleum, crude rubber, motor vehicles,
and electric power; consumption of raw textile fibers; building construction; international trade; and indexes of industrial production and business
activity. Occasional departures from downtrends were explained by special

[16]See the HES *Weekly Letter* (1930); the London and Cambridge Economic Service
publications; the CTC *Bus. Bull.* and its long charts, *American Business Activity since
1790*; the Citibank *Monthly Economic Letter*; the AT&T monthly *Summary* (esp. that of
Jan. 7, 1931); and especially W. L. Crum's reviews of the first three quarters of 1930 and the
year as a whole in *Rev. Ec. Stat.*, May, August, and November 1930, 12:49–55, 100–108,
149–55; February 1931, 13:1–14.

[17]In his annual address as chairman of the National Mutual Life Assurance Society on
Jan. 29, 1930. He also went so far as to say that the storm center was not in the United
Kingdom or the United States, but in the countries producing new materials overseas.
Economist, Feb. 1, 8, 1930, pp. 230, 268, 289–90; Citibank, *Monthly Economic Letter*, March
1930, p. 47; and Sir Roy Harrod, *The Life of John Maynard Keynes* (New York: Harcourt
Brace, 1951), pp. 289, 300–301, 481–82. See also Citibank, *Monthly Economic Letter*, July
1930, pp. 136–37; HES, *Weekly Letter*, Nov. 29, 1930, p. 298; and Royal Economic Society,
Memorandum 28, February 1931.

[18]AT&T, *Summary*, Oct. 6, 1930, p. 2; FRS, *Hist. Chart Book, 1971*, pp. 98, 100–104.

[19]F. W. Hirst, *Wall Street and Lombard Street: The Stock Exchange Slump of 1929 and
the Trade Depression of 1930* (New York: Macmillan, 1931), esp. pp. 108–22, 152–55, and
Hodson, *Slump and Recovery*, pp. 34–36, 55–58.

[20]Hodson, *Slump and Recovery*, pp. 40–50; M. K. Bennett, Helen C. Farnsworth, and
A. E. Taylor, "Wheat in the First Year of the Agricultural Marketing Act," in *The World
Wheat Situation, 1929–30: A Review of the Crop Year*, Wheat Studies of the Food Research
Institute 7 (Stanford, Calif.: Food Research Institute, 1930), pp. 145–64; the first two annual
reports of the Federal Farm Board, esp. 1930, pp. 26–44, and 1931, pp. 48–58; and W. S. Myers
and W. H. Newton, *The Hoover Administration: A Documented Narrative* (New York:
Scribner, 1936), pp. 37, 56–58.

factors.[21] The volume of mining, which fluctuates much more than that of manufacturing, dropped sharply from December 1929 to March 1930; after recovery in April, the decline was resumed and reached new lows late in the year.[22] Freight car loadings, both total and miscellaneous, leveled off in January-April 1930 but declined strongly in May-December.[23] Such shrinkage in traffic sharply reduced railway income, forced contraction in capital expenditures, and started the descent of railroad companies into serious financial difficulties. Truck competition was an additional but relatively minor factor.[24]

U.S. agriculture in 1930 conspicuously failed to live up to expectations voiced late in 1929 (see Chapters 6 and 7). On the contrary, farmers were hard hit by severe declines in prices of farm products and in farmland values per acre, by bank failures and mortgage foreclosures, and by a midsummer drought that affected large numbers.[25] The president's ambitious farm program and the Farm Board's price stabilization measures were snowed under by the drastic contraction in business, employment, and exports.[26] The Canadian Wheat Pool system, which had reached its peak of success in 1928–29, came to grief in 1930, and late in the year was virtually put under receivership.[27] Russian wheat exports, which had begun on a small scale in the preceding months, reached sizable dimensions in August-November 1930, but were smaller in the later months of the crop year.[28]

[21]See AT&T, *Summary*, July 7, 1930, p. 5.

[22]HES, *Weekly Letter*, Apr. 26, Aug. 9, Nov. 22, 1930, pp. 106–7, 200, 286–90; July 25, Dec. 26, 1931, pp. 135, 226–27.

[23]See charts in AT&T, *Summary*, July 6, 1931, pp. 15, 17.

[24]CTC, *Bus. Bull.*, Mar. 15, Oct. 15, 1935.

[25]HES, *Weekly Letter*, June 14, Dec. 13, 1930, pp. 150–52, 308–14; May 23, 1931, pp. 98–100; AT&T, *Summary*, Aug. 6, Oct. 6, 1930, pp. 10–11, 2; L. C. Gray, "The Responsibility of Overproduction for Agricultural Depression," *Proc. Acad. Pol. Sci.*, January 1931, 14:376–96; *Second Annual Report of the Federal Farm Board* (Dec. 9, 1931), pp. 38–39; Louis H. Bean, "Crops, Markets, and the Agricultural Revolution," *American Statistician*, June 1967, 21(3):10–14. The 1930 drought, however, was far less severe than that of 1934.

[26]For a good brief account, see E. S. Haskell, "Stabilization Operations of the Federal Farm Board," in W. L. Holland, ed., *Commodity Control in the Pacific Area: A Symposium on Recent Experience* (London: Allen and Unwin, 1935), ch. 2, pp. 90–124. The costly Japanese government experience with rice is treated in Seiichi Tobata, "The Japanese Rice Control," in *ibid.*, ch. 4, pp. 157–97. The experience was complicated by bumper rice crops in Japan and Chosen (Korea, annexed by Japan in 1910) in 1930 and 1933. For my interpretation of the Board's actions to the end of 1930, see J. S. Davis, "The Program of the Federal Farm Board"(Dec. 29, 1930), *AER*, March 1931, suppl., 21(1):104–13, reprinted in my *On Agricultural Policy, 1926–1938* (Stanford, Calif.: Food Research Institute, 1939), pp. 155–69.

[27]Harold S. Patton, "The Canadian Wheat Pool in Prosperity and Depression," in Holland, *Commodity Control*, ch. 3, esp. pp. 125–43; and W. Sanford Evans, *Canadian Wheat Stabilization Operations, 1929–35*, Wheat Studies of the Food Research Institute 12 (Stanford, Calif.: Food Research Institute, 1936), pp. 249–72.

[28]Wheat Studies of the Food Research Institute 8 (Stanford, Calif.: Food Research Institute, 1932), pp. 199, 304–5, 492.

Early in 1931 Alonzo E. Taylor stressed the "world-wide disinclination" on the part of millers, private traders, and grain speculators to carry wheat during the crop years 1929–30 and 1930–31 as a large but unmeasurable element in the price situation.[29] For this there were several reasons. The events of 1929–30 were distinctly such as to weaken the disposition to hold wheat stocks. The crop of 1929 turned out to be larger than was anticipated early in the crop year; initial carryovers proved to be larger than was thought; the volume of international trade became strikingly small; business depression in its various aspects began to attract attention; the broad chances seemed to favor a larger wheat crop in 1930. The stock exchange crash and contemporary price declines seriously weakened confidence and generally increased "liquidity preferences." Private traders feared—rightly, as events proved—the later consequences of the accumulating and holding of huge stocks of wheat by the Canadian wheat pools and the Federal Farm Board: the time would come to "bury the corpse." The downdrift of Liverpool prices of wheat throughout 1930 reflected and intensified these fears. Confident expectations that reduced world wheat output in 1929 would lead to marked reduction in high-record stocks in mid-1929 were disappointed; only a slight reduction occurred, and stocks even rose in North America and Australia.[30] Agrarian protective measures of various kinds were greatly expanded in European importing countries.[31]

Building construction in 1930 seriously disappointed early expectations, and this failure showed up in exceptional unemployment in the building trades. By mid-September it was clear that the real estate market had been depressed by a large volume of mortgage foreclosures[32] and that there was no shortage of housing accommodations such as had given a powerful stimulus to expansion in 1921. Hopes rested on rapid obsolescence, extremely easy money, the lowest prices of building materials in postwar years, and increased labor efficiency in construction, which had lowered the Tuttle index of building costs from 193.5 to 166 in May alone;[33] but these hopes proved vain. Belatedly, the Harvard Economic Society

[29]*Speculation, Short Selling, and the Price of Wheat*, Wheat Studies of the Food Research Institute 7 (Stanford, Calif.: Food Research Institute, 1931), pp. 231–66, esp. p. 241. An appendix (pp. 262–66) dealt with selling futures for Russian account on the Chicago Board of Trade in September 1930—a minor episode that was blown up to unwarranted proportions.

[30]M. K. Bennett and others, *The World Wheat Situation, 1929–30*, Wheat Studies of the Food Research Institute 7 (Stanford, Calif.: Food Research Institute, 1930), pp. 89–184, esp. pp. 90, 95, 104–10, 132–36, 177–78.

[31]*Ibid.*, pp. 114–19, and n. 69 below.

[32]N. J. Silberling, in his *Dynamics of Business* (New York: McGraw-Hill, 1943), pp. 197–200, stressed the peculiar significance of the acceleration of housing foreclosures, and showed two indexes on his chart 28b (p. 189).

[33]HES, *Weekly Letter*, Sept. 13, 1930, pp. 226–28.

acknowledged early in November 1930 that heavy losses in real estate, "where unsoundness had long been evident," had occurred.[34] The shrinkage of bond values first became serious in real estate bonds.[35]

The year 1930 witnessed a drastic shrinkage in corporate profits from the peak level of 1929, which was broadly progressive during the year. Fabricant's 1934 study showed a decline in rates of return on the book value of stock equity from 6.2 to 2.2 percent for all corporations, and from 8.3 to 2.6 percent for manufacturing companies.[36] For some months dividend rates were maintained out of surplus, but they were generally reduced after mid-1930, when early recovery was despaired of.[37] Nevertheless, for all corporations combined, later aggregate balance sheet figures showed little change between 1929 and 1930 in the excess of surplus and undivided profits over deficits, which in the next two years shrank heavily (by $20 billion).[38]

Efforts of the banks to strengthen their reserve positions led to calling demand loans and refusals to extend maturing commercial loans; this in turn led to distress selling of goods and materials by debtor concerns, which hastened declines in commodity prices.[39] This cycle was increasingly manifest as the post-crash optimism faded.

As late as the end of September 1930, the Harvard Economic Society mentioned among the favorable factors "a banking system not only sound but strong."[40] This was an illusion, shortly revealed as such by a veritable epidemic of bank failures.[41] On December 12, after strenuous and concerted efforts were made in vain to save one of the smaller state banks in New York City with the over-impressive name of "Bank of United States,"

[34]*Ibid.*, Nov. 1, 1930, p. 266; B. M. Anderson, *Economics and the Public Welfare: Financial and Economic History of the United States, 1914–1946* (New York: Van Nostrand, 1949), pp. 197, 205, 219.

[35]R. W. Goldschmidt [Goldsmith], *The Changing Structure of American Banking* (London: Routledge, 1933), p. 106.

[36]Citibank, *Monthly Economic Letter* for 1930–31; *Rev. Ec. Stat.*, Mar. 15, 1934, 16:50–53; Solomon Fabricant, *Recent Corporate Profits in the United States* (New York: NBER, Apr. 18, 1934); and Schumpeter, *Business Cycles*, 2:833, 1000–1007.

[37]CTC, *Bus. Bull.*, Feb. 15, 1932. Despite the sharp reduction in corporate earnings in 1930, reported interest and dividend payments increased to $8 billion, as compared with $7.6 billion in 1929. Paul H. Douglas and Aaron Director, *The Problem of Unemployment* (New York: Macmillan, 1931), pp. 485–86, citing Standard Statistics Company, *Statistical Bulletin*, Nov. 15, 1930, Jan. 15, 1931.

[38]*Hist. Stat. U.S.*, ser. V 84–85, 93–96.

[39]C. A. Phillips, T. F. McManus, and R. W. Nelson, *Banking and the Business Cycle: A Study of the Great Depression in the United States* (New York: Macmillan, 1937), p. 167.

[40]HES, *Weekly Letter*, Sept. 20, 1930, p. 234. Friedman and Schwartz say of the period January–October 1930: "There was no sign of lack of confidence in banks by the public or of unusual concern by banks about their own safety." Milton Friedman and Anna J. Schwartz, *A Monetary History of the United States, 1867–1960* (Princeton, N.J.: Princeton University Press, 1963), p. 392. Yet they date the first banking crisis as October 1930–January 1931.

[41]Monthly data are given in the annual report of the Federal Reserve Board for 1930.

it closed its doors, with the largest liabilities of any U.S. bank failure up to that time.[42] This failure accentuated the first serious banking crisis of the interwar period; depositors' confidence in many other banks was sadly shaken, and runs on banks and currency hoarding ensued.[43] Since scandalous practices were heavily responsible for this failure, it is discussed below in Chapter 14; briefer mention is also made there of similar runs on French banks late in 1930, when the Oustric scandals were exposed.[44] In Great Britain, with its highly developed branch banking system, the public trusted the banks implicitly, no runs took place, no failures occurred; losses were absorbed by hidden reserves, and bank dividends were maintained.[45] Much the same was true also in Canada.

Business liquidation in 1930 seemed extraordinary, though it was to become much more severe. The annual average failure rate per 10,000 concerns was 122, as compared with 104 in 1929.[46] R. G. Dun and Company's seasonally adjusted data for the first two months of 1931 were the highest in the four decades for which monthly figures had been recorded.[47]

As we have seen (Chapter 4 above), U.S. unemployment in 1929 was considered tolerably low, though reliable data were lacking then and later; yet in the moderately depressed building trades, where labor unions were relatively strong, union figures indicated sizable percentages of the membership out of work.[48] Employment unquestionably shrank in the last quarter of 1929; unemployment continued substantial in the first quarter of 1930, and many workers were put on shortened hours per week. The first unemployment census was taken, at President Hoover's direction, with the population census of April 30, 1930, a date when farm employment was about at a seasonal peak. It was not considered very reliable, and preliminary reports, which first became available late in June, were misleading.[49] The final census figures showed 3,187,647 unemployed, of whom about one-fourth had jobs but were temporarily laid off without pay, as well as

---

[42]Perhaps because of overzealous proofreaders, highly respected authorities have erroneously termed this the "Bank of *the* United States," and many errors have appeared in accounts of its failure. See Chapter 14 below.

[43]AT&T, *Summary*, Jan. 7, 1931, p. 4, Feb. 6, 1931, p. 3; J. B. Hubbard, "Hoarding and the Expansion of Currency in Circulation," *Rev. Ec. Stat.*, Jan. 15, 1932, 14:30–37; Friedman and Schwartz, *Monetary History*, pp. 308–13, 342–43.

[44]HES, *Weekly Letter*, Nov. 29, 1930, p. 297; Hirst, *Wall Street and Lombard Street*, pp. 89–90.

[45]Paul Einzig, *The Fight for Financial Supremacy*, 2d ed. (London: Macmillan, 1931), p. v.; Hirst, *Wall Street and Lombard Street*, pp. 80–81.

[46]*Hist. Stat. U.S.*, ser. V 2. It rose to 133 in 1931 and to the all-time high of 154 in 1932.

[47]HES, *Weekly Letter*, May 16, 1931, pp. 94–96, with chart from January 1919.

[48]Citibank, *Monthly Economic Letter*, June 1930, p. 90, with a comparison of April figures for 1928–30.

[49]AT&T, *Summary*, July 7, 1930, p. 6; Douglas and Director, *Problem of Unemployment*, pp. 9–13; Hoover, *Memoirs*, 3:48–50.

273,585 with jobs but idle because of sickness or disability.[50] Many, however, were employed on short time.[51] The number of families under strain in June was estimated at 1 to 1.5 million, not much larger than in the previous December-April.

In the second half of 1930 unemployment and short-time employment increased more considerably as business contraction proceeded.[52] By the end of the year the estimated number unemployed approached 7,000,000,[53] and the illusion of "permanent prosperity" was at last dispelled.[54] Later official estimates gave 4,340,000 as the average for the year—8.7 percent of the labor force, as compared with 3.2 percent in 1929, and the largest since the depression year 1921.[55] The impact was moderated by several factors: many families had more than one worker, and many had money savings, considerable stocks of goods, generous or trusting friends and relatives, and credit standing. The actual and potential seriousness of unemployment was recognized when the President's Emergency Relief Organization was set up on October 21, 1930, initially under Colonel Arthur Woods.[56] In his second annual message to the Congress on December 2 the president asserted: "We have as a nation a definite duty to see that no deserving person in our country suffers from hunger or cold."[57]

In September 1921, in his chairman's address to the President's Conference on Unemployment, Secretary Hoover had set forth "principles, policies, and methods" for dealing with the unemployment crisis then current. These involved federal leadership, no direct federal aid to individuals, and a decentralized system supplemented by enlarged public works and

[50]U.S., Department of Commerce, Bureau of the Census, 15th census of the U.S., 1930, Unemployment, 1:6. Other categories included persons out of a job and (a) unable to work or (b) not looking for work, and persons having jobs but (a) voluntarily idle or (b) drawing pay though not at work (e.g., on vacation). Short-time workers were not covered. Cf. Douglas and Director, Problem of Unemployment, pp. 14–17.

[51]Reflected in AT&T charts (e.g., Summary, Jan. 7, 1931, pp. 8, 15) showing much sharper declines in factory payrolls than in employment indexes.

[52]Douglas and Director, Problem of Unemployment, pp. 17–22. The two sets of figures for the U.S. given in the League of Nations Monthly Bulletin of Statistics, October 1932, 13:480, indicate fairly continuous shrinkages of employment and payrolls in manufacturing in 1930, however, than in the last quarter of 1929.

[53]AT&T, Summary, Apr. 6, 1931, p. 6. A special census of unemployment in nineteen cities in January 1931 led the Census Bureau to estimate the total number wholly unemployed at 6,050,000, excluding another 2,000,000 laid off without pay, of whom a large proportion were probably working part time.

[54]Leo Wolman, "Unemployment," Yale Review, December 1930, pp. 234–48.

[55]Hist. Stat. U.S., ser. D 46–47. Much higher estimates from 1929 through 1939 are given in International Labour Review, October 1939, 40:542–44.

[56]Wilbur and Hyde, Hoover Policies, pp. 370–89, citing various references to Hoover, State Papers. This body was continued throughout the Hoover administration, under Walter S. Gifford from Aug. 19, 1931, and under Fred C. Croxton from Aug. 6, 1932. It developed a far-flung organization of state and local committees, through which the unemployment and relief positions were appraised at intervals.

[57]Hoover, State Papers, 1:431.

various other measures. President Hoover held to these principles in 1930–33 as the problem grew, for the most part succeeded in fending off attempts to substitute other principles and methods, and appraised the results as successful in various significant senses.[58]

Confronted by the rising number of unemployed and only dim prospects for increasing employment, the Hoover administration stepped up deportations of convicted aliens, illegal entrants, and other "undesirables" and, as of September 9, 1930, drastically restricted entry of quota and nonquota immigrants. Net immigration declined from 210,000 in 1929 to 191,000 in 1930 and to 35,000 in 1931; and in 1932 there was a net emigration of 68,000.[59] This striking result was the joint effect of worsening employment opportunities and of administrative actions. Even so, unemployment increased.

In Western Europe, where unemployment had been much larger than here in 1929, increases generally were more serious, though their impact was cushioned by established relief and unemployment insurance systems, most notably in Great Britain. Increases in the last quarter of 1929 and the second half of 1930 were extreme in Germany.[60]

International   The United States was a giant component of the world
Repercussions   economy, representing nearly 40 percent of the consumption of primary goods.[61] Since prosperity elsewhere depended heavily upon it, the rest of the world was profoundly impressed, in the late 1920s, by the notion that Americans had learned the secret of making prosperity permanent. As Herbert Feis well said much later: "Prices, debt structures, trade flows all rested on the stimulus of our demand and our investment. Both fell abruptly."[62] The drastic shrinkage in U.S. business activity in 1929–30 was a major cause of setbacks in other countries, and its continuation in 1931–33 shockingly dispelled the illusion that the United States was invulnerable to depressive forces.[63] To quote the 1940 annual report of the BIS:

---

[58]Wilbur and Hyde, *Hoover Policies*, pp. 370–401, with citations to Hoover, *State Papers*.

[59]Wilbur and Hyde, *Hoover Policies*, pp. 140, 143–45; Hoover, *Memoirs*, 3:42, 47–48, 314; *Hist. Stat. U.S.*, ser. C 115, 145, 152–57. Myers and Newton went too far in saying that the president announced his determination to stop all immigration. *Hoover Administration*, pp. 44–45; relatives of residents were excepted.

[60]Unemployment data in League of Nations, *Monthly Bulletin of Statistics*, e.g., October 1932, 13:479–80, and in the London and Cambridge Economic Service report published in Royal Economic Society, *Memoranda, Reports on Economic Conditions*. Cf. also Sir William H. Beveridge, "Lessons for the Present from British Experience with Unemployment," Nov. 8, 1933, *Proc. Acad. Pol. Sci.*, January 1934, 15:378–84.

[61]BIS, *Eighth Annual Report*, May 9, 1938, p. 6.

[62]*Diplomacy of the Dollar*, p. 62. Cf. Moritz J. Bonn, *Prosperity: Myth and Reality in American Economic Life* (London: Martin Hopkinson, 1931), ch. 3, "The End of Permanent Prosperity," and Hodson, *Slump and Recovery*, pp. 54–56.

[63]Sir Henry Clay, *Lord Norman* (London: Macmillan, 1957), ch. 9.

"The decline in the autumn of 1929 was probably at first merely an example of an ordinary downward turn in the business cycle, but it released depressing forces which soon became overwhelming and brought upon the world a financial crisis and a series of monetary convulsions such as had never before been known in times of peace. Regarded historically the consequent setback in material progress was of crucial importance."[64]

"The psychological effect of the collapse," M. J. Bonn wrote in 1931, "was stupendous throughout the world."[65] He meant not merely the stock market crash but also, and even more important, the Great Contraction that followed in 1930–31. The conviction of U.S. business leaders that the great boom had been "the fruit of their own creative genius" gave way to the bitter realization that they had cherished illusions, which deflated the arrogance they had displayed. Abroad, as well as at home, disillusionment spread, and in the next few years the excoriation of businessmen was no longer limited to those whose crookedness or egregious misjudgments had been revealed.

The sudden and drastic shrinkage of U.S. demand for Latin American, Asian, and Australasian primary products such as coffee, copper, tin, rubber, wool, silk, jute, nitrates, and guano accentuated the price debacle which these areas had already begun to experience, and led to economic crises and political revolutions there.[66] It also brought general recognition of excessive world commodity stocks and overproduction of many commodities,[67] and led to conservative buying with an eye to uncertainties and possible further price declines. Hence the drastic fall of commodity prices throughout 1930 was an outstanding feature of the year.

To a degree previously unappreciated, the world commodity price structure had become highly vulnerable by 1929.[68] Technological progress in agriculture and industry had facilitated cost reductions by efficient

[64]BIS, *Tenth Annual Report*, May 27, 1940, p. 7.

[65]*Prosperity*, pp. 147–50.

[66]*Ibid.*, pp. 177–82, 187–88; Crum's quarterly reviews in *Rev. Ec. Stat.*, May and August 1930, 12:49–54, 101–5; Hirst, *Wall Street and Lombard Street*, pp. 108–22; and Moritz J. Bonn, *Wandering Scholar* (New York: John Day, 1948), p. 311.

[67]Keynes had devoted serious attention to statistics of commodity stocks in the 1920s, and had been the author or joint author of six memoranda on this subject published by the LCES between April 1923 and August 1929. The seventh, *Stocks of Staple Commodities*, by J. M. Keynes, J. W. F. Rowe, and G. L. Schwartz, appeared as Royal Economic Society *Memorandum 24*, October 1930; the trenchant comments on pp. 3–4 are impressive. Tables, with few comments, appear in later LCES reports on current economic conditions.

[68]See a brief discussion of "Price Stability and Economic Flexibility" in Frederick C. Mills, *Economic Tendencies in the United States* (New York: NBER, 1932), pp. 323–32, with a tabulated "Summary of Valorization Schemes." On that topic there is an enormous literature. For Keynes' summary views, see his *Treatise on Money*, 2 vols. (New York: Harcourt Brace, 1930), 2:141–42. Cf. Lionel Robbins, *The Great Depression* (London: Macmillan, 1934; preface dated June 1934), pp. 61, 64–65.

producers and put their more numerous, less efficient competitors in difficulties. The genuine plight of the latter led to political efforts in many
countries to check declines in prices of farm products. It also served to encourage various kinds of steps by producers to undertake price-raising or
price-supporting actions (often termed "stabilization" or "valorization"),
with or without government help, that led to holding back stocks by the
organized group. Typically the price objectives were such as to stimulate
production by nonparticipants and economies by industrial consumers
(e.g., rubber reclamation). In some important instances—wheat, for example—importing countries multiplied their restrictions on imports to protect their high-cost producers from the flood of cheap imports.[69]

Large unsold stocks and overstimulated production in sugar, coffee,
wheat, rice, cotton, silk, wool, rubber, tea, and copper[70] affected a great
many countries. In some instances the situation was made worse in 1929–
30 by exceptionally good crops, as with European grains, Japanese and
Chosen rice, and Brazilian coffee. When the onset of depression led to reduced consumption, stocks tended to rise and prices to weaken; and in the
course of 1930 most of the control schemes broke down,[71] to make matters
still worse. Efforts of the hitherto successful Canadian Wheat Pools and
the new Federal Farm Board, like the Hawley-Smoot Tariff Act, were futile
or worse, as soon became evident.

A complicating factor in 1930 was the new phenomenon of Soviet
dumping. Large quantities of Russian coal, timber, cement, textiles, and
even wheat were exported, despite shortages of these items in the
U.S.S.R.[72] Though some observers attributed this to a Soviet desire to
damage the economies of other countries, it primarily represented a
desperate effort to ensure continuing Soviet imports of urgently needed
goods when credits were well-nigh impossible to obtain.

Partly because of price declines in staple foodstuffs and raw materials, depressed conditions came to prevail in nearly all commercial
countries, advanced and backward alike, but appeared rather earlier in

[69]The intensification and increased complexity of the French and German systems of pro-
tecting their grain producers in the 1930s, and their price effects, are summarized in long
perspective in Helen C. Farnsworth and Karen J. Friedmann, "French and EEC Grain Policies
and Their Price Effects, 1920–1970," *Food Research Institute Studies* 7 (Stanford, Calif.:
Food Research Institute, 1967), pp. 5–15, 69–70, 126, and app. table 1; and Karen J. Friedmann, "German Grain Policies and Prices, 1925–1964," *ibid.*, 5 (1965), pp. 31–98, esp. pp. 32–
40.
[70]On the copper case, and the gyrations of copper prices in 1929–31, see F. E. Richter's two
brief articles in *Rev. Ec. Stat.*, February 1931, 13:15–18; Jan. 15, 1932, 14:27–29.
[71]E.g., AT&T, *Summary*, May 7, 1930, p. 9, Aug. 6, p. 6, Oct. 6, p. 2, Jan. 7, 1931, p. 1;
N&A, Apr. 19, 1930, p. 74; and Hodson, *Slump and Recovery*, pp. 40–52.
[72]Paul Einzig, *The World Economic Crisis, 1929–1931*, 2d ed. (London: Macmillan, 1932),
pp. 151–54. Paul Haensel, then of Northwestern University, made some pertinent comments
on Russian dumping in 1930 in his discussion of the papers on international economic relations at the AEA meeting on Dec. 30, 1930. *AER*, March 1931, suppl., 21(1):167.

many countries overseas than in the United States and Canada. Seriously adverse developments abroad reinforced and complicated the worsening domestic deterioration to an astonishing degree. The almost universal adoption of the gold exchange standard in the middle and late 1920s had seemed an important achievement at the time; but it ensured a worldwide shrinkage in income and prices in 1929–31, as conditions making for price declines in one country were transmitted to others.[73]

Keynes was one of the first to discern and forthrightly assert the true character of the economic contraction. In his London weekly of May 10, 1930, he wrote: "The fact is—a fact not yet recognized by the great public—that we are now in the depths of a very severe international slump, a slump which will take its place in history amongst the most acute ever experienced. It will require not merely passive movements of Bank rate to lift us out of a depression of this order, but a very active and determined policy."[74] He stressed the "very extreme and universal" fall of commodity prices, and remarked that "enterprise and confidence have collapsed." His over-bold prescription for the recovery of international prices and trade was that "New York and Paris should absorb foreign loans up to the full extent of their capacity"; yet he extravagantly condemned the Young Plan for "mobilization of German Reparations" as "one of the stupidest enterprises conceivable." As had often happened before and would happen again, his strongly worded and often cutting opinions were neither well received nor persuasive.[75]

On May 31 the Harvard Economic Society reported the conclusion of the London and Cambridge Economic Service that "Great Britain is now in a major business depression."[76] The shrinkage of purchasing power and prosperity of countries exporting foodstuffs and raw materials and the

---

[73]Friedman and Schwartz, *Monetary History*, pp. 359–62. China, on a silver standard, with silver prices falling in terms of gold even more than commodity prices in general, was hardly affected internally by the widespread economic contraction that swept the gold standard world, just as Germany had been insulated by her hyperinflation and floating exchange rates in 1920–21. Indeed, China first experienced depression after Great Britain left the gold standard in September 1931, when the Chinese yuan sharply appreciated as the pound depreciated.

[74]"The Industrial Crisis," *N&A*, May 10, 1930, pp. 163–64. One may question only his use of the word "depths." Harrod (*Keynes*, p. 398) quoted only this excerpt. Keynes' preceding passage is illuminating, and well-nigh accurate, although his optimistic cable of Oct. 24, 1929, was sent six and a half months before his article here quoted. The *Economist* soon asserted that "the world as a whole is passing through the throes of a major trade depression." Monthly supplement, May 31, 1930.

[75]This Keynes admitted in the preface (dated Nov. 8, 1931) to his *Essays in Persuasion* (New York: Harcourt Brace, 1932).

[76]HES, *Weekly Letter*, May 31, 1930, pp. 133–37. The LCES *Report on Current Economic Conditions* dated Apr. 22, 1930, already implied that the depression was "of a worldwide nature," and the next one, dated July 18, said: "The international depression is one of major dimensions." "It is clear that hopes of an early mitigation . . . would be premature." Cf. Clay, *Lord Norman*, pp. 367–69.

drop in the volume of international trade seriously affected British exports, shipping activities, and returns from overseas investments. Early in July 1930 young Harold Macmillan came to believe the British economic situation "so serious that it will lead to the breakdown of the whole party system"; and Winston Churchill said that Lord Beaverbrook's Empire free trade campaign was ruining the country.[77] At the end of August 1930 the HES review of British economic conditions frankly recognized the "intensification and spreading of the depression," the unchecked decline in commodity prices, and the fact that "the prospect of an upward movement in prices in Great Britain is remote."[78] Late in November, the crisis was called the worst in Britain's history; Parliament was considered incapable of dealing with it, and a bad smash seemed in the offing.[79] Oswald Mosley, an influential figure, left the Labour Party to launch a new party in 1930-31 with support from his then warm friend Harold Nicolson and other younger men and with encouragement from others (including Keynes) who did not join it.

In mid-June 1930, after fourteen months of congressional consideration, the Hawley-Smoot Tariff Act was passed and signed.[80] President Hoover was a firm believer in the protective tariff, and regarded tariffs on farm products as an essential part of his farm program.[81] He had called Congress into special session in mid-April 1929 primarily to deal with this program, to which he had devoted much attention in his 1928 campaign speeches, whereas Democratic speakers had largely ignored the tariff issue. The House committee made a halfhearted attempt at the limited revision Hoover had urged.[82] But the Senate committee was headed by Reed Smoot, an able and experienced high-protectionist senator of the most in-

[77]Nigel Nicolson, ed., *Harold Nicolson: Diaries and Letters*, vol. 1: *1930-1939* (New York: Atheneum, 1966-68), pp. 51-52 (diary for July 2 and 6, 1930).

[78]HES, *Weekly Letter*, Aug. 30, 1930, p. 213.

[79]Nicolson, *Harold Nicolson*, 1:61 (diary for Nov. 30, 1930).

[80]See F. W. Taussig, "The Tariff, 1929-30," *QJE*, February 1930, 44:175-204. The Senate's final vote was 44-42 (June 13). Though Roosevelt in his campaign speeches called it "the Grundy tariff," super-high-protectionist Senator Grundy of Pennsylvania had persistently opposed it, and the negative votes included those of some senators who thought its rates too low and its flexible provision dangerous.

[81]Herbert Hoover, *The New Day: Campaign Speeches of Herbert Hoover, 1928* (Stanford, Calif.: Stanford University Press, 1928), passim; Wilbur and Hyde, *Hoover Policies*, pp. 181-92, 506-23; and Hoover, *Memoirs*, vol. 3, esp. pp. 290-96. As late as Apr. 28, 1933, Iowa Senator L. J. Dickinson asserted, in the face of bitter experience: "A protective tariff is the very foundation of farm relief." *Proc. Acad. Pol. Sci.*, June 1933, 15:309.

[82]Senator Borah was reported to have said on Feb. 29, 1930, that if, in June 1929, the president had agreed to limit the tariff revision to farm products, the bill would have been passed within ninety days. *Review of Reviews*, April 1930, p. 55. Lippmann later wrote that President Hoover did not take the chance offered, in June 1929, to fight moves to broaden the bill, and that thereafter the special interests felt safe in ignoring him. Walter Lippmann, *Interpretations, 1933-1935*, ed. Allan Nevins (New York: Macmillan, 1936), p. 67 (June 5, 1933); Marian C. McKenna, *Borah* (Ann Arbor: University of Michigan Press, 1961), pp. 263-68. Perhaps they were right, but one cannot be sure.

tolerant stamp, and his influence prevailed in expanding the scope of the bill and increasing rates of duty.[83]

The general character of the bill was fairly clear before the stock market crash, and it was the subject of many protests and some retaliation in advance by a number of foreign countries.[84] In its final form it was a general revision, with substantial increases in many rates, though Hoover adduced figures to show that the level of protection was only moderately raised. With great difficulty and delay, he had won two key points: inclusion of the socalled "flexible provision," authorizing the new bipartisan Tariff Commission to consider complaints and recommend to the president raising or lowering rates;[85] and exclusion of the export debenture plan strongly urged by the National Grange.[86]

Though the final bill by no means pleased him, the president felt constrained to sign it (June 17, 1930)[87] and defended it then and later.[88] In so doing he rejected the plea for a veto signed by more than 1,250 economists.[89] He appears to have given little or no weight to the fact that, with commodity prices declining and business contraction increasing, the new rates would come into effect at a most critical time.[90] He rejected not only the general views of his Harvard friend and leading academic tariff authority F. W. Taussig, former head of the Tariff Commission, but also

[83]F. W. Taussig, *The Tariff History of the United States*, 8th ed. (New York: Putnam, 1931), p. 184.

[84]E.g., AT&T, *Summary*, Apr. 4, 1929, p. 12, June 5, 1930, p. 8, with special reference to the new Canadian tariff act; *C&FC*, July 13, Sept. 7, 1929, pp. 180, 1535, Aug. 30, 1930, pp. 1357–58; *Economist*, Aug. 31, 1929, pp. 391–94; League of Nations, *World Economic Survey of 1932*, pp. 61–66; and at great length in Joseph M. Jones, Jr., "Tariff Retaliation; Repercussions of the Hawley-Smoot Bill" (Ph.D. diss., University of Pennsylvania, 1934).

[85]On May 3, 1930, the House rejected the Senate amendments providing for the export debenture plan (231–131) and deleting the flexible provisions (236–134). *Review of Reviews*, May 1930, pp. 33–35. For his views on the Tariff Commission's work in 1931–32, see Hoover, *State Papers*, 1:148, 251–52; 2:34, 398, 472–73. On Apr. 28, 1933, John Lee Coulter, a member of the Tariff Commission, told the New York Academy of Political Science how the Commission had dealt with about 225 applications for action under the flexible and related provisions of the Tariff Act of 1930. More than 90 out of the 135 which had been formally investigated had been disposed of, and the majority had led to formal reports to the president. But he did not summarize the president's actions. "The Tariff Commission and the Flexible Clause," *Proc. Acad. Pol. Sci.*, June 1933, 15:317–26.

[86]See Hoover's letters to Senator Charles L. McNary, Apr. 22, 1929, and to Congressman John Q. Tilson, May 1, 1930, in Hoover, *State Papers*, 1:39–42, 296–97; J. S. Davis, *The Export Debenture Plan for Wheat*, Wheat Studies of the Food Research Institute 5 (Stanford, Calif.: Food Research Institute, 1929), pp. 301–46, and *The Farm Export Debenture Plan* (Stanford, Calif.: Food Research Institute, 1929), published in December.

[87]The decision was unquestionably difficult, but I distrust the account in Allen and Pearson's (initially anonymous) highly partisan *Washington Merry-Go-Round* (New York: Liveright, 1931), pp. 51–76, esp. pp. 65–66. The American Farm Bureau Federation, which at times was critical of such measures, eventually urged that the bill be signed.

[88]Wilbur and Hyde, *Hoover Policies*, pp. 185–92; Hoover, *State Papers*, 1:314–18; Hoover, *Memoirs*, 3:287–306, 405.

[89]See Chapter 15 below.

[90]T. W. Lamont, who had urged a veto, made this point in his Nov. 14, 1930, address, "Phases of the World Depression," *Proc. Acad. Pol. Sci.*, January 1931, 14:299–308.

Taussig's specific point that attempts to base tariff rates on differences in costs of production would be worthless if applied and virtually impossible to apply.[91] He also largely ignored the well-established view that higher tariff rates on export products, such as export types and grades of wheat, would be ineffective.[92] He would not openly admit any basic incompatibility between a high tariff policy and an insistence on repayment of Allied war debts.[93] He seems to have minimized the possibility that other countries would follow the U.S. example when they saw that the United States had enjoyed high prosperity with high tariffs.[94]

The Hawley-Smoot Tariff Act failed to benefit agricultural and industrial interests significantly and contributed, both directly and indirectly, to the contraction of business activity and international trade after mid-1930. Among other things, it must have helped move British policy toward greater protectionism.[95] Yet the extent of its influence has never been satisfactorily assessed.

W. C. Mitchell, speaking in the spring of 1931, rated it important, saying that raising tariff duties had "never made more trouble for this and other countries than in the last three years."[96] Salter soon expressed similar views, which he modified years later.[97] B. M. Anderson, ever a sharp critic of high tariffs, called this act "the crowning financial folly of the whole period from 1920 to 1933."[98] Schumpeter, on the other hand,

[91] F. W. Taussig, "Cost of Production and the Tariff," *Atlantic*, December 1910, pp. 721–29, reprinted in his collected essays, *Free Trade, the Tariff, and Reciprocity* (New York: Macmillan, 1920), pp 134–48.

[92] This was abundantly shown in many of the wheat studies of the Food Research Institute, and was a major part of the argument for farm relief measures (such as the export debenture plan) to "make the tariff effective for agriculture."

[93] See his campaign address at Boston, Oct. 15, 1928, in *New Day*, pp. 137–39.

[94] J. W. Angell made this point in his paper of Nov. 14, 1930, "America's Role in the International Situation," *Proc. Acad. Pol. Sci.*, January 1931, 14:289.

[95] On July 4, 1930, a Bankers' Manifesto favoring further tariff protection for Great Britain was published in London, and among the signers was Keynes' good friend Sir Reginald McKenna, former chancellor of the exchequer, Britain's leading banker, and a director of the Bank of England. *Economist*, July 12, 1930, pp. 59–60; Clay, *Lord Norman*, p. 368. This document did not mention any influence from the new U.S. tariff act, nor did Keynes, in his "Proposals for a Revenue Tariff," written eight months later "somewhat in desperation" for the *New Statesman and Nation*, Mar. 7, 1931, pp. 53–54 (reprinted in his *Essays in Persuasion*, pp. 271–80). The *New Statesman* had recently absorbed the *Nation and Athenaeum*, of which Keynes had been chairman for a decade.

[96] *Proc. Acad. Pol. Sci.*, June 1931, 14:398.

[97] *Recovery: The Second Effort* (New York: Century, 1932), pp. 197–99; and Lord Salter, *Memoirs of a Public Servant* (London: Faber, 1961), p. 198: "It seemed at the time a wanton blow at the world's hopes for a more stable foundation for the expansion of international trade and general increase of prosperity. A little later it was seen to be only a significant reflection of much more powerful disruptive forces." Cf. also Robbins, *Great Depression*, pp. 68–69, and League of Nations, *Raw Materials Problems and Policies* (Geneva: League of Nations, 1946), pp. 49–50.

[98] *Economics and the Public Welfare*, pp. 224–25. In March 1931 he had even urged unilateral tariff reductions as an important remedy for the depression. *Chase Economic Bulletin*, Mar. 23, 1931, pp. 7–12.

rightly complained in 1939 that the influence of tariffs was commonly either ignored or exaggerated; but I think he went too far in concluding that "protectionism as such played but a minor role in the cyclical process of the postwar epoch."[99] Carl Snyder, late in 1931, held (I believe rightly) that James Harvey Rogers had ascribed to tariffs and war debts too large a role in the contraction and "scarcely adequate recognition of the world-wide effect of our fantastic speculative boom in stocks."[100] John H. Williams was broadly correct, I believe, in asserting that U.S. tariff policy was "unsound in principle, extreme in degree, and bad in effect," that the so-called "scientific" "cost-equalization" principle was actually absurd, and that "European tariffs and other trade restrictions have hurt Europe more than our tariff."[101] But I think he went too far in saying that if U.S. tariffs had remained unchanged after 1913 the postwar experience would have been much the same as it was. In March 1953 Rufus S. Tucker, then a General Motors economist, who had been an assistant to Taussig, told a National Industrial Conference Board panel discussing the economics of tariffs that Taussig's last remark to him was "that he was convinced that the effects of the tariff, both good and evil, had been vastly exaggerated." Tucker, though always opposed to protective tariffs, also expressed his firm conviction that the common assertion "that our tariffs hindered the transfer operations in war debts" was absolutely untrue.[102]

Nevertheless, in spite of this wide range of opinion, it seems safe to say that the almost universal multiplication of trade barriers in the early 1930s, through tariff measures and many other devices, figured significantly in throttling down international trade, accelerating price declines, and curtailing economic activity all over the world; but there were many other important factors.[103]

Fiscal, Monetary, and   The federal treasury fiscal year ended June 30,
Financial Developments   1930, with a surplus of $184 million, virtually
in the United States   as large as in fiscal year 1929. Income tax col-
lections for 1929–30, despite the small cut in rates late in 1929, totaled $2.4 billion, 3.4 percent higher than in 1928–29. The interest-bearing public debt was reduced by $717 million to $15.9 billion, the lowest figure

[99]*Business Cycles*, 2:705–8, 915. Folke Hilgerdt in 1933 pointed out how ingeniously elaborated tariffs in the 1920s helped accentuate the boom and aggravate the depression, thus tending to destabilize domestic industrial activity. Folke Hilgerdt, in *Economic Essays in Honour of Gustav Cassel* (London: Allen and Unwin, 1933), pp. 281, 285–90.

[100]Snyder, review of Rogers, *America Weighs Her Gold* (New Haven, Conn.: Yale University Press, 1931), in *Yale Review*, December 1931, pp. 399–401.

[101]"The United States Tariff and Our International Financial Position," Apr. 28, 1933, *Proc. Acad. Pol. Sci.*, June 1933, 15:278–84.

[102]NICB pamphlet, July 1953, p. 67.

[103]See three series of papers, given in April and November 1932 and April 1933, *Proc. Acad. Pol. Sci.*, May 1932, January and June 1933, 15:1–32, 224–38, 276–367; Condliffe, *Commerce of Nations*, esp. pp. 447, 479–504; and Robbins, *Great Depression*, pp. 65–69.

since September 1918.[104] But state and local governments were already feeling the impact of reduced revenues,[105] and after mid-1930 their expenditures on public works were steadily and substantially reduced.[106] The 1933 low was only 36 percent of the 1927 high.

As already noted (Chapter 8 above), Federal Reserve authorities eased money decisively during and after the crash and further in the first quarter of 1930, either leading or following the market. But the drastic decline in short-term rates during the rest of the year was due mainly to shrinkage of demand for loans. In June 1930 open market money rates reached their lowest for any month since October 1924; and the offering rate for ninety-day prime eligible-member-bank acceptances fell to 1.875 percent, "the lowest rate for this maturity in the history of the American acceptance market." On June 20 the New York Federal Reserve Bank cut its rediscount rate to 2.5 percent, a new low in the history of the System.[107] Short-term rates sagged further in the second half of the year. The average renewal rate on call loans, which had been 8.56 percent in September 1929, was only 2 percent in October and November 1930. Yet the low rates, both in the United States and abroad, utterly failed to provide the confidently anticipated stimulus to check economic contraction and to induce business recovery.[108]

Anderson criticized the easy money policy of 1930, as reflected in lowering of rediscount rates and buying rates for bankers' acceptances, and the large-scale buying of government securities by Reserve Banks. He said in 1949, "We renewed in 1930 many of the illusions which the stock market crash of 1929 should have dispelled."[109] On the other hand, more recently Friedman and Schwartz have held that more vigorous expansionary measures in January-October 1930, such as the purchase of $1 billion instead of the actual $150 million of government securities, would have drastically changed the monetary situation, lessened the severity of the economic contraction, made the capital markets easier, reduced the likelihood of a banking crisis such as came in the fall, and

[104]So reported in AT&T, *Summary*, July 7, 1930, p. 3; slightly revised in *Hist. Stat. U.S.*, ser. Y 254-57, 265-66, 372.

[105]Lewis W. Douglas, "Economy in Federal Government," and George McAneny, "Economy in State and City Government," *Proc. Acad. Pol. Sci.*, January 1933, 15:172-78, 178-88.

[106]Leo Wolman, Nov. 18, 1932, in *ibid.*, p. 208. A. D. Gayer gives estimates of annual totals by years for 1923-35 in his *Monetary Policy and Economic Stabilization: A Study of the Gold Standard*, 2d ed. (London: Black, 1937), pp. 215-16.

[107]AT&T, *Summary*, July 7, 1930, pp. 2-8.

[108]HES, *Weekly Letter*, Dec. 6, 13, 20, 1930, pp. 300-301, 307, 316-19; FRS, *Hist. Chart Book, 1971*, pp. 26-28, 36; W. R. Burgess, "The Money Market in 1930," *Rev. Ec. Stat.*, February 1931, 13:19-25.

[109]Anderson, *Economics and the Public Welfare*, pp. 222-23; C&FC, Dec. 27, 1930, pp. 4091-92.

at least reduced its magnitude and its aftereffects.[110] The New York Bank strongly favored more expansionary open market operations but, after mid-year 1930, was unable to induce the other Bank governors or the Federal Reserve Board to agree. Eugene Meyer, Jr.—the new head of the Board when Roy A. Young succeeded the late W. P. G. Harding at the Boston Bank in September 1930—favored expansionary action, as Young had not.[111]

Though I am reluctant to take exception to the strong and divergent views of such men on this controversial issue, a careful reading of a mass of contemporary literature and an analysis of economic and financial developments in 1930 yield little or no support for the views (a) that Federal Reserve policy in that year was open to serious criticism, or (b) that flooding the money supply by the Federal Reserve System would have effectively checked the contraction or moderated the current and ensuing collapse.[112] With enterprise "collapsed," the forces making for contraction were too strong to be overcome by the stimulus of artificially reducing short-term money rates below the very low levels actually reached.

Long-term money rates showed no striking declines in 1930.[113] Yields on long-term U.S. bonds were lower than in most of 1929, and declined slightly in 1930, and high-grade corporate bond yields were moderately lower also.[114] But the reductions were not large, presumably because the risk component kept increasing.

In the midst of the world-wide slump Keynes wrote late in 1930, with questionable insight, that "the greatest evil of the moment and the greatest danger to economic progress in the near future are to be found in the unwillingness of the Central Banks of the world to allow the market-

[110]Friedman and Schwartz, *Monetary History*, pp. 392–93. Cf. Keynes, *Treatise on Money*, 2:369–74; and chart in Robbins, *Great Depression*, p. 18.

[111]On this succession, see Friedman and Schwartz, *Monetary History,* pp. 229n, 376n; Anderson, *Economics and the Public Welfare*, p. 223n; *C&FC*, August-September 1930, pp. 1355, 1507, 1654. President Hoover rated both men high, but Meyer higher.

[112]A. J. Hettinger, Jr., does not discuss this specific point in his "Director's Comment" on the Friedman-Schwartz book (*Monetary History*), pp. 809–14. I read between the lines that he would agree with my position. Cf. also E. W. Kemmerer, "The Gold Standard in the United States," in J. G. Smith, ed., *Facing the Facts: An Economic Diagnosis* (New York: Putnam, 1932), pp. 32–33. In his *Treatise on Money* (2:207, 260, 287), Keynes called the Federal Reserve System's monetary management "singularly ineffective" in 1920, perhaps because the Reserve Banks then lacked "adequate ammunition," successful from 1922 to 1928, and wrong in 1929: "The struggle in 1929 between the Federal Reserve Board and Wall Street was, in part, a misguided effort on the part of the former to prevent the rate of interest from finding its natural level," but he declined to endorse most criticisms of its behavior in 1929 and was silent on its policy in 1930.

[113]Not only in his *Treatise on Money* (e.g., 2:377–87) but also in other outlets, Keynes was much concerned over this fact and urged policy moves to accelerate the decline which he was confidently predicting.

[114]FRS, *Hist. Chart Book, 1971*, pp. 23–24; AT&T, *Summary*, Jan. 7, 1931, p. 12.

rate of interest to fall fast enough."[115] His prognosis was gloomy: "we cannot hope for a complete or lasting recovery until there has been a very great fall in the long-term market-rate of interest throughout the world towards something nearer pre-war levels."[116]

Partly in response to low short-term money rates in this country,[117] new issues of securities in New York rose in the first half of 1930 from the low level of November and December 1929.[118] The peak in May 1930 was exceeded only by that of May 1929; and public utility issues, including a huge AT&T stock offering, reached a record high. In April the general bond market seemed to be returning to vigorous health; but new offerings were overdone, and in May and June increasing accumulations of unsold issues remained in dealers' hands. In the second half of the year the volume of flotations declined, influenced by deepening pessimism over the economic outlook at home and abroad. For 1930 as a whole, excluding U.S. Government issues, new security offerings (about $6.9 billion) were 30 percent below those of 1929 and the smallest since 1924; and the December offerings were the smallest since August 1920.[119]

A fresh slump in stock prices began late in April. Despite further easing of money rates and large flotations of new securities in the first half year, most domestic business news grew more or less unfavorable, and foreign news became much worse. Price indexes of common stocks fell sharply in June and more drastically later in the year. At the low points reached on December 10, 1930, the Standard Statistics indexes of 20 utilities, 50 industrials, and 20 railroads were at levels far below those of November 1929 and were comparable to those of the spring of 1927, before the superboom got under way.[120] While the renewed collapse of stock market prices in the last two-thirds of 1930 contributed to an accentuation of business contraction, it was the intensification of economic deterioration in the United States and abroad which was primarily responsible for that collapse.

Late in 1931 Salter wrote: "When the speculative boom collapsed and the economic depression began, the investor swerved sharply from exces-

[115]Keynes, *Treatise on Money*, 2:207.

[116]*Ibid.*, p. 383; *Economist*, Oct. 11, 1930, pp. 670–71. Actually, in the United States long-term interest rates as reflected in high-grade bond yields fell to prewar levels in the mid-1930s before recovery was far under way, and continued to decline before recovery was completed. FRS, *Hist. Chart Book, 1971*, p. 23.

[117]Clay, *Lord Norman*, pp. 360–61.

[118]See chart of monthly data, 1900–38, in Leonard P. Ayres, *Turning Points in Business Cycles* (New York: Macmillan, 1939), p. 127.

[119]AT&T, *Summary*, issues for May–December 1930; Citibank, *Monthly Economic Letter*, issues for April–December 1930, esp. pp. 64, 80, 95–96, 128, 142, 156, 180–81, 193; Phillips, McManus, and Nelson, *Banking and the Business Cycle*, pp. 162–63.

[120]AT&T, *Summary*, Jan. 7, 1931, p. 5. Cf. Hirst, *Wall Street and Lombard Street*, pp. 67–73.

sive rashness to extreme prudence."[121] The initial downswing was short-lived. It was in mid-1930, not in the fall of 1929, and then by degrees rather than suddenly, that this most important shift occurred.

Foreign securities flotations in New York were sharply higher in February-June 1930 than in the preceding seven months, but they then dropped to a low level in July-October.[122] Stagnation in international loan markets was "an important cause for the prolongation of the crisis in raw materials."[123] Among the basic reasons for this stagnation were the failure of many raw material controls, the weakening of private and public credit in the producing countries, disappointing European developments, the poor market record of the new international loan to Germany, and the reluctance of owners of capital to lend freely, but not shortage of loanable funds.

The Young Plan for German reparations, only slightly revised from the form in which it had been signed in June 1929, was approved at a second conference at The Hague by representatives of Germany, France, Great Britain, and twelve other countries on January 20, 1930.[124] Though the chief German delegate (Dr. Schacht) had resigned his presidency of the Reichsbank on March 7, declaring that Germany could not fulfill her commitments under the plan, and had made speeches against it, the Reichsrat ratified it on March 11.[125] The French Senate ratified on April 3, by a vote of 294-8. The plan was put into effect on May 17, and the last obstacle to the issue of the external loan was thus removed.

This outstanding foreign issue, floated on international markets on June 12, 1930, was the $300 million, thirty-five-year German External 5.5's. The U.S. third (tranche) was floated in New York on a 6.2 percent basis.[126] Secretary Mellon warmly endorsed it as marking "a fundamental change in the situation . . . an act of confidence in Germany's good faith and financial integrity"; and the National City Company (New York)

[121]"The World Financial Crisis," Yale Review, December 1931, pp. 217-32, esp. p. 228.

[122]HES, Weekly Letter, Nov. 29, 1930, p. 293.

[123]The view of the London and Cambridge Economic Service, reported in ibid., Nov. 1, 1930, p. 267.

[124]At the first Hague Conference, Aug. 6-31, 1929, Chancellor of the Exchequer Snowden had won popular acclaim for insisting on raising the British share, contrary to the concession that Stamp had made with great difficulty; but definite approval was deferred to the second conference (Jan. 3-20, 1930). J. Harry Jones, Josiah Stamp, Public Servant: The Life of the First Baron Stamp of Shortlands (London: Pitman, 1964), pp. 249-52. Cf. Harold Nicolson, King George the Fifth, His Life and Reign (London: Constable, 1952), pp. 440-41; Charles L. Mowat, Britain between the Wars, 1918-1940 (London: Methuen, 1955), p. 374.

[125]Ivar Kreuger's offer of a substantial private loan to Germany provided the plan be ratified (see Chapter 8, n. 154, above) may have influenced the German decision. Robert Shaplen, Kreuger: Genius and Swindler (New York: Knopf, 1960), p. 129: Economist, Mar. 1, 1930, pp. 460-63.

[126]AT&T, Summary, July 7, 1930, p. 4; BIS, first annual report dated Mar. 30, 1931, p. 9, with no hint of crisis ahead; Anderson, Economics and the Public Welfare, p. 226.

advised its clients that this issue was "the beginning of a widening demand for German bonds, both in this country and abroad."[127] But the bankers who had floated the foreign *tranches* had trouble placing the bonds with investors, and here and abroad these fell to discounts below the issue prices: on January 2, 1931, the dollar quotation in New York was $69.50, compared with the issue price of $98.15.[128]

The Wall Street crash had occurred before the Young Plan was formally accepted in January 1930, but the prevailing view then was that the U.S. contraction would be short;[129] and it was generally believed that Germany would prove able to carry the burden imposed by the plan, and that under it she could grow and prosper at a reasonable rate.[130] Within a few months both views were gravely altered by the persistent fall of commodity price levels and the deepening of the depression in the United States and abroad. While the breakdown of the plan was deferred until 1931–32, its promise was seriously weakened not only by the economic contraction but also by Dr. Schacht's persistent hostility to it and the increased power of its German political opponents, as shown in the results of the elections of September 14, 1930;[131] fears of its failure were reflected in increasing discounts on German bonds as the year came to a close.

Nevertheless, most of the eminent speakers before the New York Academy of Political Science on November 14, 1930, on the Young Plan and the new Bank for International Settlements were hopeful of their success.[132] Sir Charles Addis spoke of several favorable elements in the menacing world situation and said: "Above all, . . . there is being engendered in Europe . . . a new international spirit which rejects the arbitrament of war and is seeking in common agreements a more secure foundation for peace than all the bloated and competing armaments of the past have ever . . . been able to effect." But he gravely warned that the world credit structure was in jeopardy and might break down. Such gloomy forebodings soon proved better founded than the hopes.[133]

[127]Feis, *Diplomacy of the Dollar*, p. 45. Mellon coupled with this a reiteration that Allied war debt obligations were unconnected with German reparation payments.

[128]Eleanor L. Dulles, *The Bank for International Settlements at Work* (New York: Macmillan, 1932), pp. 387–88; Clay, *Lord Norman*, p. 366.

[129]M. J. Bonn supported the new plan in an early book, *Der Neue Plan als Grundlagen der deutschen Wirtschaftspolitik* (Munich: Duncker and Humblot, 1930; foreword dated June 16), which was reviewed by Charles R. Whittlesey in *JPE*, August 1931, 39:560–62, with no evident awareness of the past year's developments. This book was not mentioned in Bonn's later discussion of the Young Plan in his *Wandering Scholar*, pp. 306–9.

[130]Angell, *The Recovery of Germany* (New Haven, Conn.: Yale University Press, 1929), ch. 11, "The Young Plan and Germany's Future," esp. pp. 342–48.

[131]*Ibid.*, pp. 306–10; Dulles, *BIS*, pp. 304–7, 387–88.

[132]*Proc. Acad. Pol. Sci.*, January 1931, 14:299–328, esp. p. 309. The speakers included the BIS president and vice president (McGarrah and Addis) and Thomas W. Lamont, Jeremiah Smith, Jr., and Walter W. Stewart. Smith had contributed an earlier article on the BIS in *QJE*, August 1929, 43:713–25. Cf. Bonn, *Der Neue Plan*, pp. 93–103.

[133]Mowat, *Britain between the Wars*, pp. 372–78.

The British government in particular, under Prime Minister MacDonald, enlisted financiers and economists to aid in policy decisions. The Committee on Finance and Industry, with Hugh P. Macmillan (Lord Macmillan from 1930) as chairman and a galaxy of members among whom Keynes was prominent, was appointed in November 1929. It took reams of testimony, but did not report until mid-1931. On January 27, 1930, an Economic Advisory Council was set up, with numerous subcommittees, two of which (with overlapping membership) were chaired by Keynes and Stamp, respectively. The Council was to report only to the prime minister.[134]

Discussion of these bodies is deferred to later chapters, but three points may be noted here: (1) most of them revealed new hard facts or estimates; (2) in several there was a serious divergence of opinion among highly competent men; and (3) the rapid course of events soon rendered much of their analyses and recommendations obsolete. As Eleanor Dulles said of the first of a series of conferences of economists of the central banks held at the BIS in September 1930, which discussed theoretical issues relating to the bank's work: "The variety of opinion expressed as to the general basis of action prevented any clear-cut result."[135] This was also true of the first interim report (summer 1930) of the League of Nations Gold Delegation, of which Bonn was an unhappy member.[136] Moreover, as Salter much later pointed out with reference to the post-1930 years, even when unanimous secret reports were made to the prime minister by an exceptionally able group of economists, these were ignored, largely because of the fixed opinions and power of the British Treasury and Bank of England, coupled with the fact that the group's views were given no publicity.[137]

Psychological Deterioration into Year-End Gloom On February 1, 1930, the Harvard Economic Society had reported: "Pessimism is clearly being replaced by confidence." But on June 14 and 21 it said: "Recent weakness and irregularity in the stock market reflect the pessimism and uncertainty of business sentiment. . . . Current business sentiment is apprehensive and, in many quarters, pessimistic."[138] The president was soberly optimistic in his major address to the U.S. Chamber of Commerce on May 1.[139] A week later Governor Young of the Federal Reserve Board admitted that the country was in "what appears to be a business depression"; but on May 28 Hoover "was reported as predicting that business would be normal by fall."[140] Midyear reviews of business

---

[134]*Ibid.*, pp. 260–62, 267–70, 359; Jones, *Stamp*, pp. 272–73.

[135]Dulles, *BIS*, p. 114. See also Hirst, *Wall Street and Lombard Street*, pp. 162–75.

[136]Bonn, *Wandering Scholar*, pp. 311–14, 319.

[137]Arthur Salter, *Slave of the Lamp* (London: Weidenfeld and Nicolson, 1967), pp. 87–88.

[138]HES, *Weekly Letter*, pp. 32, 137, 149, 154–56; and AT&T, *Summary*, July 7, 1930, pp. 1–2.

[139]Hoover, *State Papers*, 1:289–96.

[140]Quoted in Allen, *Only Yesterday*, p. 334.

prospects varied from moderate optimism to pessimism, but sober middle-of-the-roaders agreed that, while deflation was not yet complete and re-adjustment required time, pessimism was unwarranted.[141] On August 2 the HES reported: "There is increasing confidence, and increasingly frequent expression of confidence, in a prompt beginning of business revival." Until after the end of August, however, it resisted "a drastic revision of expectations."[142] The Food Research Institute's appraisal had been optimistic as late as May 1, but in August it noted the "atmosphere of pessimism in the business world."[143] Bonn, then en route across the country to take up a visiting professorship at Stanford, found gloom "descending everywhere."[144] This deepened with the banking crisis in the fall, and the year ended with indexes of business activity below estimated normals by more than they had been at their worst in 1921,[145] with stock price indexes far below the lows following the crash of late 1929, and with unemployment far higher than at the end of 1929.[146] As evidence of widespread economic deterioration accumulated and signs of incipient recovery proved shortlived, investors, enterprisers, and consumers turned strongly pessimistic, and the remarkable forward momentum of the late 1920s was gradually replaced by a vicious downward spiral. Extraordinary psychological depression unquestionably increased the severity of the business depression.[147]

In mid-September 1930 the Harvard Economic Society made a candid, realistic appraisal of depressed business conditions, in which it acknowledged the disappointment of its earlier expectations but gave reasons for expecting an upturn in the United States. The letter included

[141]The wide spread of opinion was reflected in a symposium reported in *Review of Reviews*, July 1930, pp. 34–37. Bethlehem Steel chairman Schwab said that business was a lot healthier than it had been six to nine months earlier, and saw 1930 as "a year of normal progress." Babson predicted "no panic but prolonged depression," probably for two or three years—another good "hit" for the "sage of Wellesley."

[142]HES, *Weekly Letter*, Aug. 2, 30, 1930, pp. 188, 212–14. Crum wrote late in the year (*Rev. Ec. Stat.*, November 1930, 12:149) that "depression levels were reached unmistakably by the middle of the summer." He put first among the principal causes the worldwide slump in raw materials prices, intensified by the sharp drop in silver prices. See also R. A. Gordon, *Business Fluctuations*, 2d ed. (New York: Harper, 1961), p. 430, citing A. Ross Eckler and J. B. Hubbard in *Rev. Ec. Stat.*, May 1933, 15:75–81; February 1936, 18:16–23.

[143]Wheat Studies of the Food Research Institute 6 (Stanford, Calif.: Food Research Institute, 1930), pp. 326–27, 379, 388, 410.

[144]Bonn, *Wandering Scholar*, p. 313.

[145]AT&T, *Summary*, Jan. 7, 1931.

[146]Brokers' loans shrank rapidly in 1930, and those by nonbank lenders largely disappeared; the totals shrank further to mid-1932. See AT&T *Summary*, various issues; Schumpeter, *Business Cycles*, 2:875 (chart LII).

[147]This point was made by Einzig in both the 1931 and 1932 editions of his *World Economic Crisis*, pp. 69 and 81, respectively, and by W. C. Mitchell and H. A. E. Chandler in discussing other papers in the spring of 1931. *Proc. Acad. Pol. Sci.*, June 1931, 14:397, 451.

this significant paragraph: "If business recovery in this country depended chiefly, or even largely, upon a prior improvement of conditions in the rest of the world, the outlook would be dark indeed. Fortunately, however, our experience in 1921, when conditions were far worse than they are today, showed that in a country as large and rich as the United States, enjoying such diversity of resources and activities, industry may recover even from worse conditions than prevail at present without the stimulus of improvement in foreign trade and simply as the result of remedial forces of purely domestic origin."[148] The president said in his State of the Union address in early December: "our country is today stronger and richer in resources, in equipment, in skill, than ever in its history. We are in an extraordinary degree self-sustaining, we will overcome world influences and will lead the march of prosperity as we have always done before."[149] Such views were widely held in influential quarters; but, as was the case a year earlier, they failed to take due account of unrecognized weaknesses in the U.S. economy and, in particular, the possibility of serious repercussions from the outside world. With the utmost reluctance the Society abandoned its declarations of confidence in the next few months, though it repeatedly pointed to encouraging signs.[150]

In October 1930, in the midst of "a bad attack of economic pessimism" in Great Britain and elsewhere, Keynes spoke glowingly of the "Economic Possibilities for our Grandchildren"; he reasoned that "mankind is solving its economic problem" and predicted that "the standard of life in progressive countries one hundred years hence will be between four and eight times as high as it is today."[151] Realistically, he asserted: "The *pace* at which we can reach our destination of economic bliss will be governed by four things—our power to control population, our determination to avoid wars and civil dissensions, our willingness to entrust to science . . . matters which are properly the concern of science, and the rate of accumulation as fixed by the margin between our production and our consumption; of which the last will easily look after itself, given the first three."[152] Though only forty-odd years of Keynes' century have elapsed, the indications thus far are that he was conservative in his long-term prophecies,

[148]HES, *Weekly Letter*, Sept. 20, 1930, p. 234.

[149]Hoover, *State Papers*, 1:428–40, esp. p. 429.

[150]HES, *Weekly Letter*, July 19, Aug. 2, 16, 30, Sept. 20, Oct. 4, 18, Nov. 15, 22, 29, Dec. 20, 27, 1930, pp. 180, 188, 201, 212–14, 233–34, 242, 255–58, 279–82, 295, 315–18, 322.

[151]*N&A*, Oct. 11, 18, 1930, pp. 36–37, 96–98, reprinted in Keynes' *Essays in Persuasion*, pp. 358–73. He attributed the modern trend toward rising levels of living to increasing accumulation of capital and the growth of technology. He suggested that, in a past period not clearly specified (perhaps since 1800), "the average standard of life in Europe and the United States has been raised . . . about fourfold," despite "an enormous growth in the population of the world," which he expected to be smaller in future (p. 363).

[152]*Ibid.*, p. 373.

even though his first two conditions have not been met. But the bright future he pictured stands in sharp contrast to the near future in which the boys he addressed were to grow up.

Industrial contraction, widening unemployment, and declining profits made for social unrest and political reversals generally.[153] In September-November 1930 various political consequences of the depression appeared. The National Socialist (Nazi) and Communist parties made great gains in the German elections of September 14, and the Argentine and Brazilian governments were overthrown; one result was to weaken prices of German and Latin American bonds.[154] In his inaugural address President Hoover had included among the "mandates" from the recent election "the direction of economic progress toward prosperity and the further lessening of poverty."[155] By the fall of 1930 it was clear that "our abounding prosperity" had vanished for the time and that poverty had gravely increased as a result of unemployment. In the November elections the Democrats won such sweeping victories in both House and Senate that the president had only minority support for the rest of his term.[156] There was a glaring contrast between the sad state of the country and "the fantasies of a 'new era' of unending prosperity so widely prevalent" little more than a year earlier.[157] This in itself represented a shocking disillusionment.

James Truslow Adams, more perceptive than most, wrote late in 1930: "There are many signs that our world is approaching a new and critical stage. . . . The nation as a whole is entering upon a new era in which all the conditions will be different from any experienced heretofore."[158] But to Adams this new era, unlike its predecessor, would presumably not be "one of shallow and unlimited optimism."[159]

Morgan partner Lamont, speaking on November 14, 1930, interpreted "the general consensus" as attributing the current severe depression chiefly to six causes: (1) overproduction of many basic commodities and manufactured products; (2) widespread efforts to support prices of specific products artificially, and their subsequent collapse; (3) the fall in the price

---

[153]This point was made in Citibank *Monthly Economic Letter*, May 1930, p. 75.

[154]HES, *Weekly Letter*, Oct. 11, Nov. 1, 1930, pp. 248, 267.

[155]Hoover, *State Papers*, 1:11.

[156]Myers and Newton, *Hoover Administration*, pp. 44–45, 50, 54–56. The Democratic leaders assured the president of their cooperation, but in his view they failed to give it.

[157]Carl Snyder, "The World-Wide Depression of 1930," *AER*, March 1931, 21(1):174. Cf. *C&FC*, Dec. 27, 1930, pp. 4105–7: "We have learned, from actual facts and events that our dream of 'perpetual prosperity' was *only* a dream. . . . Our studies in economics have been more full than fruitful."

[158]James Truslow Adams, "Our Changing Characteristics," first published in *Forum*, December 1930, pp. 321–28, and included in his book *Tempo of Modern Life*, pp. 34–54, esp. pp. 35, 53.

[159]*Ibid.*, p. 142, in his essay "Emerson Re-Read," first published in *Atlantic*, October 1930, pp. 484–92.

of silver;[160] (4) the almost unprecedented international shift in gold hold-ings; (5) current political unrest, notably in India, China, and South Amer-ica; and (6) "a spirit of rampant speculation." But he also stressed the psychological factors—"over-confidence and unreasonable optimism at one point in the cycle, and . . . under-confidence, undue pessimism and a gen-eral fear of vague, impending disaster" at another. Lamont himself was hopeful at this stage. In getting "back to a sober sense of realities," he held, the situation was far sounder than it had been fourteen months earlier. He cited several points of great strength, exulted in "the spirit of steadfastness and cooperation which our own community is showing in its difficulties," and concluded that "we *are* winning through."[161] On the other hand, Albert H. Wiggin, top officer of the Chase National Bank, frankly told its shareholders in mid-January 1931:

> We attempted, as a matter of collective policy, to hold the lines firm follow-ing the crash of 1929. Wages [wage rates] were not to be reduced, buying by railroads and construction by public utilities were to be increased, prices were to be maintained, and cheap money was to be the foundation. The policy has had a thirteen month test. It has failed. Each industry and each enterprise must study its own problems and adjust itself to the markets.
>
> It is bad policy for a government, or for an industry by concerted action, to try to keep prices permanently above the level which the supply and demand situa-tion justifies. We have recently seen this in copper, wheat, coffee and other commodities. We must keep the markets open and prices free.

The Year-End   Despite some encouraging developments in the first four
Position   months of 1930, the year as a whole was disastrous in almost every respect. The record-breaking characteristics of 1930, in sharp contrast with those of 1929, were all bad. At the turn of the year the de-pression in the United States was recognized as "distinctly the most severe in modern economic history";[162] and most of the rest of the world (Sweden

---

[160]The price of silver, which had fallen ominously in early 1930, fell to a new low in early 1931 and remained through most of the year at less than 50 percent of its 1926 average. See chart in AT&T, *Summary*, Dec. 7, 1931, p. 4. On this period and its background, see H. M. Bratter, "Silver—Some Fundamentals," and Frank D. Graham, "The Fall in the Value of Silver and Its Consequences." *JPE*, June and September 1930, 39:321–68, 425–70; Silberling, *Dynamics of Business*, p. 327.

[161]Thomas W. Lamont, "Phases of the World Depression," *Proc. Acad. Pol. Sci.*, January 1931, 14:299–305.

[162]The AT&T *Summary* dated Jan. 7, 1931, gave an excellent review of the year 1930 with numerous charts. See also the chart of indexes of industrial production, mostly on a 1929 base, in BIS, *Tenth Annual Report, 1939–40*, p. 7. Hoover's later statement (*Memoirs*, 3:58) that in 1930 "the country was steadily and successfully readjusting itself despite some adversities and much licking of wounds" must reflect both a biased memory and failure to check available data. He was right in saying that "even the stock speculation, the other domestic readjustments, and our weak banking system, could not have created the degree of

and Denmark were exceptions[163]) was in the throes of a major depression. Addis, in a New York address on November 24, termed it "the most serious in over one hundred years."[164] World unemployment grew from an estimated five million in the autumn of 1929 to a number estimated at nineteen to twenty-two million at the end of 1930.[165] In December Keynes wrote: "The world has been slow to realize that we are living this year in the shadow of one of the greatest economic catastrophes of modern history." But in the next breath he said, in a burst of amazing optimism, "This *is* a nightmare, which will pass away with the morning." He thought that the slump was probably somewhat exaggerated because of psychological factors, and that an upward reaction might come at any time, but that real recovery required bridging the wide gap between the disparate ideas of lenders and productive borrowers. He suggested that the most effective remedy would be for the Federal Reserve System, the Bank of France, and the Bank of England to join together in a bold scheme to restore confidence to the international long-term loan market. This action would revive enterprise and activity everywhere, and would restore prices and profits, so that in due course the wheels of world commerce would turn again; but if France preferred to stand aside, he said, Great Britain and the United States could do the trick![166] For various reasons, this was a wildly impractical proposal.

In a radio broadcast in mid-January 1931 Keynes went further, stressing "the extreme gravity of the situation, with about a quarter of our working population standing idle" and probably a total of twelve million unemployed in Great Britain, Germany, and the United States. But he considered it obvious that the great mass of the British people were living better than ever before, and that the slump could be cured by individual and national boldness and enterprise.[167]

---

ultimate wreckage that occurred in the United States, had we not had the panic in Europe." *Ibid.*, 3:15. But this statement omits recognition of the large U.S. responsibility for the European financial crises of 1931.

[163]Einzig, *World Economic Crisis*, pp. 147–48.

[164]*C&FC*, Dec. 6, 1930, pp. 3648–50 (cf. *ibid.*, Oct. 18, 1930, pp. 2436–37). Snyder, after quoting this in his AEA paper of Dec. 31, agreed merely that "this is the most world-wide depression, if not the most severe, of which we have any record." "World-Wide Depression of 1930," pp. 172–78.

[165]Discussed at length by Karl Pribram, then a professor at the University of Frankfurt, and by E. J. Phelan of the Irish Free State, an important official of the International Labour Office, in their lectures at the University of Chicago in late June 1931. Quincy Wright, ed., *Unemployment as a World Problem* (Chicago: University of Chicago Press, 1931), pp. 43–248, esp. pp. 45–46, 160–62. Though the volume then seemed "terrible," it increased further in the next two years.

[166]"The Great Slump of 1930," *N&A*, Dec. 20, 27, 1930, pp. 402, 427–28, reprinted in his *Essays in Persuasion*, pp. 135–47.

[167]*Ibid.*, pp. 145–56.

Yet the BIS itself, in its second annual report,[168] said that on March 31, 1931, "the depression, although characterised by an unusually sharp fall of prices, still showed, in most respects, the main tendencies of an ordinary downward business trend."[169] Schumpeter's "tentative diagnosis" late in December 1930 conformed to this view, and he too rashly concluded that "there is no difficulty in devising" remedies, "both general and particular," only adding that "the difficulty lies in the fact that our patients will not take what we might be able to prescribe."[170]

The responsibility of the Wall Street boom and crash for the ensuing contraction and depression largely ended with the year 1930.[171] Yet their insidious residual effects on the world economy were coupled with the evil influences of higher barriers to trade, rising unemployment, financial strain, and political changes for the worse. President Hoover may have been right in saying, in his message of December 2, 1930, that "the major forces of the depression now lie outside of the United States, and our recuperation has been retarded by the unwarranted fear and apprehension created by these outside forces," but there was far more warrant for apprehension than he would publicly admit; and he was seriously misleading in saying, earlier in that message, that "the fundamental strength of the Nation's economic life is unimpaired."

The position of various foreign countries around the turn of the year 1930–31 must be briefly summarized.[172]

Great Britain had not fully emerged from industrial depression in the late 1920s, for unemployment never fell below one million and her older industries (coal, iron and steel, shipbuilding, textiles) had been chronically depressed before 1930.[173] Costly expenditures for relief (the "dole"), however, seemed to make some such level of unemployment tolerable. In the

---

[168]*Second Annual Report, 1930–31*, p. 11 (issued May 10, 1932).

[169]Hoover quoted this, more or less exactly, in his *Memoirs* (3:79), and went even further to say (also wrongly, I believe): "The depth of our recession during the first seventeen months did not constitute a major depression" (*ibid.*, 3:4).

[170]*AER*, March 1931, 21(1):179–82. In his *Business Cycles* (2:911–17) Schumpeter took a soberer view.

[171]In the preface to his *Wall Street and Lombard Street*, completed at about this time, Hirst spoke of "the colossal slump of Wall Street" as "a national catastrophe which was to turn the whole economic and political world upside down" (p. vi). On p. 154 he said "that the great Wall Street collapse, striking a world financially crippled by the Great War and staggering under a load of reparations, war debts and war taxation was not merely an occasion but a cause of the depression that swept over trade."

[172]See esp. appendixes to Einzig, *World Economic Crisis*; Royal Economic Society, *Memorandum 27*, February 1931, "Report on Economic Conditions in Europe," Selected statistical tables were appended to Robbins, *Great Depression*, pp. 203–38. Chapter 15 of Schumpeter's *Business Cycles* contains much information on England and Germany; he was impressed by the mildness of the British depression (pp. 966, 970) and by the rapid recovery from severe depression in Germany in 1933–38 (pp. 971–83).

[173]Mowat, *Britain between the Wars*, esp. chs. 5–7.

spring of 1929 British voters rejected Lloyd George while the Labour Party "annexed" his bold program for absorbing the unemployed. After the Labour government came into power it set up a committee to draft proposals but rejected them in May 1930, and Oswald Mosley, their prime mover, resigned and was later expelled from the party.[174] André Siegfried, a perceptive Frenchman who published early in 1931 his diagnosis of England's "crisis," argued that the British were closing their eyes and ears to the basic deterioration in their country's position,[175] and could not long escape the consequences. But strong unions effectively resisted efforts to reduce wage rates and unemployment relief.[176] When the 1930 contraction occurred, the situation demanded the utmost flexibility and adaptability, but in practice rigidity prevailed.[177]

The British industrial production index (prepared by the LCES) reached its post-1920 peak in the last quarter of 1929, at 114.8.[178] A year later it was 19 percent lower, at 92.7 (revised down from 93.5). Employment had declined much less because of increases in short-time work; but the number of insured persons unemployed in Great Britain and Northern Ireland had risen every month by a total of 70 percent (fourth-quarter averages).[179] Exports of manufactures had shrunk about 33 percent in value and about 25 percent in volume. Even so, it appeared early in 1931 that there was "no serious distress except in some special districts," and that other countries had "in some respects suffered greater losses." And it seemed that the depression had "reached, but not passed, its worst phase for the present," but with "no certainty that there will not be a further set-back."[180] Late in April 1931 Nicolson reported Keynes as saying that "England is really richer than she has ever been before; . . . succeeding in bearing a burden of taxation, debts and standard of living which is at least twice as great as that of any other country [including the U.S.A.?]. . . . What is wrong with us is that owing to circumstances we are only putting forth two-thirds of our productive power."[181]

[174]*Ibid.*, pp. 350, 358–63, 371–72, 412; Harold Macmillan, *Winds of Change, 1914–1939* (New York: Harper and Row, 1966), pp. 242–47.

[175]Siegfried, *England's Crisis* (London: Jonathan Cape, 1931). In his Halley Stewart lecture early in 1932, Stamp admitted some validity in the points made by Siegfried and other foreign critics, but stressed others as essential parts of the whole truth, including important gains in employment through 1929. Salter et al., *The World's Economic Crisis and the Way of Escape* (London: Allen and Unwin, 1932), pp. 48–67.

[176]Robbins, *Great Depression*, chs. 4–5, esp. pp. 60–62, 93–94.

[177]Royal Economic Society, *Memorandum 25*, October 1930.

[178]LCES data in Royal Economic Society, *Memorandum 26*, January 1931, pp. 3, 8, 12–18, 27, slightly modified by later revisions. See also HES, *Weekly Letter*, May 3, 31, Oct. 4, Nov. 1, 29, 1930, pp. 113, 137, 143–44, 296; Jan. 3, 31, 1931, pp. 5, 29.

[179]Royal Economic Society, *Memorandum 30*, April 1931, p. 23.

[180]*Ibid., Memorandum 26*, January 1931, p. 3.

[181]Nicolson, *Harold Nicolson*, 1:71–72 (diary for Apr. 29, 1931). At the time he had hopes of Oswald Mosley's new party, which Nicolson was then actively supporting. Henry Clay's view early in 1932 was similar. See Chapter 10 below.

Germany, after an encouraging early start,[182] experienced crucial deterioration in 1930, despite the adoption of the Young Plan in January, its ratification in March-April, its formal coming into effect in May, and the floating of her $300 million international loan in June. Reduced international trade and the drying up of private loans weakened the competitive power of her "irrationally rationalized" industries, and the short-run effect was increased unemployment. Attempts to cut wage rates led to numerous strikes. Dumping of Soviet grain worsened the already weak position of German agriculture. Confidence in the stability of the reichsmark and in the workability of the Young Plan was weakened. Business failures rose to a record high, and unemployment reached staggering dimensions. The unexpectedly marked rise in the National Socialist vote in the September 14 elections was in large part a result of these conditions and, in turn, did much to aggravate them.[183]

Italy's economic position also deteriorated in 1930, despite the iron discipline imposed by the Fascist regime. Deepening depression in the United States and elsewhere reduced tourist traffic and cut down emigrant remittances. Contraction of work permits by France and bad economic conditions in Latin American countries cut down emigration and helped swell unemployment. Rigid support of the lira, stabilized at an excessive level, led to a fall in the price level. The Banca Agricole Italiana, weakened by large loans to enterprises of its leading figure (Signor Gualino), had to be liquidated.[184]

France, in August 1930 rated by the *Economist* "economically perhaps the strongest country in Europe," was slow to feel the impact of the economic contraction.[185] She was exceptionally self-sufficient. Her modernized industries were effective competitors, and the decline in industrial activity in 1930 was only moderate. Undervaluation of the franc continued to give an artificial stimulus to exports, and an export surplus continued to

[182]See the *Economist*'s German correspondence, esp. Jan. 18, Mar. 1, 8, 22, 1930, pp. 107, 462–63, 519–20, 644–47. Early in March he noted the optimistic quarterly report of the Institut für Konjunkturforschung that in its opinion Germany had nearly reached the low point of her economic depression.

[183]Royal Economic Society, *Memorandum 20*, February 1930, pp. 8–16; D. B. Copland, "The Australian Problem," *EJ*, December 1930, 40:638–49; Einzig, *World Economic Crisis*, 1st ed., pp. 141–43; Hodson, *Slump and Recovery*, pp. 61–62; C. W. Guillebaud, *The Economic Recovery of Germany from 1933 to the Incorporation of Austria in March 1938* (London: Macmillan, 1939), ch. 1; and Clay, *Lord Norman*, p. 369.

[184]Einzig, *World Economic Crisis*, pp. 144–46.

[185]William F. Ogburn and William Jaffe, *The Economic Development of Post-War France* (London: Oxford University Press, 1930), reviewed in *Economist*, Aug. 16, 23, 1930, pp. 310–11, 354–58; Percy Phillips and S. J. Wolff, in *New York Times Magazine*, Feb. 9, 23, 1930, with special reference to Tardieu; Einzig, "The Crisis in France," *World Economic Crisis*, app. 3; HES, *Weekly Letter*, Jan. 4, Mar. 1, May 3, Aug. 2, Nov. 29, 1930, pp. 6–8; 58–59, 114–15, 190–91, 297–98; Alexander Werth, *Which Way France?* (New York: Harper, 1937), pp. 28–32; and Michel Huber, in Royal Economic Society, *Memorandum 77*, February 1939, pp. 11–16.

the end of 1930. The debt burden, reduced by the 1926–28 devaluation of the franc, was no longer excessive, and substantial German reparation payments were used for debt redemption and building up of reserves abroad. Increases in unemployment were retarded by nonrenewal of permits to foreign workers.

In the autumn of 1930, however, the French economic position weakened. The fall in world commodity prices gradually eliminated the hitherto favorable disparity between French and foreign prices. Deepening depression in the United States and Europe cut down exports of French luxuries and the profitable tourist traffic. A banking crisis, precipitated by the collapse of the Oustric group in October, led to runs on small provincial and big Paris commercial banks, brought extensive liquidation, and upset the Tardieu government on December 2, 1930.[186] The price index of ten metal shares fell nearly 40 percent from its peak of 440 in September 1929 to 226 in October-November 1930. Wine-producing areas experienced a bad vintage year as well as reduced export prices. Unemployment reached substantial levels late in the year. Political instability and worsening of relations with Germany and Italy complicated the economic situation.

Moreover, the relations among the League's principal member states had deteriorated. One of its key senior personnel, Sir Arthur Salter, depressed by this trend and eager to regain his "national roots," announced his resignation in mid-July and left Geneva at the end of 1930.[187] The Young Plan, from which so much had been hoped and even expected, was already in jeopardy, and its bonds had fallen well below their issue prices.[188] Despite the successful inauguration of the Bank for International Settlements on May 20, 1930, international cooperation among the central banks diminished rather than increased.[189]

W. L. Crum began his review of the year 1930: "The course of our general business curve was continuously downward in 1930, and by midsummer depression levels had clearly been reached. By December, the decline had, in duration and intensity, become one of the most severe on record. In May a renewed price decline began. Then followed a series of adverse developments," Crum said. He listed political unrest in India; prolonged internal strife in China; excessive supplies of raw materials and recognized ineffectiveness of artificial price maintenance schemes, which

[186]C&FC, Dec. 27, 1930, p. 4104.
[187]Economist, July 19, 1930, p. 116; Salter, Memoirs of a Public Servant, pp. 200–201, 206; Salter, Slave of the Lamp, p. 108.
[188]See chart of high and low monthly prices of the U.S. issue into early December 1931 in AT&T, Summary, Dec. 7, 1931, p. 2. After some recovery into May 1931, they fell drastically in the ensuing months.
[189]Sprague had emphasized the necessity of increased cooperation in November 1929, as already noted (Chapter 8 above), and Addis did so in his address of Nov. 14, 1930 (Proc. Acad. Pol. Sci., January 1931, 14:300–315, esp. pp. 309, 312).

aggravated the difficulties; realization that the Washington conferences of late 1929 had made no lasting contribution to restoring prosperity; enactment of the new tariff act, increasing the difficulty of restoring a stable balance in international commerce and finance; severe drought in the United States; dumping and anticipated dumping by the Soviet Union; a new balance of power in Germany following the election, and revolutions in some South American countries, impairing confidence in foreign bonds; the election results in the United States, which indicated a widespread spirit of discontent and protest; renewed security liquidation, exposing the weakened position of many individual investors and financial houses; prolonged liquidation of general business, causing waves of bank failures, including some large institutions. Crum concluded: "That some of these developments were the inevitable accompaniments of the worldwide depression is obvious; but that they all, or any great number of them, should occur with such intensity in a single year is an example of the large part which chance occasionally plays in controlling the course of economic conditions."[190]

In the first few months of 1930 it was widely believed that the U.S. economy was basically sound, that its banking system was strong and sound, that the factors causing the slump in prices and protection were temporary, and that natural restorative forces would soon bring about obvious recovery under the stimulus of lower interest rates and presidential leadership. As the months wore on, all these expectations were exposed as illusory. Commodity price levels relentlessly shrank, agricultural conditions everywhere worsened, and business curves renewed their declines. President Hoover's valiant efforts had not arrested economic downtrends for long, and events destroyed the credibility of his assertions and forecasts. Moreover, as price levels kept falling and international trade kept shrinking, the very bases on which the Young Plan had been constructed were eroded. The rising burden of unemployment, here and abroad, gravely weakened the political structure in this country, Great Britain, Germany, and elsewhere. People lost faith in democratic governments and in the League of Nations. A deterioration of spirit and of cooperation was manifest. A vicious downward spiral replaced the beneficent upward spiral of 1925–29, and as it gained momentum the ablest men had no idea how to check and reverse it.

A Brief Hopeful Interlude, Early 1931   Nevertheless, around the turn of the year prominent U.S. appraisals of the outlook were at least mildly encouraging. The Harvard Economic Society reasoned that the coming year in agriculture would be appreciably better, and

---

[190]"Review of the Year 1930," *Rev. Ec. Stat.*, February 1931, 13:1–14. Cf. also C. J. Bullock and W. L. Crum, "The Harvard Index . . . 1929–31," *ibid.*, Aug. 15, 1932, 14:137.

expected general business activity to cease to decline in the first quarter or half of 1931, with a gradual revival in the rest of the year.[191] The dean of American business forecasters concluded that business was "dragging bottom," that the worst was near, and that the upturn was not far distant; indeed, he forecast an upturn in February-April 1931.[192] The AT&T expected recovery to be apparent by the second quarter of 1931 and the year as a whole to be "undoubtedly . . . a year of recovery," though normal activity would not be attained and the average level for the year would be lower than in 1930.[193] Keynes, in his annual chairman's address to the National Mutual Life Assurance Society late in January, was much less cheerful and confident, and could as yet see no end to the greatest slump in economic history.[194]

Early in 1931 several developments gave support to the hopes.[195] Bond prices recovered from the sharp drop in December caused by heavy bank sales. The Standard Statistics index of 404 stocks (monthly averages of weekly figures) rose from late December into March,[196] and member bank investments increased. Seasonally adjusted department store sales rose. Business sentiment improved. A number of important industries expanded output, and unemployment reported by trade unions even declined by 4 percent in March. But the wholesale commodity price index declined further, and agricultural prices were especially affected. Four years later Ayres attributed the favorable upturn of early 1931 in part to huge veterans' bonus payments (under legislation passed over President Hoover's veto), the working of natural forces making for recovery, and simultaneous improvement in England, Belgium, Germany, and Japan.[197] Actually, after reaching an all-time low in January 1931, the AT&T index of general business rose in the next three months to above the level of December 1930, and the contemporary *Annalist* index and the Cleveland Trust Company index of industrial production were broadly similar in indicating a lessening of the depression.[198]

[191]HES, *Weekly Letter*, Nov. 2, Dec. 13, 20, 1930, pp. 295, 314, 318. John D. Black, a highly respected agricultural economist, must have written the agricultural discussion.

[192]Warren M. Persons, *Forecasting Business Cycles* (New York: McGraw-Hill, 1931), p. 44; see also p. 82, which agrees with Crum's views noted above. Schumpeter later noted (*Business Cycles*, 2:907-8) that Persons only recognized short cycles, for which his forecast was not wrong, but that "he overlooked—as businessmen did—the drift of things below the surface movement, *i.e.*, the longer cycles and their phases."

[193]AT&T, *Summary*, Jan. 7, 1931, pp. 3-4.

[194]*Economist*, Jan. 31, 1931, p. 262.

[195]AT&T, *Summary*, issues of Jan. 7 through June 6, 1931.

[196]The Harvard Curve A ("Speculation") even reached its interim peak in April. By mid-1930 it had fallen below the low of November 1929, and it fell much further in the next six months. *Rev. Ec. Stat.*, February 1931, 13:1, May and Aug. 15, 1932, 14:84, 137.

[197]CTC, *Bus. Bull.*, Jan. 15, 1935. Cf. Wilbur and Hyde, *Hoover Policies*, pp. 193-200.

[198]E.g., CTC, *Bus. Bull.*, Feb. 15, 1932. The 1940 edition of the CTC index of industrial production also showed considerable improvement from December through March, then very

March 1931, however, marked the onset of a second banking crisis in the United States. The public resumed hoarding of currency, and banks resumed the sale of assets to strengthen their reserves.[199] Late March and April, moreover, were marked by heavy liquidation in the stock market and "the largest failure of a Stock-Exchange house in history" (Pynchon and Company), followed by the failure of another house and by "several thoroughgoing reorganizations." In the last week of April the Standard Statistics index of prices of 404 stocks was at its lowest point since July 1926.[200]

moderate retrogression in April and May. Recent editions of the CTC index of business activity (e.g., April 1971), however, show virtual stability from December 1930 through May 1931.

[199]Friedman and Schwartz, *Monetary History*, pp. 313–15, 343–44.

[200]AT&T, *Summary*, Feb. 6, 1931, p. 1, May 6, 1931, pp. 1, 4.

CHAPTER 10

EUROPEAN FINANCIAL CRISES AND THEIR CONSEQUENCES, 1931-32

AGAIN IN 1931, as in 1930, the hopeful interlude of the first few months was followed by severe economic contraction. With little warning,[1] financial crises in quick succession struck Austria, Germany, and Great Britain in May–September 1931.[2] If 1930 was an extremely disappointing year, 1931 was truly a "tragic year" of widening and deepening depression, and of extraordinary financial collapse,[3] out of which no way could be seen. In general, the worst was reached in 1932, but in the United States

---

[1]The relevant passages in President Hoover's message of Dec. 2, 1930, were not taken as seriously as they deserved to be. In March 1931, when Governor Norman visited the United States, "no urgent sense of crisis" was in evidence, and his main purpose was to discuss the ominous shrinkage of world trade and possible ways of reversing this. Sir Henry Clay, *Lord Norman* (London: Macmillan, 1957), p. 375. The Citibank *Monthly Economic Letter* for April 1931 spoke of "important . . . improvement in the foreign situation." The valuable papers given as late as Apr. 24, 1931, before the Academy of Political Science in New York at its session on depression and revival were strangely silent on this subject. *Proc. Acad. Pol. Sci.*, June 1931, 14:329–457. As late as May 20, when President Hoover "called in Federal Reserve officials to discuss our threatened economy," they assured him that "nothing was going on that they and our banks could not handle easily." Hoover, *The Memoirs of Herbert Hoover*, vol. 3: *The Great Depression, 1929–1941* (New York: Macmillan, 1952), p. 65.

[2]Especially valuable are Eleanor L. Dulles, *The Bank for International Settlements at Work* (New York: Macmillan, 1932), with a "Chronological Table of Events Relating to the B.I.S. and Reparations," 1918–33, on pp. 500–522; and John W. Wheeler-Bennett, *The Wreck of Reparations* (New York: Morrow, 1933).

[3]W. L. Crum, "Review of the Year 1931," and J. B. Hubbard, "European Economic Conditions in the Year 1931," *Rev. Ec. Stat.*, Feb. 15, 1932, 14:12–24; Dulles, *BIS*, ch. 14 and pp. 517–23; Sir Arthur Salter, "A Year and a Half of Crisis," *Yale Review*, December 1932, pp. 217–33; Sir Arthur Salter, *Recovery: The Second Effort* (New York: Century, 1932), pp. 30–32; B. M. Anderson, *Economics and the Public Welfare: Financial and Economic History of the United States, 1914–1946* (New York: Van Nostrand, 1949), ch. 33; Lord Salter, *Memoirs of a Public Servant* (London: Faber, 1961), pp. 172, 192, 196–98; R. A. Gordon, *Business Fluctuations*, 2d ed. (New York: Harper, 1961), p. 432. Milton Friedman and Anna J. Schwartz, though mentioning the European financial crises in *A Monetary History of the United States, 1867–1960* (Princeton, N.J.: Princeton University Press, 1963), pp. 314–17, inadequately emphasized their powerful adverse influence; and Friedman, in *A Program for Monetary Stability* (New York: Fordham University Press, 1960), failed to mention them and ignored what I consider ample evidence when he said: "In the summer of 1931 there were many signs of recovery" (p. 19). C. P. Kindleberger's generally favorable review (*AER*, March 1968, 58:211–13) of Dudley Dillard, *Economic Development of the North Atlantic Community* (Englewood Cliffs, N.J.: Prentice-Hall, 1967), nevertheless termed "his account of the 1931 financial collapse overwritten."

a combination of serious banking difficulties and exceptional political complications deferred the start of genuine recovery until well into 1933.

Background of   The sources of the financial crises were numerous. Huge
the Crises   foreign loans floated on U.S. and British markets from
mid-1924 to mid-1928, and impressive U.S. prosperity for another year or more, had promoted vigorous but often imprudent expansion in Europe and Latin America. The Wall Street superboom rudely checked this capital outflow and instead drew short-term funds and speculative investment capital from Europe into this country. The severe stock market collapse and subsequent economic contraction in the United States, coupled with the Hawley-Smoot Tariff Act of June 1930, reduced U.S. markets for foreign goods, services, and securities, with drastic consequences all over the world. A huge volume of short-term funds was subject to international shifts in response to fresh fears and hopes of whatever origin, and as the months passed fears recurred and swelled while hopes were repeatedly dashed. The currency stabilization measures of the 1920s proved too hurriedly taken, and the new structure was unequal to the strains imposed upon it in 1930–31.[4] Mistakes and malfeasance were rife abroad as well as in the United States (see Chapter 14 below), and political institutions proved unequal to the task of preparing for unexpectedly severe strains. The impasse over reparations and war debts continued despite the Young Plan, which was devised on the false assumption of continuing, if not "permanent," U.S. prosperity.

The European financial crisis thus had their roots in international developments in 1927–30, for which the Wall Street superboom and the ensuing crash bore no small part of the responsibility. Other powerful influences were the economic, financial, and political deterioration which progressed inexorably in 1929–30 and was far from completed in the spring of 1931. In these crises the newly founded Bank for International Settlements was called upon to play a substantial role, which it did; but its own resources proved inadequate, as did the cooperation of central banks and of private international bankers.

The seeds of serious financial trouble included a vast increase in short-term international indebtedness; its volume was gravely underestimated[5] and its dangers were ill understood at the time. Of the many

---

[4]J. A. Schumpeter later wrote in *Business Cycles: A Theoretical, Historical, and Statistical Analysis of the Capitalist Process* (2 vols. [New York: McGraw-Hill, 1939], 2:910): "The provisional solution that had been arrived at for the problem of international payments was bound to break down in any major depression and, before doing so, to accentuate its difficulties."

[5]As of the beginning of 1931 it was later estimated by the BIS at more than $10 billion, though as late as July 23, 1931, it had been believed to be less than half that figure. Hoover, *Memoirs*, 3:78–79. Cf. J. H. Rogers, "Foreign Credits and International Trade," Apr. 13,

causative factors, a few need to be mentioned here.[6] High rates of interest on long-term loans, and the sharp diminution in U.S. long-term lending after mid-1928, induced expansion of short-term credits, which were available at especially low rates in 1930 and 1931. Ill-coordinated currency rehabilitations, which overvalued some currencies (such as the pound sterling) and undervalued others (such as the French franc), had created gold exchange standards in many countries, in which dollar and sterling balances (*Devisen*) could serve along with gold in central bank reserves.[7] Repatriation of French capital after de facto stabilization of the franc late in 1926 facilitated keeping large French funds on deposit in London and New York, subject to call by French owners. These deposits drifted into the hands of French banks, and especially the Bank of France. That Bank thus came into a position to exert pressure on the British government by withdrawing gold from the Bank of England, which operated on a very slender gold reserve, and on the German government by similar pressure on the Reichsbank. Though heatedly denied, it appears to be true that such pressures were on various occasions exerted with political motives.[8]

The "flight of capital" from one country to another, whenever confidence was shaken and fears for safety came to dominate, had repeatedly complicated international affairs in the 1920s. One of the latest examples occurred in April-May 1929, when a breakdown of the Young committee's work was seriously threatened.[9] In mid-November 1929 one highly competent observer viewed the U.S. market for short-term funds as "a more disturbing factor in the international situation than ever before."[10] The initiative was sometimes taken by foreigners who withdrew short-term funds or sold securities or real property in the threatened country, and sometimes by its nationals who sought safer locations for their funds. Such episodes

1932, in *Proc. Acad. Pol. Sci.*, May 1932, 15:6–12. For 1934 the BIS estimated the total at 29 to 30 billion Swiss francs, roughly treble the prewar figure. Schumpeter, *Business Cycles*, 2:910n.

[6]Cf. Lionel Robbins, *The Great Depression* (London: Macmillan, 1934), ch. 5, esp. pp. 88, 99.

[7]League of Nations, *International Currency Experience* (Geneva: League of Nations, 1944), pp. 116–17, 122–27.

[8]See various books by Paul Einzig, in whose influential "Lombard Street" column in the London *Financial News* these charges were initially made: *Behind the Scenes of International Finance* (London: Macmillan, 1931; 2d printing, 1932), pp. v–xv et passim; *The World Economic Crisis, 1929–1931*, 2d ed. (London: Macmillan, 1932), chs. 8, 9, 15; *World Finance, 1935–1937* (London: Macmillan, 1937), p. 3; *In the Centre of Things* (London: Hutchinson, 1960), pp. 67, 128–35. See also Sir Josiah Stamp, in *Economic Essays in Honour of Gustav Cassel* (London: Allen and Unwin, 1933), pp. 600–603.

[9]Succinctly discussed in Shepard Morgan, "The Political Aspects of War Debts and Reparations," Apr. 13, 1932, *Proc. Acad. Pol. Sci.*, June 1932, 15:94–103, esp. pp. 97–98.

[10]O. M. W. Sprague, in *Proc. Acad. Pol. Sci.*, January 1930, 13:524–30. Not until June 1932 did this appear to be ended. See Federal Reserve Bank of New York, *Monthly Review*, June 1932: AT&T, *Summary*, July 6, 1932, pp. 1–2.

became much more numerous in 1931, and intensified the European financial crises; but they continued throughout the 1930s.

Furthermore, the thorny problem of war debts and reparations constituted, despite the success of the Dawes Plan and the eventually abortive agreement on the Young Plan in 1929–30, "one of the major continuing causes of disturbance in the postwar world," responsible for tension in European affairs and between the United States and European debtor countries.[11]

The Austrian   On March 21, 1931, a period of comparative calm in inter-
Crisis   national affairs was dramatically broken by the announcement of preliminary conversations looking toward the establishment of an Austro-German customs union. The proposal had economic merit, but proved a colossal political blunder.[12] It promptly aroused deep apprehension in France, where it was interpreted as the forerunner of a political union forbidden by the Treaty of Versailles—the ground on which a narrow majority of the Hague Court of International Justice declared it void early in September.[13] In the five-and-one-half-month interval this proposal caused growing irritation and concern which led to heavy withdrawals of foreign short-term assets from Germany. The ultimate withdrawal of the proposal was, as Schumpeter later observed, "a fatal blow to the prestige of the last German cabinet [Brüning's] that believed in action within existing treaties."[14]

[11]Frank Altschul, a partner in Lazard Frères, in his New York address on Apr. 13, 1932, in *Proc. Acad. Pol. Sci.*, June 1932, 15:53–64. Similarly strong expressions can be found in Clay, *Lord Norman*, p. 194 et passim, and Salter, *Memoirs of a Public Servant*, p. 172 et passim. Cf. an excellent review of "Reparations and War Debts" in *Economist*, suppl., Jan. 23, 1932, pp. 1–10.
      Governor Norman of the Bank of England had written Governor Strong of the Federal Reserve Bank of New York on May 3, 1921: "This question of reparations is not as it should be, and as Mr. Keynes assumes it to be, a purely economic question. It is almost entirely a political question over which the French government is forced to tug in one direction and the German government in another." Clay, *Lord Norman*, p. 196. The French diplomat Louis Aubert had devoted much of his lectures at the Institute of Politics in the summer of 1924 to elaboration of the economic and political aspects of reparations and other topics of the day and of the contrast between the British and French viewpoints, one stressing the economic and the other the political. Louis Aubert, *The Reconstruction of Europe* (New Haven, Conn.: Yale University Press, 1925).
      [12]Anderson, *Economics and the Public Welfare*, pp. 232–36; M. J. Bonn, *Wandering Scholar* (New York: John Day, 1948), pp. 315–16; Clay, *Lord Norman*, p. 378. Bonn stressed the weaknesses of the Weimar Republic government: "bad teamwork between departments, arbitrary action of relatively subordinate officials, and ambiguity on the part of their heads, who let them act independently."
      [13]Dulles, *BIS*, pp. 238–39, 309, 377, 517, 519. Lippmann wrote in his column on Briand dated Mar. 9, 1932, that the attempt "was utterly destructive to his influence." Walter Lippmann, *Interpretations, 1931–1932*, ed. Allan Nevins (New York: Macmillan, 1932), p. 346.
      [14]*Business Cycles*, 2:930–31. In his 1935 article ("The Analysis of Economic Change," *Rev. Ec. Stat.*, May 1935, 17:2–10) he attributed "the breakdown of the distinct upward

Despite the successful financial rehabilitation of Austria under League of Nations auspices in the mid-1920s, with notable support from leading individual nations and central banks, the economic and financial "viability" of this truncated country continued to be doubtful. Its strength and stability were undermined by socialistic imprudence in the late 1920s, then were severely strained by the stock exchange and trade slump of 1929–31. Its leading bank, the Austrian Kreditanstalt—founded by the Rothschilds in 1855—had had to rely on foreign funds in financing the precarious Central European economic system. On October 7, 1929, it had taken over the Boden-Kreditanstalt, with branches throughout Central Europe, whose affairs suffered severe financial deterioration in the first half of that year. This operation had important support from a syndicate of New York, London, and Brussels private banking houses, headed by the Rothschilds of Vienna, and from a guarantee of certain of its investments by the Austrian government. By the end of 1930, however, the Kreditanstalt's shareholdings had drastically depreciated. On the verge of collapse on May 11, 1931, it experienced an unforeseen run, amid rumors of impending financial disasters in continental Europe. Serious efforts were made to give prompt aid through a consortium of U.S., British, and French banks and the BIS; but divisions of opinion prevented timely, adequate actions. On May 29 the Austrian parliament voted an important guarantee, but the Austrian government's credit was so shaken that even a second 100-million-schilling credit from the BIS on June 6 and an advance of 150 million schillings from the Bank of England on June 16 could not avert its failure; and it had to be completely reorganized.[15]

The Austrian crisis had repercussions throughout Central and Eastern Europe, and had adverse effects on Western European countries as well. After the Wall Street crash, while long-term foreign loans were still obtainable only at high cost and with difficulty, if at all, a worldwide plethora of short-term funds permitted banks and corporations to borrow for limited periods in anticipation of floating bonds later.[16] When foreign creditors withdrew or refused to renew these loans, and the prospect of borrowing long-term funds vanished, the debtor banks, firms, and government were seriously embarrassed, and delinquencies and failures multi-

---

movement" early in 1931 to "a string of events arising out of the flutter caused by the reopening of the question of the union of Austria to Germany and the movements of short balances incident thereto." Robbins (*Great Depression*, p. 92) mentioned this but belittled its weight, and cited Nicholas Kaldor, "The Economic Situation of Austria," *Harvard Business Review*, October 1932, 11:23–24.

[15]*Economist*, Nov. 30, 1929, p. 1018, and later issues; Dulles, *BIS*, pp. 84, 90, 379–82, 405–9, 463, 478–79; H. V. Hodson, *Slump and Recovery, 1929–1937* (London: Oxford University Press, 1938), pp. 64–66, 96, 118–19; Clay, *Lord Norman*, pp. 179–93, 371–77.

[16]Cf. Einzig, *World Economic Crisis*, 2d ed., pp. 155–56.

plied; and the creditor banks, firms, and nations in turn lost, suffered from frozen assets, and were under pressure to "send good money after bad."

The German Crisis and   After Austria, Germany was the next and far
the Hoover Moratorium   more important victim of a financial crisis.
Her impressive recovery of 1926-28 had been checked in 1928 and then seriously reversed in 1930 and the first half of 1931. Bonn later remarked that the Germans responded nobly to stress and tribulations but could not stand prosperity. Overextension, manipulation, and fraud became prevalent. Unemployment expanded greatly.[17]

The "rationalization" movement of the late 1920s, carried too far too fast, had thrown out of work large numbers who could not be absorbed in other activities. More important, the spiraling contraction of industry and trade independently reduced employment.[18] Angell, writing in 1929, had credited the rationalization movement in 1924-27 with bringing about "a great gain for the German economy as a whole," without any reservations.[19] Though M. J. Bonn was among Angell's German consultants, his contrary opinions on this matter found no reflection in that book. Bonn was a persistent critic of the "irrational rationalization" movement.[20] In the foreword to his *Prosperity* he referred to "that precipitate policy of rationalization . . . , which is not only one of the causes of the existing unemployment in Germany, but also, in consequence of the misuse of capital, has contributed very substantially to the disorganization of German finance, both public and private."[21] Robert A. Brady, writing in mid-1932, concluded that "rationalization, as carried out, must bear a considerable share of responsibility for the debacle."[22]

[17]Paul Einzig, *Germany's Default: The Economics of Hitlerism* (London: Macmillan, 1934), chs. 2-4; Royal Economic Society, *Memorandum 35*, LCES "Report on Economic Conditions in Europe," February 1932, pp. 7-14; Hodson, *Slump and Recovery*, pp. 66-71; Schumpeter, *Business Cycles*, 2:930-36; Bonn, *Wandering Scholar*, pp. 314-24; Clay, *Lord Norman*, pp. 377-83.

[18]Robert A. Brady, *The Rationalization Movement in German Industry* (Berkeley, Calif.: University of California Press, 1933).

[19]J. W. Angell, *The Recovery of Germany* (New Haven, Conn.: Yale University Press, 1929; preface dated Aug. 16, 1929), pp. 78-79, 83-84, 95, 104, 187-89.

[20]Brady twice (*Rationalization Movement*, pp. 52, 374) cited Bonn's *Das Schicksal des deutschen Kapitalismus* (1930), but none of his other writings.

[21]He later elaborated in his memoirs: see his *Wandering Scholar*, pp. 301-6, 317. C. Bertrand Thompson, author of *The Theory and Practice of Scientific Management* (Boston: Houghton Mifflin, 1917), after fifteen years' experience as a management engineer in France, Germany, and Italy, was also critical of the German movement in his contribution to *Harvard College Class of 1908, Twenty-Fifth Anniversary Report* (Cambridge, Mass.: privately printed, 1933), pp. 700-701. He also remarked that "England really does not exist from the point of view of modern organization."

[22]Brady, *Rationalization Movement*, p. xii.

The Heinrich Brüning government, in office from March 28, 1930, took unpopular austerity measures to lessen the strain on the Reich budget, without adequate sensitivity to the political necessity of placating public opinion.[23] And Dr. Luther, Schacht's successor as Reichsbank president, lacked vision and savoir-faire, and was caught unawares by the crisis.[24]

After mid-1930 unemployment and government measures to balance the budget and maintain a surplus in external trade accentuated discontent in Germany. Her public finances and currency were under special strain from the time of the flight of capital following the disconcerting increase in the representation of the National Socialists and the Communists in the Reichstag election of mid-September 1930. The BIS board on October 10 discussed Germany's difficulties, and next day the Kreuger loan of $125 million was arranged with Lee, Higginson and Company of Boston.[25]

German financial houses were deeply involved in those of Austria and Hungary; the shock to confidence due to the Kreditanstalt collapse affected German credit; and a number of important financial failures occurred. The obligation to pay reparations under the Young Plan, when the inflow of capital had stopped and international commodity prices kept falling, caused foreign creditors grave uneasiness. Short-term funds were withdrawn, and foreign-held German securities were heavily sold in May, as foreign creditors were awakened to serious political dangers. The Reichsbank lost much gold and nearly reached the end of its tether. German banks, ill-prepared for disaster, suffered runs at the end of May. On June 19 a panic occurred in Berlin, as complete financial collapse threatened.

On June 20, 1931, President Hoover electrified the world by boldly proposing a one-year moratorium on all payments on reparations and other intergovernmental debts, in the hope of "checking the slide into general international insolvency." President Hindenburg had made him an urgent appeal; Secretary Mellon had conferred in London with top British officials and Governor Norman; and Hoover had consulted congressional leaders and won their approval. Germany and Great Britain promptly agreed, but the French government initially insisted on unacceptable conditions, and agreement was not reached until July 6. This unfortunate delay of two and one-half weeks prevented the dramatic move from establishing international confidence in Germany's ability to surmount the crisis, and permitted

---

[23]Public opinion polling in Germany has undergone a notable development since World War II, and recent pollsters "point out that if a generation ago the Brüning government had had advance indication . . . that the Nazi Party would jump from six to 100 seats in the 1930 elections, it could have taken decisive action to blunt the grievances that motivated this sudden movement to the right." Lewis F. Gittler, in *Interplay*, October 1967, p. 6.

[24]Bonn, *Wandering Scholar*, p. 315.

[25]Dulles, *BIS*, p. 515; Clay, *Lord Norman*, pp. 368–69.

serious further financial deterioration.[26] On July 7 the Reichsbank's gold reserve was exhausted and Germany's largest textile firm failed—Nordwolle, or North German Wool Combing Corporation—and on the 13th the first of the great German bank failures occurred—the Danat, i.e., Darmstädter und National—and the Berlin bourse was closed.

Representatives of seven governments (including five finance ministers) met in London to discuss the German crisis on July 20, 1931. Their communiqué dated July 23—seventeen days after France eventually accepted the Hoover moratorium—called the lack of confidence in Germany unjustified by her economic and budgetary situation, and assured the world of their readiness to cooperate as far as possible to restore confidence.[27] The bankers did so throughout.

The decline of the German economic and financial situation from a peak of prosperity in 1927–28 was assessed by two committees of international financial experts which the BIS convened, first at Basel on August 8, 1931, under New York banker Albert H. Wiggin and including Sir Walter Layton of Britain, and then in Berlin on December 7, 1931, under Italian Professor Alberto Beneduce.[28] The Wiggin committee recommendation of a six-month "standstill" agreement, signed by German bankers on September 9, was generally accepted by creditors of German banks all over the world. But crucial decisions with respect to reparations and interallied debts were deferred to the Lausanne conference eventually held June 16–July 9, 1932, where it was agreed virtually to end reparations on the condition that the United States would appropriately revise her war debt settlements. By that time, however, the political atmosphere made such a U.S. decision impossible. In effect, this was a sorry end to payments on reparations and interallied debts.

In a New York address in mid-April 1932, the German consul general in New York called the BIS committee reports "classic" statements. Dr. Kiep frankly added that the preceding three months had shown further industrial and business contraction, increased unemployment, reactions in public and private finance, and continued withdrawal of funds by

---

[26]Salter, *Recovery*, pp. 51, 170–71; Dulles, *BIS*, ch. 14, esp. pp. 383ff.; Alexander Werth, *France in Ferment* (New York: Harper, 1934), pp. 30–31; W. S. Myers and W. H. Newton, *The Hoover Administration: A Documented Narrative* (New York: Scribner, 1937), pp. 89–99; R. L. Wilbur and A. M. Hyde, *The Hoover Policies* (New York: Scribner, 1937), pp. 408–13; Hoover, *Memoirs*, 3:63–80. The U.S. Senate ratified the moratorium on Dec. 22, 1931, six days after Undersecretary of the Treasury Ogden Mills announced that the United States was "unequivocally opposed to reduction of War Debts." Dulles, *BIS*, p. 528.

[27]Anderson, *Economics and the Public Welfare*, pp. 239–43. Anderson asserted, with perhaps undue assurance: "If the governments had acted that winter [1931–32], Hitler would never have come into power, and we should have saved the democratic regime in Germany" (p. 242).

[28]Reports partially quoted in *Fed. Res. Bull.*, July 1931, 17:374–79; January 1932, 18:21–43.

all methods, "as a result of progressive weakening of confidence at home and abroad."[29] Yet he expressed the conviction that "with the aid of ever more stringent measures of control" by the Reichsbank, "and with the generous cooperation of the foreign private creditors united in the so-called 'standstill agreements,' " the technical, psychological, and even political bases for confidence in Germany's credit existed. But he acknowledged that "this new structure is threatened and already a new demoralizing influence is at work on it in the governmental control and interference enacted by the emergency decrees since the crisis of last July"—a disease spreading far beyond Germany.

Bonn wrote early in 1932 an illuminating article on the crisis in Germany.[30] The center of gravity of the great international crisis, he said, had shifted from the United States to Germany. He stressed the psychological aspect of the war guilt clause of the Treaty of Versailles and the evil influence of the reparation problem. He called the Young Plan (which initially he had warmly commended) a monument to the folly of politicians and businessmen, contributing to the electoral success of the Nazi Party. He noted the serious delay in accepting the Hoover moratorium, the adverse effects on Germany from the British departure from gold, and the persistently heavy unemployment.

Actually, revolt against the austerity measures, and the conditions which gave rise to them, led to the political overturn which brought Hitler into the chancellorship late in January 1933. In Brady's introduction to his extensive study, *The Rationalization Movement in German Industry* (preface dated August 1932), he soberly stated: "A temporary dictatorship (since given semipermanent status) was found imperative to prevent the financial crisis from degenerating into a general economic panic and to avert the growing threat of revolution. There is little in the picture to make the near future look more promising."

The British Crises   Upheavals on the Continent brought crises in Great Britain.[31] The financial crisis began in mid-July, close on the heels of Germany's, which was by no means over. Indeed, the efforts by the Bank of England to help other European countries surmount their crises[32]

---

[29]O. C. Kiep, "The Basis of German Credit," *Proc. Acad. Pol. Sci.*, May 1932, 15:84–93. Cf. Richard von Kühlman's article with the same title in *Foreign Affairs*, January 1932, pp. 201–11.

[30]*Yale Review*, March 1932, pp. 549–65.

[31]See J. M. Keynes, "The Prospects of the Sterling Exchange," *ibid.*, pp. 433–47; Hodson, *Slump and Recovery*, pp. 71–85; Charles G. Dawes, *Journal as Ambassador to Great Britain* (New York: Macmillan, 1939), pp. 376–82, 386–410; Clay, *Lord Norman*, pp. 375–98; C. L. Mowat, *Britain between the Wars, 1918–1940* (London: Methuen, 1955), pp. 379–406.

[32]Moreover, in mid-1931 the French banks had left large deposits in England to avoid upsetting the financial stability of Europe, and lost heavily when the Bank of England suspended gold payments. Central European bankers were disillusioned as they realized

sapped its own financial strength. After heavy gold drains, on September 20, 1931, it had to ask the government to approve its suspension of gold payments, contrary to its firmly announced intentions.[33] "The immediate cause of our failure," the able editor of the London *Economist* said in New York on April 28, 1933, "was the withdrawal of foreign balances on a tremendous scale while our foreign assets were frozen."[34]

In August 1931 a long-threatened political crisis erupted in the midst of midsummer holidays. The Labour government fell on the 23d and was succeeded on the 26th by a three-party National government, in which MacDonald remained prime minister but was deserted by most of the Labour Party, and the Conservative Stanley Baldwin became the dominant figure. On the advice of bankers and the prestigious Sir George May Committee on National Expenditures, the new government pledged the most "galling" economies. It undertook to cut the unemployment "dole" and resort to other austerity measures to balance the budget and avert devaluation. Yet the Conservatives overwhelmingly won the election of October 27, 1931, and MacDonald and Baldwin continued to head the second National government.[35] In his *Lord Norman* (1957), Sir Henry Clay observed with reference to the British financial crisis of August-September 1931 (page 397): "More important than any errors of judgment of bankers was the slow pace of Parliamentary democracy, which made every step taken in the crisis too late to effect its object, and, underlying the crisis, the destructive action of world depression."

The British government's abrupt abandonment of the gold standard astounded and shocked the world.[36] Sir Arthur Salter learned of the action as he was about to speak in an opposite vein at the League of Nations.[37]

losses as a result of following suggestions for the general welfare made at international conferences. The extreme loss of confidence tended to paralyze economic activity in 1932. Dulles, *BIS*, pp. 484–85, 491–92. Cf. Hodson, *Slump and Recovery*, p. 87.

[33]Governor Norman, who often had bouts of illness, was confined to his home, most of the time in bed, for all but one day (August 5) from late July until mid-August, when he sailed to Canada for a complete rest; he returned only on September 23. Clay, *Lord Norman*, p. 385. Norman's illness and absence may have been crucial.

The British devalued the pound sterling from $2.80 to $2.40 on Nov. 18, 1967, in the face of the strongest assertions (e.g., "unalterable determination") from spokesmen at the highest levels of the government that no devaluation would occur. See "Good Intentions, Economic Laws," *WSJ*, Nov. 21, 1969, p. 14. Businessmen and speculators have learned that "irrevocable decisions" will be revoked when pressures become powerful enough.

[34]Sir Walter Layton, "International Coöperation in the Economic Crisis," *Proc. Acad. Pol. Sci.*, June 1933, 15:347–67, esp. pp. 350–51.

[35]Well discussed in Harold Nicolson, *King George the Fifth, His Life and Reign* (London: Constable, 1952), chs. 26–27. Cf. also William McElwee, *Britain's Locust Years, 1918–1940* (London: Faber, 1962), ch. 8; Nigel Nicolson, ed., *Harold Nicolson: Diaries and Letters, 1930–1939* (New York: Atheneum, 1966–68), p. 85; and Harold Macmillan, *Winds of Change, 1914–1939* (New York: Harper and Row, 1966), chs. 9, 10.

[36]"This event suddenly convinced the world that no currency was to be trusted." Schumpeter, *Business Cycles*, 2:937.

[37]Salter, *Memoirs of a Public Servant*, p. 229.

To many this seemed an utterly dishonorable step,[38] explainable only on grounds that foreign runs on sterling balances had made it unavoidable.[39] Keynes, who in March had opposed such a move as "disastrous,"[40] now called it "a most blessed event . . . charged with beneficent significance over a wide field." Sir William Beveridge was more representative in saying, "it marks the failure of ten years' effort to restore the financial order under which the world grew rich before the war."[41] Schumpeter later observed: "Social and economic data, in England and the world at large, being what they were, going off gold was an economically rational thing to do."[42] Anderson's mature opinion was: "England, although supported by ready cooperation on the part of New York and Paris, and by great forbearance in Amsterdam and other minor financial centers, made no fight at all."[43] Here is one of many examples of serious divergences of opinion among experts of high repute.

Deeper reasons lay behind this failure.[44] British financial and political leaders in the decade after the war were overconfident of Britain's strength, and their overconfidence was shared in the United States. They thought Britain was strong enough to maintain higher levels of living and leisure than her continental neighbors,[45] to be generous in her war debts

[38]Bonn, *Wandering Scholar*, pp. 318-19; Anderson, *Economics and the Public Welfare*, pp. 253-57.

[39]Einzig initially considered that the French maneuverings had "gradually undermined confidence in sterling and were ultimately responsible" for it; but he later recognized that a whole complex of factors was involved. See his *Bankers, Statesmen and Economists* (London: Macmillan, 1935), pp. 121-30, and *Centre of Things*, pp. 128-35. Robbins held to the latter view. *Great Depression*, pp. 92-99.

[40]*New Statesman and Nation*, Mar. 7, 1931; *Economist*, Mar. 14, 1931, pp. 549-50; *Evening Standard*, Sept. 10, 1931; *Sunday Express*, Sept. 27, 1931; J. M. Keynes, *Essays in Persuasion* (New York: Harcourt Brace, 1932), pp. 276, 283, 288-94.

[41]Sir Arthur Salter et al., *The World's Economic Crisis and the Way of Escape* (London: Allen and Unwin, 1932), pp. 78, 167.

[42]*Business Cycles*, 2:955-58.

[43]*Economics and the Public Welfare*, ch. 34. Anderson was presumably right in saying that the Bank of France gave orders to six New York banks on September 18 each to sell £1 million, and thus broke the price of sterling (p. 247), but mistaken in attributing to Governor Norman the unqualified assurance by Bank of England officials to Dr. Vissering of the Netherlands Bank that it could safely hold its sterling assets (pp. 246-47). Sweden, as well as France and Holland, took heavy losses on sterling balances (pp. 256-57).

[44]The English translation of André Siegfried's *England's Crisis* (London: Jonathan Cape, 1931), published in the spring, before they occurred, dealt not with the financial and political crises of 1931, but with Britain's chronic economic disequilibrium. Stamp discussed this, without mentioning Siegfried's name or book, in his Halley Stewart lecture early in 1932. Salter et al., *World's Economic Crisis*, pp. 47-56.

[45]Late in April 1931 Keynes told his friend Harold Nicolson that the English standard of living was at least twice as high as that of any other country, and said that she was really richer than ever before, despite her heavy burden of debts and taxation and the fact that only two-thirds of her productive power was being utilized. At the time Keynes had hopes that Oswald Mosley's short-lived "new party," to which Nicolson was devoted at the time, would

policy, to bring the pound sterling back to its prewar par (April 1925), and to shoulder an undue share of the world's financial burdens in 1928–31 (especially in June-July 1931).[46] For various reasons British bankers in the later 1920s had continued to float long-term foreign loans to an extent that eventually overstrained their resources, and then resorted to short-term borrowing abroad to ease the strain.[47] These proved serious misjudgments, and went far to account for Great Britain's all too limited recovery in the 1920s and her increasingly critical financial plight in 1929–31.

The British economic and financial structure had grown weaker in the years before the crisis, despite the relatively good year 1929.[48] Important industries, notably coal mining and shipbuilding, which had expanded during the war (particularly in the north of England, Scotland, and Wales), were depressed. Despite important gains in employment in new industries and service fields, particularly in London and the south of England, unemployment was chronic, though variable. Strong unions, buttressed by unemployment insurance, kept wage rates above economic levels, though work stoppages, which had been extremely serious in 1919–26, were much less so after 1926, except in cotton textiles.[49] Price-fixing and other intercompany agreements limited competition. Business management was generally backward, though in some fields increased efficiency reduced employment. Credit was progressively extended beyond safe levels, and foreign interests had come to hold excessive sterling balances. British exports had seriously declined under the impact of foreign competition and of various forms of protectionism abroad. British income from shipping and overseas investment had suffered a "catastrophic decline."

The Bank of England aid to Austria in her crisis, when division of opinion prevented prompt, adequate, concerted action, was insufficient and unsuccessful. The German financial crisis and the standstill agreements of August-September 1931 considerably overstrained British financial resources. Furthermore, the U.S. stock market boom, the resulting high

mobilize the other third. Nicolson, *Harold Nicolson*, 1: 72 (diary for Apr. 29, 1931). Cf. A. J. Youngson, *The British Economy, 1920-1957* (Cambridge, Mass.: Harvard University Press, 1960), pp. 65–67, 135–40.

[46]Sir William Beveridge's Halley Stewart lecture, late in February 1932, in Salter et al., *World's Economic Crisis*, p. 166.

[47]Lester V. Chandler, *Benjamin Strong: Central Banker* (Washington, D.C.: Brookings Institution, 1958), p. 307.

[48]Keynes, "The Prospects of the Sterling Exchange," pp. 435-36; Robbins, *Great Depression*, chs. 1-6, esp. ch. 5 ("Great Britain and the Financial Crisis"); *Britain in Depression: A Record of British Industries since 1929* (London: Pitman, 1935), the product of a committee chaired by J. Harry Jones, appointed by the Council of the British Association for the Advancement of Science; Mowat, *Britain between the Wars*, chs. 4, 5, 7; Anderson, *Economics and the Public Welfare*, chs. 33-34, and esp. p. 235; Youngson, *British Economy*, chs. 2, 3, 6, esp. pp. 241–50.

[49]*Britain in Depression*, pp. 59–79.

interest rates in 1928-29, and the consequent drain of gold reserves from Europe made it difficult for Britain and other countries to maintain the gold standard, as did the French return to gold at a parity that under-valued the franc.[50] For years the trading account between Britain and the rest of the world was out of balance, and an enormous fall in British exports occurred in 1930-31. In mid-1931 foreign bankers and speculators finally lost confidence in her ability to regain equilibrium, and a flight of capital from Britain ensured the breakdown.[51]

Aftermath and Consequences of the European Crises, 1931-32   There were almost unchallenged predictions that suspension of gold payments would be a major disaster for Great Britain as well as the rest of the world. Actually, the British public accepted the fact with surprising calm.[52] Confidence in British banks was not impaired.[53] Tensions were relaxed. Industrial relations were relatively peaceful. Otherwise, neither beneficent nor maleficent changes were readily discernible, and no sustained recovery followed in 1931-33. Yet Clay, much like Keynes a few months earlier, asserted early in 1932 that the British were relatively better off than any other people as compared with 1929.[54] If this was true, it was partly because the drastic fall in world prices of foodstuffs, raw materials, and elementary luxuries enabled Britain, as a major importer and exporter, to consume and produce more cheaply. The cost of living had declined much more than wages.[55] Keynes' hope and expectation that freedom from the burden of maintaining sterling at the old parity would be used to develop bold policies to spur and speed recovery were sorely disappointed. The principal policy change was a bitterly contested turn to increased protection, with Empire preference, expressed in the Ottawa Agreements of August 1932; this reshaped Britain's foreign trade without significantly increasing its volume.[56]

---

[50]In *Monetary Stability*, p. 17, Friedman laid more stress on Federal Reserve policies ("gold sterilization" in the 1920s and "tight money" in 1928-29) than I consider warranted. See Chapter 5, n. 20, above.

[51]See G. C. Clark, "Statistical Studies Relating to the Present Economic Condition of Great Britain," *EJ*, September 1931, 41:343-69, and n. 34 above. The circumstances were similar in the autumn of 1967, before the Wilson government most reluctantly devalued the pound sterling (see n. 33 above).

[52]Einzig, *World Finance*, p. 89; Sir Basil Blackett, in Salter et al., *World's Economic Crisis*, p. 105; Schumpeter, *Business Cycles*, 2:954-71; Clay, *Lord Norman*, pp. 399-400.

[53]Einzig, *The World Economic Crisis*, 2d ed., p. 133; Einzig, *Bankers, Statesmen and Economists*, p. 185.

[54]In his Halley Stewart lecture, in Salter et al., *World's Economic Crisis*, p. 145.

[55]See chart of monthly data for 1925-34 in *Britain in Depression*, p. 20.

[56]Hodson, *Slump and Recovery*, pp. 85-96; Mowat, *Britain between the Wars*, pp. 415-19, 436-37; Clay, *Lord Norman*, pp. 367-75.

The major repercussions were outside Britain. A period of chaotic international exchanges followed.[57] Prices of securities fell all over the world, and most European bourses were promptly closed for varying periods. Central banks raised their rates sharply. Scandinavian countries and several British dominions soon went off gold, and others did so after some delay. The German and Austrian crises were intensified. Widespread banking difficulties were created by the depreciation of sterling. Further, it increased the burden of international private and public indebtedness, tended to depress the gold prices of commodities, accentuated agricultural depression, and extended the industrial depression to some countries that had thus far been relatively immune. Tendencies toward exchange restrictions, increased tariffs, embargoes, and bilateral trade agreements were strengthened; and the universal heightening of trade barriers made far more difficult the payment of international debts.[58]

The early consequences of the British action were most serious in Germany.[59] To meet British competition, Germany had to cut prices on her exports in order to pay for essential imports. Devaluation of the mark was avoided lest it bring fresh price inflation, which the Germans feared above all, and lest it upset the negotiations to shrink or end reparations. The Brüning government undertook the seemingly less dangerous course of reducing prices, wages, and interest rates by decrees, which prolonged the strain, yet seemed to bear fruit for a time.

France had withstood the financial crises and economic contraction of 1929–31 better than most countries. But Lucien March, Paris correspondent of the London and Cambridge Economic Service, wrote on January 25, 1932, in a sober account of the disastrous year 1931, that "bankruptcies multiplied, and large undertakings whose administration had been unsound have been swept away."[60] There were financial losses, increased unemployment, and shrinkages of tourism and export trade. Yet the country remained *relatively* prosperous into 1932. This helped to bring about belated French acceptance of the Hoover moratorium in July 1931 and the Lausanne Agreement of July 9, 1932, after the postponement of the Lausanne conference from January to June had contributed to the fall of the Brüning government.[61]

[57]AT&T, *Summary*, Jan. 7, 1932, pp. 1–2.

[58]Hodson, *Slump and Recovery*, pp. 97–114; Schumpeter, *Business Cycles*, 2:954–63; Silberling, *Dynamics of Business*, p. 326; League of Nations, *International Currency Experience*, pp. 122–31; Clay, *Lord Norman*, pp. 399–402, 409–10.

[59]Cf. Bonn, *Wandering Scholar*, pp. 322–23; Anderson, *Economics and the Public Welfare*, p. 256.

[60]Royal Economic Society, *Memorandum 35*; LCES, "Report on Current Economic Conditions in Europe," February 1932, pp. 1–7.

[61]See four books by Paul Einzig, *World Economic Crisis*, 2d ed., pp. 138–40; *France's Crisis* (London: Macmillan, 1934), pp. 1–2; *Germany's Default*, pp. 4–7; *World Finance*,

Great Britain did not devalue the pound but let her exchange rate "float," and long resisted pressures to establish a new gold parity. The consensus among leading British economists was that an internal price level must be found which would enable business to function profitably and "the country with its various rigid factors to function to its maximum possibilities," without increases in money wages. They believed that eventually, when price levels had reached stability at home and abroad, rates of exchange between sterling and other currencies would be found at which the return to the gold standard could be made without the risk of being thrown off it.[62] Meanwhile, a number of countries chose, promptly or with more or less delay, to tie their currencies to the pound sterling, thus making up the "sterling area." Another group of countries, loosely termed the "gold bloc," led by France with her huge gold reserve, held fast to the gold standard for some time despite the severe price deflation thereby entailed. The United States also stuck to gold until the change of administration in March 1933.

The Austrian crisis, the Hoover moratorium, and the German crises had resulted not only in a flight of capital to the United States, adding to her huge gold stock, but also in the freezing of short-term obligations of foreign banks held by U.S. commercial banks. These developments made U.S. bank depositors uneasy, gravely weakened the banking position as a whole, and helped bring on a new banking crisis in August. Britain's abandonment of the gold standard, a lead followed by twenty-five other countries within a year, led in turn to such heavy foreign drains on U.S. gold stock as to reduce it by the end of October 1931 to about the average level of 1929.[63] The Federal Reserve System reacted sharply, as it had not responded to the preceding internal drain upon New York banks. The Federal Reserve Bank of New York raised its rediscount rate from 2 to 2.5 percent on October 9 and to 3.5 percent on October 16. The gold drain and increased rediscount rates greatly intensified domestic financial difficulties, as the System's holdings of government securities were slightly reduced by the end of October instead of being increased.[64] Indeed, though

pp. 47, 57. The most serious French crisis came in 1933–34 (see Chapter 14 below). See also HES, *Weekly Letter*, Nov. 20, 1930, p. 197; and Wladimir Woytinsky, *The Social Consequences of the Economic Depression* (Geneva: International Labour Office, 1936), pp. 96–105.

[62]Sir Josiah Stamp, Apr. 13, 1932, in *Proc. Acad. Pol. Sci.*, May 1932, 15:138–39. See also Bonn, *Wandering Scholar*, p. 323.

[63]Anderson (*Economics and the Public Welfare*, pp. 259, 282) stresses the point that domestic hoarding of gold was "absolutely negligible," and that it became heavy only early in 1933, when persistent rumors spread that Roosevelt would take the country off the gold standard, as he did. Friedman and Schwartz (*Monetary History*, pp. 349–50) agree.

[64]Friedman and Schwartz, *Monetary History*, pp. 313–19, 345–49, 355–59. The monthly index of bond prices shown on the bars of the CTC chart of *Business Cycles since 1831*

the System bought $500 million of bankers' acceptances to counter the outflow of gold, it failed to expand its holdings of government securities until mid-December 1931, while domestic financial difficulties were being intensified.[65] But the serious fall of bond prices brought on and reinforced a second epidemic of bank failures in the United States, which reached fresh peaks after Britain left gold and tapered off in the first two months of 1932.[66] The foreign drain on U.S. gold lasted, with interruptions, until June 1932.

An unforeseen consequence of the British departure from the gold standard was that the people of India broke their age-long habit of hoarding. Indeed, they dishoarded gold on a scale that greatly helped Great Britain to get on her feet financially[67] and India to start toward economic recovery in the early months of 1932.[68]

While the European crises were reaching their climax in September 1931, a different one was emerging in the Far East.[69] Japan had suffered severely from the world economic contraction of 1929–31, which seriously reduced her exports and earnings from shipping. Britain's abrupt departure from gold caused prices to collapse on the Tokyo Stock Exchange, and it was soon closed. More important, the brutal progress of the world depression brought to an end a decade of restrained, peaceful, and friendly foreign policy and gave the militarists strong public support. On September 18, 1931, on the pretext of local disorders and alleged Chinese actions, Japanese military forces suddenly occupied Mukden and the zone of the

slumped from 94.4 in August 1931 to 72.0 in December, fell to 65.1 in June 1932, and barely exceeded 80 in only two months from then until June 1933. The reciprocal course of bond yields is charted in FRS, *Hist. Chart Book 1971*, p. 30.

Royal Meeker, speaking on Apr. 13, 1932, in *Proc. Acad. Pol. Sci.*, May 1932, 15:42–44, thought the "malevolent," "diabolical" mania for liquidating had gone too far for the Federal Reserve to "pull us out of the pit very, very rapidly."

[65]Anderson (*Economics and the Public Welfare*, ch. 35, pp. 260–64) argued that the Federal Reserve Banks had previously exhausted their ability to buy government securities. Friedman and Schwartz (*Monetary History*, pp. 407–19) adduce quite different reasons while rejecting this one.

[66]Anderson, *Economics and the Public Welfare*, p. 268; Friedman and Schwartz, *Monetary History*, pp. 309, 312, 320, 351–59.

[67]J. H. Rogers and Sir Josiah Stamp, Apr. 13, 1932, in *Proc. Acad. Pol. Sci.*, May 1932, 15:8, 131. In the three and a half years ending March 1935 India exported £173 million of gold. Hodson, *Slump and Recovery*, p. 276.

[68]In his Halley Stewart lecture, given in February 1932 and published in May, Keynes observed that Australia, and perhaps Argentina and Brazil, had "turned the corner" in the second half year, and that there had been "an extraordinary improvement in India." Salter et al., *World's Economic Crisis*, p. 79.

[69]Henry L. Stimson, *The Far Eastern Crisis* (1936); Wilbur and Hyde, *Hoover Policies*, pp. 599–603; Hodson, *Slump and Recovery*, pp. 87, 92, 346–55; Dawes, *Journal as Ambassador*, pp. 410–30; Henry L. Stimson and McGeorge Bundy, *On Active Service in Peace and War* (New York: Harper, 1948), ch. 9, esp. pp. 220–39; Winston S. Churchill, *The Second World War*, vol. 1: *The Gathering Storm* (Boston: Houghton Mifflin, 1948), pp. 86–88; Mowat, *Britain between the Wars*, pp. 419–22; Macmillan, *Winds of Change*, pp. 342–45.

South Manchurian Railway, and then proceeded to take over all of Manchuria, in seeming violation of several treaties. Henry L. Stimson, U.S. secretary of state, was exceptionally well informed and on excellent terms with his Tokyo counterpart, Baron Shidehara, who was deemed to have been confronted by the fait accompli of the Japanese army. Stimson sought to help Shidehara get control of the situation and to give the League of Nations Council the maximum U.S. cooperation possible. On September 30 the Council called for the removal of Japanese troops from Manchuria, and on October 24 set a deadline of November 16. When this was not met, no agreement on effective pressures on Japan could be reached. On November 24, however, the Council accepted a Japanese proposal for a commission of inquiry. On December 10 this was appointed under the Earl of Lytton (with a U.S. representative), and all coercive measures were postponed indefinitely. The very next day, the liberal Japanese cabinet fell and a militarist-dominated one succeeded. The Japanese advance continued, and on January 2, 1932, Chinchon was occupied, destroying the last remnant of the Chinese Republic's authority in South Manchuria.[70]

[70]These facts were clearly recognized in two able summaries published soon after the year ended which might have been cited at several points in this chapter: Arnold J. Toynbee, *Survey of International Affairs, 1931* (London: Oxford University Press, 1932), and Walter Lippmann and William O. Scroggs, *The United States in World Affairs: An Account of American Foreign Relations, 1931* (New York: Harper, for the Council on Foreign Relations, 1932).

CHAPTER 11

DESCENT INTO THE DEPRESSION TROUGH, 1932–33

SOME SLACKENING of the economic contraction was evident in many countries in the early weeks of 1932, but again, as in 1930 and 1931, it was shortlived. These were only brief interruptions in a protracted descent into deep depression.

The Harrowing Descent   In the United States wholesale price indexes continued their persistent decline, prices of bonds and stocks shrank appallingly, farm conditions were at their worst, and most economic indicators kept falling until midyear. Confidence evaporated. Indeed, from the spring of 1931 to the middle of 1932 the U.S. economy went dishearteningly from bad to worse,[1] and the rest of the world, with few exceptions, followed suit.[2] The CTC index of American business activity (100 = estimated normal), which had been 20 in March-April 1931, fell to –51 in July 1932, and ranged from –44 to –50 through April 1933. Several significant series showed much more extreme declines.[3] Both contraction and depression were unprecedented in severity. The sequel to the greatest boom in the 1920s was the greatest slump in the nation's economic history. It was worse than that of any other substantial economy, and exerted a deadening influence on the rest of the world.

The CTC "international business index" fell almost continuously from the third quarter of 1929 to mid-1932, by a total of almost 50 percent,

---

[1]B. M. Anderson, *Economics and the Public Welfare: Financial and Economic History of the United States* (New York: Van Nostrand, 1949), ch. 36. Cf. AT&T, *Summary*, monthly for 1931–33. The first quarter of 1932 showed some slackening of the contraction, but it was sharply resumed in April. Indexes of department store sales declined fairly steadily from late in 1929 through 1930 and irregularly thereafter to their low in early 1933. See chart in S. H. Slichter, "The Adjustment to Instability," *AER*, March 1936, suppl., 26(1):199.

[2]See LCES, "Report on Current Economic Conditions," in Royal Economic Society, *Memorandum 35*, February 1932, and later ones through October 1933.

[3]An index of U.S. output of producers' goods fell from 113 in 1929 (1925–29 average = 100) to 29 in 1932. A monthly index of machine tool orders, which had reached 336 in February 1929 (1922–29 average = 100), fell to 13 four years later. Extraordinary declines were registered in 1929–32 in new construction contracts, steel production, and factory sales of passenger cars, motor trucks, and buses. League of Nations, *World Production and Prices, 1925–1932*, pp. 1–56; C. A. Phillips, T. F. McManus, and R. W. Nelson, *Banking and the Business Cycle: A Study of the Great Depression in the United States* (New York: Macmillan, 1937), pp. 122–27, 162–64.

Table 1. CTC Index of American Business Activity.

Month	1927	1928	1929	1930	1931	1932	1933	1934	1935	1936	1937	1938	1939
Jan.	10	5	17	4	-21	-37	-46	-37	-29	-22	-8	-33	-24
Feb.	10	5	16	3	-22	-39	-46	-33	-28	-24	-7	-35	-24
Mar.	12	7	16	1	-20	-41	-50	-30	-28	-24	-4	-35	-24
Apr.	9	4	17	0	-20	-45	-45	-30	-30	-20	-4	-36	-27
May	9	6	19	-2	-21	-47	-38	-29	-30	-18	-5	-38	-26
June	9	8	20	-4	-25	-49	-28	-31	-29	-16	-7	-37	-24
July	6	8	20	-10	-25	-51	-23	-36	-29	-14	-5	-34	-23
Aug.	6	10	20	-12	-29	-49	-25	-36	-27	-15	-7	-30	-21
Sep.	4	11	17	-15	-31	-46	-31	-40	-24	-13	-10	-29	-16
Oct.	4	13	15	-17	-35	-44	-34	-38	-23	-12	-16	-28	-11
Nov.	1	15	10	-19	-35	-44	-38	-38	-22	-9	-25	-25	-10
Dec.	3	17	4	-21	-35	-46	-38	-34	-20	-6	-31	-24	-10

Source: Cleveland Trust Company, *American Business Activity since 1790,* 1971 ed.

to about 70 percent of its 1924 level.[4] Great havoc was wrought "by bank failures, depreciating currencies, moratoria and exchange restrictions," and the resulting forced liquidations and freezing of credits not only intensified the economic contraction but constituted "a tremendous obstacle in the way of recovery."[5] Another obstacle was persistently heavy expenditures on arms, even in the United States.[6] From 1929 to 1932 the value of world trade declined by nearly 60 percent, and that of the United States by about 75 percent; declines in terms of volume, though much smaller, were still substantial.[7]

In the United States and most of Western Europe, as employment shrank further after 1930, unemployment gathered momentum in 1931

[4]CTC, *Bus. Bull.,* Oct. 15, 1932 (1924 = 100), Apr. 15, 1934 (1927-29 average = 100). The eight countries included were the United States, Canada, Great Britain, France, Belgium, Germany, Italy, and Japan. On France, see Paul Einzig, *France's Crisis* (London: Macmillan, 1934; preface dated September), esp. ch. 1. Wladimir Woytinsky, *The Social Consequences of the Depression* (Geneva: International Labour Office, 1936), pp. 332-36, gives available data for various countries for the years 1929-35, but the figures are by no means fully comparable.

[5]BIS, *Eighth Annual Report,* May 9, 1938, pp. 15-17.

[6]Cf. "The Burden of Armaments: A Major Obstacle to Recovery," New York Trust Company, *Index,* September-October 1933, 13:153-59. In his first State of the Union message (Dec. 3, 1929) President Hoover observed that our total expenditures for national defense exceeded "those of the most highly militarized nations of the world." Hoover, *The State Papers and Other Public Writings of Herbert Hoover,* ed. William Starr Myers, 2 vols. (Garden City, N.Y.: Doubleday Doran, 1934), 1:141. His efforts to reduce these expenditures met with very limited success.

[7]AT&T, *Summary,* Dec. 6, 1932, pp. 7-8, with charts. Cf. Percy W. Bidwell, "Trade, Tariffs, the Depression," *Foreign Affairs,* April 1932, pp. 391-401. Between 1929 and 1933 trade between the United States and Canada fell to the lowest level since 1910, in money value by more than two-thirds. Herbert Feis, "A Year of the Canadian Trade Agreement," *ibid.,* July 1937, pp. 619-35.

and 1932.[8] In the United States (according to Lebergott's later careful estimates) the average number of unemployed rose from 4.34 million in 1930 to 8.02 million in 1931, to 12.06 million in 1932, and to 12.88 million in 1933, nearly one-fourth of the civilian labor force.[9] Much higher percentages were reported in Great Britain and Germany, but even there the data were incomplete and imperfectly comparable from year to year and with those of other countries.

July was the worst month of 1932. At year end, at least in some respects and in some countries, stability or improvement seemed near, if not at hand. Speaking in New York in mid-November 1932, Sir Arthur Salter said that a crucial stage had been reached in which much would depend on wise choice of policies. "It seems to me that there are some signs, possibly illusory, certainly precarious, that now the purely natural movement of the trade cycle is perhaps beginning to turn upward."[10] But he spoke of the future with great caution: this was fully justified during the next few months.

The Standard Statistics index of 60 U.S. corporate bonds declined by 25 percent from mid-1931 to mid-1932, and its index of 421 stocks fell by about 65 percent in approximately the same period. The latter index had shown declines of 30 percent in the calendar year 1930 and 48 percent in 1931. The low points were reached in late June or early July 1932,[11] when the AT&T index of general business reached its all-time low of about 61 percent below normal.[12] Business corporation profits reached their lowest point in the second quarter of 1932.[13]

[8]Quincy Wright, ed., *Unemployment as a World Problem* (Chicago: University of Chicago Press, 1931), consisting of lectures on the Harris Foundation by J. M. Keynes, Karl Pribram, and E. J. Phelan; *Britain in Depression* (1934); Joseph A. Schumpeter, *Business Cycles: A Theoretical, Historical, and Statistical Analysis of the Capitalist Process*, 2 vols. (New York: McGraw-Hill, 1939), 2:945-46; and Woytinsky, *Social Consequences of the Depression*, esp. pp. 133-53.

[9]The shrinkage of employment in a number of selected U.S. industries in 1929-32 is shown graphically by monthly indexes in AT&T, *Summary*, Nov. 7, 1932, p. 4. Cf. *Hist. Stat. U.S.*, ser. D 46-47; Hoover, *The Memoirs of Herbert Hoover*, vol. 3: *The Great Depression, 1929-1941* (New York: Macmillan, 1952), pp. 150, 155.

[10]"Steps toward Recovery," *Proc. Acad. Pol. Sci.*, January 1933, 15:266-75. B. M. Anderson, in an address on Nov. 15, 1932, rashly asserted: "Confidence has returned." *Chase Economic Bulletin*, Nov. 17, 1932, 10(6):6-8. Later he ascribed the failure of the economy to revive to the impact of the election campaign and the lack of cooperation between the outgoing and incoming presidents. Anderson, *Economics and the Public Welfare*, chs. 37-38; Hoover, *Memoirs*, 3:vii, 176-93.

[11]Anderson, *Economics and the Public Welfare*, pp. 268-72. See chart covering 1926-32 in AT&T, *Summary*, Jan. 6, 1933, pp. 3-4, 10.

[12]*Ibid.*, Sept. 7, 1932. Beginning with the next issue (*ibid.*, Oct. 6, 1932, pp. 2, 9) the AT&T substituted its index of Industrial Activity as Related to Long Term Growth (continued to early 1970), for which the July 1932 figure was −54.1. A slightly lower figure (−55.5) was registered in March 1933, when the CTC index all but equaled the July 1932 figure.

[13]Schumpeter, *Business Cycles*, 2:1006n. For annual figures on corporate net income and on individual income returns, see *Hist. Stat. U.S.*, ser. Y 280-310.

As the contraction progressed, U.S. banks were increasingly reluctant to risk lending for capital uses.[14] By the end of 1932 total loans and investments of member banks were lower than in the 1921–22 depression; commercial loans of all banks were less than half what they had been in 1928, and 36 percent less than in 1922. Thus all the bank credit "inflation" of 1922–28 was wiped out in the three years 1930–32. Successive waves of bank failures, moreover, further contributed to business stagnation and the commodity price debacle. "No economic system could withstand such wholesale bank failures and such loss of monetary purchasing power without suffering continued prostration."[15]

The number of U.S. business concerns shrank from 2,213,000 in 1929 to 1,961,000 in 1933. The number of failures per 10,000 concerns rose from 104 in 1929 to a peak of 154 in 1932 (it fell to 100 in 1933), while average liabilities per failure rose from $21,100 to their 1932 high of $29,200.[16] New business of life insurance companies fell sharply from the 1929 peak to a low in 1933. There was a "tremendous volume of surrenders and lapses," reaching highs in 1932 and 1933; and loans on policies, which had been 12.3 percent of all assets in 1924, increased to 18.4 percent in 1932.[17] The number of foreclosures on nonfarm mortgaged real estate, which had nearly doubled in 1926–29, rose from 134,900 in 1929 to an all-time peak of 252,400 in 1933.[18]

The growth of the U.S. automotive industry had been an outstanding feature of the 1920s and a large factor in the nation's prosperity. It shrank disastrously, if erratically, in 1929–32 and was slow to recover. The 1929 peak of factory sales of automobiles (4,458,178) was not exceeded until 1949, and sales of motor trucks and buses (881,909) were their largest until 1941. In mid-March 1929 R. C. Epstein considered it likely that in the next three years the annual output would not average more than 4.75 million. Actually, 1932 sales of both categories were roughly one-fourth of those in 1929, and in 1930–32 only 5,839,177 passenger cars and 1,235,929 motor trucks and buses were sold.[19] Registrations of cars declined by 10

[14]Lippmann observed on Apr. 8, 1932: "Not much hope can be placed on a policy of expanding credit while the nations are engaged in the suicidal efforts to strangle the trade which would justify the use of credit." Walter Lippmann, *Interpretations, 1931–1932*, ed. Allan Nevins (New York: Macmillan, 1932), p. 21.

[15]Phillips, McManus, and Nelson, *Banking and the Business Cycle*, pp. 167–69.

[16]Dun and Bradstreet data in *Hist. Stat. U.S.*, ser. V 1–3.

[17]*Ibid.*, ser. X 441–44, 455; *1966 Life Insurance Fact Book*, pp. 62–63, and *1971 Life Insurance Fact Book*, p. 85; and David McCahan at a December 1932 session of the American Economic Association, in *AER*, March 1933, suppl., 23(1):12–14.

[18]*Hist. Stat. U.S.*, ser. N 189. By 1946 it had shrunk to an extreme low of 10,433. For later data, see *Stat. Abstr. U.S., 1973*, p. 695.

[19]Epstein, in *JASA*, June 1929, 24:186–87; Automobile Manufacturers Association, *Automobile Facts and Figures, 1937*, p. 65, and *ibid., 1969*, p. 3. Though sales in 1933 were considerably larger than in 1932, they were less than in any other year since 1921 or 1922.

percent in 1930–33 and those of motor trucks by 6 percent in 1930–32, while motor bus registrations increased by more than 7 percent.[20]

The disastrous spring of 1932 was marked by the exposure of a number of examples of both egregious misjudgments and outright criminal behavior (see Chapter 14 below). The prestigious Swedish international financier Ivar Kreuger shot himself in his Paris apartment on March 7. Renowned as an extraordinary financial genius, he was later revealed as a swindler on a gigantic scale who had duped highly reputable victims. Soon after, the mammoth and extremely complex utility "empire" of Samuel Insull crashed in consequence of a series of monumental misjudgments by its head and of ruthless moves by powerful financial interests. Extensive financial wreckage from these two conspicuous failures, and the revelations that accompanied and followed them, drastically shook confidence in financiers and the whole financial system. Many other instances soon came to light. On April 11, 1932, the Senate Committee on Banking and Currency opened the first of its series of hearings on Stock Exchange practices, with Richard Whitney, the president of the New York Stock Exchange, as its first witness. Hearings were resumed in February 1933, with the redoubtable Ferdinand Pecora as the Committee's new counsel, and its report was issued in 1934. These exposures did much to destroy reputations, further weaken enterprise, deepen the depression, and retard recovery.

As usual, there was a tendency to exaggerate the direct financial effects of the stock market crash and subsequent collapse.[21] Undoubtedly several million shareowners saw great shrinkage in the wealth that they thought they possessed, the holdings of a considerable proportion of them were wiped out, and some shareowners were rendered destitute. Even so, it was less of a disaster than had overtaken the great majority of Germans in the postwar hyperinflation. Yet the shock to public confidence in business and financial leaders, in common stocks as an investment, and in the Federal Reserve System, the Republican administration, and President Hoover[22] can hardly be exaggerated. This change only began in the autumn of 1929. It continued as hopes were repeatedly raised only to be

[20]*Hist. Stat. U.S.*, ser. Q 315–17.

[21]Without questioning their literal accuracy (except for the final sentence quoted), one must discount the impression given by E. W. Kemmerer's statements in "The Gold Standard in the United States," in J. G. Smith, ed., *Facing the Facts: An Economic Diagnosis* (New York: Putnam, 1932), pp. 8–9: "Enormous declines were suffered by all classes of stocks and reached every class of people throughout the country. . . . Some widely distributed stocks with many thousands of stock holders have declined to less than one per cent of their October 1929 prices. Bonds have also suffered heavy declines, particularly those of foreign governments. . . . The shocks which these declines have given the American people have been terrific. For literally millions the accumulated savings of a lifetime have been wiped out."

[22]Warren termed the Insull crash (Apr. 14, 1932) "catastrophic for the Hoover Administration." H. G. Warren, *Herbert Hoover and the Great Depression* (New York: Oxford University Press, 1959), p. 82.

dashed, as bank failures mounted, as more and more crookedness was un-
covered, as recoveries in business and the stock market were followed by
fresh declines, and as widening unemployment spread first pessimism and
then despair.

The drastic shrinkage in the market values of common stocks during
the late 1929 crash, and the prolonged collapse in the next three years,
almost certainly led to a radical decline in the number of individual stockholders, though this inference cannot be conclusively supported. Many
had been wiped out; others were disillusioned. These processes cannot be
reliably traced, and we shall never know how low the numbers fell, even
when the low was reached, or just when the renewed growth after World
War II began.[23]

One striking feature of the 1930s was the extremely low level of new
issues of stocks.[24] This reflected (1) the bitter experience of investors and
bull speculators with purchased stocks, stock dividends, and split-ups that
went "sour"; (2) the extreme pessimism that succeeded the excess of
optimism; (3) the revelations of business crookedness, exaggerated by the
investigations of the mid-1930s; (4) the New Deal administration's generally anti-business attitude; and (5) excessive restraints imposed by the new
securities regulations. Ayres' long-period studies brought out the fact that
in earlier cycles business recoveries had been "largely financed in this
country by the sale of new issues of stock, and in only small degree by increases in the funded debt of corporations and by bank borrowings."[25]
Certainly the extremely low money rates in the depression years failed to

[23]Cf. Leo Wolman on the diffusion of stock ownership and employee holdings, in *Recent
Economic Changes in the United States* (New York: McGraw-Hill, 1929), 2:488–90. At the
request of the New York Stock Exchange, Lewis H. Kimmel made a valuable study, *Share
Ownership in the United States* (Washington, D.C.: Brookings Institution, 1952). Kimmel
reached the conclusion that in late 1951 or early 1952 there were 6,490,000 individuals who
owned shares in publicly owned stocks traded on organized stock exchanges or over the
counter (pp. 124–28). In an appendix (pp. 129–31) he gave some attention to trends in number
of shareholdings and shareowners in 1930–50. His study of fifty stocks showed a marked increase in the number of individual shareowners in the 1930s but attributed this mainly to a
shift of holdings from brokers' names (extremely common in the boom years) to individual
name registration. While this evidence does not support my inference, it by no means refutes
it.

I can give little credence to Edwin Burk Cox's summary table of what he calls "all of the
available reliable estimates." Cox, *Trends in the Distribution of Stock Ownership* (Philadelphia: University of Pennsylvania Press, 1963), pp. 32–33. These showed lows of 5.3 million
in 1948 and 4.8 million in 1950. I accept the New York Stock Exchange's postwar estimates
(covering all publicly owned common and preferred stocks) as reasonably trustworthy; these
show a rise from 7.5 million in 1954, to 8.6 million in 1956, to 12.5 million in 1959, to 17.0
million in 1962, to 20.1 million in 1965, and to 30.8 million on Jan. 1, 1970. *Stat. Abstr. U.S.,
1972*, p. 457, and earlier issues.

[24]See Leonard P. Ayres, *Turning Points in Business Cycles* (New York: Macmillan, 1939),
diagram 17, p. 127.

[25]*Ibid.*, p. 129.

induce such heavy bank borrowing and business revival as pre-crash reasoning had led able economists to expect.[26]

In the politico-economic climate of the period, enterprise was notably scarce, as Keynes and many others observed. A partner in an important London issuing house which managed to emerge unscathed from the crash included in his autobiography disappointingly few comments relevant to this book; but he did say of the post-crash period: "There was a lack of enterprise in industry, no inducement to take on new commitments, and in these conditions bankers do not thrive. It was a terrible period for everybody and it was not aided by a lamentable fall in all commodity prices."[27] There were exceptions, of which perhaps the most important was the British housing boom of the 1930s.[28]

The striking weakening of financial confidence in 1930–32 was reflected in a spectacular widening of the spread between prices and yields of Moody's Aaa and Baa corporate bonds. Started in the fourth quarter of 1930, this trend accelerated in 1931 and reached its peak in mid-1932.[29] Selected monthly data on the yield spread (in percentages) are: June 1930, 1.25; December 1930, 2.19; June 1931, 3.0; December 1931, 5.10; June 1932, 6.11.[30]

The passage of the Revenue Act early in June 1932, the end of gold outflow from the United States, the successful British conversion operation late in June, and the surprisingly "triumphant" Lausanne Agreement early in July[31] seemed to mark the turn of the disastrous tide, and there was an almost incredible improvement in sentiment for a short time. July and August saw a strong upturn in indexes of corporate stock and bond prices in New York and London, and in the Harvard index of sensitive commodity prices.[32] The CTC index of American business activity rose from its ex-

[26]R. G. Hawtrey, "The Credit Deadlock," in A. D. Gayer, ed., *Lessons of Monetary Experience: Essays in Honor of Irving Fisher* (New York: Farrar and Rinehart, 1937), pp. 129–44, esp. p. 130 (quoted in Chapter 15 below). Cf. Hawtrey's earlier conviction in his *Good and Bad Trade* (1913), p. 185.

[27]W. Lionel Fraser, *All to the Good* (Garden City, N.Y.: Doubleday, 1962), esp. p. 100.

[28]See pp. 293–94 below.

[29]FRS, *Hist. Chart Book, 1971*, p. 30; Milton Friedman and Anna J. Schwartz, *A Monetary History of the United States, 1867–1960* (Princeton, N.J.: Princeton University Press, 1963), pp. 304, 323, 453–56. Cf. AT&T, *Business Conditions*, August 1967: "Financial confidence as reflected by the ratio of prices of Baa bonds to Aaa bonds and the ratio of capital goods stocks to stock prices generally, has improved steadily since the credit squeeze of 1966."

[30]*Bolton-Tremblay Bank-Credit Analysis*, March 1967, pp. 26, 29–30, 32.

[31]New York Trust Company, *Index*, July 1932, 12:129–32; AT&T, *Summary*, August 8, pp. 1–3, Dec. 6, 1932, p. 1. In his review (*EJ*, March 1968, 78:133–34) of *Carl Melchior: Ein Buch der Gedenkens und der Freundschaft* (Tübingen: Mohr, 1967), Guillebaud termed this Jewish banker from Hamburg (who died in 1933) "one of the most outstanding Germans of the post-First World War period," a man of "first-class financial ability" and noble character marked by integrity and modesty, who won "the trust and esteem of friend and foe alike," and credited the successful outcome of the Lausanne conference largely to his efforts.

[32]*Rev. Ec. Stat.*, Sept. 15, Nov. 15, 1932, 14:149–53, 170–77.

treme low of –51 in July to –44 in October. But for "the whim of the political calendar" in the United States, mid-1932 might well have marked the definitive turn from contraction to recovery here and abroad.[33]

Unfortunately, improvement was shortlived. The exceptionally bitter presidential campaign played a large role.[34] It was exceptionally full of misrepresentations by the Democratic candidate, the Democratic National Committee, and their supporters. Most of the reasoned arguments of Hoover and the Republicans will stand scrutiny; but Hoover's reputation was disastrously deflated, and the severely depressed public was in no mood to be convinced by reliable facts and sound reasoning. In the interval between Hoover's overwhelming defeat at the polls on November 7, 1932,[35] and the end of his term on March 4, 1933, the United States was virtually leaderless politically. Strenuous efforts to win cooperation between the outgoing and incoming presidents on domestic and foreign issues proved futile.[36] This failure did much to intensify the latest U.S. banking crisis, to nip in the bud the nation's economic revival, and to hamper the early stages of recovery abroad. And negotiations for disarmament and preparations for the world economic conference were stalled.

One contributing factor deserves passing mention. Early in January 1933 House Speaker Garner (the vice president-elect) insisted on publishing detailed information on RFC loans made prior to July 21, 1932, which his amendment to the act of July 17, 1932, had required to be made in a confidential communication to the House and Senate. This publicity focused suspicion on all banks that had received loans, regardless of their strength, and contributed much to the banking panic that ensued.[37] And as bank failures multiplied and bank holidays spread in the first two months

[33]Schumpeter, *Business Cycles*, 2:954–55; Anderson, *Economics and the Public Welfare*, ch. 38.

[34]Hoover, *Memoirs*, vol. 3, chs. 19–30, with many quotations and citations. Cf. Friedman and Schwartz, *Monetary History*, pp. 331–32.

[35]*Hist. Stat. U.S.*, ser. Y 28–31.

[36]Henry L. Stimson and McGeorge Bundy, *On Active Service in Peace and War* (New York: Harper, 1949), ch. 11; W. S. Myers and W. H. Newton, *The Hoover Administration: A Documented Narrative* (New York: Scribner, 1936), pt. 1, chs. 15–19; Hooover, *Memoirs*, 3:vii and chs. 17–18; E. E. Robinson, *The Roosevelt Leadership* (Philadelphia: Lippincott, 1955), ch. 4; A. M. Schlesinger, Jr., *The Crisis of the Old Order, 1919–1933* (Boston: Houghton Mifflin, 1957), chs. 34–35, and *The Coming of the New Deal* (Boston: Houghton Mifflin, 1958), p. 4; and Herbert Feis, *1933: Characters in Crisis* (Boston: Little Brown, 1966), pt. 1, "From Hoover to Roosevelt," pp. 3–91. There were faults on both sides, but the basic defect was the obsolete constitutional provision delaying inauguration until March 4, which was altered if not wholly corrected by the Twentieth Amendment finally ratified on Feb. 6, 1933.

[37]Myers and Newton, *Hoover Administration*, pp. 324–26; R. L. Wilbur and A. H. Hyde, *The Hoover Policies* (New York: Scribner, 1937), pp. 433–35; Anderson, *Economics and the Public Welfare*, pp. 277–79; Hoover, *Memoirs*, 3:110–11, 198–99; Friedman and Schwartz, *Monetary History*, pp. 324–25. In August 1932 Garner had instructed the clerk of the House to make public each month the names of banks to which the RFC had made loans in the preceding month.

of 1933, bafflement and fear engulfed all classes of society. As Schumpeter well wrote later, "the psychic framework of society, which till then had held up well, was at last giving way."[38]

The president-elect was keenly aware of the complete loss of confidence in Hoover and his policies on the part of the electorate, and was unwilling to risk alienation of the voters by commitments in advance of his inauguration. Indeed, he seemed not averse to seeing the situation grow worse during the interim, the better to make a spectacular show of vigorous action in his first hundred days after taking office.

Federal Actions and Efforts, 1931-32   The descent into the deep trough of depression in the United States occurred in the face of important federal moves which helped prevent worse disasters but failed to bring about sustained recovery. When the Congress convened on December 7, 1931, President Hoover put forward a "most stupendous program" of government action, to which he added later in the session.[39] The Hoover-sponsored private National Credit Corporation had "performed a vitally needed service at a critical time"[40] but had soon become disappointingly ineffective. Early in 1932 the Congress set up the Reconstruction Finance Corporation (for its first six months chaired by Governor Eugene Meyer of the Federal Reserve Board), primarily to check the devastating consequences of widespread bank failures.[41] The Glass-Steagall Act of February 27, 1932 (initially to be in force for a year but extended annually until it was made permanent in 1935), sponsored by the Treasury and the White House, greatly enlarged the collateral eligible for loans from Federal Reserve Banks and enabled them to meet any prospective demands originating at home or abroad. Hoover viewed this act as a major anti-depression move to facilitate normal credit expansion and to free the gold standard from danger.[42] By the time it was passed, however, "the forces of deflation had gathered so much momentum that central-bank policy was not sufficient to arrest it."[43] Yet something was achieved. An able economist,

[38]Schumpeter, *Business Cycles*, 2:943-44.

[39]Myers and Newton, *Hoover Administration*, pp. 147-58; Wilbur and Hyde, *Hoover Policies*, pp. 422-27; Hoover, *State Papers*, 2:41-57.

[40]Anderson, *Economics and the Public Welfare*, pp. 266-67.

[41]Pierre Jay, in *Proc. Acad. Pol. Sci.*, January 1933, 15:152; Wilbur and Hyde, *Hoover Policies*, pp. 419-21, 427-36; Hoover, *Memoirs*, vol. 3 passim; Friedman and Schwartz, *Monetary History*, pp. 320-24.

[42]Wilbur and Hyde, *Hoover Policies*, pp. 446-48; Hoover, *State Papers*, 2:128-29; Friedman and Schwartz, *Monetary History*, pp. 191, 321-24, 363, 403-6, 422, 434-42, 447. Opposition by Senator Glass unfortunately resulted in bottling up Steagall's bill to establish a system of bank deposit insurance, which the House had passed in May 1932, and this legislation had to wait until 1934.

[43]E. A. Goldenweiser, *American Monetary Policy* (New York: McGraw-Hill, 1951), pp. 124, 126, 161.

speaking in mid-November 1932, expressed his conviction that, had it not been for the RFC, "virtually every non-member bank would have been closed by now."[44]

The President's Unemployment Relief Organization was expanded in August 1931 when Walter S. Gifford, president of the AT&T, replaced Colonel Woods as chairman; when the Congress failed to provide for its expenses Hoover raised the money from private sources and drew on his personal funds. After considerable delay, on July 17, 1932, the Congress accepted Hoover's recommendation of May 31 to authorize the RFC to lend the states up to $300 million to aid relief through the established committee system. But with strong Republican support he stoutly resisted heavy pressures to have the Treasury take over the relief burden, which threatened huge "pork barrel" outlays. Hoover also got authorization for $1.5 billion in RFC loans for useful "reproductive" or self-liquidating public works, but resisted pressures to extend it to wholly "nonproductive" works.[45] The Emergency Relief and Construction Act of 1932 (signed July 21) seemed a "colossal" program for relief and reconstruction, but accomplished little because of restrictive clauses. The Federal Home Loan Bank Act (signed July 22) set up, with initial RFC aid, the important system still in operation for promoting residential construction,[46] but could not be expected to yield prompt beneficial results.

In April 1932, under strong pressure from the Congress, the Federal Reserve embarked (belatedly, many felt) on a bold program of buying government securities in unprecedented volume to offset gold outflows, build excess bank reserves, and thereby promote credit expansion. This was viewed in some quarters as one of the most successful experiments in central banking ever undertaken, but it only diminished the pressure for credit contraction. The policy, however, did not have unanimous support from the Federal Reserve Banks and failed to stimulate expansion; purchases were tapered off in the summer and ended on August 10, after the Congress had adjourned late in July.[47] About mid-June the long period of foreign gold withdrawals had come to an end, as the amount of American short-term funds abroad became barely sufficient for working balances.

[44]Robert B. Warren, in *Proc. Acad. Pol. Sci.*, January 1933, 15:190.

[45]Myers and Newton, *Hoover Administration*, pp. 204–11, 221–23; Wilbur and Hyde, *Hoover Policies*, pp. 156, 370–401, 425, 451–62; Hoover, *State Papers*, 1:609–11, 3:221 et passim (see index s.v. "Unemployment"); Hoover, *Memoirs*, 3:149–54; and Schlesinger, *Crisis of the Old Order*, ch. 21, "The Contagion of Fear."

[46]AT&T, *Summary*, Sept. 7, Oct. 6, 1932, and Jan. 6, 1934; Wilbur and Hyde, *Hoover Policies*, pp. 334–36, 396–99; Schumpeter, *Business Cycles*, 2:940–42; Friedman and Schwartz, *Monetary History*, pp. 320n, 321–22, 325n.

[47]E. A. Goldenweiser, *Monetary Management* (New York: McGraw-Hill, 1949), pp. 57; Friedman and Schwartz, *Monetary History*, pp. 383–89. See comments by H. A. E. Chandler, R. B. Warren, T. W. Lamont, and Sir Arthur Salter, in *Proc. Acad. Pol. Sci.*, January 1933, 15:143–50, 192, 249, 266–67.

By this time France and the United States each held about 30 percent of the world's central gold reserves.[48] When the severest banking crisis reached panic proportions early in 1933, the System's portfolio of government securities was actually reduced, and it was only slightly increased in the three weeks ending February 15.[49]

President Hoover, at first mildly but then with increasing urgency, had sought banking reform measures.[50] But the Congress, with Senator Glass the virtual dictator of banking legislation, was loath to act on his recommendations, some of which were eventually embodied in the Emergency Banking Act of 1933. In an Indianapolis address of June 25, 1931, Hoover said: "It is obvious that our banking system must be organized to give greater protection to depositors against failures." In December and January he returned to this subject. At the very end of his administration, in February 1933, he and Treasury Secretary Ogden Mills were more specific, but the majority of the Federal Reserve Board resisted his urging.[51] The Board in 1932 was unanimous that "the establishment of a unified system of banking under national auspices is essential to fundamental banking reform."[52] On neither issue, however, would the Congress pass the requisite legislation.

Public opinion, well represented in Congress, baffled Hoover's efforts to break the impasse over the war debts owed the United States. The Hoover-Laval joint statement of October 25, 1931, at the conclusion of their conference, included a paragraph recognizing the need for some agreement regarding war debts to be made before the Hoover moratorium expired, and concluded: "The initiative in this matter should be taken at an early date by the European Powers principally concerned, within the framework of the agreements existing prior to July 1, 1931."[53] With this in view, Hoover on December 10 urged the revival of the World War For-

[48]AT&T, *Summary*, July 7, 1932, pp. 1–2, and Federal Reserve Bank of New York, *Monthly Review*, June 1932.

[49]Friedman and Schwartz, *Monetary History*, pp. 324–32, 363, 384–91, 399–406, 414–15. These authors, unlike E. A. Goldenweiser, "do not believe a shortage of free gold exerted any major influence on Federal Reserve policy" (p. 401).

[50]Hoover, *State Papers*, 1:154–55, 572–77, 2:46–51, 84, 400, 500–502, 597; Wilbur and Hyde, *Hoover Policies*, pp. 332–43.

[51]Hoover, *Memoirs*, 3:210–16.

[52]FRB, *Annual Report, 1933*, pp. 26, 229–59.

[53]Hoover, *State Papers*, 2:19–21; Anderson, *Economics and the Public Welfare*, pp. 242–43. Paul Einzig asserted, in the spring of 1932: "Under the concealed threat of bringing about a collapse of the dollar by the wholesale withdrawal of official French deposits, President Hoover was induced, on the occasion of M. Laval's Washington visit, to relinquish the initiative as to war debts and reparations in favour of France." *Finance and Politics* (London: Macmillan, 1932; preface dated April 1932), pp. 20–21, 53–62. Cf. ch. 16 of his preceding book, *Behind the Scenes of International Finance* (London: Macmillan, 1931, 1932; prefaces to first and second printings dated October 1931 and January 1932); and J. W. Wheeler-Bennett, *The Wreck of Reparations* (New York: Morrow, 1933), pp. 118–23.

eign Debt Commission. But on the 18th the Democrat-controlled Ways and Means Committee refused, and the Congress passed instead (on the 23d) a joint resolution which forbade even reduction of the debts.[54] Persistent efforts of the British and French to secure at least temporary adjustments were stubbornly resisted, and the president and president-elect were unable to reach agreement on this and other matters.[55]

In February 1931 President Hoover urged a complete overhaul of bankruptcy law and practice, on the basis of an exhaustive report by the Departments of Justice and Commerce; but partisan opposition prevented prompt congressional action on what the president considered one of the most important measures he had proposed. Even when his urgent recommendations eventually led to legislation, there were serious delays and often only partial enactment.[56]

The federal deficits of fiscal 1931 and 1932, after years of surpluses, gave rise to confusion and alarm, and the Hoover administration held to the then-dominant view that balancing the budget was the key to restoring confidence, which in turn was prerequisite to economic recovery.[57] President Hoover urged drastic reductions in federal expenditures and freely exercised his veto power, for the most part successfully, saying, "We cannot squander ourselves into prosperity." He also sought tax rate increases, but the Congress approved fewer increases than he favored.[58] The Revenue Act of 1932 lowered personal income tax exemptions, raised the rate of corporation income tax, and added many excise taxes. In the following year there was a slight reversal, but in the rest of the 1930s effective rates were far higher than in the second half of the 1920s. Federal deficits nevertheless continued, reaching a peacetime peak of $4.4 billion in fiscal 1936.[59]

[54]The resolution is quoted in full in Wheeler-Bennett, *Wreck of Reparations*, pp. 166–68.

[55]Hoover, *State Papers*, 2:73–75; Myers and Newton, *Hoover Administration*, pp. 153–55, 229–30, 280–97; Wilbur and Hyde, *Hoover Policies*, pp. 511–23; Stimson and Bundy, *On Active Service*, pp. 202–19, 285–96.

[56]Myers and Newton, *Hoover Administration*, pp. 42, 180–81, 321–24; Wilbur and Hyde, *Hoover Policies*, pp. 421–27, 278–94; Hoover, *State Papers*, 1:361–62, 2:126–27, 134–36, 567–68; Hoover, *Memoirs*, 3:143–49; and Joseph Dorfman, *The Economic Mind in American Civilization*, vols. 4–5, *1919–1933* (New York: Viking, 1959), 5:614. Hoover also vainly sought abolition or modification of the capital gains tax, which he had come to consider "viciously" promoted both booms and depressions. Hoover, *State Papers*, 1:438, 581–82, 2:60; Hoover, *Memoirs*, 3:135–37n.

[57]Herbert Stein, *The Fiscal Revolution in America* (Chicago: University of Chicago Press, 1969), esp. chs. 2–6. The contrary view, that in depression the government should tax less and spend more, had already become commonplace in respected circles but had not won public acceptance. *Ibid.*, esp. p. 145. Both 1932 party platforms pledged budget balancing, and President Roosevelt for a considerable time adhered to this objective, to which he returned in 1937. See also Harley L. Lutz, "Budgets, Bonds and Ballots," in Smith, *Facing the Facts*, ch. 2, esp. pp. 41–44; Schlesinger, *Coming of the New Deal*, pp. 3–11, 289–93; Dorfman, *Economic Mind*, 5:610–12; and Friedman and Schwartz, *Monetary History*, pp. 321–22.

[58]Wilbur and Hyde, *Hoover Policies*, pp. 450–85; Hoover, *State Papers*, 2:104–6 et passim; Hoover, *Memoirs*, 3:98, 132–42, 145–46, 159–63.

[59]See tables in *Hist. Stat. U.S.*, ser. Y 254–57, 321–32.

By the end of 1932 increases in federal interest-bearing debt (short- and long-term combined) in two years had canceled out almost half of the reduction from the peak reached on August 31, 1919.[60] Hoover later took pride in the fact that the increase in the national debt during his administration was held to $3.5 billion, of which $2.4 billion was in recoverable loans.[61]

In sum, Federal Reserve and administrative actions in 1931-32 included some important constructive moves as well as some ill-advised ones, but others were left out, in part because of unreconciled differences between the president and the Congress. It is clear that they neither prevented the descent into the depths of depression nor brought about a sustained upturn.

The Depression Trough, 1932-33   It is hard to exaggerate the plight of the world in the wake of the economic "hurricane" or "blizzard," and the profound disillusionment and despair that prevailed in the depths of depression in 1932-33.[62] "Never before," Keynes had written in August 1931, "has there been such a world-wide collapse over almost the whole field of money values of real assets as we have experienced in the past two years."[63] This continued and went further. After two winters in which conditions seemed so bad that they could only get better, that of 1932-33 was the worst that most people could remember. "Wherever we look in the world today," Sir William Beveridge said in a radio talk to the United States early in 1932, "we see distress. We see trade strangled, factories idle, farmers ruined, ships laid up, men by millions rotting in unemployment."[64] International finance was paralyzed. Resources were idle on a huge scale. Unemployment was of unprecedented severity nearly everywhere and of staggering dimensions in the more industrialized countries. Misery was widespread in the midst of abundance, and relief activities of unprecedented extent were wholly inadequate. The world seemed to face the greatest "climacteric" in history, with no experts or leaders who

[60]AT&T, *Summary*, Dec. 6, 1932, pp. 1-2.

[61]Wilbur and Hyde, *Hoover Policies*, pp. 468-70.

[62]The International Labour Office in 1936 published Woytinsky's valuable study *Social Consequences of the Depression* with extensive statistical tables, charts, and summaries. See also H. V. Hodson, *Slump and Recovery, 1929-1937* (London: Oxford University Press, 1938), ch. 4, "The Depression"; E. R. Ellis, *A Nation in Torment* (1970), chs. 7-16; and Louis Terkel, *Hard Times: An Oral History* (New York: Pantheon, 1970). The political and social effects of the Great Depression are briefly summarized in Kenneth E. Boulding, *The Economics of Peace* (New York: Prentice-Hall, 1945), pp. 124-26. Tables and charts of the "world," which cannot be wholly trusted because of inadequacies of data summarized, can also be found in the BIS *Annual Report* and in the Woytinsky book cited above.

[63]First published in his *Essays in Persuasion* (New York: Harcourt Brace, 1932), pp. 168-78, esp. p. 172. Surprisingly enough, real estate values had continued comparatively firm in Great Britain and France (p. 174).

[64]*New York Times*, Jan. 11, 1932, quoted in Sir Arthur Salter et al., *The World's Economic Crisis, and the Way of Escape* (London: Allen and Unwin, 1932), pp. 164-65.

could be trusted.[65] The very foundations of civilization seemed to have crumbled, and a descent into utter chaos came to be feared.[66]

It is unnecessary here to summarize the very different ways and degrees in which the trough of the Great Depression manifested itself in various countries of the world.[67] A few observations with reference to two leading ones must suffice.

In the United States unemployment of unprecedented severity prevailed in the trough of the depression, and many of those employed worked shortened hours. Labor union membership in 1933 was at its lowest level since 1917, and the unions were extremely weak.[68] Increasing proportions of workers faced a fourth winter of unemployment. Personal financial resources of the unemployed and their families were largely exhausted. Private charitable resources were limited. At least double the relief funds spent in 1931 were needed to meet admittedly meager standards of relief, but state and local governments faced huge debts and high levels of taxes. In city and country alike, poverty reached extremes which contrasted strikingly with the prosperity of the later 1920s. In 1932, with congressional approval, Federal Farm Board surpluses of wheat and cotton were drawn upon for relief use through the American Red Cross and local agencies, and substantial sums for relief use were loaned to the states by the Reconstruction Finance Corporation.[69]

President Hoover favored liberal federal policies for sick and disabled veterans and took steps in this direction; but he strongly resisted several other bills otherwise favoring veterans and vetoed several bills, two of which were passed over his veto—in the spring of 1930 and early in 1931. The widely publicized "bonus marchers" who assembled in Washington in May-July 1932 to press for legislation (which the American Legion did not support) included many nonveterans. This unhappy incident, in which federal troops under Chief of Staff General MacArthur acted decisively but smoothly after some of the District police had blundered, was the source of angry representations in the press and the political campaigns.[70] In the exceptionally turbulent period of the early 1970s we can better

[65]Cf. Harold Macmillan, *Winds of Change, 1914-1939* (New York: Harper and Row, 1966), ch. 10, "Salvage," esp. pp. 236-74, and ch. 13, "Fateful Years: 1931-5."

[66]Sir Arthur Salter, *Recovery: The Second Effort* (New York: Century, 1932), pp. 324-25.

[67]The Woytinsky book and others cited above and below give useful information, and many more could be cited.

[68]Irving Bernstein, *A History of the American Worker, 1920-1933: The Lean Years* (Boston: Houghton Mifflin, 1960), pt. 2, esp. chs. 8-9.

[69]Leo Wolman, "The Problem of Unemployment," Nov. 18, 1932, *Proc. Acad. Pol. Sci.,* January 1933, 15:207-13; George McEneny, in *ibid.,* pp. 178-88; Wilbur and Hyde, *Hoover Policies,* pp. 377-85.

[70]Hoover's side is given in Wilbur and Hyde, *Hoover Policies,* pp. 193-206, 452-56, 459, 480; Hoover, *Memoirs,* 3:225-32, 239. Cf. also Schlesinger, *Crisis of the Old Order,* pp. 256-65; Gene Smith, *The Shattered Dream: President Hoover's Gallant Fight To Save the America He Cherished* (New York: Morrow, 1970), ch. 6; and Ellis, *Nation in Torment,* ch. 12.

appreciate the baffling problem that this affair presented to the Hoover administration.

The early weeks of 1933, Allan Nevins wrote three years later, constituted "one of the darkest moments in American life. The banking system was in collapse, agriculture was prostrate, factories were chill and smokeless, fourteen million workers were unemployed, the mass of want and misery had become appalling. Half paralyzed, frightened as never before in time of peace, knowing not where to turn, the American people seemed . . . at the point of desperation."[71] The middle class was demoralized by loss of homes through mortgage foreclosures, which in early 1933 were averaging more than a thousand a day; and the real estate market and construction industry seemed headed for collapse despite the new Federal Home Loan Bank system.[72]

In its review of 1932 the AT&T observed: "The high morale of the American people in the face of the hardships entailed by the depression is essentially a tribute to the basic soundness and virility of our institutions."[73] Even then, morale was breaking down. The upswing that preceded election day faded in the ensuing interregnum; sharp declines in stock prices occurred in February 1933; there was increasing fear of growing economic chaos, even of revolution; and insistent demands came from the Middle and Far West for mortgage moratoria, tax reductions, and inflationary actions. In mid-November President Henry I. Harriman of the U.S. Chamber of Commerce had asserted that the plight of the farmer could not be overestimated, and set up a special committee to probe the farmers' situation and recommend practical steps to rehabilitate agriculture. In mid-February the *New York Times* printed a five-column front-page story by Russell Owen, headed "Danger of Revolt Cited by Farmers in Plea for Relief." Senators and congressmen were deluged with pathetic and denunciatory letters full of demands.[74] State legislatures were similarly bombarded, and numerous incidents of rural violence occurred. By March 1, after heavy withdrawals by depositors, bank holidays declared in several states, and bank failures coming thick and fast, the whole banking structure seemed to be crumbling. Confusion and panic were in the air, and citizens of all classes were demoralized.[75] In New York in January 1933, Harold Nicolson wrote in his diary: "The depression is dreadful. All

[71]Preface to Walter Lippmann, *Interpretations, 1933–1935* (New York: Macmillan, 1936), p. viii.

[72]Schlesinger, *Crisis of the Old Order*, esp. ch. 26, "The Crisis of 1932."

[73]AT&T, *Summary*, Jan. 6, 1933, p. 2. A similar statement could have been made about Great Britain.

[74]*Ibid.*, Feb. 6, Mar. 6, 1933; A. B. Genung, *The Agricultural Depression . . . and Its Political Consequences. . . . 1921–1934* (Ithaca, N.Y.: Northeast Farm Foundation, 1934), chs. 7–11. The violence continued in 1933. See Henry A. Wallace, *New Frontiers* (New York: Reynal and Hitchcock, 1934), esp. pp. 188–89.

[75]Schumpeter, *Business Cycles*, 2:944.

the hotels are bankrupt. Most apartments are empty. The great Rockefeller buildings, and the two theaters, are to close down." On March 2 he wrote, "The whole country seems close to a smash."[76]

The widespread defaults on U.S. private loans as well as the war debts, the collapse of financial institutions, and the severe economic depression led disillusioned investors to look back upon their exuberant foreign lending and investment in the 1920s as a grave error and to vow "never again." Herbert Feis later wrote: "The sense of duty to assist in the material improvement of other countries perished in the depths of American troubles and losses."[77] The rest of the world suffered greatly in consequence, and Germany was especially hard hit.

Black as conditions were in the trough of the depression, a few favorable developments must not be overlooked. U.S. mortality statistics showed substantial improvement in 1929–33.[78] Age-adjusted death rates and infant and maternal mortality rates, which are important if incomplete indicators of real levels of living, improved substantially among whites and nonwhites of both sexes. The life expectancy at birth of industrial workers, which had risen only slightly in the 1920s, rose significantly and steadily in the 1930s until in 1940 it was roughly the same as for the mass of the population.[79] There were also significant gains in education.[80] Americans who were fortunate enough to be employed, moreover, were able to take advantage of reduced prices of new household equipment and expanded their stock considerably,[81] and large consumer stocks of durable goods constituted important cushions against the impact of unemployment.

In Great Britain the depression was extremely severe, but the recent contraction was much smaller than in Germany and the United States, where employment dropped far more sharply from pre-contraction peaks of 1928 and 1929 and unemployment increases were much larger both absolutely and relatively.[82] The "depressed," "distressed," or "special" areas that had suffered in Britain's chronic depression in the 1920s were

[76]Nigel Nicolson, *Harold Nicolson*, 1:133, 140. The new president's inaugural address brought him high prestige and drastically improved the atmosphere. *Ibid.*, pp. 141–43.

[77]*Foreign Aid and Foreign Policy* (New York: St. Martin's Press, 1964), pp. 46–48.

[78]*Hist. Stat. U.S.*, ser. B 92–154, with rare exceptions. Hoover made this point at the time and later. Wilbur and Hyde, *Hoover Policies*, pp. 383, 389; Hoover, *Memoirs*, 3:152, 154–55.

[79]See also "Fifty Years of Health Progress" and "Progress in Longevity since 1850," in Metropolitan Life Insurance Company, *Statistical Bulletin*, January 1961, pp. 1–7; July 1963, pp. 1–3.

[80]*Hist. Stat. U.S.*, ser. H 223–32. The percentage of the population aged seventeen graduating from high school rose in the 1930s more markedly than in the 1920s.

[81]Detailed evidence for one city is shown in consumer surveys conducted by the *Milwaukee Journal*. G. D. A. MacDougall, in *Britain in Recovery* (London: Pitman, 1938), pp. 30–36, cited indications of more or less continuous expansion in every man's luxuries in 1929–37, and the same may well have been true in other countries.

[82]See LCES reports, e.g., in Royal Economic Society, *Memorandum 30*, April 1931, and later ones. This point was made by Schumpeter in 1939 (*Business Cycles*, 2:917–24, 927, 966), and is stressed in H. W. Richardson's *Economic Recovery in Britain 1932–39* (London:

hardest hit in 1930–33. There were some "hunger marches," but British workers seemed inured to depression and poverty, and neither social nor political revolt occurred. The number of insured persons unemployed was just under 3 million from August 1931 to January 1933, when the peak of 2.95 million was recorded in the incomplete figures.[83] Many of these, of course, shifted between employment and unemployment, but many were continuously out of work for one to five years. What was termed "the dole," provided for unemployed under sixty-five and relief of older persons, may have reduced individual incentives to hunt for jobs and to move to where jobs could be found, but it served to keep discontent from exploding into revolution. The British Fascist movement, born in 1926, became significant under Sir Oswald Mosley in 1931–32, and reached its "height of menace" in 1934, when the total membership was estimated at twenty thousand; but Britons were shocked by the brutality shown at the Olympia mass meeting on June 7, 1934, and the news of Hitler's bloody purge three weeks later ended hopes of large public support for the movement.[84]

Of profound importance to Britain in the critical years was the electrical industry. Construction of its "Grid" had begun in 1927, and it was pushed strongly under the Central Electricity Board in the worst slump years. It proved largely immune from the general depression, in contrast to the experience in Germany, France, and the United States. It contributed powerfully to the development of small industry and to improvement in levels of living in city and country alike.[85]

The British economy drive of 1931–33 brought to a standstill state-aided housebuilding under the Wheatley Act of 1924 and slum clearance under the Housing Act of 1930. Yet under private enterprise, with important aid from building societies, a housing boom got strongly under way in the fall of 1932. Low wage rates, low-cost imported materials, declining interest rates and eventually cheap credit, a whetted public appetite for better housing, and more efficient construction methods combined to make residential construction "the mainspring of Britain's recovery" in 1934–36.[86] Thanks to low-cost imports, most items of food supplies per head rose in 1929–32, some substantially. The number of workers in distributive

Weidenfeld and Nicolson, 1967), critically reviewed by R. R. Mitchell in *EJ*, March 1968, 78:129–30, and by William Woodruff in *AER*, March 1968, 58:251–53. Cf. Woytinsky, *Social Consequences of the Depression*, pp. 73–83, 308, 312–13, 315–22.

[83]According to *Britain in Recovery*, p. 95, the number out of work including uninsured persons may have been as high as 3,747,000 at its peak.

[84]C. L. Mowat, *Britain between the Wars, 1918–1940* (London: Methuen, 1955), pp. 294, 360–61, 473–75.

[85]Anon., "The Electrical Industry," *Britain in Recovery*, pp. 251–79; MacDougall, in *ibid.*, pp. 43, 63.

[86]See esp. Mowat, *Britain between the Wars*, pp. 176, 365, 432, 434, 470–75, 508–9; A. C. Bossom, in *Britain in Depression*, pp. 325–38; Sir Harold Bellman, in *Britain in Recovery*, pp. 395–437. Cf. Beveridge's comments on Apr. 28, 1933, in *Proc. Acad. Pol. Sci.*, June 1933, 15:408.

tasks rose every year. The cost of living index fell by 15 percent in 1929–32 while the index of wage rates fell only 5 percent, implying no small gain in real wages.

Despite widespread distress due to unemployment and inadequate mitigation of the plight of the poor, Britain seemed to close observers to be weathering the depression better than most other countries; but at the time there were no trustworthy indexes of those levels of living about which Keynes and others spoke with assurance.[87] There were "two Englands," one persistently and severely depressed, the other thriving. But the upward trend in the *Economist's* index of consuming power of the working class for 1924–37 showed its worst break in 1926, the year of the coal strike, a mere slowing in 1927–32, and strong gains in 1933–37.[88] The possession of radios, telephones, private cars, houses, and other durable consumer goods expanded almost continuously in the depression years, as prices dropped and real wages of the employed rose.[89]

Einzig, after surveying the worldwide economic crisis in 1932, called it the worst in modern history and said that the losses it had inflicted were far greater than in any previous one; but he added: "The sufferings inflicted upon mankind are less severe. . . . Even in Germany, with its unemployment of over four millions, the average citizen is not suffering physically to the same extent as he was in 1923, when industries enjoyed apparent prosperity due to inflation." The depreciation of "fictitious wealth" in the contraction was less than "the wholesale destruction of fictitious wealth caused by post-war inflation."[90]

But in Germany the growth of extremism was the "byproduct of the slump." The distress and bitterness of the populace, and especially of young people, was skillfully played upon by the Nazis. The downfall of the Weimar Republic began in May 1932, when a palace revolution engineered the replacement of Chancellor Brüning by Franz von Papen, a charming but irresponsible politician.[91] Its death knell was sounded when Hitler came to power eight months later.

Disillusionment and Rampant Pessimism, 1932–33   The wholly unexpected descent of the United States, the mightiest world power, from a pinnacle of prosperity in 1929 to the depths of depres-

---

[87]E.g., Keynes and Clay, speaking early in 1932, said that "even today Great Britain is decidedly the most prosperous country in the world. . . . We are . . . better off than any other country in the world compared with a couple of years ago." Salter et al., *World's Economic Crisis*, pp. 80, 145.

[88]*Economist*, Jan. 1, 1938, pp. 13–14; MacDougall, in *Britain in Recovery*, pp. 26–28, 33.

[89]MacDougall, in *Britain in Recovery*, pp. 34–35.

[90]*The World Economic Crisis, 1929–31*, 2d ed. (London: Macmillan, 1932; preface dated December 1931), pp. 82–83; cf. *ibid.*, 1st ed. (1931), pp. 69–70.

[91]Hodson, *Slump and Recovery*, p. 62; M. J. Bonn, *Wandering Scholar* (New York: John Day, 1948), pp. 336–37.

sion in 1932–33 was a terrifying spectacle long and painfully observed. In the aftermath of the great boom, some sober thinkers as well as irresponsible writers termed the recent prosperity "illusory," "sham," or "phony." This it was not; it was real, if very uneven and often exaggerated. Truly illusory, however, were the widespread convictions that it would persist indefinitely with only minor setbacks; that the economy was so strong and well-balanced that it could withstand all prospective shocks and strains; and that great economic resources, a huge gold stock, a strong Federal Reserve System, and the experience, wisdom, and determination of President Hoover gave ample assurance against economic disasters. The convincing exposure of these illusions[92] in 1929–32, in this country and abroad, was a shattering experience;[93] and it gave rise to extreme pessimism that helped to deepen and prolong the depression, as excessive optimism had enlarged and prolonged the preceding boom.[94]

The disillusionment began late in 1929, increased in 1930, reached a high in 1931,[95] and kept growing worse. Writing in the spring of 1931, Einzig commented on the abrupt reversal of public sentiment from the pre-slump conviction that "prosperity . . . could go on increasing for ever" to the post-slump impression that "the present crisis . . . will go on for ever." Writing late in 1931, he amended this sentence by adding "and will result in a complete collapse of civilization, the establishment of Soviet Republics all over the world, or at least a permanent reduction in the standard of living."[96] As early as September 8, 1931, Lippmann wrote that "we are in the midst, not of an ordinary trade depression, but of one of the great upheavals and readjustments of modern history."[97] Time and again it appeared that conditions were so bad that they could not get worse, but they did. Each winter from 1930 to 1933 was worse than the one before it.

M. J. Bonn's *Prosperity: Myth and Reality in American Economic Life* was published in German and English editions in the fall of 1931, and Harold J. Laski promptly acclaimed it as "the wisest book on America that

[92]In his letter to his wife on Apr. 18, 1932 (quoted above, p. 11), Wesley Mitchell used the term "delusion."

[93]On his visit to Japan in 1934, President Garfield of Williams College was impressed by the statements of Count Kabayama Aisuke of the House of Peers, to the effect that the world war shook Japanese faith in Europe, and that the 1929 crash shattered their belief that the United States was "the dominating force in the world." H. A. Garfield, *Lost Visions* (privately printed, 1944), pp. 91–92.

[94]"The present pessimistic view of an everlasting depression is unjustifiably responsible for the accentuation and prolongation of the crisis . . . There can be little doubt that the crisis is due more to psychological than to material causes." Einzig, *World Economic Crisis*, 1st ed., p. 69, and *ibid.*, 2d ed., pp. 81, 86.

[95]William Miller, in *A New History of the United States* (New York: Braziller, 1958), spoke of "the famine, fear, and futility astride the prostrate United States in 1931" (p. 371). There was no famine, and fear, a sense of futility, and frustration did not reach their climax until 1932–33, when they were increased by political propaganda.

[96]*World Economic Crisis*, 1st ed., p. 69, and *ibid.*, 2d ed., p. 81.

[97]*Interpretations, 1931–1932*, p. 5.

has been published in many years. . . . No one since Tocqueville has written with greater insight."[98] In his introduction to the American edition, with the title altered to *The Crisis of Capitalism in America*, George S. Counts went beyond Bonn in referring to our "pathological form of prosperity" which was "built on economic sands," but said: "We are witnessing today, not just another economic depression, but a crisis of private capitalism in America."[99] Bonn himself had entitled his sixth chapter "The Crisis of Capitalism," and ended the preceding chapter thus: "The crisis of economic policy may very easily become a crisis of the economic system."

The inordinate respect and admiration for big businessmen and financiers which had reached its zenith in 1929 was gravely eroded in 1929-30 and all but vanished in 1931-33, as one after another impressive figure "bit the dust."[100] This was true not only of those who were adjudged (by their fellow men, if not by the courts) guilty of criminal conduct, egregious misjudgments, or both, such as Clarence Hatry, Ivar Kreuger, Samuel Insull, and Charles E. Mitchell, but also of many others whose integrity was never impugned, such as Owen D. Young, Montagu Norman, and Herbert Hoover. Doubtless Keynes had some following in castigating bankers as "by nature blind," hopelessly stupid, with obsolete ideas, "bent on suicide."[101] In fact, bankers were only among the many who failed to foresee the seriousness of the economic contraction of 1929-31, displayed mistaken optimism in 1929-30, and lost standing in consequence.

It is hard to overstate the profound and far-reaching distrust of businessmen, financiers, economists, forecasters, and statesmen which pervaded this country and others in the depths of the depression. The former idols had all proved to have clay feet. Whom could one trust? For the time, the answer seemed to be: "You can't never trust nobody nohow." Thus the stage was set for the rise of charismatic political leaders who, claiming to have the secret of salvation for the masses, could win and hold the confidence of electorates. The public mood was such that bold or even rash experimentation was welcome, though the new leaders often paid lip service to orthodox objectives such as "sound money" and "balanced budgets."

Despite assurances that were repeatedly violated, the Japanese military expansion in Manchuria continued. Secretary Stimson's efforts to get British support for his strong protest to the Japanese government on January 7, 1932, were rebuffed by Foreign Secretary Sir John Simon. By mid-January Japan had won complete military and diplomatic success. After China refused demands for dissolution of Chinese associations that were

---

[98] *New Statesman and Nation*, Dec. 26, 1931, p. 877.
[99] Published in New York by John Day in 1933.
[100] Cf. Einzig, *World Economic Crisis*, ch. 10, "The Moral Factor."
[101] E.g., see *Essays in Persuasion*, pp. 176, 178. In his Halley Stewart lecture early in 1932 Keynes substantially moderated this view. Salter et al., *World's Economic Crisis*, pp. 87-88.

enforcing an effective boycott of Japanese goods, Japanese marines were landed north of the International Settlement at Shanghai on January 28. When the Chinese Third Route Army offered unexpectedly stubborn resistance, the Japanese bombed the area. This aroused world opinion against Japan and brought a degree of cooperation from the British Foreign Office, and after a truce arranged on May 5 Japanese forces were withdrawn from occupied areas north of Shanghai. A British draft of a policy of nonrecognition of Japanese takeovers was adopted by the League Council on February 18 and endorsed by the Assembly on March 11. Two days earlier Japan established the puppet state of Manchukuo and formally recognized it on September 15. The Lytton commission report, published on October 2, expressed sympathy for Japanese grievances in Manchuria but condemned the Japanese moves, refused to accept Manchukuo's independence, and proposed for Manchuria an autonomous regime under Chinese sovereignty. After long delay, the League Council adopted the report in full on February 24, 1933. A month later, Japan gave notice of her withdrawal from the League. None of the leading powers was willing to reinforce moral disapproval with economic sanctions or military force.[102]

One by one the international institutions built and agreements concluded since the end of 1918 failed in 1931-34. Nations were spending on arms sums exceeding $4 billion a year.[103] Viscount Robert Cecil wholeheartedly endorsed President Hoover's repeated assertions that restoration of world confidence depended chiefly on the success of the World Disarmament Conference. Convened in Geneva on February 2, 1932, this "dragged wearily along its ineffective life" until June 1934.[104] The Kellogg-Briand Pact to outlaw war, signed in August 1928 with many explicit and implicit reservations, and joined later by more nations, soon proved a toothless failure. The League of Nations became virtually impotent not only to check aggressions and ensure peaceful settlement of threats to war, but even to promote international solution of pressing economic problems.

Currency rehabilitation broke down under the strain of the economic contraction. The Bank of England, the sheet anchor of monetary stability, gave way. The BIS proved a weak reed instead of a powerful bulwark. The

[102]Stimson and Bundy, *On Active Service*, pp. 253-63; Mowat, *Britain between the Wars*, pp. 420-22.

[103]Viscount Cecil, "Facing the World Disarmament Conference," *Foreign Affairs*, October 1931, pp. 13-22, esp. pp. 15, 17.

[104]Stimson and Bundy, *On Active Service*, ch. 10, "The Tragedy of Timidity"; Mowat, *Britain between the Wars*, pp. 423-26; Macmillan, *Winds of Change*, pp. 269, 352-59; Arnold A. Offner, *American Appeasement: United States Foreign Policy and Germany, 1933-1938* (Cambridge, Mass.: Harvard University Press, 1969), pp. 20-53, 58, 73, 298. For perspective see Donald R. Brennan, ed., *Arms Control, Disarmament, and National Security* (New York: Braziller, 1961), pp. 13-15 (Jerome Wiesner), 19-21 (Brennan), 68-70 (William R. Frye), and 446-50 (Jules Moch).

promising Young Plan for a "final settlement" of the supremely vexing reparations problem was an early victim of the depression, and its demise was recognized in the Lausanne Agreement of July 1932. The war debt problems were not really solved when payments came to a graceless end in 1932–33, leaving a residue of international bitterness.[105]

In the spring of 1932 Sir Josiah Stamp, addressing a New York audience, noted that in the past year or two there had been a great loss of confidence in the institutions of government, finance, and education, in men previously considered infallible, and in slogans.[106] In the face of the sorry spectacles in many countries, people sourly recalled the wartime slogans "a war to end war," "make the world safe for democracy," and "a nation fit for heroes to live in," and the discredited peacetime slogans "world disarmament," "collective security," "renouncement of war as a national policy," and "safe as the Bank of England." The vision of a "United States of Europe," which even Montagu Norman found appealing, proved a vain dream.[107]

Narrowly nationalist trade policies reinforced the economic contraction, shrinking international trade drastically; and when the "strangulation of trade had progressed so far that a return to free trade seemed impossible,"[108] even Great Britain, long the satisfied exponent of relatively free trade, finally joined the protectionist circle. National policies of many kinds were strikingly discordant, and international reconciliation of them was proving impossible.

Intellectual leaders in private and public life were all at sea; their diagnoses were divergent, and most of their prescriptions were impossible for political leaders to accept and implement. Business and economic forecasting, in which high hopes had been reposed, was utterly discredited.[109]

Under these circumstances it is no wonder that the Great Depression revived the despairing pessimism that had followed the Great War. As early as August 12, 1931, Keynes privately expressed extreme views: a general breakdown was inevitable; the United States would revert to "a Texas type of civilisation"; France and Germany would go to war; Russia

[105]Wilbur and Hyde, *Hoover Policies*, pp. 513–23; Hoover, *Memoirs*, 3:171–73, 178–91.

[106]Sir Josiah Stamp, "Control or Fate in Economic Affairs," Apr. 13, 1932, in *Proc. Acad. Pol. Sci.*, May 1932, 15:123–40, esp. p. 130. Stamp added, "heaven help America when she loses faith in slogans!"

[107]Edouard Herriot, *The United States of Europe*, trans. R. J. Dingle (New York: Viking, 1930), reviewed by Harry D. Gideonse in *JPE*, June 1931, 29:417–18; Sir Henry Clay, *Lord Norman* (London: Macmillan, 1957), p. 232. For a sober summary of the abysmal attitudes in Great Britain in the trough of the depression, see Macmillan, *Winds of Change*, pp. 266–68, 273–79.

[108]See William Orton's paper and B. H. Beckhart's discussion, Apr. 13, 1932, in *Proc. Acad. Pol. Sci.*, May 1932, 15:27–37.

[109]See Chapter 15, n. 24, below.

would starve; and the British, though impoverished, might just survive. On December 11 his pessimism was slightly modified, but his predictions were no less wild.[110]

Early in 1932 Keynes gloomily painted the prospect of preventing "an almost complete collapse of the financial structure of modern capitalism." He found grounds for hope chiefly in the "remarkable capacity of the system to take punishment," as in the United States and Germany. He no longer felt that a cheap money policy would suffice, and urged that Britain set the example of boldness in promoting and subsidizing new investment.[111] Actually, timidity rather than boldness characterized Great Britain's course in 1931-37, not only in the economic sphere but also, and more markedly, in meeting the drift toward another great war; and it was Hitler who conspicuously displayed boldness.

Blackett, following Keynes, went so far as to say that "modern civilization finds itself on the brink of chaos owing to the inability of human beings to manage the machine they have brought into being." He plumped for "conscious cooperative planning" as "an unavoidable necessity if we are to save the economic structure . . . from disaster, . . . steering a wise course between tyrannous compulsion and anarchic individualism."[112]

Salter's able and justly popular book *Recovery: The Second Effort*, published soon after the Halley Stewart lectures ended, gave an excellent comprehensive analysis in good perspective. It concluded with a program of action which began with an extremely sober sketch of "The Task of 1932." He predicted default on most private and public debts, for lack of timely actions; thought it likely that "we shall touch bottom sometime, and the upward turn will come"; but he noted that the bottom had "unhappily lost its upward resiliency" and saw the possibility that "before recovery comes there will be revolution and social disintegration" with cataclysmic consequences.[113]

Lippmann's column of July 22, 1932, opened: "In the past ten years there has appeared a large literature prophesying the end of our civilization." In the wake of economic and financial breakdowns he saw "a vast disillusionment not only with the existing order but with its idealism over liberty, democracy, nationalism, and progress . . . the things which the pre-war generation held to be the most precious of motivations."[114]

---

[110]Nicolson, *Harold Nicolson*, pp. 87, 98.

[111]Salter et al., *World's Economic Crisis*, pp. 71-88.

[112]*Ibid.*, pp. 91, 98-99. In his earlier lecture in this series, Salter insisted that, despite the bleak outlook, the problems were "essentially capable of human solution." *Ibid.*, p. 39. Cf. also Clay, in *ibid.*, pp. 117-58.

[113]*Recovery*, pp. 326-46.

[114]Lippmann, *Interpretations, 1931-1932*, pp. 334-37. He went on to stress the "purgative effects of a great depression."

In campaign addresses in September and October 1932, Roosevelt conveyed the impression that America had reached a sort of limit to its development, and that it faced the tasks of adjusting production to consumption, and distributing wealth more equitably, rather than discovering and exploiting natural resources and producing more goods. Hoover vainly challenged this as a "counsel of despair."[115] But in the later 1930s, as the U.S. depression proved obstinately resistant to forces of recovery and population growth appeared to be approaching an end, the doctrine of "secular stagnation" won prominent adherents for a time.[116]

An experienced agricultural economist concluded his intimate account of U.S. agriculture and agropolitics in 1921-34, replete with episodes of violence in the worst years, by saying, "at the time it seemed that things had gone to the very verge of chaos."[117] An outstanding U.S. economist wrote in the trough of the depression: "The peculiarly grave and threatening character of the present emergency needs no proof. As to how close it has brought us to a complete collapse of our economic system economists, like others, can only conjecture."[118] The reputable authors of a significant book published as late as 1937 quoted from Clark, and from T. E. Gregory's gloomy statement of 1921, and went on:

Certainly ours is a weary and disillusioned generation. The tragedies of the War and the sufferings and disappointments of subsequent years have left the occidental world cynical and despairing. Old ideals, old values, old institutions, old faiths—all have crumbled, leaving stretches of barren wastes all too receptive to the seeds scattered so freely by economic charlatans and political medicine-men. Partial economic disintegration has been accompanied by the collapse of democratic governments. With the remaining ruins as foundations, with a frantic energy born of despair, no inconsiderable fraction of mankind has set about attempting to construct new shelters in the form of totalitarian states, to be entrusted to the custodianship of authoritarian dictators.[119]

And Schumpeter wrote in 1939: "Capitalism and its civilization may be decaying, shading off into something else, or tottering toward a violent death. The writer personally thinks they are."[120]

---

[115]Hoover, Memoirs, 3:243-44, 251-52.

[116]Anderson, Economics and the Public Welfare, pp. 497-500; R. A. Gordon, Business Fluctuations, 2d ed. (New York: Harper, 1961), pp. 447-49.

[117]Genung, Agricultural Depression, p. 141.

[118]J. M. Clark, Strategic Factors in Business Cycles (New York: NBER, 1935; introduction dated November 1933), p. 4.

[119]Phillips, McManus, and Nelson, Banking and the Business Cycle, pp. 1-2.

[120]Schumpeter, Business Cycles, 2:908. He went on, however: "But the world crisis does not prove it and has, in fact, nothing to do with it. It was not a symptom of a weakening or a failure of the system. If anything, it was a proof of the vigor of capitalist evolution to which it was—substantially—the temporary reaction."

In the last chapter of his *Great Depression*, published in mid-1934, Lionel Robbins went so far as to say: "The basis of recovery in the United States is gravely jeopardised by the policy of the Government. The conditions under which the dollar has been stabilised may lead to an inflation there, or most severe difficulties, financial and political, in continental Europe. There is danger of war and civil disturbance." He found "the prospects of enduring recovery . . . not bright." Even if the next few years should be "years of comparative revival . . . it is impossible to feel any confidence in the continuance of stability. . . . The probability of peace and progress in the next half-century is not very great. . . . The tendencies making for instability . . . have been strengthened." While Robbins was unwilling to despair, his outlook was the gloomier because he felt convinced that "men of intellect and good will" had gradually persuaded their fellows of the virtues of socialistic ideas and monetary policies which he considered tragically wrong.

Several of those whose gloomy opinions have been mentioned retained their basic confidence in a bright future for their country and even the human race. Keynes, Lippmann, Noyes, and Salter were among these. But I have not found that any one at that time quoted Adam Smith's calm response to his friend Sinclair, who, after Burgoyne's surrender in 1777, thought Britain about to be ruined: "Be assured, my young friend, there is a great deal of ruin in a nation."[121]

[121]Quoted by Charles F. Bastable, in *Journal of the Royal Statistical Society*, December 1894, 57:626, quoting Sinclair's *Memoirs*, 1:87.

CHAPTER 12

UNCOORDINATED ECONOMIC RECOVERY AND GRADUAL DRIFT TOWARD WORLD WAR II, 1933–39

FOR THE PURPOSES of this book it is unnecessary to discuss at length the erratic and uncoordinated progress out of severe depression in the highly complex period 1933–39, when the militarists were dominant in Japan, Hitler in Germany, Mussolini in Italy, Stalin in the USSR, Stanley Baldwin and Neville Chamberlain in Great Britain, and Roosevelt in the United States. The personalities and moves of these very different men interacted with impersonal forces to shape the history of this fateful period.[1] But it seems essential to set forth many highlights of the tangled course of events.

Disappointing   For most countries the vicious spiral of **International Cooperation** economic contraction and price deflation ended in mid-1932, with low points typically reached in June-August, but the depression trough lasted well into 1933,[2] which brought a whole series of alarming events. The surprisingly successful Lausanne conference in June-July 1932 seemed to mark a major turning point, but early expectations were soon disappointed. The agreement on July 9 to end reparation payments (suspended by the Hoover moratorium of a year earlier) was contingent on U.S. governmental action on interallied debts; since no such move was made, the agreement was never formally ratified.[3] Nevertheless, as most payments soon ended and the creditors did not press their

---

[1]See Sir Arthur Salter, *Personality in Politics: Studies of Contemporary Statesmen* (London: Faber, 1947), esp. p. 18, and his earlier book, *Security: Can we Retrieve It?* (New York: Reynal and Hitchcock, 1939); Bruce Bliven, *The World Changers* (New York: John Day, 1965); and Harold Macmillan, *Winds of Change, 1914–1939* (New York: Harper and Row, 1966). This installment of Macmillan's memoirs is of value throughout this chapter.

[2]CTC, *Bus. Bull.*, June 15, 1933; Robert A. Gordon, *Business Fluctuations*, 2d ed. (New York: Harper, 1961), pp. 642–44, and sources therein cited.

[3]Walter Lippmann, *Interpretations, 1931–1932* (New York: Macmillan, 1932), pp. 147–86 (his column of June 24, 1932, was enthusiastic); J. W. Wheeler-Bennett, *The Wreck of Reparations: Being the Political Background of the Lausanne Agreement 1932* (New York: William Morrow, 1933), including apps. 1 and 2; BIS, *Third Annual Report*, May 8, 1933, p. 6; H. V. Hodson, *Slump and Recovery, 1929–1937* (London: Oxford University Press, 1938), pp. 138–45, 172; C. W. Guillebaud, *The Economic Recovery of Germany from 1933 to the Incorporation of Austria in March 1938* (London: Macmillan, 1939), pp. 30–31; Herbert Hoover, *The Memoirs of Herbert Hoover*, vol. 3: *The Great Depression, 1929–1941* (New York: Macmil-

claims, these thorny problems ceased to bedevil international relations as they had in most of the previous years since the war. The alleged world shortage of gold, which some had blamed for the financial crises of 1929–31, vanished in the next few years, as India disgorged huge quantities of her hoards and gold production rose sharply under the stimulus of falling costs of gold mining.[4]

For several months hopes centered on the League-sponsored World Monetary and Economic Conference agreed upon at Lausanne. After unfortunate politically necessitated postponements, this was finally held in London from June 12 to July 27, 1933.[5] In the course of painstaking preparations, Hitler had become chancellor of Germany (January 30, 1933) and Roosevelt president of the United States (March 4). By a series of steps in March-May President Roosevelt had deliberately taken the country off the gold standard, though it was not until January 31, 1934, that the official price of gold was raised by presidential proclamation from $20.67 to $35 per fine ounce.[6] Deep disagreements insured the wreck of the conference. To this outcome Roosevelt contributed decisively by rejecting (July 3) a declaration on currency stabilization which had been based on a resolution, drafted with the aid of the U.S. delegation in line with a Roosevelt message circulated on May 16, and introduced by one of its members.[7] The

lan, 1952), pp. 171-73, 178-91; and William McElwee, *Britain's Locust Years, 1918-1940* (London: Faber, 1962), pp. 204-6. McElwee called the Lausanne conference "a failure," and the disarmament conference "the most important failure" of 1933, *Ibid*, pp. 206 9.

[4]G. Findlay Shirras, in A. D. Gayer, ed., *Lessons of Monetary Experience; Essays in Honor of Irving Fisher* (New York: Farrar and Rinehart, 1937), pp. 328-45, esp. pp. 332-34; interim and final reports of the League of Nations Gold Delegation, 1930-32; and BIS, *Annual Report*, esp. the tenth, May 27, 1940, pp. 66-71.

[5]Hodson, *Slump and Recovery*, ch. 6, pp. 172-206; M. J. Bonn, *Wandering Scholar* (New York: John Day, 1948), pp. 323-26.

[6]Lionel Robbins, in *The Great Depression* (London: Macmillan, 1934), adverted to "the incredible confusion into which the world has been thrown by the exchange policy of the United States" in 1933 34 (p. 164). Cf. Joseph A. Schumpeter, *Business Cycles: A Theoretical, Historical, and Statistical Analysis of the Capitalist Process*, 2 vols. (New York: McGraw-Hill, 1939), 2:996-98.

[7]Hodson, *Slump and Recovery*, pp. 205-6. Salter's later comment was: "It may be, of course, that the Conference would have failed in any case, but as it is the responsibility for its failure clearly rests with this decision." *Personality in Politics*, pp. 180-81. In a valuable paper, "The Foreign Exchanges, 1932-1937," in *Britain in Recovery* (London: Pitman, 1938), pp. 149-50, N. F. Hall conceded that while "American monetary experiments . . . wrecked the World Conference, . . . London overplayed its hand during the period of Washington's impotence and must share with the new administration the responsibility for the break-down of the World Conference and subsequent difficulties which are resulting from the high price for gold which was adopted by the American administration at the end of January, 1934."

In his second volume of *The Age of Roosevelt, The Coming of the New Deal* (Boston: Houghton Mifflin, 1959), A. M. Schlesinger, Jr., included two chapters (12 and 13) dealing with this conference. The American part of the story is a shabby one, from the appointment of the mostly ill-qualified delegation to the end. Though not dissatisfied with the negative outcome, Schlesinger aptly said (p. 229): "Unquestionably, Roosevelt's day-to-day management of American policy at the Conference was deplorable."

principal positive products of the conference, Senator Key Pittman's silver resolutions and a committee recommendation for commodity control moves, were of minor significance.[8]

This new blow to the prestige and influence of the League of Nations ended serious efforts toward general international cooperation "to bring order out of the fast developing nationalistic chaos."[9] Dr. Schacht, again president of the Reichsbank, asserted at the conference: "International co-operation cannot become a practical reality unless countries stop relying upon the help of others and start to do their utmost to master the economic crisis by their own endeavours."[10] By choice or by necessity, thereafter, individual nations made their moves in divergent ways, for the most part regardless of their effects on other countries, and international currency disorders kept plaguing world trade.

In the 1920s, under the lead of Governor Norman of the Bank of England and Governor Strong of the Federal Reserve Bank of New York, an increasing amount of cooperation among central reserve banks had developed without formal meetings of their heads. With encouragement from national governments, these contacts had facilitated widespread currency rehabilitation and the general establishment of the gold exchange standard.[11] This movement culminated in the opening of the Bank for International Settlements in May 1930 at Basel, as provided in the Young Plan for settlement of German reparations. Unfortunately, the hopes and expectations that this rehabilitation would pave the way for world eco-

An excellent account by a participant is given in Herbert Feis, *1933: Characters in Crisis* (Boston: Little Brown, 1966), pt. 3, pp. 169-258. See also Milton Friedman and Anna J. Schwartz, *A Monetary History of the United States, 1867-1960* (Princeton, N.J.: Princeton University Press, 1963), p. 469; Mowat, *Britain between the Wars, 1918-1940* (London: Methuen, 1955), pp. 440-41; Macmillan, *Winds of Change*, pp. 270-71. Cf. also Arnold A. Offner, *American Appeasement: United States Foreign Policy and Germany, 1933-1938* (Cambridge, Mass.: Harvard University Press, 1969), pp. 37-42, 299.

[8]Hodson, *Slump and Recovery*, pp. 199-203, 230-65, 447-67. Pittman introduced the silver resolutions, but they were "largely formulated and advocated by Sir George Schuster, then Finance Member of the Executive Council of the Viceroy of India" (p. 202n). In response to strong political pressures to "do something for silver," the United States had already made with Great Britain the "London Silver Agreement," which expired at the end of 1937, and soon passed the Silver Purchase Act of 1934, under which the U.S. Treasury bought domestic silver at above market prices and silver mined abroad at Treasury-fixed prices. Cf. Schlesinger, *Coming of the New Deal*, pp. 248-52.

[9]B M. Anderson, *Economics and the Public Welfare: Financial and Economic History of the United States, 1914-1946* (New York: Van Nostrand, 1949), ch. 72; J. B. Condliffe, *The Commerce of Nations* (New York: Norton, 1950), p. 497.

[10]Quoted in Hodson, *Slump and Reocvery*, p. 205. Cf. Hjalmar Schacht, *Confessions of "The Old Wizard"* (Boston: Houghton Mifflin, 1956), ch. 40. In his book *The British Economy, 1920-1957* (Cambridge, Mass.: Harvard University Press, 1960), p. 120, A. J. Youngson said that the conference "foundered largely on President Roosevelt's unexpected insistence that for each country improvement must begin at home."

[11]See R. H. Meyer, *Bankers' Diplomacy: Monetary Stabilization in the Twenties* (New York: Columbia University Press, 1970).

nomic stability were soon dashed. Einzig later wrote that, "given the circumstances in which the currencies were stabilized between 1925 and 1929, a crisis of first-rate gravity was a mere question of time."[12]

In mid-November 1929, Sprague had rightly asserted that postwar conditions required still more cooperation among, and more conscious efforts by, central banks and "the adoption of concerted policies based upon intelligent foresight and adopted well in advance of the appearance of emergencies."[13] The breakdown of the gold exchange standard under the stress of economic contraction and the financial crises of 1931 prevented such cooperation.[14] After the British suspended gold payments in September 1931, the Bank of England was eclipsed by the various chancellors of the Exchequer, Governor Norman's influence was gravely curtailed, the BIS failed to mature into major significance, and international financial cooperation shrank rather than expanded.[15] Contributing to this end were the illness and death of Governor Strong in 1928, the subsequent weakening of the influence of the Federal Reserve Bank of New York, and the shift of the center of financial power from New York to Washington under the New Deal.

After Great Britain went off gold without specific devaluation, many countries chose to follow suit and link their currencies to sterling—several promptly and others (e.g., Greece, Turkey, and South Africa) after more or less delay. In several continental European countries the bitter experience with hyperinflation in the early and middle 1920s had left a legacy of determination to avoid a repetition. Deflation seemed far more tolerable, and devaluation was popularly identified with inflation.[16] When efforts to arrive at fresh currency stabilization failed at the World Conference of mid-1933, and the Roosevelt administration chose to go it alone, a few European countries stubbornly resisted devaluation.[17] What was loosely termed the "gold bloc" was led by France, with her huge gold reserve. "Defense" of their gold-based currencies entailed serious deflationary measures, with increased unemployment. These moves took a variety of forms: cuts in public expenditures, including those on public works and unemployment

---

[12]*World Finance, 1914-1935* (New York: Macmillan, 1935; preface dated April 1935), p. vi et passim. For Schumpeter's similar opinion, see his *Business Cycles*, 2:910.

[13]O. M. W. Sprague, "The Working of the Gold Standard under Present Conditions," Nov. 14, 1929, *Proc. Acad. Pol. Sci.*, January 1930, 13:524-30.

[14]Cf. Eleanor L. Dulles, *The Bank for International Settlements at Work* (New York: Macmillan, 1932), chs. 16-17; and Meyer, *Bankers' Diplomacy*, esp. ch. 7.

[15]N. F. Hall, writing in November 1937 in *Britain in Recovery*, pp. 149-61.

[16]League of Nations, *International Currency Experience* (Geneva: League of Nations, 1934), esp. pp. 11, 23-26, 167, 220-21. Alexander Loveday, Salter's successor in the League's senior staff, wrote a penetrating paper, "Collective Behavior and Monetary Policy," in Gayer, *Lessons of Monetary Experience*, pp. 425-39, esp. pp. 427-28.

[17]See various writings of Paul Einzig, especially his *World Finance, 1935-1937* (London: Macmillan, 1937; preface dated March 1937), and Hodson, *Slump and Recovery*, passim.

relief; reduced wage rates for public and private employees; increased tax rates; and restrictions on imports and subsidization of exports. Devaluations lightened the burden of public and private debts, thus favoring debtors at the expense of creditors. Public opinion, nevertheless, typically opposed devaluation, yet everywhere accepted it calmly when it eventually came. .

Restrictions on the transfer of funds from Germany under the standstill agreements of 1931-32, by the Hitler regime after 1932, and by other countries under various schemes embarrassed banks and other creditors in the financially stronger countries—including Switzerland, an important international banking center. The relative overvaluation of the Swiss franc rendered its banks vulnerable and also cut into the important tourist business, but devaluation was strongly resisted. Belgium, technically the weakest member of the gold bloc, was the first important one to desert it, on March 30, 1935, under the courageous banker Premier Paul van Zeeland.[18] About this time Italy adopted drastic exchange restrictions and the lira was allowed to depreciate gradually, though formal devaluation was deferred until October 1936. Poland had devalued early in 1936. France, after desperate struggles, finally devalued late in September 1936, with the aid of a flimsy tripartite agreement with Britain and the United States and the complementary three-power pact of October 12.[19] The Netherlands and Switzerland soon followed, in order to avoid prompt depletion of their gold reserves. Germany, never a member of the gold bloc, experienced disguised currency depreciation but resisted formal devaluation and refused to align her currency with that of any other country.[20]

Toward mid-1934 Robbins wrote: "If democracy goes by the board altogether, among the chief States of Continental Europe, the chaos of international exchanges since 1931, although by no means the only cause, will have played a not unimportant rôle in bringing about the disaster."[21] The Financial Committee of the League reported to the Council on September 22, 1936, that the disparity between internal and external currency values was the greatest obstacle to worldwide recovery.[22] Some improvement followed the demise of the gold bloc. Writing early in 1937, Einzig rashly said that "by the end of 1936 there was *de facto* stability practically all over the civilized world." But he rightly added that "this almost uni-

---

[18]Einzig, *World Finance, 1935-1937*, chs. 6, 11, 37, 41. In *ibid.*, chs. 4, 16, Einzig rated the devaluation of the Belgian belga ("which marked the beginning of the death struggle of the Gold Bloc") with the unpegging of the Allied exchanges in 1919, the British return to the gold standard in 1925, the stabilization of the franc in 1927-28, and the suspension of the gold standard in Britain in 1931 and in the United States in 1933 ("turning the international tide") as outstanding monetary events of the interwar period.

[19]*Ibid.*, chs. 5-14, 20, 23-44; Hodson, *Slump and Recovery*, chs. 10-11.

[20]Einzig, *World Finance, 1935-1937*, chs. 18, 40-41.

[21]*Great Depression*, p. 163.

[22]Hodson, *Slump and Recovery*, p. 413.

versal stability . . . covers a state of disequilibrium."[23] In 1937–38 there occurred a series of gold and dollar scares; these gave rise to renewed hoarding of gold in Europe and America, and heavy speculative international movements of funds, in the course of which a number of reputable experts lost their reputations. The French franc was again twice devalued, in June 1937 and in May 1938—in too small doses and spread over too long a period; and successive crises of the franc coincided with cabinet crises.[24] Interventions by central banks and exchange stabilization funds then brought a degree of stability in international exchange rates up to mid-August 1939, when the imminence of war caused a general breakdown.[25]

In short, nothing like normal relations between devalued currencies and price levels had been achieved when World War II opened with the German blitzkrieg on Poland on September 1, 1939. With pardonable exaggeration, Salter wrote in 1939: "The history of post-war Europe could almost be written in terms of currency depreciation and deflation."[26] Time and again, in each of the countries of Western Europe, fateful decisions were made, or wise decisions were delayed or prevented, under pressures arising in part from currency disorders. The most serious such events were the paralysis of British policy when Japan invaded Manchuria in September 1931 and the failure of France to take military action when Germany reoccupied the Rhineland in March 1936.[27] Tensions and uncertainties over the international political situation and outlook rendered hopeless the achievement of monetary stability.

After the defaultless record of foreign loans in the 1920s, the first half of the 1930s registered a record number of defaults. By 1935, more than one-third of all outstanding foreign bonds were in default, though one later comprehensive investigation found satisfaction in the fact that interest was paid in full throughout the period 1930–35 despite the severity of the depression.[28]

---

[23] *World Finance, 1935–1937*, p. 309; but cf. averages of daily rates in London in LCES, "Report on Current Economic Conditions," Royal Economic Society, *Memorandum 80*, September 1939, p. 26; New York rates in *Fed. Res. Bull.*

[24] BIS, *Eighth Annual Report*, May 9, 1938, pp. 37–38, 44–63, 78–81, and *Ninth*, May 8, 1939, p. 5; and Paul Einzig, *World Finance, 1938–1939* (London: Kegan Paul, 1939; preface dated March 1939), chs. 4, 7, 9, 17, 36.

[25] BIS, *Tenth Annual Report*, May 27, 1940, p. 18 et passim.

[26] *Security*, p. 152.

[27] Churchill, *The Second World War*, vol. 1: *The Gathering Storm* (Boston: Houghton Mifflin, 1948), ch. 11; Einzig, *World Finance, 1935–1937*, ch. 24; *ibid., 1938–1939*, esp. chs. 40–41; Mowat, *Britain between the Wars*, pp. 419–22, 563–65.

[28] Ilse Mintz, *Deterioration in the Quality of Foreign Bonds Issued in the United States, 1920–1930* (New York: NBER, 1951), esp. pp. 2, 30–31, 42–44. Mintz constructed a "default index" to measure the impact of changing conditions in the 1920s on the "quality" of new issues of foreign bonds in this country, viewed according to their status at the end of 1937. See also J. T. Madden, Marcus Nadler, and Harry Sauvain, *America's Experience as a Cred-*

On the world scene, the drastic fall of commodity prices in 1929–33, and currency depreciations in 1931–33,[29] had led to "a tangled network of defensive measures . . . resulting in a progressive strangulation of international trade," with disastrous effects on agriculture, industry, trade, and employment. By the spring of 1933 the volume of world trade was at best one-fourth, and its value only one-third, of the respective 1929 levels.[30] Per capita, combined U.S. exports and imports were $80 in 1929, $58 in 1930, $27 in 1931, $24 in 1932, and even lower in 1933.[31] In 1933–39 political considerations increasingly dominated commercial policy, and it proved "impossible for a truly international currency system to function under conditions of economic warfare and aggressive bilateral bartering."[32] The U.S. program which Secretary of State Cordell Hull pushed with vigor and hope in 1934–38, under the Reciprocal Trade Agreements Act of June 12, 1934, was a sound effort, but it had yielded only limited results before war came.[33]

Under the impact of the breakdown of the gold bloc in 1935–36, the end of deflationary measures, a few steps toward freer trade despite Britain's turn to increased protectionism in 1931–33, some further expansionary efforts, and the gradually rising armaments boom, commodity prices staged a marked advance from mid-1936 to a dangerous peak in March-April 1937, with great differences among commodities and among countries. This advance was sharply reversed in 1937–38, and price levels in 1939 were considerably lower.[34] During the later 1930s international trade increased in real terms and much more, of course, in terms of depreciated currency values; but even under the stimulus of widespread "feverish" rearmament in 1938–39, its growth failed (except temporarily)

---

itor Nation (New York: Prentice-Hall, 1937), pp. 105–20; Cleona Lewis, *America's Stake in International Investments* (Washington, D.C.: Brookings, 1938), esp. p. 39 and chs. 18–19; and BIS, *Eighth Annual Report*, pp. 68. 79.

[29]James W. Angell, "Exchange Depreciation, Foreign Trade, and National Welfare," Apr. 28, 1933, in *Proc. Acad. Pol. Sci.*, June 1933, 15:285–96; G. P. Auld, in *ibid.*, p. 312; and CTC, *Bus. Bull.*, Nov. 15, 1936 (chart).

[30]J. H. Williams and J. G. Rogers, in *Proc. Acad. Pol. Sci.*, June 1933, 15:284, 328.

[31]G. R. Parker, "Import Quotas and Other Factors in the Restriction of Trade," *ibid.*, pp. 297–302.

[32]League of Nations, *International Currency Experience*, p. 209. Yet Condliffe (*Commerce of Nations*, p. 504) went perhaps too far in saying that "the decade preceding the second World War was one of economic breakdown and economic warfare."

[33]Hodson, *Slump and Recovery*, pp. 269–70, 437–38; Schumpeter, *Business Cycles*, 2:1026; *Foreign Affairs*, October 1937, January 1938, pp. 103–14, 417–29, July 1939, pp. 782–83; Schlesinger, *Coming of the New Deal*, ch. 15, "The Triumphs of Reciprocity." The nineteenth agreement, with Great Britain, was belatedly reached on Nov. 17, 1938, too late to make much difference. *Economist*, Nov. 26, 1938, pp. 414–15 ("a decisive act of economic statesmanship") and special supplement.

[34]See log-scale charts for eight countries, 1926–38, in AT&T, *Summary*, Nov. 2, 1938, p. 2; Hodson, *Slump and Recovery*, ch. 12, esp. p. 439; BIS, *Tenth Annual Report*, pp. 8–9; for details, see Royal Economic Society memoranda and LCES reports on current economic conditions.

to match the rise in industrial output.[35] World shipping continued in the doldrums until the boom of 1936–37 temporarily boosted ocean freight rates to a sharp peak in September 1937.[36]

International commodity agreements (ICA's), often with intergovernmental support, to regulate the international flow of several important foodstuffs and raw materials (e.g., sugar, coffee, tea, tin, rubber) had had a dismal record in the 1920s. Most of those which survived until 1930 collapsed under the strains of the economic contraction of 1929–30. The Macmillan report in mid-1931 pointed out that individual commodity restriction schemes, as Beveridge put it a few months later, "have nearly always, in the end, broken down, and in breaking have added to the difficulties of our time."[37]

The two-year international tin control scheme, which became effective on March 1, 1931, inaugurated a monopolistic restrictionist scheme, backed by the governments of leading tin-producing countries, exploitive of processors and consumers, which was continued with modifications. The Chadbourne Sugar Agreement among producers' associations in seven sugar-exporting countries was signed May 9, 1931, but broke down before it expired on May 31, 1935. Other agreements for tea, coffee, sugar, wheat, rubber, silver, and lumber were established in 1933–39. Those for tea, tin, and rubber—all under able Anglo-Dutch leadership—were considered successful by their sponsors, and their success gave rise to plans to expand the role of international commodity agreements in the postwar world. However, ICA operations did not prevent a severe decline in international prices in 1937–38, their net contribution to economic recovery was limited, and, as a whole, the interwar ICA experience was discouraging from the standpoint of genuine economic progress.[38]

---

[35]See chart in BIS, *Tenth Annual Report*, p. 41.

[36]League of Nations, *Monthly Bulletin of Statistics*, 1933–39; Royal Economic Society, *Memorandum 63*, October 1936, p. 23, and *Memorandum 80*, September 1939, p. 25 (indexes of ocean freight rates in LCES reports of current economic conditions); BIS, *Eighth Annual Report*, pp. 31–32, 36; and Mowat, *Britain between the Wars*, pp. 434–35, 446.

[37]Sir William Beveridge, in Sir Arthur Salter et al., *The World's Economic Crisis and the Way of Escape* (London: Allen and Unwin, 1932), p. 182.

[38]Eugene Staley, *Raw Materials in Peace and War* (U.S. Memorandum 1, prepared for the American Coordinating Committee for International Studies, June-July 1937), esp. ch. 7 and app. C; "Stocks of Staple Commodities," Royal Economic Society, *Memorandum 69*, November 1937; Hodson, *Slump and Recovery*, pp. 40–52, 199–203, 230–66; Sir Andrew McFadyean, ed., *The History of Rubber Regulation, 1934–1943* (London: Allen and Unwin, 1944); Joseph S. Davis, "Experience under Intergovernmental Commodity Agreements, 1902–45," *JPE*, June 1946, 54:193–220, and *International Commodity Agreements: Hope, Illusion, or Menace?* (New York: Carnegie Endowment for International Peace, Committee on International Commodity Policy, 1947), esp. pp. 5–24, 79–81, and references therein cited, including books by K. E. Knorr and V. D. Wickizer. National and international cartels, the most important of which was the European steel cartel, also affected coal and many manufactured products. Edward S. Mason, *Controlling World Trade: Cartels and Commodity Agreements* (New York: McGraw-Hill, 1946).

Table 1. Federal Reserve Index of Industrial Production in the United States
(1947-49 average = 100)

Month	1927	1928	1929	1930	1931	1932	1933	1934	1935	1936	1937	1938	1939
Jan.	51	50	57	53	42	35	31	38	44	50	61	46	54
Feb.	51	50	57	53	42	34	31	40	45	45	62	45	54
Mar.	52	51	57	52	43	33	29	42	45	49	64	45	54
Apr.	51	50	58	52	43	31	31	42	44	52	64	44	52
May	51	51	59	51	43	30	36	43	44	53	64	43	53
June	51	52	60	50	41	29	42	42	45	55	63	44	55
July	50	52	60	47	41	28	45	39	45	56	64	46	56
Aug.	50	53	60	46	39	29	44	39	46	56	63	49	57
Sept.	49	54	59	45	38	31	41	37	48	47	64	50	61
Oct.	49	55	58	44	36	32	39	38	49	58	51	51	65
Nov.	48	56	56	43	36	32	37	38	51	60	51	53	65
Dec.	49	57	53	42	36	31	37	41	51	62	47	54	66
Year	*50*	*52*	*58*	*48*	*40*	*31*	*37*	*40*	*46*	*55*	*60*	*47*	*56*

Source: *Federal Reserve Bulletin*, December 1959, 45: 1469.

Irregular Economic   The second half of 1932 marked the upturn from the
Recovery   bottom of the depression in most countries of the
world,[39] with the United States the most conspicuous laggard—initially
because of the hobbling of presidential leadership in the four months between election and inauguration. From the trough of 1932-33 there was a
gradual but irregular climb out of severe depression into more or less vigorous activity and a good deal of feverish prosperity late in the decade. As
reflected in indexes of industrial production in leading industrial countries,
the expansion was greatest in Germany, most erratic in the United States
(Table 1), least in France. From 1935 on, rising armaments expenditures
provided important economic stimuli. By 1937 most countries except France
and the United States had exceeded their 1929 peaks, and Germany, Japan,
and the United Kingdom had considerably exceeded their more moderate
1929 levels. In fact, Germany, Austria, and Japan increased industrial out-

[39]For valuable summaries with charts and comments, see BIS annual reports (published
each May for the preceding April-March year), e.g., *Tenth*, pp. 7, 1-10 (industrial production
in 1929-39 for eleven countries). See also CTC, *Bus. Bull.*, Jan. 15, 1935; League of Nations,
Monthly Bulletin of Statistics, 1932-39; League of Nations, *Economic Stability in the Post-
War World: The Conditions of Prosperity after the Transition from War to Peace—Report of
the Delegation on Economic Depressions, Part II* (Geneva: League of Nations, 1945), p. 89,
diagram 12.
    The irregularity in recovery in various countries is well brought out in LCES reports on
economic conditions in Europe, e.g., Royal Economic Society *Memorandum 51*, February
1935. Thus in The Netherlands, where three years earlier the economic situation had been
"judged relatively favourable compared with several other countries" (cf. *ibid.*, no. 40, February 1932, pp. 21-22), "1933 brought improvement in various departments" but "1934 was
definitely bad—on the whole not better, and in some respects rather worse, than 1932" (p. 18).

put in 1937–38, when production contracted sharply in the United States (see the table), considerably in Britain, moderately in France and Canada, and slightly in Sweden. By 1938 the League of Nations index of industrial production for the world as a whole was 11.5 percent above that of 1929, and national indexes showed increases much higher for Japan and a number of smaller countries and (on the basis of questionable data) far higher for the Soviet Union.[40] Unemployment concurrently diminished but remained high in Great Britain and abnormally high in the United States, where the New Deal administration fell short of achieving its avowed objectives of raising commodity price indexes to their 1926 or 1929 levels, eliminating unemployment, and balancing the budget. Harry Hopkins' expressed confidence in early November 1933 that through the Public and Civil Works administrations (PWA, CWA) "this relief business" would be wiped out was never realized.[41]

World stocks of primary commodities (foodstuffs and raw materials) had risen in 1925–27, remained high in 1928, climbed strikingly in 1929–31, and rose further to extreme highs in early 1933. There was a slight decline in 1933 and a slight rise in the first eight months of 1934. Then followed a sharp decline to about the 1928 level in mid-1937, as recovery proceeded and rearmament got under way. Under the influence of severe business contraction in the United States, however, world stocks of primary commodities rose sharply in 1937–38 and then declined moderately for a few months, only to rise again as governments built up defense stocks.[42]

Taking over the presidency in the depths of the depression, in the midst of a severe banking crisis, Roosevelt dramatically injected a new spirit into the nation, got a docile Congress to enact a remarkable series of acts in its first hundred days,[43] and boldly pushed a program of recovery and reform including both rash and wise experiments, with mixed results.[44] Over-reacting to Hoover's devotion to "fiscal integrity," Roosevelt

[40]League of Nations, *International Currency Experience*, p. 196.

[41]*Proc. Acad. Pol. Sci.*, January 1934, 15:449–51.

[42]BIS, *Ninth Annual Report*, pp. 46–50, and *Tenth Annual Report*, p. 9; Royal Economic Society, *Memorandum 24*, October 1930, and *Memorandum 69*, November 1937.

[43]Schumpeter (*Business Cycles*, 2:986–96) later termed most of this legislation "both uncontroversial and unimportant," though it helped to steady the situation, and rated the influence of the NRA and AA Act on the whole "corrective rather than constructive"; but others he rated important. Cf. Schlesinger, *Coming of the New Deal*, ch. 1, which lists on pp. 20–21 fifteen of the more important actions with dates; and E. R. Ellis, *A Nation in Torment*, ch. 17, "March 1933."

[44]Lippmann's cogent and intelligent comments are readily accessible, with Nevins' helpful footnotes, in Walter Lippmann, *Interpretations, 1933–1935* (New York: Macmillan, 1936), esp. pp. 1–79. A careful appraisal of New Deal legislation and its administration would have been appropriate but has been excluded for various reasons. Beyond the brief mention in this chapter, I merely cite as examples two papers by George J. Benston: "Interest Payments on Demand Deposits and Bank Investment Behavior," *JPE*, October 1964, 72:431–49, in which he found to have "no basis in fact" the belief that paying interest on demand deposits, forbid-

conspicuously flouted it in some respects, yet was not ready to abandon it. Wobbling New Deal policies were not conducive to smooth and sustained progress and instead contributed much to the "go-stop-go" course of the U.S. economy.

The recovery following the banking crisis of March 1933 was one of the most rapid ever experienced, but shortlived. It ended in July, as the excessive initial enthusiasm quickly cooled, and the ensuing setback in industrial production and business activity lasted until May 1934. The course of the economy in 1934 was erratic; 1935 was somewhat better on the whole, and a moderate gain was made in the second half. What seemed like a sustained recovery gathered momentum after March 1936. The boom continued into the spring of 1937, when the CTC index registered –4, the best since June 1930.[45] The stock market collapse that began in mid-August was followed by a sharp contraction into severe depression. The growing threat of war led the country to start rearming in late 1937, and defense expenditures contributed heavily to the significant, if incomplete, recovery in 1938–39.

There were radical contrasts in personality and tactics between Hoover and Roosevelt which rendered effective cooperation between them impossible in the critical interval between election and inauguration. But Roosevelt did share his predecessor's novel conviction that the federal government must shoulder the responsibility for bringing about economic recovery, utilized the RFC and other machinery that Hoover had built up, and in most respects pursued the same objectives[46] and was hampered by certain similar limitations.

President Roosevelt skillfully retained his popularity with the voters, and is rightly credited with many achievements.[47] Yet he did not succeed

den by the new banking legislation, impelled banks to make unsafe investments; "Required Disclosure and the Stock Market: An Evaluation of the Securities Exchange Act of 1936," *AER*, March 1973, 63:132–55, in which he concluded: "There appears to have been little basis for the legislation and no evidence that it was needed or desirable."

[45]The CTC index (Table 1, p. 278) rose from –50 in March to –23 in July 1933, then fell to –38 in November-December. The old Federal Reserve index of industrial production (1923–25 = 100) rose from 60 in March to 100 in July; it then dropped to 72 in November. In the CTC *Bus. Bull.* for Dec. 15, 1935, business sentiment was appraised as "far too optimistic" in believing that full recovery could not be long delayed. Early in 1937 Phillips, McManus, and Nelson warned that "the present recovery must ultimately prove as illusory as the New Era of the 'twenties." *Banking and the Business Cycle: A Study of the Great Depression in the United States* (New York: Macmillan, 1937), p. 213.

[46]Walter Lippmann forcefully pointed this out in an article in the June 1935 issue of the *Yale Review*, which was reprinted in his little book *The New Imperative* (New York: Macmillan, 1935), pp. 8–37. B. M. Anderson, who was far more critical of both presidents, went so far as to say that the New Deal began in 1929–30; see his *Economics and the Public Welfare*, esp. ch. 31.

[47]Salter's essay on "Franklin Roosevelt: Courage and Improvisation," in his *Personality in Politics*, pp. 175–89, is a perceptive, forthright commentary by a key Englishman who first met Roosevelt in 1917, spent a day with him at the time of the 1932 election, and was in Washington as head of the British Shipping Mission in the crucial months before Pearl Har-

in bringing about full economic recovery,[48] despite the prevalence of very low interest rates (the result less of policy than of shortage of demand), a notable increase in the money supply, and the ending of the flood of bank suspensions[49] (in large part the result of the unexpectedly successful institution of bank deposit insurance, which the Congress imposed on the administration). Many factors contributed to this failure.

The New Deal administration attempted too much and expected too quick results; excessive hopes were raised, and soon dashed. The overambitious National Recovery Administration (NRA) proved an overall failure before its brief career was ended by an adverse decision of the Supreme Court on May 27, 1935. The Agricultural Adjustment Administration (AAA) survived a crippling decision of January 6, 1936, but had a very mixed record. The president's attempt in 1937 to pack the Supreme Court dismally failed; but later Court decisions were less hampering to his programs, and several supported both major and minor New Deal moves, though often by narrow margins.[50]

No comprehensive rationale for the devices and somewhat inconsistent policies for recovery and reform was ever worked out, and several New Deal measures called for exceptional operative skills that were not yet developed. In general, too much was expected of the federal government, and the private economy was not encouraged to play a large role in economic recovery. Undue stress was laid on raising wages and increasing consumer purchasing power, and too little stress was laid on increasing incentives to private investment, which tended to lag. Labor demands were typically supported, and union membership tripled in 1933–41. But after a

---

bor, when the destroyer deal and the Lend-Lease Act were among the moves that facilitated U.S. aid to the Allies without violating our Neutrality Acts. Schlesinger summed up his views on Roosevelt in the last three chapters of *The Coming of the New Deal*. Cf. also Edgar Eugene Robinson's *The Roosevelt Leadership* (1956); Bruce Bliven's chapter on Roosevelt in his *World Changers*; and James M. Burns, *Roosevelt: The Lion and the Fox* (New York: Harcourt Brace, 1956), and *Roosevelt: The Soldier of Freedom* (New York: Harcourt Brace Jovanovich, 1970).

[48]In his *Economic History of the United States*, 1st ed. (New York: McGraw-Hill, 1941), pp. 1006–8, C. W. Wright suggests reasons for the failure to achieve full recovery. The point is not discussed in S. E. Morison's monumental *Oxford History of the American People* (New York: Oxford University Press, 1956), pp. 985–87—"Conclusion to the New Deal"—in which he gives the president and administration high praise. See also F. D. R.'s remarks to Young Democrats at Baltimore, Apr. 13, 1936, in Roosevelt, *Public Papers*, 5:164, quoted in Herbert Stein, *The Fiscal Revolution in America* (Chicago: University of Chicago Press, 1969), p. 101.

[49]*Stat. Abstr. U.S., 1972*, p. 444.

[50]In addition to Schlesinger's chapters and his extensive citations, see two books summarizing Brookings Institution studies: Leverett S. Lyon and Associates, *The National Recovery Administration: An Analysis and Appraisal* (Washington, D.C., 1935), and E. G. Nourse, J. S. Davis, and J. D. Black, *Three Years of the Agricultural Adjustment Administration* (Washington, D.C., 1937). Friedman and Schwartz's *Monetary History* sheds valuable light on important points. E. R. Ellis' *A Nation in Torment*, chs. 19–20, illuminates the atmosphere.

decade of "remarkable industrial tranquility," labor disturbances were far more numerous than in 1920-33, and at times, notably in 1936-37, they reached very serious proportions.[51] Moreover, presidential utterances and administration moves increasingly alienated businessmen (and many other prominent persons), to the detriment of recovery.[52]

The divergence of responsible opinion on economic problems and policies which had characterized the period 1929-33 continued in 1933-39, and this divergence handicapped government leaders in democratic countries in playing their enlarged roles in promoting recovery, as well as in facing the growing threat of war. The Roosevelt administration ignored sober recommendations of representative professional economists[53] and turned instead to unorthodox thinkers such as Cornell agricultural economist George F. Warren on monetary policy. His chosen advisers were able individuals, full of bright ideas not easily brought into harmony. Despite his engaging personal qualities, F. D. R. proved a very difficult man to work with and for, and many of his lieutenants sooner or later quit or were eased out. Moreover, the complexities of the situation multiplied faster than economic and political "intelligence" could grow, and even those closest to the new developments were often at odds in their interpretations and had to revise their forecasts frequently.[54] The public held stubbornly to its distrust of Europe and to its unwillingness to readjust war indebtedness, to become involved in other collective decisions, or to abandon its traditional devotion to budget-balancing.

Pigou, in a memorandum written in April 1936, noted that in Great Britain "substantial progress towards recovery from the great depression has been made."[55] Nevertheless, it was far from complete in 1935. In shipbuilding, despite a 40 percent contraction in the number of persons belonging to the industry, 43 percent were unemployed. In coal mining the corresponding percentages were 22 and 32. In construction, heavy unem-

[51]See two valuable volumes by Irving Bernstein entitled *A History of the American Worker*, both published by Houghton Mifflin, Boston: *The Lean Years, 1920-1933* (1960) and *The Turbulent Years, 1933-1941* (1970).

[52]See a candid, illuminating editorial in the *Economist*, July 2, 1938, pp. 2-3; and Stein, *Fiscal Revolution*, pp. 108, 479, for Keynes' unsolicited letter to F. D. R. of Feb. 1, 1938.

[53]See the letter to the president-elect signed by twenty-four representative economists early in 1933, published in *C&FC*, Jan. 7, 1933, p. 71, and reprinted in Anderson, *Economics and the Public Welfare*, pp. 302-3.

[54]This point is well illustrated in Paul Einzig's numerous books, in Offner's recent *American Appeasement*, and in other works too numerous to cite.

[55]A. C. Pigou and Colin Clark, "The Economic Position of Great Britain," Royal Economic Society, *Memorandum 60*, June 1936. This brought up to date Pigou's pamphlet with the same title published in 1927. Schumpeter in 1939 (*Business Cycles*, 2:966-68) stressed the gentleness of Britain's descent into deep depression and the steadiness of her recovery, and attributed her failure to attain full employment to "the fact that in modern capitalism the worker is a free and very powerful citizen." Mowat wrote: "Recovery, despaired of in 1931, was in the air by 1933, obvious by 1935." *Britain between the Wars*, p. 432.

ployment persisted in spite of a very large expansion in employment, and in fishing, entertainment, and sport, despite a considerable expansion (page 16). Pigou pointed to the fact (subject to some qualification) that in 1932–35 the loss in aggregate real income and in real income per head had been more than made good (page 21). He emphasized the great improvement in the "terms of trade" (i.e., the amount of imports that a representative unit of exports would buy) in 1929–33 and 1933–35 (pages 26–28), and also the grave effects of depression-induced trade restrictions in forcing British productive resources into involuntary idleness (pages 28–29). Despite steady improvement from the worst month (January 1933), the percentage of insured persons unemployed in Great Britain and Northern Ireland averaged 15.6 in 1935 (page 34). Between June 1932 and December 1935 the number working rose by over 1.3 million, but the number of insured unemployed rose by 300,000 (page 37). Great expansion in housebuilding in 1931–35 had by no means solved the housing problem, particularly for the very poor (page 41).

Neville Chamberlain, who succeeded Philip Snowden as chancellor of the Exchequer in November 1931, pursued a cheap-money policy from June 1932, when a large conversion operation was successful and the bank rate was cut to 2 percent (where it remained until August 13, 1939). Lower costs of construction stimulated the remarkable residential building boom of 1931–37, largely under private enterprise.[56] Early in 1935 urgent rearmament requirements led Chamberlain reluctantly to turn to limited deficit financing, though British rearmament lagged.

In the second half of 1936 economic progress became nearly general in Great Britain. Without important stimulus from rearmament, the iron and steel industry had emerged from its long depression before increasing rearmament brought boom conditions in 1937–39. Late in January 1937 the *Economist* reported British prosperity at "an advanced stage" and world economic activity "at a higher level than ever before." The pronounced boom seemed even to threaten general catastrophe. In a series of articles in the *Times* (London), Keynes stressed this danger, and argued that unemployment had fallen so low that expansionist measures were no longer necessary. In February–April President Roosevelt publicly recognized the same threat. The U.S. government's net contribution to national income, which had been dominant since late 1933, was drastically reduced in 1936–37, and the Federal Reserve System announced increased reserve requirements effective March 1 and May 1.[57]

[56]Einzig, *World Finance, 1935–1937*, ch. 17; and Mowat, *Britain between the Wars*, pp. 455–61.

[57]*Economist*, January–March 1937, esp. pp. 1–2, 33, 108, 221, 236, 344–45, 460, 585, 641, 682–88, 697, Apr. 3, 17, 1937, pp. 14, 144–45; June 25, 1938, pp. 754, July 2, 1938, pp. 2–3; E. D. McCallum, in *Britain in Recovery*, pp. 361–74; *Fed. Res. Bull.*, 1937, passim; Board

Actually, however, the momentum of recovery was gravely overestimated. Keynes failed to mention that, despite the marked downtrend of unemployment from its peak of early 1933, some 10 to 12 percent of the British insured labor force was still unemployed.[58] The speculation-fed boom soon ended in a sharp fall in wholesale prices affecting nearly every internationally traded commodity.[59] Wall Street prices of stocks weakened in mid-March, and U.S. business activity reached its post-crash peak in that month. August saw the beginning of the U.S. slump that lasted for nearly a year. From August 14, 1937, to the end of March 1938 Wall Street experienced one of the most violent declines in its history.[60] Severe weakening of business confidence was reflected in the sharp widening of yields on corporate Aaa and Baa bonds, which reached its maximum in the spring of 1938.[61] Despite official and unofficial forewarnings, advance preparations for coping with the brief but drastic depression of 1937-38 were limited and inadequate, and the varied proposals for action were in some respects contradictory. Recovery began only when the administration reluctantly returned to huge spending.[62]

To a generally lesser degree, this slump was paralleled in various other countries, but there too it was shortlived.[63] In the United States there was a striking advance in business activity from the low point of May 1938

of Governors, FRS, *Annual Report*, 1937; BIS, *Eighth Annual Report*, esp. pp. 9, 25-32, 89-91; *Ninth*, pp. 5-10, 46-48, 78-89, 106; Schumpeter, *Business Cycles*, 2:1027-50; Roosevelt's utterances of Feb. 11, Mar. 9, Apr. 2, 1937, the last two in *The Public Papers and Addresses of Franklin D. Roosevelt* (New York: Macmillan, 1941), 1937 vol., pp. 123, 140-43; Kenneth D. Roose, *The Economics of Recession and Revival* (New Haven, Conn.: Yale University Press, 1954), esp. pp. 45-47, 238-39; Friedman and Schwartz, *Monetary History*, pp. 543-45, 699.

[58]H. W. Robinson, in *Britain in Recovery*, pp. 64-65; and Royal Economic Society, *Memorandum 73*, September 1938, pp. 26-27. The lowest monthly figure, in August 1937, was 1,357,000 unemployed, representing 9.9 percent of the insured labor force in Great Britain and Northern Ireland. The 1929 averages had been 1,262,000 and 10.1 percent, respectively. Cf. D. Graham Hutton, "The Economic Progress of Britain," *Foreign Affairs*, January 1938, pp. 279-93. The *Economist*, Dec. 31, 1938, trade supplement, p. 19, gave a chart ("The Anatomy of Unemployment, 1927-1938") dividing the unemployed into three groups: cyclical, special, and normal. This chart was brought up to date in later issues.

[59]The authors of Royal Economic Society *Memorandum 69*, November 1937 ("Stocks of Staple Commodities," p. 4), attributed this mainly to the fact that "output of most raw materials is expanding and is expected to expand further in the near future, while consumption shows signs of slower expansion and in some cases of a certain diminution."

[60]Anderson, *Economics and the Public Welfare*, pp. 438, 447-57, 469.

[61]FRS, *Hist. Chart Book, 1971*, p. 30.

[62]BIS, *Ninth Annual Report*, pp. 1-7, 35, 106, et passim; Anderson, *Economics and the Public Welfare*, chs. 66-68, 70; Marriner Eccles, *Beckoning Frontiers: Public and Personal Recollections*, ed. Sidney Hyman (New York: Knopf, 1951), esp. pp. 287-323; Stein, *Fiscal Revolution*, pp. 89-90, 100-114. Morison barely mentioned the important 1936-38 boom and contraction in his *Oxford History*, chs. 56-57.

[63]See the able summary in LCES, "Report on Economic Conditions in Europe and North America," Royal Economic Society, *Memorandum 77*, February 1939.

to a far higher one in the last quarter of 1939; the CTC index rose from –38 to –10. In Europe, intensive rearmament brought about important economic advances and, largely as a result, "the economic pulse of the world was quickening rapidly" in 1938–39. Germany's course under Hitler is dealt with below. Even in Britain, where some areas and industries continued depressed, and unemployment failed to fall below a million workers, levels of living had risen far above prewar levels when war finally came.[64]

Early in 1932 Keynes had said: "In the past, . . . we have not infrequently had to wait for a war to terminate a major depression. I hope that in the future we shall not adhere to this purist financial attitude, and that we shall be ready to spend on the enterprises of peace what the financial maxims of the past would only allow us to spend on the devastations of war. At any rate I predict with an assured confidence that the only way out is for us to discover *some* object which is admitted even by the deadheads to be a legitimate excuse for largely increasing the expenditures of someone on something!"[65] At the time, however, he gave no hint that rearmament would be the major object of largely increased public expenditures, or that the boldness which he deemed essential would be displayed by Japan and Germany, not by Britain. Indeed, though all that Keynes wrote was eagerly read, his advice in these years was seldom followed, even in Britain.[66] In

---

[64]*Economist*, trade supplement, Sept. 30, 1939, p. 17. This outstanding journal had developed an index of business activity for Great Britain, which in its experimental form was fully described in *Economist*, supplement, Oct. 21, 1933, with a chart on a 1929 base covering 1924–33. Later the index was shown on a 1935 base. See also Mowat, *Britain between the Wars*, pp. 205–8, 451–55, 490–96, 502–16, and sources therein cited.

I consider misleading, despite its element of truth, Boulding's assertion: "It is no exaggeration to say that Great Britain experienced a continuous depression from 1932 to about 1938." Kenneth E. Boulding, *The Economics of Peace* (New York: Prentice-Hall, 1945), p. 124. In 1937 Hawtrey had said much the same thing of 1921–29. Gayer, *Lessons of Monetary Experience*, p. 131. Cf. McElwee, *Britain's Locust Years*, pp. 249–52, 451–55, 490–96; Macmillan, *Winds of Change*, ch. 7, "Life in the Twenties," esp. p. 181.

Keynes, who repeatedly stressed Britain's relatively high level of living, ignored not only the American position but also the extent of poverty and undernourishment in Britain, which all social workers well knew. Macmillan, *Winds of Change*, pp. 429–30, 451. Yet there had been impressive gains since prewar days in the reduction of poverty and in improvements in housing, household equipment, and recreation. Colin Clark wrote in 1937 (*National Income and Outlay*): "Even the employed man with a family was better off in the thirties than the unskilled laborer in full work in 1913." Quoting this, Mowat added (*Britain between the Wars*, p. 492): "For a time of depression this was a remarkable and unexpected phenomenon." Cf. also B. Seebohm Rowntree, *Poverty and Progress* (1941) and Youngson, *British Economy*, pp. 65–67, 135–40.

[65]In his Halley Stewart lecture (given Feb. 11, 1932), in Salter et al., *World's Economic Crisis*, pp. 85, 88. Cf. McElwee, *Britain's Locust Years*, p. 202.

[66]Stein, in ch. 7 of his *Fiscal Revolution*, explored at length Keynes' influence on American thinking and policies in the interwar period. In sum, it was limited. Even in Britain, where he was widely read, in great demand as a speaker and adviser, and honored, "his advice was not taken" (p. 141). D. H. Winch, in his recent book *Economics and Policy* (London: Hodder and Stoughton, 1969), comes to conclusions similar to Stein's, as reported by the

retrospect, it is impressive that the return to or toward prosperity was due less to government policies aimed at economic recovery than to "natural" recuperation, mostly on private initiatives, and to the consequences of government policies with other objectives.

Generally, economic recovery had been only moderate, and financial rehabilitation was far from complete, in 1935-36 when three wars erupted— Japan vs. China, Italy vs. Ethiopia, and civil war in Spain—and the growing threat of another world war led to extensive rearmament in Europe. In Japan, indeed, rearmament had begun to be of importance in 1931-32; and in Italy and in Germany, which soon set the pace, it was of increasing importance, if more or less sub rosa, in 1932-35. In the later 1930s the key problem was no longer how to speed recovery from varied degrees of depression but rather how to cope with a vastly grimmer danger. From 1935 on, widespread rearmament broke the back of the depression and became the major factor in world economic recovery. Large demands for raw materials brought prosperity to much of Latin America, and frozen international indebtedness gradually thawed.[67] The United States was exceptionally slow to rearm and consequently lagged in recovery.

The Rise of Militaristic Dictators   The Great Depression, Bailey later wrote, "generated the New Deal at home [and] accelerated the rise of power-hungry dictators abroad: Hitler, Mussolini, and the Japanese war lords."[68] Unquestionably true and important as this was, other factors were involved in each of these cases.[69]

The Japanese militarist actions from late 1931 on were indeed promoted by contractions in Japanese domestic business, foreign trade, and shipping in 1929-31. But her military and economic aggressions in Manchuria and China proper in 1931-39, for which Chinese actions afforded excuses, must be partly explained by expansionary ambitions, heightened

---

reviewer in *EJ*, June 1969, 80:355. Youngson earlier wrote that "the ideas of Keynes had almost no effect on Government policy in this country before 1939." *British Economy*, p. 259. Only later, when his ardent disciples streamed into government offices in and after 1938, did Keynes exert extraordinary influence.

[67]Einzig, *World Finance, 1935-1937*, chs. 48, 53. "The whole continent of South America has recovered economically and financially during 1936 far beyond the most optimistic expectations" (p. 303). Cf. BIS, *Ninth Annual Report*, p. 16, for chart, "Trend of National Defence Expenditures of the World," comparing 1932-38 with selected earlier years.

[68]T. A. Bailey, *The American Spirit* (1963), p. 822. Mussolini had been in power since 1922, but until 1935 was reasonably cooperative internationally.

[69]Here, as to a lesser degree in earlier chapters and in the later sections of this one, Churchill's first volume in his series on World War II, *The Gathering Storm*, is of major importance. Among many later works of special value are the first of three volumes of Harold Nicolson's *Diaries and Letters*, covering the years 1930-39, edited by his son Nigel Nicolson (New York: Atheneum, 1966), and the first volume of Harold Macmillan's memoirs, *Winds of Change, 1914-1939*.

by foreign restraints on Japanese exports, and exacerbated by humiliations at the Paris Peace Conference, by anti-Oriental land laws in some western states and by federal restrictions on Oriental immigration. Widespread pacifism in the democracies, weak leadership in Britain, and U.S. unwillingness to venture far to support the League all combined to prevent effective action after the admirable Lytton report. For the first time, "the League Covenant was successfully flouted by a first-class power."[70]

Mussolini's unconscionable aggression on Abyssinia (Ethiopia) late in 1935, after years of international cooperation and two years of inconspicuous preparation, was traceable less to ravages of the depression than to his ill-advised commitment at Pesaro on August 26, 1926, to "defend the lira to the last drop of our blood" and to the strains imposed by the deflationary policies that this decision entailed.[71] Here too, however, past humiliations and imperialistic ambitions played important parts—Bliven has called the venture "a piece of naked imperialism." Italy was able to complete her conquest by May 1936, despite the League's ineffective invocation of "sanctions." This outcome, however gratifying to Italian pride, had serious international consequences: the British-French-Italian agreement at Stresa in the spring of 1935, which had offered a possible safeguard to peace in Europe, broke down; Hitler's influence in Austria and Hungary was strengthened and he was able to occupy the Rhineland in March 1936 without resistance.[72]

Germany's desperate economic and financial plight at the end of 1932 and the massive unemployment her people were experiencing were major factors in giving Hitler his chancellorship. But the festering wounds

[70]Henry L. Stimson, *The Far Eastern Crisis* (New York: Harper, 1936); Hodson, *Slump and Recovery*, pp. 87, 92, 104, 345–55; Paul Einzig, *The Japanese "New Order" in Asia* (London: Macmillan, 1943); Henry L. Stimson and McGeorge Bundy, *On Active Service in Peace and War* (New York: Harper, 1948), ch. 9; Churchill, *Gathering Storm*, pp. 86–88; Mowat, *Britain between the Wars*, pp. 419–22; McElwee, *Britain's Locust Years*, pp. 212–19; and Macmillan, *Winds of Change*, pp. 342–45.

[71]On a visit to Italy in October 1932, Einzig was impressed by the improvements since his previous visit in 1922, by the atmosphere of order and prosperity in Milan, and by evidence of "progress and stability in Italy . . . in sharp contrast with the depression in Britain and other democratic countries." In 1933 he published *The Economic Foundations of Fascism* (London: Macmillan, 1933), in which, as he later admitted, he somewhat overpraised "the economic efficiency of the system of planned economy on the basis of the results achieved in Italy." Einzig, *In the Centre of Things* (London: Hutchinson, 1960), ch. 15, esp. pp. 148–52. Bliven's chapter, "Mussolini: Jackal in the Lion's Skin" (*World Changers*, pp. 251–79), needs to be supplemented by Einzig's 1933 book. Cf. also Herman Finer's more balanced presentation in his *Mussolini's Italy* (New York: Holt, 1935), based partly on stays in Italy from January to September 1933 and in March and April 1934.

[72]Einzig, *World Finance, 1935–1937*, chs. 19–22, esp. pp. 119, 129, 131; Hodson, *Slump and Recovery*, pp. 386–402; Churchill, *Gathering Storm*, pp. 132–34; McElwee, *Britain's Locust Years*, pp. 236–42; Bliven, *World Changers*, pp. 269–70; Macmillan, *Winds of Change*, ch. 15, "Doubts and Distractions"; and Nicolson, *Harold Nicolson*, 1:103, 212, recording on Aug. 21, 1935, Prime Minister MacDonald's comment that this was the worst crisis since 1914.

of national humiliation, Chancellor Brüning's drastic deflationary moves, crucial delays in holding the Lausanne conference, successful political machinations against Brüning which induced the aged and senile President Hindenburg to force his cabinet's resignation late in May 1932, and Stalin's order that German Communists ruthlessly attack Social Democrats: these were among the factors collectively responsible for Hitler's fateful opportunity.[73] For the later progress of his regime, factors other than the world depression were of major importance.

The depression was not a significant factor in starting the terrible civil war in Spain, which erupted in mid-July 1936 when right-wing General Franco led what was eventually a successful revolt against the leftwing Republican government established in Madrid. Officially, nonintervention was early agreed upon as the policy of Great Britain, France, Germany, Italy, and the Soviet Union, and Churchill strongly endorsed it; but Britain alone adhered strictly to this policy. Hitler and Mussolini sent men, equipment, and funds to support Franco, though the German involvement began to be liquidated late in 1937. The U.S.S.R. gave the Republic military aid on a major scale for a period of several months, but only limited economic aid thereafter. The French, to a much smaller extent, supported the Republic, and volunteers from the United States and elsewhere did likewise. But this bloody, disastrous war dragged on for thirty-three months before the rightists won.[74]

The weaknesses of Euoprean democratic governments and parliamentary deadlocks in the 1920s had led to what Bonn called "the clamor for a dictator."[75] These weaknesses accounted, at least in part, for the rise of Mussolini to power in Italy in 1922-24, for the occasional delegation of powers to legislate by decree in France and Germany, for the administration of economic and financial reforms in Austria and Hungary in the mid-1920s under League of Nations foreign officials, and for the subjection of Germany to foreign controls under the Dawes Plan in 1924-29. Hitler came to power early in 1933 after the German electorate had come to despair of emerging from extreme economic depression under parliamentary government and were ready to gamble on a self-styled *Führer* who was

[73]Salter, *Security*, ch. 3, "The Psychology of Defeat"; Churchill, *Gathering Storm*, pp. 64-65, 68-69; Bonn, *Wandering Scholar*, pp. 336-39; Adolf Hitler, *Mein Kampf* (New York: Reynal and Hitchcock, 1939), p. 370n; Ralph H. Lutz, "The Collapse of German Democracy under the Brüning Government, March 30, 1930-May 30, 1932," *Pacific Historical Review*, March 1941, 10:1-14 (Brüning's own story appeared in a letter to the *Deutsche Rundschau*, July 1937); Bliven, *World Changers*, pp. 199, 219.

[74]Churchill, *Gathering Storm*, pp. 212-15, 244-49; George F. Kennan, *Russia and the West under Lenin and Stalin* (Boston: Little Brown, 1960), pp. 294, 308-12, 317-18; Macmillan, *Winds of Change*, pp. 433-38, 470; Nicolson, *Harold Nicolson*, 1:270.

[75]M. J. Bonn, *The Crisis of European Democracy* (New Haven, Conn.: Yale University Press, 1925), pp. 82, 88, 93.

sure that he knew how to lead his people out of their slough of despond into a thousand-year Reich. In this decade many westerners became enamored of four- and five-year plans of the Soviet and German types,[76] but public planning met with only limited success. In the 1930s, as in much of the 1920s, France was notorious for the instability of its governments, and no political leader emerged who could long hold the support of the Chamber of Deputies, as Poincaré had in 1926–29. It was in Great Britain, however, that the record of political democracy in the crucial decade of the 1930s was conspicuously and dishearteningly bad.[77]

The deepening world depression in 1929–33 and the rise of Hitler to power in 1933 drastically changed the international political situation for the worse, and the League of Nations was reduced to virtual impotence in 1933–38.[78] Far too much had been expected of it; its major disarmament efforts crumbled within months after Hitler suddenly withdrew the German delegation from the disarmament conference in October 1933; and the failure of the League to halt the Japanese and Italian aggressions and German rearmament both reflected and publicized its almost complete futility. Three important League members announced their withdrawal: Japan on March 27, 1933, Germany on October 21, 1933, and Italy on December 11, 1937.[79] Though withdrawal was not legally effective until two years after notice, their active participation ended with these announcements. The accession of the Soviet Union on September 18, 1934, proved inadequate to offset these defections, for Stalin soon abandoned his support of collective resistance to Hitler's aggressive moves and launched a series of "blood purges" which gravely weakened the Red Army, undermined Soviet bargaining power, disrupted the new united fronts of the Socialist and Communist parties in Europe, and eventually led to the amazing Nazi-Soviet (Ribbentrop-Molotov) Nonaggression Pact of August 23, 1939.[80]

[76]Even Paul Einzig, no admirer of Hitler, Stalin, and their policies, argued that economic planning was the basic instrument for recovery and advance. See especially his *Economic Foundations of Fascism*, esp. ch. 12. Cf. Macmillan, *Winds of Change*, pp. 331–32.

[77]See pp. 322–23, 337–42, below.

[78]Salter, *Security*, pp. 145–62, and *Memoirs of a Public Servant* (London: Faber, 1961), pp. 200–201, 206; Churchill, *Gathering Storm*, pp. 87–88, 170–87; Macmillan, *Winds of Change*, pp. 417, 425. As early as November 1933 Einzig wrote: "The trend of evolution in Europe points inexorably towards another world war in the lifetime of our generation. . . . The victory of Hitler, its circumstances and its consequences, have made another war most likely, if not inevitable." *Germany's Default: The Economics of Hitlerism* (London: Macmillan, 1934), p. 100. While he continued to hold this view, as late as March 1939 Einzig was in error in believing war in the next twelve months to be unlikely. *World Finance, 1938–1939*, p. 300.

[79]Several lesser members, mostly Latin American, had announced their withdrawal in 1924–37, and Austria ceased to be a member after her forced reunion with Germany in 1938.

[80]Kennan, *Russia and the West*, chs. 20–21, "The Struggle against Hitler, and the Purges" and "The Nonaggression Pact"; Bliven, "Stalin: Caligula in a Sack Suit," *World Changers*, pp. 183–250.

Hitler and Resurgent   Adolf Hitler, thus far disastrously underestimated,
Germany   was the key actor on the world stage from the
time of his appointment as chancellor of Germany on January 30, 1933. In
the presidential election of April 10, 1932, he had run a poor second to
President Hindenburg—pitiably aged but still greatly admired, an extremely
reluctant candidate—and well ahead of the Communist Party candidate,
Ernst Thälmann, who had run third in 1924 as well.[81] Hitler had been a
potent political agitator from the time of Germany's humiliating defeat in
World War I. While serving a prison sentence (April–December 1924) for
his large share in the bloody but abortive Munich beer-hall *Putsch* of
November 9, 1923,[82] he wrote the first volume of *Mein Kampf*—"a propa-
gandist essay by a violent partisan"—in which he undertook to set forth the
objectives of the Nazi movement and project the course of its development.
The two volumes were first published in 1925 and 1927, respectively.
Though read more and more widely in Germany from 1930 on, this "most
important political tract" was not translated into English until 1933, and
then in a severely abridged version;[83] the first U.S. edition—unabridged,
richly annotated, and sponsored by a group of respected citizens—did not
appear until 1939.[84]

Until the very eve of his elevation to supreme power, Hitler seemed
to most observers, including Germans with large political experience, an
almost negligible figure.[85] This was a tragic blunder. He was one of the
world's greatest demagogues, who repeatedly evinced charismatic ability
to arouse men to a "fever pitch of personal devotion and enthusiasm."
His able young minister of armaments recently termed him a "charming
monster."[86] He was backed by a party with "fantastic powers of organization, . . . inspired by a fanatical stormy determination to let nothing stand
in its path." To outsiders he often gave the impression of being "only a mad,

---

[81]Lutz ("Collapse of German Democracy," p. 8) gives the votes on the first and second
ballots; Nicolson, *Harold Nicolson*, 1:103–4, 108, 114.

[82]Churchill, *Gathering Storm*, pp. 54–57; Hitler, *Mein Kampf*, pp. 803n, 813–15n.

[83]E. T. S. Dugdale, ed., *Adolf Hitler, My Battle* (New York: Houghton Mifflin, 1933).

[84]Hitler, *Mein Kampf*. Second in the list of ten was Sidney B. Fay, who had written an
authoritative study, *Origins of the World War*, 2 vols. (New York: Macmillan, 1928; rev. ed.
1930), in which the war guilt issue was convincingly dealt with. The official *British Documents
on the Origins of the War, 1908–1914*, in ten volumes edited by G. P. Gooch and Harold
Temperley, were published in 1937–38. Pierre Renouvin's able review of these in *Foreign Affairs*, October 1938, pp. 111–27, ends with this paragraph: "In July 1914 England merely
followed her traditional policy. But her peaceful intentions and her hesitations brought about
the very result she wished to avoid." Much the same could be said of the United States in
1933–39.

[85]Salter, *Personality in Politics*, pp. 242–43; Anderson, *Economics and the Public Welfare*,
pp. 227–28; Sir Andrew McFadyean, *Recollected in Tranquillity* (London: Pall Mall Press,
1964), p. 213; Nicolson, *Harold Nicolson*, 1:108, 174–75 (diary for Jan. 24, 1932, June 12, 1934).

[86]Albert Speer, in a candid interview in Heidelberg on July 5, 1970. See also his *Inside
the Third Reich: Memoirs* (New York: Macmillan, 1970).

vicious fool." Paranoiac, hypochondriac, and monomaniac though he was, he was "bold and resolute in his decisions" in a period when so many leaders were timid and irresolute. He had no conventional scruples, and occasionally made "great strategic mistakes," most notably during the war. But time and again, in 1933–39, his actions in the face of strong opposition from his military and civilian staff proved justified by events, partly "because he had correctly estimated the timidity and vacillation" of others.[87]

From the outset Hitler ruthlessly repressed Communists, Jews, and liberals. He forced out of high German academic positions outstanding Jews such as Moritz J. Bonn[88] and outspoken liberals such as young Karl Brandt. In 1933–35 the Nazis interfered with the productive work of the German and Austrian institutes for research on business cycles (both established in 1926) before they could profit from Keynes' *General Theory*, and several key members of the institutes emigrated to England or the United States.[89] But Hitler was able to draw into his service, by various means, such prominent democrats as Hans Luther, a former chancellor, such a financial wizard as Hjalmar Schacht, Luther's predecessor and successor as Reichsbank president,[90] and such able nonpolitical persons as the young architect Albert Speer, as well as seasoned Nazis such as Hermann Wilhelm Göring, Joseph Paul Göbbels, and Heinrich Himmler. And he even charmed several notable foreigners.[91]

[87]William L. Shirer, *Berlin Diary: The Journal of a Foreign Correspondent, 1934–1941* (New York: Knopf, 1941), passim; Kennan, *Russia and the West*, pp. 319, 334; Bliven's excellent chapter "Hitler: The Madman as Leader," in *World Changers*, pp. 128–82; Macmillan, *Winds of Change*, p. 354 et passim.

[88]Bonn, *Wandering Scholar*, ch. 19. On Oct. 1, 1931, Bonn had been elected by his colleagues Rector Magnificus of his Berlin College (Handelschochschule), when it celebrated the twenty-fifth anniversary of its founding. In the spring of 1933 he felt it necessary to resign as rector and was soon forced to retire from his lifetime professorship, but he managed to escape into Austria in time.

[89]E. Coenen, *La "Konjunkturforschung" en Allemagne et en Autriche 1925–1933* (Louvain: Editions Nauwelaerts, 1964), reviewed by C. T. Saunders in *EJ*, December 1967, 77:892–94. The emigrants included the Austrian Institute's first two directors, F. A. Hayek and Oskar Morgenstern, and Fritz Machlup, one of its senior staff.

[90]Hjalmar Schacht, *Confessions*, pp. 256–61, 275–80, et passim. The London edition, entitled *My First Seventy-Six Years*, had appeared in 1955.

[91]Mowat, *Britain between the Wars*, pp. 591–92. "It is no mean feat to have deceived . . . such varied and distinguished men as [George] Lansbury, [Lord]Lothian, [Lord] Rothermere, Arnold Toynbee, [Lord] Londonderry, [Clifford, later Lord] Allen, Tom Jones, and Lloyd George." Macmillan, *Winds of Change*, pp. 361, 420–25, 450.

Sir Josiah Stamp, who met Hitler on a visit to Nuremberg in December 1935, "was obviously impressed by the latter's personality and the results that he had achieved," and considered him a "statesman and demagogue combined." To the distress of many friends and admirers, Lord Stamp attended the Nazi Party conference in Nuremberg in early September 1938, and was impressed afresh. He then went on to Prague, and later publicly defended Walter Runciman's proposals, which were "anathema to most people" in Britain. J. Harry Jones, *Josiah Stamp, Public Servant: The Life of the First Baron Stamp of Shortlands* (London: Pitman, 1964), pp. 326–27, 331–32; Mowat, *Britain between the Wars*, pp. 606–16.

Early in February 1933 Communist Party meetings and demonstrations were forbidden, and a nationwide roundup of secret arms belonging to individual party members began. The day after the Reichstag fire of February 27—blamed on the Communists but almost certainly instigated by the Nazis—President Hindenburg signed a decree curtailing civil liberties, and members of the Central Committee of the Communist Party were among the four thousand persons arrested overnight. Thanks to Göbbels' skill and zeal in organizing the campaign for the election on March 5, the Nazis won 44 percent of the popular vote and 288 seats in the Reichstag, while the opposition parties won a total of 251 seats. On March 24, however, with the support of Hugenberg's Nationalists, Hitler was given complete emergency powers for four years by a vote of 441-94.[92] On July 14, the Nazi (National Socialist German Workers') Party was decreed the only legal political party in Germany.[93] After the death of Hindenburg on August 2, 1934, under a law passed the day before, Hitler became chief of state as well, and a plebiscite on August 18 overwhelmingly confirmed this.[94]

The economic position of Germany in 1932-33, when Hitler came to power, was extremely bad, in spite of the generous cooperation of her creditors after the financial crisis of mid-1931.[95] The breakdown of the Weimar Republic is reflected in the fact that in 1932 there were three successive unpopular chancellors—Brüning, Von Papen, and General Schleicher—and five Reichstag elections.[96] Keynes' younger colleague Guillebaud, visiting various parts of Germany in the fall of 1932, found conditions very similar to those on his visit in the spring and summer of 1919—"the factories idle, the streets full of beggars; and unemployment, poverty and decline everywhere apparent." Employment reached its lowest point and unemployment its highest in calendar 1932. The low points for the decade in crude birth rate, excess of births over deaths, and new issues of securities came in 1933. In January 1933 there were 6 million on the official unemployment register, and nearly another million were non-

[92]Hitler, *Mein Kampf*, pp. 570-72n; M. J. Elsas, in LCES, "Report on Economic Conditions in Europe," Royal Economic Society, *Memorandum 45*, February 1934, p. 7; Churchill, *Gathering Storm*, pp. 69-71; Offner, *American Appeasement*, p. 13.

[93]Pierre Accoce and Pierre Quet, *A Man Called Lucy, 1939-1945*, 1st American ed. (New York: Coward-McCann, 1967), p. 34.

[94]Churchill, *Gathering Storm*, p. 105; Offner, *American Appeasement*, p. 98.

On Aug. 30, 1933, in an affable letter to Prime Minister MacDonald, President Roosevelt expressed his concern over events in Germany and his feeling that "an insane rush to further armaments in Continental Europe is infinitely more dangerous than any number of squabbles over gold or stabilization or tariffs." Schlesinger, *Coming of the New Deal*, p. 232. Actually, there was no such rush, sane or insane, except subtly in Germany, for two years.

[95]Guillebaud, *Economic Recovery of Germany*, pp. 43-46, 275, 277.

[96]Churchill, *Gathering Storm*, pp. 62-70.

registered unemployed;[97] indeed, according to the *Economist* (Sept. 2, 1939, pp. 447–48), in the winter of 1932–33 no less than eight million, or one-half of the industrial labor force, were out of work. The unemployment insurance system, started in 1927, had broken down, benefits were drastically cut, and most of the unemployed were subsisting on small poor relief doles.[98] Despite relief from reparation payments after July 1932, the public finances were in a deplorable state; the capital market was completely disorganized, interest rates were very high, savings and investments were negative, and the banks were extremely illiquid. The wholesale price index continued to fall in the second half of 1932, but it was virtually stable in the first quarter of 1933 and began to rise in May.

The Nazis came to power pledged to cure unemployment, yet this objective was only part of their broad program for "national salvation," initially outlined by Gottfried Feder and Hitler as early as February 1920 and elaborated in *Mein Kampf*. It included not only wiping out the humiliating provisions of the Treaty of Versailles, most of which (except frontier alterations) had already been conceded before Hitler took over,[99] but also suppressing Communists and Jews, thoroughgoing rearmament, expanding the Reich to include German minorities abroad, putting the state above individual private interests, and replacing the national inferiority complex by a national superiority complex.[100] By and large, this program was successfully carried out, though of course not in every detail.[101]

At the outset the new regime gave lip service to the principle of international cooperation. Hitler's address to the Reichstag on March 21, 1933, "was moderate, even conciliatory: pacific intentions were proclaimed; and even international industrial warfare was repudiated, when it was asserted that the 'exchange of goods' between the peoples of the world remained imperatively necessary."[102] On April 28, Hans Luther—then

[97]Guillebaud, *Economic Recovery of Germany*, pp. 30n, 32. See also Dr. M. J. Elsas' "Review of the Year 1933," in Royal Economic Society, *Memorandum 45*, February 1934, pp. 7–12.

[98]Guillebaud, *Economic Recovery of Germany*, pp. 3n, 16, 24, 26, 226n; Otto Nathan, "Some Considerations on Unemployment Insurance in the Light of German Experience," *JPE*, June 1934, 42:289–327.

[99]Lippmann, *Interpretations, 1933–1935*, p. 321 (Mar. 16, 1933). By April-May 1933, however, Hitler's drastic moves had "ended all possibility of a pacific revision of frontiers." *Ibid.*, pp. 325–29 (Apr. 28, May 12, 1933).

[100]Einzig, *Germany's Default*, app. 4, "The Official Programme of National Socialism"; Salter, *Security*, chs. 3, 5; Churchill, *Gathering Storm*, ch. 4, esp. pp. 53–57. Though the American translation of *Mein Kampf* was based on the first edition, its editorial sponsors noted in their introduction that the changes in later editions, referred to in their notes, were "not as extensive as popularly supposed." The authorship of the Party program was ascribed to Feder (pp. 116–18n), who was quoted as saying: "For many, perhaps for himself, Hitler is the German Messiah."

[101]Hitler, *Mein Kampf*, pp. 686–94n.

[102]*Ibid.*, p. 652n.

German ambassador to the United States—assured the Academy of Political Science in New York: "The German Government is surpassed by no other in its eagerness for international cooperation."[103] He quoted the chancellor's recent statements to this effect. But whenever such cooperation hampered or threatened to hamper pursuit of Nazi goals, it was quickly abandoned. Treaties were repeatedly treated as "scraps of paper."

The Nazi methods employed included far-reaching controls, amounting to regimentation, over labor, business, foreign trade and exchange, capital, and agriculture; maximization of domestic production, including development of substitutes for imported goods; virtual default on foreign loans; bilateral clearing agreements; and controlled inflation to finance public works and rearmament while isolating internal prices from world prices.[104] In line with Keynes' views, but by characteristically ruthless methods, long-term interest rates were reduced.[105]

In *Mein Kampf* Hitler had cited the swelling flood of Allied propaganda in 1915-18, handled "with really unheard-of skill and ingenious deliberation."[106] By comparison, he said, German counteractions "failed completely." As early as 1921 he took over the management of the German Workers' Party propaganda, which he considered the party's most important job. Propaganda to the masses, concentrating heavily on little and big lies and on stirring up hatred, became a powerful instrument in Nazi hands. Goebbels, an unprincipled opportunist of high intelligence, directed it with devilish ingenuity.[107]

Initially, the new regime concentrated on measures calculated to increase employment. That was done mainly by public works, emergency employment, and compulsory employment. Pending the absorption of the unemployed into regular employment, workers were given "substitute employment," mostly on land drainage and other land improvements, for which they were supplied food and equipment; by March-April 1934 the

---

[103] *Proc. Acad. Pol. Sci.*, June 1933, 15:361-67.

[104] Stephen H. Roberts, *The House That Hitler Built* (New York: Harper, 1938); Elizabeth Wiskemann, "The 'Drang nach Osten' Continues," *Foreign Affairs*, July 1938, pp. 764-73; Royal Economic Society, *Memorandum 76*, October 1938, pp. 13-15; Hitler, *Mein Kampf*, pp. 751-55n, 686-94n; Salter, *Security*, pp. 48-64; Guillebaud, *Economic Recovery of Germany*, pp. 213-33. Roberts, an Australian professor of history at Sydney University, spent several months in Germany investigating the Nazi regime. He was given unusual privileges, and soon published his perceptive article "The Rise of Hitler," in which this "portrait" appeared.

[105] Guillebaud, *Economic Recovery of Germany*, pp. 74-80. The BIS *Ninth Annual Report*, pp. 109-11, shows the five-fold increase in the public debt in 1932-38 with illuminating comments.

[106] P. 228. For the British, this was directed by the powerful "press lord" Northcliffe; it was run for the Americans by George Creel, head of the Committee on Public Information.

[107] Hitler, *Mein Kampf*, pp. 108-11, 227-43, 463-77, 572-73, 686, 693n, 697, 846-67; Guillebaud, *Economic Recovery of Germany*, p. 269; Salter, *Security*, pp. 312-13; Macmillan, *Winds of Change*, p. 361.

number so employed had risen to about one million.[108] From 1935 on, the primary object was to build up what was called the "defense economy" (*Wehrwirtschaft*) but was really the capacity for armed aggression, to be used if Nazi objectives could not be achieved without it. In 1935–37, when emergency relief work had shrunk into insignificance, about two hundred thousand men were retained in the Labor Service for training in physical work. Under orders of June 28, 1938, however, hundreds of thousands were drafted from their usual occupations to intensify rearmament and, in particular, to fortify the western frontier of Germany with all possible speed.[109]

The German economic recovery under Hitler's dictatorship in 1933–36 was spectacular: unemployment sharply declined, industrial activity increased, trade revived, and frozen credits were liquidated.[110] Ambitious public works schemes were undertaken; rearmament was pushed with increasing openness; resources of commercial and savings banks and insurance companies were commandeered; import trade was subjected to rigid government control; levies were made on domestic industries to finance export subsidies; and experts such as Dr. Schacht were induced to manage these operations even if contrary to their convictions.[111] Even before the occupation and remilitarization of the Rhineland in March 1936, economic recovery and vigorous rearmament in Germany heightened the prospect that she would plunge the world into another war. This prospect became almost a certainty as rearmament and related activities were intensified under the second Four-Year Plan (October 1936)[112] and as Germany absorbed first Austria and then Czechoslovakia, and dominated much of southeastern Europe by bilateral agreements.[113]

Schumpeter in 1939 briefly discussed the state-directed economy of Germany up to the spring of 1938.[114] In terms of industrial output and

[108]Hitler, *Mein Kampf*, p. 652n; Guillebaud, *Economic Recovery of Germany*, pp. 37–38, 46–47.

[109]Guillebaud, *Economic Recovery of Germany*, pp. 225–28.

[110]*Ibid.*, ch. 2. An early summary is given in Paul Einzig, *Bankers, Statesmen, and Economists* (London: Macmillan, 1935), pp. 37, 336–40. This was a revision of Einzig's illuminating earlier book, *Germany's Default*. As early as 1934, said Einzig (*Bankers*, p. 45), "Germany had become decidedly the strongest continental power and probably the strongest world power." A chart in BIS, *Ninth Annual Report*, p. 8, compares actual working hours per week in Germany, France, and the United States in 1931–38 and shows the sustained uptrend in Germany in the period 1932–38, reaching peak levels in 1938, when hours in the other two countries were much lower.

[111]Einzig, *World Finance, 1935-1937*, p. 112, said that Hitler was understood to have told him when Schacht tendered his resignation that the alternative was the concentration camp. Cf. Schacht, *Confessions*, passim, and n. 119 below.

[112]Guillebaud, *Economic Recovery of Germany*, ch. 3.

[113]See Royal Economic Society, *Memorandum 76*, October 1938, pp. 13–15 ("Trade with South-Eastern Europe").

[114]*Business Cycles*, 2:971–83.

reduction of unemployment he found its success outstanding; but the consumption level had merely returned to about that of 1929, and in freedom of producer, worker, and consumer the results were negative.[115] Schumpeter pointed out that "income-generating expenditure . . . was primarily pump-priming or additive until about the first quarter of 1935 and primarily substitutive after that."[116] He also stressed certain similarities to the New Deal program in the United States.

The Nazi regime went all out to win support from the largely disaffected youth and from women. By and large, the German people accepted the program with either enthusiasm or docility.[117] This was partly because it was so extremely harsh—not only on Communists and Jews, but even on those of Hitler's close associates who were suspected of disloyalty to him or of plots against him.[118] However, as the eloquent anti-Nazi Rauschning said, "there was something majestic about Hitler's plans and ideas" which "made it possible for so many intelligent people to fall under his spell."[119] The regime's remarkable record of successes fed the national pride. But there was a substantial undercurrent of discontent, and several abortive plots against Hitler's life attested the existence of extreme hostility to him. No less significant is the fact that the deeply patriotic German Rudolf Rössler was able to enlist ten officer friends in Germany who "abhorred Nazism and hated the Führer" to cooperate with him in Switzerland in 1939-44 in his extraordinary anti-Nazi spy-ring, eventually to the disastrous disadvantage of the Nazi cause.[120] Yet it is sobering to read, in a recent article by the editor of the *American-German Review*, that in the early

---

[115]This is fully brought out in Guillebaud, *Economic Recovery of Germany*, ch. 4, "Prices, Wages, and the Standard of Living." See also Otto Nathan, "Consumption in Germany during the Period of Rearmament," *QJE*, May 1942, 56:349–84.

[116]*Business Cycles*, 2:974. Cf. Einzig, *World Finance, 1935-1937*, p. 112: "From 1935 onwards . . . the main object was to rearm as rapidly and as extensively as possible."

[117]Minnesota sociologist Clifford Kirkpatrick wrote, on the basis of a sabbatical year in Germany in 1936–37, his illuminating *Nazi Germany: Its Women and Family Life* (Indianapolis, Ind.: Bobbs-Merrill, 1938). Cf. Karl Dietrich Bracher, *Die Deutsche Diktatur* (Cologne: Kiepenheuer, 1969). *Foreign Affairs* (October 1969, p. 191) called this book "the first scholarly synthesis of all aspects of the Nazi phenomenon, by Germany's leading expert on the subject. Judicious, thorough and incisive, this study, likely to become a standard work, offers a further commentary on the precariousness of modern democracy and the ways by which it can be perverted."

[118]A prominent instance was the bloody purge of June 10, 1934, which liquidated Ernst Röhm, one of Hitler's earliest Nazi comrades and close friends, who had been for seven years chief of staff of the S. A. ("Storm Troops" or "Brown Shirts"), and hundreds of others including General Schleicher, who had preceded Hitler as chancellor. Churchill, *Gathering Storm*, pp. 54–55, 59–61, 68–69, 96–100; Mowat, *Britain between the Wars*, p. 477; Schacht, *Confessions*, pp. 293–95.

[119]Hermann Rauschning, *The Redemption of Democracy* (New York: Literary Guild, 1941), pp. 195–96, 205–6. He also said that "so hardened a skeptic as President Schacht of the Reichsbank has said more than once that he comes out from each audience with Hitler refreshed and invigorated."

[120]Accoce and Quet, *A Man Called Lucy*.

1950s a majority or near-majority of the German people, according to newly developed public opinion polls, (1) believed that they had been best off in 1933–39, (2) rated Hitler with Bismarck as the German statesmen who had done the most for Germany, and (3) considered that Germany was not responsible for World War II.[121]

In February-March 1938 ex-President Hoover revisited the democracies of Central and Western Europe, which gave him the red carpet treatment in grateful recognition of his great relief work in behalf of their peoples in 1915–21. In the course of a stopover in Berlin, he could not avoid meeting with Hitler, Göring, and other leading Nazis, and Dr. Schacht, whom he had known since 1914. He was much impressed by Germany's economic and military progress under the Nazi regime but profoundly depressed by the human costs of it all.[122]

The Treaty of Versailles (Arts. 159–213) had exacted drastic reductions in German military and naval power and imposed severe restrictions on German armaments. These restrictions were never effectively enforced. Even in the 1920s, chiefly under the lead of General Hans von Seeckt but with support from civilian leaders, a great variety of devices were employed to evade the Treaty restrictions.[123] Even before the Treaty of Rapallo (April 17, 1922), by which Germany and the U.S.S.R. re-established diplomatic relations, secret agreements were made under which twenty thousand selected German combat veterans were trained as officers and noncommissioned officers at three large bases in the Soviet Union, and prototypes of war planes and tanks, developed in secret German workshops, were shipped to the U.S.S.R. for mass production in Soviet plants.[124] These made possible a far more rapid increase in Germany's armed strength when Hitler openly pressed rearmament. On December 16, 1926, the Social Democratic leader Philipp Scheidemann "startled the cabinet and the Reichstag with a scathing speech in which he charged that Germany was openly violating the disarmament clauses" and gave details "of the Army's clandestine dealings with the Soviet Union and the Red

[121]Lewis F. Gittler, "Probing the German Mind," *Interplay*, October 1967, pp. 4–8. Gittler pointed out that although such opinions had been greatly modified in the past fifteen years recent polls had indicated that, while 62 percent regarded this recent period as Germany's best, 34 percent believed that Hitler would rank as one of Germany's greatest statesmen had it not been for the war.

[122]Louis P. Lochner, *Herbert Hoover and Germany* (New York: Macmillan, 1960), chs. 8–9. Lochner accompanied Hoover on this trip.

[123]Churchill, *Gathering Storm*, pp. 42–51, 58–61; John W. Wheeler-Bennett, *The Nemesis of Power: The German Army in Politics, 1918–1940* (London: Macmillan, 1964). Macmillan later wrote: "It is clear, . . . from his papers, that Stresemann actively abetted this process of rearmament and was guilty of making Briand his dupe." *Winds of Change*, p. 345. Sir Andrew McFadyean, who knew Stresemann well in 1924–28, wrote me in 1969 that he still held the contrary belief, which he expressed in his memoirs (*Recollected*, p. 119).

[124]Churchill, *Gathering Storm*, pp. 113–14; Accoce and Quet, *A Man Called Lucy*, pp. 22–26.

Army."[125] This outraged Stresemann, then foreign minister, who believed that political parties should leave the Army a free hand. Yet in January 1927, in the period of optimism following the Locarno agreements of 1925, the Allies withdrew the Inter-Allied Control Commission and left to the League of Nations the responsibility of trying to enforce the Treaty provisions,[126] which proved even less effective. By 1931, military formations not officially admitted as such (the "Black Reichswehr") numbered at least sixty thousand men, with their own arms depots and training regulations, surreptitiously financed by funds diverted from other purposes.[127] Under Hitler the treaty restrictions were soon openly flouted.[128]

Moreover, throughout the Weimar Republic, from the days of Walther Rathenau to those of Heinrich Brüning, reconstructed and new factories were designed for speedy conversion into war plants,[129] and stocks of machine tools were secretly accumulated. Under Hitler, the output of the Volkswagen plants was turned exclusively to military purposes, and the grand new superhighways were designed as part of the defense economy,[130] as was later true in the United States.

Successive German governments made persistent efforts to gain the right to equality in armaments, seemingly promised in Article 8 of the League covenant and the Preamble to Part V of the Treaty of Versailles.[131] Even before Hitler, Germany insisted that other powers must disarm to her level or that she be allowed to rearm to theirs. The British were willing to concede this, but the French were not. By early 1932 it was well known that German rearmament had gone beyond the imposed treaty limits. Failure to win timely concessions helped cause the fall of Chancellor Brüning at the end of May 1932. His successor, Von Papen, announced his government's withdrawal from the disarmament conference on September 16. Germany returned after a five-power conference at Geneva in December at which she was conceded "equality of rights in a system which would provide security for all nations." In March 1933, a week before Hitler was granted dictatorial powers, the conference received a British

---

[125]H. A. Turner, *Stresemann and the Politics of the Weimar Republic* (Princeton, N.J.: Princeton University Press, 1963), pp. 227–28. Turner says that Stresemann "had long known all the essential facts of Germany's rearmament but . . . did not feel that Germany was morally bound to adhere to the letter of the disarmament clauses of the Versailles Treaty . . . and felt that . . . the Army should be free from all political interference."

[126]Churchill, *Gathering Storm*, pp. 44–47.

[127]*Ibid.*, p. 66; Hitler, *Mein Kampf*, p. 786n.

[128]Churchill, *Gathering Storm*, ch. 7, "Air Parity Lost" (esp. p. 118), ch. 8, "Challenge and Response, 1938"; Guillebaud, *Economic Recovery of Germany*, pp. 73–74.

[129]Churchill, *Gathering Storm*, pp. 49–50.

[130]Though I believe this to be true, I have not found a source to cite.

[131]Well summarized in Alec France, "The Quest for German Equality of Armaments," *Interplay*, November 1967, pp. 58–60. As that writer pointed out, the issue had again become important.

plan which, after Hitler had made a highly conciliatory speech on May 17, was approved in principle before the conference adjourned in June. When it reconvened on October 14, however, Hitler announced Germany's withdrawal and her intention to withdraw from the League, and the German electorate overwhelmingly approved the decision on November 12. Serious efforts to reach a disarmament agreement were made in the ensuing months, when France was racked by scandals. In April 1934 German budget proposals included large rearmament provisions; in May Norman Davis, U.S. ambassador-at-large, formally advised the Geneva commission that this country would participate in no political negotiations and make no commitment to use armed forces for settling disputes anywhere; and failure of disarmament efforts was finally admitted. Mowat wrote years later: "The necessary efforts for peace, whether in Europe or the Far East, were inhibited by the depression, by the lack of harmony between Great Britain and France, by apathy, and by pacifism among the British people, and by the opportunism of Sir John Simon at the Foreign Office."[132]

Hitler's prestige was enhanced when, in conformity to a 90.3 percent vote of the inhabitants in the plebiscite held under international supervision on January 13, 1935, the Saar Basin was quietly returned to Germany after sixteen years under French control, as the Treaty of Versailles had provided (Arts. 45–50 and Annex thereto), with no opposition from the French government. Soon thereafter, Hitler officially recognized the existence of a German air force (March 9), announced the introduction of conscription (March 16), and told the British foreign secretary, Sir John Simon, that Germany had attained air power parity with Britain (March 24). For some time this was a disputed question, but when war came British military aircraft numbered barely half those of Germany. The League Council on April 15–17 voted unanimously to condemn these unilateral breaches of the Treaty, and referred the conscription issue to the Plenary Assembly. This verbal protest was inconsequential, since no power or group of powers was prepared to contemplate use of force, even as a last resort.[133] German rearmament, in all its phases, was now "pushed on openly and with feverish haste."[134] Under the law of May 21, 1935, the Reichswehr became the Wehrmacht, and every soldier swore loyalty to the person of Hitler.[135] In mid-1935 an Anglo-German naval agreement was

[132]Churchill, *Gathering Storm*, pp. 73–77, 102–3; Mowat, *Britain between the Wars*, pp. 423–25; Macmillan, *Winds of Change*, pp. 352–60; Offner, *American Appeasement*, pp. 31–33, 46–50, 74.

[133]Churchill, *Gathering Storm*, chs. 7 ("Air Parity Lost") and 8 ("Challenge and Response"); esp. Mowat, *Britain between the Wars*, pp. 538–41 (Mowat's page references to Churchill are to the 1949 edition, mine to that of 1948); Macmillan, *Winds of Change*, pp. 345–67; Offner, *American Appeasement*, pp. 110–17.

[134]Guillebaud, *Economic Recovery of Germany*, pp. 73–74.

[135]Churchill, *Gathering Storm*, p. 143.

signed; although it limited the German fleet to 35 percent of the British, this was an appeasement move which permitted the German navy to expand as fast as was physically possible—a serious blunder on the part of Britain.[136] In mid-October, the German staff college was reopened in defiance of Versailles Treaty clauses, and on November 7 the young men born in 1914 were called up for military service, swelling the German army to nearly seven hundred thousand.[137]

In March 1936, in open violation of the Locarno agreements as well as the Versailles Treaty, and despite the opposition of his military advisers, Hitler's troops reoccupied and then remilitarized the Rhineland; no prompt or effective resistance which would have led to their withdrawal was offered.[138] From this point forward, Germany seemed to become unbeatable, as Colonel Lindbergh stated after visits to Germany and the U.S.S.R. in September 1936 and May and September 1938.[139] Thereafter, British fears of German air attacks well-nigh paralyzed British foreign policy.

On the first page of *Mein Kampf*, written in 1924, Hitler asserted: "German-Austria must return to the great German motherland." This the Treaty of Versailles had forbidden (Art. 80). The customs union proposed in March 1931 failed because of strong French pressures and a close but adverse decision of the World Court. In mid-1934 the Austrian Nazis, armed and financed by Germany, carried on vigorous propaganda and terrorist activities which culminated in the assassination of Engelbert Dollfuss, the Austrian chancellor. When Mussolini, furious, openly supported Austria by sending three divisions to the Brenner Pass, Hitler backed down for the time.[140] In the Reichstag on March 21, 1936, Hitler declared: "Germany neither intends nor wishes to interfere in the internal affairs of Austria, to own Austria, or to conclude an Anschluss."[141] On July 11 he signed a pact with Austria reinforcing these commitments, but they were promptly violated by secret instructions to the Austrian Nazi Party and to the German general staff. In February-March 1938, however, Hitler induced Mussolini to raise no objection to the German takeover of Austria; and Chancellor Kurt von Schuschnigg was soon compelled to submit to

[136]*Ibid.*, pp. 137–40, 195, 318, 359–61; Mowat, *Britain between the Wars*, pp. 540–41; Macmillan, *Winds of Change*, pp. 366–67, 543.

[137]Churchill, *Gathering Storm*, p. 144.

[138]*Ibid.*, ch. 11, "Hitler Strikes"; Einzig, *World Finance, 1938-1939*, ch. 24. Another version is given in Macmillan, *Winds of Change*, pp. 422–25. Rudolf Rössler ("Lucy"), the key man in the anti-Nazi spy ring, announced the Rhineland occupation on March 7, 1936, in his Swiss pamphlets, a month in advance. Accoce and Quet, *A Man Called Lucy*, pp. 37–38.

[139]Mowat, *Britain between the Wars*, p. 608; Nicolson, *Harold Nicolson*, 1:272, 343 (diary for Sept. 8, 1936, May 22, 1938); Charles A. Lindbergh, *The Wartime Journals of Charles A. Lindbergh* (New York: Harcourt Brace Jovanovich, 1970), pp. 279–80 et passim.

[140]Churchill, *Gathering Storm*, pp. 90–92, 103–4; Nicolson, *Harold Nicolson*, 1:155–66 (diary for Feb. 5, 1934).

[141]Churchill, *Gathering Storm*, pp. 205–6.

virtually complete absorption by Germany, accompanied by Nazi atrocities.[142] The subjugation of Czechoslovakia followed in the next nine months, culminating in the humiliating Chamberlain-Daladier-Hitler agreement at Munich on September 30.[143] On April 28, 1939, Hitler denounced the Anglo-German Naval Agreement reached in June 1935 and the German-Polish Non-Aggression Pact of January 20, 1934. On August 23, 1939, the German-Soviet Nonaggression Pact was signed.[144] The attack on Poland, opening World War II, followed nine days later.

The Drift toward World War II The victorious Allies had made a grave blunder in compelling Germany to sign the Treaty of Versailles with a statement (Art. 231) accepting for herself and her allies their sole responsibility for World War I (Art. 231). While German responsibility was very substantial, the "guilt" was shared by other nations, as Sidney B. Fay and other historians later showed convincingly. Hitler's positive share in the responsibility for World War II was much larger than that of Kaiser Wilhelm II for World War I twenty-five years earlier. This time, however, the role of other nations was largely negative, in that they failed to thwart Japanese, Fascist, and Nazi moves in time. The United States pursued a largely isolationist policy. President Hoover cherished ambitions to cooperate in maintaining peace but was determined to avoid U.S. involvement in another war. President Roosevelt realized the menace of Hitlerism earlier than most, but did not utilize his great popularity to reverse isolationist sentiment until very late. France weakened in her will to see that restraints in the growth of German military, naval, and air power were enforced; at a crucial time in the spring of 1936 she was in the midst of a political crisis and the "defense of the franc"; and she let her armament become obsolete. In these crucial years Britain was almost paralyzed; Italy was drawn into the Hitler orbit after her Ethiopian adventure; and the Soviet Union was eventually immobilized by Hitler's diplomatic maneuvers.

Germany's course under Hitler fully justified the strong French fears of a resurgent Germany which had induced her wartime leaders—Clemenceau, Foch, and Poincaré—to make security their primary demand at Paris in 1919 and to insist on the armament restrictions that were written into the Versailles Treaty. These fears also explain, although they do not

---

[142]See M. W. Fodor, "Finis Austriae," Charles Rist, "The Financial Situation of France," and Walter Hildebrand, "The Austrian Contribution to German Autarchy," *Foreign Affairs*, July 1938, pp. 587–600, 601–11, 719–22; Churchill, *Gathering Storm*, pp. 261–64, 267–74; and Nicolson, *Harold Nicolson*, 1:322–23, 328–31, 347–48.

[143]Churchill, *Gathering Storm*, chs. 16–19. On Apr. 18, 1939, Germany declared a protectorate over Bohemia and Moravia. See also R. W. Seton-Watson, "The German Minority in Czechoslovakia," *Foreign Affairs*, July 1938, pp. 651–66.

[144]Churchill, *Gathering Storm*, pp. 140–360, 392–95; Kennan, *Russia and the West*, pp. 300, 315–30; Mowat, *Britain between the Wars*, pp. 642–44.

justify, overly harsh French demands for reparations, on the fragile assumption that heavy exactions would weaken Germany. By the early 1920s, however, the wartime unity of the victorious Allies had vanished and their political leaders were weak; problems of economic recovery and financial rehabilitation had become dominant; hopes of "collective security" under the League of Nations, and visions of disarmament removing both the causes of war and ability to wage it, were widely cherished; and pacifist sentiment rose to extraordinary heights in Britain and France. Even in support of League efforts, the commitments that peoples and leaders would tolerate invariably stopped short of the use of armed force. The painful truth that extreme toughness by peaceful nations is sometimes essential to avert major war was too unpalatable to swallow. Churchill later put it thus: "Virtuous motives, trammeled by inertia and timidity, are no match for armed and resolute wickedness. A sincere love of peace is no excuse for muddling hundreds of millions of humble folk into total war. The cheers of weak, well-meaning assemblies soon cease to echo, and their votes soon cease to count. Doom marches on."[145]

The resurgence, rearmament, and aggressions of Nazi Germany in 1933–39 were unquestionably the positive forces that brought on World War II. By the end of August 1939 Italy was virtually a German ally, Austria had been absorbed, Czechoslovakia was under Nazi control, the Soviet Union was a neutralized power, and Japan was a limited ally (formally one from September 27, 1940). Time after time in the 1930s, the democracies lost or fumbled opportunities to restrain, halt, or reverse the dangerous drift toward war.[146]

Harold Macmillan contributed an article to the *Star* on March 20, 1936,[147] in which he charged that Baldwin and MacDonald, who had been in power jointly or singly for almost thirteen years, had shirked the country's social and economic problems ("so that we find ourselves to-day almost at the top of an industrial boom with two million men unemployed and nearly half our population undernourished"), and that in foreign affairs the country was also "drifting," with "no strong and forceful direction of policy." "They have elevated inactivity into a principle and feebleness into a virtue." "The mood of the people in Britain and throughout the Commonwealth was for peace at almost any cost. To some extent, this defeatism was mingled with true idealism; to some extent it was exhibitionism." By late 1937, Macmillan later wrote, "the growing sense of impotence and almost despair . . . pervaded the whole nation."[148] Salter

---

[145]*Gathering Storm*, p. 190.
[146]Churchill, *Gathering Storm*, passim; Nicolson, *Harold Nicolson*, 1:215, 242, 247–51.
[147]Partially quoted in *Winds of Change*, pp. 429–30.
[148]*Ibid.*, p. 450.

put it thus in the spring of 1939: "The leaders of the democracies suffered from lethargy and a paralysis of the will."[149]

Churchill, the outstanding Cassandra of this period, later credibly called World War II "the unnecessary war." "Up till 1934 at least," he said, "German rearmament could have ben prevented without the loss of a single life. . . . France, unaided by her previous allies, could have invaded and reoccupied Germany. In 1936 there could be no doubt of her overwhelmingly superior strength. . . . Up till the middle of 1936, Hitler's aggressive policy and treaty-breaking had rested, not upon Germany's strength but upon the disunion and timidity of France and Britain and the isolation of the United States."[150]

Churchill's outspoken warnings, most of which proved accurate, were disbelieved, in part because he had earned the distrust of the British public as well as of political leaders, and he was kept out of the government until the war came—and was rejected as a peacetime prime minister in 1945 after it was won. The MacDonald-Baldwin-Chamberlain governments of 1923-39 catered to a shortsighted, pacifistic public opinion until late in the period, and their ill-judged moves and inaction at crucial points in foreign affairs more than offset skillful handling of a few domestic issues, such as the abdication of King Edward VIII late in 1936.[151]

Gross divergence of expert opinions rendered impossible any approach to consensus in all the leading democracies. Rigid pursuit of narrow objectives, such as the maintenance of the gold standard in the gold bloc countries until 1935-36, not only interfered with economic recovery but also diverted attention from urgent problems in foreign relations. France was bogged down in a political morass. In March 1936, facing an early election, deeply involved in her latest "battle of the franc," fearful of incurring the heavy costs of mobilization, and failing to get assurances of British cooperation in using her still strong military power, France lacked the will to move independently. The Netherlands and Belgium soon chose a neutral status, fearing that alliance with France and Britain would be less a safeguard than a menace.[152] Thereafter, as Rauschning wrote in

[149]Salter, *Security*, p. 374. Elsewhere in that book much evidence on this point is given. Churchill summed up his devastating criticism of the British political parties and leaders in the closing paragraph of his chapter, "The Locust Years, 1931–35," in *Gathering Storm*, p. 89. He was no less critical of Baldwin's government in 1935–37 and of Neville Chamberlain's in 1937–40. *Ibid.*, pp. 220–22, 240.

[150]Churchill, *Gathering Storm*, pp. iv, 15–18, 41, 51, 92, 118, 211.

[151]It is surprising, however, that McElwee gave most of the credit to MacDonald and Baldwin for creating "the unity, stamina, and moral courage of the nation which stood firm behind Churchill in 1940." *Britain's Locust Years*, p. 249. I cannot endorse this conclusion.

[152]Churchill, *Gathering Storm*, pp. 381, 472–73; Rudolph Binion, *Defeated Leaders: The Political Fate of Caillaux, Jouvenel and Tardieu* (New York: Columbia University Press, 1960), p. 332. Belgium's neutral status was recognized in an Anglo-French declaration of Apr. 24, 1937.

1941, "every level of the French people went on strike. . . . the substance of the nation had evaporated."[153]

The United States, under Presidents Hoover and Roosevelt, for the most part remained aloof and pursued its isolationist course regardless of untoward international consequences, out of deference to powerful public opinion. What Offner properly called "crimes of omission" weakened Britain and France and abetted Hitler's aggressive moves.[154] President Roosevelt occasionally showed awareness of the grave dangers abroad, but could not arouse the nation to join "a quarantine upon the aggressors" (his Chicago speech of October 5, 1937, was abortive), to say nothing of stronger steps.[155] An effort made early in 1938 to get representatives of Britain, France, Italy, and Germany to confer in Washington on "the underlying causes of present differences" failed because of Chamberlain's coolness to the idea; and Roosevelt's personal appeal to Hitler and Mussolini on April 15, 1939, was ignored by them.[156] The neutrality acts which Roosevelt halfheartedly signed between 1935 and 1939 "played right into the hands of the aggressor nations," as he later observed.[157] As keen an observer as Paul Einzig wrote in the winter of 1937: "Anyone who has an elementary knowledge of the American attitude must be aware that there is not the least likelihood of any active intervention of the United States in any European war. Not only would the United States give no military sup-

[153]Rauschning, *Redemption of Democracy*, pp. 109–14. Several books by the prolific Paul Einzig, in which he dealt particularly with French political finance, have already been cited. See esp. *World Finance, 1938–1939*, ch. 17. Alexander Werth was the able Paris correspondent of the *Manchester Guardian* (1931–40) and other journals. His three books, *France in Ferment* (1934), and *Which Way France?* or *The Destiny of France* (1937), and *France and Munich* (1939), all published by Harper and Brothers in New York and London, illuminate the tumultuous course of events in France in 1933–39 and go far to explain the instability of French governments and the ultimate French collapse in June 1940. In the epilogue to his fourth book, *The Last Days of Paris: A Journalist's Diary* (London: Hamish Hamilton, 1940), pp. 215–74, Werth discusses the reasons for the humiliating collapse. Cf. William L. Shirer's later book, *The Collapse of the Third Republic: An Inquiry into the Fall of France in 1940* (New York: Simon and Schuster, 1969).

[154]Extensively set forth in Offner, *American Appeasement. Foreign Affairs* (October 1969, p. 186) termed this "one of the best books on a tragic chapter in the history of the Western democracies." In concluding this well-documented book, Offner observed (p. 278) that "Secretary Hull's responses to the crises and chaos of his era were excessively cautious," and that President Roosevelt, though "able, shrewd, and farsighted, . . . expended most of his energy on domestic problems and belatedly and without daring or dash turned to foreign policy" and "demonstrated his naiveté about the Third Reich and international problems. . . . Further, to a shocking degree those responsible for planning and executing their nation's foreign policy did not heed Messersmith's charge that they were responsible for informing and guiding the public in its own interest." The last point, however, is applicable also to earlier and later administrations. Cf. Herbert Feis, *Foreign Aid and Foreign Policy* (New York: St. Martin's Press, 1964), pp. 7, 47–48.

[155]Mowat, *Britain between the Wars*, pp. 590, 596–97, 641, 647; Bliven, *World Changers*, pp. 53–55.

[156]Churchill, *Gathering Storm*, pp. 251–55, 354–55.

[157]Morison, *Oxford History*, pp. 991–92. See excerpts from George W. Ball's testimony before the Senate Foreign Relations Committee, in *WSJ*, Aug. 5, 1971, p. 6.

port to France or Great Britain against a German aggression, but, owing to the deadlock over the war debts, even financial support would not be forthcoming this time."[158] Lippmann, more prescient, vainly undertook to dispel this widely cherished illusion in an article on the (Johnson) Neutrality Act of 1937.[159]

Ex-President Hoover, in a press interview on March 19, 1938, newsreel remarks on March 29, and prepared addresses in New York on March 31 and in San Francisco on April 8, summed up his recent observations in fourteen European countries. He emphatically asserted that the United States should display an "inflexible determination to keep out of other people's wars and European age-old quarrels. Our job is to cleanse our democracy, raise our moral standards, and keep alive the light of free men in the world. . . . We can make war but we do not and can not make peace in Europe."[160] These statements echoed the convictions that he had expressed in 1919, and foreshadowed his vigorous campaign in 1939-40 to keep the nation out of World War II.[161]

What Einzig termed the "rich man's revolt" was a prominent feature of 1937 which became endemic in 1938 in Britain, France, and the United States. It defeated Chamberlain's efforts to revive the wartime excess profits tax and for a time helped to slow the pace of British rearmament. It figured in the overthrow of the Popular Front in France late in 1938. It was among the factors that led the Roosevelt administration belatedly to seek to appease businessmen.[162]

Great Britain eventually awoke to the grim necessity of organizing to resist the burgeoning forces led by Hitler before they could achieve overwhelming superiority. Why did she sleep so long?[163]

[158]*World Finance, 1935-1937*, p. 227.

[159]Walter Lippmann, "Rough-Hew Them How We Will," *Foreign Affairs*, July 1937, pp. 587-94, partially quoted in Salter, *Security*, pp. 34-35. Joseph P. Kennedy, U.S. ambassador in London, expressed a similar view on Sept. 12, 1938. Offner, *American Appeasement*, p. 254.

[160]Lochner, *Hoover and Germany*, p. 200. To the end of his life, I am reliably informed, Hoover took special pride in having said this.

[161]See Chapter 2 above; Herbert Hoover, *Further Addresses on the American Road* (New York: Scribner's, 1940), pp. 85-179.

[162]Einzig, *World Finance, 1938-1939*, pp. 6-7, 109-10, 284.

[163]See Winston S. Churchill, *While England Slept* (New York: Putnam, 1938), and John F. Kennedy, *Why England Slept* (New York: Wilfred Funk, 1940). The latter book, to which Henry R. Luce wrote a commendatory foreword, was written as a Harvard senior's honors thesis in the first year of World War II, while the author's father, Joseph P. Kennedy, was U.S. ambassador in London. In his recent memoirs George F. Kennan noted the adverse reaction of the Prague embassy staff when Ambassador Kennedy asked their help in facilitating John's investigatory visit in 1939. *Memoirs, 1925-1950* (Boston: Little Brown, 1967), pp. 91-92. The son did not share his father's defeatist views.

On Feb. 29, 1940, Nicolson noted in his diary that Sir Robert Vansittart (chief diplomatic adviser to the foreign secretary, 1938-41), who on Sept. 15, 1939, had given him the impression that Britain could not win, was very worried by the return of Kennedy, saying that he "has been spreading it abroad in the U.S.A. that we shall certainly be beaten and he will use his influence here to press for a negotiated peace. In this he will have the assistance of the old

Weak political leadership was a major part of the answer, but attitudes of the British people exerted powerful influence.[164] They were strongly committed to world peace and to the League of Nations and disarmament as means to this end. Superactive British consciences obfuscated clear thinking. Macmillan said of Ernest Brown, minister of labour from June 1935 to September 1939: "To use a phrase of Samuel Butler, he was a good man in the worst sense of the word."[165] There were many such. The pacifist movement swelled to a peak in 1935. In a vigorous speech at the Labour Party conference at Brighton in that year, Ernest Bevin said that pacifism meant "a world safe for Hitler."[166] Repeatedly moves were made to appease the dictators, whose appetites "grew with eating," and Churchill was long excluded from cabinet office, lest his appointment antagonize Hitler. In the later 1930s well-founded fears of air attacks, and of defeat such as overtook France in June 1940, became powerful negative forces.[167]

In retrospect, Great Britain could take small pride in her political leadership in the interwar years.[168] Lloyd George had been a great minister before and early in the war, a great wartime prime minister, and for a time after peace a towering world leader. But he then lost his popularity with the voters and never held office in any government after 1922. He was deeply distrusted, feared, and hated by Baldwin and Chamberlain. While active at intervals in the declining Liberal Party, he lost his following even in it, and was ineffective in opposition. In September 1936 he visited Hitler, and returned much impressed by both his work and his peaceable intentions.[169]

---

appeasers, of Minsky [Soviet ambassador in London, 1932–43], and of the left-wing pacifists." On Dec. 3, 1940, Nicolson's diary reported a conversation with Lord Halifax, then foreign secretary, regarding "Joe Kennedy and his treachery to us and Roosevelt. The general idea is that he will do harm for the moment but not in the end. How right I was to warn people against him. I was the first to do so." Nicolson, *Harold Nicolson*, 2:33, 60, 130.

[164]Einzig, *World Finance, 1938–1939*, passim; Hodson, *Slump and Recovery*, pp. 403–11; Churchill, *Gathering Storm*, esp. ch. 11, "Hitler Strikes," pp. 191–99; Mowat, *Britain between the Wars*, pp. 470, 564–68; McElwee, *Britain's Locust Years*, chs. 11–12; Macmillan, *Winds of Change*, pp. 429–30.

[165]*Winds of Change*, p. 453.

[166]Kingsley Martin, "The 'United' Kingdom," *Foreign Affairs*, October 1937, pp. 114–28, esp. p. 120. This article well brings out the agonizing transformation of the political disunity of the early 1930s into effective unity in mid-1937.

[167]The gloomy defeatism that pervaded Britain in the last year of worried peace carried over into the early months of the war, as the second volume of Nicolson's diaries makes abundantly clear. Nicolson, *Harold Nicolson*, 2:19, 33–36, 61–62, 123, 148, 155, 163. In his *Economic Warfare, 1939–1940* (London: Macmillan, 1941; preface dated February 1941), Einzig may have been right in saying (p. viii) that wishful thinking was by far a bigger factor than defeatism in Great Britain.

[168]The lists of British cabinets with their members are given in Mowat, *Britain between the Wars*, pp. 665–73, based on lists in the official *Annual Register*.

[169]Salter, *Personality in Politics*, pp. 38–53; Churchill, *Gathering Storm*, p. 89; Mowat, *Britain between the Wars*, pp. 10, 534, 554, 562, 591, 640, 654; Macmillan, *Winds of Change*,

After Lloyd George's downfall in the autumn of 1922, from which the Liberal party never recovered, Britain had notably weak leaders until Churchill became prime minister in May 1940.[170] Andrew Bonar Law held the top office for only 209 days, from October 1922 until May 1923, when grave illness forced him to resign.[171] Then followed fourteen years of the MacDonald-Baldwin regimes, in which Stanley Baldwin was the dominant political figure whether he held the chief office or not.

Ramsay MacDonald, though prime minister for ten months in 1924 and again in 1929–35, never had an independent Labour majority. In 1931–35, heading the coalition government, he was deserted by the majority of his own party. His physical and mental deterioration began as early as the fall of 1930 and progressed until he resigned in June 1935.[172] Yet he remained prime minister throughout this critical period in British and world history.

Baldwin, who bore the major responsibility for British political leadership in 1930–37 and for its failure in crucial respects, was an effective politician who sought to avoid taking unpopular positions, but was an indecisive leader.[173] He concentrated on domestic matters without seriously trying to solve difficult problems of the economy, and neglected important matters of foreign policy.[174] Bonn later aptly wrote of him: "No man was perhaps a more passionate friend of peace . . . and no man was more

pp. 237, 289–90, 450. Lloyd George and most of the Liberal Party and Clement Attlee and the Labour Party opposed conscription in peacetime when Chamberlain announced it in April 1939.

[170]Mowat, *Britain between the Wars*, p. 142. A keen appraisal of British prime ministers in 1922–39, from Lloyd George to Churchill, is given in Bonn, *Wandering Scholar*, pp. 362–64. Of this period Bonn says: "A curious torpor seemed to have seized the British people. A highly emotional flabbiness prevailed. The classic representative of this spinelessness was Ramsay MacDonald." Baldwin, MacDonald's alternate, mentor, and successor, was "a very astute politician" who "possessed that mellow seductive lack of principle which is so disconcerting to non-Britishers," and who "kept his ear carefully to the ground in the way American presidents are apt to do." Cf. Macmillan, *Winds of Change*, pp. 285–92.

[171]Robert Blake, *The Unknown Prime Minister: The Life and Times of Andrew Bonar Law, 1858–1923* (London: Eyre and Spottiswoode, 1955), chs. 29–32.

[172]Salter, *Personality in Politics*, "Ramsay MacDonald: The Tragedy of Success," esp. pp. 59–65; Salter, *Memoirs of a Public Servant*, pp. 248–49; Churchill, *Gathering Storm*, p. 37. In his diary for Oct. 8, 1930, Harold Nicolson, a loyal younger friend, noted that MacDonald could not remember Canadian Premier Bennett's name when he tried to introduce him to Nicolson's wife, and added: "He makes a hopeless gesture, his hand upon his white hair: 'My brain is going,' he says, 'my brain is going.'" Nicolson, *Harold Nicolson*, 1:56.

[173]By contrast, in postwar Germany Chancellor Adenauer carried out measures which current opinion polls showed to be distinctly unpopular, such as master plans of reconciliation with France and with the Jewish world community, and persuaded the people afterward that his way had been the right one. Gittler, "Probing the German Mind," p. 8.

[174]On Baldwin, see also Churchill, *Gathering Storm*, p. 215; McElwee, *Britain's Locust Years*, pp. 227–28; Nicolson, *Harold Nicolson*, 1:288; K. Middlemass and J. Barnes, *Baldwin: A Biography* (London: Weidenfeld and Nicolson, 1969); K. Middlemass, *Thomas Jones: Whitehall Diary*, 2 vols. (London: Oxford University Press, 1969). The last two books are reviewed by D. E. Moggridge in *EJ*, June 1970, 80:356–60, and the biography undertakes to habilitate Baldwin's reputation.

responsible for the coming of the war. He saw the danger but did nothing to make color-blind pacifists visualize it."[175] Yet he won an overwhelming Conservative victory in the 1935 elections, long held the confidence of the electorate, survived several shocking disclosures,[176] and, late in 1936, won acclaim for his handling of the delicate matter of King Edward VIII's abdication.[177] He was worn out when, in late May 1937, he accepted an earldom and left to his successor, Chancellor of the Exchequer Neville Chamberlain, what Churchill rightly termed "a ghastly mess."[178]

Chamberlain, a stronger personality, dominated his cabinets as MacDonald and Baldwin never dominated theirs. He did not neglect foreign policy; on the contrary, he played rather too large a role in its formation and execution, to the serious detriment of the Foreign Office, whose "permanent" head, Sir Robert Vansittart, he promoted early in 1938 to an "honorific but powerless post," an act which was soon followed by Foreign Secretary Eden's resignation. But Chamberlain was so strongly impressed with Britain's military weakness and the necessity of avoiding war that he carried appeasement ("the Conservative brand of pacifism"[179]) far beyond rational lengths until March 1939, when he belatedly reversed his policy after Hitler forcibly took over Czechoslovakia. He tried "summitry" with disastrous results. "Never for over a century," wrote Salter in the spring of 1939, "has Great Britain sustained such a series of humiliations as in the last four years."[180] Yet "the overwhelming mass of British opinion enthusiastically endorsed the Chamberlain government's every move."[181]

Each of these three prime ministers was responsible for significant positive achievements, which were eventually overshadowed by failures. MacDonald and Baldwin received cheering ovations when they resigned;

[175]Bonn, *Wandering Scholar*, pp. 363-64.

[176]Important ones included: (1) his admission in November 1936 that the East Fulham election of a pacifist Labour candidate in a supposedly safe Conservative district on Oct. 25, 1933, had restrained his rearmament efforts in the next three years, despite his solemn pledges (Churchill, *Gathering Storm*, pp. 111, 215-16); (2) his confession in the House of Commons on May 22, 1935, that he had gravely underestimated the pace of German rearmament when he flatly contradicted Churchill on that subject in late November 1934 (*ibid.*, pp. 118-19, 123, 126); and (3) his post-election reversal of approval of the Hoare-Laval agreement on Abyssinia on Dec. 9, 1935, in response to a public outcry (*ibid.*, pp. 181-85).

[177]Salter, *Security*, pp. 194-98; Churchill, *Gathering Storm*, pp. 217-21, 287; Mowat, *Britain between the Wars*, pp. 583-86; Nicolson, *Harold Nicolson*, 1:278-87; Lord Beaverbrook, "How the Duke of Windsor Lost His Throne," *Saturday Evening Post*, Jan. 25, 1966, pp. 38-51.

[178]Mowat, *Britain between the Wars*, chs. 8, 10; Churchill, *Gathering Storm*, pp. 113, 119, 123, 128, 175-81, 184-85, 197-98, 215-16, 220-21; McElwee, *Britain's Locust Years*, chs. 10-11, esp. p. 231; Nicolson, *Harold Nicolson*, 1:278-79, 295, 330, 332-37, 338-41. Repeatedly Nicolson could not decide how to vote, and often decided just to lie low. *Ibid.*, pp. 331, 341, 344, 345-46, 359, 377, 390-91.

[179]McElwee, *Britain's Locust Years*, p. 228.

[180]*Security*, pp. 24-25. Cf. Macmillan, *Winds of Change*, chs. 17-18.

[181]Mowat, *Britain between the Wars*, ch. 11; Salter, *Personality in Politics*, pp. 66-85; Salter, *Memoirs of a Public Servant*, pp. 248, 251; Churchill, *Gathering Storm*, pp. 220-22, 240-43, 250-51, 333-35, 342-43; Macmillan, *Winds of Change*, p. 495.

yet in their last years they were bitterly attacked by disillusioned Britons.[182] Chamberlain died six months after Churchill became prime minister.

Churchill, who had held government posts in 1925–29, broke with MacDonald and Baldwin in 1929–31 on the issue of self-government for India.[183] He was increasingly outspoken on the danger of another world war and the importance of British rearmament. As early as June 1931 he spoke at Oxford on the topic, "Wake Up, England!"[184] This was his favorite theme for the rest of the decade; in 1938 he published his *While England Slept*. But he was out of tune with the British voters and their political leaders, was blamed for grave wartime and peacetime blunders (including the April 1925 restoration of the gold standard with sterling at prewar parity with the dollar, which he came to regard as his worst mistake), and gave what many considered wild, irresponsible, scaremongering and warmongering speeches, all the more dangerous because he was so skilled an orator. Had he died in the mid-1930s, he might have been "recorded in history as a brilliant, erratic, unstable man whose great talents had never come to fruition."[185] In the House of Commons Harold Nicolson, a man of brains, experience, and charm, remained loyal to MacDonald though fully aware of his increasing weakness, and refused to join Churchill's circle, while keeping on good terms with him. He later sadly wrote of Churchill and the years 1931–35: "Such prophets were denounced as cynical, selfish, out-of-date, militaristic and anxious to promote the very conflict against which, in agonised impotence, they sought to warn their countrymen."[186]

From mid 1935 on, Churchill was a member of the newly formed Committee of Imperial Defence, in air defense research, but he was left free to debate policy and program issues connected with the air services. His old friend Professor Frederick Lindemann of Oxford (later Lord Cherwell), his chief adviser on various aspects of modern warfare, was appointed to its Technical Subcommittee at Churchill's insistence. This research work proved of high significance; notable results included the development of radar and the "asdics" system of submarine detection.[187] When Germany attacked Poland on September 1, 1939, Chamberlain at last asked Churchill to become a member of the war cabinet, and soon

[182]Mowat, *Britain between the Wars*, p. 588; McElwee, *Britain's Locust Years*, pp. 93–249; Nicolson, *Harold Nicolson*, 1:301.

[183]Churchill, *Gathering Storm*, pp. 32–33, 67–68, 78–79. The background is well summarized in Harold Nicolson, *King George the Fifth, His Life and Reign* (London: Constable, 1952), pp. 502–9.

[184]Nicolson, *Harold Nicolson*, 1:77 (diary for June 8, 1931).

[185]Bliven, "Churchill: The Last Bulldog," *World Changers*, pp. 75–127, esp. p. 102.

[186]Nicolson, *George the Fifth*, p. 519; Nicolson, *Harold Nicolson*, 1:328 (diary for Mar. 2, 1938); Blake, *Bonar Law*, pp. 55–56. In his diary covering the war years, Nicolson repeatedly recorded his glowing admiration for Churchill (see index s.v. "Churchill"), and said that his "magnificent" message to the Italian people (December 1940) showed that "he was not a war-monger but a heroic pacifist" (2:131).

[187]Churchill, *Gathering Storm*, pp. 79–80, 148–54, 163–64, 224, 386–87, 411, 468.

gave him the Admiralty post as well.[188] But it was not until May 10, 1940, that Churchill succeeded Chamberlain as prime minister, at the head of a coalition government which he formed.[189]

In almost every country, indeed, the record of conflicting opinions and advice among social scientists and responsible leaders, which had been painfully conspicuous in the late 1920s and became worse in the depression years, continued in the later 1930s.[190] Repeatedly, national and international situations were incorrectly appraised, confident forecasts proved wrong, crises were not foreseen, serious preparations for coping with them were not made, and the best minds were baffled. It is therefore not surprising that economic recovery was so spotty and erratic; that government measures were neither timely nor consistent;[191] and that the drift toward another great war proceeded inexorably.[192] And it is ironic that widespread pacifist sentiment in the democratic countries[193] promoted that drift, and that rearmament made the major contribution toward the revival of general prosperity.

The Wall Street superboom of the late 1920s and the ensuing crash and collapse played a large role in starting and intensifying the grave depression that engulfed the world in the early 1930s. That depression, which was notably severe in Germany, contributed heavily to Hitler's rise to power early in 1933, and had some part also in the dominance of the militarists in Japan. For the time these two countries succeeded amazingly well in emerging from depression while the pacifistic, divided democratic countries, under the spell of ideas that proved impractical, recovered more slowly and less completely. The relative power of the two groups had altered so drastically that, when Germany opened World War II in September 1939 and intensified it in June 1940, the achievement of her goal of

[188]*Ibid.*, pp. 405-10.

[189]*Ibid.*, pp. 658-67.

[190]See Chapter 15 below. In ch. 8 of his *Great Depression*, tentatively sketching conditions of recovery, Robbins touched repeatedly upon the lack of agreement among economists, and his own discussion well illustrated it.

[191]G. McCrone's recent book *Regional Policy in Britain* (London: Allen and Unwin, 1969), which came out about seven weeks before the Hunt Committee Report on the Intermediate Areas (Cmd. 3998), spoke of the interwar efforts to reduce very high rates of unemployment in the distressed areas as "a confused rag-bag of interventions in which political, social and economic objectives are variously intermingled" (words of the reviewer, A. Beacham, in *EJ*, December 1969, 79:920-22).

[192]A recent book by D. F. Fleming (*The Origins and Legacies of World War I* [London: Allen and Unwin, 1968]) cites no work published after 1938 except one book published in 1949. It lays the responsibility for World War II on failure of leadership in the League of Nations, referring principally to the United States and secondarily to Britain and France. *EJ*, December 1969, 79:1017. Though containing an element of truth, this seems far too simplistic an interpretation.

[193]Morison wrote (*Oxford History*, p. 988): "Never since Jefferson's time had America, and never in recorded history had England, been in so pacifist a mood as in 1933-39. Hitler was canny enough to play upon this."

European domination seemed assured; and by late 1941 the Japanese felt such confidence in their competence that they assaulted Pearl Harbor. The fumblings and blunderings in the 1930s on the part of their intended victims only gradually gave way to effective mobilization of their enormous potential to win World War II, first in Europe and then in the Pacific.

PART III

ANALYSIS AND INTERPRETATION

CHAPTER 13

WEAKNESSES UNDERRATED
OR IGNORED

THE STOCK MARKET crash in the fall of 1929 broke on a world full of confidence and hope. The U.S. economy seemed strong and sound. The Federal Reserve System seemed to have matured in the postwar decade, and was seen as a powerful bulwark against recessionary forces and an important engine of recovery. A great social engineer was in the White House. Continuance of the forward momentum seemed assured, and the ending of the speculative and investment boom was expected to entail only a temporary setback.

Most of those who were confident of the soundness of the U.S. economy in 1929 neglected to give due weight to the speculative fever, the credit strain that it brought, and the distortions to which it contributed, here and abroad, even before the final frenzy in the summer months. Our "acquisitive society"[1] had become truly ill; but most victims of the disease were only dimly aware of their illness, and most "doctors" failed to recognize and diagnose it. All too few recognized the increasing vulnerability of the economy or drew attention to potential sources of adverse developments. Numerous weaknesses and ominous signs were commonly underrated, if recognized at all.[2] Comparable but somewhat different elements of weakness in major foreign countries also were inadequately recognized or underrated. This multifaceted failure was important among the factors responsible for the breadth, length, and severity of the ensuing worldwide depression.

A Summary Basic, though hardly of major importance, was the notable
View slowing down of U.S. population growth in the 1920s, in consequence of severe restrictions on immigration early in the decade

---

[1] This phrase was coined by Richard H. Tawney in *The Acquisitive Society* (New York: Harcourt Brace, 1920); but this book shed little light on American problems of the ensuing decade.

[2] Galbraith listed five weaknesses in the U.S. economy that "seem to have had an especially intimate bearing on the ensuing disaster": the bad distribution of income, the bad corporate structure, the bad banking structure, the dubious state of the foreign balance, and the poor state of economic intelligence. *The Great Crash 1929* (Boston: Houghton Mifflin, 1955), pp. 182–91. The first of these I have explored at length, with the aid of several later studies, without being able to satisfy myself that it deserves to be included; but see Herman P. Miller, *Income Distribution in the United States: A U.S. Census Monograph* (Washington, D.C.: U.S. Government Printing Office, 1966; preface dated March 1966), pp. 1, 17, 27. The others are dealt with in this chapter and the next.

and the decline in births that took place almost unnoticed in the second half. Specialists did see and stress this, but their somewhat discordant views did not win widespread credibility, and failure to recognize the implications for growth of demand was general and serious.

The decline in nonfarm residential construction from its postwar peak in 1925–26[3] was recognized but underweighted. Its main causes were catching up with wartime arrears, the falling off in family formations, and the shortage of mortgage credit in competition with speculative borrowings in 1928–29.

In addition, current consumer demand for automobiles and several types of durable household goods had subtly approached saturation, a process which was widely underestimated.[4] The danger in the notable expansion of installment debt incurred for such purchases had been overrated,[5] but the extent to which this debt might shrink if and when unemployment spread was largely overlooked.

The recent growth in "inventories" and stocks of important commodities was seriously underrated, and their potential for forcing price declines was inadequately realized until months after the Wall Street crash.

The construction of industrial, commercial, and public utility plant had continued[6] at a pace that contributed heavily to current high employment, profits, and prosperity; but this created actual or latent surplus capacity which any significant curtailment of demand was sure to reveal as serious.

The remarkable strength of many large corporations obscured the vulnerability of many small corporations, for which the vaunted prosperity was "profitless" in its later stages. More important, the recent buildup of holding companies, most notably in public utilities, had made them subject to extreme stress if the overoptimistic expectations of their promoters were not borne out.[7]

[3] *Hist. Stat. U.S.*, ser. N 4, 31, 61–67, 106, 189.

[4] Cf. Stuart Chase, *The Nemesis of American Business and Other Essays* (New York: Macmillan, 1931), pp. 14–16, 78–81, 93–94, 169.

[5] E. R. A. Seligman, *The Economics of Installment Selling* (New York: Harper, 1927); Melvin T. Copeland, in *Recent Economic Changes in the United States* (New York: McGraw-Hill, 1929), 1:390–402, 424; N. J. Silberling, *The Dynamics of Business* (New York: McGraw-Hill, 1943), pp. 480–87; B. M. Anderson, *Economics and the Public Welfare: Financial and Economic History of the United States, 1914–1946* (New York: Van Nostrand, 1949), pp. 174–75.

[6] *Hist. Stat. U.S.*, ser. N 6, 7, 10–13; Silberling, *Dynamics of Business*, pp. 222, 236–38.

[7] Georges F. Doriot, "Our Sick Industries," *Yale Review*, March 1931, pp. 442–55; HES, *Weekly Letter*, May 16, 1931, p. 95; Silberling, *Dynamics of Business*, pp. 291–92; J. A. Schumpeter, *Business Cycles: A Theoretical, Historical, and Statistical Analysis of the Capitalist Process*, 2 vols. (New York: McGraw-Hill, 1939), 2:832–34. Chester W. Wright, in his monumental *Economic History of the United States* (New York: McGraw-Hill, 1941), correctly observed that the highly competitive struggle among big holding companies for choice additional operating companies has led to "a top-heavy pyramiding of security

Debt expansion was carried much too far. In particular, the large volume of mortgage debt on individually owned nonfarm homes and rental properties imposed heavy fixed charges on incomes that were subject to substantial shrinkage. There was inadequate awareness that this contraction could go so far as to make debt charges critically burdensome, and the doubling of the number of mortgage foreclosures in 1926–29[8] was little realized and taken too lightly.

The enormous swelling of stock market loans despite the fact that rates on call loans were generally over 6 percent from mid-1928 through October 1929 was well publicized but diversely interpreted, and its true significance was ill appreciated. These loans proved to entail no great losses to lenders; but they were subject to great shrinkage, very costly to borrowers, if nonbank lenders chose to liquidate their huge loans, as they did soon after the Wall Street crash.

A subtle decline in the *quality* of domestic and international credits, which had been so liberally extended, was little recognized.

A structure of commodity prices that seemed to contemporary observers remarkably stable was not responding smoothly to the increasing abundance of several important commodities. Private and public efforts were mistakenly directed toward preventing truly appropriate price declines, and crumbling of prices was not seriously considered possible.

The volume of bank credit was expanded in 1922–29 far beyond the needs of commerce, and huge amounts flowed into inappropriate channels such as capital additions, real estate bonds, and loans on securities. The weaknesses thereby created were generally overlooked.

The U.S. banking system, reinforced by the Federal Reserve System, was erroneously deemed a great source of strength. In reality almost chaotic and inherently weak, it was subject to special strains if the commodity and security price structures were undermined. The power of the FRS to put on brakes or provide stimuli when needed, and its readiness to use such powers effectively, were both overrated.

The nation's agricultural economy had made progress in readjustment after its severe postwar depression, but was so heavily burdened by debt as to be vulnerable to substantial declines in farm prices and incomes, to a degree that few realized in 1929.

International trade was progressively hobbled in the later 1920s, first in agricultural products, as European countries sought to protect their domestic agriculture and their balance of payments, and then more generally, as economic nationalism ran rampant. Yet dominant political leaders

values on the basis of net earnings which, even if only moderately impaired, threatened serious disaster" (p. 983). The collapse of the huge Insull empire (see pp. 375–77 below) was one of several instances of the fateful outcome. Cf. Galbraith, *Great Crash*, pp. 183–84.

[8] *Hist. Stat. U.S.*, ser. N 150–57, 189; Silberling, *Dynamics of Business*, pp. 188–89, 262.

were moving toward raising U.S. tariff barriers still higher, as was done in June 1930 over the protests of a large group of economists.

While it was generally accepted that "booms" threaten "busts," that maladjustments develop during prolonged expansions,[9] and that curbing excesses during prosperous periods was vital to avoiding depressions, actions were inhibited by widespread fears of checking prosperity and weakening confidence. Despite the existence of the Federal Reserve System and the efforts made under Secretary Hoover's leadership to find ways to ensure full employment and the stability of the economy, the federal government did not seriously try to moderate the boom or correct manifest abuses.[10]

The potential consequences of a fairly severe stock market break were viewed with undue complacency, with little awareness of its strong adverse influence on the economy and on the extraordinarily high level of confidence. The proved resiliency of the U.S. economy was thereby overrated.

Little recognition was given to the serious damage done to European financial structures by the high money rates in this country which the stock market superboom had brought about.[11]

Incomplete economic recovery in Western Europe was coupled with a flimsy foundation for the currency stabilizations that had been achieved by arduous efforts; and the dangers inherent in the huge volume of short-term international indebtedness were not rightly appreciated.

Political weaknesses in Great Britain, France, Italy, and Germany, as well as many smaller countries, were also largely ignored and their evil potential very inadequately appreciated. In the United States the constitutional threefold division of functions and an ill-developed bureaucracy rendered the government poorly equipped to undertake the radical extensions of federal authority to cope with contraction and speedy recovery attempted by Presidents Hoover and Roosevelt.

Although progress had been made in enlarging statistical data and in analyses of the overall U.S. economy, its major segments, and European economic and financial developments, these provided an inadequate basis

[9]Citibank, *Monthly Economic Letter*, May and June 1930, pp. 76, 89–90; Clark Warburton, "Plateaus of Prosperity and Plains of Depression," in *Economic Essays in Honor of Wesley Clair Mitchell* (New York: Columbia University Press, 1935), pp. 497–516; Schumpeter, *Business Cycles*, 1:148–49; Anderson, *Economics and the Public Welfare*, pp. 390–91. Many other sources could be cited.

[10]In the past, Eccles wrote early in 1937, "we have made virtually no preparation for economic disasters. . . . Stable prosperity can be attained only if we are aware of the problem, if we are willing to tackle it vigorously, and if we can develop a broad, positive program designed to correct economic distortion and unbalance." Marriner S. Eccles, "Controlling Booms and Depressions," in A. D. Gayer, ed., *Lessons of Monetary Experience: Essays in Honor of Irving Fisher* (New York: Farrar and Rinehart, 1937), pp. 3, 12. Cf. Chapter 15 below.

[11]E.g., see HES, *Weekly Letter*, Mar. 15, 1930, pp. 73–74.

for reliable judgments and forecasts. Yet excessive faith in economic fore-casting was generated and the crucial need for foreseeing a major contraction was not met (see Chapter 15, esp. n. 26).

In the aggregate, these weaknesses made the U.S. economy highly susceptible to shocks and created conditions favorable to them; and ignoring or underrating them helped to swell the excessive expectations which the increasingly widespread New Era psychology had created. Several of the foregoing points listed call for amplification here.

Population growth. Intensification of the long-term downtrend in the rate of U.S. population growth was noted by specialists in 1920–28.[12] On the whole, they regarded this trend as normal, but its implications were little explored. Louis I. Dublin, the eminent statistician of the Metropolitan Life Insurance Company who was president of the American Statistical Association in 1924, organized a program at the ASA annual meeting on population problems in the United States and Canada. In his introductory chapter to the published volume of the papers there given Dublin wrote: "We must be prepared at a comparatively early date for a stationary population, unless we completely change our present attitude toward the foreigner and modify our approval of small families. Such a reversal is not probable, because as a nation we like to indulge our sense of exclusiveness and superiority."[13] Other contributors to the program voiced no direct dissent from this view, and none forecast the upsurge of population that came in the 1940s. E. B. Reuter, though stressing the "continuous and uniform decline" in the rate of natural increase in 1870–1920 (pp. 22–29), nevertheless concluded (p. 32) that "prediction concerning the rate of population increase even in the immediate future [is] an extra-hazardous

[12]Raymond Pearl and Lowell J. Reed published their famous logistic curve paper in June 1920 (*Proceedings of the National Academy of Sciences*, 6:275–88). Edward M. East's alarmist *Mankind at the Crossroads* came out in 1923 (New York: Scribner). Frederick Jackson Turner, famous for his 1893 paper on the American frontier, complacently observed in a 1925 paper reprinted in his Pulitzer-Prize-winning book *The Significance of Sections in American History* (New York: Holt, 1932), p. 41: "We, like the European nations, are approaching a saturation of population." Paul H. Douglas in 1933 remarked: "The prospects are that the populations of the United States and Western Europe will become virtually stationary within the next three or four decades." See his paper in *Economic Essays in Honour of Gustav Cassel* (London: Allen and Unwin, 1933), p. 115. Most scholars appear to have welcomed this prospect, but O. E. Baker, who made population projections for the Bureau of Agricultural Economics in the 1920s and 1930s, found it alarming. P. K. Whelpton published his initial forecast in September 1928 (*American Journal of Sociology*, 34:253–70). On Mar. 15, 1933, I sent Baker's chief, Dr. O. C. Stine, at his request, several comments on Baker's draft report on population prospects. One sentence reads: "Personally, I should not be surprised if the next thirty years should bring to light some factor that would alter these trends in significant measure; and I am inclined to doubt that the United States will actually reach a stationary population by 1960 or decline after 1970."

[13]*Population Problems in the United States and Canada* (Boston: Houghton Mifflin, 1926), p. 10.

type of speculation." Subsequent history fully bore out this warning.[14] Reread in 1970–74, these nineteen papers reveal a sorry mixture of truth, error, and blindness. The diversity of views expressed helped to account for their limited impact on thinking at the time.

Reduction in the absolute increase in U.S. population in the second half of the 1920s—a new fact, of importance if it should persist[15]—was recognized in Wesley Mitchell's chapter in *Recent Economic Changes.* The retardation was due to drastic immigration restrictions and to an absolute decline in births, which averaged 2,955,000 a year in 1920–24 and 2,761,000 in 1925–29,[16] in a decade when marriage rates trended strongly downward[17] and wants for durable goods competed heavily with wants for babies. Mitchell, however, merely touched upon "certain prompt economic consequences" of the population trend, without exploring its full significance. It was not until late December 1938 that A. H. Hansen, in his famous presidential address before the American Economic Association, stressed the "profound change" in the nation's economic prospects in consequence of the "drastic decline in the rate of population growth."[18] Had such views been arrived at and published a decade earlier, they might have helped to restrain the excessive optimism so prevalent in 1929. Actually they persisted even through the 1940s, in part because current published data were inadequate and belated, in part because firmly entrenched ideas proved very hard to reverse.

Consumer demand. By mid-1929 the demand for durable consumer goods was approaching saturation,[19] to a degree that was underrated. The

[14]J. S. Davis, *The Population Upsurge in the United States,* Food Research Institute War-Peace Pamphlet 12 (Stanford, Calif.: Food Research Institute, 1949), esp. charts on pp. 4, 18, 28–29, 48, 64–65, and comments on pp. 57–58, 70–73, 78–84; and J. S. Davis, "Our Changed Population and Its Significance," *AER,* June 1952, 42:304–25. Cf. Asher Achinstein, *Introduction to Business Cycles* (New York: Crowell, 1950), esp. pp. 422–23.

[15]In his *Full Recovery or Stagnation?* (New York: Norton, 1938), A. H. Hansen wrote that "decline in population growth is a new fact that differentiates our age from that of the nineteenth century—a fact of profound significance for investment outlets" (p. 313).

[16]As estimated much later; see *Hist. Stat. U.S.,* ser. B 6.

[17]The number of marriages showed a horizontal trend in the 1920s, and the five-year moving average of marriages per thousand population declined almost continuously and substantially throughout the decade. *Hist. Stat. U.S.,* ser. B 8; Davis, *Population Upsurge,* p. 4.

[18]"Economic Progress and Declining Population Growth," *AER,* March 1939, 29:1–15. Hansen relied heavily on the seemingly authoritative report of the outstanding Committee on Population Problems, *The Problems of a Changing Population* (Washington, D.C.: National Resources Committee, 1938). Early in 1937 J. M. Keynes had given his Galton lecture, "Some Economic Consequences of a Declining Population," published in *Eugenics Review* (London), April 1937, 39:13–17. By 1939, however, a fresh population upsurge had already quietly begun, and it rendered such analyses irrelevant for the time. Chapter 2 in Silberling, *Dynamics of Business,* reflected the "wrong ideas too well learned and illusions too long cherished." Cf. J. S. Davis, "The Population Upsurge and the American Economy, 1945–80," *JPE,* October 1953, 61:369–88.

[19]A. J. Youngson, *The British Economy, 1920–1957* (Cambridge, Mass.: Harvard University Press, 1960), pointed out (pp. 239–50) that evidence given before the Macmillan com-

enormous expansion of passenger car ownership and of automotive exports had not exhausted potential demand; but such a large proportion of the latent demand had been met that saturation was near at hand, pending the deterioration of the huge stocks of relatively new and longer-lived cars and trucks, and the rise of new crops of buyers.[20] Much the same was true of durable household goods, in view of the recent decline in home building and the slowing increase in the number of married couples.

Commodity stocks. It was a fairly common view in 1929 that commodity inventories were moderate, not excessive as they had been in 1920.[21] The basis for this view was very weak, for data were available only for certain groups of products, and those were none too satisfactory. The Harvard Economic Society, after emphasizing this point in mid-October 1929, asserted that while stocks of cotton goods, leather, and bituminous coal were moderate, they were large "for the time of year," and by comparison with other recent years in the chief non-ferrous metals, petroleum, rubber and rubber manufactures, automobiles, cement, and food products —even after reduction over recent months in holdings of some of these goods. It went on: "There are no indications of shortage in any important direction, and surpluses are evident in some lines."[22] Nevertheless, the real inventory position became ominous only after the general assumption that the business level would continue high, even after a moderate contraction, proved false.

Later investigation revealed that, while stocks of manufactured goods showed only a moderate uptrend in 1923–29 (and even in 1930), warehouse stocks of raw materials (metals, chemicals and allied products, foodstuffs,

---

mittee in 1930 found the explanation of the "crisis" in (1) price instability, (2) structural maladjustment, and (3) "gluttability" of wants, which D. H. Robertson particularly stressed.

[20]Gordon rightly emphasized the great expansion in motor vehicle production and use in the 1920s, and the fact that even for the peak output of 1929 (when sales were double those of 1922) the industry was overbuilt. R. A. Gordon, *Business Fluctuations*, 2d ed. (New York: Harper, 1961), esp. pp. 411, 426. Relevant data are available in *Hist. Stat. U.S.*, ser. Q 310–21, and two annuals published by the Automobile Manufacturers Association: *Automobile Facts and Figures* and *Motor Truck Facts.* Cf. R. C. Epstein in *Recent Economic Changes*, 1:59–62; F. Leslie Hayford, "The Automobile Industry," *Rev. Ec. Stat.*, February 1934, 16:37–40.

[21]Cf. *Recent Economic Changes*, 1:292–93, 302–3, 343–64, 350–61; 2:508–9, 865, 915. Stress was laid on the successful efforts of businessmen to avoid the mistakes of 1919–20. Cf. C. A. Phillips, T. F. McManus, and R. W. Nelson, *Banking and the Business Cycle: A Study of the Great Depression in the United States* (New York: Macmillan, 1937), p. 64: "The fact that there was no increase of inventories during the late boom was iterated and reiterated by almost every writer up to the time of the crash."

[22]HES, *Weekly Letter*, Oct. 19, 1929, pp. 250–51. In the issue of May 18, 1929 (pp. 122–23), the HES had mentioned "some evidence . . . that stocks of goods are now accumulating" but that "actual figures upon the size of inventories are extremely defective." And the *Brookmire Forecast* of July 22 stated: "The automobile industry became overextended; mounting stocks of cars in dealers' hands, and curtailment of manufacturing operations suggest that the turn has now come here too."

and textile materials) rose impressively in January-August 1929. Then, after a brief contraction, they went up irregularly to new highs; in the first half of 1932, they were more than 75 percent above the 1923–25 averages.[23]

Until after the Wall Street crash there was very inadequate awareness of the extent of the buildup of stocks of staple commodities—wheat, coffee, rubber, copper—and such manufactured products as tires, gasoline, and paper, which contributed to the unexpectedly sharp decline in prices in 1929–30 and later.[24] Moreover, almost no attention was given to the noteworthy size of stocks of durable consumer goods in consumer hands as a result of the huge sales in the long prosperity period and the rising life expectancy of these goods.

Excess capacity. In mid-May 1925 the Harvard Economic Service had called attention to the "existence of a considerable excess of capacity in many branches of industry, especially in those producing basic materials or staple commodities intended for sale to ultimate consumers."[25] But the HES seldom sounded this note in the next four years, as industrial, commercial, and public utility construction and purchases of industrial and transport equipment (including motor trucks) rose to 1929 peaks.[26] Much of this investment was undertaken to supply future needs in the expectation of continuing increases in population, demand, and the level and profits of business, without regard to accumulating relevant evidence. When these expectations were disappointed, the fact of overinvestment became painfully obvious.

It is not surprising that this element of vulnerability was poorly appraised in the late 1920s, in view of inherent difficulties in the concept and measurement of excess capacity, the divergent views of competent specialists,[27] and serious inadequacies in data. In retrospect, however, I

---

[23]CTC, *Bus. Bull.*, Nov. 15, 1932; Phillips, McManus, and Nelson, *Banking and the Business Cycle*, pp. 189–90.

[24]See Citibank, *Monthly Economic Letter*, March 1930, p. 49; J. S. Davis, *The World Wheat Problem*, Wheat Studies of the Food Research Institute 8 (Stanford, Calif.: Food Research Institute, 1932), pp. 409–44, esp. pp. 428–33; "Wheat and the World Depression" (July 6, 1933), reprinted in my *On Agricultural Policy, 1926–1938* (Stanford, Calif.: Food Research Institute, 1939), pp. 180–93, esp. pp. 183–85; and Davis, "Wheat, Wheat Policies and the Depression," *Rev. Ec. Stat.*, April 1934, 16:80–88. Like most others, I had not been wise enough to see and say these things four or five years earlier.

[25]HES, *Weekly Letter*, May 16, 1925, pp. 149–50.

[26]*Hist. Stat. U.S.*, ser. N 28, 85–105.

[27]E.g., see E. G. Nourse and Associates, *America's Capacity To Produce* (Washington, D.C.: Brookings Institution, 1934), and succeeding volumes in this four-part series; Willard L. Thorp, "The Problem of Overcapacity," in *Economic Essays in Honor of Wesley Clair Mitchell*; and Schumpeter, *Business Cycles*, 2:509, 754, 801–3. Kuznets' 1938 figures led Schumpeter to conclude that real "investment" in the 1920s was much more modest than was then generally believed and to question current overinvestment theories; and he quoted Mitchell's 1936 opinion that "the partial character of the liquidation effected during mild contraction" largely accounted for the violence of the convulsions in 1907–8, 1920–21, and 1929–33.

lean to Gordon's view that the economic downturn in mid-1929 was due in considerable part to overinvestment in relation to the demand for final products, in the sense that in numerous lines capacity had been expanding at a rate that could not be indefinitely maintained.[28]

Bulging indebtedness. The ebullient 1920s witnessed a vast increase in public and private indebtedness. Additions to state and local public debts more than overbalanced the marked reduction in the federal debt. Private debts of almost all sorts rose by leaps and bounds, though many large corporations took advantage of the stock market boom to retire bonds through stock issues. Individuals, investment-rating agencies, and the marketplace all underrated the increasing risks involved.[29]

Outstanding consumer debt, in an inclusive sense, rose strikingly in the nine years 1921–29, from some $12 billion to $32 billion (end year data, 1920–29).[30] Mortgage debt rose from $5 billion to $14 billion, as total nonfarm residential mortgage debt, including real estate bonds and mortgages on rental properties, rose from $9.4 billion in 1922 to $29.4 billion in 1929.[31] Consumer security loans more than trebled, from $3 billion to over $10 billion at the end of 1928, and the October 1929 peak was much higher. Installment debt more than trebled, to over $3 billion. All other consumer debt roughly doubled, to nearly $6 billion in 1929.

Grave weaknesses in the mortgage situation were not widely apparent until the crash came. The huge expansion of loans on securities in 1928–29 was increasingly recognized as abnormal and dangerous, but there was much disagreement about this. Careful studies by Seligman and Copeland yielded reassurances about consumer installment loans without giving adequate consideration to the possibility of severe economic contraction.

Altogether, the buildup of huge indebtedness, which had contributed much to the prosperity of the 1920s, was carried so far that it rendered both debtors and creditors vulnerable to shocking losses when the bottom dropped out of the real estate and stock markets and commodity price levels.[32]

Deteriorating credit quality. In the later 1920s, as the boom was prolonged and optimism became well-nigh universal, the quality of credits so freely granted underwent subtle deterioration. This was later shown by several studies of mortgage credits, foreign loans, and corporate bonds.[33]

[28]Gordon, *Business Fluctuations*, pp. 444–46.

[29]Arthur F. Burns, "Business Cycle Research and the Needs of Our Times," *The Frontiers of Economic Knowledge* (Princeton, N.J.: Princeton University Press, 1954), pp. 178–79; Anderson, *Economics and the Public Welfare*, p. 197 ("Mob Mind in Manhattan Real Estate").

[30]FRS, *Hist. Chart Book, 1965*, pp. 61, 119.

[31]*Hist. Stat. U.S.*, ser. N 150–57. Cf. Frederick C. Mills, *Economic Tendencies in the United States* (New York: NBER, 1932), pp. 452–53.

[32]Cf. Schumpeter, *Business Cycles*, 1:146–48, 2:793–94, 909–10.

[33]Geoffrey H. Moore, "The Quality of Credit in Booms and Depressions," *Journal of Finance*, May 1956, 11:285–309; Max Winkler, *Foreign Bonds: An Autopsy* (Philadelphia:

Years later, Friedman and Schwartz rightly warned against exaggeration of this point and questioned the degree to which it had occurred;[34] but that it was significant and generally overlooked seems clear. To a surprising extent, investment-rating agencies failed to recognize these increasing risks.

As early as 1927, a few keen observers in the United States voiced concern over weaknesses in the foreign loan situation. Reichsbank President Schacht and the agent general for reparation payments (S. Parker Gilbert) warned that lending to Germany was going too far. The marked contraction of foreign bond issues here after mid-1928, due to other causes, was welcomed in some quarters. Yet, with confidence in the future of America and Europe still dominant, and with the widely accepted prospect of nothing worse than a brief and minor recession here, the danger of numerous defaults was given little serious attention. Overcompetition and irresponsibility on the part of some investment bankers, and gullibility on the part of investors, were paving the way for extensive defaults on foreign and domestic bonds floated in 1927–29 and for rising delinquencies on urban mortgage loans. In 1929–32 the drastic shrinkage of commodity prices, real estate values, and general confidence, which had been largely unforeseen, expanded the disaster.

Price stability. The U.S. price level, following its sharp fall in 1920–21, was relatively stable in 1922–29, while important technological developments were reducing real costs in agriculture and industry. Private and private-public efforts such as international commodity agreements and cartels, and government steps by tariffs and otherwise, were aimed at resisting the normal tendency for prices of particular commodities to decline as abundance succeeded scarcities. The idea of stabilizing the price level as a means of smoothing out the business cycle won wide support. The Federal Reserve System would not endorse proposed legislation to make this a primary objective of its monetary management, but it did include it among' its objectives. For a few years these moves seemed to have succeeded. The BLS index of wholesale prices showed a peak in the excep-

Ronald Swan, 1933); George W. Edwards, *The Evolution of Finance Capitalism* (New York: Longmans Green, 1938); R. J. Saulnier, *Urban Mortgage Lending by Life Insurance Companies* (New York: NBER, 1950); Ilse Mintz, *Deterioration in the Quality of Foreign Bonds Issued in the United States, 1920–1930* (New York: NBER, 1951), esp. pp. 45–48, 76–78; Carl F. Behrens, *Commercial Bank Activities in Urban Mortgage Financing* (New York: NBER, 1952); W. Braddock Hickman, *Corporate Bond Characteristics and Investor Experience* (Princeton, N.J.: Princeton University Press, 1958). Cf. also Silberling, *Dynamics of Business*, pp. 287–89; Moritz J. Bonn, *Wandering Scholar* (New York: John Day, 1948), pp. 304–5. Anderson later observed (*Economics and the Public Welfare*, p. 6): "There was no such qualitative deterioration of credit preceding the panic of 1907 as there was preceding the panic of 1929."

[34] Milton Friedman and Anna J. Schwartz, *A Monetary History of the United States, 1867–1960* (Princeton, N.J.: Princeton University Press, 1960), pp. 245–49, 355.

tional year 1925 and a slight downtrend in 1923–29;[35] but this was not regarded as ominous or as inconsistent with virtual stability. From time to
time a few observers showed awareness of maladjustments in the commodity price structures, and held that a stronger but gradual downtrend
was possible or even likely; but it was widely assumed that the degree of
stability achieved would persist. Even in mid-March 1930, after a sharp
decline in commodity prices, the Harvard Economic Society saw some
reason for expecting "international cooperation in stabilizing commodity
prices."[36] And in their book on unemployment published in May 1931 Paul
H. Douglas and Aaron Director devoted chapter 17 to "Stabilization of
Prices and the Business Cycle" and ventured the very "iffy" opinion "that
we may expect for the near future a decline in the price level of between
one and two percent a year."[37]

Bank credit inflation. Late in 1928 Carl Snyder, in his impressive
presidential address before the American Statistical Association, observed
that "in all boom periods, save that of the present, the amount of possible
credit expansion has . . . soon reached the end of its tether."[38] From
mid-1922 to April 11, 1928, roughly its culmination, U.S. commercial banks
expanded their deposits by about $13.5 billion and their loans and invest-
ments by $14.5 billion—close to 40 and roughly 44 percent, respectively. The
huge gold stock and the operations of the Federal Reserve System were
responsible for this extraordinary expansion, greater than in World War I
and far beyond the requirements of commerce. Much flowed into the real
estate and stock markets, and contributed heavily to notable advances of
prices there, while commodity price indexes continued reasonably stable.[39]

[35]*Fed. Res. Charts*, Nov. 9, 1939, p. 32. Wholesale price indexes weakened in 1928 and
1929 in Great Britain and Germany also, and in 1929 most sharply in France.

[36]Of the voluminous literature on this subject I select for citation only the following:
HES, *Weekly Letter*, June 10, 1922, pp. 133–40, Mar. 15, 1930, pp. 70–75, July 3, 1931, pp.
122–23; W. L. Crum, *Interpretation of the* [Harvard] *Index of General Business Conditions*
(supplement to *Rev. Ec. Stat.*, September 1929, with data through July 1929; see Chapter
15 below); Phillips, McManus, and Nelson, *Banking and the Business Cycle*, ch. 8; Silberling,
Dynamics of Business, chs. 4–6, 24, esp. chart 7b, p. 51.

[37]*The Problem of Unemployment* (New York: Macmillan, 1931; preface dated Feb. 26,
1931), pp. 186–246.

[38]*JASA*, March 1929, 24:11.

[39]Anderson, *Economics and the Public Welfare*, ch. 18. Anderson, in the *Chase Economic
Bulletin*, and H. Parker Willis, in the New York *Journal of Commerce* and elsewhere, protested repeatedly in vain. Cf. Friedman and Schwartz, *Monetary History*, pp. 298, 699. These
authors do not recognize or discuss what I have called (I believe rightly) bank credit inflation.
Indeed, by relying on what I consider an unduly narrow concept of "inflation," they denied
the "widespread belief that the 1920's were a period of inflation," and went so far as to say:
"Far from being an inflationary decade, the twenties were the reverse. And the Reserve System, far from being an engine of inflation, very likely kept the money stock from rising as
much as it would have if gold movements had been allowed to exert their full influence." In
my considered view, these authors exaggerated the "gold sterilization" and unduly discounted
important "inflation" that did not manifest itself in commodity price indexes.

Snyder computed a much more inclusive index of the "general price level," which rose from 152 (1913 average = 100) in 1922 to 183 in 1929.[40] This was truly inflation, though many contemporary observers failed to recognize it as such.[41]

Banking weaknesses. Late in 1928 Snyder had called the U.S. banking system "now centralized and unified." In his first State of the Union message in early December 1929, President Hoover found satisfaction in "the strong position of the banks" in the Wall Street crash, and they indeed met the strains of the early stock market liquidation remarkably well. On the eve of the first of three "epidemics" of bank failures in the last quarter of 1930, the Harvard Economic Society termed the system "not only sound but strong," and in the ensuing difficult weeks it found repeated evidence of its soundness. Actually, to a degree that was largely unperceived in 1928–30, the "system" was chaotic, poorly integrated, and shot through with grave weaknesses despite elements of strength. Under pressure it proved, as Eccles and Hoover later observed, "one of the weakest links in our economy," and its eventual collapse "tremendously intensified" the great depression.[42]

There were serious defects in structure. In addition to national banks chartered under federal laws and required to belong to the Federal Reserve System, there were thousands of state banks and trust companies chartered under the laws of forty-eight competing states and the District of Columbia, which were subject to highly variable state bank examinations.[43] State-chartered institutions had the option of joining the FRS; many did, but most did not. Banks could and did shift from one category to another. The great majority, many with capital as low as $10,000 or $25,000, were too small to attract or hold good managers or to diversify their loans

[40]Carl Snyder, "New Measures of the Relations of Credit and Trade," *Proc. Acad. Pol. Sci.*, November 1929, 13:468–86, and "Commodity Prices versus the General Price Level," *AER*, September 1934, 24:385–400.

[41]Phillips, McManus, and Nelson, *Banking and the Business Cycle*, ch. 8, esp. pp. 191–99; Silberling, *Dynamics of Business*, chs. 11–12.

[42]Carl Snyder, Dec. 27, 1928, in *JASA*, March 1929, 24:14; HES, *Weekly Letter*, Sept. 20, Nov. 29, Dec. 13, 1930, pp. 234, 294–98, 307, Jan. 3, 1931, pp. 3–4; Herbert Hoover, The *State Papers and Other Writings of Herbert Hoover*, ed. William Starr Myers, 2 vols. (Garden City, N.Y.: Doubleday Doran, 1934), 1:145, 154–55; Jacob Viner, in *AER*, March 1936, suppl., 26:106–19; Paul H. Douglas, in *Economic Essays in Honor of Wesley Clair Mitchell*, p. 116; Marriner S. Eccles, in Gayer, *Lessons of Monetary Experience*, pp. 3–22, esp. pp. 19–20; Phillips, McManus, and Nelson, *Banking and the Business Cycle*, esp. chs. 5, 8; Silberling, *Dynamics of Business*, pp. 193–205, 236–37, 239–62, 272, 320–21; B. M. Anderson, *Economics and the Public Welfare*, chs. 24–25, 29–30, 39; Hoover, *Memoirs*, 3:15, 21–28; Friedman and Schwartz, *Monetary History*, esp. pp. 240, 244–45, 270, 299, 351–53, 420, 693–95; Gottfried Haberler, *Prosperity and Depression: A Theoretical Analysis of Cyclical Movements* (New York: Atheneum, 1963), p. 458.

[43]The comptroller of the currency had a corps of bank examiners to check national banks, and the Federal Reserve Board had others who examined state banks that had joined the FRS.

and investments. Moreover, their rural and small-town clienteles were adversely affected by the financial difficulties of farmers and the growth of chain stores and mail-order houses, and improved roads increased bank competition. Strong public prejudice in favor of "unit" banking led to severe legislative restrictions on branch banking, and the substitute evolution of group and chain banking came too late and too slowly.[44]

Even during the prosperous twenties unprecedented numbers of banks failed or were saved from suspension only by merger with others, and the profitability of others was marginal.[45] Yet such was the prestige and glamour of a few large banks that their stocks were among those boosted in the frenzied superboom. The bad record of bank failures in the prosperous 1920s was regularly shown in annual reports of the Federal Reserve Board,[46] but was largely ignored by it and by the Federal Reserve Banks.[47] The Economic Policy Committee of the American Bankers Association summarily said in its October 1927 report: "In the supremely important matter of safety the recent record of the American system of independent unit banking has been conspicuously unsatisfactory."[48] But this report led to no action. In general, public opinion attributed the failures to bad luck, inadequate reserves, poor management, dishonesty, or some combination of these, and experiments with state guaranty or insurance of bank deposits seemed to confirm the belief that this would only make matters worse.[49]

There were other important sources of banking weakness.[50] The volume of commercial credit failed to expand in the 1920s, and the banks sought other channels for their funds and services indeed, attempted to become department stores of finance. This involved greater risks, most notably in real estate loans and bonds, in corporate stocks and bonds, and in investment and speculative operations. These played a large role in in-

---

[44]These and later points are well discussed in a book by Belgian-born R. W. Goldschmidt (later Goldsmith), *The Changing Structure of American Banking* (London: Routledge, 1933; preface dated September 1933), written before the author emigrated to this country. His appendix tables are useful.

[45]W. E. Spahr, "Bank Failures in the United States," *AER*, March 1932, suppl., 22:219, 235.

[46]E.g., that of 1929, pp. 21–24, 123–25, 197–98.

[47]Friedman and Schwartz, *Monetary History*, pp. 358–59.

[48]*C&FC*, October 1927, suppl., pp. 79–80.

[49]Goldschmidt, *American Banking*, pp. 272–74.

[50]Others of lesser importance deserve only passing mention or none. Bank acceptances based on goods stored abroad or moving between foreign countries swelled greatly in 1925–29 (*Hist. Stat. U.S.*, ser. X 315–21), and many were later frozen. The Federal Reserve System drastically reduced collection charges on checks, one of the sources of profits to rural banks. It was widely believed that the common practice of paying interest on demand deposits induced banks to take undue risks to earn higher profits, though years later George J. Benston's study convinced him that this was mistaken ("Interest Payments on Secured Deposits and Bank Investment Behavior," summary in *JASA*, June 1964, 59:582).

flating prices of real estate (which doubled in the decade) and in common stocks, and in promoting the sale of second and third mortgages, all without adequate realization of possible shrinkage of values. The activities of bank affiliates in floating stocks rose to scandalous proportions in 1928–29.[51]

Though individual criticisms of the banks were numerous in the 1920s, it is not too much to say that their multifarious weaknesses were largely unperceived. The great contraction of 1929–33, to which these heavily contributed, revealed them and their tragic consequences, and led to reforms in the banking acts of 1933 and 1935 without creating a unified system. As late as mid-November 1932, a former chairman of the board of the Federal Reserve Bank of New York gave a paper before the Academy of Political Science in which he gave no hint of the severe banking crisis ahead and did not specifically recommend federal guaranty of banking deposits,[52] which unexpectedly proved a key measure.

Agricultural and wheat situations. American farm prosperity during World War I and overenthusiastic purchases of farms shortly thereafter led to striking advances in farmland values, which reached a peak of $66.3 billion in 1920, and also in farm mortgage indebtedness, which is estimated to have reached $10.2 billion on January 1, 1921. The subsequent drop in prices of farm products led to severe declines in farm income and, in turn, to a drastic shrinkage of farmland values—to $48 billion in 1927–29; this was in striking contrast to the upward sweep of such values in prewar decades. Meanwhile, taxes and interest charges rose. Farm mortgage debt rose to a peak of $10.8 billion early in 1923 and declined slowly thereafter to $6.6 billion on January 1, 1940. The number of foreclosures per thousand farms rose from a 1919 figure of 3.2 to a high of 18.2 in 1926, and declined only to 14.8 in 1928, after which it rose to the peak of 38.8 in 1932.[53] Moreover, the increasing use of the automobile, the truck, and motor-driven farm equipment drastically shrank the farm market for draft animals and feed grains. Nevertheless, enough readjustment had been made by 1929 for the outlook for farmers to be optimistically appraised in mid-June and mid-December of that year, and unduly roseate forecasts were made by competent persons in the face of accumulating adverse evidence into the spring of 1931.[54]

[51]J. G. Smith, "Banking and the Stock Market," ch. 6 in J. G. Smith, ed., *Facing the Facts: An Economic Diagnosis* (New York: Putnam, 1932), pp. 153–85.

[52]Pierre Jay, "The Structure of the Banking System," *Proc. Acad. Pol. Sci.*, January 1933, 15:151–61.

[53]*Hist. Stat. U.S.*, ser. K 4, 116, 162, 201–4, X 431, and later U.S. Department of Agriculture data. "Foreclosures" include "assignments, bankruptcies, and related defaults, occurring in the 12 months ended March 15 of the year following that indicated."

[54]HES, *Weekly Letter*, June 15, Dec. 14, 1929, pp. 146–48, 298–303 (predicting "that the economic position of agriculture would not change greatly for some years to come"); *ibid.*, June 14, Dec. 13, 1930, pp. 150–52, 308–10 (predicting that 1931 would be a better year for agriculture); and *ibid.*, May 23, 1931, pp. 98–100 (renewing the last prediction).

Meanwhile, after European agricultural output had largely recovered by 1925, agrarian protectionism flourished in European importing countries and made for widespread overproduction of staple products, restriction of U.S. exports, and piling up of surpluses—all of which were intensified in 1929-31. The basic difficulties of U.S. farmers, so amply publicized, bore little responsibility for the crash or the subsequent economic contraction. But the increasing vulnerability of the farm commodity price structure was very inadequately realized before it was revealed and accentuated by the crash.

Early in 1961 the International Wheat Council rightly stated: "The dominant feature of the present world wheat situation is the persistence of production in excess of effective demand, as reflected in the large and increasing stocks of wheat."[55] This problem had its origin in 1925-29 when natural, economic, and political forces were jointly responsible for the bumper world crop of 1928 and record grain crops in Europe in 1929, for world wheat stocks of unprecedented volume in mid-1929, and for their persistence for several years. Many of the elements in this situation were more or less correctly appraised by specialists of the day, but with such caution that there was no general appreciation of their ominous significance. Indeed, it was not until three to five years later that they were adequately sized up and interpreted.[56]

Wheat prices in exporting countries and Great Britain had tended downward from their exceptional peaks in 1924-25. In 1928-29 they seemed distinctly low, but were by no means fully adjusted to the abnormally heavy supplies. Indeed, prospects for a small Canadian crop led to a shortlived price advance in June-July 1929. When European importing countries harvested excellent food and feed crops in 1929, the stage was set for a crumbling of the wheat price structure. The stock market crash and the ensuing business contraction accentuated this decline, here and abroad; and the Federal Farm Board intervention in U.S. wheat markets on October 26 and December 20 gave temporary support to domestic prices but severely restricted exports and weakened the disposition of private holders to hold wheat for better prices. In short, the wheat position in 1928-29 proved far more vulnerable than was widely realized at the time, even by those who were most deeply involved.

Prices of many other internationally traded foodstuffs and raw materials also weakened in the late 1920s, and fell faster in the two years following the stock market crash, as business depression widened in

[55] Here quoted from the Australian *Wheat Board Gazette* (Melbourne), January-February 1961, p. 1.

[56] See my papers cited in n. 24 above; my book *Wheat and the AAA* (Washington, D.C.: Brookings Institution, 1935), ch. 1; and V. P. Timoshenko, *Monetary Influences on Postwar Wheat Prices*, Wheat Studies of the Food Research Institute 14 (Stanford, Calif.: Food Research Institute, 1938), pp. 263-318.

Europe and deepened in the United States.[57] Interactions of commodity markets, the course of business, and the stock market were mutually destructive of the confidence and optimism that predominated as late as the summer of 1929. "From the general standpoint," moreover, as the Economic and Financial Committee of the League of Nations said in 1931, "we are forced to the conclusion that the general result of National measures to cope with the effect of the crisis is almost inevitably to prolong and seriously aggravate it."[58]

Threatening world forces. The degree of economic recovery and financial rehabilitation in Western Europe was generally exaggerated, and it was far too little realized that world forces threatening monetary chaos were at work, in the face of which superficial money-market manipulations could not be expected to be effective. Before the Wall Street crash it should have been clear that the world was heading for an impasse and a breakdown of trade and international debt service. The growing surplus of major foodstuffs and raw materials, increasing agricultural protectionism in continental European importing countries, financial stringency in Latin American food-exporting countries, the development of synthetics, higher tariffs in Latin America, and the first stages of currency devaluations, coupled with the excessive hopes of payments on German reparations and U.S. war debts—each of these was noted by some observers, but their combined significance was not generally perceived.[59]

Moreover, far too little attention was given to the dangers inherent in the vast increases in the underestimated volume of short-term international indebtedness in the 1920s and to the "restlessness" of international capital, which raised international transfers on capital account to many times the prewar figure. For this many factors were responsible: the early chaos of currencies and exchange rates; reckless speculation in foreign exchange; the "flights of capital" that accompanied decisions to stabilize currency units at specific values and the threat that crucial negotiations on the Young Plan would fail; and, after long-term borrowing became difficult in mid-1928, governments' resort to excessive short-term borrowing in anticipation of easier terms later.[60] And the financial leadership in

[57]See index charts and tables in M. K. Bennett and Associates, *International Commodity Stockpiling as an Economic Stabilizer* (Stanford, Calif.: Food Research Institute, 1949), pp. 426ff.; and FRS, *Hist. Chart Book, 1965*, pp. 96–104.

[58]Quoted in Davis, *World Wheat Problem*, p. 432.

[59]Silberling (*Dynamics of Business*, pp. 291–97) went so far as to attribute "the ensuing catastrophic difficulties" ultimately to the inability "of the raw-material countries to find markets to maintain prices and income levels, and to validate their foreign and domestic debts."

[60]Paul Einzig, *The World Economic Crisis, 1929–1931*, 2d ed. (London: Macmillan, 1932), pp. 50, 155–56; BIS, *Second Annual Report*, May 10, 1932, p. 11; J. H. Williams, in Quincy Wright, ed., *Gold and Monetary Stabilization* (Chicago: University of Chicago Press, 1932), pp. 146–48; and Phillips, McManus, and Nelson, *Banking and the Business Cycle*, pp. 52, 54.

London and New York was unequal to the extraordinarily difficult tasks that had to be faced.[61] "The gathering international storm" of 1928–31 was most imperfectly recognized.[62]

[61]See Sir Josiah Stamp's list of distinctive interlocking weaknesses in the monetary affairs of the United Kingdom in his paper "The Monetary Question in Great Britain," in *Economic Essays in Honour of Gustav Cassel*, pp. 600–603.

[62]Silberling, *Dynamics of Business*, ch. 13.

CHAPTER 14

MISJUDGMENTS AND MALFEASANCE

THE EXUBERANT optimism of the later 1920s, the inadequacy of the best economic intelligence of the decade, and the stock market boom itself gave rise to multifarious misjudgments, multiplication of objectionable practices, and admixtures of the two. These contributed substantially to the excesses of the business and stock market booms and the severity of the contraction and depression.

Serious Misjudgments   The whole interwar period was marked by a large number of critical misjudgments which bore evil fruit. Of major importance was President Wilson's conviction that the American people would follow his lead in approving the Treaty of Versailles, despite its faults, and that the United States would become an active member of the new League of Nations and an influential participant in the work of its agencies. The nation's relapse into isolationism was crucial, and the consequent absence of U.S. representation on the Reparation Commission was a major factor in its inability to play a beneficent role in dealing with reparation questions in 1919–23, on which Wilson had counted.

One of the greatest misjudgments in the first postwar decade, in Britain, the United States, and elsewhere, was the overestimation of the strength and resiliency of the British economy. Almost as serious was the overconfidence in Germany's ability to regain her economic, financial, and political equilibrium and her forward momentum. These errors of judgment go far to account for the harshness of the British-U.S. debt settlement, the April 1925 return of the pound sterling to prewar parity with the dollar, excessive lending abroad by Britain, and the flood of private U.S. loans into Germany in the late 1920s. Related misjudgments grew out of the insensitiveness of the American public to the well-based French obsession with security and unwillingness to consider the feelings of the French and British over issues of war debts and reparations.

What proved serious misjudgments were also made in setting new currency parities in 1925–28. The pound sterling and the Italian lira were overvalued, necessitating downward adjustments in domestic price levels. These handicapped their export industries in international competition, retarded British recovery from sticky postwar depression, and forced Italy into a depression from 1926 onward, while other countries were generally prospering or at least improving economically. France, on the other hand, undervalued her franc, built up a huge gold stock, and exercised her financial power toward political ends.[1]

The most widely shared misjudgments in mid-1929 were these: (1) that the U.S. economy was fundamentally sound and strong, and that its future was entirely secure; (2) that even Germany was firmly embarked on an economic uptrend; (3) that European financial reconstruction was solidly based and would continue; (4) that, while stock speculation had gone to unhealthy extremes, the speculative mania would have to run its course and would breed its own correctives without important damage to the economy; and (5) that the Federal Reserve System and the Hoover administration could and would effectively check any recession, provide ample credit to facilitate rapid recovery, and supply stimuli adequate to ensure its completion.

After the contraction got well under way in 1930, three further major misjudgments were made: (1) that the depression of 1930 would be only a brief setback, much less serious than that of 1920–22 and nothing like as severe as the depression of the 1890s; (2) that the Young Plan would definitely settle the thorny problem of reparations; and (3) that the prime essential of policy was to maintain confidence and to restore it when shaken.

Such erroneous convictions were expressed by a great many business and financial leaders, in whom the public had come to have inordinate confidence, and were shared by multitudes of other businessmen, petty financiers, investors, and speculators. They were also shared by high government personnel, who were influenced by the superoptimism of the times and by political considerations as well. At the time they were not adequately challenged by economists and political scientists.

Among the fruits of these misjudgments were: (1) the notable insensitivity to alarmist warnings such as that of Sir George Paish late in October 1929; (2) the remarkable revival of bullishness in stocks in the wake of the October-November crash, and seemingly authoritative expression of bullish convictions by outstanding men; (3) the persistence of at least relatively optimistic economic forecasts, by most of those who were practicing this art, during the next two years;[2] (4) imprudent further expansion of debt by corporations and individuals, and overinvestment in railroad and utility plant, both before the crash and in 1930 in response to President Hoover's initiative; and (5) the wrecking of the Young Plan for reparations.

[1]See various books by the prolific Paul Einzig, e.g., on Italy—*The World Economic Crisis, 1929–1931,* 2d ed. (London: Macmillan, 1932), pp. 147–50—and *World Finance, 1935–1937* (London: Macmillan, 1937), pp. 119–22.

[2]The less widely known Silberling Economic Service (Berkeley, Calif.), on Dec. 21, 1929, found the outlook dark for the next six months but was confident that recovery would come after mid-1930.

In the course of the great contraction and depression other misjudgments were serious. Excessive faith was reposed in the League of Nations, in the practical possibilities of disarmament, and in such weak reeds as the toothless Kellogg-Briand Pact for outlawing war. The need to counter deflationary forces by bold monetary expansion and foreign lending was far too little appreciated. Adolf Hitler was almost universally underrated, before and long after he came to power; he was trusted to keep his promises even after he had violated them repeatedly; and his enormous power for evil was persistently underestimated. Such errors of judgment, coupled with continued U.S. unwillingness to risk taking strong stands in · foreign affairs, to say nothing of other factors, led inexorably toward World War II.

One of the major misjudgments of the 1930s was exaggerating the necessity for budget balancing; relief operations in the United States and vigorous rearmament, first in Europe and ultimately here, eventually overrode this common obsession. Also, too long ignored was the fact that persistence of severe depression and its attendant unemployment favored the dictators.

In a notable address in New York in April 1932, Sir Josiah Stamp rightly observed that "an error of human judgment can do more damage in aggravating conditions in this complex civilization than it would in a simpler state of society. . . . Psychology plays an infinitely greater part than it ever could have done in a more primitive state."[3]

Altogether, misjudgments contributed far more to the excesses of the boom of 1927–29, to the crumbling collapse of 1929–33, to delays in recovery, and to the drift toward war than did outright dishonesty and all sorts of reprehensible practices. Yet these were rife and contributed much to aggravate the boom and collapse; and a surprising number were taken as a matter of course.

Malfeasance in   Astute observers remarked—mostly after the stock
Myriad Forms   market crash—on the tendency of booms and active speculation to breed ill-advised, reckless, and fraudulent undertakings and practices which could not stand the test of even a moderate recession, and which the severe contraction that occurred turned into disaster.[4] Hyperinflation in Germany and Austria led to the meteoric rise of Hugo Stinnes and others, whose fortunes vanished with the stabilization of the reichsmark and the

---

[3]Apr. 13, 1932, published in *Proc. Acad. Pol. Sci.*, June 1932, 15:132.
[4]Lionel Robbins, *The Great Depression* (London: Macmillan, 1934), pp. 62, 92; J. A. Schumpeter, *Business Cycles: A Theoretical, Historical, and Statistical Analysis of the Capitalist Process*, 2 vols. (New York: McGraw-Hill, 1939), 1:146–49.

krone.[5] The flush period of U.S. lending abroad in 1925–28 witnessed not merely irresponsible flotations but several instances of bribery and misrepresentation, which helped turn public opinion strongly against foreign lending and were factors in subsequent defaults in the depression years.[6] Alfred Loewenstein, a spectacular Belgian financier who had founded the Hydro-Electric Securities Corporation and the International Holdings and Investment Company, fell out of his private airplane (whether accidentally or intentionally was never determined) on July 4, 1928. His death led to a sharp fall in the prices of these securities.[7] Before the Wall Street crash, here and in European countries, scores of vulnerable positions were built up in part through fraudulent activities. Sooner or later many of these concerns collapsed, with heavy losses to disillusioned investors. One consequence, as Snyder wrote late in 1928, was "a distinct transfer of wealth and income from the many to the few, from the ignorant and improvident to the . . . sagacious, the farsighted and the crafty."[8]

Gross malfeasance exerted significant adverse influence on the course of events at crucial times in 1929–30. In August 1929 confidence in the German financial situation suffered a severe shock from the sudden collapse of a big Frankfurt insurance company with large outstanding foreign claims; its losses were due to "business alien to insurance and expressly disallowed."[9] In September 1929 the notorious Clarence Hatry failure in London, attributable to scandalous practices, triggered the setback in Great Britain and contributed to the crash in Wall Street.[10] On December 11, 1930, a New York state bank which had "departed to an incredible degree from sound commercial bank practices" was forced to close its doors.[11]

[5]Einzig, *World Economic Crisis*, ch. 10, "The Moral Factor." He did not mention Sweden, for Ivar Kreuger's spectacular fall from eminence occurred after the second edition of this book went to press.

[6]Max Winkler, in *New York Tribune*, Mar. 27, 1927, and Winkler, *Foreign Bonds: An Autopsy* (New York: Roland Swain, 1933), esp. chs. 4–5; Walter Lippmann, *Interpretations, 1931–1932*, ed. Allan Nevins (New York: Macmillan, 1932), pp. 54–57; Eleanor L. Dulles, *The Bank for International Settlements at Work* (New York: Macmillan, 1932), p. 218; Ilse Mintz, *Deterioration in the Quality of Foreign Bonds Issued in the United States, 1920–1930*, NBER Publication 52 (New York: NBER, 1951), chs. 4–6.

[7]*C&FC*, July 7, 21, 28, 1928, pp. 38, 317–18, 347, 482–83; *Economist*, July 14, 1928, pp. 75–76, 136–42; W. Lionel Fraser, *All to the Good* (Garden City, N.Y.: Doubleday, 1963), pp. 98–99. Loewenstein had failed to win his battle with Dr. Henry Dreyfus, chairman of British Celanese, over acquisition of companies producing artificial silk, which had slumped in price.

[8]Carl Snyder, in his ASA presidential address, Dec. 27, 1928, *JASA*, May 1929, 24:1–14, esp. p. 13.

[9]A brief account was given by Moritz Elsas of Frankfurt, German correspondent of the LCES, in Royal Economic Society, *Memorandum 20*, February 1930, p. 9. The company was the Frankfurter Allgemeine Versicherungsgesselschaft. See Chapter 8, n. 31, above.

[10]See Chapter 8 above.

[11]See pp. 373–75 below.

The raging economic blizzard of the next two years upset all sorts of calculations, impelled desperate efforts to avoid the consequences of earlier imprudence, gave rise to a rash of embezzlements, and increased the magnitude of the collapse of Insull, Kreuger, and others which came belatedly in 1932, and of Richard Whitney in 1938. One who was in a good position to judge said late in 1932:

The real sources of many of the recent troubles in the field of securityship were localized in point of time before rather than after the beginning of the depression. The depression aggravated these pre-existing conditions and serious trouble resulted. A few examples may be cited. The frenzy of speculation which swept this country during the bull market caused more than one person occupying a position of trust to "borrow" money that was not rightfully his. Everyone was "in the market" and everyone was getting rich. The money would double and treble in no time and it could then be returned with no one the wiser. A sure thing if there ever was one! Many were tempted and could not resist the temptation. Money was embezzled, securities or real estate were bought on margin, deal after deal was successfully negotiated—and then the market broke! As values collapsed, the scheme by which the deception was practiced could no longer be concealed. The result was exposure and a claim against the bonding company under a fidelity bond or some form of blanket bond. There were, of course, other causes for fidelity and blanket bond claims, but speculation in one form or another undoubtedly accounted largely for the abnormal losses of the recent period.[12]

If, as was widely believed in 1929–30, standards of business ethics had risen greatly in recent decades, the level reached was still low. In his book published just before the crash, Charles A. Dice admitted that the former market leadership had been "much more largely of a predatory nature," but argued that the "new leadership" was so able and enlightened that it had not only won but earned the confidence of the public.[13] This was far too rosy a view: the ability and enlightenment of the new leaders were grossly exaggerated, and the confidence won was not truly earned. As the stock market kept rising the public continued remarkably gullible,[14] most "independent" auditors gave support by omission to corporate financial

[12]G. F. Michelbacher, at a session of the annual meeting of the American Economic Association, in *AER*, March 1933, suppl., 23(1):16.
[13]*New Levels in the Stock Market* (New York: McGraw-Hill, 1929), pp. 8–10. Cf. John T. Flynn, "Dishonest Business," *Forum*, December 1929, pp. 551–55; Julius Klein, "The Dividends of Honesty in Business," *ibid.*, March 1930, pp. 129–33.
[14]Thus Harvard's able accountancy expert W. M. Cole began his article on "Our Outdated Accounting" (*Harvard Business Review*, July 1933, 11:478–89): "No one disputes the statement that among the causes of the crash of 1929 was the speculation preceding. Sufficient emphasis has not been placed, however, on the fact that speculation was carried on largely by people who were buying a pig in a poke, or were hoping to sell in a poke a pig that they knew something about. So far as the general public was concerned, all the pigs were in pokes; and even for the professional dealers in pigs the pokes were not more than half transparent."

abuses, responsible business leaders issued few warnings, and government authorities continued to be complacent, opportunities for irresponsible and disreputable actions naturally multiplied, and much advantage of them was taken. Colonel Ayres later listed "malefactors of great wealth" first among the factors that did *not* cause the depression.[15] Yet he surely would have agreed that many wealthy men actively or passively helped to carry the boom to extremes in 1929 and thereby to intensify the subsequent collapse and depression.

Manipulation, bull operations and bear raids in particular stocks, rigging markets, flagrant misrepresentations, and insider preferences were accepted features of the 1920s, as a chapter in Dice's popular textbook on the stock market elucidated.[16] In his annual report for fiscal 1928 (dated November 20, 1928) Secretary Mellon referred to "the activities of powerful groups of speculators" (page 5), but he neither took nor suggested any steps to curb them. Pool activities were extremely common. On August 5, 1929, for example, Insull stocks crashed on the Chicago Stock Exchange, which temporarily suspended trading in Insull Utility Investments. At the time the fall was attributed to pool operators who had "worked the issues to meteoric heights" and then suddenly withdrawn the "props."[17] But this transitory event attracted little comment at the time, and is not mentioned in McDonald's recent biography of Insull.

Shortly after the stock market crash, J. H. Hollander of Johns Hopkins inveighed against "the grossest and most impudent pool operations in the stock exchanges of the land— . . . simply bare-faced, strong-arm manipulations for the rise, to which the stock exchanges either lent themselves or in connection with which they were unwittingly used."[18] No doubt this accentuated the frenzied boom and the severity of the collapse. Albert W. Atwood, commenting on this paper, got Hollander to concede

[15]L. P. Ayres, *The Economics of Recovery* (New York: Macmillian, 1933), p. 14.

[16]N. J. Silberling, in *The Dynamics of Business* (New York, McGraw-Hill, 1943), pp. 401–7, well summarized the stock manipulation practices that were prevalent in the 1920s and that were curbed, but by no means eliminated, under subsequent legislation. Cf. John Lloyd Parker, *Unmasking Wall Street* (Boston: Stratford, 1932); Barney F. Winkelman, *Ten Years of Wall Street* (Philadelphia: Winston, 1932); and various books by John Brooks, one of which is cited in n. 48 below.

[17]*C&FC*, Aug. 10, 1929, pp. 901–2.

[18]"Panics and Pools," *Proc. Acad. Pol. Sci.*, January 1930, 13:455–58. The earlier part of the paragraph reads: "In essentials an exhibit of hysteria, the panic of 1929 and the feverish months leading up to it are certain, however, to be associated in the mind of the future historian with certain provocative causes. For months, when all the signals pointed to a developing speculative mania, we sat by in altruistic sympathy with Europe's monetary troubles and refused to raise discount rates until the speculative bit was hopelessly lodged between the public's teeth. For months we gave receptive ear to financial ballyhoos, perched on high places, who perverted a widespread public confidence in America's economic future into high-pressure selling of anything, anywhere, at any price. Most of all, for months we remained childlike witnesses to the grossest and most impudent pool operations in the stock exchanges."

that manipulation had accompanied the flotation of many undigested securities, but Hollander insisted that, in general, "the manipulation occurred in the evaluation of relatively sound securities sponsored by unusually sound agencies."[19] This way of putting the matter blurs the distinction between misjudgments and malfeasance, but tends to put the stress on misjudgments, where it belongs.

Tieups of commercial banks with investment affiliates, and of banking houses with "trading corporations" and investment corporations or trusts, became common. (The latter grew at an extraordinary pace in 1927–29: at the beginning of 1927 160 were estimated to be in existence; in the next three years 140, 186, and 265 were successively added.[20]) Such tieups afforded fantastic opportunities for promotion of new investment trusts and flotation of huge issues of their stocks. A notorious example was the respected banking firm of Goldman, Sachs and Company.[21] Late in 1928 it formed the Goldman Sachs Trading Corporation; most of its stock was sold to the public while the firm kept control through a management contract and directorships. The Trading Corporation soon merged with one investment trust and spawned two others—the Shenandoah and Blue Ridge corporations. It also acquired a number of smaller ones and the American Trust Company. These were gravely irresponsible moves with a disastrous sequel, regardless of the technical legality and correctness of the procedures employed; and the lines between responsible and irresponsible utterances and actions, and between legitimate and illegitimate ones, were badly blurred.

A young Boston investment banker who was treasurer of the State Street Investment Corporation testified in 1928 before a committee of the New York Stock Exchange on current abuses in the investment trust movement. Cabot attributed them to "dishonesty," "inattention and inability," and "greed." In March 1929 he published an illuminating article elaborating these points, and specifically discussed two common abuses other than pyramiding: trusts "being run for ulterior motives and not primarily for the best interests of the shareholders," and trusts "being used as a depository for securities that might otherwise be unmarketable." He cited an example:

In my opinion there is to-day in this country a large and well-known investment trust whose shares are selling for far more than their intrinsic or liquidating value, which has continually managed its portfolio so that it can show the greatest possible profits and thereby obtain the greatest market value for its shares, regardless of their real worth. Generally speaking, in this trust during the past year the

[19]*Ibid.*, pp. 497–98.
[20]J. K. Galbraith, *The Great Crash 1929* (Boston: Houghton Mifflin, 1955), pp. 53–56.
[21]*Ibid.*, ch. 5, "In Goldman, Sachs We Trust."

good securities that have appreciated in value have been sold and the poorer ones retained or increased, simply to show profits.[22]

After speaking of "pyramiding" and other abuses which were rampant in the investment trust mania in Britain in the late 1880s, and the long period of difficulty for the trusts which the Baring crisis of 1890 inaugurated, Cabot correctly forecast that "unless we avoid these and other errors and false principles we shall inevitably go through a similar period of disaster and disgrace. If such a period should come, the well-run trusts will suffer with the bad as they did in England forty years ago. Of course, the honest and ably managed companies would emerge from the difficulties eventually." But Cabot overoptimistically considered publicity and education to be adequate remedies: "If the investment trusts pursue this policy of complete information, bad practices, simply by revelation, will be eliminated" (page 407). Correction of such abuses was the object of much New Deal legislation.

The extraordinary increase in concentration of control in the electric power industries, chiefly through the expansion of holding companies[23] and the formation of certain types of investment trusts, opened the way "for abuses through manipulation of accounts, secrecy as to financial conditions, concealment of assets, liabilities, profits or losses, diversion of profits to controlling interests through excessive salaries and clandestine transactions between companies or individuals."[24]

A Few Notorious Examples Large numbers of U.S. commercial banks failed in the 1920s (nearly 6,000 in 1921–29), and in 1931 the number reached the peak figure of 2,294.[25] Most of these were small, and the majority were chartered under lenient state laws and operated under inadequate public supervision. The public and the Congress strongly favored the "unit banking system" and were hostile to the branch banking system that was predominant in Great Britain and Canada. Embezzlement

---

[22]Paul C. Cabot, "The Investment Trust," *Atlantic*, March 1929, pp. 401–8. He had just succeeded Charles Francis Adams as treasurer of the Harvard Economic Society, when Adams became President Hoover's secretary of the navy. In 1948, still an officer of the same investment trust, Cabot became treasurer of Harvard College, which in 1930 had 20 percent of the book value of its investments in common stocks, and since 1954 had more than 50 percent of the market value in commons. Paul C. Cabot, "Chasing the Budget: My Twelve Years as Treasurer," *Harvard Alumni Bulletin*, May 25, 1963, pp. 634–37. Cabot resigned this post in 1965, as Harvard's endowment fund reached $100 million.

[23]Ralph L. Dewey, "The Failure of Electric Light and Power Regulation and Some Proposed Remedies" (Dec. 31, 1930), *AER*, March 1931, suppl., 21(1):242–58, esp. pp. 244–45.

[24]*Ibid.*, p. 246, quoting W. E. Mosher, ed., *Electrical Utilities: The Crisis in Public Control* (New York: Harper, 1929), p. 90.

[25]Federal Reserve Board, *Annual Report*, 1935, p. 176.

and other forms of malfeasance were not prominent among the many factors that accounted for the rash of bank failures in 1920–34. More important were insufficient capital, inexperienced or imprudent management, too little diversity of loans, competition from banks in larger centers as automobile use and hard-surfaced roads expanded, shrinkage of prices of farm products and farmland, local droughts and other agricultural disasters, and real estate excesses such as the Florida land boom. Even in 1924–29, when financial conditions encouraged reckless plunging, most bankers kept their heads, stuck to sound banking practices, and adhered to the moral standards of the times, but there were a few notable exceptions.[26] The disappointing record of several state systems of deposit guaranty insurance was largely attributable to causes other than crookedness; and banking opinion long opposed adoption of a federal system lest it reduce incentives for due care and sound judgment on the part of individual bank managers.[27]

One glaring though relatively minor pre-crash instance deserves brief mention, that of the City Trust Company, a small bank chartered by New York State. It had been formed in 1928 by merger of the Harlem Bank of Commerce and the Atlantic State Bank of Brooklyn, and closed ten days after the death of its founder-president, Francesco M. Ferrari, on February 1, 1929. Most of its seventeen thousand depositors were Italian-Americans. Governor Alfred E. Smith had appointed Frank H. Warder superintendent of banks in 1926, though his only financial experience had been as a staff member of the state banking department since 1920. Contrary to custom, Warder did not resign when Smith's term ended in 1928, and Governor Franklin D. Roosevelt allowed him to retain the office, which he resigned ten weeks after the City Trust Company failed. By gifts of cash, liquor and other consumables, and securities, Ferrari had induced Warder to close his eyes to the bank's weakness, bad practices, and illegal actions, thus making himself partially responsible for its failure. In Roosevelt's temporary absence, Acting Governor Herbert Lehman appointed Robert Moses to investigate the relations between the bank and the state banking department which had taken it over. On July 10 Moses submitted an exceptionally able and comprehensive report to Governor Roosevelt. Roosevelt, who had previously clashed with Moses and nursed a grudge against him, virtually ignored the report and its urgent recommendations for reorganization of the state banking department and tightening the state banking law. The

    [26]B. M. Anderson, *Economics and the Public Welfare: Financial and Economic History of the United States, 1914–1946* (New York: Van Nostrand, 1949), pp. 228–30, 310–15; Milton Friedman and Anna J. Schwartz, *A Monetary History of the United States, 1867–1960* (Princeton, N.J.: Princeton University Press, 1960), pp. 235, 240, 249, 278, 299, 308, 321, 324, 351–57, 434–37. Some conspicuous exceptions are mentioned below.
    [27]See Chapter 15 below.

Joint Committee to which it was referred was unwilling to go so far. Roosevelt appointed a special committee, including a director of the Bank of United States, and in April 1930 signed the much more lenient bills that it had recommended. Warder, however, was tried, convicted of accepting a ten-thousand-dollar bribe, and sentenced to Sing Sing for five to ten years.[28]

Bank of United States. A far more conspicuous exception to the rule of careful bank management was the Bank of United States in New York City, which was forced to suspend operations in a critical period on December 11, 1930.[29] Chartered by New York State in 1913, its impressive name was presumably deliberately chosen to mislead the public. The then state superintendent of banks, George C. Van Tuyl, Jr., resigned that office, became one of the bank's directors, and served throughout its seventeen years of unsound banking practices speckled with unsavory, illegal, and criminal actions.[30] The bank mushroomed in 1924–29, and eventually had sixty-one branches in New York City. Through special-interest or "thrift" deposit accounts it attracted large numbers of poor and ignorant recent immigrants on the East Side. On October 17, 1930, it had some 413,000 depositors, with total deposits of $212 million. Insiders knew of the bank's deep troubles, and by the time it suspended operations its deposits had shrunk to $161 million.[31]

This bank had loaned large sums on second and third mortgages. It also accommodated persons engaged in speculative activities who could not get what they wanted from competing banks. Its affiliate, the Bankus Corporation, engaged in many questionable transactions, including manipulation of its own stock. In March 1933, its president and executive vice president (Bernard K. Marcus and Saul Singer) went to Sing Sing to serve sentences of three to six years, after the New York Court of Appeals upheld their conviction on charges of misapplying funds of a subsidiary, the Municipal Safe Deposit Company.[32]

[28]Condensed from summary in E. R. Ellis, *A Nation in Torment: The Great American Depression, 1929–1939* (New York: Coward-McCann, 1970), pp. 104–8.

[29]I have found no complete account of this bank, its operations, and its failure, though abundant materials are available in New York newspapers, the *C&FC*, and New York State documents and court records. Reliable summary accounts are in Anderson, *Economics and the Public Welfare*, pp. 203, 228–30, 269; J. G. Smith, ed., *Facing the Facts: An Economic Diagnosis* (New York: Putnam, 1932), p. 167; and Friedman and Schwartz, *Monetary History*, pp. 167–68, 308–12, 355–57, 376–77. Many respected authors (including E. R. Ellis) have miscalled it the "Bank of *the* United States," and a few have otherwise distorted the story, e.g., W. S. Myers and W. H. Newton, *The Hoover Administration: A Documented Narrative* (New York: Scribner, 1936), pp. 59, 64; and W. E. Leuchtenburg, *The Perils of Prosperity, 1914–32* (Chicago: University of Chicago Press, 1958), p. 256.

[30]*Who Was Who in America*, 1:1273; *C&FC*, Oct. 24, 1931, p. 2639.

[31]*Ibid.*, Nov. 29, Dec. 13, 20, 27, 1929, pp. 3047, 3945–46, 3982–83, 4156.

[32]*Ibid.*, Mar. 18, 25, 1933, pp. 1833–34, 2012.

Though one of the smaller banks in New York City, the Bank of United States was much the largest bank in the nation to fail up to that time. Under the lead of a new state superintendent of banks (1929–34), the respected Joseph A. Broderick,[33] with support from the Federal Reserve Bank of New York, strenuous efforts were made in the fall of 1930 to rescue the bank by merging it with the Manufacturers Trust Company and two others. When success seemed assured, the New York Clearing House Association declined to put up $30 million, and a last-minute alternative plan also failed because the bank's condition seemed so bad.

The failure of this bank reflected lax supervision by state and federal authorities and reluctance to check bad practices which had grown up over a period of years and which were known to the Federal Reserve Bank of New York.[34] Indeed, on July 13, 1929, the bank's books were studied by a flock of examiners from the state banking department and the Federal Reserve Bank of New York, who found its policies and condition highly questionable and were very critical of its key officers; but no action was taken.[35] Broderick, who should have acted promptly, was later indicted by a New York County grand jury for neglect of duty in not closing the bank earlier; but he was acquitted on May 28, 1932,[36] and went on to higher responsible positions.

Gradually assets of the Bank of United States were liquidated, stockholders, directors, and officers were assessed, and depositors repaid in installments. Two-thirds of its adjusted liabilities as of the date of suspension were paid off within two years, and the eventual losses to depositors were only about one-sixth of their claims. Much of the credit for salvaging and prosecuting has been given to Carl J. Austrian, who was counsel for the state superintendent of banks from 1930 to 1943.[37]

A banking crisis registered in mounting bank failures had begun in October 1930, and the November total of deposits in suspended banks was more than double the highest recorded since monthly data were started in 1921. This crisis was accentuated by the sensational failure of the Bank of United States and the disclosures which followed. These precipitated a series of bank runs and widespread resort to currency hoarding for a time.

[33] *Who Was Who in America*, 3:105.

[34] The unpublished minutes of the Federal Reserve Board, 14 (pt. 3), pp. 142–43, record a letter from Governor Strong dated Aug. 23, 1927, regarding "certain apparently crucial violations of the law" by the bank's president, and the reasons why he had not reported them to the U.S. district attorney. After its failure the board of directors of the Federal Reserve Bank of New York pondered seriously the lessons of its debacle. Friedman and Schwartz, *Monetary History*, pp. 357–58.

[35] The reasons for inaction are not clear, but the peculiar "climate" of July–November 1929 explains numerous instances of excessive caution by officials.

[36] *C&FC*, Oct. 24, 1931, pp. 2699–2700, May 21, June 4, 1932, pp. 3742–47, 4086–87.

[37] *Ibid.*, Jan. 14, Feb. 11, 1933, pp. 277–78, 462–63; *Who's Who in America*, 21:112; and *New York Times*, June 26, 1970.

The immediate crisis was soon over. The stock and bond markets reached their lowest points in mid- and late December, then rose in the next three months, before another major relapse started.

The Harvard Economic Society *Weekly Letter* of December 13 (page 307) overoptimistically reported that the difficulties had been met in such a manner as to give "renewed evidence of the soundness of the general banking situation." The AT&T's next monthly summary (January 7, 1931, page 4) reported that "the rapidity with which the Federal Reserve System was able to increase the circulating currency demonstrated its strength and ability to deal with such emergencies." A very different view has recently been forcefully urged: that, in the absence of the FRS, restriction of convertibility of deposits into currency, such as had occurred in 1907 under the former system, would surely have come at this time (if not in October 1929); that it would have "quickly ended bank suspensions arising primarily from lack of liquidity"; that even the Bank of United States might have been able to reopen as the Knickerbocker Trust Company had in 1908; and that "it would have prevented the collapse of the banking system and the drastic fall in the stock of money that were destined to take place."[38] While I cannot fully endorse this judgment, I do believe that the HES and the AT&T badly misjudged the situation, and that the FRS, like the Bank of England, mistakenly carried resistance to liquidation of weak positions much too far, with unfortunate consequences.

Insull. The admixture of misjudgments, malfeasance, and bitter conflicts with other powerful financiers is well illustrated in the story of the amazingly dynamic and constructive genius Samuel Insull.[39] London-born, he immigrated to this country early in 1881, and was closely associated with Thomas A. Edison and his enterprises until June 1892. Thereafter he built a huge and far-flung midwestern utility network, and had won national and international acclaim by the mid-1920s. In 1926–30, driven by greed for wealth and power, he involved himself and his extraordinarily complex "empire" in fateful financial excesses. After struggling valiantly to rehabilitate it during the collapse of the stock market, he suffered a spectacular business failure in April 1932, which entailed huge

[38]Friedman and Schwartz, *Monetary History*, pp. 167–68, 308–13.

[39]Forrest McDonald, *Insull* (Chicago: University of Chicago Press, 1962). The reviewer of this book in *Economist* (Apr. 6, 1963, p. 58) termed it "a remarkable story, remarkably well told and documented, a true thriller for economists," and did not dispute the claim that the collapse of Insull's empire was perhaps "the most spectacular business failure in the history of the world." A brief, racier account is in Ellis, *Nation in Torment*, ch. 3. Insull was one of a number of "empire-builders" in the 1920s who gave way to "organization-builders" in the 1930s; see Harold L. Willensky, "Intelligence in Industry," *Annals of the American Academy of Political and Social Science*, March 1970, 388:52–53. I am indebted to a long-time friend who had large responsibilities for liquidating parts of the Insull empire after its collapse; he kindly read a draft of this chapter and made valuable comments.

losses to investors who had trusted him implicitly. With others he was indicted in October 1932 and bitterly excoriated. He came to trial after considerable delay because he had fled the country. The prosecution made an incredibly weak case, and he eventually won acquittal on all charges brought; but he was undoubtedly guilty of gross misjudgments and bribery as well.

Insull was a prodigious worker, lacking in personal charm, but a brilliant egoist whose egomania contributed substantially to his successes and was probably the major factor in his downfall. His major malefaction was lending his name to Insull Utility Investments, Inc. (IUI), and using his wholly-owned sales outlet with its huge retail staff to peddle the stock from door to door (on the installment plan) to inexpert, low-income savers who bought solely because of their confidence in the Insull name.

Such were the loose standards of the 1920s that it was not generally held against Insull that he contributed liberally to both parties in Chicago elections, slipped money to the chairman of the Illinois regulatory commission, and encouraged the formation of an Illinois committee that, as Ellis much later asserted (page 50–52), "spewed out . . . facts, half-truths, quarter-truths, and outright lies" to newspapers, schools, and service clubs. But he also made serious blunders before, during, and after the Wall Street crash. Initially, in 1926, he declined Prime Minister Baldwin's request that he chair a commission to build a government-operated, unified power system for England, on the model of his own system, and instead set out to found a huge dynasty for his only son, recently married. Soon he resorted to "pyramiding," creating two interlocking investment trusts—Insull Utility Investments (December 1928) and Corporation Securities Company of Chicago (Corp, September 1929)—to perpetuate the existing management of the Insull group.[40] By various operations he incurred the bitter enmity of the New York financial club, the Morgan group, whose two simple rules[41] he had repeatedly violated. His worst mistake, however, was to underestimate the severity of the 1929–32 collapse.

---

[40]The New York correspondent of *Economist*, writing on Aug. 21, 1929 (Aug. 31, 1929, p. 394), must have been referring to the Insull trusts and others when he said: "The popularity of the investment trusts is a not unnatural consequence of the long-sustained bull market in shares. Some misgivings are created in conservative minds, however, by the manner in which some of these holding companies and trusts are being 'pyramided.' The holding companies purchase shares of subsidiaries. The rise in the subsidiaries thereupon stimulates strength in the shares of the holding company. Frequently the holding company will then sell more of its own shares to the public at the higher prices and then repeat the process by buying more of the shares of the subsidiaries. Instances are not lacking in which this holding company 'pyramiding' has been carried through several stages with an accumulation of paper profits throughout. The practice has been much more prevalent in the utility field than in any other, and is to considerable degree responsible for the low yield and earnings[-price] ratios at which utility shares are selling."

[41]McDonald put them thus: "Do not upset the order of things. Look to New York for financial leadership." *Insull*, p. 247.

When Wall Street crashed Insull demonstrated his self-confidence, strength, and prestige. He rescued thousands of employees caught with low-margined accounts by personally supplying additional collateral;[42] he opened the palatial Civic Opera House in Chicago; he began construction of a huge natural gas pipeline from the Texas Panhandle to Chicago; he saved the City of Chicago from bankruptcy; he tackled the job of bailing out, integrating, and modernizing the city's transportation industries; and he undertook to rehabilitate the textile and shipbuilding industries in upper New England. "Supremely confident that this depression would be neither longer nor more severe than those he had weathered in the past, Insull geared his own business operations to that expectation. As a result, in 1930 he did three things that considerably weakened his position; he expanded far more than turned out to be prudent, he returned to debt financing, and he bought [Cyrus S.] Eaton's holdings."[43] These moves proved disastrous, and eventually Insull was so overextended that, after a drastic market collapse, for lack of $20 million he had to lose control of his empire to his chief enemies.[44] Yet he retained his heroic status in the public eye for two full years, and never lost the affectionate admiration of the great majority of the employees of his companies.[45]

Whitney. The stock market collapse and the subsequent contraction of stock values exposed not merely the weaknesses of the economy but also the speculations and malpractices of men of high repute. These only gradually came to light, and many who lost their reputations did so only in the aftermath of the crash. Prominent examples in the United States were the presidents of two big New York banks—Charles E. Mitchell of the National City and Albert H. Wiggin of the Chase—and the president of the New York Stock Exchange, Richard Whitney, whose shocking misconduct over more than a decade came to light only in early March 1938.[46] Richard was the personable younger brother of George Whitney, who since 1917 had been a partner in Wall Street's most prestigious firm, J. P. Morgan and Company. With family money Richard had bought a seat on the New York Stock Exchange in 1912, and in 1916 had formed the firm of Richard Whitney and

[42]*C&FC*, Nov. 2, 1929, p. 2816.
[43]McDonald, *Insull*, p. 284.
[44]*Ibid.*, esp. ch. 10, "The Enemies," and ch. 11, "The Fall of the House of Insull."
[45]For a time even some who lost through his disaster were charitable. The New York correspondent of *Economist* (Apr. 30, 1932, pp. 975–76), after reporting "The Insull Failure"—the greatest utility failure in U.S. history—broken "on the rocks of the distressing decline in security prices," added: "Criticism of the Insulls is milder than might have been expected in view of the large losses investors must suffer. The opinion is widely held that they merely erred with the rest of the market in over-estimating the value of future possibilities, and were carried away by ambition to reach too far." Cf. *ibid.*, Apr. 23, 1932, p. 925, and Oct. 8, 1932, p. 652.
[46]Galbraith, *The Great Crash*, pp. 140, 152–61.

Company, bond specialists. For years this firm handled many Morgan transactions on the Exchange. Vice president of the Exchange in the spring of 1929, Whitney became acting president when E. H. H. Simmons took a long vacation, and late in November received the high commendation of its Governing Board for rare qualities of leadership and efficient actions during "the recent disturbances."[47] In the spring of 1930 he was elected to succeed Simmons, and continued to serve as president for five years. After Charles R. Gay was elected his successor in May 1935, Whitney was continued a member of the Governing Board and was soon given a glowing testimonial signed by almost two thousand employees of the Exchange and its luncheon club. On December 26, 1935, he was unanimously elected to a four-year term as one of six trustees of the Stock Exchange Gratuity Fund. He held several other responsible positions reflecting high confidence in his probity and judgment. Like his predecesor, he made many addresses as Wall Street's symbol and spokesman, including one in April 1931 on "Business Honesty."

Actually, Richard Whitney's admirable qualities were mixed with utterly reprehensible ones. He lived extravagantly, speculated unwisely (notably in accumulating stock of Distilled Liquors Corporation), borrowed huge sums from many sources, and used as collateral for secured loans securities of others to which he had access as executor, treasurer, or trustee. Surprisingly he long managed to keep his partners, his brother, and many more in the dark about his financial status and operations, which under stress he falsified. His injudicious and criminal actions, and his deep personal financial troubles, had extended over a long period before their exposure in March 1938 led to his admission of insolvency, expulsion from the Stock Exchange, and arrest and indictment for misappropriation of funds, to which he pled guilty. On April 11 he was sentenced to five to ten years in Sing Sing, where he was a model prisoner and from which he was released on parole in August 1941. His property holdings were liquidated, and his brother George made good what he had borrowed or stolen from others.

Whitney's downfall paved the way for transforming the exchange from a virtually private club to a public institution, ending a protracted struggle with the Securities and Exchange Commission. On May 9, 1938, under new rules providing for more democratic procedures, a predominantly liberal board of governors was elected, headed by young William McChesney Martin, who had been elected to it in the stormy voting of 1935. Under a new constitution soon adopted, on June 30 Martin became the first paid president of the Exchange, with broad executive powers.[48]

[47]*C&FC*, Nov. 30, 1929, p. 3444.
[48]The main facts are given in Galbraith, *The Great Crash*, pp. 107-8, 114-17, 121-24, 161-72. Fifteen years later John Brooks published a much fuller account, *Once in Golconda:*

Kreuger. From a world standpoint, even more serious if less spectacular than the Insull failure was the collapse of the vast, complex, even fabulous empire that had been built up by the renowned Swedish engineer and international financier Ivar Kreuger. He committed suicide in Paris on March 12, 1932, when he had reached the end of his rope.[49] Robert Shaplen aptly entitled his biography *Kreuger, Genius and Swindler.* He was both, and a man of great personal charm as well. At the time of his death the obituaries were highly laudatory, and his enormous financial operations were viewed as the result of great financial and intellectual ability, courage, and astonishingly constructive genius. Prominent among his activities was his buildup of a series of national match monopolies and integrating them into the International Match Corporation. The collapse of so much of the world financial structure in 1931, and widespread defaults by borrowing governments to which he had made loans in return for monopoly concessions, led to the crash of his enterprises. Salter believed (as late as 1967) that, if these had not occurred, "Kreuger would have lived out his natural span of life, honoured and respected by all those who knew, or knew of, him."[50] Perhaps so; but the more one learns of his operations, the more one tends to believe that he was bound to come a cropper sooner or later.

Misjudgments made a major contribution to Kreuger's undoing, and a few out of many must be mentioned. After the Wall Street crash he was sanguine about the economic future of Germany and France despite their dismal political outlook. While he rightly recognized the stock market boom as crazy, he expected the foolish public to become still more crazy. Even in the spring of 1931 he retained marked confidence in the recovery prospects of the United States.[51]

Only as his tangled affairs were unraveled and his life was intensively studied did it become clear that he was a basically amoral man whose truly constructive acts went hand in hand not merely with bribery and juggling of balance sheets but also with a variety of other indefensible actions even before the severe depression led him into rash speculation, forgeries, and counterfeitings on a grand scale. Extemely secretive about his business affairs, he outdid even Calvin Coolidge in his dedication to silence on principle, and kept his closest business and financial associates in the dark. Yet

---

A True Drama of Wall Street 1920–1938 (New York: Harper and Row, 1969), in which Richard Whitney is the central figure. See also Robert Sobel, *The Big Board: A History of the New York Stock Market* (New York: Free Press of Glencoe, 1965).

[49]See Isaac F. Marcosson, "The Match King," *Saturday Evening Post,* Oct. 12, 1929, pp. 3–4, 233–46; *Time,* Oct. 1, 1928, pp. 32, 34, and Oct. 28, 1929, cover and pp. 43–46.

[50]Sir Arthur Salter, *Personality in Politics: Studies of Contemporary Statesmen* (London: Faber, 1947), pp. 201–4, and *Slave of the Lamp* (London: Weidenfeld and Nicolson, 1967), pp. 39–42. The contrast with Stavisky (see below, pp. 380–81) was marked, though Alexander Werth somewhat misleadingly remarked, "Kreuger became a crook *at the end*, he did not *start* as a crook." *France in Ferment* (New York: Harper, 1934), p. 222.

[51]Shaplen, *Kreuger: Genius and Swindler* (New York: Knopf, 1960), pp. 128–33.

he managed to retain their confidence and that of the public long after this was warranted. His American underwriters were Lee, Higginson and Company, an old and respected Boston firm which was conspicuous among the victims of his collapse. Kreuger and Toll, the Swedish-American Investment Corporation, and the International Match Corporation were among the many others. The crumbling of such pillars of the international financial structure made a major contribution to the deepening of the financial decline and the depression in the spring of 1932, and gave the final blow to public confidence in financiers and businessmen, which did much to retard financial and economic recovery.

Stavisky. Crookedness as well as misjudgments played a part in every country in the pre-depression and depression periods.[52] In selecting only one more example for brief discussion I do not mean to imply that it was the worst.

French taxpayers were notorious for wholesale evasion of income taxes, and corruption in the press and political life in France was widespread in the interwar years. Periodic scandals involved prominent politicians, judges, and civil servants, and frequently jeopardized stability and caused a dangerous atmosphere of demoralization. They brought on recurrent political and financial crises, and were viewed with anxiety in England and with great satisfaction in Berlin, where France came to be regarded as hopelessly decadent.[53] The masonic organization known as the Grand Orient was large, influential, and the mainstay of the parties of the Left because of members who held key positions in the Ministry of Home Affairs and the Sûreté Générale (the French Scotland Yard). But some leading politicians of the Right used their official position to gain financial advantage for themselves. Few political leaders except Poincaré and Gaston Doumergue (who succeeded Camille Chautemps as premier in January 1934) were considered above suspicion.

One of the most flagrant and wide-reaching scandals was that of Sacha Alexander Stavisky, which came to its climax early in 1934.[54] Stavisky, born in 1886 in Kiev, had come to Paris with his parents as a small boy and was given a good education. When still young he started as a small crook in the Paris underworld. By 1926 he had come to be called "the king

---

[52]Robbins (*Great Depression*, p. 92) spoke of the German banks of the pre-1931 years as "weakened by practices which for years had been the admiration of foreign financial experts— active participations in industrial financing—and honeycombed with the jobbery and graft characteristic of the Kreuger period."

[53]Paul Einzig, *France's Crisis* (London: Macmillan, 1934), ch. 8, "The 'Crise Morale,'" pp. 77–87; see also pp. 15–18.

[54]*Ibid.*, pp. 83–86. The story is told in considerable detail in Werth, *France in Ferment*; and Rudolf Brock, *Stavisky: Der grösste Korruptions-Skandal Europas (aus dem Französischen)* (Berlin: Eden-Verlag, 1934).

of crooks." Finally arrested that spring, he managed to arrange his release in November 1927 before his case had come to trial. Then he went on to bigger deals. With many aliases and links with underworld figures, French officialdom, and the venal press, he engaged in a succession of large and increasingly complicated operations. These culminated late in 1933 in a Bayonne swindle that mulcted insurance companies and the Social Insurance Fund of over 500 million francs.[55] His arrest early in 1934 was shortly followed by his suicide or murder by the police. The resulting explosion led to the fall of the six-week-old Chautemps government, when some of its ministers were shown to be implicated in Stavisky's affairs.

The Stavisky scandal was really a whole series of scandals—legal, police, press, administrative, and parliamentary. It came to light in a period of hard times, great political instability, and serious international crises. A thorough inquiry by a parliamentary committee soon revealed corruption and negligence in all phases of French public life and inherent vices in public administration "which facilitated the corruption and often accounted for the negligence."[56]

The Exposures and   In the later 1920s few voices were raised to attack
Their Consequences individual and corporate malpractices. One was that of W. Z. Ripley of Harvard, a recognized authority on railroads, corporations, and trusts. In articles and a book he candidly discussed a variety of reprehensible actions.[57] President Coolidge, mildly concerned over the matter, called Ripley to the White House for a conference early in 1926, but characteristically took no action on the moderate suggestions for reform which Ripley offered.[58] Only after the "prosperity decade" ended in collapse and depression were misjudgments and malfeasance extensively exposed, reputations mercilessly deflated, and belated remedies formulated and in part legislated.

Ferdinand Pecora became counsel for the Senate Banking and Currency Committee early in 1933, assembled an expert staff, and vigorously pushed the investigation of financial practices which had made little progress in April-December 1932.[59] Many of the disclosures of the Pecora investigation were calculated to inflame public opinion against financiers

[55]Werth (*France in Ferment*, pp. 62, 72) points out that "as a financial swindle it was mediocre," but that "it fell on soil rich with anxiety and discomfort."
[56]*Ibid.*, ch. 11, "What the Stavisky Inquiry Showed."
[57]*Atlantic*, September-November 1926, pp. 380-99, 667-87; *Main Street and Wall Street* (Boston: Little Brown, 1927). See also George W. Alger, "Other People's Money," *Atlantic*, December 1930, pp. 730-39.
[58]Joseph Dorfman, *The Economic Mind in American Civilization*, vols. 4-5: *1919-1933* (New York: Viking, 1959), 4:52-54, citing Ripley Papers, Feb. 10, 1926.
[59]Ferdinand Pecora, *Wall Street under Oath* (New York: Simon and Schuster, 1939); Schlesinger, *Coming of the New Deal*, ch. 27, "Alienation of the Financial Community."

and prominent Republicans and Democrats. It was revealed that, thanks largely to legally deductible capital losses, J. P. Morgan paid no federal income tax in 1930-32; that the total tax paid by all the members of his firm was under $50,000 in 1930 and that they had paid none in 1931; and that many prominent persons on Morgan's "preferred list" were able to buy Allegheny Corporation shares at the initial offering price of $20 a share when it was selling on the Exchange at $31 to $35,[60] which at the time was accepted practice. The investigations also brought to light many forms of outright crookedness and indefensible practices, including bribery, huge bonuses received by financiers, stock market pools run or rigged, bad investments sold to a trusting public, and all sorts of culpable actions and inaction.[61] These exposures helped to pave the way for much New Deal legislation, including the Truth-in-Securities Act signed on May 27, 1933, the Banking Act of June 15, 1933, and the Securities Exchange Act signed on June 6, 1934.

Here it is unnecessary to recapitulate these scandals further. Details can readily be found in the 1932-34 congressional hearings and reports on stock exchange practices and in the 1939 report of the Securities and Exchange Commission on Investment Trusts and Investment Companies, and Galbraith devoted a good deal of space in his book to them. Unquestionably the record is a sorry one. In this country and others, indefensible practices did much to increase individual losses before, during, and after the collapse, and helped to wreck the foundations of confidence, not only of investors. Yet one must not exaggerate their extent and their influence on the course of events, nor, by implication, should we overrate the degree of improvement in the past forty years with the aid of corrective and preventive measures adopted in the 1930s and later. The *Wall Street Journal* made this pertinent comment in reviewing two books on Wall Street in its issue of August 29, 1962: "Both books make much of the same instances of proven or merely problematical skulduggery. . . . Though the specific criticisms of Mr. Fuller and Mr. Cormier of specific happenings are well taken, the roll of dishonor is not extremely impressive when stacked up against the entire volume of transactions recorded by the various exchanges."[62] Such a comment could appropriately have been made on the more vitriolic exposures of the 1930s.

---

[60]Schlesinger, *Coming of the New Deal*, pp. 435-37; Hillel Black, *The Watch Dogs of Wall Street* (New York: Morrow, 1962), pp. 8-10.

[61]Cf. S. E. Howard's chapter in the Princeton essays, in Smith, *Facing the Facts*, esp. pp. 125-27, 146; and Schlesinger, *Coming of the New Deal*, ch. 29, "Controlling the Stock Exchanges," pp. 456-70. Joseph P. Kennedy was the first chairman of the Securities and Exchange Commission, which was set up to administer this act and the Truth-in-Securities Act of 1933; he was soon succeeded by James M. Landis.

[62]Frank Cormier, *Wall Street's Shady Side* (Washington, D.C.: Public Affairs Press, 1962; introduction by Ferdinand Pecora); John G. Fuller, *The Money Changers* (New York: Dial Press, 1962).

In today's perspective, widespread misjudgments and ill-founded honest utterances were far more responsible for the disasters that were then experienced. The SEC and other watchdog agencies have proved of value, but have utterly failed to deter, much less eradicate, all of the evils with which they were designed to cope. The hard fact remains: tendencies to large and small misjudgments and to petty and flagrant malfeasance are perennial evils that must be continually struggled with but can never be wholly overcome. Elimination of either cannot be expected in our fallible human world. The enduring problem is not to perfect, but to improve so far as possible, the level of judgment and ethical behavior in business, government, and elsewhere.

CHAPTER 15

INADEQUATE ECONOMIC AND POLITICAL INTELLIGENCE

THE WORD "INTELLIGENCE" has many meanings. Here it is used in the sense of accurate information, penetratingly interpreted, and made readily available to businessmen, labor leaders, public officials, and the general public in many countries. Perfect knowledge is of course unattainable, and truly adequate economic and political intelligence is far too much to expect; but the role of inadequacies in these areas merits more emphasis than it has received. Some of these, but by no means all, are remediable.

The Postwar Flowering and its Disappointing Results World War I and its troubled aftermath gave a great stimulus to the development of economists, many of whom were drawn into national and international service.[1] The postwar period saw a notable expansion of the network of intelligence.[2] It also witnessed the rise of organized research inside and outside of universities,[3] employment of economists by banks and business corporations, and enlargement of financial and economic data. Under Secretary Hoover, the Department of Commerce and its Census Bureau greatly expanded their collection and publication of significant data and interpretations. So did the federal Bureau of Labor Statistics (BLS) and the U.S. Department of Agriculture. The Federal Reserve Board made major contributions to available statistics, and its monthly *Bulletin* also published valuable documents (or excerpts from them) on both domestic and international developments. Several big commercial banks and most of the Federal Reserve Banks had able staffs and issued useful monthly reviews or letters. The monthlies published by the Cleveland Trust Company, the National City Bank of New York, and the Ameri-

[1]Wesley C. Mitchell, *Economic Research and the Needs of the Times*, 24th Annual Report (New York: NBER, 1944), pp. 8–11.
[2]Conspicuous contributors were the *Economist* (London), the *Manchester Guardian* and its *Commercial* (Manchester), the *Frankfurter Zeitung* (Frankfurt) and the *Commercial and Financial Chronicle* (New York), but there were many other weeklies and dailies.
[3]Leonard P. Ayres devoted his presidential address before the American Statistical Association late in 1921 to "The Nature and Status of Business Research." *JASA*, March 1922, 17:33ff. An excerpt was quoted by N. J. Silberling in his *Dynamics of Business* (New York: McGraw-Hill, 1943), pp. 583–85, at the end of his ch. 22 on business forecasting. See also Z. C. Dickinson, "Bureaux for Economic and 'Business' Research in American Universities," *EJ*, September 1925, 35:398–415.

can Telephone and Telegraph Company were exceptionally valuable. Late in 1930 Keynes pointed with admiration to all "the pioneer work—and in the last five years much of it of the highest quality" which had been done in the United States under various auspices.[4]

Attention was especially focused on business cycle research by the Harvard University Committee on Economic Research (established in 1917), the National Bureau of Economic Research in New York (1920), and private and governmental organizations in Great Britain and several continental European countries. The Harvard group and several business services undertook to develop and practice forecasting techniques. The Institute of Economics (1922) of what in 1927 became the Brookings Institution in Washington studied urgent current problems and published many volumes to enlighten the general public.

Governmental and political problems also were given serious attention. The Institute for Government Research (1916) antedated the Institute of Economics and also became part of the Brookings Institution. The Royal Institute of International Affairs in Great Britain (1921) and its counterpart, the Council of Foreign Relations in New York (1921),[5] not only published excellent journals, *International Affairs* (1922) and *Foreign Affairs* (1922), but also fostered many other studies. The Foreign Policy Association (1921) and its regional groups held monthly luncheons, organized conferences, and published reports and other studies.[6] The Institute of Politics (1921) conducted annual conferences at Williamstown, Massachusetts, with participants of high repute from this country and abroad. These sessions were extensively reported in the daily press (especially the *New York Times*) and many volumes grew out of them.[7] There were also laudable attempts in the 1920s and 1930s to interpret to one another the tone and temper of leading peoples. The Academy of Political Science (New York) held one-day sessions at which current topics were ably discussed by those in a good position to know. The annual meetings of many professional associations were prolific of papers, most of which were soon published.

These were among the extraordinary efforts to enlarge business, professional, and public understanding of the problems that faced mankind in

[4]*A Treatise on Money*, 2 vols. (New York: Harcourt Brace, 1930; preface dated September 14, 1930), 2:407. Cf. Harold L. Reed, *Federal Reserve Policy, 1921-1930* (New York: McGraw-Hill, 1930; preface dated August 1930), p. 197.

[5]See Anon., *The Council on Foreign Relations: A Record of Fifteen Years, 1921-1936* (New York: Council on Foreign Relations, 1937).

[6]In his recent autobiography, *After Five Million Words* (New York: John Day, 1970), Bruce Bliven gives personal observations on the FPA (pp. 239-40, 304-6) and the Twentieth Century Fund (pp. 306-10, 313), which became important after its founder, E. A. Filene, died in 1937. Bliven served on the boards of directors of both organizations.

[7]See Harry A. Garfield, *Lost Visions* (privately printed, 1944) and its 1931 appendix (pp. 245-77) in which Arthur H. Buffinton sketched the Institute's history from its origin in 1913 through 1930. Bernard M. Baruch supplied essential financial support.

the turbulent interwar years. They yielded valuable fruits. The collapse of the booms and the U.S. monetary and banking systems, the extended economic and financial contractions here and abroad, and the severe and protracted depression nevertheless revealed a surprisingly "poor state of economic intelligence."[8]

In the spring of 1931, shortly before the grave financial crisis broke, the London financial journalist Paul Einzig wrote:

It is a commonplace of economic text-books that the function of economic science is to explain and foresee economic phenomena. The view is widely held that, in the case of the present world economic crisis, economic science has failed deplorably to fulfill its task. . . . The uninitiated public complains—and not altogether without reason—of having been left in the dark as to the causes of the world-wide depression.[9]

A little earlier a U.S. economist charged: "The business depression points an accusing finger at professional economists."[10] Late in 1931, after the crises which he himself had not foreseen, Einzig wrote without exaggeration of the failures to recognize the gravity of world developments.[11] Fair or unfair, such accusations continued to be made as the depression widened and deepened.

In the spring of 1933 a mock-trial of "the economists" was staged at the London School of Economics, Robert Boothby, M.P., representing "the state of the popular mind," charged the economists with "conspiring to spread mental fog," declaring that they "were unintelligible; that they had in general proved wrong; and that in any case they all disagreed." Four men of high standing (Sir William Beveridge, Sir Arthur Salter, Professor T. E. Gregory, and Hubert Henderson) discussed Boothby's charges without wholly refuting them. It was sagely observed: "Much of the public's distrust of economics arises from the fact that the economist is compelled to act both as physiologist and doctor at once." In fact, economists had not been trained to be "economic doctors" or "social engineers," and very few persons had acquired such competence.[12]

---

[8]Galbraith used this phrase in *The Great Crash 1929* (Boston: Houghton Mifflin, 1955), pp. 187–91, and was extremely critical, but hardly dealt adequately with the subject.

[9]*World Economic Crisis, 1929–1931* (London: Macmillan, 1931; preface dated May 1931), chs. 1-3, esp. p. 19; and the 2d ed., 1932, pp. v–ix, 5–11, 23–24. I cannot ascribe much weight to what Einzig called the "main reason"—"that most attempts aiming at the explanation of the crisis are partisan, either because those who put them forward strive to establish or support a theory of their own or because they are too eager to use the facts of the crisis to defend or attack certain political or economic interests."

[10]Broadus Mitchell, "A Blast against Economists," *Virginia Quarterly Review*, April 1931, p. 186.

[11]*World Economic Crisis, 1929–1931*, 2d ed. (London: Macmillan, 1932; preface dated December 1931), pp. 5–11, 23–24.

[12]See "Economists on Trial," *Economist*, June 17, 1933, p. 1291; and my paper of 1936, "Statistics and Social Engineering," reprinted in J. S. Davis, *On Agricultural Policy, 1926–1938* (Stanford, Calif.: Food Research Institute, 1939), pp. 51–59.

The dean of the Harvard Graduate School of Business Administration wrote in mid-1933: "The inability of business and political leadership to rise to the new heights required by an unprecedented situation is the most disturbing fact of the three and a half years ending March 4. Nor were our universities any better. Business men handled the affairs of their particular concerns in most cases with amazing skill, but in the larger aspects of the depression business men, politicians and university professors almost universally assumed that things would right themselves."[13]

The record of economic intelligence and analysis in the years following the trough of the depression was seriously marred by the wide divergence of supposedly expert opinion on procedures appropriate to speed recovery, even after widespread recognition of the necessity for government intervention, and then by the crucial failure to appraise the forces leading toward World War II and to support appropriate and timely moves to get them under control. Many of these forces were primarily political. But the drastic economic setback of 1937–38 also took the world by surprise. During these critical times sharp differences developed in the banking community, the Federal Reserve Banks, the Board of Governors, and high government circles as to appropriate Federal Reserve actions.[14]

There was, in short, a deplorable failure to foresee and forecast coming crises, to gauge their significance after they had arrived, to provide adequate explanations of the worldwide depression, and to give appropriate guidance in recovery. The responsibility was shared by many individuals in universities, banks, business corporations, and governments. The best that the professions involved did—indeed, were capable of doing—was not nearly good enough, as a number of participants admitted at the time and later.[15] In one of his humble moods, Keynes wrote late in 1930 of world management of monetary affairs: "We do badly; but we do not know how to do better. I do not think that practical bankers are primarily blameworthy for this." He went on to comment on the immature state of economic thinking and the inadequacy of data.[16]

---

[13]Wallace B. Donham, "The Failure of Business Leadership and the Responsibility of the Universities," *Harvard Business Review*, July 1933, 11:418–35.

[14]Marriner S. Eccles, *Beckoning Frontiers* (New York: Knopf, 1951), pt. 5, ch. 3, "The Recession of 1937–38." C. A. Phillips, T. F. McManus, and R. W. Nelson published their valuable *Banking and the Business Cycle: A Study of the Great Depression in the United States* (New York: Macmillan, 1937; preface dated Feb. 28, 1937). This dealt mainly with the period through 1933, but in their last chapter they were critical of the recovery program, and averred that recovery was being engineered largely by the same means which produced the last boom and depression, with the difference that the government, and not the banking system, was producing, not "an investment credit inflation" but "a consumption credit inflation" (pp. 212–15). But they did not specifically predict the collapse of 1937–38.

[15]See pp. 414–16 below.

[16]*Treatise on Money*, 2:405–8.

Why the Record   In his foreword (dated January 27, 1927) to Paish's
Was So Bad   *Road to Prosperity*, Sir Josiah Stamp set forth
cogent reasons for the current failure to appraise the economic situation
aright, especially in the international sphere. He began:

> Prior to the war, there was a sufficient balance and stability in economic af-
> fairs, for a competent economist or observer to have an informed and reasoned
> opinion upon most important questions of his times. To-day, there are separate
> problems of industry, finance, and international economico-political relations in
> each country, so different in magnitude from former times as to be almost differ-
> ent in kind, and they all change their relative positions and importance with be-
> wildering rapidity. It seems impossible for any one person to have a clear grasp of
> them all. It needs an army of skilled observers, led and generalled by a group of
> penetrating analytical thinkers, to cope with the merely intellectual problem as a
> whole satisfactorily. Neither the numbers nor the equipment exist, for there only
> are a mere handful of writers and thinkers who have a new post-war apparatus of
> thought and principle sufficiently incisive for the purpose. It needs, too, a position
> of *practical* power and influence to drive unpalatable truths through the thick
> undergrowth of particularist interest and prejudice, and the bogs of political
> obscurantism, into the field of objective reality. This position the handful—some
> of them moving mainly in academic circles—do not occupy.[17]

Schumpeter, in defense of those responsible for seriously erroneous
views of the outlook for the first half of 1930, had this to say in 1939:

> It is of the utmost importance to realize this: given the actual facts which it was
> then possible for either business men or economists to observe, those diagnoses—
> or even the prognosis that, with the existing structure of debt, those facts plus a
> drastic fall in price level would cause major trouble but that nothing else would—
> were not simply wrong. What nobody saw, though some people may have felt it,
> was that those fundamental data from which diagnoses and prognoses were made,
> were themselves in a state of flux and that they would be swamped by the torrents
> of a process of readjustment corresponding in magnitude to the extent of the in-
> dustrial revolution of the preceding 30 years. People, for the most part, stood their
> ground firmly. But that ground itself was about to give way.[18]

The baffling complexity of the world situation and the array of diverse
opinions concerning it were well reflected in General Dawes' opening address to the Reparation Commission in mid-January 1924, in Stamp's ad-

---

[17]Sir George Paish, *The Road to Prosperity* (London: Benn, 1927). Stamp continued:
"But hopes now centre in two potent possibilities—the Economic Section of the League of
Nations, and the International Chamber of Commerce, at whose conferences rival absurdi-
ties which live lusty lives in isolation, may be brought face to face to refute each other, and
where competent observation and thinking may get a more powerful leverage on practical
affairs and policy." Both institutions did valuable serivce, but not nearly enough.

[18]J. A. Schumpeter, *Business Cycles: A Theoretical, Historical, and Statistical Analysis
of the Capitalist Process*, 2 vols. (New York: McGraw-Hill, 1939), 2:793–94.

dress in New York in the spring of 1932,[19] and in other papers at this and earlier and later sessions of the Academy of Political Science, as well as at annual conventions of several professional associations. Even those who were considered most competent differed widely on causes, prospects, and appropriate actions.

In the later stages of the slump in 1931–32, after the gravity of the world crisis was widely recognized, in the slightly moderated depression of 1933–35, and in the boom and contraction of 1936–38 the errors, inadequacies, and divergences in economic thinking in academic, banking, business, and government circles were again distressingly revealed, as they had been in 1927–31.[20] In the absence of common convictions as to what was basically wrong, the welter of ideas as to what could and should be done paralyzed "the hands of authority on both sides of the Channel and of the Atlantic."[21] Some urged wise moves that had little or no chance of adoption in the near future. Some advocated one bold action or another, such as cancellation of both reparations and war debts, devaluation of currencies, "pump-priming" on a huge scale, and numerous intergovernmental commodity arrangements—almost all in vain. Some, in desperation, were ready to try anything once. Some threw up their hands and frankly admitted that they had no clear advice to offer. It is therefore not surprising that timely actions were not taken, that many which were taken proved bad mistakes, that some worked at cross-purposes with others, and that governments took steps that injured other nations and failed to take steps that could have helped themselves and other nations.[22]

[19]Charles G. Dawes, *A Journal of Reparations* (London: Macmillan, 1939), pp. 27–78; Sir Josiah Stamp, "Control or Fate in Economic Affairs," Apr. 13, 1932, *Proc. Acad. Pol. Sci.*, May 1932, 15:123–40. Stamp's lecture in the Halley Stewart series earlier in 1932 (see p. 397 below) was not very illuminating, and reflected his own uncertainties. Sir Arthur Salter et al., *The World's Economic Crisis and the Way of Escape* (London: Allen and Unwin, 1932), pp. 44–67.
The bafflement of and divergence among important thinkers is also well illustrated in several contributions to the *Economic Essays in Honour of Gustav Cassel* (London: Allen and Unwin, 1933), e.g., A. H. Hansen, "The Maintenance of Purchasing Power" (pp. 253–54); E. M. Patterson, "The United States and the World Economy" (pp. 479–90); and Josiah C. Stamp, "The Monetary Question in Great Britain" (pp. 599–603). Cf. also Joseph Dorfman, *The Economic Mind in American Civilization*, vols. 4–5: *1919–1933* (New York: Viking, 1959), 5:479, on Frank H. Knight.

[20]Cf. Myron W. Watkins, "The Literature of the Crisis," *QJE*, May 1933, 47:504–32; and Leo Rogin, "The New Deal: A Survey of the Literature," *ibid.*, February 1935, 49:325–55. At the request of the editor, I contributed to this journal several reviews of the literature on the agricultural situation and policies.

[21]Keynes, "The Great Slump of 1930," *N&A*, Dec. 20, 27, 1930, 48:402, 427–28, reprinted in his *Essays in Persuasion* (New York: Harcourt Brace, 1932), pp. 135–47.

[22]For indications that the same has been true in recent years, see J. O. N. Perkins, *International Policy for the World Economy* (London: Allen and Unwin, 1969), and Sidney Dell's review of it in *EJ*, September 1970, 80:698–700.

Before examining other evidence, let me attempt a brief summary of the reasons why the record was so bad.

1. There was no consensus then—if, indeed, there is today—that the main task of economics is to explain and foresee economic phenomena in all their bewildering manifestations. The term "economic science" was a grossly exaggerated expression for the organized and tested knowledge at hand in the period, as most professionals well realized,[23] and perfecting such a structure was accorded a very low priority even in the Social Science Research Council. Moreover, neither the older economists of the day nor the growing number of younger ones viewed their role in Einzig's ambitious terms or presumed to be able to perform such tasks reliably.[24]

2. Individual researches, which greatly predominated, were heterogeneous and little coordinated; organized research, private and governmental, was in its infancy; and events moved far faster than the researchers could mature their products.[25]

3. Limitations of data and techniques continued to be serious, especially in the new and vital field of economic and business forecasting, and this was among the reasons why forecasts turned out badly.[26] Even where statistical data were most highly developed (in the United States, Great Britain, and Germany), serious deficiencies handicapped the all-too-limited number of skilled investigators.[27] Inadequate data prevented accurate

---

[23]The *Economist* of June 18, 1932 (pp. 1358–59), rather harshly reviewed Lionel Robbins' new book, *An Essay on the Nature and Significance of Economic Science*. In his most influential book, *The General Theory of Employment, Interest and Money* (New York: Harcourt Brace, 1936), Keynes wrote (p. 146): "The fact that the assumptions of the static state often underlie present-day economic theory, imparts into it a large element of unreality." Susan Howson concluded her 1973 article (cited in Chapter 3 above): "Keynes was always very much the optimist over the period of time involved in a real world economic process." My own slight contribution was given on June 7, 1946, in "Whither Now?" in *Economic Research and the Development of Economic Science and Public Policy* (New York: NBER, 1946), pp. 171–88.

[24]After long study Dorfman concluded (*Economic Mind*, 5:770): "In retrospect, the economists who reached professional maturity after World War I appear to have reacted to the Great Depression in substantially the same way as did their older colleagues."

[25]See Lippmann's column dated Apr. 29, 1932, in Walter Lippmann, *Interpretations, 1931–1932*, ed. Allan Nevins (New York: Macmillan, 1932), p. 15.

[26]The following references are useful but by no means inclusive: Louis I. Dublin, ed., *Population Problems in the United States and Canada* (Boston: Houghton Mifflin, 1926; preface dated December 1925), esp. chs. 6–8; C. O. Hardy and G. V. Cox, *Forecasting Business Conditions* (New York: Macmillan, 1927); *JASA*, March 1930, suppl., 25 (169A): 31–35; Warren M. Persons, *Forecasting Business Cycles* (New York: Wiley, 1931); Silberling, *Dynamics of Business*, ch. 22, "Business Forecasting"; Phillips, McManus, and Nelson, *Banking and the Business Cycle*, esp. pp. 146–53; H. Theil, *Economic Forecasts and Policy* (Amsterdam: North Holland, 1958), reviewed by Robert Dorfman in *Rev. Ec. Stat.*, August 1961, 43:310–11; and Robert A. Gordon, *Business Fluctuations*, 2d ed. (New York: Harper, 1961), ch. 17.

[27]This point is repeatedly made in *Britain in Depression* (1935) and *Britain in Recovery* (1938) and in publications of the Harvard University Committee on Economic Research and the London and Cambridge Economic Service.

assessment of commodity stocks, unemployment, and excess capacity. The available indexes of wholesale prices and the cost of living tended to be used for more than they were worth.[28] And contributions of psychology, which were urgently needed to supplement economic analysis, were not ripe for use in interpreting the overoptimism and the speculative mania of the late 1920s and the overpessimism that developed in the following years.[29]

4. Several basic concepts (e.g., New Era, equilibrium, the state of confidence, momentum, stabilization, inflation, deflation, capacity to pay, soundness of the economy, standards of living) and assumptions were not subjected to careful analysis, even after events had shown their inadequacy; for lack of this and of precision in the use of terms much of the research suffered, and the public was misled or confused.

5. Noneconomic developments were given wholly inadequate study. In particular, important political elements in the ever-changing situation were inherently difficult to understand and were inadequately recognized, reported, and studied,[30] despite the valuable work of many groups, institutions, and journals such as those mentioned above. Far too little attention was given to what may be termed festering sores or smoldering fires in international relations and to the problems of restoring and maintaining a right spirit among nations. The "disposition in the several human parts to work in harmony together," which the Committee on Recent Economic Changes in 1929 had stressed as essential, was weak enough in the United States in 1928–33 and conspicuously weak in international relations in the interwar years. Personality conflicts at high levels, within national governments and between leaders of the democracies, were important through most of the two decades, and defects in channels of formal communication were too slowly repaired by establishment of heterodox informal ones.[31]

6. Divergence of seemingly responsible opinion prevailed over wide areas and on salient and lesser issues, including the alleged "gold scarcity" and "gold sterilization." Indeed, conflicting theories of the business

[28]Cf. *Westminster Bank Review*, April 1931, pp. 3–7; and Charles Rist and Sir Henry Strakosch in *The International Gold Problem* (London: Oxford University Press, 1932), pp. 213–14, 221–22.

[29]See a relevant discussion in Keynes' *General Theory of Employment, Interest, and Money* (New York: Harcourt Brace, 1936), ch. 12, "The State of Long-Term Expectation," esp. pp. 154–63.

[30]Understandably, U.S. diplomatic reports from Germany in the spring of 1933 "were a conglomeration of certainty and guesswork, hope and despair, incisiveness and blindness. American policy moved accordingly, sometimes showing initiative and strategy—as in the case of Roosevelt's May 16 disarmament appeal—but far more often moving listlessly and without design." Arnold A. Offner, *American Appeasement . . . , 1933-1938* (Cambridge, Mass.: Harvard University Press, 1969), p. 57.

[31]For one illuminating example based on newly discovered evidence, see Donald Watt, "The Secret Communications of Chamberlain and Roosevelt," *Interplay*, January 1971, pp. 45–49. Others are mentioned earlier in this book.

cycle itself were prevalent.[32] All too few efforts were made to reach something like a consensus.[33] The contemporary influence of reputable scholars was accordingly limited.[34] One notable exception was the able plea for a presidential veto of the Hawley-Smoot tariff bill, signed by more than 1,250 economists out of about double that number who were circularized in the spring of 1930 on the initiative of Paul H. Douglas and Clair Wilcox;[35] this appeal attracted wide attention but failed to convince President Hoover (see Chapter 9 above).

7. In the United States certain ideas were strongly entrenched in the minds of the public and of high officials, e.g., distrust of the British and continental Europeans, stubborn insistence on payment of war debts, support of tariff protection, belief in balanced federal budgets, and a near-obsession with maintaining prosperity, with insufficient regard to the consequences. Similar or comparable fixed ideas were prevalent in other countries. The result was strong resistance to evidence and reasoning that might otherwise have been helpful in modifying policies. Receptiveness to unpalatable truths was conspicuously low in the late 1920s and early

[32]For example, see Johan Åkerman, "Saving in the Depression," in *Economic Essays in Honour of Gustav Cassel*, pp. 11–31; Phillips, McManus, and Nelson, *Banking and the Business Cycle*, chs. 4, 6, 7; and Murray N. Rothbard, *America's Great Depression* (Princeton, N.J.: Van Nostrand, 1963), esp. pp. 72–75.

[33]Schneider remarked, shortly after the Wall Street crash, that "the bitter controversy over the past few years has not tended to promote clear thinking or judicious conclusions." Franz Schneider, Jr., *Proc. Acad. Pol. Sci.*, January 1930, 13:568–69. See also R. S. Tucker's observations at the same session (*ibid.*, pp. 533–37). A valuable guide to the somewhat confused evolution of American thought on economic issues in 1929–33 is provided in part 2 of vol. 5 of Dorfman, *Economic Mind*. In the three professional associations in which I was active in the interwar period, the members seemed to delight in disagreement and to resist attempts to arrive at agreement.

[34]Einzig wrote early in 1933 that none of the numerous suggestions "put forward by economists and statesmen of international reputation carried much conviction," and that the present crisis "has exploded the myth of the superman in industry and finance." Paul Einzig, *The Economic Foundations of Fascism* (London: Macmillan, 1933; preface dated April 1933), pp. 112, 118.

In his "Assessment of Accomplishments," Dorfman (*Economic Mind*, 5:771–76) warned (perhaps too charitably) against "the impression of a nation bogged down in chaotic disagreement" and stressed the progress toward substantial agreement on a number of issues. See also his ch. 22, "The Response of the Profession," including even "some form of guarantee of bank deposits."

Much later, in the spring of 1937, Harold Macmillan remarked: "The writings of leading economists were now more generally studied by Members of Parliament, although they found difficulty in disentangling the essentials from the mass of complicated jargon which was more and more coming into fashion." *Winds of Change, 1914–1939* (New York: Harper and Row, 1966), p. 451. Cf. Milton Friedman and Anna J. Schwartz, *A Monetary History of the United States, 1867–1960* (Princeton, N.J.: Princeton University Press, 1963), pp. 409–11; and Herbert Stein, *The Fiscal Revolution in America* (Chicago: University of Chicago Press, 1969), chs. 6–7, esp. pp. 102–3, 147–48.

[35]Frank W. Fetter, "The Economists' Tariff Protest of 1930," *AER*, June 1942, 32:355–56. For the statement and full list of signers, see *Congressional Record*, May 5, 1930, 72:8327–30. Cf. Dorfman, *Economic Mind*, 5:673–74.

1930s; and in every country people were highly susceptible to propaganda of many kinds and degrees of trustworthiness.

8. Moreover, most economists were heavily influenced by the pervading optimism of the 1920s and, indeed, by the whole "climate of intellectual opinion."[36] Many found it hard to abandon firmly held opinions after events had shown them to be illusory or obsolete.[37] Examples were the convictions that depression was a desirable and necessary means of curing the inefficiencies and weaknesses developed in the boom,[38] that the Federal Reserve System had solved problems of liquidity, and that "easy money" would prevent falling into and promote recovery from depression; and there were many others.[39] In one of his arrogant moods, Keynes said in April 1931 that would-be experts "talk much greater rubbish than an ordinary man can ever be capable of."[40] Schumpeter later referred in passing to "all those undoubtedly very competent judges of business who [in early 1930] were unable to account for or to predict anything but a brief recession."[41]

9. Economists and businessmen were typically cautious in their appraisals of the economic situation, less than penetrating in their consideration of weaknesses and vulnerabilities, and far from forthright in pointing out dangers ahead.[42] In some important instances (e.g., Carl Snyder, W.

---

[36] Friedman and Schwartz, Monetary History, pp. 299–304, 407–11, 691.

[37] Friedman and Schwartz (ibid., p. 529) mention Governor Harrison of the Federal Reserve Bank of New York, who revised in 1937 a long-held position, as "a striking illustration of how difficult it is for anyone—whether in practical affairs, politics, industry, science, the arts—however able and disinterested, as Harrison was in unusual measure, to reverse a strongly held intellectual position."

[38] As late as mid-May 1932 A. C. Miller, the Federal Reserve Board member whom Hoover considered the ablest, held that the government should rely mainly on letting nature cure the sick economy. Dorfman, Economic Mind, 5:609, citing Hearings before the Senate Committee on Banking and Currency, May 18, 1932, 72d Cong., 1st sess., p. 225.

[39] Dorfman says (ibid., p. 412) of Mitchell's March 1921 review of David Friday's recent Profits, Wages and Prices: "Mitchell, like the vast majority of students, could not go along with Friday's unprecedented (for the time, but currently acceptable) view that the war had stimulated a considerable increase in the country's total productive capacity." Cf. Friedman and Schwartz, Monetary History, pp. 408–9.

[40] Quoted in Stein, Fiscal Revolution, p. 145, citing New York Times, Apr. 13, 1931. Professional economists showed a common disposition to look down upon or ignore popular economic and financial writers such as Stuart Chase, W. T. Foster and Waddill Catchings, Paul Einzig, A. D. Noyes, and Sir George Paish, instead of reading their voluminous output with discrimination. Walter Lippmann's columns maintained a high level of penetration and accuracy, though of course they were not without slips. The two volumes of Interpretations edited by Allan Nevins cover the years 1931–35; I have not sought out his earlier comparable writings. Stewart Alsop, in his recent book, The Center (New York: Harper and Row, 1968), pp. 180–81, recognized Lippmann's prestige despite the fact that many officials and former officials and some journalists believed his "judgments on international affairs have been consistently and demonstrably wrong."

[41] Business Cycles, 2:411–15.

[42] Some exceptions are noted in Chapter 7. Brilliant, nimble-witted Keynes was clearly exceptional in this respect, but his many changes of opinion help to explain why his influence

Randolph Burgess, E. A. Goldenweiser), the constraints of official position must have been a significant factor.[43] Awareness of their own limitations, fear of being conspicuously wrong, and reluctance to face criticism or to "rock the boat" all contributed to this common tendency, especially in the overoptimistic period before and shortly after the Wall Street crash. A few economists were unduly outspoken on occasions, presuming to know more than they did or could. Keynes was conspicuous among these. B. M. Anderson, who was one of Keynes' severe critics,[44] at times displayed similar brashness and lost influence thereby. The "happy mean" is perennially difficult to achieve.

10. Poor vision was extremely prevalent in the late 1920s and persisted in the 1930s, in a great many respects, of which I select only one. Keynes wrote in August 1931: "Banks and bankers are by nature blind. They have not seen what was coming."[45] This extreme statement, whatever its degree of truth, was pointed too narrowly. Though he had better vision than most, even Keynes failed to see what was coming. So did Einzig, a well-informed and perspicacious financial writer. In his 1939 summary of world finance since 1914, he observed: "In 1929 came the inevitable slump, followed by the inevitable series of financial crises from 1931 onwards."[46] But in his 1931 book on the world economic crisis he had not foreseen or forecast these "inevitable" events.[47] Time and again respected analysts overlooked or underweighted signs of weakness or danger, went wrong in their forecasts, omitted or muted timely warnings,[48] and evinced

on British policy in the interwar period was so slight. Sir Josiah Stamp, in his letter to President Coolidge on July 3, 1926, had voiced his conviction that "it is no good making public utterances on these subjects unless one speaks out fearlessly one's conclusions, particularly in the case of an economist who had given prolonged study to the question and cannot always speak those smooth sayings which are welcomed by politicians and governments." He added: "There is nothing I have so much at heart as the relations between England and America but these will never be properly served by misconceived reticence on economic issues." J. Harry Jones, *Josiah Stamp, Public Servant: The Life of the First Baron Stamp of Shortlands* (London: Pitman, 1964), p. 307.

[43]In reviewing Burgess' valuable book, *The Reserve Banks and the Money Market* (New York: Harper, 1927), in *JASA*, December 1927, 23:470–72, George W. Dowrie noted: "Dr. Burgess is not critical of anything in the Federal Reserve mechanism or the way in which it is operated. He chronicles accurately what he finds, and seems to assume that 'whatever is, is right.' " The *Economist* expressed similar views.

[44]B. M. Anderson, *Economics and the Public Welfare: Financial and Economic History of the United States, 1914–1946* (New York: Van Nostrand, 1949), ch. 60 ("Digression on Keynes"). Much of this had appeared in Anderson's earlier papers in the *Chase Economic Bulletin*.

[45]In a paper first published in his *Essays in Persuasion*, p. 176.

[46]*World Finance, 1938–1939* (London: Macmillan, 1939; preface dated March 1939), p. 21. See also the two last paragraphs of ch. 7 in Friedman and Schwartz, *Monetary History*, esp. p. 419.

[47]*World Economic Crisis*, 1st ed., pp. 11–15. In its section on "Future Prospects," they were not even mentioned, and this was left unchanged in the second edition of this book, published early in 1932.

[48]It was too much to expect strong warnings against the excessive speculation in stocks and real estate in the late 1920s from those who had been active speculators or speculative

ill-founded hopes. Especially serious were the failures to analyze effectively the credit inflation, the superoptimism, and the speculative orgy of the 1920s and their consequences at home and abroad; the various domestic and foreign weaknesses that accumulated in the prosperity period; and the interconnection between political and economic forces that were so imperfectly understood.

11. Finally, while exploration of minutiae and development of improved techniques were necessary and appropriate, very few persons found the time to amass the knowledge and acquire the skills to deal with global issues and present the results in ways that business and political leaders could utilize. Specialists multiplied, but there was a dearth of competent generalists, and too many of those who essayed that role gave the unjustified impression of certainty in their assertions.

British and International The human resources for grappling with inter-
Illustrations war problems were most abundant in Great
Britain. There a number of able individuals and important councils, commissions, and committees investigated fiscal, financial, and economic developments in 1929–32 and made diagnoses and recommendations.

On January 27, 1930, Prime Minister MacDonald set up an Economic Advisory Council which met under his chairmanship. It was composed of prominent businessmen, politicians, labor leaders, and men outside politics including Keynes, Stamp, R. H. Tawney, and G. D. H. Cole, with a staff of five including three economists (H. D. Henderson, H. V. Hodson, and Colin Clark). The Council survived until World War II It functioned mainly through ad hoc and standing committees, on which Britain's leading economists served. Keynes was chairman of the first standing committee, set up on July 24, 1930. Stamp was chairman of the second, which prepared some twenty long reports on the economic situation. MacDonald and Chamberlain took the reports seriously, while Baldwin did not, but it accomplished little. Disagreements within the committees and Council unquestionably figured in the disappointing outcome, but other important factors were the secrecy of the reports and the entrenched power of the Treasury and the Bank of England, which stubbornly maintained differing views.[49]

The prestigious fourteen-member Committee on Finance and Industry, chaired by Hugh P. (later Lord) Macmillan, with Keynes an outstanding member, had been appointed on November 5, 1929, during the

investors, such as Baruch, Keynes, Governor Roosevelt, and Al Smith's 1928 campaign chairman John J. Raskob, or from candidate Hoover, who was under the constraint of political ambition.

[49]Charles L. Mowat, *Britain between the Wars, 1918–1940* (London: Methuen, 1955), p. 359; R. F. Harrod, *The Life of John Maynard Keynes* (New York: Harcourt Brace, 1951), pp. 397, 426, 432; Jones, *Stamp*, pp. 296–303; Arthur Salter, *Slave of the Lamp* (London: Weidenfeld and Nicolson, 1967), p. 87.

Wall Street crash. It took reams of testimony over an extended period while the economic contraction developed apace and financial complications multiplied. Its report, dated June 23, 1931, was published on July 13, when the financial crises had reached an advanced stage.[50] The Macmillan committee was unanimous that there could be no question of Great Britain departing from the gold standard; when this departure took place nine weeks later, Keynes reversed his position to acclaim it. Formidable difficulties presented by the great two-year fall of commodity prices and the huge volume of contractual obligations to rentiers were emphasized, but no solutions were offered except by minority dissenters. A number of these (including Keynes) favored tariff remedies. Sir Robert Brand held that a rise of world prices was essential to any normal solution of Britain's difficulties, and that wiping out reparations and interallied debts would be "the greatest single step towards recovery." Lord Bradbury dissented almost in toto. Altogether, this committee's contribution to recovery policy was negligible.[51]

Late in 1929 the Royal Institute of International Affairs assembled a distinguished group of forty-five or more leading representatives of various British interests, with at least one each from France, Germany, and the United States.[52] The group met at intervals from December 3, 1929, to February 11, 1931, to discuss the international gold problem. Its collected papers and reported discussions were published in 1932.[53] "The readers of this volume," the introduction stated, "will find that threads of thought run through it which, if followed, will lead him to the world monetary crisis of 1931." But none of the several crises of that year was clearly foreshadowed by any of the participants, and diversity of views was so prevalent that the book made little contribution to the "well-instructed

[50]Cmd. 3897 (1931), summarized with editorial comment in the *Economist*, July 18, 1931, pp. 106–12. Cf. Mowat, *Britain between the Wars*, pp. 260–62, 267, 269–70, 380, 385, 456–57. The *Minutes of Evidence* were published soon. Robertson's not highly perceptive memorandum, "The World Slump," submitted to the committee in April 1930, was printed in A. C. Pigou and D. H. Robertson, *Economic Essays and Addresses* (London: King, 1931), pp. 16–38. Cf. Clay, *Lord Norman*, p. 389 et passim.

[51]A. J. Youngson, *The British Economy, 1920–1957* (Cambridge, Mass.: Harvard University Press, 1960), ch. 7, "Economic Thought and Policy between the Wars," devoted pp. 235–55 to discussions before the Macmillan committee.

[52]The incomplete list of forty-five, given on the page preceding the contents, included Blackett, Brand, Einzig, Keynes, Salter, Stamp, and Strakosch, as well as Melchior Palyi, Charles Rist, and O. M. W. Sprague.

[53]*The International Gold Problem* (London: Oxford University Press 1932). D. E. Moggridge, reviewing the papers of a recent conference (R. A. Mundell and A. K. Swoboda, eds., *Monetary Problems of the International Economy* [Chicago: University of Chicago Press, 1969]) in *EJ*, September 1970, 80:696–98, commented that "the meetings appear to have been fairly successful in stimulating the participants," but "except in the case of a few papers, its results seem to have been rather negative." This has been all too typical, and the comment is clearly applicable to the papers just mentioned.

public opinion" which seemed necessary to the "creation of a sound policy." One member, Joseph Kitchin, was the leading international authority on gold supply and demand whose views were widely sought, but his forecasts in the 1920s and early 1930s soon proved inaccurate and misleading.[54]

The League of Nations Gold Delegation, of which M. J. Bonn was an unhappy member and Sir Henry Strakosch the most brilliant, made interim reports in June 1930 and December 1931 and rendered its final report in June 1932. Disagreements within the group, early blindness to the effects of price declines in stimulating gold production, other unexpected changes in the situation studied, and compromises to reach an agreed version resulted in largely futile products. The *Economist* termed the final report "a disappointing document . . . calculated to mystify rather than educate public opinion."[55]

In February 1932 six leading Englishmen intimately concerned with and experienced in economic and financial affairs gave successive papers on the world economic crisis.[56] In this notable series Sir Arthur Salter, Sir Josiah Stamp, J. M. Keynes, Sir Basil Blackett, Henry Clay, and Sir W. H. Beveridge each said much that was worth saying; but they fell far short of agreement on either diagnosis or prescription, and they acknowledged their inability to point to a practical way out of the universal "slough of despond" (Blackett, page 113). In the final lecture Beveridge said: "The way of escape from world crises is barred and doubly barred by disagreement among economists, and by the lack of international will among Governments. Only a world dictator could break his way out now" (page 188).[57] In his *Recovery* book, published soon after, Salter wrote:

Ours is a problem of the impoverishment that comes from plenty. It comes from defects in human organization and direction, from imperfect planning, from weakness in our financial and distributive systems—from essentially remediable evils and essentially removable causes. . . . If we are to avoid a period of misery and

[54]His articles in the *Encyclopaedia Britannica*, 11th to 14th editions, and in *Rev. Ec. Stat.*, July 1926 and May 1929, are listed in the bibliography to *The International Gold Problem*, pp. 225–26.

[55]League of Nations publications 2, Economic and Financial (1930), 2A.26,34; *ibid.*, 1931, 2.A2; *ibid.*, 1932, 3.A.12; *Economist*, June 11, 1932, pp. 1277–78; *EJ*, September 1932, 42: 502–3. Cf. Paul H. Douglas and Aaron Director, *The Problem of Unemployment* (New York: Macmillan, 1931), pp. 184–88; A. D. Gayer, *Monetary Policy and Economic Stabilisation: A Study of the Gold Standard*, 2d ed. (London: Black, 1937), pp. 27, 85–86, 99, 135–36, 147–50, 204n, 267–68; M. J. Bonn, *Wandering Scholar* (New York: John Day, 1948), pp. 311–14, 319.

[56]*World's Economic Crisis*. Cf. *Economist*, Feb. 13, 1932, pp. 341–42, June 11, 1932, p. 1297.

[57]In his book, *The Economics of Peace* (New York: Prentice-Hall, 1945), Kenneth Boulding somewhat condescendingly elaborated on the illusions, myths, fetishes, fears, and confusions that were prevalent in the interwar years, and added (p. 206): "It is the irresponsibility of nations that leads to war, and it is their attempt to be independent that leads to international chaos." The "chaos of 1918–1939" is among several exaggerations that I have noted (pp. 124, 186, 190, 191).

disruption which may threaten the fabric of our present civilization, we need a renewed effort of searching analysis and constructive reform in our Western world, comparable in boldness and in determination to that which is now being witnessed in Russia, however different to be the goal and the method.[58]

Lionel Robbins was younger than the Halley Stewart lecturers but equally competent. In mid-1934, after four years of activity in various groups, he set forth his reasoned views on the background, genesis, and development of the depression and the conditions of recovery.[59] He staunchly supported continued free trade. He favored some degree of stabilization of the foreign exchanges as the first essential of world-wide recovery. He considered the objective of raising prices to the 1929 or 1926 level as "not merely illusory, but positively harmful," and opposed "reflationary" efforts to raise price levels by "deliberate monetary manipulation." He strongly urged moves to remove the "grosser obstacles" to international trade. In many of his views he differed strongly with Keynes, whom he nevertheless greatly admired.[60]

That outstandingly brilliant, prolific, mercurial, many-sided man—much more than an economist—had powerfully influenced public opinion in many countries in 1919-32, but his strongly worded views were a mixture of right and wrong, and his influence on the course of policy was limited[61] and frequently harmful rather than helpful. This record continued in 1933-39. If Keynes sensed the menace of Hitler and Nazism, I have looked in vain for evidence of it.[62] His junior colleague Guillebaud, in his 1938 book on Germany's economic recovery through 1937 and in a December 1940 article ("Hitler's New Economic Order for Europe"), offered no criticism of Hitler's aims and policies. When that article aroused Einzig's ire, Keynes accepted Einzig's redrafted article and a later one expressing a very dif-

---

[58] *Recovery: The Second Effort* (New York: Century, 1932, pp. 8-9), mentioned in *Economist*, Apr. 16, 1932, pp. 836-37, and briefly reviewed in *ibid.*, June 11, 1932, p. 1287. In his Philadelphia address on May 20, 1932, Lippmann spoke on "The Paradox of Poverty and Plenty" and asserted: "This is the first great economic depression in which every thinking person has been conscious of such a paradox." Lippmann, *Interpretations, 1931-1932*, p. 1.

[59] Lionel Robbins, *The Great Depression* (London: Macmillan, 1934; Preface dated June 1934). The quoted phrases are on pp. 161, 163, 185. Mitchell's review of this book (*QJE*, August 1935, 49:503ff.) was highly critical. In his recent *Autobiography of an Economist* (London: Macmillan, 1971), pp. 154-55, Lord Robbins expressed strong regret at having published this book.

[60] Cf. Harrod, *Keynes*, p. 323, and Jones, *Stamp*, pp. 299-301. Apropos of a serious clash in 1930, Jones observed: "The world of economists was split almost beyond repair." The rift or gulf between the London and Cambridge economists must have adversely affected the London and Cambridge Economic Service, one of Keynes' special interests, which Harrod failed to mention.

[61] Youngson later wrote (*British Economy*, p. 252): "The ideas of Keynes had almost no effect on Government policy in this country before 1938." Cf. Bertil Ohlin's review of Keynes' *Essays in Persuasion* in *EJ*, April 1932, 42:258-62, and Stein, *Fiscal Revolution*, esp. ch. 7.

[62] Cf. Harrod, *Keynes*, pp. 479-80.

ferent viewpoint, but avoided giving his own opinion. "Considering Keynes' immense influence on official opinion, expert opinion and public opinion," Einzig later wrote in his autobiography, "I felt very glad that I had been successful in influencing him against supporting appeasement."[63]

Woytinsky concluded his 1936 study of the social consequences of the depression with these well-founded assertions: "A comprehensive view of the whole problem is an indispensable condition for success in a task as complex as that of overcoming a depression in the capitalist system as at present constituted. It was the lack of such a comprehensive view in recent years that made so many isolated efforts and legislative measures abortive."[64] The social scientists of the interwar period were not equipped to perform such a gigantic task. Even if they had been, one may doubt whether their analyses would have been accepted, whether they or anyone else could have drafted measures to cure the disease in its earlier or later stages, and whether, if they had, the recommendations would have been implemented by those in power.

Organized Economic Research in the United States   The many useful studies of the productive Brookings institutes in the 1920s, notably those of the Institute of Economics, were for the most part deliberately designed for the general reader.[65] They dealt capably with a large number of selected foreign and domestic subjects without attempting to come to grips with many issues of theory and policy, as they came to do in the 1930s.[66] For example, Owens and Hardy made an extensive 1925 study of the influence of the money market on the stock market, mostly using monthly data for the years 1872–1922 and daily data for 1906, 1908, and 1910.[67] They found no substantial support for the commonly accepted theory that daily, seasonal, and cyclical variations in interest rates (most specifically on call loans) caused inverse variations in speculative activity and prices of common stocks. They made no attempt to deal with issues of Federal Reserve policy, as Hardy did in his 1932 book, *Credit Policies of the Federal Reserve System*. Several of the later studies unquestionably

[63]*EJ*, December 1940, 50:449–60; April 1941, 51:1–18; June-September 1942, 52:176–85; Paul Einzig, *In the Centre of Things* (London: Hutchinson, 1960), pp. 168–70.

[64]Wladimir Woytinsky, *The Social Consequences of the Economic Depression* (Geneva: International Labour Office, 1936), p. 306.

[65]These are summarily covered in Charles B. Saunders, Jr., *The Brookings Institution: A Fifty-Year History* (Washington, D.C.: Brookings Institution, 1966), esp. ch. 2, "Early Years: The Vision of the Founders."

[66]*Ibid.*, ch. 3, "The Thirties: Depression and Controversy."

[67]Richard N. Owens and Charles O. Hardy, *Interest Rates and Stock Speculation: A Study of the Influence of the Money Market on the Stock Market* (New York: Macmillan, 1925; rev. ed., 1930). Monthly average rates on call loans were given for 1866–1924 (pp. 135–38) and daily rates for 1906, 1908, and 1910 (pp. 149–64). See also n.107 below.

exerted influence, but on some crucial issues they failed to convert the public, and a few evoked strong criticism from economists.

The Food Research Institute was primarily concerned with national and world problems of food and agriculture, and concentrated heavily on important commodities. It pioneered in interdisciplinary research; it attempted some forecasting, in particular of wheat prices and in some special studies as well; and it grappled with various issues of agricultural policy. It sought to maintain sound geographic, historical, and economic perspectives within the limited scope of its program but did not undertake to go outside that scope.[68]

In dealing with relevant politicoeconomic problems of 1929–33, the FRI's best efforts were useful but often inadequate and unsuccessful. My own detailed analysis of wheat policies and the depression did not appear until the spring of 1934. My conclusions then ran:

The world wheat situation was exceedingly vulnerable in 1929. This fact and belated recognition of it played a substantial role in the crisis. Developments in the wheat situation already under way helped to intensify the recession. Various national policies have tended to prevent early readjustment and rather to prolong the wheat depression. The obstinacy of the wheat maladjustment has been a factor impeding recovery. In creating and maintaining an ill-balanced and vulnerable wheat situation Nature played no small part; but ill-judged private actions and public policies have been even more important.[69]

Far too little of these conclusions appeared in the institute's publications in the crucial preceding years.

The Harvard Group. The most intensive analyses of current economic and financial developments, and the most ambitious attempts at business forecasting, were undertaken by the Harvard University Committee on Economic Research. It published the *Review of Economic Statistics* (1919) (which the Department of Economics took over in May 1935) and the *Weekly Letter* of its Harvard Economic Service and Society in 1922-31. The *Letter* was terminated, for financial reasons, after the collapse and contraction had revealed grave errors and deficiencies in appraising the economic position and outlook.[70] The *Review* has continued, with a slight

---

[68]See my paper, "The Bending of the Twig," in the recent Food Research Institute booklet *Dedication Addresses*, Apr. 6, 1970.

[69]"Wheat, Wheat Policies, and the Depression," *Rev. Ec. Stat.*, Apr. 15, 1934, 16:81. V. P. Timoshenko's valuable historical study *Monetary Influences on Postwar Wheat Prices* did not appear until 1938: see Wheat Studies of the Food Research Institute 14 (Stanford, Calif.: Food Research Institute, 1938), pp. 263–318. See J. S. Davis, Helen M. Gibbs, and Elizabeth B. Taylor, *Wheat and the World Economy: A Guide to Wheat Studies of the Food Research Institute* (Stanford, Calif.: Food Research Institute, 1945).

[70]See the Harvard Economic Society's letter to members and subscribers, dated Nov. 14, 1931. Reviewing in the NBER annual report for 1944 the interwar period in the development of economics, Mitchell adverted to the "misadventures of 'business forecasting' " as reflect-

change of name in January 1948. Like much of the business and professional literature of the period, the Harvard studies (apart from valuable historical ones) were heavily focused on short-run developments and gave too little consideration to the intermediate future[71] in which serious weaknesses were to bear evil fruit. Moreover, the staff, though able, was too small to deal adequately with the enormous complexity of the world economy and its problems,[72] and two of its key members (Persons and Vanderblue) left for investment trust positions in New York shortly before the Wall Street crash.[73]

In September 1925 W. L. Crum published a lengthy interpretation of the Harvard index of general business conditions. Four years later this was substantially revised with data through July 1929 and reprinted in a separately paged supplement to the *Rev. Ec. Stat.*[74] If one rereads today this very able analysis, however, he is amazed that Crum could have failed to realize the ominous significance of the ballooning Curve A (Speculation) and the strongly rising Curve C (Money) in the basic index chart[75] and the downtrend in its weekly sensitive price index from early 1928 to mid-1929; that near the end of that crucial summer he could consider it "unlikely that a prolonged decline of the general price level will develop within the next few years";[76] and that he could have concluded:

The conditions which ordinarily precipitate strain and crisis have not appeared since 1919–20, and it is impossible now to foresee the termination of the

ing reckless efforts of some investigators. This was a natural remark from the leader of the cautious National Bureau of Economic Research, but it failed to do justice to the pathbreaking enterprise led by Bullock and Persons.

[71]This point is seldom mentioned. In early December 1929, however, Stamp emphasized the high importance of the "medium run" as compared with the short run and the long run. *International Gold Problem*, pp. 1–2.

[72]My contributions to the *Review* and *Weekly Letter* on European economic and financial developments (many of which are cited in Chapters 2 and 3) ceased in mid-1925, and this subject thereafter received inadequate staff attention.

[73]See editorial announcement in *Rev. Ec. Stat.*, August 1929, 10:152.

[74]*Rev. Ec. Stat.*, September 1925, 7:217–35; *Interpretation of the* [Harvard] *Index of General Business Conditions* (reprint supplement to *Rev. Ec. Stat.*, September 1929). The quoted passages in the rest of this paragraph are, in order, from pp. 14, 2, and 21 of this reprint.

[75]The indexes were repeatedly revised; e.g., see W. L. Crum in *Rev. Ec. Stat.*, November 1928, 10:202–12. In an unpublished memorandum dated May 27, 1963, Geoffrey H. Moore of the National Bureau reported his finding that "the sequence upon which the Harvard ABC curves [1903–41] were based has persisted over a long period," extending from 1879 to 1961 (exclusive of the cycle turns during and immediately following two world wars) with only minor exceptions. One exception was crucial: stock prices, which reached their peak in September 1929, failed to give their usual advance warning of the economic downturn.

[76]In mid-1922, and again late in 1925, the Harvard Economic Service had taken pains to appraise the outlook for the level of commodity prices over the next few years. *Weekly Letter*, June 10, 1922, pp. 133–40; Nov. 28, 1925, pp. 358–60. In both instances the provisional conclusion was that a horizontal trend was probable, around a level about 50 percent above the prewar level. This conclusion was not seriously modified in an extended discussion of the commodity price level in *ibid.*, Mar. 15, 1930, pp. 72–73, when it was held that prospective easy money would "presently stabilize commodity prices and then lead to an upturn of prices."

present business cycle. Although for many months there has been exceptionally active speculation in securities, with a consequent development of credit strain, the existence of abundant credit reserves and the probable continuance of regulatory control of credit have given confidence that these financial conditions would not usher in a period of general business depression. . . . the present situation contains no elements which clearly forecast an early termination of the prosperity phase of the present longer [than prewar] business cycle.

This notable forecasting experiment failed despite its early successes and many valuable contributions. Its "barometers" were particularly influential, but only experience revealed the dangers in their oversimplified presentation of exceedingly complex events. In 1928–31 the HES proved seriously misleading, and it was especially slow to modify its view of the outlook in 1930. It recognized the speculative inflation or craze, but did not point to the danger of a severe shock to the economy that a Wall Street crash might bring about.[77] It unwittingly gave support to the New Era psychology, and failed to unveil the illusions that were prevalent. It did not emphasize, and only inadequately recognized, the credit inflation which B. M. Anderson saw clearly and wrote of in the 1920s. It did not pursue the implications of the belatedly recognized foreign impact of the tight money caused by excessive stock speculation in the late 1920s. It showed inadequate awareness of the precariousness of the continental European currency stabilizations and of the unfavorable international developments of 1928–30. Cooperation with its British, French, and Italian counterparts added little to its grasp of European developments in these years, and the London and Cambridge Economic Service itself was similarly disappointing, despite some distinct contributions. Not infrequently, ominous developments were briefly reported without their significance, if realized, being emphasized.[78] On the whole, the HES concentrated too heavily on statisti-

[77]In its *Weekly Letter* of Apr. 30, 1927, pp. 110–11, the HES had discussed the cause and probable duration of the general prosperity that began about mid-1922, for which it found a precedent in 1886–92. Its excellent concluding paragraph read: "In the past, periods of active business have always given way to periods of depression, and it is hazardous to conclude today that general prosperity is going to last indefinitely. In particular, we should not expect the federal reserve system to prevent depression from ever occurring, since central banks in Europe were never able to accomplish such a thing. Moreover, the extraordinarily strong position of our banking system has been chiefly the result of the accumulation of gold in this country, and there is no assurance that world economic conditions may not later lead to a substantial outflow. Nor is there any assurance that, if most people come to the conclusion that depressions are impossible, an old-fashioned boom might not speedily develop and bring with it the old-fashioned sequel—a depression. Clearly, however, such developments are not in immediate prospect; and we believe that business (despite intermediate fluctuations like those of recent years) will remain generally active so long as easy money continues." Somehow this wise counsel was not well heeded.

[78]E.g., in *ibid.*, Oct. 11, 1930, p. 248: "The increase in the discount rate of the German Reichsbank apparently reflects disturbed political conditions in Germany, which have led to the transfer of funds to other countries. Political unsettlement in Germany and revolution in Brazil have adversely affected prices of German and Latin American bonds in this country."

cal materials and analysis and on historical studies and failed to assemble enough additional information to provide the basis for sound judgments on domestic and foreign developments, economic and political.[79]

The National Bureau and Recent Economic Changes. The National Bureau of Economic Research concentrated mainly on basic research in business cycles, and studiously avoided forecasting and policy recommendations. It held to these principles when it was drawn into service to the federal government, first in its 1922 survey *Business Cycles and Unemployment*, then, more notably, in the preparation of the impressive series of monographs that were written in 1928–29 for the Committee on Recent Economic Changes and published with the committee's report in June 1929 (see Chapter 6 above). From the viewpoint of the needs of the time, these principles were seriously restrictive, and the speed with which the volumes were produced did not permit the necessary maturing of their massive contents. The following comments on two of these papers illustrate their shortcomings.

Two able economists, O. M. W. Sprague of Harvard and W. Randolph Burgess of the Federal Reserve Bank of New York, coauthored an important fifty-page chapter in *Recent Economic Changes*. The manuscript was completed in the fall of 1928, well before the bull market reached its more advanced stages. The authors rightly pointed out the recently ended easing of the money market, the rapid increase in bank credit, the relatively high rates on brokers' loans, the unusually large volume of savings, the ease with which securities had been marketed, the heavy investment by the public in the security markets, the wide diffusion of ownership of bonds and shares, and the spectacular advance in stock prices (pages 674–81). Several mild incidental warnings merit quoting (pages 672–88):

it is yet to be seen whether the recent increase [in bank credit] has sowed seeds of trouble which have not yet fully grown. . . . we may say of recent foreign as of domestic investments that only the future can determine whether or not they have been shrewdly made, with advantage to borrowers and with but negligible losses to those who have supplied the funds. . . . In some instances, the capital structure in the course of time will doubtless prove defective. . . . There is also the possibility that unfortunate results, in the long run, may follow the separation of management and control from ownership which, whether by design or not, is apt to be found when a business is owned by wide circles of investors. . . . sudden contraction on a large scale is possible with no class of loans, and under a well-organized banking

[79]A candid, illuminating internal appraisal was soon published: C. J. Bullock and W. L. Crum, "The Harvard Index of Economic Conditions: Interpretation and Performance, 1919–31," *Rev. Ec. Stat.*, Aug. 15, 1932, 14:132–48. Cf. C. J. Bullock, W. M. Persons, and W. L. Crum, "The Construction and Interpretation of the Harvard Index of Business Conditions," *ibid.*, April 1927, 9:74–92, and the promotional brochure, *Harvard Economic Service* (Cambridge, Mass.: HES, 1923).

system is never necessary. . . . It is, of course, entirely possible that much of the ample supply of capital may have been placed in feeble hands, and that certain industries may prove to have been overdeveloped. . . . Discounting the future in the security market may be carried to excess with resulting unhappy consequences, and it is an important limitation upon the significance of this survey that it covers a period that witnessed only the economic, social, and financial effects of a rising market for securities. . . . That security prices should have further advanced in 1928, with an accompanying increase in brokers' loans and in spite of a sharp advance in rates, may perhaps be regarded as symptomatic of unrestrained speculation. But even though an over-extended situation in the security market should not develop and be followed by a disastrous reaction, it may be said that the recent experience in the functioning of the money market, as it is affected by the Stock Exchange demand for credit, raises new and perplexing problems. In the past, the bulk of brokers' loans has been furnished by banks and bankers. Under the influence of rates for call loans ruling generally above rates on all other classes of loans, the funds of investors and surplus funds of business enterprises have been attracted into the market in such volume that they now provide very nearly one-half of the total supply. The outcome of this practice remains for the future to disclose. . . . The possibilities of effectually restraining intense speculative activity through sharp and even drastic action have not been tested.

But the warnings were not given the stress that they deserved, and they were partly offset by the recital of favorable factors and by a few specific reassuring statements (e.g., pages 669, 681) that soon proved wrong: "now the monetary affairs of the world are again stabilized. . . . the abundant supply of funds, seeking investment at declining rates, seems to have exerted an influence favorable to the strengthening of the financial structure of business during the course of the period covered by the survey."

In ending their chapter, Sprague and Burgess emphasized "the need for suspending judgment as to final conclusions" (page 705):

Business has continued for extended periods above any computed normal growth line, with only brief recessions. There has been an extraordinarily large volume of building, of new financing, of automobile production, and of consumption. There has been a huge volume of speculation, accompanied by striking increases in prices of securities. This has been made possible, in part, by gold imports and the resulting comparatively easy money conditions.

It is possible that in some one or more of these directions an unsound economic structure has been built up, the dangers of which are not now obvious. Only the test of a longer period of time can yield convincing results.

In his long review chapter in *Recent Economic Changes* (pages 841–910) Wesley C. Mitchell rightly stressed the maze of economic changes, the diversities of fortune, the hardships that accompanied improvements in industrial technique and business methods, and the retardation in population growth. But he took satisfaction in much of the evidence, including the spirit of caution among businessmen, the relative stability of business, and the fact that, while business cycles had not been ironed out, the amplitude of cyclical fluctuations had been reduced. He referred in the same sentence to the Florida land boom of 1925 and the stock market "adventure" of 1928, and adverted to optimists who were saying that we need fear no serious reaction in the future. But he went on: "The forecast in this statement we may leave for the future to test, reserving our attention to what has already happened."

Mitchell's final paragraphs, like the chapter by Sprague and Burgess, contained significant reservations, as the following passages illustrate (pages 909–10):

> Forecasting the future is no part of the present task. But we should not close the record without noting that recent developments may appear less satisfactory in retrospect than they appear at present.
>
> Even on the face of affairs, all is not well. . . . The condition of agriculture, the volume of unemployment, the textile trades, coal mining, the leather industries, present grave problems not only to the people immediately concerned, but also to their fellow citizens. How rapidly these conditions will mend, we do not know. Some may grow worse.
>
> Nor can we be sure that the industries now prosperous will prolong indefinitely their recent record of stability. That we have not had a serious crisis since 1920 or a severe depression since 1921 is no guarantee that we shall be equally prudent, skillful and fortunate in the years to come. . . . The credit structure must be kept in due adjustment to the earnings of business enterprises. Security prices must not outrun prospective profits capitalized at the going rate of interest. Commodity stocks must be held in line with current sales . . . Perhaps errors are being kept within the limits of tolerance. Perhaps no serious setback will occur for years to come. But we are leaving 1921 well behind us, and there are signs that the caution inspired by that disastrous year is wearing thin.

These scholars touched upon most of the real weaknesses in the situation which, added together, should have made it difficult (even in the winter of 1928–29, to say nothing of later months) to assert that the economy was fundamentally sound. Whether because of their own spirit of caution, lack of courage or perspicacity, or reluctance to rock the boat and undermine the prevailing confidence, however, they lost the opportunity to sound strong warnings and even to temper significantly the overoptimistic tone of the committee report. And such recommendations as they ventured to suggest were couched only in vague and general terms, which are reflected in the final paragraph of the committee report (quoted in Chapter 6 above). Similar considerations, strongly reinforced by political ones, seriously restrained the utterances of leaders in the federal government and the Federal Reserve System.

It is hard to escape the inference that President Hoover influenced the tone of the volumes, probably through the committee secretary, Edward Eyre Hunt, at least to the point of insisting that clear evidence—inherently difficult to marshal—be cited for any strong warnings. Mitchell's natural caution was reinforced by the National Bureau's principle of avoiding forecasting. From a letter he wrote to his wife on April 16, 1932, I infer that, while the *Recent Economic Changes* manuscripts were being completed and hurriedly reviewed in 1928–29, he had serious misgivings about the prevalent "delusion" and "emotional unbalance." If so, those were muted in his review chapter.[80]

Hoover repeatedly demonstrated high confidence in Gay and Mitchell, the National Bureau's codirectors of research. Yet they were not trusted to provide the interpretation of the mass of facts yielded by their collaboration. The last paragraph of the foreword read: "While the National Bureau is solely responsible for the basic survey, the committee is solely responsible for the interpretation of the facts set out in the following brief report."[81]

In a critical review of these two volumes late in 1930, a British economist observed, with the advantage of information from the fifteen eventful months since their publication:

Nowhere in the 943 pages is there any strong suggestion that the crisis of late 1929 was blowing up, or that the tremendous increase in industrial capacity and output in 1928 and 1929 was anything save an acceleration normal and proper and capable of being maintained, provided due caution were exercised. . . . In a work dealing with American economic life as wide-sweeping as this, it is rather surprising to find that there is, save incidentally, no mention of the effects of the tariff; that the "theory of high wages"—so intriguing to European observers—gains only passing notice; that the problem of over-capacity appearing in many industries is almost ignored, and that no attempt is made to assess the net economic effects of phenomena peculiar to this society, such as intensive advertising, "high-pressure" salesmanship, the legal maintenance of competition or the social consequences of the growth of large-scale production.[82]

Jewkes also found the committee's report most disappointing. Its optimistic view on the balance attained in production and consumption, he said, "hardly squares with the general complaint that is heard in practically all industries of increasing over-capacity." Such complaints were doubtless heard in 1930, but in the spring of 1929, when the committee was putting the finishing touches on its report, the prevailing view was that excess capacity was limited to only a few industries (see Chapter 13 above). The committee's view that equilibrium had been fairly well maintained seemed to Jewkes hardly "consistent with a period when intense

[80]Lucy Sprague Mitchell, *Two Lives: The Story of Wesley Clair Mitchell and Myself* (New York: Simon and Schuster, 1953), p. 388, quoted on p. 11 above.

[81]In the *Survey Graphic* of June 1, 1929, Beulah Amidon gave a brief account of the committee's procedures.

[82]J. Jewkes, in *EJ*, December 1930, 40:650–57.

speculation was bringing in its train crisis and industrial regression, in which banks and investment banks were forcing into existence many mergers which had no economic justification save the profits to be made in floating their securities and in which agriculture was the increasingly poor relative of industry." This view, which the severe contraction of 1929–30 encouraged, was doubtless held by a few in 1928–29 but was seldom voiced, and never stressed, at that time. To have embodied it in the committee report would have required far more trenchant analyses and forthright utterances in the detailed chapters.

It must be added, however, that correction of these defects would have taken so long that the volumes could not have come out in time to exert significant influence on the course of the economy or the stock market, which by mid-1929 were far along the road to disaster. The social science professions were insufficiently matured to dampen, in time, the exuberance that developed in the 1920s. A search of the relevant literature strongly reinforces this conclusion, as a few examples will indicate.

Evidence from   Soon after the 1928 election a reputable mid-
Contemporary Literature   western economic historian wrote an article on the economic problems confronting the president-elect, in which he made no mention of speculation, unemployment, or a possible retreat from prosperity.[83]

Carl Snyder, a key staff man in the Federal Reserve Bank of New York, discussed the problem of prosperity in his presidential address before the American Statistical Association late in 1928. He reviewed the general sequences of prosperity, boom, collapse, depression, and recovery since the Civil War, with special reference to the depressions of the 1870s and 1890s and the preceding "high industrial and constructional activity . . . accompanied by a period of intense speculative activity which approached, at times, a national mania." "It seems not improbable," he went on, "that this seizure of the national mind has been one of the chief contributing causes to the disasters and disillusionments which followed."[84] Instead of saying "here we are now" and urging early moves to avert catastrophe, however, Snyder found comfort in "a parallel outburst of the statistical mania" and rashly expressed his belief that "the Cinderella of the sciences may offer a solution." Statistical investigation had made an important contribution to economic theory in showing that an excess of the rate of credit expansion over the growth of production and trade, which we had learned to measure, "results merely in the familiar forms of overstimula-

[83]E. L. Bogart, in *Yale Review*, December 1928, pp. 227–45.
[84]*JASA*, March 1929, 24:1–14.

tion, inflation and speculation."[85] But he was silent as to steps that the system should take under this "working rule of banking and credit policy."

In the late 1920s and early 1930s the receptiveness to unpalatable truths was notably low, especially in official circles. Churchill may have been right in saying that the few who in 1929 correctly saw what lay ahead were "cowed into silence by what they foresaw."[86] At least twice, Secretary Hoover was enraged by the findings of Brookings studies. When Moulton's analysis of the French war debt problem led the Debt Commission to scale down the U.S. claims on France, Hoover told a press conference that Moulton "represented a liability to the United States to the extent of $10 million a year in perpetuity."[87] The six-year Brookings study of the St. Lawrence Seaway proposal (1929), which gave cost estimates five times those of the government, helped to thwart Hoover's efforts to get this favorite project through the Congress.[88]

Late in 1930 James Truslow Adams, who published many forthright critical essays in 1927–34, stressed the common "refusal to face the truth or even to search for it."[89] He saw the "cultivation of emotion in the child instead of the power of critical thought" as "a source of the greatest possible danger to us in the modern world." Because of the refusal to think, he said, "everyone is now paying a far higher price than they otherwise would have for the cost of a normal and severe trade reaction." "The America of 1930 cannot afford to trust to a blind optimism," as could the earlier America of the agricultural era. He endorsed Sir Josiah Stamp's recent statement that we cannot live in "the golden age of economic organization and the stone age of economic thought."

Speaking before the American Economic Association late in December 1930, when the worst of the depression was still to come, Snyder quoted Sir Charles Addis' recent characterization of it as "the most serious in over one hundred years" and agreed: "This is the most world-wide depression, if not the most severe, of which we have any record." This he found "an astonishing and sinister portent . . . in ironic contrast to the fantasies of a 'new era' of unending prosperity, so widely prevalent but little more than a

[85]Elaborated in his paper of Nov. 22, 1929: Carl Snyder, "New Measures of the Relations of Credit and Trade," *Proc. Acad. Pol. Sci.*, January 1930, 13:16–34. Dorfman observed that David Friday in 1928–29, "like so many economists, took the view that in boom times government agencies should not attempt to restrain enthusiasm." *Economic Mind*, 5:402–14, esp. p. 413.

[86]Churchill, *The Second World War*, vol. 1: *The Gathering Storm* (Boston: Houghton Mifflin, 1948), p. 32.

[87]Saunders, *Brookings*, p. 31.

[88]*Ibid.*, pp. 45–46.

[89]See especially *The Tempo of Modern Life* (New York: Boni, 1931). The quoted words are from "Pollyanna, Our Patron Goddess," *Forum*, November 1930, pp. 237–62. Many similar statements can be found in this collection, both earlier and later in date, and in his subsequent books.

year ago": "The collapse of the speculative mania in the United States last year, puncturing conditions of overexpansion in some important lines, reacted then upon a world in none too buoyant a condition and in which many countries were directly dependent upon these United States, either through our immense purchases of raw materials or through loans of billions of dollars, for such well-being as they had enjoyed."[90]

Snyder was brutally frank in calling the gold inflation after 1921 a dominant factor in U.S. prosperity and "certainly the strongest factor in the tremendous speculative boom"; blaming high money rates on the "speculative madness"; and stressing the generally adverse impact of these factors on the rest of the world and the fall in commodity prices "of almost catastrophic severity" for some countries. He rejected the popular belief in general overproduction but was baffled by "the phenomenon of the general debacle, when these drastic declines come all together, in a sort of ill-omened unison." One could wish that Snyder had spoken as trenchantly late in 1928.

The American Statistical Association held several dinner meetings in New York in 1928 and 1929 at which issues and prospects were dealt with. In retrospect, the speakers seem singularly lacking in penetration. Much the same obtains of papers given at the ASA annual meeting late in 1929, several of which merit brief summary.[91]

Garfield V Cox of the University of Chicago School of Business undertook to appraise economic forecasts prior to the 1929 crash.[92] His broad conclusion was that "a representative group of forecasters appear to have stood the test of these appraisals with a sufficient degree of success to prove that they have been, on the whole, helpful to business men; and the increasing use of scientific methods of analysis promises improvement in the future." That the collapse of stock prices had not been predicted was

[90]*AER*, March 1931, suppl., 21 (1):172–78. Schumpeter's discursive "tentative diagnosis" at the same sessions (pp. 179–82) was not one of his best papers, and he too rashly concluded that "there is no difficulty in devising," on the basis of this diagnosis, remedies "both general and particular." But he added that "the difficulty lies in the fact that our patients will not take what we might be able to prescribe."

[91]The New York dinner meetings of Oct. 25 and Dec. 6, 1928, and of Mar. 14 and May 9, 1929, are well summarized in *JASA*, 1929, 24:69–74, 182–87, and 307–11. The annual sessions are reported in *ibid.*, March 1930, suppl., 25 (169A).

[92]Various services operating in the mid-1920s were discussed in Hardy and Cox, *Forecasting Business Conditions*. Cox's *An Appraisal of American Business Forecasts* [1918–28] (Chicago: University of Chicago Press, 1929), published in December 1929, was the basis of his own leading ASA paper. His brief concluding chapter included these revealing and amazing sentences (p. 70): "The error which marred most seriously the record of these services was the failure to foresee the industrial recession of 1923–24, and this mistake appears to have been due primarily to an overemphasis upon the power of abundant bank credit to sustain business at a high level. . . . Finally, the study seems to indicate that minor cycles are harder to predict than major ones. If this is true, and if, as many believe, we are facing a period in which the only business fluctuations to be forecast will be of moderate proportions, the job of the business forecaster may prove a difficult one. . . ."

not stressed by Cox. One discussant (John G. Thompson of Simonds Saw and Steel Company) argued, on the basis of nearly a decade of forecasting experience, that a major upswing of money rates, such as had occurred in the preceding two years, was invariably followed by a decline in business activity beginning nine to eighteen months later. Had this truth been widely recognized and acted upon, he made bold to say, the stock market crash would not have occurred.

J. L. Snider of the Harvard Graduate School of Business Administration, reviewing production and prices in 1929, interpreted the production data to indicate that the current decline would be "at least slightly more severe than the decline in 1924," and considered significant the near-stability of domestic commodity price indexes, which had fallen only "moderately during the recent months of declining production."

Thomas S. Holden of the F. W. Dodge Corporation gave a realistic review of the building situation, noting that "construction was the most important manufacturing industry that suffered considerable losses in 1929 as a more or less direct result of our stock market spree." But he held that the decline in residential building had largely corrected the oversupply of housing, and he awaited recovery with considerable confidence. He lamented the serious setback in the country's program of civil engineering development, which he attributed to the continued decline in the municipal bond market. He looked forward to the inauguration of a program of public building and public works and expected expansion to be resumed in 1930.

E. Dana Durand of the Department of Commerce reviewed the foreign trade of 1929, for which data were incomplete. He adverted to the stock market in connection with the international gold movements, markedly reversed late in the year, and to the fact that capital movements, which had "played a great part in recent years . . . , are exceptionally difficult to measure, especially those connected with stock market and banking transactions." He pointed with pride to the very marked increase in exports of manufactures in practically every year since 1921. He noted the moderate reduction in exports of agricultural products since 1926 (notably cotton, tobacco, barley, and rye); the increased exports of meats, lard, corn, and fruits and nuts; and the more or less marked declines in prices of major import commodities such as rubber, coffee, silk, sugar, and tin. But his conclusion was unreservedly optimistic (quoted in Chapter 8 above).

Of the three general forecasts for 1930, only that of Paul Clay of the United States Shares Corporation was published in the ASA proceedings. His view, which he thought to be the consensus, was that July 1930 would mark the bottom of the minor depression in progress. He thought a "secondary boom" of "plodding prosperity" would follow, and that the stock market would advance long before July.[93]

---

[93]For views that Clay had expressed on Mar. 14, 1929, see Chapter 7 above.

James F. Hughes of Otis and Company briefly discussed security prices. He called the market of mid-October to mid-November 1929 the most chaotic in U.S. history, but dealt mainly with technical points and attempted no forecast. Carl Snyder realistically discussed the "prodigious rise" in brokers' loans and the "pyramiding of credit," but, after likening the experience to the Mississippi and South Sea bubbles, he cautiously concluded: "Our Wall Street financiers seemed to see no limits to which the fiction of 'new values' could be carried. What repercussion the collapse will have upon the industry and employment of the country remains to be seen." Irving Fisher briefly discussed the stock market panic, anticipating his book then in press (*The Stock Market Crash—and After*). His paper ended: "In short both the bull movement and the crash are largely explained by the *unsound financing of sound prospects*"—one of his typical over-statements.

Leland Rex Robinson of the Second International Securities Corporation illuminatingly discussed the role of investment companies in the security markets of 1929. These companies were of several types, and their financial practices were so varied that he considered broad generalizations more misleading than helpful; but he found no valid reason for holding that as a group they were responsible for the speculative boom or its collapse. The fundamental causes of the "extremely buoyant stock market of the past few years" he summarized thus:

Emphasis for several years upon the qualities of common stocks for long-term investment, the increased volume of business and larger earnings of leading corporations; the preaching of the "new economic era" with its promise of greater steadiness and better coordination in the vast network of the nation's industries; the ample supply of gold and the country's comfortable reserve position; the growth in investment capital coupled with a widespread interest in and knowledge of the characteristics of junior as compared with senior securities—all these and many other factors have to be reckoned with as basic causes, without losing sight of the mob psychology which in the later stages of the recent bull market broke past all barriers of reason.

More than most writers, Robinson rightly stressed the international interactions before and during the crash: "tight money artificially created by the omnivorous appetite of Wall Street"; the "general decline in European stocks . . . partly due to the heavy drain toward Wall Street"; and then the large withdrawals of foreign capital which "helped to undermine further the highly unbalanced security price structure in this country and to start the processes of acute demoralization."[94]

[94]Robinson's *Investment Trust Organization and Management* (New York: Ronald, 1926), an elaboration of his earlier government bulletin, had been reviewed by A. Vere Shaw in *AER*, March 1927, 17:105–6; Shaw rated this "the most comprehensive book" on the subject but weak from the investor's viewpoint. The revised edition (1929) appeared shortly before Robinson spoke before the ASA.

Marcus Nadler of New York University, reviewing Europe ten years after the war, noted important progress in reconstruction and reorganization—fiscal, financial, and commercial. However, he considered the reparations problem still unsolved, the budget balancing more apparent than real, unemployment a serious problem not only in Germany and England but in four other countries, and military expenditures a heavy burden reflecting the great uneasiness and uncertainty and the injustices of the treaties of peace. "Economically," he concluded, "the face of Europe is changing rapidly and is assuming an entirely different aspect from that of pre-war days. What the outcome of these developments will be, only the future can tell."

Robert B. Warren, one of the best informed and most perceptive of the younger economists, ventured this impressive prophecy in his comment on Nadler's paper:

Now, unemployment, from which we have been so free over the past decade [sic], seems to be one of the inherent risks of an industrialized society. Sooner or later, it is not unlikely that we shall find our economic life paralleling more closely that of Europe; the happy freedom not only from unemployment, but from an unemployment "problem," which has been peculiar to us among industrial nations, may pass, and we may find ourselves confronted with it. This may indeed develop within the coming decade; and if and when it does, its victims will take refuge in political action, like their industrial counterparts in Europe and their agricultural counterparts here. Indeed, if one wished to assume one of the risks of the statistical profession, and, on the basis of the past decade venture to a guess about the coming decade, he might suggest that in this country over the next ten years industrial relief, whether old age pensions, unemployment insurance or what not, may replace farm relief as a major topic of political-economic discussion.

But Warren did not predict the enormous increase in unemployment in the three years immediately ahead.

In sharp contrast to Nadler's rightly somber and reserved outlook on Europe was J. W. Angell's book on Germany,[95] written for the Council on Foreign Relations, to which Nadler made no reference. In his concluding chapter Angell recognized that various factors would hinder future growth in a number of directions, but confidently asserted that the country's expansion would continue. "The road marked out for Germany through the com-

---

[95] *The Recovery of Germany* (New Haven, Conn.: Yale University Press, 1929). In the preface (dated Aug. 16, 1925) Angell said that the book had been read in manuscript by E. F. Gay, W. C. Mitchell, and Charles P. Howland (who wrote the introduction), and the concluding chapter ("The Young Plan and Germany's Future") by John Foster Dulles. Angell also acknowledged aid from a large number of well-known men including Paul M. Warburg of New York, M. J. Bonn and Melchior Palyi (both then of the Berlin Handelshochschule), Josef Schumpeter (then of the University of Bonn), Ernst Wagemann and Otto Nathan of the German Federal Statistical Office, and "various members of the staff of the Office for Reparation Payments, Berlin."

ing decades is not easy, but it is a road which climbs steadily upward, and at its end lies the prize of assured national strength and prosperity." W. J. Dawson, reviewing Angell's book in the spring of 1930, called it "a sound piece of workmanship," adding that "in both diagnosis and prognosis Dr. Angell is backed by most well-informed opinion abroad."[96] Nine months later Dawson praised Sir Andrew McFadyean's 1930 book *Reparation Reviewed* as "an exceptionally well-balanced piece of work,"[97] and noted that Sir Andrew endorsed Angell's opinion "that Germany can only meet her indebtedness by constantly increasing her exports of industrial products, which means ever-growing competition in the world markets, and particularly in the markets of her creditors." None of these four men, however, gave any advance hint of Germany's virtual collapse in the next three years.[98]

An enlarged and revised edition of Angell's book was published within three years, with a new preface dated February 7, 1932. He left the bulk of it unchanged except for a number of minor corrections, though he frankly acknowledged that "a number of the observations and estimates presented in the last half of Chapter XI now seem, if not flatly wrong, at least seriously overoptimistic." He added a short postscript chapter summarizing developments since 1929, but could still find no grounds for pessimism.

Though a few economists were sufficiently prescient to favor a federal system of insurance or guarantee of bank deposits, which proved a great success in 1934–39, most supported bankers in strongly opposing this bold innovation.[99]

J. M. Clark's *Strategic Factors in Business Cycles*, published by the National Bureau in 1935, was one of several later studies sponsored by the Committee on Recent Economic Changes,[100] which provided an introduction dated November 1933. Two of Clark's several cogent observations (esp. pages 98–101, 111–16) merit quoting here: "Stock prices during the great boom were capitalizing not current earnings but future increases of a sort which any systematic analysis should have revealed as beyond all

[96]See Chapter 6 above.

[97]W. J. Dawson, in *EJ*, March 1931, 41:94–97; McFadyean's book was written in 1929 after the completion of the Young committee report, with a preface dated Sept. 13, 1930, but not brought up to date before publication.

[98]The *Economist* review of 1929, issued Feb. 15, 1930, reported that German economic indexes "show very clearly that something is still out of joint in the economic mechanism."

[99]Cf. Chapter 13 above; Dorfman, *Economic Mind*, 5:683–84, and index under "bank deposit insurance." R. W. Goldschmidt (Goldsmith), in his generally excellent book *The Changing Structure of American Banking* (London: Routledge, 1933; preface dated September 1933), termed this provision of the Banking Act of 1933 mistaken, "unsound," and "most dangerous" (pp. 273–74).

[100]In the list of members Shaw's name appears as chairman, that of Samuel E. Reyburn is added, and those of Brown and Hoover are omitted.

human possibility. . . . Buyers who thought of the matter at all were typically convinced that the country had entered upon a 'new era' in which
deluges were not to be permitted." If Clark saw this in 1928–29, he seems
not to have said it publicly. Even in his ASA paper late in 1931,[101] he made
only a brief reference to "our late 'new era' delusion and the present reversal of it."

Much more evidence could be cited to show that, in the main, the
economic analyses in the late 1920s and early 1930s were insufficiently
penetrating and either too optimistic or too cautious in appraising the outlook. One of the most disagreeable and sobering lessons to be learned from
the experiences of these years, and indeed of the two interwar decades, is
that a whole generation of able scholars can be seriously wrong in interpreting the present and sizing up the future.

Admissions of   Some of the economic analysts in these crucial years, to
Errors   their credit, scrutinized the record and frankly acknowledged errors that had been made. On the morrow of the stock market
crash, Professor Henry R. Seager of Columbia said, "As we review what
has happened must we not agree that we all shared in responsibility for the
phenomenal boom and for the inevitable crash which followed it?"[102] A
few others deserve mention.

Stuart Chase had written early in 1929: "If we should cease to buy
automobiles at the present rate, what would happen to prosperity; would it
go down like a house of cards?"[103] In a later 1929 book he voiced no doubt
as to the reality of our prosperity and could not foresee its early end.[104]
In the spring of 1931 he wrote: "Many of us at the time saw no reason why
a stock market collapse should necessarily undermine business, and indeed
there was none; but what most of us did not see was the extent of the black
cloud over Detroit which had been gathering all summer."[105]

Two years after the crash, an astute observer who was active in Wall
Street spoke at a dinner meeting of the American Statistical Association
on "The Role and Responsibility of Academic Delusion in the Depression."[106] Before the crash, Sachs pointed out, the profession laid undue

---

[101]"Business Cycles: The Problem of Diagnosis," *JASA*, March 1932, suppl., 27 (177A):212–
17.

[102]"Some Remedies for Stock Gambling," Nov. 22, 1929, *Proc. Acad. Pol. Sci.*, January
1930, 13:505–7. At the end of 1930 Colonel Ayres acknowledged the error of his forecast a
year earlier; this I recall but have not verified.

[103]Stuart Chase, *Men and Machines* (New York: Macmillan, 1929), p. 228.

[104]*Prosperity: Fact or Myth?* (New York: Boni, 1929).

[105]Stuart Chase, *The Nemesis of American Business and Other Essays* (New York: Macmillan, 1931), p. 14.

[106]Alexander Sachs, then economist of Lehman Corporation, an investment company;
his talk was summarized by Willford I. King in *JASA*, March 1932, 27:87–89, reporting the
meeting on Nov. 24, 1931.

stress on monetary factors as the prime determinants of the business cycle, and put undue faith in the ability of the Federal Reserve System to eliminate extreme cyclical movements and in the effectiveness of low interest rates in stimulating business. Hence the "almost universal confidence that no serious depression was likely to occur in the immediate future." Statisticians, moreover, tended to trust trend lines too far, commonly overlooked the increased durability of new products such as automobiles, tires, and refrigerators, and therefore failed to anticipate slackened demand for these. In addition, the undermining of the railway business by improved highways, high-voltage electric lines, and long-distance pipe lines was little noted. Failure to understand the true situation during the boom led to drastic errors in prediction when unforeseen strains developed.

Another experienced economist humbly acknolwedged the shortcomings of the profession in the pre-crash years. Hardy ended his 1932 book on Federal Reserve policies with this sentence: "The responsibility of the Reserve system in this matter must be shared with legislators, and with all serious students of public affairs; for we all failed to detect in time of prosperity the inadequacy of our precautions against a time of adversity."[107] As already noted, Bullock and Crum critically examined the record of the Harvard group, and undertook to explain how they had gone wrong, but even their searching examination was far from complete.[108]

In mid-1934 Robbins wrote: "It is agreed that to prevent the depression the only effective method is to prevent the boom. But how this is to be done is not a matter on which there exists unanimity."[109] Machlup later wrote that Keynes "really believes that it is possible to perpetuate the boom." Machlup also said: "The dogma that one can avoid the downswing only by avoiding the upswing, which was widely held a few years ago, has recently fallen into disrepute. I still hold to that idea, not as a dogma, but as a statement of an extremely high 'probability value.' I believe that the upswing breeds a host of disproportionalities in the production and price structure, which turn out to be untenable and result in a depression."[110] Alvin Hansen said in mid-1937: "we shall never achieve reasonable economic stability unless we learn to master the boom. For the boom is the progenitor of the depression."[111] Marriner Eccles, then the key man in the Federal Reserve System, wrote in April 1937: "The time to prepare

[107]Charles O. Hardy, *Credit Policies of the Federal Reserve System* (Washington, D.C.: Brookings Institution, 1932), pp. 88, 348.

[108]*Rev. Ec. Stat.*, Aug. 15, 1932, 14:132–48, cited in n.79.

[109]Robbins, *Great Depression*, p. 171.

[110]Fritz Machlup, *The Stock Market, Credit and Capital Formation* (New York: Macmillan, 1940), pp. 195, 294–95. His reference is to Keynes, *General Theory*, p. 322.

[111]"Monetary Policy on the Upswing," in A. D. Gayer, ed., *The Lessons of Monetary Experience: Essays in Honor of Irving Fisher* (New York: Farrar and Rinehart, 1937), pp. 89–98.

for economic disasters is when things are going smoothly. . . . we have
made virtually no preparation for economic disasters in the past."[112] Unhappily, the uncontrolled boom then under way soon rose to its climax
with wholly inadequate preparation to deal with its consequences. R. G.
Hawtrey, an eminent English economist with the British Treasury in 1904–
45, confessed in 1937: "Perhaps the most notable of all the lessons to be
derived from the years of depression is to be found in the prolonged failure
of the accepted methods of credit regulation to induce revival."[113]

The huge increase in brokers' loans in the late 1920s gave rise to a
vast amount of confused thinking and many wrong ideas. These were only
partially clarified until the end of the 1930s, notably in Machlup's 1940
book *The Stock Market, Credit and Capital Formation*—a translation of
a revised and enlarged edition of his book with a similar title first published in German in 1931, with a preface dated May 1931. In 1940 he was
quite positive on many points, e.g.:

No boom can develop unless optimism is supported by increased supply of money
capital (page 90). A lasting boom can result only from an inflationary credit supply
(page 92). . . . figures giving the sum total of brokers' loans tell us absolutely
nothing about the absorption of credit by the stock market (page 128). . . . a fall
in prices which is due to increased productivity need not give rise to economic depression (page 190). The boom on the stock exchange undoubtedly involves a
cheapening of industrial credit. The cheapening which took place in the United
States in the years 1927–29 was . . . the result of an inflationary expansion of
credit (page 279).

But in his preface he confessed: "There are a few things of which I have
become more certain than I was eight years ago; but there are many things
of which I was cocksure then—and am very uncertain now. My views
have changed not only concerning the truth-value or probability-value, but
also concerning the practical significance of many a statement" (page v).
Many others might well have made similar admissions.

This chapter certainly does not do justice to the positive contributions made by "social scientists" in the interwar period. It nevertheless
is essential to an understanding of the misjudgments that were in considerable measure responsible for the onset and protraction of the depression
and the coming of World War II. Since 1946 we have continued to be afflicted by many of the same problems that bedeviled the previous decades, and a later generation of social scientists has not proved notably better equipped for the job than their predecessors. As one of the contributors

[112]"Controlling Booms and Depressions," *Fortune*, Spring 1937, reprinted in *ibid.*, pp.
3–22. One looks in vain through these papers by highly respected economists and bankers for
recognition of the imminence of the severe contraction of 1937–38.
[113]"The Credit Deadlock," in *ibid.*, p. 130.

to an important series of articles, "Lessons and Legacies 30 Years After," wrote in mid-1961: "The 1960s can hardly sneer at the 1930s. . . . The problems that did the most damage in 1931 are still those that free societies have done least to solve."[114] In my own paper published late in 1972 I presented later evidence to this effect,[115] and *Time*'s issue of January 14, 1974 (page 62), adds more up-to-date testimony.

[114]*Economist*, June 17, 1961, pp. 1263–87, esp. pp. 1266–67.

[115]Joseph S. Davis, *America and the World, 1946–71, in the Perspective of 1914–39* (Stanford, Calif.: Food Research Institute, 1972), esp. pp. 13–16.

CHAPTER 16

CONCLUDING OBSERVATIONS

IMPORTANT technological advances, much international cooperation, and varied gains in levels of living marked the turbulent interwar
decades. Yet the Great Depression and the onset of World War II frustrated
high hopes that were widely entertained in 1919 and 1929. Long study has
convinced me that these monumental failures were inevitable, though inherently preventable. This unhappy conclusion is in harmony with Morison's mid-1922 answer to the question: was the American Revolution
"inevitable"? He said:

most of the few Englishmen who have thought about it have the decided opinion
that it was not—that the Revolution was due to a temporary misunderstanding, and
to a series of blunders by George III, or to a certain obliquity of vision and pervers-
ity of performance on the part of colonial leaders. I think that the Revolution was
due to a variety of causes which rendered it, humanly speaking, inevitable; that is
to say, inevitable without imaginative statesmanship of an order seldom attained by
historians, and never attained in practice by politicians.[1]

Similarly, Keynes wrote late in 1930 of the grave slump then under way:

The causes to which we have assigned it were the outcome of policy; and, in a sense,
therefore, it was avoidable. Yet it is evident that the policy could not have been
radically different, unless the mentality and ideas of our rulers had also been greatly
changed. That is to say, what has occurred is not exactly an accident; it has been
deeply rooted in our general way of doing things.[2]

Like many historians and economists, here Keynes overstressed policy
aspects and did not probe into manifold defects in our way of doing things
or the reasons for them. I cannot accept such simplistic conclusions as that
the war of 1914–18 and avoidable blunders at the Peace Conference made
another great war inevitable; that errors in Federal Reserve and presidential policies in the 1920s ensured the coming of a severe, prolonged depression; and that this depression and Adolf Hitler were the causes of World
War II. Each of these played only a part in the intricate chain of causation.
If we are to learn aright the lessons that the history of 1919–39 has to teach,
broader and deeper understanding is essential.

A bewildering array of "causes" has been put forward, in those years
and later. Despite agreement on a few points, no consensus has been reached

[1]Samuel Eliot Morison, *A Prologue to American History: An Inaugural Lecture Delivered
Before the University of Oxford, on 1 June, 1922* (Oxford: Clarendon Press, 1922).
[2]John Maynard Keynes, *A Treatise on Money*, 2 vols. (New York: Harcourt Brace, 1930),
2:385.

on why two grave disasters became inevitable. The preceding chapters contain many elements of my answer to that basic question, which I refrain from summarizing but must supplement here. Behind the misjudgments, blunders, malfeasances, and policy ineptness were fundamentals that were commonly unstressed, if recognized. Three were of special importance: (1) the complexity of the real world of the period; (2) the heterogeneity of its inhabitants; and (3) imperfect understanding of persons, peoples, institutions, situations, and trends, which rendered trustworthy forecasts impossible to make.

1. Interlinked as never before, the world between the wars was inordinately complex—always in a state of flux and so beset by tensions that it sometimes seemed more chaotic than it actually was.[3] The several nations were of very different size. China was one only in the loosest sense: India a conglomerate component of the British Empire, Africa a congeries of nations, colonies, and protectorates. Several large and populous nations, and many small ones as well, were more or less isolated from the rest of the world through most of the interwar years. With rare exceptions the most nearly unified nations were made up of diverse groups with different traditions, customs, and languages or dialects, and several had more or less rebellious minorities. Civil wars often threatened, and several raged for months and even years. Groups that shared a broad viewpoint could not consistently agree on leaders, policies, or specific moves, and majorities shifted amid continuous wrangling. Modes of governance varied widely, even among the remaining monarchies, and none worked well, yet the trend was toward enlarging the role of governments in economic and social affairs. The democracies, notably Italy before Mussolini, France, and Germany, were racked by political instability. Communist and fascist dictatorships seethed with unrest even when dissent was ruthlessly repressed. Nominally democratic governments were repeatedly upset by coups and replaced by dictators. National objectives were mostly confused, and, while some were capable of being harmonized with difficulty, others were wholly irreconcilable. The "national economies" were at different stages of development, from primitive to relatively advanced, with very different levels of education, income, and living. The "world economy," sometimes depicted as an

---

[3]My researches in 1919–25, aided by visits to Europe in 1921 and 1924, revealed the extraordinary complexity of Europe and its economic and financial developments and the extreme difficulty, but also the possibility, of tracing their course with a fair approach to accuracy, as I did in published papers cited in Chapter 3 above. In concluding my review of 1923–24 (*Rev. Ec. Stat.* 6:240) 1 noted "a pronounced tendency, in certain quarters, to use extravagantly picturesque terms and phrases in describing European conditions—the existence of widespread 'chaos,' the 'ruin of Germany,' the imminence of farreaching 'catastrophes,' the big debts as 'millstones around Europe's neck,' and so on." I went on: "Such characterizations are unsupported by the evidence, of the past as well as the present. Abnormal though the situation has been, such language presents a grotesque caricature of the real Europe."

intricate and delicate machine, was imperfectly articulated, with its parts in various stages of disrepair, obsolescence, or both. Never in stable equilibrium, it repeatedly faced the necessity to adjust both to continuous change and to unexpected shocks of various kinds and degrees. Nationalism had virtues and serious vices.[4] Switzerland had kept out of World War I and, despite incessant internal friction, survived as a democratic republic with German, French, and Italian cantons; Geneva therefore seemed the logical choice for headquarters of the League of Nations, ambitiously superimposed on a disorderly world.

2. Individual human beings in these years were complex combinations of strengths and weaknesses, with good and bad traits and tendencies only gradually modified by education, experience, and self-discipline. Their intelligence, knowledge, and morality varied through an incredible range; but the most perceptive could exhibit egregious blindness, and the brainiest and best-informed often made foolish statements and did stupid things. Conscientious exercise of great talents did much good and much harm. Command of vast knowledge did not ensure wisdom, and exceptional understanding could coexist with grave ineptness.[5] Very few well-balanced, nicely integrated, wholly admirable persons attained or long retained high position. Viscount Grey of Fallodon (the former Sir Edward Grey, British foreign secretary in 1914) wrote perceptively in his memoirs:

One of the most exasperating features of working in close contact with remarkable men is the defects of those who have great qualities. The very greatness of the qualities makes the defects so plain and so provokingly inconsistent. We are all apt to be conscious of each other's shortcomings. This is not because we have none of our own; our own may be even worse than those of others; but they are not the same, and we see most clearly the faults from which we are ourselves free. Equally exasperating is the perception that those who are free from the defects that we deplore are often without the qualities that we admire. In war we must have the men with the qualities essential to success. We cannot have the benefit of these great qualities without the defects that accompany them.[6]

Outstanding leaders, with or without such charisma as Wilson, Roosevelt, and Hitler possessed, aroused great admiration and bitter enmity, commanded strong support and excited venomous attack. Great buildups

    [4]Hans Kohn, author of *Nationalismus* (1922), *The Idea of Nationalism* (1944), and *Nationalism, Its Meaning and History* (1955), long argued that nationalism was the leading and decisive force of our age, for good to some extent but especially for ill. Cf. also C. J. H. Hayes, *Nationalism: A Religion* (New York: Macmillan, 1960).
    [5]In his *Personality in Politics: Studies of Contemporary Statesmen* (London: Faber, 1947), Arthur Salter wrote that Clemenceau "hated Poincaré and despised Briand. . . . The well-known aphorism of Lloyd George, 'Poincaré knows everything and understands nothing; Briand understands everything and knows nothing,' is not quite accurate, though it throws an illuminating light on all the three men concerned and their reactions to each other" (pp. 193, 197).
    [6]*Twenty-Five Years, 1982–1916*, 2 vols. (New York: Stokes, 1925), 2:245.

of reputations repeatedly evoked counter-efforts to tear them down. Intense publicity magnified strong points and good moves but also pitilessly exposed weaknesses and blunders. Personalities counted heavily, and clashes of strong personalities were recurrent sources of intranational and international friction.[7] There were never enough harmonizers (such as Morrow, Salter, Cecil, D'Abernon, Stamp, Monnet, and Stresemann) to help divergent minds meet. While complete sanity may be normal, it was rare; blurred vision, warped minds, distorted judgments, and defects of many types and degrees were prevalent in these years. Hitler and Stalin may have been, as many currently believe, victims of well-known types of insanity; but they long dominated their great nations with powerful public support, repeatedly outwitted the leaders of other nations, and for years achieved exceptional success despite unbelievable cruelties. In the real world as it was, at all levels, from couples and families to nations, people found it impossible to get along smoothly together.

The press and radio rendered both great service and disservice— informing and misinforming, clarifying and distorting, exaggerating and minimizing, soothing and inflaming, building up hopes, fears, good will, and hatreds.[8] Hence the public was often confused, prejudiced, and exceedingly volatile. United States participation in the war was highly popular while it lasted, but was soon roundly condemned.[9] Wartime sentiment in Britain and the United States was strongly pro-French and anti-German; within three years it was reversed. The standing of the United States abroad went through astounding reversals, as did the reputations of national leaders. Official and popular attitudes toward communism and Soviet Russia, and Russian attitudes toward other peoples, varied over a wide range.[10] The socioeconomic counterparts of hypertension—hypercriticism, hyperinflation, hyperpessimism, and hyperoptimism—did vast damage in the interwar years.

[7]This point and others in this paragraph are abundantly illustrated in *An Ambassador of Peace: Lord D'Abernon's Diary*, vols. 2–3 (London: Hodder and Stoughton, 1929–30), and in A. J. P. Taylor, *Beaverbrook* (London: Hamish Hamilton, 1972). Both lords were extraordinary men with distinctive personalities.

[8]Three powerful "press lords"—Irish-born Harmsworth brothers Lords Northcliffe and Rothermore and Canadian-born Lord Beaverbrook—had counterparts in other countries. In his recent *Autobiography of an Economist* (New York: Macmillan, 1971), Lord Robbins adverted to Beaverbrook's "capricious enthusiasms and venomous hatreds—especially of America and Americans" (p. 204). Dawes wrote early in 1923: "Public sentiment all over the world at the end of the war was like molten lava from a volcano, it was uncontrollable and not plastic. It has not yet had time to cool off everywhere." C. G. Dawes, *A Journal of Reparations* (London: Macmillan, 1939), pp. 78–79. Late in 1931 Maryland Governor Albert C. Ritchie spoke of the "chaos of fears, perplexities, uncertainties, and demoralization" that confronted Americans. *Proc. Acad. Pol. Sci.*, January 1932, 14:593. These persisted and contributed to intensifying and prolonging the depression.

[9]Samuel Eliot Morison, *The Oxford History of the American People* (New York: Oxford University Press, 1965), p. 886.

[10]Henry Shapiro brought this out in a series of eight newspaper articles in December 1972, which grew out of his nearly forty years in Moscow, mostly as a newspaper correspondent.

3. The complex world of 1919–39 and its varied peoples were inherently hard to understand. Despite excellent work by such international interpreters as Moritz Bonn and André Siegfried, even the British, French, Germans, and North Americans failed to understand themselves and one another with anything like accuracy and adequacy. The workings of Russian, Indian, Oriental, and African minds were far less comprehended elsewhere. Basic misunderstanding and misinterpretations persisted for years. Prolonged and seemingly thorough investigation led to some major decisions that proved seriously mistaken.[11] Highly respected "authorities," presuming to know more than they could know, confidently expressed opinions that were to prove quite wrong. At the time and later, attempts were made, some of them with wholly unwarranted assurance, to explain how the collapse of 1929–33 and the ensuing depression could have been prevented.[12] Pride was properly taken in advancing technology and expanding education, but it was too little realized that these facilitated both social progress and all sorts of skulduggery and crime, and that an unemployed educated class could easily fall prey to demagogues, of whom Hitler and Goebbels were extreme examples.

In retrospect, it seems clear that such fundamentals were accorded too little attention and emphasis. Inadequate account was taken of the prevalence of ignorance and shortsightedness; of slowness to learn and unlearn; of addiction to wishful thinking, illusions, and veritable manias; of quickness to blame other individuals and nations while overlooking positive and negative defects of one's own; of tendencies to go to excess and to swing from one extreme to another; and of reluctance to make painful choices and decisions, allowing deep sores to fester and knotty problems to build up to explosive proportions. A satisfactory blend of idealism and realism was seldom reached. Too much was expected of leaders, institutions, and governments, of economics and economists; the

[11]Moggridge concluded after exhaustive investigation that the British decision in April 1925 to return the pound sterling to gold at prewar parity with the dollar—one noteworthy example—was unfortunate from every point of view and "despite all the emphasis on the long run, represented a triumph of shortrun interests and conventional assumptions over long-term considerations and hard analysis." D. E. Moggridge, *The Return of Gold 1925: The Formulation of Economic Policy and Its Critics* (London: Cambridge University Press. 1969), p. 88.

[12]For example, this statement appeared in the highly regarded Citibank *Monthly Economic Letter* of July 1972 (p. 7): "Today, in retrospect, it is readily apparent that the Great Depression resulted from a grave misunderstanding of the workings of monetary and fiscal policy." There was such misunderstanding, and it was partly responsible for inept policy, but to attribute the depression to this alone is indefensible. It ignores well-established facts of great importance, notably in the international sphere, as well as fundamentals discussed above. Furthermore, I cannot accept the implication that this whole matter is now well understood by all eminent economists, to say nothing of all those who have hard decisions to make. Even if it were thoroughly understood, various obstacles could prevent appropriate and timely action.

public's ability to understand complex issues and arrive at sound decisions was overrated, as was the feasibility of making reliable knowledge available to those needing it. Actions were taken as if people were largely homogeneous, basically good and reasonable,[13] and able to see what their long-run interests were. The difficulties of reaching agreement on tough and complicated issues—by diplomacy, in mammoth conferences, and in small groups of selected "experts"—were gravely underestimated; and it was mistakenly assumed that agreements reached would be kept, good resolutions followed through, and broad commitments honored. Unforeseeable vagaries of nature sometimes played a significant part for better or worse. Of much greater importance were illnesses, health breakdowns, mental deterioration or derangement, and premature deaths (from disease or violence) of key individuals at critical times.[14]

Much more could be added, but perhaps enough has been said to support my conviction that failure to give due recognition to such fundamentals and inadequate effort to overcome basic weaknesses contributed greatly to bringing on successive crises and eventual tragedies in 1919–39. In the subsequent thirty-five years the complexity of the world has surely increased, the diversity of its peoples has not diminished, and deep understanding of both has not been achieved. Vast improvements in communication have increased the interdependence of nations but failed to bring about a well-integrated world. A holocaust has indeed been avoided, and impressive progress has been made on many fronts, but the danger of inherently preventable disasters still looms large. These sober conclusions challenge the world as it enters the last quarter of the twentieth century.

[13]In an intimate paper given on March 3, 1938, before a little club of which he had long been a member, but published only after his death, by express instruction to his executors, that marvelous man Keynes said: "I remain, and always will remain, an immoralist." This, he explained at length, involved repudiating customary morals, conventions, and traditional wisdom. Yet he admitted that he had come to realize that this attitude was "flimsily based . . . on an *a priori* view of what human nature is like, both other people's and our own, which was disastrously mistaken. . . . I still suffer incurably from attributing an unreal rationality to other people's feelings and behavior (and doubtless my own, too)." John Maynard Keynes, *Two Memoirs: "Dr. Melchior: A Defeated Enemy" and "My Early Beliefs"* (London: Rupert Hart-Davis, 1949; introduction by David Garnett), pp. 73–100, esp. pp. 78–81.

[14]Friedman and Schwartz, who properly gave much weight to fundamentals that I have discussed, expressed agreement with Carl Snyder's emphatic opinion (in his *Capitalism the Creator*, 1940, p. 203) that if Benjamin Strong (the highly influential governor of the Federal Reserve Bank of New York) had remained in vigorous health, the depression might have been ended in 1930. Milton Friedman and Anna J. Schwartz, *A Monetary History of the United States, 1867–1960* (Princeton, N.J.: Princeton University Press, 1963), p. 692. Though I would not minimize the negative influence of Strong's 1928 illness and death, Snyder's conclusion seems far too strong.

INDEX